ESSEX THE REBEL

ESSEX THE REBEL

The Life of Robert Devereux, the Third Earl of Essex

1591-1646

by

Vernon F. Snow

UNIVERSITY OF NEBRASKA PRESS · LINCOLN

Publishers on the Plains
UNP

MANUFACTURED IN THE UNITED STATES OF AMERICA

Contents

List of Illustrations

List of Maps

Preface

On Thursday, 10 September 1646, Robert Devereux, the third Earl of Essex, the semiretired lord general who had led the Parliamentary army through the early years of the Civil War, suffered an apoplectic stroke while hunting in Windsor Forest. He was rushed to Essex House, his mansion in London's West End, and placed under the care of Dr. John Clarke, one of England's foremost physicians. Essex lay in semiconsciousness for four days, and in the evening hours of 14 September, after another stroke, the former general expired in the arms of his cousin and political ally Henry Rich, the Earl of Holland. Trumpets soon announced his death to the people of London and Westminster.

Essex had lived a full and eventful life. From the day of his baptism in Walsingham House to the hour of his demise in Essex House he remained in the public eye. To some he was the son of a traitor, to others the son of a martyr, but to all he was a leader by virtue of his name, noble birth, and family connections. His personal life was filled with tragedy, reversals, and disappointments. Essex was forced to marry the vivacious daughter of a rival family. Later, in one of the age's most scandalous divorce trials, he was publicly humiliated and compelled to give up the marriage. His second marriage, though it began with affection, ended in infidelity and separation. His public career was equally checkered and complex. He was hated by Queen Elizabeth, admired by James I, and detested by Charles I. During the reign of Queen Elizabeth, Essex, though born an aristocrat, lost his birthright as a result of his father's treason and the ensuing attainder; in the reign of James I, after being reinstated and reconciled, Essex entered the ranks of the opposition faction; during Charles I's reign, after several demonstrations of loyalty, he was proclaimed a rebel for his resistance to the sovereign. He remained a rebel until his death.

To reconstruct the life of one who has been dead for centuries is never simple, and several factors have made the task irritatingly complicated and difficult in Essex's case. Essex was first and foremost a man of action. He did not keep a diary or write an autobiography, as did many of his contemporaries. His published words were few, ephemeral, and limited to political and military matters. Excluded from national office and the Court for most of his adult life, Essex left no record as an administrator, judge, diplomat, councilor, or courtier. His incoming correspondence, which was voluminous, did not survive the crucial years of the Puritan Revolution. To the Royalists, especially the King, Essex was a rebel, exempt from general pardon. To the Puritans of Cromwell's stripe he was a dangerous risk because of his peacemaking gestures and mediative activities. Very likely Essex, caught between the extremes of a revolution, destroyed his private papers dating from the Civil Wars. It is also possible that Essex's sister the Marchioness of Hertford destroyed some of his correspondence or that the executors of the estate did not deem it advisable to preserve the literary effects of their compatriot. If Essex had not been the last of his line, he probably would have bequeathed to posterity a better record of his life.

Fortunately, Essex was a prominent enough figure, especially during the Puritan upheaval, to evoke attention and comment from his contemporaries. From 1640 to 1645 his actions were always newsworthy. His parliamentary speeches and public pronouncements invariably found their way into the semiweekly newsbooks. His decisions, particularly those of a military nature, drew comments and criticisms from his friends, allies, and enemies. His day-by-day military exploits in the Civil War were recorded by his scoutmaster general, Sir Samuel Luke. Essex's activities in the House of Lords, the Committee of Both Kingdoms, and the Westminster Assembly were faithfully reported. More important, many of Essex's personal letters and dispatches were considered significant and preserved by their recipients. Some of these papers have been sold or transferred to private and public depositories in England, Scotland, and the United States; others remain in private collections. Most significant is the fact that the executors of his will preserved some of Essex's last effects, including several manuscripts, some letters dating from the pre–Civil War period, and an inventory of his library and his personal holdings. The documents, in turn, became the property of William Jessop, a lawyer who represented the executors, and his heirs. Only recently Jessop's descendants deposited the papers with the British Museum.[1]

To date, the third Earl of Essex has had no biographer. Robert Codrington and Arthur Wilson, two of his contemporaries, wrote short laudatory sketches of his life. These accounts and a plethora of eulogies, which covered the military aspects of his career and were published shortly after Essex's death, formed the basis for the article on Essex in *Biographia Britannia* (London, 1793) and subsequent reference works. In 1853, W. B. Devereux pieced together a family history of the Devereux Earls of Essex and included the hitherto unpublished letters of the third Earl.[2] This new material enabled S. R. Gardiner to write for the *Dictionary of National Biography* the most authoritative account of Essex's career ever composed.[3] The only substantial pieces of critical research on Essex's career written since the publication of the *Dictionary* have been three articles published by Godfrey Davies[4] during the first part of this century and two articles I wrote.[5]

Throughout the ensuing biography I have attempted to portray Essex as dispassionately as possible. This work is not intended to be an apology for or a depreciation of the subject. I have not consciously sought to make Essex either a hero or a villain. I have, however, made every effort to understand him—his character, his ideals, his personality, his ambitions, his motivations, his aims, his limitations, and his shortcomings—considering the changing background of the tempestuous times in which he lived. I have deliberately sought to portray him both as a member of the aristocratic class, which was in a state of crisis, and as a leader of those

[1] These are catalogued under Additional MSS, MSS 46,188–46,193.

[2] Walter Bourchier Devereux, *The Lives and Letters of the Devereux Earls of Essex*, 2 vols. (London, 1853).

[3] *Dictionary of National Biography*, 22 vols. (London, 1885–1900), 5: 890–97 (hereafter cited as *DNB*). Unless otherwise noted, references are to this first edition.

[4] "The Parliamentary Army under the Earl of Essex, 1642–1645," *English Historical Review* 49 (1934): 34–54; "The Battle of Edgehill," *English Historical Review* 36 (1921): 3–44; and "Documents illustrating the First Civil War, 1642–1645," *Journal of Modern History* 3 (1931): 64–71.

[5] "Essex and the Aristocratic Opposition to the Early Stuarts," *Journal of Modern History* 32 (1960): 224–33; and "The Lord General's Library, 1646," *Transactions of the Bibliographical Society* 21 (1966): 115–23.

peers who were closely allied with the opposition in the House of Commons.[6] For these reasons I have focused my attention upon the House of Lords; aristocratic rights, privileges, and grievances; and the role of the aristocracy in the rising opposition to the early Stuart monarchs. It is hoped not only that this emphasis will elucidate the career of one opposition leader but that it will serve to give a more balanced view of the events preceding and during the English Civil Wars.

Without the services and courtesies of many attendants and officials in public and private libraries and archives on both sides of the Atlantic, the problems of locating, perusing, and copying the published and unpublished materials relating to Essex would have been insurmountable. I am indebted to the British Museum, the Public Record Office, the House of Lords Record Office, the Institute of Historical Research, the Scottish Record Office, the William Salt Library in Stafford, the Victoria and Albert Museum and Library, the Kent Archive Office, the Bodleian Library, the Folger Library, the Henry E. Huntington Library and Art Gallery, and numerous county archives in England. I am particularly grateful to Maurice F. Bond, Clerk of the Records, who assisted me in locating and copying manuscripts; to archivist F. B. Stitt, who gave me the benefit of his knowledge of Staffordshire history and made accessible to me the manuscripts in the William Salt Library; and to the late Godfrey Davies, who shortly before his death encouraged me to attempt this study of Essex and the aristocratic opposition to the early Stuarts. Financial assistance from the American Philosophical Society enabled me to visit some of the battle-fields mentioned and to copy relevant material for this biography. Both the University of Nebraska and the University of Montana provided me with research funds and time to complete the writing of this book. To those past and present scholars who have written about the early Stuart era I owe more than I can acknowledge. To several mentors and many colleagues who gave me wise counsel and encouragement I am very grateful. I am most indebted to Professor Melvin C. Wren of the University of Toledo, who read several chapters and helped me avoid some pitfalls; to Professor William L. Sachse of the University of Wisconsin, who read the

---

[6] For a definitive treatment of the aristocracy as a class in this period, see the superb study by Lawrence Stone, *The Crisis of the Aristocracy, 1558–1641* (Oxford: Clarendon Press, 1965).

entire manuscript and rendered valuable criticism; and to both Helen Gray and Professor Glenn Gray of the University of Nebraska, who read the whole manuscript and graciously permitted me to use their transcript of the D'Ewes diary. My wife, Jean, has as always been my most faithful critic and assistant.

ESSEX THE REBEL

CHAPTER 1

Son of a Traitor

I

IN THE EARLY HOURS of 11 January 1591 the Countess of Essex gave birth to a son.[1] Eleven days later in Walsingham House, Dr. Lancelot Andrewes, a learned divine who served the Archbishop of Canterbury as chaplain, performed the baptismal rites. The witnesses were equally distinguished: great-grandfather Sir Francis Knollys, the aged treasurer of the Queen's household; Lady Ursula Walsingham, the recently widowed maternal grandmother; the Countess of Leicester, the paternal grandmother; and Lord Robert Rich, the wealthy husband of the infant's aunt Lady Penelope Rich (nee Devereux). The infant was given his father's name, Robert Devereux, and was called Roben by the Countess. The event was subsequently recorded in the register of Saint Olave's, Hart Street, the parish church located near Walsingham House.[2]

From his father, Roben inherited a distinguished Norman surname and an ancient lineage. Before coming to England with William the Conqueror, the Devereux lived in the vicinity of Évreux, a cathedral city in Normandy. From there the Count of Rosmar and Mantelake, who was related to the powerful Duke of Normandy, sent two sons, Edward and Robert d'Evereux, with William to assist in the Norman conquest of England in 1066. Edward, the elder of the two knights, secured several estates in Wiltshire and took the surname of De Salisburie, from Salisbury, where his principal manor was located. Robert secured estates in the Marches of Wales, where he settled and retained the family

1 Parish register, Saint Olave's, Hart Street. Charles Lethbridge Kingsford claims in "Essex House," *Archaelogia*, 2d ser. 23 (1922–23): 13, that Robert Devereux was born in Essex House, but this is not borne out by facts.

2 W. B. Bannerman, *The Register of St. Olave Hart Street* (London: Roworth and Company, 1916), p. 14.

1

name. His descendants, many of whom were knighted and ennobled, acquired more estates and remained in the area throughout the medieval era. Many served as sheriffs; some attended the Parliaments called by the Angevin monarchs; a few attained international fame. King John created Almeric de Evereux the Earl of Gloucester as a reward for his military services rendered on the Continent, but the title became extinct. Over a century later Sir John Devereux, a member of Parliament for Herefordshire, brought much honor to his house by fighting on the Iberian Peninsula in 1360 and attending the Black Prince in Gascony and Angoulême. For these and other services he was appointed governor of Leeds Castle, named a Knight of the Bath, and summoned to Parliament as Lord Devereux. Though this title also became extinct in the following generation, other branches of the family prospered in local politics during the next century. Sir Walter Devereux of Weobly served the Lancastrian monarchs as sheriff of Herefordshire, and his eldest son, Sir William, was knighted by Edward IV in 1461 and summoned to Parliament as Lord Ferrers of Chartley. He received this title as a result of his marriage to the late Lord Ferrers's heiress.[3]

During Tudor times the Devereux rose steadily to greater prominence in national affairs. The members of the family slowly increased their land holdings in Staffordshire and Ireland. They proved their loyalty to the Tudor monarchs through meritorious military service and support of the reformed religion. They secured places in the higher echelons of government and won many honors. In 1501, Walter Devereux, Lord Ferrers of Chartley—the son of Sir William—succeeded to his father's title and the ancestral lands in Staffordshire and Herefordshire.[4] The new Lord Ferrers took part in Henry VIII's wars on the Continent, sat in Parliament and the Council of Wales, and served as a Privy Councilor during the reign of Edward VI. It was in Edward's reign, on 2 February 1550, that he was elevated and summoned to Parliament as Viscount Hereford. Because his eldest son, Richard, died before him, Lord

[3] Much of the genealogical data comes from the *DNB;* W. R. Williams, *Parliamentary History of the County of Hereford* (Brecknock, 1896), pp. 26–34; Josiah C. Wedgwood and A. D. Holt, *Biographies of the Members of the House of Commons, 1439–1509,* 2 vols. (London: His Majesty's Stationery Office, 1936–38), 1: 271–74; and G. E. Cokayne, *Complete Peerage of England, Scotland, Ireland,* ed. Vicary Gibbs, 13 vols. (London: St. Catherine Press, 1910–49), various entries under the headings of "Ferrers," "Hereford," and "Essex."

[4] Devereux, *Lives of the Devereux,* 1: 6.

Hereford was succeeded, during the last year of Queen Mary's reign, by his grandson Walter Devereux, who was destined for even greater achievements during the reign of Elizabeth I.

Lord Hereford's marriage to Lettice Knollys, daughter of Sir Francis Knollys, bound the Devereux fortune firmly to the Protestant cause and promoted their interests at Court.[5] Sir Francis had experienced hardships during the rule of Queen Mary, but instead of compromising his religious principles by bending with the times, as some other Englishmen had, he sought refuge on the Continent and became a convert to the doctrines of John Calvin. Upon returning to England soon after Queen Elizabeth's accession, he became a spokesman and patron for the more advanced Protestants who demanded further reforms in the Anglican establishment. The fact that his wife was a cousin of the Queen gave him a great deal of influence in the political and social circles of Elizabethan England. Lettice and her husband benefited greatly from these close connections with royalty.

The Queen came to regard Lord Hereford, Roben's grandfather, as one of her favorite and most dependable courtiers. In 1569, Elizabeth called upon him to subdue the rebels in the North, and in 1576 she empowered him to reduce and colonize Ireland. She also showered him with honors, in 1572 elevating him to the earldom of Essex, an ancient title previously held by such distinguished families as the Mandevilles, the Bohuns, and the Bourchiers. This promotion gave the Devereux higher precedence in the affairs of state and greater prestige in Parliament.[6] Four years later, the very year he was appointed Earl Marshal of Ireland, the first Earl of Essex died in Dublin Castle, and the Devereux titles and estates descended to his heir, nine-year-old Robert Devereux.

The second Earl of Essex, Roben's father, was the eldest son among the four surviving children.[7] Both his sisters were older— Penelope was thirteen and Dorothy eleven—and his brother, Walter, was seven. His mother, one of the Queen's Maids of

[5] Devereux's *Lives of the Devereux* remains the best biographical study of the first Earl of Essex; for additional information on his life see H. E. Malden, *Devereux Papers with Richard Broughton's Memoranda*, Camden Society (London: Royal Historical Society, 1923).

[6] Cokayne, *Complete Peerage*, 5: 131–49.

[7] The best biography of the second Earl remains G. B. Harrison's *The Life and Death of Robert Devereux, Earl of Essex* (New York: H. Holt and Company, 1937).

Honour, had not accompanied her husband to Ireland; she had instead followed the royal Court to Kenilworth and participated in the celebrated revels associated with that castle. After learning of her husband's death, the Countess of Essex took her family from Kenilworth to Chartley, their principal residence in Staffordshire, and not long before the Christmas holidays they witnessed the interment of the late Earl in the nearby parish church at Stowe. The funeral effigy depicted the first Earl of Essex as a bearded soldier, dressed in heavy armor and a cape, with his sword at his side. The sturdily built tomb, graced with the Devereux shield, still stands.

In the years following the death of the first Earl of Essex, the female members of the Devereux family attracted much public attention. In 1568 the widowed Countess secretly married the great Earl of Leicester; when the Queen found out, in a fit of anger she imprisoned her favorite.[8] Only after his friends informed the Queen that the marriage, though secret, was completely lawful was Leicester excused and released. The jealous sovereign never forgave the new Countess of Leicester, however. Lettice's two daughters, meanwhile, commenced troublesome marital careers.[9] Penelope became secretly betrothed to Charles Blount but was compelled to break this entente and marry the opulent Lord Rich. Dorothy, at seventeen, caused something of a sensation in 1583 when she married Sir Thomas Perrot, son of the lord deputy of Ireland, in a clandestine service performed under dubious circumstances. In 1595, after Perrot's death, Dorothy married Henry Percy, ninth Earl of Northumberland.

The second Earl of Essex, meanwhile, went to Cambridge University and began his studies at Trinity College under the direction of its master, Dr. John Whitgift.[10] Essex remained at Cambridge for five years, taking a master's degree in 1581, and then retired to his house at Llanfydd in Pembrokeshire, where he read and hunted for three years. Yielding to the appeals of his mother, he then went to

[8] Milton Waldman, *Elizabeth and Leicester* (Boston: Houghton Mifflin Company, 1945), pp. 157–60.

[9] For information about Penelope see Hoyt H. Hudson, "Penelope Devereux as Sidney's Stella," *Huntington Library Quarterly* 7 (1935): 89–129; and Cyril Falls, *Mountjoy: Elizabethan General* (London: Odhams Press, 1955). For a discussion of Dorothy see Harrison, *Essex*, pp. 256–58.

[10] Harrison, *Essex*, pp. 2–7.

London for his public debut. The seventeen-year-old nobleman was led into the Presence Chamber by his stepfather and presented to Queen Elizabeth. Essex immediately attracted her attention and rapidly supplanted other young courtiers, including Sir Walter Raleigh, as a royally favored attendant. His charming manners and his urbanity as well as his handsome features appealed to the aged Virgin Queen.

In the ensuing years Essex continued to rise in the Queen's favor.[11] She allowed him to serve under his stepfather, Leicester; in fact, she commissioned him General of the Horse. In 1585 the young general crossed to the Continent and traveled with his stepfather in the Low Countries, and during the following months he tasted war for the first time. He assisted in the bombardment and capture of Doesburg and helped restore order among the plundering troops. In 1586, Essex moved off to attack Zutphen, accompanied by his brother-in-law Sir Thomas Perrot and Sir Philip Sidney, who was severely wounded during the charge in the early morning hours of 22 September. The Earl of Essex performed valiantly in this, his first real battle. After several more skirmishes, he was made a knight banneret along with other officers who had distinguished themselves at Zutphen.[12]

Essex's bosom friend and subordinate Sir Philip was becoming increasingly ill.[13] His wounded leg did not respond to treatment, and gangrene set in. His wife, Lady Frances, who had come to Flushing earlier in the summer, rushed to him and remained at his side, while the Earl of Leicester, visibly grieved over the fate of his nephew, stayed nearby. Resigned to his fate, Sir Philip prepared to die. After forwarding a final message to his Queen, he turned to poetry, and like a medieval knight, composed a deathbed sonnet. He also wrote his last will and testament, leaving his lands and revenues to his wife and then to his brother Robert.

---

[11] Ray Haffner, "Essex, the Ideal Courtier," *English Literary History* 1 (1934): 23–44.

[12] Harrison, *Essex*, pp. 13–22.

[13] The material on Sir Philip Sidney has been garnered from the following works: Arthur Collins, *Letters and Memorials of State . . . from the Originals at Penshurst*, 2 vols. (London, 1746); John Buxton, *Sir Philip Sidney and the English Renaissance* (London: Macmillan and Company, 1954); Malcolm W. Wallace, *The Life of Sir Philip Sidney* (Cambridge: At the University Press, 1915); and Fulke Greville, *The Life of the Renowned Sir Philip Sidney*, ed. Nowell Smith (Oxford: Clarendon Press, 1907).

His literary friends Sir Edward Dyer and Sir Fulke Greville would receive his books, and Sir William Russell his best armor.

Sir Philip reserved his most highly treasured possessions, however, for Robert Devereux. With memories of the past and thoughts of the future, Sidney asked Essex to marry his pregnant wife and protect his young daughter. The young Earl promised to fulfill the wishes of his dying friend. To seal this verbal covenant, Sir Philip made one of his last bequests:

> I give to my beloved and much honored
> Lord, the Earl of Essex, my best sword.[14]

With this sword the Virgin Queen had dubbed him a Knight of the Bath. With it Sidney had hoped to win a title, military glory, and immortality. In Essex's possession it would continue to promote his cause and preserve the memory of his life and death. After making his final peace with God and bidding his friends a final adieu, Sir Philip died in the arms of a servant.

Shortly thereafter Essex returned to England. He paid his respects to the Queen and retired to Essex House, thoroughly dissatisfied with the indecisive wars in the Low Countries. "If God give me leave," he vowed, "these legs of mine shall never go again into Holland. Let the States get others to serve their mercenary turn, if they will make themselves rich, for me they shall not have."[15] Instead he turned to domestic politics and personal matters. Essex attended the flamboyant funeral ceremony and procession of Sir Philip Sidney. He began to appear regularly at Court, participate in the tiltings and royal fetes, and play cards with the Queen and chat with her into the small hours of the night. Before long he became the royal favorite.

Essex also took measures to fulfill his promise to the late Sir Philip Sidney. He allied himself with the anti-Spanish interests in Elizabeth's government. He cultivated the friendship of Sir Francis Walsingham, the Queen's principal secretary, and sought a permanent alliance with him. More important, Essex directed his attention to Sir Francis's only daughter and heir, the widowed Lady Sidney.

14 Albert Feuillerat, *The Complete Works of Sir Philip Sidney* (Cambridge: At the University Press, 1922–26). See Appendix I for Sidney's will.
15 Harrison, *Essex*, p. 22.

II

ROBEN DEVEREUX's mother, Frances Walsingham, was born in London in 1567.[16] Her father, Francis Walsingham, after receiving a genteel education at King's College, Cambridge, entered the Queen's service through the patronage of Sir William Cecil and thereafter devoted his energies to affairs of state. Her mother, Ursala St. Barbe, was a well-to-do heiress who descended from a Somersetshire landowning family. After their marriage in 1566 the Walsinghams purchased a substantial residence in London and established a household in the country. In 1577, Francis was honored with a knighthood for service rendered to the Queen as secretary of state.

In 1583, after much negotiating between their parents, Frances Walsingham married Sir Philip Sidney.[17] The wedding ceremony took place behind closed doors, probably because the match did not meet with the Queen's approval, but this secrecy only increased the royal displeasure. Nevertheless the couple remained in London and resided at Walsingham House. There in early November 1585, shortly before her husband went to war in the Low Countries, Lady Frances gave birth to her first child, christened Elizabeth after the Queen, her godmother.[18] Within a year Lady Frances was a widow.

She did not remain a widow very long, however, for within six months she secretly married the Earl of Essex, a political ally of her father. During her late husband's last days Lady Frances often had seen Essex, who tried to console her, and no doubt she knew of Sir Philip's deathbed request. Her father welcomed the match, for it meant that his daughter would be a Countess and that his son-in-law would be the Queen's favorite courtier.[19]

For more than three years the marriage remained a well-kept secret. The new Countess of Essex stayed out of the public eye, living a quiet life with her young daughter and mother in Walsing-

[16] Conyers Read, *Mr. Secretary Walsingham and the Policy of Queen Elizabeth,* 3 vols. (Oxford: Clarendon Press, 1925), 1: 26–28.

[17] *Ibid.*, 3: 167.

[18] Sir Philip's only daughter married the Earl of Rutland, a ward of the second Earl of Essex, and was the subject of a poem written by Ben Jonson. See Wallace, *Sidney,* pp. 333–35.

[19] For a complete discussion of Essex's marriage to Lady Sidney see Harrison, *Essex,* p. 46 and the extended note on pp. 332–33.

ham House, while her husband resided in grand style at Essex House and assumed a larger hand in public affairs. He spent countless hours with the Queen and her intimates and expended his energies on military matters. In successive years, beginning in 1587, he became Master of the Queen's Horse, helped defend England against the Spanish Armada, participated in an unsuccessful crusade against the Duke of Alva in Portugal, and began preparations for an expedition against the Catholic League.

Amidst these preparations, on 6 April 1590, the Countess of Essex's father died after a brief illness. He went to the grave much embittered and perturbed by his poverty. At one time he had been a man of considerable wealth, but his assumption of Sir Philip Sidney's financial obligations and his large expenditures for secret service had so weakened his estate that shortly before his death he was compelled to sell some property to satisfy creditors. He had willed his daughter a small annuity, and his wife the residue of his estate—after his creditors were paid—but whether there would be enough in his depleted estate to fill these bequests was then uncertain. Even worse, his papers were impounded and his body was secretly buried at night in Saint Paul's Cathedral.[20]

Soon after her father's death the Countess became pregnant. By autumn 1590, no longer able to conceal her condition, she confessed that she was secretly married to the Earl of Essex. He acted shrewdly, denying neither the marriage nor the fatherhood of Lady Frances's unborn child. Neither did he contest the Queen's indictment that the marriage lowered the dignity of the Devereux family. Instead, he contritely acknowledged all, continued to attend Court, and acted as though nothing had happened to modify his relationship with the Queen. The strategy worked well, for with little loss of royal favor, he was soon forgiven and recovered any ground he might have lost because of the Queen's displeasure.

But a different fate awaited the Countess, who was caught between Elizabeth and Essex. The jealous Queen never forgave her. Twice Frances Walsingham had snatched handsome admirers from under Elizabeth's eyes and secretly bound their wills with marriage contracts. Twice she had borne them children. Twice she had defied the royal will. Frances was not good enough; she lacked dignity and noble bearing, despite her beauty and appeal. The

20 Read, *Walsingham*, 3: 442–48.

Countess soon felt the full impact of Her Majesty's wrath. She was banished from Court and forbidden ever to set her eyes upon the Queen's person. All subsequent attempts to win royal favor and recover her lost position failed miserably. Stigmatized forever by the Queen's expressed disapproval, she confined herself in Walsingham House and waited for a more promising day.[21]

III

ROBEN DEVEREUX, Viscount Hereford, spent his earliest years with his mother in Walsingham House. Here, in the section of London known as Old Jewry, land was scarce, the streets were narrow, the air was always thick with coal smoke, and the inhabitants were anything but blue in blood or aristocratic in bearing. The magnificence of Tower Ward lay in the past; the semiluxurious houses that once graced some of the lanes were giving way to multistoried tenement houses designed to hold London's burgeoning population. Here in London's East End, where commerce reigned, stood the docks, the wharves, the naval warehouses, the Royal Customs House, Ironmonger's Hall, and Galley Row. Here, too, lived overseas merchants, grocers, artisans, and some laborers. Toward Aldgate stood Northumberland House, which was used for bowling, dicing, and unlawful gaming. The Baynings and the Knollyses, both rising mercantile families with significant political ties, lived in Tower Ward; but they proved exceptions, for the tombstones and monuments in the parish churches bore the names of few men of genteel birth.[22]

Across the street from Walsingham House stood Saint Olave's, Hart Street, the parish church where members of the Walsingham household fulfilled their religious obligations. Its records reveal that the population was motley, including many aliens of Portuguese, Italian, Spanish, and Dutch origins. Most of the parishioners earned their livelihood as tradesmen, tailors, feltmakers, silkweavers, sailors, blacksmiths, and porters. Some few lived in the decrepit almshouses near the Tower. The parish population was increasing as a result of metropolitan migration; yet nearly twice as many souls were buried as baptized. Infant mortality remained very

[21] Harrison, *Essex*, pp. 46, 253, 332.
[22] H. B. Wheatley, *Stow's Survey of London* (London: J. M. Dent and Sons, 1912), pp. 118–25.

high. The incidence of plague and pox deaths was higher than in the West End. Life in the populous wharf district, where foreigners and middle-class Englishmen mingled indiscriminately, involved risks for all ages and stations in society.[23]

Southeast of Walsingham House rose the awesome Tower of London, with its manifold functions and ghastly associations. It was the royal mint, the royal arsenal, the national archives, the royal museum, and the state prison. Inside were housed historic mementos and relics, torture machines, exotic beasts from Africa, the royal jewel box, and bears and dogs for baiting. Here royalty once lived and fought and died—some famously, some infamously—and here countless nobles awaited their fates. Outside the Tower, on the hill which sloped down toward Walsingham House, stood a large scaffold and gallows, ready for the next traitor destined to pay with his life for his crimes against the state.

In the confines of the Walsingham household young Roben spent his childhood years in an environment unbefitting his station.[24] The death of his maternal grandfather, Sir Francis Walsingham, still darkened the family circle. Although left relatively poor, Lady Walsingham maintained a fair-sized household staff for her distinguished daughter and grandson. The staff's salaries plus the normal needs of the Countess's growing family and the extraordinary entertainment of friends and relatives made the widow dependent on her creditors, Essex, and the Queen for both money and mercy.

The beautiful manor Barn Elms made existence more tolerable for the Countess and her children.[25] Picturesquely situated along the south shore of the Thames, several miles upstream from Westminster, Barn Elms afforded easy escape from the evils of metropolitan life. Although not so magnificent as the Cecil establishment at Theobalds nor so pretentious as some of the Elizabethan country

[23] This information comes from Alfred Povah, *The Annals of the Parishes of St. Olave Hart Street and All Hallows Staining* (London, 1894); and Bannerman, *Register of St. Olave Hart Street.*

[24] The Countess of Essex spent some time at Essex House, as evidenced in letters to and from Robert Sidney, but stayed at either Walsingham House or Barn Elms most of the time between 1591 and 1601. See Collins, *Letters and Memorials,* 1: 1–175; *Historical Manuscript Commission* [hereafter cited as *H. M. C.*] *De Lisle Manuscripts,* 2: 152–74; and *Calendar of State Papers Domestic* [hereafter cited as *C. S. P. Dom.*] *1596–1597,* p. 101.

[25] Read, *Walsingham,* 3: 430–33.

houses in Buckinghamshire, Barn Elms more than satisfied the needs of Lady Walsingham's coterie, and the banished Countess of Essex spent much time there.[26] She and her newborn son summered there in 1591 while Essex fought in Normandy. During the catastrophic plague of 1593, which took the lives of over ten thousand Londoners, and during the merciless smallpox epidemic of 1594, she lived at the manor with her mother and children. Again in 1595 and in 1597, Lady Walsingham's circle spent their summers at Barn Elms. Quite frequently the visitors included the Sidneys, the Talbots, Lady Penelope Rich, and Lord Mountjoy. Occasionally Essex himself went there to be with his family.

In the early days of 1592 the Countess gave birth to another child, Walter, but like countless other infants in those days, he did not survive the first month. Early death also befell Penelope, born in 1593 and buried in 1599, and Henry, who was born in 1595 and died the following year. Two other children, Frances, born in September 1599, and Dorothy, born shortly before Christmas the following year, like their elder brother were baptized in Walsingham House. Except for Essex's bastard son, Walter, Viscount Hereford remained the only potential inheritor of the earldom.[27]

Because of his father's station, Roben inherited the privileges and rights of nobility. From his birth until his father's death, Roben bore the title Viscount Hereford. When he became of age he could claim a seat in the House of Lords and could carry the family banner wherever he wished, demanding the full respect of those inferior to him. In peacetime he could bear arms to protect the weak and preserve order; in war he could expect to be granted a command and, mounted on a horse and armed with a sword, to fight the enemy. In public processions and ceremonies of state he could claim the right of precedence, which would place him near Her Royal Majesty. No one could possibly mistake him for a commoner.

The Earl of Essex, busy man of state that he was, relegated his responsibility for Roben's early education to the Countess.[28] The details of the child's earliest education in Lady Walsingham's

[26] H. M. C. De Lisle Manuscripts, 2: 152, 156, 174, 268, 288.

[27] For information about the Countess's children see Harrison, Essex, p. 333; and Josiah C. Wedgwood, Staffordshire Parliamentary History, William Salt Archaeological Society, vol. 2, pt. 1 (Stafford, 1920–22), p. 52.

[28] H. M. C. Salisbury Manuscripts, 4: 169.

household are unknown. Probably his grandmother or Elizabeth
Sidney (Sir Philip's daughter), who was six years older, taught him
from a hornbook and read the traditional nursery rhymes to him.
In all likelihood he received his first religious instruction from the
family chaplain, Lawrence Thompson, a Puritan who had served
Sir Francis for many years.[29]

Lord Hereford spent his childhood years in a social environment
dominated by women. The nurse, the personal attendants of the
Countess, and many of the household servants were women.
Masculine influences were minimal. His grandfathers were dead.
His mother, moreover, had no male kinsmen, and his only uncle,
Walter Devereux, died before Roben's first birthday. His father,
preoccupied with public affairs, still lived in Essex House and spent
most of his time at the head of military expeditions, around the
council table, or in the Presence Chamber of Her Majesty.

Viscount Hereford's initial conception of authority involved a
matriarchal sovereign who hated his mother and doted upon his
father. Women taught him to be a gentleman. Commoners schooled
him in the essential qualities of nobility. The image of his noble
father, whom he was supposed to mirror, must have appeared
blurred. Most important, he matured amidst a vicious love-hate
triangle involving his parents and Queen Elizabeth. He personally
symbolized, not merely the marital tie between his parents, but the
hatred persisting between his mother and Her Majesty. His future
was inextricably related to the complex personal relationship
between Elizabeth and Essex.

IV

MEANWHILE, the fortunes of Viscount Hereford's father rose and
fell like the action of a Greek tragedy. Despite his marriage to a
commoner and his rash activities, the Earl of Essex continued to
enjoy the Queen's patronage and support. His following in the
Court and in Parliament increased proportionately. In 1593 he was
sworn into the Privy Council; in 1596 he sailed to Spain and led

[29] See Read, *Walsingham*, 2: 261. Thompson, who had served as Sir Francis's
confidential secretary, had supported Travers in the controversy with Richard
Hooker. He was one of several Puritans in Walsingham's household. Thompson
died in 1599, the same year that young Roben was placed under the tutelage of
Sir Henry Savile.

a successful assault against the port of Cádiz; the next year he led a similar expedition to Portugal. In 1599 he commanded the English army in northern Ireland. Some of these ventures turned out to be financial and military fiascos, but he succeeded in capturing the imagination of countless Elizabethans. By patronizing poets and subsidizing essayists, he secured a good press. Essex seemed well on his way to everlasting fame, greatness, and immortality.[30]

The breach between the Queen and the Countess proved to be final, however. Try as he might, Essex could not persuade Elizabeth to relent and allow the Countess to attend Court. The climax of this situation came in 1599 when Essex himself suffered the Queen's displeasure. The Countess, hoping to aid her husband's cause as well as her own, sent a costly jewel to the spiteful sovereign, who promptly refused it. A few days later, openly defying her ban, Lady Essex went to Court to talk with Her Majesty. By appearing in an inexpensive, unbecoming black dress, which was completely incongruous with her station, the Countess irritated the Queen and shocked the gossipy peers. The Queen not only refused to grant her a royal audience but ordered her away from the Court. "My Lady Essex rises almost every Day, by Day light," wrote Rowland Whyte to Sir Robert Sidney in December 1599, "to goe to my Lord Treasurers and Sir John Fortescue; for to this Court she may not come."[31] As long as Queen Elizabeth ruled, the Countess would remain persona non grata—a relationship that could only breed mistrust, insecurity, and revenge for all concerned, including her son.

Essex's adulterous activities further strained his marriage. Stories about his amours passed from mouth to mouth. He was linked romantically with the mysterious "Mistress B." and was obliged to acknowledge the fatherhood of a son, Walter, born to Mistress Southwell and subsequently turned over to Essex's mother, the Countess of Leicester, for upbringing. Essex made love to Lady Mary Howard, one of the ladies-in-waiting, who soon incurred the Queen's rebuke, and he also courted the Viscountess Purbeck on several occasions. Ribald rumors even linked Essex with Queen Elizabeth herself.

The Countess, aware of her husband's infidelity, reciprocated by

[30] Throughout this section on the second Earl, I have relied heavily upon Harrison, *Essex*, pp. 69–210.
[31] Collins, *Letters and Memorials*, 2: 149.

accepting the attentions of Lord Richard Burke, the handsome heir of the Irish Earl of Clanricarde. Essex learned of the affair and apparently disparaged the honor and character of his rival. To defend his name and honor, Lord Burke, in turn, challenged Essex to a duel. News of this rivalry and challenge spread rapidly throughout Court circles and the City. Queen Elizabeth promptly forbade the two to duel. They refused to obey the royal command, however, and fought secretly, using the traditional armor. Essex lunged at his rival's heart, pierced his shirt, but did not draw blood. Burke wounded Essex, forced him to the ground, and could have killed him. Instead, he spared the life of his adversary and walked away the victor. Some Englishmen believed, with reason, that Essex's fall before the sword of Lord Burke was a portent of things to come.[32]

If Essex failed to protect his wife from the amorous advances of a competitor, he also failed to provide his family with economic security. Most of his lands were mortgaged. His inheritance had been meager compared to that of his social equals. His marriage portion had not lasted long. He secured from the Queen the lease on French wines, which helped his financial status, but his long-standing debts and high living consumed cash and capital alike. In 1599 he was more than twenty thousand pounds in debt. The Earl was forced to dismiss many of his servants and aides. Only the Queen stood between him and his other creditors.[33]

Essex's rivals relished the thought of his fall from favor. Older and wealthier families such as the Howards and the Talbots resented and envied his overmightiness. Powerful advisers like Sir Robert Cecil and Thomas Sackville, Lord Buckhurst, regarded Essex as a threat to their power and patronage. Sir Walter Raleigh, who had been a royal favorite with a bright future until Essex appeared on the scene, bore special animosity toward his rival and strove desperately to bring him low. He labeled Essex a tyrant and conspired with Sir Robert Cecil against him. When these individuals bound by common fears and hopes, united against their common enemy, Essex's lease on favor lessened considerably.

32 For a discussion of the Burke incident see Philip Caraman, *John Gerard, the Autobiography of an Elizabethan* (London: Longmans, Green and Company, 1951), pp. 176–79.

33 See William Murdin, *Collection of State Papers . . . Left by William Cecil, Lord Burghley*, 2 vols. (London, 1740–59), 2: 656 ff.; and *H. M. C. Salisbury Manuscripts*, 7: 283.

The decisive step which led directly to the executioner's scaffold was Essex's own doing. In 1601 the erstwhile favorite—now defeated, bankrupt, humiliated, outwitted, and outmaneuvered—attempted a palace revolt. In the early morning hours of 8 February, Essex and his dwindling faction tried to seize the Queen, secure London, and force their competitors out of their places. The attempted coup was a failure. The people of London did not rally around Essex's banner. Some of his followers confessed. The chief conspirators, caught in their own trap, gave up with little fighting, and the royal troops rounded up the rest of the traitors and sent them to the Tower and to Newgate.[34]

In the political trial which followed, Essex defended himself against his enemies. The evidence was damning, however, and he was no match for orators such as Bacon and Sir Edward Coke. Essex was condemned to die for treason. In the eleventh hour, after unsuccessfully defending his actions, he finally confessed his crimes and begged for clemency, but the confession came too late. His crime was too dangerous to go unpunished, his enemies too powerful and vengeful; the Queen could not afford to give him one more ounce of mercy. Cruel necessity ruled.[35]

On Ash Wednesday, 25 February 1601, about eight o'clock in the morning, a tall, handsome figure mounted the scaffold erected on the green near the Tower. The second Earl of Essex played the role of the gallant Christian knight to the last moment of his short life. He prayed for strength to carry him through the ordeal. He politely took off his hat, bowed before the assembled lords, and then launched into a studied speech in which he confessed his recent crimes and sins, defended himself against the charges of atheism and popery, and begged for charity and forgiveness. Just as Essex was about to remove his ou,er gown, one of the divines reminded him to grant forgiveness to his enemies. "I thank you for it," Essex said, and then turning to the spectators he announced, "I desire all the world to forgive me even as I do freely from my heart forgive all the world."[36]

After these formalities, the waiting executioner gave Essex the necessary instructions and then sought forgiveness for his forth-

[34] Harrison, *Essex*, pp. 276–93.

[35] David Jardine, *Criminal Trials*, 2 vols. (London, 1882), 1: 313–65. For Coke's role in the trial see Catherine Drinker Bowen, *The Lion and the Throne* (Boston: Little, Brown and Company, 1956), pp. 139–59.

[36] Harrison, *Essex*, pp. 315–25.

coming act. "I forgive thee with all my heart, thou are the true executioner of justice," responded Essex, after which he promptly removed his black doublet, placed it on the floor near his feet, and stood momentarily before the spectators in his scarlet waistcoat. He knelt, repeated the Lord's Prayer, and again prayed for fortitude. Finally, the Earl laid his neck on the block, saying, "Lord Jesus, into thy hands I commit my spirit," and waited for the blow. When the executioner hesitated, Essex cried, "Strike, strike." Finally, the axe fell and the head was severed from the body of Robert Devereux, the second Earl of Essex.

After the spectators left, Essex's remains were sealed in a coffin and carried into the Tower. He was buried in Saint Peter's Chapel near the grave of Anne Boleyn, Queen Elizabeth's mother. The aged Queen supposedly wept upon hearing that Essex was dead. And, if one contemporary account is reliable, his image haunted her mind long after the interment.

V

Essex's enemies reaped advantages from his death, as his followers paid dearly for supporting his cause. Sir Robert Cecil, the secretary of state, secured his relationship with the Queen and strengthened his ties with James VI of Scotland, and his cautious, pacifistic policy continued. Essex's execution opened new avenues for the Howards and the Sackvilles and gave fresh hope to by-passed courtiers such as Raleigh. On the other hand, conspirators Sir Christopher Blount, Sir Charles Danvers, Sir Gelly Meyrick, and Henry Cuffe were, like their leader, tried and put to death for treason. William Shakespeare's patron, Henry Wriothesley, Earl of Southampton, was confined indefinitely to the Tower. The remaining conspirators, including Roger Manners, the youthful Earl of Rutland, were spared but heavily fined. Some of the survivors continued to meet periodically and a few even commemorated the death of their former leader.[37]

The Countess and her children felt the full impact of Essex's eclipse and his death on the scaffold. The law treated traitors and their survivors very harshly. "Implied in the judgment is," to quote

[37] During the Christmas season of 1602 several Essexians, including Sir Robert Sidney and the Earls of Bedford, Rutland, and Pembroke, met at Sir John Harington's home. See A. L. Rowse, *An Elizabethan Garland* (London: Macmillan and Company, 1953), p. 73.

from prosecuting attorney Coke's legal handbook, "first the forfeiture of all his manors, lands, tenements, and hereditaments in fee simple or fee-tail of whomsoever they be holden. Secondly his wife to lose her dower. Thirdly, he shall lose his children for they become base and ignoble. Fourthly he shall lose his posterity, for his blood is stained and corrupted, and they cannot inherit to him or any other ancestor. . . ."[38] Soon the heavily mortgaged estates became the property of the Crown. The late Earl's library, linens, silver plate, wardrobe, and personal effects were seized by royal agents and sold to pay off outstanding debts. The Countess was left with an income so small that she became dependent upon her relatives.

During the months following the ordeal the Countess became very despondent and was acutely aware of her reliance on others. "The weight of God's finger hath been so heavy upon me," she wrote, "as I daily expected no further cumbersome to any friends or the world than in performing my last funeral duties."[39] The widow's friends and relatives rendered what assistance they could, her mother appealed to the Queen for merciful treatment, and the Countess herself pleaded with Sir Robert Cecil. These appeals apparently produced no results, and the unfortunate widow became more depressed and desperate. After Lady Walsingham sold Walsingham House, probably to help Frances, the Countess of Leicester permitted her widowed daughter-in-law to live in Essex House.

The Countess of Essex experienced the severity of insolvency. Her children, she complained, were left "without one penny for their education and maintenance."[40] Only the Queen could remit some of the forfeited estates and thus provide her with adequate means. Yet Elizabeth would not allow her an audience, so the Countess turned to her late husband's enemy. "I entreat you to intercede on my behalf to her majesty that she may graciously remit those forfeitures," she wrote Sir Robert Cecil, "without which favour my son is like never to possess one foot of his father's inheritance."[41] This appeal seems to have accomplished little, for by the summer months the Countess's financial condition was just as bad as it had been, if not worse.

[38] E. M. Tenison, *Elizabethan England*, 12 vols. (Glasgow: At the University Press, 1932–60), 12: 147.

[39] *H. M. C. Salisbury Manuscripts*, 11: 157.

[40] *Ibid.*, p. 546.

[41] *Ibid.*, p. 157.

It was the Countess's first-born son who suffered most from Essex's fall. Roben was dispossessed of his titles. His blood was deemed corrupt—stained by his father's infamy—and his name was stigmatized. He lost his aristocratic rights and privileges, the earldom of Essex, and the family estates. To redress these wrongs against her son, the Countess again appealed to Cecil for lenient treatment, reminding him that Roben "in conscience and equity deserves to bee favoured"; but this and similar pleas came to nought.[42]

VI

ON THAT MEMORABLE DAY when his father went to the scaffold, Roben was living in the household of Dr. Henry Savile, provost of Eton, where Roben had been sent two years earlier. While at Eton, Lord Hereford heard of his father's sickness, imprisonment, trial, and death. At the time of the execution the young Viscount, according to Robert Codrington, "did suddenly, and distractedly, leap out of his bed, where he was fast asleep, and to the amazement of all, he cried out, that his father was killed, his father was dead."[43]

In the days immediately following the coup several precautionary measures were taken for the disinherited youth. To prevent any foul play, Roben was taken across the Thames River to Windsor Castle and committed to the charge of Robert Bennet, dean of Windsor. In all likelihood Cecil initiated these changes, for Bennet had once been chaplain to Sir Robert's family. Savile, having corresponded with some of the conspirators, including Roben's father, was suspected of complicity, taken into custody, and questioned about his connections with the leaders of the rebellion. Until the present dangers were past, the dean of Windsor could be trusted with the son and heir of the chief conspirator.[44]

In mid-March, after the crisis was over, Roben's case came before the Privy Council. Savile had cleared himself of all suspicions and returned to Eton. Lady Walsingham had petitioned Her Majesty and Cecil about Roben's education. After receiving several letters and hearing some discussion, the Queen decided that it would be safe for her former favorite's heir to return to Eton. The dean of

---

[42] *Ibid.*, p. 547.

[43] Robert Codrington, *The Life and Death of the Illustrious Robert, Earl of Essex* (London, 1646), p. 7.

[44] *Acts of the Privy Council* [hereafter cited as *A. P. C.*] *1600–1601*, pp. 229–31.

Windsor was ordered to surrender his charge, while Savile was reminded of his great responsibility and given brief instructions relating to Roben's education.[45]

When he was ten, the boy returned to Eton to continue his education by Savile.[46] It is doubtful whether Roben realized at the time the deeper implications of the conspiracy or fully grasped the ultimate consequences of his father's execution, yet he must have noticed certain changes and wondered about their meaning. Sooner or later he must have reasoned that his noble birthright had been canceled retroactively; that he was disinherited; that the family was disgraced; and that his changed status was due, in part at least, to those who sat in high places.

Robert Devereux matured in the aura of his father's life and death. He could not hide his name. He could not forget the fortunes of his family. He could not escape the consequences of his father's fame, his follies, and his infamies. He bore the stigma of his father's political sins and personal shortcomings and, significantly, he shared much of the shame. Eventually the taint of treason might gradually diminish, perhaps even vanish completely; but until the death of the Queen, Roben remained the son of a traitor.

[45] *H. M. C. Salisbury Manuscripts*, 10: 131.
[46] *A. P. C. 1600–1601*, p. 231.

CHAPTER 2

The Prince's Companion

I

THE DEATH OF Queen Elizabeth and the accession of James I in 1603 brought fresh opportunities and new hopes to many Englishmen.[1] For Sir Robert Cecil, the late Queen's secretary of state, it meant greater power. For the Howards and some other aristocrats it meant additional honors and more patronage. For the Scottish lairds it signalized the beginnings of a new era in Anglo-Scottish relations. For Elizabeth's enemies it presented the possibility of pardon, amnesty, and, perhaps, the return of royal favor. For the relatives, friends, and followers of the late Earl of Essex the accession of James meant restoration and reconciliation. Shortly after entering his newly acquired kingdom, James released the Earl of Southampton from the Tower.[2] Before long, the pardoned Earl received both a new patent for his title and the Order of the Garter. About the same time, he secured a new license for his dramatic company, which included one William Shakespeare, playwright.

The first meeting between Roben Devereux and James I took place on 27 April 1603 near the home of Sir Oliver Cromwell. "In his journey," reported the Venetian ambassador, "his Majesty

[1] In the following four chapters, dealing with Essex during the reign of James I, I have used the following general works: *The Five Years of King James*, published in 1643 and reprinted in the *Harleian Miscellany*, 11 vols. (London, 1810), 5: 349–403; Sir Anthony Weldon, *The History of the Court and Character of King James I* (London, 1650); Arthur Wilson, *The Historie of Great Britain, being the life and reign of King James the First* (London, 1653); Thomas Frankland, *Annals of King James and Charles the First* (London, 1681); *Truth Brought to Light or the Most Remarkable Transactions of the first fourteen years of King James Reign* (London, 1692); S. R. Gardiner, *A History of England from the Accession of James I to the Outbreak of the War, 1603–1642*, 10 vols. (London, 1884); Godfrey Davies, *The Early Stuarts* (Oxford: Clarendon Press, 1937); and D. Harris Willson, *King James VI and I* (New York: Henry Holt and Company, 1956).

[2] A. L. Rowse, *Shakespeare's Southampton, Patron of Virginia* (New York: Harper and Row, 1965), p. 173.

has destined to great rewards the Earl of Southampton and Sir
Henry Neville . . . and has received the twelve-year-old son of the
Earl of Essex and taken him in his arms and kissed him, openly and
loudly declaring him the son of the most noble knight that the
English had ever begotten." [3] In a dramatic gesture the new monarch
also commissioned the youth to bear the sword before him in the
triumphal entry into London and appointed him to be the constant
companion of his eldest son, Henry, Prince of Wales.

The coronation ceremonies took place on 25 July. In a fit of glee
the Earl of Southampton, still confined to the Tower, tossed his
hat into the air and then threw it over the wall so that all the passers-
by could perceive his jubilance. His coconspirator's son, meanwhile,
attended the formal ceremonies in Cheapside. Mounted on horseback and accompanied by his uncle the Earl of Northumberland,
Roben carried the royal sword of state.[4] Immediately after the
celebration he apparently rejoined his mother at Essex House.
Before long, he and Jack Harington joined Prince Henry's Court
and lived with the heir apparent. Reconciliation with the Crown
was well under way.

Contemporaries could not possibly have missed the meaning of
these gestures.[5] Roben's father had corresponded with the Scottish
sovereign for several years and supported his claim to the English
Crown—all of which had irritated the Cecil and the Howard
factions.[6] James I realized this only too well. He also knew that the
succession question had been more closely related to the recent
conspiracy than the official accounts indicated and that Essex had
paid a high price for his actions. Thus, to repay a political debt,
to pacify the vengeful survivors, and to appease the masses who had
idolized Essex, the new monarch endeared himself to the attainted
heir.

Nor were these measures all. In July, shortly before the coronation, James restored to the disinherited youth his noble birthright,

[3] C. S. P. Venetian [hereafter cited as C. S. P. Ven.], 1603–1607, p. 24.

[4] Devereux, Lives of the Devereux, 2: 219.

[5] Lord Cobham, who was coldly received by the King, was concerned about
these actions. "I pray you," he wrote Sir Robert Cecil, "send me word whether
the King did write for young Essex to come to him." See H. M. C. Fifteenth Report,
p. 66.

[6] As early as 1589 he had corresponded with James and continued to do so
through 1600. Raleigh was another of Essex's rivals in this secret succession
diplomacy. See Willson, James I, pp. 153–58.

his titles, and his landed inheritance.[7] The aristocratic privileges and rights were once again his, and Roben rejoined the ranks of the peerage. He was now the social equal of the aged Earl of Shrewsbury, the recently named Earl of Suffolk and Lord Mountjoy, and the reinstated Earl of Arundel. To the joy of many, but the dismay of some, the earldom of Essex reappeared on the official roll of the Barons of Parliament.[8] During the first session of Parliament the House of Lords passed a bill granting complete "restitution of the Son and Two Daughters of Robert late Earl of Essex."[9]

The third marriage of the widowed Countess of Essex, to Richard Burgh the Earl of Clanricarde, took place about the same time. "Here is a common bruit that the earle of Clanricarde hath married the Lady of Essex," wrote Chamberlain, "wherewith many that wisht her well are nothing pleased."[10] Clanricarde, a handsome young nobleman about court, so closely resembled the late Earl of Essex that Queen Elizabeth had once made some advances toward him. Although an Irishman by birth, he had an English following at the Court, including several women. He had fought valiantly on the Continent, distinguished himself at the battle of Kinsdale, won favors from the late Queen, successfully sought the love of the then-married Countess of Essex, and fought a duel with Essex to avenge his honor. His marriage to Lady Essex, seemingly, merely legalized a clandestine affair.[11] It was successful, for in 1604, Sir John Davis found the couple living happily at Athlone.[12]

This Anglo-Irish match left the Countess's eldest son virtually homeless, however. His father was dead. Sir Francis and Lady Walsingham were dead. His mother went to live in Ireland with

[7] See Violet Wilson, *Society Women of Shakespeare's Time* (New York: E. P. Dutton and Company, 1925), p. 57.

[8] John Nichols, *The Progresses, processions and magnificent festivities of King James the First*, 4 vols. (London, 1828), 1: 424.

[9] *Lords Journal*, 2: 266–74.

[10] N. E. McClure, *The Letters of John Chamberlain*, 2 vols. (Philadelphia: American Philosophical Society, 1939), 1: 194 (hereafter cited as *Chamberlain's Letters*). John Manningham dated the marriage on 8 April 1603; see John Bruce, *The Diary of John Manningham*, Camden Society (London, 1868), p. 165. The Earl of Clanricarde was, according to the diarist, "a goodly personable gentleman something resembling the late Earl of Essex."

[11] Tenison, *Elizabethan England*, 12: 155.

[12] Falls, *Mountjoy*, p. 62. At the time Clanricarde was acting president of Connaught.

an Irish "papist." The Countess's English friends and relatives were extremely displeased with an alliance that brought little honor to the Devereux name. For Roben, it meant another stigma to bear. The King was so averse to the marriage that he forbade the Countess any jurisdiction over her eldest son. Instead, he made Roben a ward of the Crown.[13]

The lot of a royal ward in Jacobean England was rather unpleasant. King James, like his Tudor predecessors, continued to exploit wardship long after the feudal custom had lost its moral justification.[14] The English sovereign was, technically speaking, the legal guardian of all under aged royal tenants like Essex, and the Court of Wards handled the details and carried out the royal will. Custom permitted the Master of Wards to sell the wardship rights if he so desired or to delegate the rights and responsibilities to a relative or family friend of the child. This custom, which changed an honored responsibility into a price-exchange commodity, bred corruption and abuses of all varieties and constantly brought the Court of Wards under attack. The victims of this antiquated practice, especially the wealthy landowners and their heirs, detested the abuse, but they were generally powerless against the King and his councilors.

Since Secretary of State Cecil was also master of the Court of Wards, he became the guardian of the son of his late rival.[15] This gave him a determining voice in young Essex's education and marriage, and empowered him to administer the estates of the Devereux heir.[16] Whether Cecil exercised his guardian rights directly

[13] See McClure, *Chamberlain's Letters*, 1: 194. This is confirmed by Tenison, *Elizabethan England*, 12: 385.

[14] For an excellent analysis of the Elizabethan Court of Wards see Joel Hurstfield, *The Queen's Wards* (Cambridge: At the University Press, 1958), especially the section on Cecil's administration, pp. 297–325.

[15] It is interesting to note that Essex had named Sir Robert Cecil an executor in his will, written in 1591. See Tenison, *Elizabethan England*, 12: 149.

[16] The King's grant of restitution, presumably, nullified the forfeiture and put into effect the late Earl's will. His unalienated lands were then administered by the Court of Wards or the guardian it appointed until Roben reached his majority. In addition to these inherited lands the young Earl's estate was increased by his mother sometime after her marriage in April 1603. The new Countess of Clanricarde repurchased for her son those lands which the second Earl had mortgaged, namely, the manors of Merevale, Rosse, and Rivington. Most of the sum of £23,940 was paid to Peter Vanlore, a financier. To raise this money, the Countess sold Vanlore her jointure and lands she had recently inherited from her

or delegated them to another is not known, for the existing evidence is not conclusive; but it is certain that James I, who took a personal interest in young Essex, had a voice in his education and marriage, and that Cecil corresponded with Essex's mother and grandmother about educational matters. Presumably the diminutive secretary simply translated the royal wishes into action. Yet it is also clear that Charles Howard, the Earl of Nottingham, exercised some jurisdiction over the Devereux estates.[17] It was he who in 1608 granted Walter Bagot, Essex's steward, permission to cut down some wood on a family manor. Since this authority generally resided with the legal guardian, it would appear that Essex's was Nottingham. Perhaps Cecil sold or gave the wardship to this new-found political ally and onetime rival of the late Earl; perhaps James I had ordered Cecil to grant it to Nottingham. Whatever the case, Essex's fate as a royal ward rested in the hands of those who had tried his father for treason.

During his fifteenth year the young Earl received several honors. In April 1605 the lawyers of the Inner Temple inducted him and several of his fellow peers into their refined ranks; the assembly which granted the special admission included Sir Edward Coke, the distinguished jurist.[18] In August, Essex participated in the festivities which accompanied Prince Henry's matriculation at Oxford University.[19] Attending the week-long ceremonies were the King, the Queen, George Abbot, the vice-chancellor of the school, and a host of lesser gentlemen. On 29 August the scholars staged an

---

mother, including Barn Elms, Walsingham House, and estates in Lincolnshire and Buckinghamshire, for £24,400. This complicated transaction enabled the recently restored third Earl to recover some of the family fortune which had been lost by his father's fall. When it was time for young Essex to take his Continental tour, he borrowed on these lands from Vanlore. For these facts see Tenison, *Elizabethan England*, 12: 383.

[17] *Ibid*, p. 149. Essex had also designated the Earl of Nottingham as an executor of his will. Yet, it is also clear from the Bagot MSS, Folger Shakespeare Library, that the third Earl had some jurisdiction over his Staffordshire estates; at least he dealt with agents between 1605 and 1616 in matters pertaining to land and legal disputes.

[18] F. A. Inderwick, *A Calendar of Inner Temple Records*, 4 vols. (London, 1898), 2: 10. Among those admitted with him were the Earl of Arundel, the Earl of Oxford, the Earl of Northampton, and several of Prince Henry's personal attendants.

[19] Nichols, *Progresses*, 1: 530.

academic debate which covered several controversial questions of the day. The next day the authorities of Merton College, acting upon the request of the King, awarded young Essex the Master of Arts degree by a special warrant.

Soon after the granting of these royal favors came reconciliation with the Cecil family. Young Essex and Secretary Cecil's eldest son, Viscount Cranborne, became the closest of friends. In August they shared academic honors at Oxford University. The next month they visited the countryside around Chesterford.[20] In October their names were linked together in plans for a marriage project involving the daughters of the Earl of Suffolk.[21] About this time Essex also began corresponding with Secretary Cecil himself.[22]

Later that year, in the night hours of 4 November, Cecil and his fellow councilors uncovered a Catholic plan to blow up Parliament House. If the gunpowder plotters had succeeded, the King, the councilors, the peers, and the commoners would have been annihilated. But William Parker, Lord Monteagle, forewarned Cecil, who then caught Guy Fawkes red-handed and exposed the infamous design. The reaction was electric. Parliament was postponed until January. An anti-Catholic hysteria soon followed. The conspirators were seized, forced to confess, tried, and eventually executed. Essex's uncle the Earl of Northumberland was implicated in the plot, tried in the Star Chamber, found guilty, fined an exorbitant amount, and imprisoned in the Tower of London. Soon after, James I demanded an antipapal loyalty oath of all Englishmen. Those families whose ancestors or relatives had connections with Roman Catholicism came under suspicion.

The Howards, who fell into the last category, had reason to be fearful. From the days when Catherine Howard was Henry VIII's fifth wife, through the trials of Edward VI's reign and the successes under Mary Tudor, to the days of Queen Elizabeth, the interests of the Howards had been identified with the old faith. For this loyalty they had paid a heavy price in blood. Although Thomas, the Earl of Suffolk, and Charles, the Earl of Nottingham, had demonstrated their undivided loyalty to the English Crown by

[20] Public Record Office, State Papers 14/15 (hereafter cited as P. R. O., S. P.).

[21] *H. M. C. Seventh Report*, p. 529; and McClure, *Chamberlain's Letters*, 1: 211.

[22] *H. M. C. Salisbury Manuscripts*, 19: 34, 150, 358.

giving outstanding service against the Spanish Armada, many of the Howards still adhered to the faith of their fathers. Lord William Howard, a bookish antiquarian, had openly joined the Church of Rome, while Henry Howard, the newly created Earl of Northampton, had Spanish sympathies and many Catholic connections. To consolidate his position at Court, the Earl of Suffolk, backed by his cousin Northampton, flattered Cecil and sought alliances for his daughters.[23]

The improvement of young Essex's financial condition made the proposed match quite attractive. The King had restored to him the lands forfeited by the attainder. Essex's mother had used her inheritance to repurchase for him lands which had been sold or heavily mortgaged by the second Earl.[24] Soon after the Gunpowder Plot, the King granted Essex a remission from paying the huge fine which he had inherited.[25] About the same time, the case of Sir Robert Dudley, the bastard son of Leicester, was settled and the result was in Essex's favor. It seems that soon after the accession of James I, Dudley, backed by several aristocratic allies, sought to legitimatize himself in the courts.[26] As the only known living son of the late Earl of Leicester, he had all to gain and little to lose by appealing to King James. Dudley was opposed vigorously, quite naturally, by members of the Devereux family, including the Countess of Leicester, Essex's grandmother. In November 1605, after much controversy, the verdict was handed down by the Archbishop of Canterbury's Court of Audience and reconfirmed the bastardy of Dudley. The Leicester estates would remain in jointure and would, upon the death of the Countess, descend to

[23] Several contemporaries mentioned this possibility. In late October one reported, "There be two great marriages shall be shortly celebrated at Court, my Lord of Suffolk's daughters with my Lord of Essex and Viscount Cranborne"; see *H. M. C. Seventh Report*, p. 529.

[24] See note 16 above.

[25] *C. S. P. Dom., 1603–1610*, p. 259. The remission was for £761, due on a lease of land in Wales valued at £190. During the four years since the late Earl's death the rent on these lands evidently had not been paid to the Crown, hence the need for a remission.

[26] Dudley's attempt to legitimatize himself had been violently opposed by Lady Rich, Essex's aunt, in 1603 (see *H. M. C. Coke Manuscripts*, 1: 45) and by the Countess of Leicester in 1604 (see *H. M. C. Skrine Manuscripts*, 1: 183). After the Court of Audience handed down a negative verdict, Dudley left England for Italy.

her heirs. The legal victory carried consequential financial and political implications, for Essex, the principal heir.

II

THE EVENTS OF 5 January 1606 proved the rumormongers right, for on that day the young Earl of Essex married Lady Frances Howard, the Earl of Suffolk's enticing daughter. At the ceremony, solemnized in the royal chapel at Whitehall, King James gave the bride away. James Montagu, dean of the chapel, officiated. The bridegroom, who "carried himself very gravely and gracefully as if he were of his father's age," afterwards received numerous gifts, including plate, jewels, and money, valued at more than four thousand pounds.[27] From his future father-in-law he received a fair-sized dowry in land.

The bride, though only thirteen, was a prize that many ambitious men about Court had hoped to win. Contemporary artists portrayed her as a fair-complexioned, well-proportioned girl with delicate features. She followed the latest fashions, wearing extremely low-necked gowns, lace, jewelry, and starched collars. She possessed "the best nature and sweetest disposition of all her father's children," according to one friendly commentator.[28] More critical observers considered her a flirt—a mischievous, changeable minx capable of much iniquity. Both friend and foe praised her beauty, however.

Lady Frances came from an old, illustrious Norfolk family whose members had served English kings for centuries and had secured several titles, claims to high offices, and lands throughout England. Her father, the Earl of Suffolk and Lord Chamberlain to James, had distinguished himself against the Spanish Armada.[29] He had competed with Essex's father for royal favor and openly opposed him on many occasions. Howard had recently allied himself with the Cecil faction, passed judgment on his rival in the

[27] Godfrey Goodman, *The Court of James the First*, 2 vols. (London, 1839), 2: 124–26; and E. F. Rimbault, *The old cheque-book of the Chapel royal from 1561–1714*, Camden Society (London, 1872), p. 161.

[28] See Devereux, *Lives of the Devereux*, 2: 139. Frances Howard was celebrated by Chapman in his *Andromeda* as a beauty and in Samuel Daniel's *Tithy's Festival* as a sea nymph. For a biographical treatment see Edward Le Comte, *The Notorious Lady Essex* (New York: Dial Press, 1969).

[29] Willson, *James I*, pp. 175–78.

conspiracy trial of 1601, and helped engineer both the Scottish succession and the Spanish peace. The Countess of Suffolk, like her husband, was very influential in the Court circles around the King and Queen Anne. Extremely ambitious, unscrupulous, and avaricious, she used her marriageable daughters to enhance her position in Jacobean society. She spotted the promising attendants, the youthful royal favorites whom James I loved to reward, and sought to marry them to her offspring. According to some sources, she promoted the match between Frances and young Essex.

After the religious ceremony, the Court witnessed one of the most magnificent revels yet seen in the Banqueting Hall. Little cost was spared. Some of the best artists in the land combined their talents to entertain the celebrants with a Court masque. Playwright Ben Jonson wrote the libretto, architect Inigo Jones provided the decor, Alphonso Ferrabasco composed the choral parts, and Thomas Giles directed the choreography. Unity in its manifold forms was the underlying theme of the intricate and highly symbolic pageant, entitled *Hymenaei*.[30] The long performance of the masque of union, as it was called, was followed by other festivities.

These harmonious activities coincided with those of Twelfth Night. To crown the festivities of the Yuletide season and complete the wedding celebration, the guests reassembled in the Banqueting Hall on 6 January for revels known as "The Barriers." This fete, which gave the members of the Court another opportunity to display their skills and trappings, was in reality an elaborate pageant modeled after the outmoded tournament of chivalry. "The Barriers" permitted the young, spirited courtiers to channel their chivalrous instincts into a harmless dramatic exercise accompanied by family insignias, arms, and other vestiges of medieval warfare.

King James, of course, fostered the marrriage that united Essex with a member of the House of Howard, and the Countess of Leicester was very pleased with the match.[31] Domestic peace

---

[30] The account of the wedding festivities is garnered from D. J. Gordon, "Hymenaei: Ben Jonson's Masque of Union," *Journal of the Warburg and Courtauld Institutes* 8 (London, 1945): 107 ff.; James Lees-Milne, *The Age of Inigo Jones* (London: B. T. Batsford, Ltd., 1953), pp. 27–30; and Ben Jonson's *Hymenaei* in C. H. Herford and Percy and Evelyn Simpson, *Ben Jonson*, 11 vols. (Oxford: Clarendon Press, 1941), 7: 203–42.

[31] Edmund Lodge, *Illustrations of British History*, 3 vols. (London, 1791), 3: 281.

demanded the intermarriage of opposing factions. If the personal union of the crowns of England and Scotland could bring tranquility to the blood-stained borderlands between the two peoples, so the marriage union of rival families might ensure the disappearance of factional strife. From the viewpoint of the Crown, then, the Devereux-Howard match represented sound statesmanship.

Personal favors and material rewards followed royal approval.[32] For a wedding gift James I gave Essex gold and silver valued at nearly one thousand pounds. Within a month the sovereign directed the tax farmer of the port of London to restore an annuity as well as all arrears to the bearer of the Essex title. Later in the year Essex and his new brother-in-law, Lord Theophilus Howard, heir to the earldom of Suffolk, received joint jurisdiction over the office of the steward of Welsh lands.

Secretary Cecil, shrewd and shifty, also stood to gain by the match. He perceived that James I thought well of young Essex and the survivors of the Essex conspiracy. At the same time Sir Robert knew only too well that the omnipotent House of Howard stood high in royal esteem. To ensure his position among both rival factions and at the same time to forestall any political revenge, he matched his son, Lord Cranborne, and Essex to daughters of the Lord Chamberlain. "The object," according to the perceptive Venetian ambassador, "is to reconcile the Earl of Essex to Lord Salisbury if possible. Essex is but little the friend of Salisbury, who is the sole and governing cause of the late Earl's execution." [33]

The teen-age couple had no choice or voice in the match. They were innocent pawns in the palms of their elders. Essex's maternal and paternal relations tried to look after his interests, but who would listen to his mother, presently married to an Irish Catholic; his aunt Lady Penelope Rich; or his uncle the Earl of Northumberland, recently incarcerated for complicity in the Gunpowder Conspiracy? Who, moreover, dared dispute the desires of James I and the decisions of Cecil? So, with little or no recourse, young Essex was married to the beauty from an enemy house. He appears to have accepted his fate stoically.

Tradition intervened at this point, however, and checked the expedience of the matchmakers and challenged the exigencies of

[32] See *C. S. P. Dom., 1603–1610*, p. 322; and *H. M. C. Salisbury Manuscripts*, 18: 53.

[33] *C. S. P. Ven., 1603–1607*, p. 308.

the moment. The couple, though matched and united by vows exchanged in the King's chapel, were forbidden to live as husband and wife until they were older and more mature. Lady Frances must learn more about the personal duties of a wife and the responsibilities of motherhood. Essex had to complete his studies and round out his education with a Continental tour before claiming his bride and consummating the marriage.

III

THE EDUCATION OF the third Earl of Essex concerned many Englishmen, including his mother and his father's friends, clerics and scholars, princes and kings; but the manifold forces and influences which molded his character and prepared him for his social role can be conveniently symbolized by a trinity of prominent figures, each bearing the name Henry. One Henry, a savant, contributed a Christian home, discipline, and an intellectual foundation based on the classics. Through the second, a prince, Essex was introduced to Court politics, intrigue, the art of patronage, the social graces, luxurious living, aristocratic recreations, unorthodox religious views, and connections with prominent political leaders. Associations with a foreign king named Henry exposed Essex to a wider political world, Continental manners and culture, cosmopolitanism, and the intricacies of international society and entangling alliances.

Essex commenced his formal education in 1599 when his father placed him, at the age of eight, in Eton College. There he enjoyed privileges consistent with his station and affluence. He was not obliged to room and dine with the poorer scholars, for whom the college was originally chartered, or with the common students. Nor did he have to learn his Latin from an unknown or mediocre fellow. Rather, he lived with and learned from Eton's distinguished provost, Henry Savile.[34]

[34] See Sir Wasey Sterry, *The Eton College Register*, 2 vols. (Eton: Spottiswoode, Ballantyne and Company, 1943), 1: 102; and Edward S. Creasy, *Memoirs of Eminent Etonians*, 2 vols. (London, 1850), 1: 102–10, for Essex's years at Eton. Both authors erroneously claim that the young heir first went to Eton in 1601, after his father's execution, at the behest of the Privy Council; but it is clear that he went earlier, presumably when his father was in Ireland, and was sent back by the Privy Council in 1601.

Elizabethans regarded Dr. Savile as the living image of the "perfect scholar."[35] "He was so sedulous at his study," one contemporary noted, "that his lady thereby thought herself neglected."[36] The Queen, recognizing his intellectual stature and liking his personality, commissioned Savile her Greek tutor and eventually the official Latin secretary. In international intellectual circles, moreover, he enjoyed a reputation which no contemporary could equal. Savile's interests and achievements were many and varied. He translated the Gospels from Greek into English, translated and annotated the *History* of Tacitus, published an edition of Euclid's *Geometry*, and collected the writings of ancient English historians for publication. During the years that young Essex lived with him, Savile wrote a treatise on the Roman military system.[37] The learned provost also lectured on diverse subjects: politics, history, astronomy, geometry, and Greek.

Savile governed Eton as an autocrat would. Order, conformity, regularity, propriety, decorum, and rigor were his standards for himself and his students. "He was a very severe governor," according to John Aubrey, the gossipy collector of lives, "the scholars hated him for his austerity."[38] Eton still clung to many of the austere medieval customs that had characterized monastic education.[39] The students rose at five o'clock in the morning and had prayers read in school by an usher. From seven to nine, under the direction of the headmaster, the students recited. After an hour's recess, there was chapel, followed by dinner at eleven. Classes from twelve to three. An hour of play. Lessons again. Supper at five. Study and class preparations from six to eight, followed by beer and bread. Latin and Greek classics, of course, dominated the entire curriculum. The masters and ushers lectured from Latin authors, including Caesar, Cicero, Terence, Sallust, Horace, Martial, Ovid, Vergil, and Lucian. At eight o'clock all the students retired, "pouring out prayers."

[35] See *DNB*, 17: 856; and Creasy, *Eminent Etonians*, 1: 52.

[36] Quoted in Bernard W. Henderson, *Merton College* (London, 1899), p. 99.

[37] This was edited by Sir Walter Scott and incorporated into his edition of *Somers' Tracts*, 13 vols. (London, 1809–15), 1: 55–61.

[38] Andrew Clark, *Aubrey's Brief Lives*, 2 vols. (Oxford, 1890), 1: 214.

[39] See Christopher Hussey, *Eton College* (London: Country Life Press, 1952); and M. H. M. MacKinnon, "School Books Used at Eton College about 1600," *Journal of English and Germanic Philology* 66 (1957): 428–33.

In January 1602, Dr. Savile returned to Oxford University, where he resumed his duties as warden of Merton College, the oldest of the colleges there.[40] Though relatively small, Merton possessed a rich academic tradition, numbering among its alumni Duns Scotus, philosopher; John Wycliffe, scholar and heretic; and Bishop John Hooper, a Marian martyr. Savile reformed Merton along several lines: he was more tolerant of Puritanism and the "New Learning" than most of his academic peers and introduced geometry into the curriculum, established a chair for the advancement of science, updated the old statutes, and promoted a new building program.[41]

The Devereux heir, at that time disinherited, was taken to Oxford by his distinguished mentor. There on 2 January 1602 he signed the subscription book of the university register and, presumably, took the customary Oath of Supremacy.[42] He matriculated as a commoner, because of his attainted title, but he continued to enjoy the privileges and rights of an aristocrat. He boarded in the Warden's Lodge and worshipped in a special pew in the age-old Chapel of Saint John the Baptist. It is not clear whether he began studying toward the traditional Bachelor of Arts degree, which required mastery of Latin grammar, rhetoric, dialectic, arithmetic, and music, or whether, under the tutelage of Savile, he began reading toward the Master of Arts. Whatever the case, Merton College granted him a master's degree in the summer of 1605, when Prince Henry matriculated at Oxford.[43]

Little is known of Essex's life at Merton. Perhaps he attended the lectures of John Hales, a promising Greek scholar recently brought to Merton, or perhaps he listened to the geometry lectures delivered by Savile. The youth was assigned a special tutor, John King, who came from East Anglia. A Merton-educated man, King instructed Essex for several years and appears to have traveled to the Continent with him.[44] No record remains telling about King's religious

[40] Henderson, *Merton*, especially pp. 95–98.

[41] Mark H. Curtis, *Oxford and Cambridge in Transition 1558–1642* (Oxford: Clarendon Press, 1959), pp. 233–35.

[42] See Joseph Foster, *Alumni Oxonienses*, 4 vols. (Oxford, 1891–92), 1: 236, 399.

[43] *Ibid.*

[44] *Ibid.*, 2: 852. He was subsequently rector of Stourton, Wiltshire; canon of Westminster; and canon of Windsor. He died in 1638 and was buried at Saint George's Chapel in Windsor.

beliefs or political views. Of his popularity a contemporary noted: "In the Universitie he spent his time, where he got both admiration, love and learning."[45]

Like many of his peers, Essex seems to have preferred the stag hunt to the dusty tomes in the Merton College library. He possessed physical prowess, according to Codrington, and excelled in riding, hunting, and jousting and other military games.[46] He conjugated his Latin and recited and profited from doing so, but he learned out of compulsion rather than delight. He fled from his studies rather than to them. Young Essex preferred action to reflection. His heroes were soldiers, not scholars.

IV

A COLORFUL CANVAS, very likely painted at the King's command, confirms the foregoing verbal speculation. Robert Peake, an artist who thrived on the commissions of posterity-conscious Englishmen, portrays the Prince of Wales, sword in hand and dressed in a decorative hunting garb, standing over a slain stag. His mount, a hunting dog, and an attendant are clustered behind him. To the Prince's right, young Essex, bareheaded and clothed in the conventional costume of the chase, is kneeling beside a dead "reined deer," the popular symbol of Elizabeth's Essex. He is grasping the large pointed antlers. Except for a slight, stoic smile on his upturned face, he appears mute, emotionless. His eyes are fixed on the naked sword which Prince Henry is replacing in his scabbard.[47]

Essex, though older by two years, was chosen by James I to be the constant companion of his son and heir apparent. The young men lived in the same household, shared some tutors and attendants, and corresponded. Together they dined, conversed, hunted, and played tennis. To fulfill his duties as the heir apparent's "eternal companion," Essex was compelled to leave the household of Dr. Savile and assume his place in the peripatetic retinue of Prince

---

[45] See Gervase Markham, *Honour in his Perfection* (London, 1624); and Tenison, *Elizabethan England*, 12: 527.

[46] Codrington, *Life and Death*, p. 8.

[47] This painting, part of the Royal Collection at Hampton Court Palace, is reprinted by Tenison in *Elizabethan England*, 12: 384. For information about Robert Peake see Roy Strong, "Elizabethan Painting: An Approach through Inscription—I. Robert Peake the Elder," *Burlington Magazine* 105 (1963): 53–58.

Henry.[48] This change, however desirable and opportune, neither freed him from his Latin conjugations nor allowed him to abandon his books even if he so wished; on the contrary, he was obliged to conform to the rigorous educational conventions and Court customs, for the Prince's coterie was in reality a royal academy designed to prepare him and his noble companions for their future roles and responsibilities. Though small and relatively unpretentious at first, the courtly college expanded rapidly.[49] Socially minded ladies and politically minded lords clamored to secure a place for their sons in the unique institution. A shadow Court, modeled after the royal one, soon blossomed into existence. Gentlemen knights by the score won honorary places in the entourage. A detailed body of rules with minute directions and complicated orders became the law of the Prince's attendants. There were morning prayers, daily confessions, weekly lectures, and monthly communions. Rules were established for the privy chamber and the mock presence chamber.

To carry out this educational experiment, James I called upon some of the most talented men in England and Scotland. He named Sir Thomas Chaloner, an able and experienced courtier, the governor, and Adam Newton the principal tutor. A native of Scotland, Newton had studied at Glasgow College under Andrew Melville, taught Greek in a French Huguenot school, and lectured at the University of Edinburgh.[50] Although inclined toward the Calvinistic theology and the Presbyterian system of church government of his teacher, Newton compromised with the Anglican establishment. Preferment and rewards were soon his. James I named him dean of Durham in 1605.

Under Governor Chaloner's careful guidance the princely academy also attracted other celebrities.[51] John Florio, the Anglicized Italian who translated Montaigne's *Essays* into English and won the support of Shakespeare's patron, Southampton, offered

[48] In October 1604, James I discharged Prince Henry's household and ordered him and Essex to remain at Court together. See *H. M. C. De Lisle Manuscripts*, 3: 138. "Prince Henry was pleased to be very conversant and familiar with him," wrote Codrington in *Life and Death* (p. 8), "being near unto him in age, but more near in affection than years."

[49] See E. C. Wilson, *Prince Henry and English Literature* (Ithaca: Cornell University Press, 1946), especially pp. 19 ff.; and Thomas Birch, *The Life of Henry Prince of Wales* (London, 1760), especially pp. 322–26.

[50] *DNB*, 14: 364.

[51] Wilson, *Prince Henry*, p. 25.

instruction in Italian and French. James Cleland, Scottish author and teacher, provided the courtly college with pedagogical principles in his *Institution of a Young Noble Man.* England's most famed contemporary composer Dr. John Bull contributed his musical talents to the Court. Thomas Giles taught dancing; Nicholas Villiard, defense and combat; Sir Robert Douglas and M. St. Antoine, horsemanship; and John Reynolds, gunnery. Also attached to the Court were playright Samuel Daniel; Sir David Murray, a popular Scottish poet; Edward Wright, navigator and mathematician; and surveyor and architect Inigo Jones.

Life in the princely academy contrasted sharply with Essex's earlier experiences at Walsingham House and Eton. The Court migrated constantly—from Saint James's Palace in London to Nonesuch, Winchester, Windsor Castle, Oatlands, and Richmond—and life in this masculine environment moved at a fast pace. There were feasts without end, dances, masques, and plays. More vigorous recreations included riding, foxhunting, hawking, cockfighting, bearbaiting, and military games designed to prepare the participants for heroic action in war. Young Essex, however, preferred the chase. "He would seldom fail to be amongst the foremost at the fall of the stag," Codrington wrote.[52] From equerries such as St. Antoine, who was Prince Henry's personal riding master, and John Alexander, the young Earl acquired a knowledge of horsemanship and a love of "martial exercises." According to Gervase Markham, "few horsemen in the Kingdome (the Gentlemen who taught him excepted) did ride better, valianter, or with more discretion and judgment."[53] Essex soon became a living symbol for the growing legend about his father.

Several contemporaries also began to proffer advice to Essex and regard him as a patron. Scottish educator James Cleland dedicated part of his *Institution* to him. Essex, on the other hand, introduced Joseph Hall, the popular satirist, eloquent preacher, and Puritan sympathizer, into royal circles. In 1607, while the Prince's Court was at Richmond, Essex helped arrange for the pulpit appearances of Hall, whose *Meditations* were already highly esteemed.[54] Chaplain Hall, in turn, dedicated one of his early

[52] *Life and Death,* p. 8.

[53] *Honour in his Perfection,* p. 32.

[54] See Joseph Hall, *Works,* ed. Peter Hall, 12 vols. (Oxford, 1837–39), 7: 146 ff.

books, *Solomon's Politics or Commonwealth*, to the Earl of Essex.[55] In this handbook, filled with hundreds of Biblical quotations, the learned divine outlined his political and economic ideals, emphasizing the ethical basis of society and calling for the application of Christian principles in politics. Monarchs should be just and merciful, councilors wise and pious, courtiers discreet and diligent, subjects reverent and obedient. Whether or not the young dedicatee read the book and digested the truths therein one cannot say, of course, but he appears to have sympathized with the popular preacher.

As the time drew near for Essex to complete his formal education by taking the traditional Continental tour, Hall honored his would-be patron with a literary epistle entitled "Advice for his Travels."[56] "Gain wisdom and enrich yourself through observation," Hall suggested, and "for God's sake, my Lord, whatever you gain, lose nothing of the truth: remit nothing of your love and piety of God, of your favour and zeal to religion . . . I need not tell you the eyes of the world are much upon you; . . . If your virtues shall be eminent like your father's, you cannot hide yourself, but the world will see you; and force upon you applause and admiration, in spite of modesty: but, if you shall come short in these, your father's perfection shall be your blemish."

V

Armed with these words of admonition and advice, in the summer of 1607 the Earl of Essex boarded a Continent-bound packet and commenced his grand tour. In the course of his peregrinations he visited France, Germany, and the Low Countries but cautiously avoided the Catholic countries of southern Europe. To finance the trip, Essex borrowed money at a high rate of interest from Peter Vanlore, a Dutch lender whose clientele included many aristocrats.[57] Essex's entourage included St. Antoine, John King, and several domestic attendants. There had been a move to place Dudley Carleton, an agent of the Earl of Northumberland, in charge of the

---

[55] *Ibid.*

[56] *Ibid.* Cleland also rendered travel advice in Chapter Six of his *Institution of a Young Noble Man* (London, 1607).

[57] Tenison, *Elizabethan England*, 12: 383.

touring party.[58] When Carleton decided to stay in England and marry Savile's daughter, the task fell to St. Antoine,[59] who proved exceptionally well equipped for the responsibility. A native of France, he knew the language, the national customs, and the Court *mores*. Essex must have applauded the choice.

In France, his first stopover, Essex received a friendly welcome.[60] Upon his arrival in Paris, Essex was greeted by Sir George Carew, the English ambassador, who was negotiating with Henry IV for a triangular alliance between France, England, and Holland.[61] Onetime lawyer, author, and follower of Elizabeth's Essex, Carew made arrangements for an audience with Henry IV. The event took place on 25 November 1607 in the Louvre. Carew made the presentation. The French monarch delivered a short eulogistic speech to which Essex responded in excellent French. "For his manner," commented Carew, "the princes and noblemen said to those that came with me, *il a bonne façon, il sent son françois*, which in their understanding is the greatest commendation that can be given and the top of pefection." [62]

In April 1608, Henry IV invited Essex to join him at Fontaine-bleau Palace, the castlelike edifice which the King was in the process of transforming into the most grandiose structure in France. At the very time of Essex's visit, Henry was busy supervising con-struction of the Grand Canal. In the palace which symbolized the triumphs of the Bourbons over their antagonists in the bloody reli-gious conflicts, young Essex dined with the Continental champion of absolute monarchy. Here, assisted by St. Antoine, Essex acquired firsthand knowledge of Franch finesse, manners, and *bienséance*. In the immense Forest of Fontainebleau nearby, the French monarch and the English Earl rode and hunted side by side.[63]

In May 1608 the Earl of Essex left the French Court and jour-neyed southward toward those parts of France that English sover-eigns had ruled during the Middle Ages. He passed through

[58] P. R. O., S. P. 14/26.

[59] See C. H. Firth, *The Life of William Cavendish, Duke of Newcastle* (London: G. Routledge and Sons, 1907), p. 105. Newcastle was one of St. Antoine's students.

[60] See John Walter Stoye, *English Travellers Abroad, 1604–1667* (London: Jonathan Cape, 1952), pp. 46–48.

[61] Birch, *Henry Prince of Wales*, pp. 104–106.

[62] Stoye, *English Travellers*, p. 47.

[63] *Ibid.*

Touraine, a province where many English knights had fought and died in the Hundred Years' War, and stopped over at Orléans and Montreuil. From the last-named town, known for its fortress-like chateau, Essex dutifully penned a letter to Prince Henry. "Most Gracious Prince," he wrote, "I do in these lines present my humblest duties to your highness. Being now entered into my travels, and intending the end thereof to attain true knowledge and to better my experience, I hope God will so bless me in my endeavors, as that I shall return an acceptable servant to your Highness." [64] This pledge of loyalty and devotion was the first of several communications addressed to the heir apparent.

Essex stayed in the Loire Basin the summer and autumn of 1608. He spent much time at the Chateau of Blois, the magnificent castle-palace associated with Joan of Arc, Francis I, Catherine de Medici, and Henry III. Before returning to his homeland, Essex spent several weeks in the Low Countries. Here he met Prince Maurice of Nassau; the famed Dutch warrior, who fulfilled William the Silent's dream of an independent Dutch nation, entertained Essex royally that November. [65] At Middleburg he was greeted and feasted by the all-important Merchant's Adventurers, who held a court in the Zeeland city. In The Hague he was entertained by Sir Ralph Winwood, England's special ambassador to the Estates General of Holland, who had recently signed a treaty between the two nations.

Essex's Continental tour undoubtedly reinforced many prejudices, particularly those relating to religion and foreign policy; but at the same time it afforded him more wisdom of the world, greater understanding of foreign peoples, new international friends and connections, and a more cosmopolitan outlook. Precisely what he contributed to the Anglo-French entente of 1609 is uncertain, but very likely his presence in the French Court and his stag hunts with the French monarch made the task of Sir George Carew somewhat easier. Throughout his travels young Essex kept in touch with his friends and relatives in England. He corresponded with Prince Henry and wrote several obsequious letters to Secretary of State Cecil, then the Earl of Salisbury. [66] If he wrote his bride, the letters have not survived. Shortly before returning to England,

[64] Devereux, *Lives of the Devereux*, 2: 233–34.
[65] *H. M. C. De Lisle Manuscripts*, 4: 68.
[66] *H. M. C. Salisbury Manuscripts*, 19: 34, 150, 358.

however, he sent his father-in-law,• the Earl of Suffolk, some wild-boar meat from Flushing.[67]

VI

IN THE EARLY DAYS of 1609, upon returning from the Continent, young Essex prepared to claim his bride of several years and assume his place in the Court of King James. Essex's prospects were indeed enviable. His connections with the King, who still felt amicable toward him, bore fruit. Not very long after Essex's return James I granted him three thousand pounds in payment for claims made by the second Earl against Queen Elizabeth.[68] Very likely the youth's association with the heir apparent would in due time give Essex a political place. His alliance with the Howards might benefit him as well as the public. The gods seemed to smile kindly upon the teen-aged noble.

Before long, however, Essex found himself plagued with several reverses and misfortunes. Nature struck the first blow. Shortly after his return from the Continent, the young Earl contracted smallpox, the much-dreaded contagion for which there were no preventive measures and certainly no antidotes to the after effects. He never completely recovered from those effects, for like most other survivors, he was left with a permanently disfigured face. This the Austrian ambassador, who saw him several years later, noted as a distinguishing feature: "*Le Conte d'Essex est de moyenne stature: un peu maigre cheveus noirs: sans barbe: la face un peu gastee de petites verroles: age, de vingt trois ans.*"[69]

Essex appears also to have suffered a psychological reaction to the dreadful disease. After recovering, he assumed a less active and conspicuous role in the social circles of England. He seems to have shunned the gay gatherings, the colorful masques, the

[67] *H. M. C. De Lisle Manuscripts*, 4: 70–72.

[68] *C. S. P. Dom., 1603–1610*, p. 654. The date here is 10 December 1610. However, Frederick Devon, *Issues of the Exchequer* (London, 1836), p. 310, lists the date as 24 December 1611. In either case the result was the same: Essex received an unanticipated windfall of three thousand pounds.

[69] Cited in Devereux, *Lives of the Devereux*, 2: 251. In his *Historie*, p. 56, Arthur Wilson wrote, "A most violent disease of a poysonous nature, imputed to, but far transcending the small pox, seized on the Earl of Essex." The following year Essex was stricken with distemper, according to William Wingfield's letter of 23 March 1610 in the Bagot MSS, Folger Shakespeare Library.

elaborate ceremonials, and numerous feasts. He even seems to have boycotted the tiltings and joustings. Perhaps he deliberately avoided the Court out of shame or from fear that he would be snubbed because of his scarred face, or perhaps he simply put into practice the warnings of his grandfather about the courtier's avenue to greatness. It is also possible that he merely preferred other company and a different type of life while preparing to assume his majority status.

This much, however, is certain: Essex emerged from his teens a man's man. He did not return to England with the affectations and mannerisms of a fawning favorite and did not display the finesse of a flatterer or the smooth policy of the perfect courtier. He was not a Raleigh or a Sidney, nor did he pretend to be. While favorites such as Sir Robert Carr and courtiers like the Earl of Worcester dominated the mixed gatherings of Court society, Essex turned his attention to country pleasures and manly recreations. He befriended the soldiers,[70] hobnobbed with adventure-seeking gallants, and associated with those who loved the chase and preferred to settle disputes with swords. On one occasion Essex opened his chamber in Whitehall to a card game.[71] In the midst of the play a verbal dispute arose between James Steward, a relative of the King, and Sir George Wharton, the son of Lord Wharton. Harsh words led to sharp blows, blows to drawn daggers, daggers to a public duel in Islington Field. The same coach which took the disputants to the field soon carried two dead bodies back to the City.

On another occasion Essex himself quarreled with Philip Herbert, the Earl of Montgomery, one of James I's cronies.[72] The two men apparently fought over a petty matter while hunting with the King at Woodstock. Essex, in fact, nearly slew his King's hunting companion. When Essex's friend William Browne heard of the dispute, he warned, "God turn this ill fortune from your house."[73] Fortunately, Essex and Montgomery resolved their differences and again became friends.

[70] In 1609, returning from his travels, he recommended Captain Michael Everarde to his father-in-law for a promotion. See *H. M. C. Buccleuch Manuscripts*, 1: 79.

[71] *H. M. C. Downshire Manuscripts*, 2: 182–85.

[72] *Ibid.*, p. 353.

[73] *H. M. C. De Lisle Manuscripts*, 4: 226. Within six weeks Essex was involved in another argument, this time with Sir John Grey, a royal dependent. See *H. M. C. Downshire Manuscripts*, 2: 370.

VII

SOMETIME after his eighteenth birthday Essex began to live with his wife. He loved her, a contemporary noted, "with an extraordinary affection, having a gentle, mild and courteous disposition, as might win upon the roughest natures."[74] Sometimes they lived at their specially assigned suite in Whitehall Palace.[75] Other times the couple stayed at Durham Palace, the magnificent structure once among the Sidney family holdings, or at Salisbury House, the city residence of the Cecils. They also visited Greenwich Palace, where James I loved to hunt in the well-stocked deer park. Occasionally they progressed westward to both Kensington and Hampton Court.

The couple generally spent their summers in the country. Sometimes they summered at Audley End, the ostentatious mansion situated along the River Cam near Saffron Walden in Essex, the favorite meeting place of the Howard family. Along the banks of the Thames at Caversham Lodge, the colorful red-brick country estate of the Knollys family, they enjoyed the hospitality of Lord Knollys (one of Essex's cousins), the ambitious treasurer of the royal household and a Privy Councilor. They also visited the aged Countess of Leicester, Essex's paternal grandmother, who lived at Drayton Basset, a pleasant Warwickshire manor house which she had inherited from her famous husband.

The royal Court, meanwhile, watched and waited for the Countess to announce the coming of an heir. But the announcement never came. Tongues began to wag about the fate of the marriage. Rumors circulated about the couple: the Countess did not love her husband; in fact, she hated him; she wanted a separation; she was trying to poison him; she really loved the new royal favorite, Sir Robert Carr, and wanted to marry him; the Earl of Essex was a cuckold, an impotent one at that. Some of the rumors were true, some false, some half true—but the whole truth remained hidden behind closed chamber doors.

[74] From Fulke Greville's *The Secret History of the Reign of James I*, edited by J. O. Halliwell-Phillipps and included in *The Autobiography and correspondence of Sir Simonds D'Ewes during the reigns of James I and Charles I*, 2 vols. (London, 1845), 2: 333.

[75] The following information has been garnered from the annulment proceedings in William Cobbett, *State Trials*, 34 vols. (London, 1809–28), 2: 786–861. For a full, but semipopular, account see Le Comte, *Lady Essex*, pp. 33–57.

Gradually, though, the facts about the strained relationship between Essex and his spouse came to be known.[76] The Countess shared her suite with her husband, but she denied him her bed; she flatly refused to consummate the marriage which had been forced upon her. Some claimed she could not tolerate her husband's scarred face. Some claimed her mind had been poisoned against Essex by the Earl of Northampton. Others contended that, an experienced coquette, she had tasted fruits of forbidden love and found them sweeter than the bitter fruits of a forced marriage. Whatever the reason, the result remained the same: she shunned Essex and tried to avoid his company. Once she escaped to Audley End, but the Earl soon followed her. She grew to hate him and detest his presence. The royally planned union, originally designed to promote peace between the rival Court factions, now seemed to have the opposite effect on the principals.

There were other factors. The Countess, dissatisfied with her husband, turned to others. Prince Henry, with whom she danced and flirted, responded to her coquetries. In the opinion of one contemporary, he gave her only a "loving glance"; another thought that he made a direct advance.[77] To Sir Simonds D'Ewes, the Puritan diarist, the Countess of Essex, encouraged by the ambitious Northampton, tempted the Prince and "prostituted herself to him, who reaped the first fruits of her virginity."[78] The Countess also flirted with Sir Robert Carr, whose fortunes increased by the day.[79] This gambit, however, brought her affair with the Prince to an abrupt end. Henry, discovering that the Countess's loyalty shifted like a weather vane, flatly rejected subsequent advances and even publicly slighted her on one occasion, when the Countess dropped her glove while dancing. A misguided but obliging soul picked it up and presented it to Prince Henry, thereby hoping to win favor. The heir apparent refused to accept the glove, however, remarking satirically, "It was stretched by another," obviously alluding to the royal favorite, Sir Robert.[80]

These triangular affairs also jeopardized the close personal

---

[76] For some of these rumors see *Truth Brought to Light*, pp. 11–12.

[77] See White Kennett, *A Complete History of England*, 3 vols. (London, 1706), 2: 686.

[78] D'Ewes, *Autobiography*, 2: 90.

[79] McClure, *Chamberlain's Letters*, 1: 377.

[80] Wilson, *Historie*, p. 95.

relationship between the heir apparent and the jealous Earl. It was an incident on the tennis court, however, which precipitated a falling out between them. While they were playing tennis one morning, a vigorous argument broke out between the two spirited youths when, in a fit of anger, the Prince supposedly impugned the integrity of his opponent by dubbing him "the son of a traitor," a phrase which the code of honor deemed duelworthy. The maligned Earl, "full of fire and courage," struck the Prince on the head with his tennis racket. The blow, unfortunately, drew blood. When James I learned of the incident, he immediately assumed the role of a Solomon, examined the evidence, and attempted to straighten out the difficulties through arbitration. He pardoned Essex without any punishment. He then admonished his son: "He who did strike him then, would be sure, with more violent blows, to strike his enemy in times to come." [81]

About this time Essex appealed to his father-in-law, the Earl of Suffolk, and asked him to exert his authority over the obstinate Countess. Suffolk, undoubtedly fearful of scandal and its consequences, concurred with Essex. "The Father," Arthur Wilson pointed out, "made use of his Paternal Power to reduce his daughter to the obedience of a Wife." [82] Suffolk was assisted, moreover, by his wife and by his son, William Howard: all three tried to induce the Countess to consummate the marriage—for their good as well as her own. Under these mounting pressures, the Countess finally reluctantly agreed to assume her marital responsibilities.

She did not surrender completely, however. To escape a bad situation which had been forced upon her by the King, her husband, and now her family, the Countess of Essex looked to less reputable persons for salvation. Confronted with the double fear of living with a man she hated and losing the one she loved, she turned to several quacks who gradually entangled her in a web of vice from which she never fully freed herself. Precisely when the Countess turned to the "black arts" for guidance or who introduced her to the master practitioners is unknown, but as early as July 1610, according to a contemporary letter writer, there was a plot to poison the Earl of Essex. [83] Fortunately, he was forewarned of the attempt to be made

[81] Codrington, *Life and Death*, p. 8. This incident prompted an exchange of written apologies, which appear in Devereux, *Lives of the Devereux*, 2: 236–37.

[82] Wilson, *Historie*, p. 98.

[83] *H. M. C. Downshire Manuscripts*, 2: 328.

on his life. Rumor claimed that the Countess was involved, but the entire truth remains hidden and it is not known who was to administer the potion, who masterminded the plot, or what the motives were.

At the time, the Countess of Essex was in direct communication with Anne Turner, a charlatan of the first order.[84] The widow of Dr. George Turner, she lived in Paternoster Row, under the protection of Sir Arthur Maynwaring. Her husband's medical reputation and her trade secrets gained her many aristocratic clients, including the Countess, who, it seems, placed her fate in the hands of this empiric. Frances even purchased and administered potions to decrease Essex's love and a love philter to increase Carr's affections. When the potions proved unsuccessful, the gullible girl informed her confidante: "My Lord is as lusty as ever he was and hath complained to my brother Howard that he hath not lain with me, nor used me as his wife. This makes me mad, since of all men I loathe him, because he is the only obstacle and hindrance that I shall never enjoy whom I love." [85] The Countess obviously was determined to have her way in love, even if she had to pawn her soul to a medicaster.

Through the auspices of Mrs. Turner, the Countess was then introduced to Dr. Simon Forman, who, under a pledge of secrecy, was informed of the strategy.[86] That the Countess implicitly trusted this celebrated charlatan who posed as a medical doctor is evident from the letters in which she addressed him as "Father." [87] She wanted him to secure Carr's love for her and to influence Essex to have no further desire to claim her as his wife. To decrease the Earl's affection, Dr. Forman prescribed a white powder which was supposed to be secretly added to Essex's food.[88] Armed with this nostrum, the Countess left London to join her husband.

In 1611 the Earl of Essex and his duplicitous bride summered

84 *Truth Brought to Light*, pp. 15–16.

85 Greville, *Secret History*, 2: 356.

86 See Mirian A. de Ford, *The Overbury Affair* (Philadelphia: Chilton Company, 1960), pp. 21–23.

87 Greville, *Secret History*, 2: 361.

88 In the British Museum's print collection there is a portrayal of Dr. Forman and his quackeries under the title *A Representation of Quackeries such as those which were alleged to have been Practised Against Robert Devereux, Third Earl of Essex*. It depicts Essex lying on his back with his head in an oven; the Countess, dressed in a tight-fitting bodice and plumed hat, is in the background.

at Chartley, the most highly prized manor among the Devereux estates. Here, in the idyllic Vale of Trent, several days' distance from the metropolis, they were virtually alone. Nearby was the little parish church of Stowe, which housed the effigy of Essex's paternal grandfather. Essex developed a strong, sentimental attachment to the home of his ancestors. Chartley symbolized past family glory and power: here Essex was truly king of his castle and lord of his tenants. In the heart of rural England the evils of urban England could be more easily forgotten. At Chartley the superficialities of the Court and the artificialities of government favorites amounted to nothing. Here, the code of chivalry, the principles of honor, and the ideals of nobility were more easily remembered.

The Countess, however, remained anything but content at Chartley. She missed her parents and her favorite uncle, the Earl of Northampton. She longed for the Court with its masques, revels, and pageants. Above all, she missed the clandestine meetings with her paramour, Sir Robert Carr. She seems to have sulked, balked, and behaved like a shrew. "When she came thither (tho' in the pleasantest time of summer) she shut herself in her Chamber," wrote Arthur Wilson, "not suffering a Beam of Light to peep upon her dark Thoughts. If she stirr'd out of her Chamber, it was in the dead of Night, when sleep had taken possession of all others but those about her. In this implacable discontented Humour she continu'd some Months, always murmuring against, but never giving the least civil Respect to her Husband; while the good Man suffer'd patiently, being loth to be the Divulger of his own Misery."[89]

If Essex failed to tame this shrew, the Countess also failed to achieve her evil ends. The drug which the Countess employed against her husband apparently did not diminish the Earl's affection or erode his patience. In fact, as one author noted: "The good Earle, carrying an extraordinary affection towards her, and being a man of milde and courteous condition, with an honest and religious love, ready rather to suffer than correct those outrages, patiently admonisheth her to a better course of life, and to remember how that all her fortunes depend upon his prosperity and therefore she in this offered more injury to her selfe than hurt to him."[90] Tenderness and tolerance, however virtuous, did not win the

[89] *Historie*, p. 58.
[90] Greville, *Secret History*, 2: 333.

Countess. She refused to submit to Essex and dismiss Sir Robert from her life.

Finally in 1612 after many distressing months at Chartley, the Earl of Essex capitulated to the will of his wife. The unhappy couple left their Midlands manor and returned to London. The Earl apparently rejoined his cronies, and the Countess returned to the arms of her lover.

VIII

FOR MANY PERSONS in high places the Devereux-Howard marriage alliance had already fulfilled its original purpose. For the Howards the tie with Essex had established some useful connections with the King and the heir apparent. The match had silenced would-be critics, especially the ones who were suspicious of the Spanish and Catholic sympathies of the Howards. The marriage had also established a valuable link between the Howards and the Cecils.

Yet the young Earl of Essex did not adhere to the politics of his in-laws. He preferred the religious sympathies of his late father and still associated and corresponded with the elder Essex's friends. Moreover, the youth's recent travels clearly revealed his position in foreign policy: he favored strong ties with France and the Dutch Republic, stood for an alliance with the Protestant princes of Europe, and associated with the anti-Spanish faction. Furthermore, Essex would soon be of legal age and, therefore, no longer dependent upon the Court of Wards and his in-laws. Free to make his own decisions and to handle his own affairs without interference from Cecil, the Howards, or the Court of Wards, Essex would no longer be a pawn.

Events at home and abroad threatened Essex's position in the Court of King James. In April 1609, after forty years of continuous war, Spain and the United Dutch Provinces had signed a truce which led to an entente between England, France, and the United Provinces. It is impossible to determine precisely what role, if any, the Earl of Essex played in the events which culminated in the triple agreement. He was, obviously, too young to have assumed any responsibility in the negotiations. The purpose of his trip abroad, moreover, had ostensibly been educational, not diplomatic; yet his presence in the Courts of Henry IV and Maurice of Nassau at the very time that ambassadors Carew and Winwood were engaged in the negotiations appears to have been more than coincidence. In all likelihood Essex served as a diplomatic instrument. His father, a champion of alliances with both the Dutch and the French, had had close ties with Henry IV and Prince Maurice; in fact, in 1591 he had fought in France for their common cause. This propensity Cecil, Carew, and others remembered only too well. It would seem, then, that the makers of English foreign policy probably used the son of Elizabeth's Essex to help cement the ties among the three nations.

Essex's role in these negotiations, however symbolic, only served to put him further at odds with the Howards. The leading proponents of the pro-Spanish faction, they stood to lose their pensions and prestige if such an alliance proved successful, for they had hoped for stronger ties with Spain, not France. They had even pushed for a marriage alliance between the royal families of England and Spain. The Earl of Northampton, the chief strategist of this faction, probably came to regard Essex, the husband of his favorite niece, as a potential threat to the family fortunes. In due time Essex began to detest the Howards. "Young Essex hated his father-in-law," wrote the Spanish emissary, Diego Sarmiento de Acuña, Count Gondomar, "because he had been the principal enemy and cause of the death of the Earl of Essex his father, who was beheaded by order of Queen Elizabeth, . . . and who was a gentleman of great valour and talents, still regarded with much affection by this people."[91]

The death of Secretary Cecil, in May 1612, did not help Essex's cause,[92] for Cecil had acted as a powerful check against excessive Howard predominance. Soon after his body was buried in the magnificent marble tomb at Hatfield House a great grab began for the offices vacated when he died. James I divided the spoils. He entrusted the treasury to a commission which included the Earls of Suffolk and Northampton and made Sir George Carew the new master of the Court of Wards. Cecil's death, consequently, further complicated both Essex's relationship with his wife and his position at Court. While Essex lacked the means to unravel his tangled state of affairs, his father-in-law, his wife, and her secret lover now had them.

Later that year Essex's stepsister and friend, Elizabeth Sidney,

[91] Quoted in Tenison, *Elizabethan England*, 12: 528.
[92] See Willson, *James I*, pp. 333–35.

Countess of Rutland, died at the age of twenty-seven, just a few
months after her husband,[93] who had participated in the Essex
conspiracy. The rumor that she had been poisoned by pills given to
her by Sir Walter Raleigh appears to have been false. For some
undisclosed reason her burial, next to her renowned father in Saint
Paul's Cathedral, was completely private.[94]

On 6 November of that same year Prince Henry, after a brief
illness, succumbed to typhoid fever at the age of nineteen. This was
truly a national tragedy; everywhere the heir apparent's death was
lamented. Essex attended the elaborate state funeral, held on
7 December. Despite his tiff with the Prince, he served as an assistant
to the chief mourner and walked between the Earls of Pembroke and
Salisbury in the public processional. During the interment ceremonies at Westminster Abbey, Essex carried Prince Henry's
gauntlet. He listened to the newly appointed Archbishop of Canterbury, Dr. George Abbott, read the text from Psalm 82, "Yea
Princes shall fall like others," and heard the primate deliver the
elegiac funeral sermon honoring the companion in whom Essex
had once placed so much hope.[95]

[93] Cokayne, *Complete Peerage*, 11: 260.
[94] *C. S. P. Dom., 1610–1618*, p. 143.
[95] Nichols, *Progresses*, 2: 490–502.

CHAPTER 3

That Great Cause

I

BY THE SPRING of 1613 the marriage of the Earl and the Countess of Essex had reached its nadir: there was still no sign of an heir; the principals lived in separate households; and the nature of the Countess's adulterous relationship with the royal favorite was guessed, if not known, by those in Court circles and by many other Englishmen. By Easter the couple, their families, and, finally, their King all concurred that it was futile to abide by the letter of the law any longer.[1]

Before initiating formal proceedings for an annulment, however, the Howards felt it necessary to dispose of Sir Thomas Overbury, a brilliant author who knew too much. Overbury, the secretary of Viscount Rochester, the title held by Sir Robert Carr, advised his patron against any permanent entente with the Countess of Essex.[2] He opposed all connections with the Howard family and their minions. He forewarned his master against supporting any annulment proceedings and prophesied disaster if his advice went unheeded. This was enough to bring the wrath of his superiors upon him, but his disparagement of the Countess proved to be his undoing. Although Sir Thomas had earlier devoted his pen to winning the love of the Countess of Essex for his patron by writing

---

[1] Goodman, *James the First*, 1: 221. He said: "About a year or two before the marriage was questioned, I did heai from a gentleman belonging to the Earl of Huntingdon, but very well known and a great servant of the Earl of Essex, that the Earl of Essex was fully resolved to question the marriage and to prove a nullity; and I am confident that if the Countess had not then at that instant done it, the Earl of Essex himself would have been the plaintiff; so then hereby I conclude that both parties were agreed and were alike interested in the business."

[2] For the following information on Overbury and Rochester see Richard Savage, *Sir Thomas Overbury: A Tragedy* (London, 1724); Edward A. Parry, *The Overbury Mystery* (London: T. F. Unwin, 1925); Beatrice White, *Cast of Ravens; The Strange Case of Sir Thomas Overbury* (New York: Braziller, 1967); and de Ford, *The Overbury Affair*.

flowery love notes and sonnets, he now refused to support a cause which he could no longer condone. He had helped the Viscount play the game of courtly love but now felt that to launch nullity proceedings with the intent to marry the Countess was a very dangerous matter. That the defendant in the case would be the Earl of Essex made Overbury's opposition more understandable, and the fact that the plaintiff would be the Countess only made a divorce seem preposterous. From Overbury's viewpoint the whole enterprise seemed folly. The Countess was, after all, the daughter of a pro-Spanish Howard, the niece of a papist, and an immodest minx not above using poison to achieve her dubious ends. Overbury considered her a "base woman," a phrase which the Countess herself heard soon.

Sir Thomas also knew too much about the clandestine love affair—too much for an open courtroom. He had read and written too many letters; he could easily remember faces and recall events and meetings which would be better forgotten in a divorce suit. His testimony could ruin everything—the proposed divorce suit, the remarriage, and the reputation of the Howards.

According to William Cobbett, on 10 April 1613 the Countess of Essex sent for Sir David Wood. This man-about-London, once swindled by Overbury, had at that time tried to provoke a duel with his avowed enemy, but Overbury had refused to fight. The Countess, knowing all this, suggested that she and Sir David work together to avenge themselves. Instead of relying on such a public and unpredictable means as a duel, however, she proposed that Sir David murder Overbury late some evening. At first Sir David appeared willing to organize an ambush, especially since he was promised one thousand pounds as a down payment, a pledge of immunity, and future favors from the Howards. After reconsidering the plan, however, he became frightened and refused to comply, claiming that he "would play hangman for nobody." [3] Balked in this enterprise, the Countess committed Overbury to Northampton, who was more adept at such matters.

The crafty Earl of Northampton drew all Overbury's enemies into a carefully constructed web before closing in on his prey. [4] He collaborated closely with the Countess, Suffolk, and Rochester. He

[3] Cobbett, *State Trials*, 2: 925.
[4] De Ford, *The Overbury Affair*, pp. 11–13, 39–44, 77–89, 114–21.

demanded, above all, secrecy. Appealing to common fears and hatreds, he drew the King, the Queen, the Archbishop of Canterbury, and the Earl of Pembroke into the periphery of his scheme. Queen Anne, in particular, bore a bitter grudge against Overbury, who had seemingly insulted her on one occasion. King James did not trust Overbury, for it was commonly reported that Rochester ruled the King and Overbury ruled Rochester. The King, who knew his logic quite well, could hardly stomach the conclusion of the syllogism.

Northampton's plan unfolded slowly. The King, who was in the process of reshuffling various ambassadorial posts, instructed Archbishop Abbot, Primate of England, to discuss with Overbury the possibility of serving as special ambassador to Russia, presumably to improve Anglo-Russian relations, which were at a low ebb.[5] It might as well have been an assignment to Cathay or Pondicherry, for Sir Thomas refused to consider the offer. Somewhat later, on 12 April 1613, the Lord Chancellor and the Earl of Pembroke visited Overbury and dangled before him a more attractive political carrot, the embassy post in either France or the Dutch Republic. They demanded his prompt decision. Refusing to be summarily pushed out of his enviable sphere of influence, the proud and strong-willed ghost writer again turned down the offer to serve his King abroad, claiming that poor French and bad health made him ill-equipped for either post. When his enemies rebutted his excuses with arguments, Overbury lost his temper and vowed that he would not leave the country for any preferment in the world.[6]

Infuriated with this decision and with the arrogant spirit of the man who made it, James I called the Privy Council into special session to deal with the matter. After discussing it, the council sent for the defiant secretary, who had much to learn about courtly politics. Instead of being called to the bar of justice to present his side of the case, Overbury was placed on the Privy Council's barge with two guards. With his head buried in his hands, he floated down the river and soon passed under Traitor's Gate into the Tower of London. A royal warrant, personally signed by James I, directed the Lieutenant of the Tower to treat Overbury as a close prisoner. "I dare pronounce of Sir Thomas Overbury," wrote Sir Henry

[5] Greville, *Secret History*, p. 365.
[6] *Ibid.*, p. 374.

Wotton, "that he shall no more on this stage." [7] Wotton was right.

With Overbury incapacitated, the divorce case between the Countess of Essex and her husband could proceed.

II

SOMETIME early in May a small conclave assembled at Whitehall—probably at the King's behest—to decide the fate of the estranged couple.[8] The Earls of Suffolk and Northampton, representing their daughter and great-niece respectively, demanded a legal annulment. An informal separation in which the Countess would be "put away" would not suffice, they insisted; for her to be allowed to remarry, it had to be nullity, nothing less. The Earl of Southampton and Lord Knollys, both close friends of the second Earl of Essex and both related to the Devereux, in representing young Essex's interests, did not confute these demands. The one condition which they imposed, that Essex's honor be fully preserved, was accepted and the strategy agreed upon.

Shortly thereafter the Countess filed her formal complaint with the Crown. King James, fully apprized of all the proceedings, considered the complaint well founded and granted her request for a nullity commission to hear her case. Thus on 12 May he called upon George Abbot to preside as ranking commissioner in the controversial case. "I did not know the ground whereupon they intended to move," the Archbishop later claimed, "but that if I were to be a judge in any such question, I would pray that the other bishops being near town and court, might be joined with me . . . that before any such thing were entered into, I might speak privately with my lord of Essex for satisfying my own mind."[9]

The next day Abbot met privately with Essex. "I found him generally much reserved in talk," the Primate noted, "but only avowing the ability of himself for generation; and that he was resolved never to lay any blemish upon himself in that way. I

[7] E. F. Rimbault, *Miscellaneous Works, in Prose and Verse, of Sir Thomas Overbury* (London, 1856), p. xlvii.

[8] *H. M. C. Mar and Kellie Manuscripts*, p. 51; and Cobbett, *State Trials*, 2: 805.

[9] Throughout this chapter I have relied heavily upon Archbishop Abbot's account of the proceedings, which is published in Cobbett, *State Trials*, 2: 805–60; and Paul A. Welsby, *George Abbot: The Unwanted Archbishop* (London: Society for Promoting Christian Knowledge, 1962), pp. 57–73.

knew not well what to make of this; for I did not then understand
that some lords met before at Whitehall on both parts . . . to settle
an order by consent, how this prosecution should be; that is to
say, that a separation should be made, and my lord's honour every
way preserved." [10] From the very start of the proceedings, then,
the Archbishop possessed many misgivings about the case.

Within a day or two Abbot encountered the Earl of Suffolk
in a gallery at Whitehall Palace and privately discussed the matter
with him. "I perceived it was like to be a matter of great difficulty,"
he wrote, and explained that there would be legal difficulties
because the Earl refused to admit a general impotency and thus
blemish himself, and the Countess's oath was not sufficient evidence
for annulment. To this warning the Earl of Suffolk responded,
"Perhaps the father's sin was punished upon the son." [11] The
Archbishop appears to have believed that a reconciliation between
the principals was still a possibility. Suffolk refused to consider
this alternative. From the very start, therefore, the Archbishop and
the Lord Chamberlain occupied opposite campsites in the nullity
battle.

Archbishop Abbot, who headed the Court of Delegates, was a
grim-faced bachelor who lived by the letter of the law. [12] Though
a staunch supporter of the episcopal system of church government,
Abbot leaned toward a Calvinistic theological position. He was at
once a powerful preacher and a patient scholar. For many years
he had studied theology at Oxford; more recently he had contributed
his knowledge of linguistics to the translation of the Holy Writ,
since known as the King James Version. He had also achieved
distinction as an educational administrator and an ecclesiastical
statesman. Although he had risen quite rapidly up the hierarchical
ladder, he had made many enemies since 1611, when the King had
appointed him Primate, in preference to several other prelates.

The Primate was assisted by nine commissioners—three ecclesiastics and six civilian lawyers and judges—in the divorce proceedings. [13] John King, Bishop of London and onetime chaplain of

10 Cobbett, *State Trials*, 2: 805.

11 *Ibid.*, p. 806.

12 See Welsby, *Abbot*, pp. 1–56.

13 The information on the commissioners has been garnered from several
sources, including *DNB*, *C. S. P. Dom.*, and Welsby's biography of Archbishop
Abbot and his study of *Lancelot Andrewes* (London: S.P.C.K., 1958).

Queen Elizabeth, continued to enjoy preferment under James I. Described as profound, pious, voluble, and grave, he was, above all, a preacher. Lancelot Andrewes, Bishop of Ely, called the "angel of the pulpit" by his contemporaries, had benefited from the patronage of Walsingham, the Earl of Huntingdon, Queen Elizabeth, Archbishop Whitgift, and, of course, James I. This translator of the Pentateuch and publisher of anti-Catholic polemics had officiated at Essex's baptism. Richard Neile had enjoyed the patronage of the Cecils and had been chaplain to both Lord Burghley and his son. After serving as dean of Westminster and Bishop of Rochester, Neile was translated to the Bishopric of Lichfield, the diocese in which Chartley and other Devereux properties were located. His loyalties were sharply divided: he had lived at Chartley and served briefly as Essex's chaplain, but he was related to the Howards.

The civilians were an able but less distinguished lot. Dr. Julius Caesar, a lawyer and Master of the Rolls, was the most experienced and noteworthy of the group. His devotion to the law was great, but his loyalty to the King was greater. Caesar's friend and colleague Thomas Parry, Privy Councilor and chancellor of the duchy of Lancaster, was an experienced bureaucrat. Similarly, Sir Daniel Donne could point to a lifetime of government work. Having served for several years as Dean of Arches, a specialized ecclesiastical tribunal which dealt with divorce, he brought to the Court of Delegates expert legal knowledge and a reservoir of experience in nullity suits. Of the three remaining civilian lawyers—Dr. Thomas Edwards, Dr. John Bennet, and Dr. Francis James—little is known.

Initially the Archbishop was, by his own admission, pleased with the composition of the Court of Delegates, but during the hearings his pleasure gradually was replaced by distrust and disapproval. The court met at Lambeth Palace, Abbot's official London residence, and adhered to the legal calendar which governed English courts. Like all other English courts, it moved slowly, especially during the summer.

On 17 May the commissioners received from Dr. Nicholas Steward, the Countess's legal counsel, a document containing ten allegations. The complaint maintained that the Countess was the legal wife of the Earl of Essex, that she had lived with her husband and shared his bed for several years, that she was still a virgin, that she was physically capable of sexual intercourse, that she had unsuccessfully sought sexual union with her husband on many occasions, and that Essex possessed the "power and ability of body to deal with other women" but could "never carnally know her, nor have that copulation in any sort which the married bed alloweth." [14] For these reasons and others, the Countess concluded, her marriage to the Earl of Essex should be declared null and void.

"When we saw it," Archbishop Abbot later claimed, "and that it contained *impotentia versus hanc* most of us, who were not acquainted with the project before, were much amazed at it. I told the counsel for my lady, 'That they had laid a very narrow bridge for themselves to go over.'" [15] With this the Bishop of London concurred. The Bishop of Lichfield, who had married the ill-fated couple, could scarcely believe what he read. Caught between two opposing sides, he hoped for a *rapprochement* between the two parties and advised caution. As he put it, "We should proceed with great wariness in this cause . . . the world looketh on us what we do; and there were not more eyes upon the earl's father losing his head, than there be upon the earl now losing his wife." [16]

The Court of Delegates then called the Earl of Essex to the bar. There, in open court with much self-composure, he responded to the charges in the libel. He admitted that the marriage had never been consummated. Asked for reasons, he replied, "When I came out of France, I loved her; I do not now, neither ever shall I." Essex answered affirmatively when he was confronted with the allegation that he possessed power to deal with other women. According to the Archbishop, when Essex was quizzed about the Countess's claims of virginity, he "smiled, and saith, 'She saith so, and she is so for me.'"

To prove her case, the Countess as plaintiff marshaled many witnesses before the court. On 2 June, Katherine Fiennes, a teen-age cousin-german of the Countess, testified that "from Mid-summer last to All-hollowtide, the earl of Essex and Lady Frances remained and kept company together as man and wife; first in the countess of

[14] Quoted at length in Cobbett, *State Trials*, 2: 785.

[15] The version I have relied upon, Philips MS 538, Folger Shakespeare Library, is substantially the same as that appearing in Cobbett, *State Trials*.

[16] Throughout this narrative of the divorce I have used the Ballard MS 56 version, entitled "Proceedings which happened between Lady Frances Howard and Robert Earl of Essex Concerning the Divorcement," in the Bodleian Library. This account, dated 1644, is virtually the same as that reprinted in Cobbett, *State Trials*, 2: 785–862, which is the source for my direct quotes.

Leicester's house at Drayton in Warwickshire; and later at the earl's own house at Chartley in Staffordshire: And that for two of the nights they lodged at Drayton, being on Sunday at night and Monday at night, they to her knowledge lay together in one chamber."[17] Elizabeth Raye, one of the Countess's domestic servants, confirmed these facts and gave additional testimony about the cohabitation of the couple at Durham House in London and at Cawsam House in Oxfordshire.[18] Another deponent, Frances Britten, a widow who had known the principals from their infancy, testified that the Countess and her husband shared the same bed at Hampton Court and Whitehall Palace.[19]

The plaintiffs produced several more Howard dependents to prove their case.[20] A girl in her teens, Catherine Dandenell, had seen the Countess and the Earl together at Audley End in Essex, Chartley, Drayton, and several residences in London. George Powell, a middle-aged domestic, revealed what he knew from more than three years' service as the Countess's attendant. The depositions of Anne Jaconian, the Countess's chambermaid, and Benjamin Orwell, another teen-age attendant, merely added details to the growing body of evidence.

The testimonies of Thomas Bamforde and William Power confirmed the earlier depositions. The former, who had known the Countess for about five years, testified that "in 1611, about the latter end of the summer, the earl of Essex and lady Frances were at the lady Corbett's house in Derbyshire, whom the deponent then did and still doth serve; that they continued there about a week, and dined or supped together in the said house, and lay together in one and the same naked bed, as it was commonly thought amongst the servants of the said house." Power, a London merchant, admitted that Sir William Button, a Howard family agent, had requested him to testify. Power told that he had attended the couple's wedding, that he spent the summer of 1611 at Chartley, and that he had "been in their lodging chamber in a morning and hath seen them in naked bed together." The nullity suit spared no one.

The plaintiffs then brought forward their star witnesses. On 10

---

[17] Cobbett, *State Trials*, 2: 789.
[18] *Ibid.*, p. 790.
[19] *Ibid.*
[20] *Ibid.*, pp. 790–94.

June the Earl of Suffolk submitted his deposition.[21] He made it clear that at the time of the wedding in 1606 both parties were of the age of consent, thus clearing himself of any antenuptial irregularities. Up to that time and since, Suffolk further related, "the earl was, in the judgment of men, of good health and strength in body, except at two times, when he was sick of the small-pox and ague; and likely to be able to have the carnal knowledge of a woman." He also testified that "the earl never had any carnal knowledge of lady Frances nor never could."

To clinch their case, the plaintiffs called for an inquest to test the Countess's chastity.[22] The Court of Delegates agreed to the proposal and appointed ten matrons and six London midwives to examine her. The matrons selected five of themselves and two midwives to conduct the inquest. On the appointed day the Countess of Suffolk and the examiners gathered at Lambeth Palace. After swearing to speak the truth, these ladies inspected the Countess of Essex, who was alone in a nearby room, and then delivered their verdicts separately and secretly to the register. They found her "a virgin uncorrupted." To make their claims more convincing, the plaintiffs secured further corroboration from seven compurgators.[23] In open court the Countess of Suffolk, the Countess of Kildare, Lady Walden, Lady Knivett, Lady Thynne, Katherine Fiennes and Dorothy Neile all swore that their kinswoman was a "virgin uncorrupted." It is interesting to note that Katherine Fiennes had already testified by deposition and that Mrs. Neile was the wife of the Bishop of Lichfield, a commissioner. Lady Knivett, later ashamed of her role in the questionable affair, claimed that she "wept all day about it."

Finally, the Countess herself was called to the bar to sign an oath drawn by her attorney: "That since the earl of Essex was 18 years of age, he and I have for a space of 3 years divers and sundry times lain together in naked bed all night. And at sundry of the said times the said earl hath purposely endeavored and attempted to consummate marriage with me, and to have carnal copulation with me for procreation of children; and I have such times, as the said earl hath attempted so to do, yielded myself willingly to the same purpose. All which notwithstanding, I say and affirm upon

21 *Ibid.*, p. 794.
22 *Ibid.*, pp. 802–808.
23 *Ibid.*, p. 808.

my Oath, that the said earl never had carnal copulation with me."
When it was time for the Countess to sign the statement, one of her
brothers reminded her to sign it correctly. She did not forget. She
signed it "Frances Howard." [24]

The pleaders for "Frances Howard" then rested their case.

III

ON 5 JULY, Essex's counsel opened the case for the defense. His
insufficiency was admitted, but the claim of general impotency
was denied. Essex, as the register recorded it, "believeth that
before and after the Marriage, he hath found an ability of body to
know any other woman, and hath oftimes felt motions and provocations of the flesh, tending to carnal copulation, but for perpetual
and natural impediments, he knoweth not what the words mean;
but that he hath lain by the lady Frances two or three years last,
past, and hath no motion to know her, and he believes never shall."[25]
Although this statement raised several questions, the Earl went
even further, claiming that "he believeth not that the said lady
Frances is a woman able and fit for carnal copulation, because he
hath not found it." This countercharge obviously was intended to
undermine the attempt of the plaintiffs to cast the cause of insufficiency solely at the feet of Essex. Both parties, contended the defense,
must be held responsible in the absence of conclusive evidence.

The Earl of Suffolk, angered with these answers, complained
privately to the King,[26] who wrote a letter of disapproval to Archbishop Abbot. Soon after, the Court of Delegates disallowed the
defense's case and ordered that "no record should remain of it,
but it should be utterly defaced." Though this action pleased the
plaintiffs, it meant that the defense would have to present different
answers and arguments. This demanded time. The Archbishop,
who considered time a boon to justice, granted the defense more
time to reconstruct its case.

At this juncture, however, Abbot was sharply criticized and
accused of using delaying tactics. "The lord chamberlain," Sir
William Button explained to the Archbishop in a private conversation, "was every way a kind father to his children; but in this of

24 *Ibid.*, p. 788.
25 *Ibid.*, p. 787.
26 *Ibid.*, pp. 808–11.

his daughter he was so passionate till it had an end, that he lay as on a grid-iron, broiling till the matter were accomplished." The nullity suit, demanded Sir William on behalf of his patron, should not be delayed.

"It shall not be delayed by me," Abbot promised.

Sir Daniel Donne also demanded speedier justice. Claiming an obligation to attend the King in progress, he requested that he be allowed to give his judgment upon the matter. Although some commissioners disapproved of this irregular procedure, the request was granted and Sir Daniel spoke. The commission, he claimed, had the right to hear the case summarily. He believed, moreover, that the annulment should be granted on grounds of a general, rather than a particular, impotency.

"In such a sentence," the Archbishop interjected, "the world will look that we should yield a reason for which we did."

To this the divorce expert replied, "It was fit to give no reason." He was seconded by Dr. Caesar, who claimed that "a judge is not to give reason of his sentence, but only to God. I would give no reason to any prince in the world."

"Well, lest it be we acquaint not the world with the reason of that which we do," rebutted the Primate, "yet is it not fit, that I who am judge and must pronounce the sentence know the grounds of that which I am to pronounce?"

Such vigorous exchanges reveal that the commissioners were sharply divided over nullity. When James I learned of these and other differences, he and the Earl of Suffolk sought to influence the commissioners.[27] Through Sir William Button they pressured Dr. Edwards, and through Viscount Fenton they attempted to change Dr. Bennet's mind. A few days later Suffolk personally contacted Caesar and Parry. The King, meanwhile, demanded that the commissioners attend him immediately to discuss the matter. He wanted a decision before the end of Trinity term. The Court of Delegates, consequently, left London and joined the King at Windsor Castle.

At the lengthy session held before the sovereign on 5 July, the last day of Trinity term, Sir Daniel again assumed the initiative in the debates, arguing on grounds of *non potuit*. Archbishop Abbot counter-charged, claiming that "*non potuit* was for lack of love,

---

[27] *Ibid.*, p. 813.

and not for want of ability." He also contended that the precedents cited by Donne had little or no bearing on the case and that the libel fell short of the cause and the proofs fell short of the libel.

"What a disgrace this will be to my Lord Chamberlain and his daughter," Sir Daniel complained, "if it should not go forward."[28]

"They should have looked to that before they did begin it," countered the English Primate. "We were not the men that set the matter on foot . . . must I, to save any man from disgrace, send my soul into hell to give sentence whereof I saw no ground? I will never do it." The Bishop of London, Edwards, and Bennet all supported Abbot in the verbal duel. Bennet, in particular, encountered much opposition from the King, who apparently tried to bend the wills of the dissenting commissioners with appeals to their loyalty.

The English monarch then revealed his personal views. He, too, found some deficiences in the libel and the procedures. He asked why the Earl of Worcester and Lord Knollys were not examined as witnesses although their names had been introduced into the hearings. Despite these misgivings, James I had already made up his mind: the Earl of Essex, he believed, "was impotent for a woman."[29]

"I would to God we might see these things legally proved," rejoined the Archbishop, who refused to yield his conscience to the royal will.

James was sorely troubled with the case as it then stood. He found himself caught between the desires of his favorite, Rochester; the demands of the Howards; and the unbendable conscience of his Archbishop. It was too late to stop the proceedings and it would be risky to launch another suit, so he too bid for time. Unable to win all the commissioners to his side, the King finally agreed to postpone the case until unanimous approval was granted in the next law term. He then commanded the commissioners to meet regularly at Lambeth Palace during the interim and to secure unanimity as soon as possible. Then, after rising from the throne of justice, the troubled monarch inveighed against child marriages and antenuptial contracts.[30]

28 *Ibid.*
29 *Ibid.*, p. 814.
30 *Ibid.*, p. 815.

The following day the Court convened at Lambeth Palace to discuss the case. The commissioners debated all morning in a closed session. The antinullity clerics resorted to authorities. The Archbishop appealed to the Scriptures as a sufficient arbiter to all controversies, especially in matters pertaining to marriage. During the afternoon session Sir John Bennet propounded the legal issues in the suit. There were at least six arguments against granting an annulment. The consensus seemed to be that the answer to the libel was neither clear nor complete. Nor had the Earl given satisfactory answers to the question posed by the Bishop of Lichfield. "This instructed me," the Primate claimed, "that the proofs were not full." [31]

At this point Abbot introduced a proposal which caused him much trouble. He suggested that the commissioners strive to reconcile the Earl and his wife. The Bishop of Ely expressed complete disapproval of this proposition, believing that it was too late for a reconciliation, which, moreover, "might be cause of poisoning and destroying one another to bring them together again." He undoubtedly knew something about the earlier poison plots.

The Court of Delegates was now completely deadlocked over the nullity suit and could not give the King the unanimous consent he demanded. They apparently agreed that more proof was needed before anything resembling a unanimous decision could be secured. They could do nothing but notify the King of their indecision and wait for further instructions, so Abbot wrote his sovereign a letter explaining the hopeless situation. He enclosed Bennet's legal objections and his own arguments and asked James to take him off the commission or relieve him from making a decision, claiming that he was, after all, a bachelor.[32]

The British sovereign, upon reading the epistle, was not pleased over the recent developments, especially the Archbishop's plan for reconciliation. He was not ready to capitulate on the matter, though. James I decided to beat Abbot at his own game. First, he postponed the proceedings until mid-September and decided to pack the commission and personally refute the Archbishop's case against nullity. To this end, while on summer progress, he studied and "wrote much with his own hands." [33]

31 *Ibid.*
32 *Ibid.*, p. 816.
33 *Ibid.*, p. 819.

Essex, meanwhile, decided to spend the remainder of the summer at Chartley. He had responsibilities to fulfill in Staffordshire: the Privy Council had recently ordered him, among others, to raise some troops for the occupation of Ireland,[34] so the beleaguered Earl petitioned the Archbishop of Canterbury for permission to leave London. The Primate, after clearing the matter with the plaintiff's counsel and two other commissioners, granted the request. Essex left, promising to "stand to and abide what the commissioners shall award."[35]

IV

James I was seeking new ways to win the Countess's divorce suit.[36] He found several. He prepared a rebuttal to the Primate's objections and decided to increase the size of the Court of Delegates by two and change its decision-making procedures. In the enlarged court eight commissioners would constitute a quorum; moreover, if three bishops and two civilians consented to the annulment, it could be granted. Thus, a minority of five could pronounce the verdict and prevail against the remaining seven.

The new commissioners, the Bishops of Winchester and Rochester, were in favor of granting the divorce.[37] The former, Thomas Bilson, a noted preacher and scholar who had been appointed to his lucrative see by Queen Elizabeth, had been involved in a disagreement several years earlier with Abbot, when the latter was serving him as dean of Winchester. James I, no doubt, hoped to use an old grudge to secure a new opinion in the divorce proceedings. The Bishop of Rochester, John Buckeridge, after successfully preaching at the Hampton Court Conference, traveled the high road of preferment. Patron of William Laud and close friend of Lancelot Andrewes, this "great dependent upon my lord Lichfield," as Abbot termed him, was a firm supporter of the royal prerogative and an avowed advocate of nullity.[38]

---

[34] *A. P. C. 1613–1614*, p. 111. Essex had been appointed lord lieutenant of Staffordshire by the Privy Council in 1612; see Bagot MS L.a.138, Folger Shakespeare Library.

[35] Cobbett, *State Trials*, 2: 809.

[36] McClure, *Chamberlain's Letters*, 1: 465–80, *passim*.

[37] Welsby, *Abbot*, p. 64.

[38] Cobbett, *State Trials*, 2: 817.

Though deeply disturbed by these royal machinations, the Primate was resolute and diligently prepared against the inevitable, refusing to compromise with his conscience. To undergird his position, he delved into the ancient authorities, the canon law of the Roman Catholic Church, and the English legal precedents. He conferred with others—lawyers, clerics, judges, and nobles—and reached the conclusion that much public opinion was behind him in the matter. His earlier suspicions about the Countess and Rochester were further confirmed when he learned about the poison plot and heard many stories which depreciated the Countess and her family. He searched his own soul and prayed to God.

The Earl of Essex, in the meantime, plunged into another conflict with the Howard dynasty. Sometime in mid-August, Henry Howard, the Earl of Suffolk's third son, aspersed Essex's loyalty or his virility, either of which would have constituted a provocation.[39] On the morning of 20 August, Essex, who considered his honor impugned, sent a challenge to his brother-in-law, who accepted it and answered with an invitation to meet at four o'clock in the afternoon. The reply, however, did not reach Essex in time for him to make the appointment, so he sent his seconds, Sir Walter Devereux and Sir Thomas Beaumont, to set a different time and place. They contacted Howard and agreed to meet in the Netherlands on 17 September, one day before the Court of Delegates would convene to pass judgment.[40]

If Essex's reaction to the defamations of Henry Howard represented the normal response of an aristocrat who deemed his honor at stake, the royal disapprobation was equally natural. The British Solomon, pressured by the Earl of Northampton, denounced dueling and tried to prevent the principals from leaving English soil.[41] Essex, Howard, and their seconds escaped the royal dragnet, however, and crossed the English Channel to meet at Flushing on 31 August. The four seconds met at Bruges to decide upon the weapons, and they moved up the duel three days, presumably to outwit those who might try to prevent it. They also changed the meeting place to Sluis. During the preparations Essex offered Howard a final opportunity to retract his statements, but Howard

[39] The best coverage of this incident is in *H. M. C. Downshire Manuscripts*, 3: 190–205.

[40] Ellesmere MSS, Huntingdon Library.

[41] *C. S. P. Dom. 1611–1618*, p. 203.

flatly refused to give him reasonable satisfaction. When this offer was turned down, Essex prepared for the dueling day.

At this point, James I appealed to Archduke Albert of Austria, governor of Flanders, to prevent the forthcoming combat,[42] and the Austrian Archduke sent a circular to his subordinates calling for the arrest of the would-be duelers. The English sovereign also sent Hugh May and Henry Gibbs, both royal messengers, to deliver royal cessation commands to the principals. Finding Essex at Courtrache, May handed him the King's command. These measures forestalled the proceedings.

One day before the Court of Delegates reconvened at Lambeth Palace to renew the nullity proceedings, Essex and Howard were summoned before the Privy Council.[43] There the Earl of Northampton and the Duke of Lennox appointed Sir Dudley North, Sir Horatio Vere, and Sir John Wentworth, to judge the points of honor which had precipitated the feud between the two men. The would-be combatants and their seconds, now confined to London, were ordered to state their cases before the judges at a later date and reconcile their differences.[44]

V

IN THE WAKE of these events the commissioners of the Court of Delegates began to gather in London for their prearranged hearing of 18 September. The Bishop of Winchester, who returned early, campaigned for nullity by entertaining the plaintiff's counsel, Caesar, and Donne at his London residence. "I expected no great good of this," complained Abbot.[45] How right he was! On the eve of the hearing the Primate received from the Bishop of Lichfield a sealed package containing a handwritten letter from James I and a copy of the King's brief. Abbot scanned the material immediately and discussed the nullity suit with the Bishop, who promising not to give his consent unless the Primate did, suggested that Essex be reexamined. Abbot then withdrew to study the papers from the King.

[42] Devereux, *Lives of the Devereux*, 2: 251.
[43] *H. M. C. Downshire Manuscripts*, 3: 205–7.
[44] For this declaration see P. R. O., S. P. 14/74, fol. 65.
[45] Cobbett, *State Trials*, 2: 819.

The Archbishop now found himself in a corner. He feared that the Anglican Church would be disgraced and become the object of smiles, perhaps scorn. His own position and personal reputation were also at stake. Early the next morning he reread the sharp words from the pen of King James. "I considered them again and again, and methought they were not altogether so bitter as I apprehended them; that they were wrung from his majesty by my lord chamberlain's importunity; that my master had deserved at my hands, that I should bear patiently twenty times more; and that all was nothing, so the clearness of my conscience might be preserved."[46]

On 17 September the Primate had heard of Sir Thomas Overbury's death in the Tower of London. (On 15 September, after surviving several other attempted poisonings, Sir Thomas died from taking a laxative administered by his keeper, a hireling of the Countess of Essex. The following day, after a rigged inquest, his corpse was buried in Tower Chapel without a funeral, and the Earl of Northampton tried to keep the entire matter secret.) This news naturally confirmed the Archbishop's earlier suspicions. Little business was transacted that day. The next day, 18 September, as planned the new commision was read and the supernumerary commissioners took their places behind the bar. The proposal that Essex be reexamined passed, the only opposition coming from Caesar. Since no formal action could be taken, Abbot decided to recess the court until Monday.

James I now vigorously opposed all delay. He flatly prohibited the commissioners from recalling Essex before the court, rightly fearing that a reexamination might undermine the plaintiff's case. He ordered Dr. Thomas James and the Bishop of Ely, both of whom had been absent from most of the earlier hearings, to rejoin the court at Lambeth Palace so that there would be a *plena curia*. Tired of the matter, he stated that the principals had the right to a verdict without further delay; the case, he demanded, should be terminated on Saturday.

The Archbishop agreed to sit both mornings and evenings, all night if necessary, so the case could go forward. The plaintiff's counsel introduced more evidence, as did the defendant's. The

[46] *Ibid.*

Bishop of Winchester, now the King's mainstay, tried to sway others to his position. As Abbot put it, "He played the advocate all that day to the great offence of the standers-by so that it was publicly spoken of in London." [47]

On Thursday 23 September confusion prevailed at Lambeth Palace. The Countess's counsel commenced to answer some objections made by the defense. Then Dr. Henry Martin, the King's Advocate, made a speech pointing out that the Earl of Essex had not been sworn in properly. This issue struck the commissioners and the plaintiff's counsels like a bolt of lightning. No one could satisfactorily answer why the Earl had not been sworn correctly. Counsel was abashed. During the afternoon session, the commissioners began to debate Bennet's six legal objections, which were primarily concerned with an imperfect libel and an incomplete examination of Essex. "Shuffling and shifting answers" were given, the Archbishop reported, and such difference of opinion arose that any hope of compromise evaporated completely.

The majority, nevertheless, ruled. Out of the confusion emerged a gambit which won the nullity battle for the Crown. "Let us put it to the question," Caesar proposed, "and let the major part of voices determine it." [48] This proposal—a radical one indeed for an absolute monarch and his civilian lawyers to espouse—was coolly received by Archbishop Abbot. "When I saw this to be the proceeding," he related, "the Lord, thought I, deliver me from such judges."

Abbot then resorted to a strange tactic for one with Calvinistic proclivities: he reverted to canon law. He cited cases from the Roman Curia and the French ecclesiastical courts. He quoted from Alexander III, the pope who had turned down Henry VIII's appeal for annulment; and he had Sir John Bennet read a case in which a Spanish archbishop granted a nullity petition similar to that of the Countess's, only to find that, upon appeal, the Sacred Roman Rota reversed the archbishop's decision. The Rota's decision was then read *en toto* to the commissioners. This maneuver proved futile, however, for as Abbot himself bemoaned, "both these were slighted, as matters of nothing, and so I think had St. Paul been, if he had been there." [49]

47 *Ibid.*, p. 823.
48 *Ibid.*, p. 824.
49 *Ibid.*, p. 825.

The next day, the Archbishop went to Whitehall to attend the King. After offering his hand to be kissed, James took the Primate aside and asked him about the state of "that great cause," as he termed the Essex divorce case. "I had not liking of it," Abbot reported, and explained why he could not in clear conscience grant an annulment to the Countess. After restating his reasons and his misgivings, he again asked to be relieved of the assignment. James I, of course, refused the request and asked the Primate if he had enough lawyers, to which the latter replied, "Yes enough, there is not an honest lawyer in England that would not be on my side." [50]

On Saturday, 25 September, the Court of Delegates gathered at Lambeth Palace for the final session. Sir Thomas Lake delivered an admonitory message from the King, which demanded that the commissioners speak briefly and not fix the blame on any particular person. The voting was as anticipated: the Bishops of Winchester, Ely, Lichfield, and Rochester, together with Caesar, Parry, and Donne, cast their votes for nullity; the Archbishop, the Bishop of London, Bennet, James, and Edwards voted against the annulment. Nullity won by the necessary vote of seven to five. [51] After pronouncing the verdict, the Bishop of Winchester returned immediately to Whitehall to inform the King that "that great cause" had been decided in favor of the Countess.

VI

As the trial before it had, the sensational divorce rapidly became a primary topic of conversation in London. Most contemporaries praised the minority commissioners for their resolute stand and criticized the majority members for their role in the decision. [52] Archbishop Abbot received commendatory messages from powerful aristocrats, bishops, university scholars, and preachers, especially those of Puritan sympathies, for his staunch position. Some courtiers and several poets supported the sentence and its anticipated

---

[50] *Ibid.*

[51] *Ibid.* For a discussion of the vote see P. R. O., S. P. 14/74, fol. 62. For the breakdown also see Folger MS V.b.211, entitled "The Proceedings which happened touching the divorcement between Lady Frances Howard and Robert Earl of Essex," especially p. 5.

[52] See *H. M. C. Downshire Manuscripts,* 3: 214.

consequences, but the great bulk of the English people disapproved of the Essex divorce. The verdict produced so much criticism and sarcasm that some of the nullity commissioners proposed to publish a book to justify their position.[53] This proposal was debated for several months, but it was finally decided that one book defending the divorce might well evoke two books denouncing it.

Though the nullity sentence tended to fix the blame on Essex for the unconsummated marriage, the sentence legally liberated both parties from the terms of their antenuptial contract. The Countess could marry Viscount Rochester. Essex also was free to do as he willed, but the revelations of the hearings, especially the doubts surrounding his sufficiency, would make any subsequent marriage, if heirless, fraudulent in the eyes of the law. The nullity sentence— indeed, the whole case—may have liberated the Countess, but it victimized the Earl of Essex. His honor and integrity had been impugned by the plaintiffs and he was not free to defend himself against the personal attacks of his adversaries. He could not exercise his aristocratic right to avenge a personal wrong with private justice. The same absolute power which had packed the Court of Delegates had intervened and squelched Essex's appeal to an ancient and honorable code of ethics.

Nor was this all. On 26 September, one day after the sentence, the special Court of Honor called by the King met under the jurisdiction of Northampton and Lennox to settle the dispute be- tween Essex and his brother-in-law.[54] The seconds, after testifying to judges Sir Horatio Vere, Sir John Wentworth, and Sir Dudley North, subscribed to a brief report based on their own testimony and subsequently turned over to the King, who took a personal interest in the affair.[55] At this point Essex disavowed the report to which the seconds, including his brother, had subscribed. According to Essex, the report which the seconds had agreed to maintain by oath, sacrament, and sword was not the same as the report read.

In answer to a summons, Essex appeared before the Privy Council on 11 October.[56] The exact details are not known, but the con- sequences provide some clues. Presumably Essex was reprimanded, perhaps rebuked. The Privy Councilors confined him to his London

[53] Cobbett, *State Trials*, 2: 832.
[54] McClure, *Chamberlain's Letters*, 1: 478.
[55] P. R. O., S. P. 14/74, fol. 65.
[56] *A. P. C. 1613–1614*, p. 231.

residence and issued a warrant for the incarceration of his brother. Two days later Sir Walter was imprisoned in the Fleet, a London prison, with no cause being stated.[57] On 15 October the Privy Council issued a royal proclamation against dueling.[58] This document, which reflected the views of the King, Bacon, Northampton, and others, aimed at ending the practice once and for all. The Earl Marshal, it stated, was empowered to settle all personal disputes involving honor. All appeals would be directed to his commissioners. The Court of Star Chamber would punish those who refused to abide by these procedures, the suggested penalty being banishment from Court for seven years.

To Essex's wounds more salt was added. Since the marriage was null and void, he was legally obliged to return the Countess's dowry—if the Howards demanded it; within six weeks the Earl of Suffolk requested repayment of the five thousand pounds, which, of course, had long since been spent.[59] To meet this demand, Essex was compelled to sell some of his woods at Adderston and borrow money. Though his grandmother, the Countess of Leicester, lent him some money to keep his estate intact, he was later forced to sell Bennington Manor in Hertfordshire. The buyer of Bennington was none other than Sir Julius Caesar.[60]

Essex was not, however, left completely bereft by these events. After several weeks had passed, he and his baseborn brother were freed from their prisons. "Essex has become a great courtier," a newsletter writer recorded early in November, "the people show to love him and already begin to speak well of him, but all is vanity and transitory."[61] Transitory or not, Essex became a popular martyr as a result of "that great cause."

VII

THROUGHOUT the first twenty-three years of his life the Earl of Essex had occupied a conspicuous but small spot on the stage of history. His role had been passive, for he had been the object of actions and the victim of events. At an early age he had been

57 *Ibid.*, p. 244.
58 Willson, *James I,* p. 307.
59 Greville, *Secret History,* p. 379.
60 *DNB,* 3: 658. Essex sold the manor for fourteen thousand pounds.
61 *H. M. C. Downshire Manuscripts,* 3: 252.

subjected to the harsh realities of public life, defeat, and personal tragedy. He had been publicly humiliated by many of his contemporaries, including the late Queen, the new sovereign, and family rivals; he had been exposed to much ridicule and scandal. During the recent nullity proceedings he had experienced the worst of royal justice, favoritism, political corruption, and human greed.

The annulment, however, changed the direction of Essex's career. No longer a passive pawn, he became a man of action. No longer allied to the Howard faction or closely associated with the royal coterie, he emerged from the affair bitterly opposed to his onetime relatives and mistrustful of the king. No longer a minor or a royal ward, he could be less subservient to the royal bureaucracy. The scandalous divorce also made Essex much wiser in the ways of the world. It enabled him to perceive his true friends, his close allies, and his real enemies. He discovered that the Archbishop, the Earls of Pembroke and Southampton, and several members of the House of Commons were all enemies of his enemies, and hence allies in the political struggles of the era.

Essex could not eradicate from his memory the traumatic experiences of his early life. He would find it difficult indeed to forget the humiliating divorce and equally difficult to forgive those who had contributed most to his humiliation. Throughout the remainder of his life he would seek to right the wrongs committed against him. In addition to redeeming his father's name and his family's reputation, Essex now had to avenge himself.

CHAPTER 4

Master of Chartley

I

IN NOVEMBER 1613 the Earl of Essex, having been confined to his residence by the Privy Council, regained his freedom, whereupon he won sympathy and support from countless Englishmen. Even Queen Anne, Gondomar noted, "gave many marks of favour to him, driving out with him in her coach . . . all in opposition to the Earl of Somerset [Rochester's new title] to whose wedding the Queen she would not go."[1] Rather than chance further humiliation at the forthcoming wedding of his former wife and her paramour, "the Earl of Essex refused to be present," the Spanish envoy continued, "and went off to his estates in defiance, alone as no one dared accompany him." Henceforth, moody and melancholic, he avoided the Court. Aloof, in semiseclusion at Chartley Manor, he no doubt hoped to eradicate bitter memories of the past and begin life anew.

The poets, however, kept alive the memory of Essex's marriage and divorce. Two of England's foremost versifiers commemorated the Countess's remarriage to Somerset. In each case Essex emerges as a character in the argument. In his *Ecologue*, John Donne, the celebrated preacher and poet, portrays Essex in thinly disguised phrases. Allophanes, finding Idios (Essex) in the country during the Christmas season, chides his absence from Court:

> Unseasonable man, statue of ice,
>   What could to countries solitude entice
> Thee, in yeares cold and decripit time?
>   Natures instinct drawes to warmer clime
> Even small birds, who by that courage dare,
>   In numerous fleets, saile through their Sea, the aire.
> What delicacie can in fields appeare,
>   Whil'st Flora herselfe doth a freeze jerkin weare? . . .[2]

---

[1] Tenison, *Elizabethan England*, 12: 529.

[2] John Donne, *Poems*, ed. John Hayward (London: Nonesuch Press, 1962), p. 107.

After this introductory dialogue, Donne proceeds to his *Epithalamion* proper, in which he describes the marriage ceremony, the feasts, the revels, and the nuptial night.

In *Andromeda Liberata*, George Chapman, the translator of Homer's *Iliad* who had been attached to Prince Henry's Court, also commemorated the recent marriage of his new patron. The author, obviously pleased with the recent annulment, cast his verses into an allegory which contained several hidden allusions to Essex, the Howards, and Somerset. He depicts Perseus's release of innocent Andromeda, who had been chained to a rock:

> Her lookes fir'd all things with her loves extreames
> Her necke a chaine of orient pearle did decke,
> The pearles were faire, but fairer was her necke:
> Her breasts (laid out) show'd all enflamed sights
> Love, lie sunning twixt two Crysolities:
> Her naked wrists showde, as if through the skie,
> A hand were thrust, to signe the Deitie.
> Her hands, the confines, and digestions were
> Of Beauties world: Love fixt his pillars there.
>   Her eyes that others caught, now made her caught,
> Who to her father, for the whale was brought,
> Bound to a barraine Rocke, and death expected. . . .[3]

Though threatened by the tide, a monster, and Neireides, Andromeda was saved from her sacrificial ordeal by "conquering Perseus," who slew the monster and then freed the chained maiden:

> He, for it selfe, with his owne end went on,
> And with his lovely rescu'd Paragon
> Longed of his Conquest, for the latest shocke:
> Dissolv'd her chaines, and tooke her from the rocke
> Now woing for his like that fled to her
> As hers in him lay: Love did not confer
> To one in both: himselfe in her he found,
> She with her selfe, in onely him was crownd.

To perceptive contemporaries the "barraine Rocke" symbolized the Earl of Essex.

This poem—especially those allusions to Essex—brought criticism to its author from several sources. Chapman, in turn, claiming that

---

[3] Phyllis Brooks Bartlett, *The Poems of George Chapman* (London: Oxford University Press, 1941), p. 312.

he was misunderstood and misrepresented, denied that Essex was the object of a malicious attack. But verbal denials were not enough. He soon felt compelled to write a prose tract entitled *Justification* and a poetic dialogue, both defending the original poem. Though Chapman often regarded his readers with contempt, he could scarcely afford to offend Essex if the offense would threaten the author's relationship with Somerset. Chapman therefore abandoned his philosophic justification of the annulment and lectured his readers on the fine points of allegory. This aftersight proved ineffectual, however, for the damage was already done: the court poets, like several bishops, had sold their souls to the high and mighty Howards.

II

IN FEBRUARY 1614, Essex returned to London to attend the marriage of Lord Roxborough and Mrs. Jane Drummond, a favorite of Queen Anne.[4] The wedding ceremony, which took place at Somerset House on 3 February, was followed by the usual entertainment. The occasion was marred, however, by an incident involving Essex and John Heydon. Their harsh words sparked a public quarrel between them.[5] Challenges were exchanged, and the principals were soon on their way to the dueling site when the Archbishop of Canterbury intervened and attempted to restrain Essex. His efforts apparently were successful, for the duel never took place. The Queen considered the fracas an affront to the whole wedding. Heydon was committed to Fleet prison, and some feared that he might even pay with his life. That very day, in a document obviously aimed at Essex and his opponent, the Privy Council issued another proclamation against, and demanding the cessation of, provocations and duels.[6]

Two months later, on 5 April, Essex made his political debut in the House of Lords.[7] At eleven o'clock in the morning he joined the long procession which paraded from Whitehall Palace to Westminster Abbey. The peers, garbed in their colorful robes, followed behind the trumpeters, officers, knights, baronets, and

[4] Nichols, *Progresses*, 2: 754.

[5] *C. S. P. Dom., 1611–1618*, p. 223.

[6] Willson, *James I*, p. 307.

[7] Thomas L. Moir, *The Addled Parliament* (Oxford: Clarendon Press, 1958), pp. 78–83.

judges. After them came the high officers of state, Prince Charles, a group of gentlemen on foot, and finally the King. After divine service James and his peers proceeded on foot to the House of Lords in Westminster Palace. There, after much waiting, the commoners went to the Upper House to hear the King's opening speech, delivered from the royal throne. Before the King sat the berobed peers and bishops. Behind them pressed a throng of bystanders and a few members from the Lower House. Although the King spoke eloquently, his words were lost upon most of the intended audience, for the majority of the commoners, lacking seats, returned to Saint Stephen's Chapel.

On 11 April, Essex was formally sworn into the House of Lords.[8] Among the eighty-four lay lords were one marquis, twenty-seven earls, two viscounts, and fifty-four barons.[9] About half these men possessed titles antedating the Tudors, while one-fourth owed their places to the creations of the present sovereign. The Earl of Oxford could point to a title dating from 1142. Several peers, including Essex, Southampton, the Earl of Arundel, and Lord Paget, sat because their titles, attainted during the reign of the late Queen, had been restored by the present monarch. Several earls, Suffolk for example, had been advanced by James from the rank of baron. Fifteen of the barons had received their titles since 1603.

In this aristocratic assembly Essex ranked eleventh among the earls. Among those above him were the Earls of Suffolk, Northampton, Rutland, Nottingham, Southampton, and Pembroke.[10] On one side of him sat the aged Earl of Hertford, on the other the young Earl of Dorset. Below him were the Earls of Exeter, Salisbury, Montgomery, and Richmond, Viscount Lisle, the bishops, and the barons. Though not at the very apex of the political pyramid, Essex occupied an eminent spot in the Upper House.

Fifteen members of the Upper House sat on the Privy Council. Of the twenty-six spiritual lords, the two archbishops and fourteen bishops owed their elevation or translation to the King. Most of the others never assumed their seats in the 1614 Parliament. All the figures who had participated in the recent annulment proceedings, however, attended the debates in Westminster Hall. The close bond between the prelates and the King, and the ties between the

8 *Lords Journal*, 2: 685.

9 See Moir, *Addled Parliament*, Appendix II and pp. 62–66.

10 *H. M. C. Hastings Manuscripts*, 4: 283.

peerage and the King, gave the Crown a distinct predominance in the Upper House.

The only significant opposition was an informal, loosely organized circle of peers associated with the Earl of Southampton, the brilliant patron of William Shakespeare and onetime ally of Elizabeth's Essex.[11] They looked to the country itself rather than the Court for support. Their attendance was uneven, and their loyalty at times vacillated. Southampton was able to gain their support for a great variety of reasons, including their desire for personal advancement. Two absentee members of the group, the Earl of Bedford and Lord Grey, entrusted Southampton with their votes in the 1614 Parliament, thus giving the opposition leader a total of three voices in the House of Lords. These, plus influence in the Lower House, gave his faction a much broader base than appears on the surface.

From the very start the Earl of Essex cast his lot with this opposition. Southampton, his father's closest friend and political ally, had looked after the Devereux interests on several occasions and in the recent annulment crisis had stood by Essex's side and helped him against the Howards. Like virtually all the other opposition peers, Southampton was hostile to the Howards and critical of the pro-Spanish faction. Because of his youth and inexperience, Essex played a relatively inconspicuous role in his first Parliament.[12] Although he attended the debates religiously, missing only four of the twenty-nine meetings, he did nothing significant enough to attract the attention of the contemporary commentators. Like most other junior members in the Upper House, he appears to have said little or nothing. On 16 April he was put on a committee—his first—which dealt with wills and entails, and on 3 May he was placed on a committee which considered a bill to preserve the woodlands of England. Of his position on these measures or his role in the committees no evidence remains.

Essex did, nevertheless, support Southampton's faction in the controversial impositions issue. The Lower House, after rejecting a proposal to first petition the King on the matter, finally decided to

[11] Moir, *Addled Parliament*, p. 65. For a discussion of Southampton's life see Charlotte C. Stopes, *The Life of Henry Third Earl of Southampton, Shakespeare's Patron* (Cambridge: At the University Press, 1922); and Rowse, *Shakespeare's Southampton*.

[12] The following facts and the resultant deductions are drawn from *Lords Journal*, 2: 685–709.

confer with the Lords in hopes of abolishing imposts. When asked for a conference on the matter, the peers drifted into a bitter debate over the royal prerogative and the whole conference method of handling legislation. When a vote was finally taken, the Crown won in the Upper House, and Southampton's opposition faction suffered a sharp setback.

These parliamentary deliberations brought to the political surface several personal animosities.[13] Early in the session the Commons protested the presence of Sir Francis Bacon, then attorney general, in their midst and succeeded in establishing the principle that thereafter the King's lawyer should never be elected to the Lower House. Similarly, Sir Thomas Parry, chancellor of the duchy of Lancaster, was ousted by his colleagues for corrupt electoral practices. Next the opposition groups in both Houses combined to bring Richard Neile, the unpopular Bishop of Lincoln, to his knees in submission. The chief spokesman of the Crown against conferring with the Lower House on impositions, he had in the course of his speeches impugned the loyalty and integrity of several leaders in the Commons. When, with a majority of the House of Lords in agreement, these leaders demanded an apology, the arrogant churchman finally complied. Southampton and the Archbishop of Canterbury, who harbored grudges against the man, swung the vote in the Upper House.

Together these three cases signify something more than pure coincidence. Bacon had once betrayed the Earls of Essex and Southampton and both Neile and Parry had opposed young Essex and Southampton in the divorce case. Parry and Southampton, moreover, were avowed enemies. These personal attacks, in brief, reveal a working alliance between disgruntled members of both Houses. Southampton's faction could not command enough support to carry the day on matters of principle and procedure, but it did muster up opposition on grounds of personalities.

To preserve the power of the Crown, James decided to dissolve Parliament.[14] Many councilors were deeply disappointed. Despite days of debating, only one bill, the naturalization of Count Palatine, became law. Even worse, several acts were allowed to lapse. The opposing sides were hopelessly deadlocked. There was no hope

[13] William Cobbett, *The Parliamentary History of England*, 36 vols. (London, 1806–20), 1: 1163.

[14] Gardiner, *History*, 2: 248.

of securing funds without surrendering a principle and a large amount of power. On 7 June the King's second Parliament came to its end. Because it had accomplished nothing, this assembly went down in history as the Addled Parliament.

Essex learned the rudiments of opposition politics in the Addled Parliament. But, in the course of his practical tutelage, he incurred the wrath of his King. As one newsletter noted: "H.M. is very angry with the ld. of Southampton, the ld. of Essex, Chandos, and divers others. All is out of frame. God put it in again." [15] Before putting his parliamentary lessons to another test, Essex would have to wait seven long years.

III

THE DAY AFTER the dissolution of Parliament the aged Earl of Northampton, attended by more than forty mounted followers, proudly paraded through the streets of London.[16] The dissolution had been a victory for him and his pro-Spanish faction. It proved to be Northampton's last triumph, for he died a week later of a tumor in his thigh.

Essex, who returned to Chartley shortly after the dissolution, benefited politically from Northampton's demise. The Earl of Northampton had been high steward of Stafford, the borough nearest Chartley. This office gave the holder a voice in local matters and in the selection of members of Parliament. Thus, in 1614, Northampton nominated Thomas Gibbs, a bureaucrat, to sit for Stafford. Through such practices the great landed families, particularly the peers, influenced the composition of the House of Commons. Essex himself had very likely used a similar device to secure a Welsh seat for his brother, Walter, in the Addled Parliament.

In June 1614, Essex made a bid for the spot vacated by his late enemy. In a personally penned letter he promised to fulfill the duties of the high steward if selected for the post. "Mr. Maior," he wrote to Matthew Cradocke, "I understand that by the death of my Lord of Northampton the high steward place of your town is become vacated; if you and your brethren would please to make he of me to supply that [position] I will take it gratefully and at your guide be ready to do you the best respect I may. And so I

[15] *H. M. C. Downshire Manuscripts*, 3: 426.
[16] Moir, *Addled Parliament*, p. 145.

rest, Your very loving friend, Ro. Essex." [17] The burgesses responded favorably to this request, and Essex was immediately appointed. Because he had become high steward, Essex then administered the oath of office to the newly elected mayor, Cradocke. Not long thereafter Essex also secured the high stewardship of Sutton Colfield in Warwickshire.

Shortly after the dissolution of the Addled Parliament the Privy Council sought benevolences to fill the empty coffers of the Lord Treasurer, but the results were so disappointing that the requests were reiterated later in the summer. Essex responded to the second request so generously that his former father-in-law, the Earl of Suffolk, who was now Lord Treasurer, responded with a letter of thanks. "My Lord," he wrote in late November, "your free gyft to the kyng may truly be called bounty for I know you have given more out of your proportion of estate than most of the lords of England whych his majesty doth well understand and howsoever the fortunes of the world have in some sort separated our persons, yet shall not my good affections departe from my wyshing you all honor and happy life as he that wyll remayne, Your lordships affectionate cosen, T. Suffolk." [18]

Northampton's death had an adverse effect on Essex's former wife and her new spouse, for while he lived, the crafty uncle of Lady Frances had kept the murder of Sir Thomas Overbury secret. If Somerset had been able to maintain his position as royal favorite, the truth might well have remained hidden, but after the marriage James had gradually forsaken him and had begun to bestow his kindnesses on others.[19] The writing on the wall became clear, and in July 1615, Somerset applied to the King for a royal pardon broad enough to cover all offenses he had ever committed. Although Somerset was supported initially by the King, Lord Chancellor Ellesmere and several other Privy Councilors set forth a strong protest based on legal grounds. The blanket pardon went unsealed.

In September several revelations about Overbury's death confirmed rumors that had been circulating for two years.[20] The details

17 Stafford Town Records and Accounts, William Salt Library. Stafford.

18 British Museum, Additional MSS 46,188.

19 Willson, *James I*, p. 350. Also see James Spedding, "A Message from King James to the Earl of Somerset in the Case of Sir Thomas Overbury," *Archaeologia* 41, pt. 1 (1867), pp. 75–98.

20 Cobbett, *State Trials*, 2: 922.

still remain obscure. Some claim that one of Overbury's servants revealed information to Sir Edward Coke. Others said that it was Overbury's kinsmen who did so. Still others claimed that the Archbishop had been so deeply suspicious of the death that he took the initiative and worked through Secretary Thomas Lake. The best surviving evidence, however, indicates that early in September, Sir Gervase Elways, lieutenant of the Tower, informed Secretary Ralph Winwood that Sir Thomas Overbury had been poisoned.[21] His motives remain a mystery, but the King demanded a further investigation. Elways subsequently confessed. On 29 September several members of the Privy Council examined Overbury's keeper, Richard Weston, who also confessed to a great deal. Not long after this disclosure the Earl of Southampton found out about the matter.[22] Somerset's fate was sealed.

Throughout October the infamous plot unfolded piece by piece, implicating more and more Englishmen in high circles. Upon further examinations by Chief Justice Coke and Justice Carew, Weston implicated Anne Turner and an apothecary named James Franklin, and Elways dragged in the name of Sir Thomas Monson.[23] Sir Thomas, when examined, revealed that he had employed Weston under orders from others higher on the social ladder. By the middle of the month the entire truth was known: Overbury had been poisoned, and all the evidence pointed to the former Countess of Essex as the prime suspect.

The murder trials of Weston, Mrs. Turner, and Elways, which came on the heels of the examinations, provided the Crown with an impenetrable case against the onetime Countess of Essex.[24] While on trial for his life Weston bared the sordid details of the crime. Similarly, Mrs. Turner told of her associations with Dr. Simon Forman and other druggists and explained how she had been persuaded by Dr. Savery to practice sorceries on the Earl of Essex. Subsequent testimony also brought out that Essex had lost his hair and fingernails because of the drugs administered to him under Mrs. Turner's guidance. Only his "youthful strength," one source explained,

[21] *H. M. C. Buccleuch Manuscripts*, 1: 162.

[22] In early October 1615, while he was at Beaulieu, the Earl of Southampton's estate in Hampshire, the King learned from Winwood of Weston's revelations and consented to further investigation.

[23] Cobbett, *State Trials*, 2: 911.

[24] *Ibid.*, pp. 912–52.

accounted for his survival.[25] All three defendants were promptly found guilty and executed.[26]

Essex soon learned of these events, although he apparently remained at Chartley through the summer and autumn months. There is no evidence that he put pressure on either Elways or Weston, even if he could have, yet he seems to have been in communication with someone about the affair. Southampton, who knew the details through Secretary Lake, probably kept Essex informed about the proceedings, for his actions betray some knowledge of them. Sometime in October, probably after Mrs. Turner's testimony, Essex requested Chief Justice Coke to examine Franklin about the whereabouts of the wedding ring he had given to Frances Howard about ten years before.[27] After the divorce, it seems, Essex had demanded that the ring be returned, but the Countess had not obliged. He suspected that she had used the ring to pay Franklin for drugs used against either Essex himself or Sir Thomas Overbury.

Franklin did not possess the ring, yet his confession proved crucial in the case against the Countess—as Essex had seemed to sense.[28] At the trial before the King's Bench on 27 November the apothecary admitted providing Mrs. Turner and Weston with poisons. More important, he confessed that he had been approached by the Countess of Essex *after* Weston's confession and was requested to admit nothing about their earlier dealings. Franklin's admissions clearly established the fact that the Countess was deeply implicated in the murder plot.

On 24 May 1616 the Countess stood on trial in Westminster Hall as an accessory to the murder of Sir Thomas Overbury.[29] Both she and her husband were tried by a specially summoned commission of peers, headed by the Lord Chancellor, and a large group of legal experts, supervised by Chief Justice Coke. Attorney General Bacon presented the Crown's evidence to the peers who acted as the jury. When asked to speak for herself, the Countess could only say, "I can much aggravate, but nothing extenuate my fault; I desire mercy, and that the lords will intercede for me to the king." [30] In

[25] C. S. P. Ven., 1615–1617, p. 61.

[26] Sir John Maclean, ed., Letters from George Lord Carew to Sir Thomas Roe, Camden Society (London, 1860), p. 19.

[27] C. S. P. Dom., 1611–1618, pp. 324, 328.

[28] Cobbett, State Trials, 2: 937–47, 990–95.

[29] Greville, Secret History, pp. 393–95.

[30] Cobbett, State Trials, 2: 951–66.

the sentence which followed, the Lord High Steward declared, "Thou shalt be carried from hence to the Tower of London, and from thence to the place of execution, where you are to be hanged by the neck till you are dead; and the lord have mercy on your soul." Three days later she was committed to the Tower to await her fate. At her own request, the Countess was not assigned to the room where Overbury had been poisoned.

Somerset's trial, which began on 25 May, proved to be a lengthy legal battle. The evidence garnered from the examinations and trials of Weston and Elways was introduced. Dozens of new witnesses—servants, friends, and relatives of Overbury—were examined and gave their depositions. Some incriminating correspondence between Overbury and Northampton and some of Somerset's letters to Overbury were read before the commissioners. The crucial examination and the confession of the late James Franklin were introduced. Bacon, who carried the burden of the case, won his points, and the Scottish-born courtier was found guilty by his peers. Though a modern legal mind might find many flaws in the case, especially in the procedures and handling of evidence, the specially summoned commission sentenced Somerset to death. When asked for his reaction to the sentence, he mustered enough courage to say, "I only desire death according to my degree." [31]

The Earl of Essex, though not a member of the high steward's commission, came to London to witness the trials of his former wife and his rival. He supposedly viewed the arraignment and sentence of the Countess but deliberately kept in the background. He also appeared as a spectator at Somerset's trial, where, a contemporary noted, "he stood in full face." [32] He had little reason to be ashamed of his presence there. Justice, however tardy, had run its course.

Both aristocratic accessories to Overbury's murder received death sentences, but neither died by the hand of the executioner. [33] Many thought that the King, who declared himself strongly committed to seeing justice prevail, would permit the sentences to be carried out. Instead, he granted the couple a reprieve, assigned them a suite in the Tower, and allowed them to live within the confines of the age-old edifice.

[31] *Ibid.*, pp. 966–1,022.
[32] Devereux, *Lives of the Devereux*, 2: 266.
[33] Maclean, *Letters from Carew*, p. 60.

IV

DURING the five years following the annulment, Essex made Chartley Park rather than London the principal center of his activities. At Chartley he could express his personal feelings without fear of being heard by an informer. There his sensitive temper would less likely be stretched to the breaking point by aspersions or provocations. He hunted so frequently during this period that the county government built a bridge over the Trent at Shugborough, thus enabling him to ride more directly to Cannock Chase, a hunting ground near Chartley.[34] He attended some state affairs, but more out of duty than choice. Though he excelled at tilting, he did not appear at the Accession Day tournaments, held annually at the Tiltyard, where the Scottish favorites, the Howards, and the King's cronies invariably carried away the honors. Essex did not participate in the masques or the royal progresses and apparently even boycotted the creation ceremonies of the Prince of Wales on 4 September 1616. Nor was he—in contrast to many of his fellow peers—admitted into the sacred ranks of the Knighthood of the Bath.

Essex nevertheless took his political responsibilities very seriously. As lord lieutenant of Staffordshire, a post to which he had been appointed by the Privy Council in 1612, he carried innumerable obligations.[35] His principal duty as the Crown's personal representative in the county was to preserve peace and maintain order. To this end he commanded the local militia and was responsible for the defense of the county. Each year troops had to be mustered, reviewed, and trained; military supplies had to be inventoried and replenished; local defenses had to be repaired; new troops had to be recruited; and reports had to be made to the Privy Council. The Earl of Essex gave these matters his personal attention instead of appointing deputies, as many peers did, and thereby secured firsthand experience in recruitment and military administration.

The Crown's most pressing need from 1613 to 1619 was gaining reinforcements for Ireland. Since the days of Essex's grandfather, England had sought to subjugate the Irish by both conquest and colonization. The English had occupied Ulster since 1603, and year

---

34 Devereux, *Lives of the Devereux*, 2: 276.

35 *A. P. C. 1613–1614*, pp. 111, 433, 555. There is some evidence, though not conclusive, that he served as Lord Lieutenant in 1612; see the Bagot MSS, Folger Shakespeare Library.

by year, occupation troops pushed back the Irish and increased the size of the Pale so that more English, Welsh, and Scottish settlers could immigrate and obtain land. To meet this perennial demand, the Privy Council relied upon the counties, particularly those in the western and midland sections, for fresh troops. Thus, in 1613 the councilors requested 100 foot from Essex;[36] in 1614 and 1615 the same number;[37] and in 1616 only 25 foot.[38] To fill these quotas was no simple task. The council, demanding able-bodied Staffordians who were to be trained and well supplied with equipment, warned Essex against levying rogues, vagabonds, and the infirm. In 1614, at his first muster, Essex secured a grass-roots knowledge of the local military problems. He discovered many deficiencies among the troops. They lacked, above all, training and experience, and needed more and better equipment. Despite these shortcomings in his troops, Essex appears to have done his duty, for the council reappointed him to the post. His later demands for a permanent staff and a professional army undoubtedly stem from his firsthand contacts with this half-medieval, half-modern military system.

During this six-year period Essex's services were sought on several occasions. In February 1615, Prince Christian of Brunswick, the administrator of Halberstadt, asked him to participate in a military campaign on the Continent.[39] Essex seems to have turned down this and similar requests. Two years later he was recommended to lead an expedition into the Mediterranean Sea against the Algerine pirates. "The Earl of Essex," the ambassador wrote the Venetian doge, "although he does not speak so freely, would be very glad to go."[40] James, however, apparently turned down Essex's request.

The master of Chartley Manor also devoted some time to pressing personal and family matters during these years. In 1616 by authority of a decree from the Prerogative Court he took possession of his landed inheritance,[41] receiving those possessions of his father's which had been supervised by the Court of Wards. Henceforth the manors in Staffordshire, Gloucestershire, Herefordshire, and Wales

---

[36] *A. B. C. 1613–1614*, p. 111.
[37] *Ibid., 1614–1616*, pp. 90, 230.
[38] *Ibid.*, p. 697.
[39] British Museum, Additional MSS, 46,188.
[40] *C. S. P. Ven., 1615–1617*, p. 210.
[41] Tenison, *Elizabethan England*, 12: 149.

would be his to oversee, and the income, the influence, and the power accruing from these lands would be at his disposal.

Despite this inheritance Essex did not remarry or even contemplate remarriage at this time. He did, however, concern himself with matches for his sisters, both of whom were in their mid-teens. Like most contemporary family heads, Essex was more concerned with the perpetuation of the Devereux line than with the feelings of the betrothed. On 10 May 1615 he arranged for the marriage of his youngest sister, Lady Dorothy, to Henry Shirley, son of Sir George Shirley of Staunton-Harrold, Leicester.[42] In an indenture signed by Sir George and Essex, a jointure was settled on Lady Dorothy. The wedding soon followed.

Two years later Lady Frances Devereux, Essex's elder sister, married William Seymour.[43] A controversial figure who gave the King no end of worry, he was the sole surviving hope of the Seymours, a powerful family in southwestern England. An illegitimate son of Edward Seymour, Earl of Hertford, he was the heir to his grandfather's title, Earl of Hertford. Since his grandmother Lady Katherine Gray also possessed a claim to the throne, William Seymour had political potentialities out of proportion to his age and legal status. Earlier his grandfather had tried to realize these potentialities by marrying him to Lady Arabella Stuart, the King's kinswoman, and thus unite two blue bloods. When James found out about the marriage plans, Lady Arabella was incarcerated in the Tower. Seymour, who fled to the Continent to escape the royal wrath, remained in exile for five years. After Arabella's death, his petition to return to England was granted. About a year later, on 3 March 1617, he married Lady Frances at Drayton Basset, the residence of her grandmother the aged Countess of Leicester.[44] It proved to be a successful political alliance for all parties concerned, Essex included.

Soon Essex's brother Walter, namesake of the first Earl of Essex, was personally knighted by the King.[45] The ceremony took place on 2 September 1617 at Ashby de la Zouch, the country estate of

---

[42] *C. S. P. Dom., 1611–1618*, pp. 286, 344.

[43] A. A. Locke, *The Seymour Family* (London: Constable and Company, 1911), p. 121.

[44] Devereux, *Lives of the Devereux*, 2: 275.

[45] Josiah C. Wedgwood, ed., *Historical Collections of Staffordshire* (London: William Salt Archaeological Society, 1920), p. 52.

the Hastings. That same year Sir Walter was appointed sheriff of Warwickshire. Whether or not Essex was instrumental in arranging for this honor is not known, but in subsequent skirmishes with the Stuarts, Sir Walter aligned himself with his more famous brother.

At Chartley the Earl of Essex surrounded himself with personal aides and household servants consonant with his station.[46] Most important was Essex's personal secretary, Arthur Wilson, who served his patron for two decades. This Cambridge-educated author, born in 1596, was a well-traveled libertine who entered Essex's household in some servile capacity in 1614. He soon secured Essex's complete confidence. Wilson wrote about an incident which occurred that first year:

Toward Michaelmas a great alarm and outcry arose in the house after dinner; some thought it was fire, some thieves, and all ran hither and thither. My Lord of Essex, and some Lords and Gentlemen with him ran out on the drawbridge, for the house had a very deep moat around it. I ran where I saw others run, into the laundry. When I came there I found the cause. One of the laundry maids rinsing clothes in the moat upon a little gallery for that purpose, she fell into the water; another coming to help her, was pulled in by her; the third to help both, was pulled in by both, which caused the shrieks and noise which begot this disturbance. The two last got out by help of poles the first comers reached unto them; but she who fell in first, with the plunging of the water, was driven without reach, or sense of taking hold. So that my Lord of Essex, and all who stood on the bridge, cried out, "Now she sinks, now she's gone!" I came, as God would have it, just as she was so, and had only a glimpse of where she sunk; and being no time to study what to do, I instantly, with a running leap, bounced into the water. My plunging then brought her up again, and holding her up with one arm, I swam with the other; the people drew her out, and with much ado recovered her. For this my Lord of Essex took me into liking, and would have me wait on him in his chamber; and he presently furnished me with clothes, which begot envy; and entrusted me with the keeping of his private purse.[47]

Essex came to depend greatly upon his new-found attendant. He took Wilson on his hunting trips and, with Sir Charles Egerton and Sir Peter Lee, they chased the stag. They fought side by side on the Continent. Essex gave Wilson special assignments and relied upon him for advice. Most of the great landed lords, like the ruling

[46] For the following information see Arthur Wilson's *Autobiography*, first published in Francis Peck, *Desiderata Curiosa*, 2 vols. (London, 1779), 2: 460–83.
[47] *Ibid.*

monarchs, had their learned personal secretaries care for private correspondence and counsel. Essex's father had employed several secretaries like Wilson. Thomas Egerton had poet John Donne; the Earl of Devonshire had philosopher Thomas Hobbes; the Earl of Montgomery had Michael Oldisworth, the legal antiquarian; and Fulke Greville had John Coke, later Principal Secretary.

Wilson wrote his own rules while serving Essex. He had economic security and many personal privileges. He wrote poetry, read philosophy, and studied history. Wilson's most ambitious project was a history of the Jacobean era entitled *Historie of the Reign of King James*.[48] This account, written at Chartley after Wilson had associated with his patron for several years, undoubtedly represents Essex's patronage and influence. Though the book is not strictly an apology, Essex received favorable treatment in its pages; the Court of King James, on the other hand, fared very badly.

To most contemporaries Wilson was a libertarian. Though baptized a Catholic, he became an Anglican and toward the end of his life professed sympathies for Presbyterianism. He had no use for the divine-right theory of kingship.[49] His plays and *Historie* reveal a man extremely critical of courtly hypocrisy, flattery, and immorality. He, like his patron, could not stomach the royal court or the obsequious hangers-on. Whether or not Essex was greatly influenced by the views of his secretary is not certain, but the fact that he tolerated Wilson for twenty years was testimony enough for most contemporaries.

In 1615, Essex appointed as his chaplain-in-ordinary Thomas Pestell, a Leicestershire poet who had taken both his B. A. and his M. A. degrees at Queen's College, Cambridge.[50] Although his poetry was mediocre, Pestell's preaching brought him wide-spread fame. In 1615 and 1623 several of his sermons were published, probably through Essex's patronage. His religious views reveal a man of Puritan sympathies. At a later date he was investigated by the Court of High Commission for refusing to conform to the Laudian ceremonies.

Essex also lent his name to the arts. In 1614, Joseph Hall honored

48 This book was published after Wilson's death in 1653.
49 This fact is evident in his play *The Swisser*, ed. Albert Feuillerat (Paris: Fischbacher, 1904), p. 14.
50 See Thomas Pestell, *The Poems*, ed. Hannah Buchan (Oxford: B. Blackwell, 1940), especially the introductory material on his life.

Essex with a political treatise.[51] Five years later Michael East, music master of Lichfield Cathedral, dedicated a collection of madrigals to Essex. "There bee few Arts of life worth," he wrote in the flowery dedicatory epistle very typical of the times, "that so much stand in neede of Patronage, as Musicke: for with the greatest part of the world, all Sciences which bring not in money, are esteemed needless and idle. . . . I beseech your Lordship therefore to bee pleased to let these Songs bee protected by the greatness of your name; for which onely no doubt all men will love them better. This name of yours in your Father, hath honoured many learned Workes, and graces many Actions, for he loved Arts, and men of Arte, both Civill and Militarie, Schollars and Souldiers, and these two (which were the true Springs from which all earthly glory is derived) made him renowned in the world so loved at home, so feared abroade."[52]

Essex was featured in *Mirrour of Majestie* in 1618.[53] In this elaborate emblem booklet, a Jacobean social register, the author honored all the officers of state and the principal peers of the realm with an explicatory poem and a representation of their escutcheon. The simply designed Devereux shield is followed by a doggerel rhyme:

> The chiefest of this Scuchion comprehends
> Three *Torteaux*, which unto all commends
> A Firme and plenteous liberality,
> Proper to you, and to your familie:
> And this one vertue, in you (cleare as day)
> All other vertues elements display.

On the next page the author-editor printed a highly figurative emblem which, in his estimation, symbolized the head of the Devereux dynasty. He portrayed Jupiter's gauntlet-covered arm stretching from the heavens and launching thunderbolts. Power, fearlessness, and valor: these traits characterized the Devereux.

[51] See above, p. 36.

[52] See the dedicatory statement in the preface to his madrigals entitled *Fourth Set of Bookes* (London, 1619).

[53] Henry Peacham, *Mirrour of Majestie* (London, 1618), p. 3. Ralph Brook's *Catalogue and Succession of the Kings, Princes, Dukes, Marquesses, Earls and Viscounts of this Realme of England since the Norman Conquest* (London, 1619), contains a section on the Essex earldom and material on the Devereux Earls of Essex, including the third Earl. In his *Horwologia* (London, 1620), Henry Holland includes information on the first and second Earls of Essex but excludes the third Earl.

The Devereux motto, *Virtutio Comes Invidia*, reveals another significant character trait.[54] To some this meant "Envy is a companion of virtue"; to others, "Envy ever follows virtue." Essex, envious or not, remained loyal to his sovereign. Though allied with the opposition peers and commons against the foreign policy and certain domestic measures, Essex opposed neither the King himself nor the monarchical system. The spark of rebellion may have lain smoldering inside him, but Essex obeyed the laws and bided his time.

V

In 1617 the King, assisted by several cronies and some of the high officers of state, toured the kingdom in the style of bygone days.[55] He progressed northward through the eastern shires to Edinburgh, where he was received by his cooling Scottish subjects with much pomp and fanfare. His return to Scotland, James claimed, stemmed from personal reasons—he wished to once again see the land of his nativity. His real motive, however, was to impose the Anglican ritual upon the Kirk. Although opposed by most of his advisers, James would not be thwarted from his aim. The Scots, in particular, vigorously protested what appeared to be a more papist approach to worship. But the strong will of James Stuart prevailed for the moment.

After touring Scotland, the British monarch began his homeward journey, returning via Lancashire, Cheshire, and Staffordshire. James passed within a few miles of Chartley Park, but he did not stop to visit Essex. The Staffordians, nevertheless, gave the King a warm reception.[56] The mayor and the common council agreed to provide James with "most royaliste" entertainment. They requested the citizens to repair their roof tops, paint their house fronts, and sand the streets. They voted money to repair Northgate, whereupon the passage was widened, a nearby barn removed, the gates adorned, and the arms of the kingdom mounted. The City Hall windows were glazed for the rare occasion, and Richard Weston, a councilor of law, was asked to prepare a suitable oration. The leaders also made sure that the Earl of Essex, their newly selected high steward, would be present for the affair.

54 The motto on the second Earl's shield read *Basis Virtutum Constantia*.
55 See Willson, *James I*, pp. 389–93.
56 Nichols, *Progresses*, 3: 415.

On 28 August a drenching rainstorm announced the arrival of the King. When the rain finally slackened temporarily, the monarch and the Earl of Arundel examined the recently repaired gate and the old city walls at Northgate. When Arundel remarked that the town was ancient, James said that it could not be, "for it is three years sithence we made them a Maior Town, for before that tyme, they could not sende Burgesses to the Parliament, but were onlye governed by Bayliffs." [57] The royal memory erred on this point: the town was old, for Stafford had sent burgesses to Westminster for centuries. James was no doubt confused by the recent modification of the charter. [58]

After this blunder the King mounted the horse of state in preparation for the formal procession through the town. The Earl of Essex, plumes and all, rode by the King's side. In a meaningful gesture, the King commissioned Essex to carry the decorative sword of state before him. It was the second time the sovereign had so honored him. Followed by the other nobles, bishops, trumpeters, and a host of lesser attendants, the two men proceeded to the center of town. Near the market place the mayor and the councilors, seated on a richly panoplied and carpeted stand, awaited the procession, while multitudes of people thronged the open square. Upon his arrival James artfully commented that Stafford was like a "Little London." [59]

Essex then formally presented the newly elected mayor, Thomas Cradocke, to the King, and the ceremonies began. After a prayer was offered, the mayor kissed the beautifully carved mace and delivered it to the King. Weston then commenced his speech, reminding the King that Staffordians were neither social upstarts nor firebrands and were not ambitious name-changers or buyers of pedigrees. As if to correct the erroneous views of the sovereign, the councilor at law also pointed out that Stafford had been incorporated during the reign of King John. His oration over, Weston presented an expensive cup to the King as a reminder of the love

[57] *Ibid.*

[58] On 15 April 1615, James I had granted Stafford a new borough charter to eliminate some conflicts between local magistrates. In his capacity as High Steward, Essex had administered the oath to the new alderman; it is entirely possible that he had used his influence to secure the revised charter. See John W. Bradley, *The Royal Charters and Letters Patents Granted to the Burgesses of Stafford* (Stafford, 1897), p. 167.

[59] Nichols, *Progresses*, 3: 415.

and loyalty of the people of Stafford. When James had accepted the gift, smiled, and thanked the speaker, the multitude replied in unison, "God Blesse your Majestie." [60]

After this demonstration of loyalty the Earl of Essex and his sovereign went their separate ways. Essex returned to nearby Chartley, and King James traveled to Ashby, where he bestowed a knighthood upon Walter Devereux and then headed for London. That James sought to win support from Englishmen of all stripes during his journey was obvious.

In the months following the royal progress several of Essex's enemies and rivals experienced reversals. The Earl of Suffolk, then Lord Treasurer, became the butt of much criticism and was compelled to resign his post. He and his wife were subsequently tried for embezzling, found guilty, and fined heavily. The Earl of Nottingham lost the Lord Admiralship, a position which he had held since the defeat of the Spanish Armada, and the office was awarded to a rising favorite, George Villiers. Suffolk's sons, Lord Howard de Walden and Sir Thomas, lost their influence among the courtiers. The Howards, clearly out of royal favor, became fair game for political attack. Lastly, in October 1618, Sir Walter Raleigh, a rival of Essex's father, was executed in Old Palace Yard, Westminster, after an unsuccessful attempt to escape from the Tower. [61]

At the time of Raleigh's death the third Earl of Essex was in his twenty-seventh year. In the seventeen years that had transpired since his father's execution, Essex had experienced the seamy side of a corrupt Court dominated by the second Earl's enemies; in fact, he had been humiliated and victimized by those enemies. Fortunately, his relatives, friends, and allies looked out for his interests and helped him recover some of his family fortune and influence. These same individuals also exposed the Howards and ousted them from their places in the Court of King James. The third Earl, though more of an innocent bystander than an active participant in these political vendettas, must have experienced some personal satisfaction from the eclipse of the Howards and the execution of Raleigh. Yet, though the beneficiary of this retributive form of justice, Essex remained ever distrustful of courtesans and aloof from the Court, placing his political hopes, instead, in Parliament.

[60] *Ibid.*

[61] A. L. Rowse, *Sir Walter Raleigh* (New York: Harper and Brothers, 1962), p. 318.

CHAPTER 5

A Defender of Old English Honour

I

THE DEATH OF QUEEN ANNE and the drift toward war brought the Earl of Essex out of seclusion. In April 1619 he left Chartley for London to attend the state funeral of the late Queen, who had shown him favor after the divorce, and to offer his condolences to the King. He arrived in the metropolis only to find that the final rites were postponed because of the King's health.[1]

Essex received his first diplomatic assignment while waiting for the funeral to take place. He was commissioned to meet and extend an official welcome to the Marquis de Tremouille, ambassador extraordinary from the French Court.[2] In conjunction with the May Day festivities Essex entertained the Marquis and his large retinue. Very likely this commission represented the influence of the Earl of Southampton, who had recently been sworn a Privy Councilor; but no doubt Essex's earlier associations with the French Court and his command of the language also explain the choice.

Two weeks later Essex took part in the funeral ceremony of Queen Anne. He joined the long procession, which led from Somerset House to Westminster Abbey, and witnessed the interment rites at the lower end of Henry VII's chapel. After fulfilling these obligations the Earl remained in London at Essex House. Within months all Europe was at war.

In the summer of 1619, one year after deposing King Ferdinand, a Catholic, the Bohemian nobility offered the vacant throne to Frederick V, Elector of Palatine and son-in-law of James I. When Frederick, a Calvinist, accepted the kingship and traveled to Prague for the coronation in the autumn, the European powers became involved in a long and bitter struggle that lasted for thirty years. The Catholic states, led by the Spanish Hapsburgs, sided with Ferdinand and promised to defend his claim to the Bohemian

---

[1] Nichols, *Progresses*, 3: 538.
[2] Devereux, *Lives of the Devereux*, 2: 276.

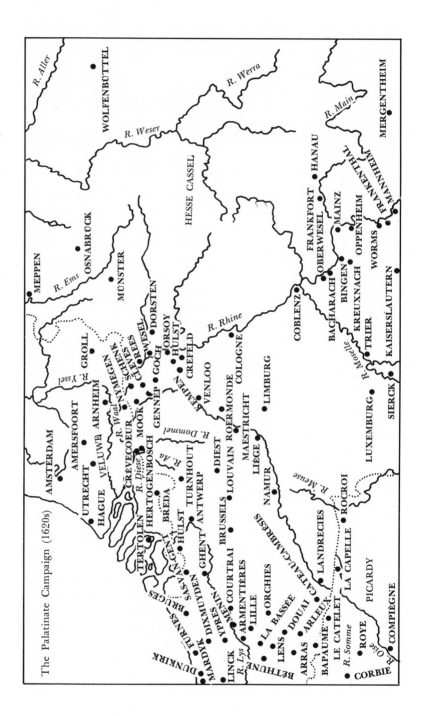

The Palatinate Campaign (1620s)

throne, while the leaders of the Protestant Union backed Frederick and offered him assistance. These events placed the English sovereign in a most awkward position. He hoped to prevent a war through mediation or by negotiation with the Spanish Hapsburgs. At the same time he felt obliged as a loving father to help his daughter and his son-in-law. Moreover, most of his subjects sympathized with Frederick and clamored for a war against the Catholic powers.

The following year, while General Ambrogio Spinola, the Italian nobleman who commanded the Spanish-paid mercenaries, prepared for his invasion of the Rhineland, enthusiasm mounted in England for the cause of Elector Frederick and the Protestant Union. Lord Doncaster, who returned from the Continent in January, proposed a crusade against the Catholics, and Sir Andrew Gray, a Scottish officer in the service of the Bohemian government, requested royal permission to borrow money from London financiers and recruit a regiment for the Elector. Archbishop Abbot, however, proved to be the principal advocate of armed intervention. In March, after warning James about neglecting the holy enterprise, he obtained permission from the English sovereign to collect a voluntary contribution from the clergy, who responded generously to the cause. Some of the nobility loaned money, but London aldermen, who really controlled the purse strings of the nation, withheld their support. Though sympathetic with the cause, they disapproved of the means, namely, the "benevolent" gifts and loans. Let Parliament be convened, they ordered, and then the Bohemian cause would secure broader support.

This demand James promptly dismissed. After living successfully without one for six years, he was not prepared to summon another Parliament, especially when he disapproved of official intervention. He held, first of all, some misgivings about his son-in-law's claim to the Bohemian crown. Secondly, he still hoped to secure a peaceful solution to the knotty succession problems in central Europe, and thus live up to his motto and his international reputation as a peacemaker.

Many Englishmen, however, wanted war. In the spring of 1620, shortly after Spinola took to the field, the clamor for armed intervention continued. Though the King refused to underwrite an expedition, he permitted the English people to provide monetary gifts. "Now we begin in London," wrote John Coke, "to raise a voluntary contribution for his [Frederick's] aid, wherein the rich proceed with caution, but the common sort with a strange heartiness and zeal."[3]

The Earl of Essex, still in London, responded eagerly to the crisis created by General Spinola's war preparations. In May he and several gentlemen representing England's leading families volunteered to join the army of the Elector as adventurers.[4] Technically, James could have easily dissuaded or prevented the volunteers from leaving English soil, if he had so desired, but such a refusal would certainly not have been well received by the host of sympathizers. Early in June, after much soul searching, James finally consented to send a contingent to assist his son-in-law.[5] He still refused to openly declare war or intervene directly in the Continental conflict, but, after consultations with his Privy Council, decided to send 4,000 volunteers to defend the Palatinate and agreed to underwrite their expenses. Gradually England backed into the Thirty Years War.

The command of the expedition was in question. General Edward Cecil, the experienced son of the late Lord Burghley, was among the best qualified. His principal rival, Sir Horace Vere, the third son of the late Earl of Oxford, hailed from an ancient family of war heroes and was equally fit for the position. Also under consideration were the Earl of Southampton and, of course, young-blooded and less experienced aristocrats, like Essex and the Earl of Oxford. James selected Sir Horace as the commanding general and Sir John Burlacy as his second-in-command. This decision, however judicious, offended Cecil's pride so much that he withdrew from the expedition.[6]

Essex secured a captaincy along with the Earl of Oxford, Lord Gerard, Lord Grey, Sir Edward Sackville, Sir William Fairfax, and Sir John Wentworth. Each of these "young and daring spirits," as Arthur Wilson called them, was commissioned to lead a regiment of 250 men,[7] and, preferably from trained and experienced gentlemen, was to recruit his own troops. "Owing to the youth of these," the Venetian ambassador reported in July, "they have nominated

[3] *H. M. C. Twelfth Report*, Appendix 1, p. 108.

[4] *C. S. P. Ven., 1619–1621*, p. 263. For additional details of Essex's decision see the Bagot MSS, Folger Shakespeare Library, especially MS L.a. 907.

[5] *A. P. C. 1619–1621*, p. 225. Also see British Museum, Harleian MSS, 5109.

[6] *Cabala sive scrinia sacra* (London, 1691), p. 173.

[7] Wilson, *Historie*, p. 135.

their lieutenants and officers, captains experienced in war, at least forty years old. By the power of money and their personal following, in addition to the general propensity of the multitude, they will easily obtain a fine levy . . . the show will be great, and one must believe that they will fight better for honor than the others in every circumstances." [8]

Despite the enthusiasm of the masses, contributions came in more slowly than expected, recruitment lagged, and the acquisition of equipment bogged down. The arms, which were defective, arrived late. Two precious months passed before the expedition could move. Then only 2,000 men—half the expected number of troops—answered the roll of the drums. Nevertheless, as the Venetian ambassador noted: "They form the finest regiment that has left this kingdom for many a year, but it cost a great deal both for the levy and the transport. The two companies of the Earls of Oxford and Essex were recruited and brought to the place of embarcation at their own expense." [9]

Essex was more fortunate than his colleagues in this, his first, crusade on the Continent. He encountered no recruitment problems. On the contrary, so many men volunteered to fight and die with him that his regiment swelled to over 300. [10] This popularity, however self-satisfying, proved costly, for Essex had to equip and maintain the additional volunteers out of personal funds.

Spinola soon struck. In August, leaving a large force in Flanders to check the Dutch, he advanced eastward toward the Rhine with nearly 20,000 men. Feigning a march into Bohemia, he crossed the Rhine at Coblenz, and in a masterly military tactic suddenly wheeled around, recrossed the Rhine, and marched into Mainz on 19 August, catching the Palatine army completely off guard. "It is now too late," lamented the Electress-mother in Heidelberg, "to doubt whether Spinola's large army is destined against the Palatinate, and it is already at our door." [11]

Essex left Gravesend early in August, crossed the Channel, and disembarked in Holland with only a middling-sized force and moderate support from the sovereign. The troops were met by

[8] *C. S. P. Ven., 1619–1621*, p. 297.

[9] *Ibid.*, p. 348.

[10] Kennett, *Complete History of England*, 2: 722.

[11] C. V. Wedgwood, *The Thirty Years War* (London, Penguin Books, 1957), p. 111.

Prince Maurice, who conducted Vere's contingent through the United Provinces and on the last day of August assisted them in crossing the Rhine on a boat-style bridge a little below Wesel.[12] Here the English joined with Prince Henry of Nassau, a brother of Maurice and future protector of the United Provinces, who had an army of 2,000 horse and 400 musketeers which he took from the garrisoned town of Jülich. The combined armies then marched parallel to the Rhine to Coblenz, where Spinola had been a month earlier.

Here, camped along the Moselle, Essex experienced gunpowder warfare for the first time. Food was scarce. Nearly 100 English soldiers were too sick to move on. On one occasion Captain Fairfax, Essex's subordinate, sent a squadron to secure bread and wine in a nearby town, but the local inhabitants greeted them with gunfire. In the fracas that followed, some natives were slain. The next day came the reprisal. "In the Halt before Coblentz," wrote Arthur Wilson, who was with his patron, "one bullet among others from the Town, past between Generall Vere, and the Earl of Essex standing together, and hit a gentleman, called, Flood, on the elbow." It was a narrow escape.

On 16 September, imitating Spinola's shrewd tactic, the combined English and Dutch armies faced eastward, feigned a crossing of the Moselle, and suddenly drew back to the Rhine. Their subterfuge, designed to confuse Spinola's scouts and keep his troops out of action, was followed by a quick recrossing of the Rhine in punts. On 24 September, just below Frankfurt, the troops crossed the Main and found themselves so close to Spinola that two alarms were sounded. The next day a long march took the army to Darmstadt, a town belonging to the Elector. Here, the conducting mission fulfilled, Prince Henry and his troops left the English and returned to Jülich to guard their homeland against surprise attack. Vere, in turn, joined an army of 1,500 men, which the princes of the Protestant Union had put into the field. On 1 October the combined armies joined the Margrave of Ansbach, who was the Elector's general, and several other Protestant leaders and their troops. Under the Margrave's command, this polyglot army, now over 12,000 men, immediately marched toward Altzi to take Spinola unexpectedly.

[12] For the following account I have relied mainly upon Wilson, *Historie*, pp. 136–51. Wilson went with Essex as an aide-de-camp.

The general was not that easily surprised, however. Realizing that the Palatinate town was indefensible, he turned about and marched toward Ansbach's army. A harmless skirmish between scouts ensued, and each army tried to secure the military advantage. Spinola occupied one hill, forcing his adversary to withdraw his horse and cannons to another. Weary from long marches, each army watched and waited for the opportune moment to attack.

Essex and his fellow officers, eager to battle, took a forward position. After surveying the situation, Vere selected 80 musketeers from each division and prepared for the attack. Dr. Cornelius Burgess, the commander's Puritan chaplain, gave them his blessing and encouragement. Thus prepared, the musketeers patiently waited for the Margrave's command to charge. But the command never came; the Margrave of Ansbach, fearing the lateness of the hour, refused to attack. Essex, Oxford, and Vere, somewhat disgusted, rode to the hilltop, only to see Spinola's army in the process of quietly marching away in the dusk. Using their wagons as shields, the foot soldiers marched away "without drum or trumpet," while the horse brought up the rear. As the last division moved out of sight, Spinola's soldiers broke into shouts of joy: they had escaped from a perilous situation. Ansbach had lost his golden opportunity to deal a decisive blow to the invincible Spinola.

The Margrave of Ansbach forfeited another tactical opportunity. Since his army was nearer Oppenheim, Spinola's headquarters, than was the Genoan himself, Ansbach should have either forced Spinola to fight or captured his headquarters. "The Earl of Essex being informed of this by some that knew the Country," wrote Wilson, "pressed the Margrave of Ansbach to it, desiring him not to let slip an opportunity so happily put into his hand. He, not well pleased to be urged to a thing so contrary to his humour, replied angerily, 'There is a Fort betwixt us and the Town, and we must pass thither under the mercy of their Cannon.'"[13] This danger the Margrave refused to risk. Vere was furious. Indecision and dissension lost for the Protestant allies.

Spinola took advantage of these blunders. He safely returned to his center of operations in Oppenheim, rested for a week, replenished his troops, and then began to play a cat-and-mouse game with his adversaries, who outnumbered him. Feigning an attack on a border

[13] *Ibid.*, p. 138.

town, he brought Ansbach's army into view but then retreated rather than risk an open battle. As Arthur Wilson wrote, "They sported with one another, as children at seek and find."

In the meantime winter set in. Frost began to cover the desolate and naked hills. The English, ill-accustomed to the Continental climate, found themselves so poorly prepared for winter that they had to burn many of their wagons to provide warmth. It grew so cold that the soldiers, Wilson noted, "lay in heaps upon the ground close together like sheep cover'd as it were with a sheet of snow." Not without reason did the English contingent go into winter quarters. Essex assumed a defensive position in the walled city of Frankendal.

II

THE EARL OF ESSEX, realizing the hopeless situation in the Palatinate, decided to return to England to raise more troops. Leaving shortly before the news of the enemy's victory at White Hill reached Vere, and accompanied by about 20 men, including the Earl of Oxford, he left Frankendal and proceeded through Lorraine and northern France. On 11 November he and Oxford received a warm welcome in London. "The return was the more joyed at," diarist D'Ewes noted, "because their families were great and noble, and they had no issue, nor were married."[14] Sir Francis Bacon, now Lord Chancellor, did not let Essex's return pass unnoticed. In a personally penned letter, written from York House, he wished Essex success in soliciting aid for the Palatinate.[15]

James was furious, not at the English leaders for returning, but at Gondomar, the Spanish ambassador, who had implied that Spinola would not advance into the Palatinate. In late September upon hearing of Spinola's conquests there, James burst into a storm of anger, realizing that he had been duped. Shortly before Essex's return the sovereign resolved to send more military aid to the Elector and the princes of the Protestant Union. His pacificism could still not allow him to declare war, but he did pronounce "an auxiliary war." On 25 October the King issued a circular letter to all nobles and bishops, asking for aid. Funds were needed immediately! There was no time to call a Parliament, he contended, hence

14 From D'Ewes's "Excerpta" in the Forster MS 48, D.12, Victoria and Albert Library, South Kensington, London.

15 *H. M. C. Twelfth Report*, Appendix 9, p. 174.

the unusual plea. The leaders of the war party resisted the "benevo-lence," one lord after another refusing to contribute. The voluntary payment was so paltry that James had no other recourse: on 6 November he finally announced that Parliament would convene on 16 January.[16]

News of the fall of Prague came about two weeks after Essex's return. It corroborated his and other reports about the critical situation on the Continent and confirmed the suspicions and warn-ings of many Englishmen, especially those sympathetic to Calvinism. London preachers castigated Gondomar, whose life was threatened, and denounced the papists and clamored for intervention. On Christmas Eve the King issued a royal proclamation intended for those who intermeddled in the affairs of state. There was entirely too much discussion of foreign affairs, the document warned, too much implied criticism of the royal foreign policy. James promised that the guilty individuals would be punished accordingly.

Despite this sour note, the Christmas season was a festive one in England. The members of the Court moved from feast to feast. At Theobalds the King entertained the Marquis of Cadenet, a special ambassador who came to propose a French alliance. Later, on Twelfth Night, the nobles banqueted in the House of Lords' chamber and danced at Whitehall. On Twelfth Day the royal company performed a masque there. Two days later Prince Charles and several nobles performed at the Tiltyard. That night Essex House was the scene of a sumptuous banquet hosted by Viscount Doncaster, Essex's cousin.[17] For a week dozens of cooks prepared for the feast, the like of which had never been seen in London. Everyone who was considered important, including the King and the Prince, came to Essex House for the affair. A masque climaxed the evening.

Essex, meanwhile, apparently spent the yuletide season in the country, at either Chartley Park or Drayton. Though one of the best tilters in England, he did not attend the Tiltyard activities. He refused to be the courtier even when he might have capitalized on glory from the campaign in the Palatinate. Either he avoided the Court or the Court boycotted him.

A few days after the festivities of Twelfth Night, however, Essex

---

[16] Gardiner, *History*, 3: 381.
[17] McClure, *Chamberlain's Letters*, 2: 333.

came forward to receive his first military honor. On 10 January the Privy Council appointed him to the newly formed Council of War—the first of its kind in English history. It also included the Earls of Leicester and Oxford, Viscount Wilmot, Lords Danvers and Caulfield, Sir Edward Cecil, Sir Horatio Vere, Sir Edward Conway, Sir Richard Morrison, and Capt. John Bingham.[18] Several of these men had served under Essex's father in either France or Ireland and some had gained military experience with the Dutch army. On 13 January the Council of War, which served as an adjunct to the Privy Council, was called to the table and informed of the procedures and the proposed strategy.[19] The King was firmly resolved to recover the Palatinate, they were told, but he needed their advice. They were to meet whenever necessary at Whitehall, five members constituting a quorum. They were instructed to consult with seasoned soldiers, especially Vere and Conway, when professional opinion was advisable. They were to make a written recommendation concerning the amount of manpower, matériel, and money essential to their objective.

Throughout the first half of 1621 the Council of War met and made plans for the "auxiliary war."[20] They produced a table of organization. In their first formal report, given on 12 February, they recommended that the King levy and equip an army of 20,000 foot and 5,000 horse—an unheard of size. But those who had fought Spinola knew only too well that a small contingent, like that sent the year before, was next to useless against the large, professional armies that the Hapsburgs could put on the field. The immediate need was for two hundred fifty thousand pounds. The total estimated cost would be about nine hundred thousand pounds.[21] Parliament would provide the funds.

III

The Parliament of 1621 was the first held since the Addled Parliament. In his opening speech James I explained his predicament to the members of both Houses.[22] The foreign situation demanded

---

[18] *A. P. C. 1619–1621*, p. 333.

[19] British Museum, Additional MSS, 46, 188. A copy of the 13 January transaction is among Essex's few surviving papers.

[20] P. R. O., S. P. 16/119, fols. 4, 93–94.

[21] *C. S. P. Ven.*, *1619–1621*, p. 543.

[22] Gardiner, *History*, 4: 25–29.

action. Elector Frederick, his son-in-law, must be freed from the menace of Spinola's army and occupation. The English would have to prepare for war. The urgent need was money. To conduct a successful campaign, James claimed, he needed supplies, which he promised to use for an expedition to the Palatinate. He pointed out the ordnance problem that awaited a solution. In return for advice and supplies James promised to reform what was amiss and deal with personal grievances.

Essex faithfully attended the debates in Westminster Hall from the King's speech to the adjournment four months later.[23] He did not surrender his vote to a proxy and rarely missed a daily meeting. The House of Lords had witnessed several significant changes since the Addled Parliament.[24] Prince Charles, now in his majority, attended the deliberations. Not since the days of Henry VII had a royal peer sat in the Upper House. King James encouraged the attendance of his heir, it seems, but discouraged any partisanship. Charles's very presence, however advisable, proved most unfortunate, for he sided with George Villiers, Duke of Buckingham, and having entered the political arena, could not avoid the thrusts and counterthrusts. Charles undoubtedly learned much about parliamentary politics, but he also made enemies, not the least of whom was Essex.

Old faces were gone. Both Lord Chancellor Egerton and the Earl of Northampton had passed away. The Howards were no longer predominant. New faces included Lord Chancellor Bacon and Lord Admiral Buckingham. Bacon, recently raised to the peerage as Viscount Saint Albans, had many rivals and enemies, some of whom regarded him as an untrustworthy, ambitious upstart. Others, though admiring his brilliance, detested his arrogance. During the days of the Addled Parliament, Villiers had been a nobody. Now the onetime page with a pretty face was both a royal favorite and the Prince's bosom friend. He had won influence, estates, titles, places, and everything else essential to the courtier.

23 From *Lords Journal*, 3: 1–140.

24 See J. L. Sanford, *Studies and Illustrations of the great rebellion* (London, 1857), p. 109; C. H. Firth, *The House of Lords During the Civil War* (London: Longmans, Green and Company, 1910); S. R. Gardiner, *Notes of the debates in the house of lords, 1621*, Camden Society (London, 1870); Lady de Villiers, *The Hastings Journal of the Parliament of 1621*, Camden Society (London: Royal Historical Society, 1953); and Cobbett, *Parliamentary History*, 1: 1178–90.

His place, Lord High Admiral, gave him precedence rights in Parliament.

In this session of Parliament, which was enlarged by several new peers, the clergy exercised a relatively smaller voice in national policy. Archbishop Abbot, now overshadowed by the Prince, Bacon, and Buckingham and his bloc of votes, did not count so much as before. Nevertheless, James counted on clerical support in most matters. Buckingham had the greatest voice, with a total of eight proxies.[25] Behind him were Pembroke with six votes, Arundel and Richmond each with four votes, and Oxford with two. Of these factions, Buckingham and Richmond, plus several other office holders, represented the Crown. Arundel and Pembroke, however, gravitated back and forth.

Southampton still headed the aristocratic opposition.[26] Although holding only Lord Morley's proxy, he usually had the support of the Earls of Warwick, Oxford, and Essex and of Lords Saye and Spencer. The Earl of Huntingdon, too, often sided with him. These men and some members of the Lower House met frequently in Southampton's residence in Holborne to plot their strategy. Although they could not prevail without assistance from Pembroke, who often held the balance of power in the Upper House, the opposition could—and did—muster as many as twenty-nine voices out of sixty-three present.

But Southampton's opposition faction, though larger, more experienced, united in opposition to several domestic policies, and critical of the royal foreign policy, still lacked the cohesiveness of a modern party. It tended to unite against personalities or particular measures rather than for certain principles. The members were united, however, on their defense of the aristocratic way of life. Not without reason were they called "the Defenders of Old English Honour."[27] Essex and his fellow champions of the social elite also enjoyed the support of innumerable country gentry, many of whom had seats in the House of Commons. Several of the peers secured seats for their sons, brothers, other relatives, and allies. In this manner the aristocratic opposition could count on support in the Lower House and vice versa. That the opposition leaders from the two chambers met in Southampton's London home was known

[25] Compiled from the proxy registrations in *Lords Journal*, 3: 1–2.
[26] See Wilson, *Historie*, p. 161.
[27] *Ibid.*

to many; in fact, James, in his opening speech, issued a thinly disguised warning against those "popular" lords who courted the support of their untitled allies.

Essex, then thirty years old, remained overshadowed by the faction's leaders, who were older and more experienced politicians. Southampton, of course, dominated the group. Lord Spencer, a fearless speaker, and Lord Saye, a tireless debater, spearheaded the parliamentary skirmishes. Essex was a faithful supporter of the opposition but lacked eloquence and debating skill. The nobleman "had ever an honest Heart," Wilson wrote, "and though Nature had not given him Eloquence, he had a strong reason that did express him better." [28]

Though taciturn, Essex secured appointments to the major committees of the session.[29] His military interests and his place on the Council of War explain his assignment to the two committees dealing with armaments. To meet the demands of war, the Upper House established a committee, with Archbishop Abbot, the chairman, to write a military preparedness bill. The original bill empowered the Council of War to rejuvenate the munitions industry and make sure that each county was properly equipped for war. Essex appears to have favored this bill, which would have expedited war preparations and centralized military authority at the expense of the lord lieutenants, but the majority in the Upper House demanded that those deputies continue to determine the military needs of their respective counties. The amended bill was passed on 14 February, thus enabling the Council of War to continue its campaign plans. Closely associated with this measure was the bill to prohibit the exportation of ordnance. Many English-manufactured armaments were shipped to the Dutch and the Spanish. Essex and his colleagues maintained that English armaments should be used to build up English—not foreign—defenses. Essex served on the committee which penned the bill designed to prevent such exportations. The bill, which designated ordnance exporters felons and demanded the death penalty, passed on 15 February. If England was ill-prepared it was no fault of aristocrats like Essex.

Throughout the first session of the Parliament of 1621 there was much talk of the honor, privileges, and rights of the peers. Early

[28] *Ibid.*, p. 162.

[29] The following information has been gathered from the *Lords Journal;* de Villiers, *Hastings Journal;* and Gardiner, *Notes of the debates, 1621.*

in the session Arundel championed the right of a nobleman to demand reliance upon his word rather than upon an oath in public matters. Backed unanimously by his fellow peers, he secured the King's promise that this principle would be followed. More significant was the establishment of the Grand Committee on Privileges, which, under the chairmanship of Huntingdon, searched the records in the Tower and elsewhere for legal precedents.[30] The nobles, now considering the House of Lords a court of record, set out to discover their ancient rights and lost privileges. The Grand Committee spent endless hours combing through legal and parliamentary documents. Although Huntingdon and Warwick devoted much time to the task, the burden of the searching fell upon antiquarians like William Hakewill and lawyers like John Selden. The result was *Remembrances of Order and Decency*, a short guidebook containing the rules, rights, and procedures of the peers in Parliament.[31] These temporary rules of order were subsequently perfected and eventually adopted as the standing rules or procedures.

From this small pivot the peers broadened their rights. Thereafter the *Lords Journal* cites innumerable cases dealing with freedom from arrest. Essex himself appealed to the bar of justice when his servant Sir James Hales was arrested.[32] The Earl presented the case before his peers, who promptly freed Hales. Soon after, the right of free speech was tested in the Upper House. When Prince Charles tried to prevent Lord Sheffield from speaking on one occasion, the Earl of Southampton and others came to Sheffield's defense. The next day the Upper House turned itself into a committee of the whole, discussed the matter, and reaffirmed their right of free speech. Aided by the antiquarians, some peers also claimed that the Upper House was the *magnum concilium*; others viewed it as the supreme court of the nation, the court of final appeal. All the peers concurred that the jurisdiction of the Upper House should be restored to its earlier preeminence and that the peers should recover all lost rights and privileges.

To Essex and like-minded noblemen honor was the hallmark of an aristocrat and should be won in battle or for long and faithful

30 De Villiers, *Hastings Journal*, p. 22.

31 For a discussion of this theme see my article, "Essex and the Aristocratic Opposition to the Early Stuarts," *Journal of Modern History* 32 (1960): 226–28.

32 See Dorothy Gardiner, *The Oxinden Letters* (London: Constable and Company, 1933), pp. 85, 106, 312.

service.[33] Titles should be granted for heroic acts and selfless achievements, not bought and sold in the anteroom of the Presence Chamber. Places should be awarded, not to the highest bidder, not to the obsequious courtiers, and above all not to the Scots, but to those imbued with *noblesse oblige*. The King, of course, did not subscribe to such exalted notions about nobility and honor. He sold titles and dignities to those who had ready cash and frequently awarded political offices to the highest bidders or to obedient courtiers. James, however, had a plan which is often overlooked. He wanted, above all, to unify England and Scotland into a greater Britain, but he had encountered bitter opposition from Parliament, the English merchants, many personal advisers, and clerics. When parliamentary and legal means failed, James resorted to the royal prerogative to unite the two peoples by backing marriages of English and Scottish aristocrats and by elevating certain Scottish peers, including Somerset and Lennox. Just before the meeting of Parliament he had designated Lucius Cary, Viscount Falkland, who bore a Scottish title, to be comptroller of the royal household.[34] The crowning blow came on the opening day of Parliament when James appointed three Scottish peers—the Earls of March, Cambridge, and Holderness, all of whom possessed English titles—to lead the earls in the processional.

In mid-February the disgruntled English aristocrats decided to register their disapproval. Twenty-six barons, led by the Defenders of Old English Honour, formulated a protest against the Scottish invasion of the English peerage. "Our humble desire," they contended, "is that with your gracious allowance we may challenge, and preserve our Birth-rights, And that we may take no more notice of these Titulars to our prejudice than the Law of this doth, but that we may be excused, if in civil courtesie, we give them not our respect or place." [35] The leaders of this bold defiance were Essex, Oxford, Huntingdon, Lincoln, Dorset, Salisbury, and Warwick —all members of Southampton's opposition faction.[36] If Southampton had not been a member of the Privy Council, very likely

[33] For a full discussion of the subject see Curtis B. Watson, *Shakespeare and the Renaissance Concept of Honor* (Princeton: Princeton University Press, 1960).

[34] McClure, *Chamberlain's Letters*, 2: 338–41; and Gardiner, *History*, 4: 37–39.

[35] Wilson, *Historie*, p. 187.

[36] McClure, *Chamberlain's Letters*, 2: 348. "There was a kind of combination among the Younger Lords to present a petition to his Majestie about the pre-

he too would have signed, for he agreed in substance with the protestation.

The King quickly ended the movement. Furious and deeply offended, he called the principals before the Privy Council on 19 February and demanded of them the original document. At first the protestors refused to surrender it, but they finally compromised by giving a copy to Prince Charles, who turned it over to the King. James, sorely troubled about the event, called in the complainants one by one to listen to their grievances. He gave them, especially the leaders, a lecture and a warning, after which he dismissed them graciously and allowed them to kiss his hand. When Essex went in, James admonished him: "I fear thee not Essex if thou wert as well beloved as thy father, and hadst 40,000 men at thy heels." [37]

Two days later Essex moved that a writ of summons be sent to William Seymour, the new Earl of Hertford. [38] Earlier in the month the previous Earl had died of palsy, leaving his title and estates to his grandson, Essex's brother-in-law by the recent marriage. A committee, headed by Southampton, was set up to deal with the complex problem brought about by this turn of events. King James, who always viewed the Seymours as potential rivals to the throne, considered declaring the illegitimacy of the late Earl of Hertford's children. Anticipating such a move, both Southampton and Oxford presented proof to demonstrate the validity of his marriage and hence the new Earl's birthright. This was enough for the Upper House: on 24 May the clerk was ordered to summon Hertford. Essex lost his proxy as a result of this action, but he and the aristocratic opposition gained a valuable ally.

Personal conflicts flourished during the session. The Earl of Berkshire was put in Fleet Prison for provoking a fight with Lord Scroope in the Lords' Chamber. Essex himself quarrelled with Lord Gerard about a petty matter, which contemporary gossips failed to report. [39] Fortunately for both parties, it was immediately

---

cedence of Scottish and Irish viscounts," wrote Chamberlain, "wherewith they found themselves agreeed, and had subscribed names to the number of five or six and thirty, but the matter was discovered before it was full ripe, and the King was much offended with it and caused the counsaille to call diverse of them before them."

[37] Devereux, *Lives of the Devereux*, 2: 290.

[38] *Ibid.*, p. 27; and Locke, *Seymour Family*, p. 122.

[39] P. R. O., S. P. 14/120.

reconciled. Later in the session Essex and Lord Digby tangled verbally over violations of the orders of the House.[40] Only the presence of the Prince prevented the nobles from resorting to blows.

On another occasion Pembroke was castigated for terming the Lord Chancellor and the Lord Treasurer "Great Lords." To Lord Spencer, who objected most vigorously, peers were peers—equals. He had enough support to pass a resolution stating that "no Lords of this house are to be called Great Lords, because they are all Peers." Sometime later he and Arundel nearly exchanged blows during a debate. The latter was urging the lords to condemn an offender without hearing his defense, whereupon Spencer, who was arguing the other side, reminded his opponent that two of Arundel's ancestors had been condemned to death unheard. Arundel took the allusion to his ancestor's attainders as a personal offense. "I do acknowledge that my ancestors have suffered," he retorted, "and it may be for doing the king and country good service, and in such time as when perhaps the Lord's ancestors that spake last kept sheep."[41] This slam at Spencer's lowly origins and recently acquired title provoked a storm of protest, and the majority of the peers came to his defense. Arundel was asked to apologize for the insult and submit to the Upper House. He refused in both instances.

On 17 May, Essex, acting as a mediator, moved that the quarrel between the two peers be ended.[42] Each man then arose in his place, rather than before the bar, and gave an explanation. Arundel still considered Spencer's remark an insult, a provocation, saying that by implication he had been referred to as a "son of a traitor." Spencer refused to apologize; he simply placed himself at the mercy of the House. After the two lords departed, the peers tried to determine the case. Most lords still sided with Spencer and eventually committed Arundel to the Tower until he would agree to submit himself to the House. Essex's attempt at reconciliation had failed then, and Spencer won a moral victory over one of the "Great Lords."

These personal clashes over rank and precedence within the Lords' House, however divisive, were overshadowed by the joint attacks of both Houses on several of the King's men: Sir Giles Mompesson, Sir Henry Yelverton, and Sir John Bennet. The issue

[40] *Ibid.*, 14/122.
[41] See Firth, *House of Lords*, p. 39, for the material in this paragraph.
[42] Gardiner, *Notes of the debates, 1621*, p. 91.

was corruption in high places, the means impeachment. In Mompesson's trial the House of Lords proceeded extremely slowly and warily.[43] The peers, acting as judges, insisted on established judicial procedures. Confessions and accusations had to be in writing. Witnesses, even peers, were required to take an oath. Although some of the commoners contended that this was contrary to privilege, Sir Edwin Sandys and Coke persuaded them otherwise. On 26 March the two Houses finally met in joint session; after a brief speech by the King, the noblemen delivered the sentence against Mompesson, who had already fled England. He was degraded, fined, excluded from all pardons, imprisoned for life, and declared an infamous person. For the first time since the troublesome days of Henry VI, the House of Lords had sat in judgment upon an indicted official. It was such a memorable occasion that the peers voted to set the trial date aside forever after as a sermon day throughout all England. Arundel even suggested that the peers erect a statue commemorating the occasion.

Parliament then proceeded to perfect its newly recovered weapon by impeaching others guilty of malversation. In April, Lord Chancellor Bacon came under the combined attack of Southampton, Arundel, Sheffield, Huntingdon, and a host of commoners in the Lower House;[44] his only advocate among his peers was Lord Admiral Buckingham. Bacon's principal crime was bribery—a common practice in Jacobean England—and the evidence was convincing. On 24 April he submitted a statement which, upon Southampton's recommendation, was judged unsatisfactory. Six days later Bacon confessed his crimes and cast himself on the mercy of the Upper House, as he had been asked to do. On 3 May the arrogant man, who had once betrayed Southampton, was fined forty thousand pounds, imprisoned at the King's pleasure, stripped of his offices, and forbidden to ever enter Parliament again. Although Southampton had not won completely—he would have also degraded Bacon and banished him from the Court—it was clearly a victory for him and his cohorts.

The next day Sir Francis Mitchell, a silver-thread extortioner, was found guilty by the Upper House,[45] imprisoned, fined one thousand pounds, and perpetually excluded from public office.

43 McClure, *Chamberlain's Letters*, 2: 355–58.

44 Gardiner, *Notes of the debates, 1621*, pp. 61–90.

45 *Ibid.*, p. 65.

On 20 June, the unfortunate man was forced to ride backwards on a horse through the streets of London, amidst jeering crowds, to Westminster Hall, where he was officially degraded by the Earl Marshal's court. Parliament, meanwhile, also gathered evidence for the extortion cases of Bennet and Yelverton, both of whom undoubtedly would have been impeached had not the King adjourned Parliament. As it was, Bennet was subsequently punished by the Star Chamber, and Yelverton was censured during the next session.

Essex participated in these historic legal battles. He was present at the debates and the sentences, served on the epochal grievance committee which worked with the Lower House in the Mompesson case, and voted with the opposition. Whether his role was major or minor, however, the result was the same. The attacks on Bacon, Yelverton, and Bennet represented the attainment of revenge: all three figures had been either personal or family enemies. Some other nobles also sought a legal means of obtaining vengeance through the trials, while to still others they meant the revival of power for the Upper House. To some commoners impeachment was an offensive weapon against the evils of absolute monarchy. Few contemporaries could foresee that these trials might be a step forward in the direction of responsible government.

On 4 June the King decided to adjourn Parliament. Both Houses, he believed, had diverted their attention from long-overdue legislation to personal attacks. Only one measure had passed both Houses—a supply bill granting the King two subsidies, of about one hundred thirty-five thousand pounds, for the next campaign. At the eleventh hour, however, the House of Commons drew up a declaration calling for the continuance of the war against Spinola and promising parliamentary support.[46] Upon hearing of this bold action, James I was so furious that he issued a proclamation telling them that he would personally take care of foreign affairs and attempt to recover the Palatinate in his own manner. He did.

First, however, James punished the opposition leaders who had thwarted his will and seized the initiative in Parliament.[47] On 16 June he demanded both the confinement of the Earl of Southampton, who was subsequently questioned about the clandestine caucuses, and the arrests of Sandys and Selden. Shortly thereafter Coke was

[46] Gardiner, *History*, 2: 129.
[47] Firth, *House of Lords*, pp. 41–47.

removed from the Privy Council and several members of the Lower
House were ordered to Ireland, a political graveyard. A month
later the Earl of Oxford was placed under arrest.

Essex escaped these counterreprisals, for although the King probably feared him secretly, he needed Essex's military talents and
popularity for the recovery of the Palatinate. The men were not on
good terms however, for as Wilson noted: "The King never affected
him, whether from the bent of his Naturall inclination to effeminate
faces, or whether from that instinct or secret Prediction that Divine
fate often imprints in the apprehension . . . the King never liked
him." [48]

IV

"ALL MEN run together to quench a fire; which is our case. Though
we are not so here; yet the Palatinate is on fire; and all other
countries on fire . . . this is the greatest cause, the greatest occasion
for a Supply, since the conquest." [49] These feelings were voiced by
Sir John Davies, M.P. from Newcastle under Lyme, a borough
where Essex enjoyed political influence. To quench the fire which
was rapidly spreading throughout Europe, the Council of War
met periodically to prepare for the summer campaign. In February
the Councilors of War had submitted a proposal for 25,000 troops
and an astronomical number of pounds sterling. To equip this huge
army, the largest ever requested, prodigious quantities of arms and
munitions were needed, so the councilors deputed men to conduct a
military census of all arms in England and to collect all the privately
owned weapons. The council thought in terms of a national army
responsible to the monarch.

Parliamentary opposition to the collection of arms, however,
proved to be too strong, so the Councilors of War resorted to other
means of achieving their ends. In March they held a special muster
in the Middlesex area and invited the members of both Houses. [50]
Many deficiencies and irregularities were discovered. Soon after,
the Venetian ambassador learned that the Council of War was
ordering equipment for only 8,000 troops. As lord lieutenant of
Staffordshire the Earl of Essex had found out that the English

48 Wilson, *Historie*, p. 162.
49 Cobbett, *Parliamentary History*, 1: 1186.
50 *C. S. P. Ven., 1619–1621*, p. 589.

recruits were ill prepared for service in Ireland; that they were more unfit for the recovery of the Palatinate he now discovered as a Councilor of War. England's need for military reform was evident: while capable of producing excellent armaments in her foundries, England lacked a large disciplined and experienced army.

The efforts of the Council of War proved fruitless, nevertheless, for King James was not prepared to discard his foreign policy. He still hoped that the Palatinate could be recovered through peaceful means. Moreover, practically speaking, he had little choice, for it would be extremely difficult to raise the money to equip a large army and maintain it in the field. The benevolences trickled in slowly and often under protest. The parliamentary grants were too meager to allow consideration of anything like the Council of War proposed. Yet James felt morally obligated to help the Elector regain his throne in the Palatinate. The monarch wrote his daughter consoling letters. He appealed to the Elector's Protestant allies for aid and troops and permitted these allies—the Dutch and the Danes, at least—to levy English and Scottish troops. James even allowed his own military leaders to volunteer for service on the Continent.

For four successive years Essex was one such volunteer. Each summer he crossed the Channel and warred against the Catholics; each winter he returned to England. Little is known about these military activities, but the evidence, however scanty, sheds some light on Essex's public career. In April 1621 the truce between Spain and the Dutch provinces came to an end. The wearisome negotiations had produced nothing, for neither side had been willing to concede. The swords were once again unsheathed. The Spanish monarch, relying upon his Austrian allies, Spinola's army, and the gold mines in the New World, hoped to beat the Dutch rebels into submission and thus regain his hereditary lands. Through diplomacy, he hoped to prevent the Dutch from receiving direct aid from the English. Promises of a Spanish marriage and well-placed pensions to English leaders, plus faint hints about the restitution of the Palatinate all kept James inactive.

Immediately after cessation of the truce, the Dutch, now fighting for their national existence, again came to the English for help. In return for assistance Prince Maurice promised to help James recover the Palatinate. Though James gave no positive answer at the time, he permitted Maurice to raise and equip eight thousand soldiers and loaned him England's experienced leaders, including Essex and General Cecil. Standing by his promise to Spain, James insisted that these troops be used only in the United Provinces and not to reinforce Vere in the Palatinate.

The war in 1621 brought little or no fighting. Spinola maneuvered his army in Flanders. Maurice, expecting the general to attack, entrenched along the Rhine at Rees, a small town in the principality of Cleves, but the assault never came. Essex and the troops near Rees, however. had to fight a more devastating enemy—the sickness which broke out in October and November among the poorly fed soldiers.[51] In December, after no decisive encounters had taken place, Maurice assigned his army to winter quarters.

Essex had returned to England for the winter months.[52] On 20 November he heard the state-of-the-nation speech at the formal opening of the second session of the "do-nothing" Parliament.[53] That same day Lord Digby gave a lengthy report on the status of foreign negotiations, and the Lord Treasurer reported on the nation's economic health. Both painted gloomy pictures. In addition the speaker of the House of Commons, acting under instructions, attacked the pacifistic foreign policy, which, he believed, benefited Spain, and criticized the royal administration for being lenient toward Catholicism.

A parliamentary battle was on. James rebutted the speaker in a blistering letter and warned the Commons against debating matters which were "far above their reach and capacity." The House of Commons retorted with a remonstrance, claiming that "the voice of Bellona must be heard, and not the voice of the Turtle."[54] But the voice of Bellona went unheard. After another royal lecture and a stormy struggle over freedom of debate in Parliament, James simply dissolved the assembly and subsequently tore a page from the House of Commons' *Journal* in a fit of anger.

In 1622 after the cessation of Parliament, Essex returned to serve under Prince Maurice.[55] Upon landing on the Continent, he rejoined

51 *Ibid.*, pp. 124–62.

52 British Museum, Additional MSS, 46,188. Essex was back in England by 16 November 1621, at which time he was ordered to raise more troops and send them to the maritime counties for transportation to the Continent.

53 *Lords Journal*, 3: 167.

54 Frankland, *Annals*, p. 61.

55 Before leaving, however, he took care of his duties as Lord Lieutenant and appointed two deputies, Sir Simon Weston and Walter Bagot, to handle matters in

the Dutch army at Rees.[56] Here warfare was completely defensive. The Rees Leaguers, as they were called, hoped to prevent Spinola from overrunning their principality and then penetrating the Palatinate again. There were no major engagements along the Rhine and the troops became soft. "The infantry with their captains," wrote the Venetian ambassador, "who serve more for appearance than use, care for little else than eating and drinking and smoking their infernal tobacco in the numerous taverns. They go to the musters more for sport and these delights than from a desire to gain experience. Accordingly out of a thousand scarce a hundred know how to manipulate the musket and pike with numerous other faults and imperfections."[57]

The campaign of the following summer went no better. Neither the Spanish nor the Dutch were in any position to fight: each suffered from food shortages and disease, and neither had money to pay the troops. Spinola left his winter quarters near Antwerp and moved toward the east as if to join Johannes Tserklaes, Baron Tilly, but instead of going to Maastricht went to Brussels, where he waited for several months for money or news of a truce. Neither came.

During the 1623 campaign Essex remained in Arnheim, the principal city of Nassau.[58] Maurice, whose health was deteriorating, spent part of the summer there, hoping to defend the eastern frontier of the United Provinces against attack. He feared, quite naturally, that Baron Tilly might strike down the Rhine and join Spinola, but Tilly crossed the Weser, moved to less than ten miles from the Dutch border, and at Stadtlohn resoundly defeated Christian of Brunswick. He did not need to attack Arnheim, however, for Elector Frederick finally yielded to the wishes of King James and signed an armistice with the Holy Roman Emperor. This gave the Elector time, if nothing else.

Essex, who had fully intended to stay three years on the Continent, returned to England prematurely, in November 1623, with little to show for his efforts.[59] He had, however, gained some renown

---

his absence. See *A. P. C. 1621–1623*, p. 226; *C. S. P. Dom.*, *1619–1623*, p. 382; and British Museum, Additional MSS, 46,188.

[56] Wilson, *Autobiography*, p. 465.

[57] *C. S. P. Ven.*, *1621–1623*, p. 433.

[58] Wilson, *Autobiography*, p. 466.

[59] *C. S. P. Dom.*, *1619–1623*. In June 1623, Essex had been given a license to travel (probably as a soldier of fortune) for three years.

among the soldiers. "He first trailed a pike," Codrington later noted, "and refused no service in the field, which every ordinary gentleman is accustomed to perform. This did much to endear him to the soldiers, and his liberality and humanity did the more advance him." [60] Essex also secured some wartime experience—certainly more than some nineteenth-century historians like S. R. Gardiner credited him with.[61]

The Earl, still shunning the Court, spent his winters in the countryside.[62] He divided his time between Chartley; Drayton in Warwickshire, the home of his grandmother, the aged Countess of Leicester; and Tottenham Court in Wiltshire, the country residence of his brother-in-law the Earl of Hertford. For recreation sometimes he played chess or catastrophe, a popular card game; frequently he or his grandmother commissioned Arthur Wilson to prepare a play or masque for the enjoyment of the family circle and their friends. Sometimes he practiced "tobacco drinking," a new fad which was fast becoming popular among the upper echelons of English society.

Essex still enjoyed riding and hunting. "My Lord would ride very hard and loved it extreamly," wrote Wilson. "He was an excellent horseman; four score or a hundred miles a day I have often ridden with his Lordship." [63] Among others, his riding and hunting cronies included Lord Cromwell, the Earl of Hertford, Sir Charles Egerton, and Sir Peter Lee. If not at Chartley, he hunted with his friends in Cheshire, Warwickshire, and Wiltshire. While progressing from one of his winter haunts to the other he preferred the saddle of a horse to the comfort of his coach.[64]

In addition to these diversions Essex also tended to his local responsibilities as lord lieutenant of Staffordshire. Each year between campaigns he had to care for local defenses and recruit troops

---

60 Codrington, *Life and Death*, p. 9.

61 "It is amusing," Gardiner wrote in his *History*, 3: 388n., "to find historians of the Civil War justifying Essex's appointment as Parliamentary General on the ground of the experience which he had acquired in the Palatinate. He saw the enemy once, but he never drew sword against him." It is clear that Essex spent three summers on the Continent, two with Prince Maurice, and three springs preparing for the respective campaigns. He was engaged in defensive actions, seemingly, but he may well have participated in offensive warfare which has not been recorded. Gardiner's remark is hardly justified in view of the evidence.

62 See Wilson, *Autobiography*, pp. 465–67.

63 *Ibid.*, p. 466.

64 *Ibid.*

for Ireland and the Continent. In 1622 he received a new obligation when the Privy Council also appointed him lord lieutenant of Essex.[65] This additional assignment led Essex to delegate his duties in Staffordshire to two deputy lieutenants, Sir Simon Weston, the scion of an old and respected Staffordshire family, and Walter Bagot, a Devereux dependent for several decades.[66] Both appointees proved to be trustworthy adherents to Essex's political circle, which was widening year by year.

V

BY CHRISTMASTIDE 1623, James I's foreign policy was completely bankrupt. His efforts to prevent Europe from plunging into a general war had proved futile. Already much blood had been spilled for the Elector's cause. The King's promise of recovering the Palatinate through negotiations with the Emperor failed to materialize. His negotiations with Spain for a marriage treaty and the restitution of the Palatinate lingered on and on. Some of the King's staunchest supporters began to entertain doubts about the royal foreign policy; in fact, after their return from Spain in 1623, both Buckingham and the Prince considered declaring war against the Spanish. Before long the English monarch found himself virtually alone in his pursuit of peace.

Gradually the King shifted to a French alliance and more direct action on the Continent. Together England and France could recover from the Hapsburgs not only the Palatinate but Valtellina as well. Perhaps a marriage treaty between Prince Charles and Princess Henrietta Maria could be arranged to cement English and French fears against Hapsburg hegemony. To determine French feeling, the English sovereign sent several ambassadors extraordinary to talk with Cardinal Richelieu and Louis XIII.

To take more direct action against the enemy, James summoned another Parliament to meet on 16 January 1624. The avowed purpose of the session was to consider the foreign situation and secure supplies necessary for armed intervention. If nothing else, this amounted to an admission of failure. But the King went even further: he invited Parliament to discuss foreign affairs. In return, as he had hoped, Parliament granted him several subsidies.

[65] *A. P. C. 1621–1623*, pp. 89, 226.
[66] British Museum, Additional MSS, 46,188.

Although the complexion of the Lower House differed little from the previous session, the Upper House witnessed several significant changes.[67] Prince Charles, now more experienced, assumed a prominent role in the deliberations. He and his favorite, the Duke of Buckingham, controlled six proxies. Pembroke, still Lord Chamberlain, held five votes in addition to his own. Northumberland, Essex's uncle who had recently been freed from the Tower, was now the ranking earl.

Essex, who held the Earl of Hertford's proxy, answered the daily roll calls with meticulous regularity, as before, but he said almost nothing.[68] He secured several important committee posts and apparently was chairman of a committee dealing with the reform of some legal abuses in the Westminster courts, for on 23 April he reported on the bill in the Lords' Chamber. When put to the question, after the third reading, the bill passed. Later in the session he was appointed to committees dealing with such matters as the exportation of wool and fuller's earth, relief for the feltworkers of London, and the repair of Colchester Haven.

Essex also participated in the impeachment of Lionel Cranfield, a successful London merchant and able administrator who had secured from King James the office of Lord Treasurer and the newly created earldom of Middlesex.[69] His meteoric rise to power—he was second to the Prince on the precedence list—when coupled with his common origins, offended Essex and fellow Defenders of Old English Honour. His policies of retrenchment and reform and his acceptance of bribes were denounced in the house of Commons. Although most of the accusations were made in the Lower House, as was the practice in impeachment cases, it was Essex who opened the deliberations of 9 April with a short speech in which he questioned some inflammatory statements, really counteraccusations, made by the Lord Treasurer and demanded an explanation of them.[70] Some peers sided with Essex on this matter, while others defended the Lord Treasurer. Cranfield came to his own defense and requested forgiveness, a request which was honored.

---

[67] See Samuel R. Gardiner, *Notes of the Debates of the House of Lords 1624–1626*, Camden Society (London, 1879); *H. M. C. Buccleuch Manuscripts*, 3: 228; *Lords Journal*, 3: 220; and Cobbett, *Parliamentary History*, 1: 1165–86.

[68] The following facts have been garnered from *Lords Journal*, 3: 220–379.

[69] See Menna Prestwich, *Cranfield* (Oxford: Clarendon Press, 1966), pp. 423–67.

[70] Gardiner, *Notes of the Debates 1624*, p. 60.

Both Houses of Parliament spent much time in the impeachment trial of the Lord Treasurer. Several committees were set up; joint conferences were held. Members of the House of Commons gathered evidence and examined witness after witness. On 7 May, after much wrangling, the Lord Treasurer was called to the bar of the Upper House to stand trial for bribery, extortion, and misdemeanors. Four days later he sent word that he was ill and could not attend the trial. Since several lords believed that he was feigning sickness, Essex, Southampton, Cromwell, Saye, and a few other peers were selected to verify his claim. They took a physician, who found him bedridden but not seriously ill. Cranfield was evidently greatly fatigued. Upon returning to Parliament, Essex reported: "For a Man to be thus followed Morning and Afternoon, standing Eight Hours at the Bar, till some of the Lords might see him ready to fall down; Two Lawyers against him, and no Man his Part was such a proceeding as never heard of; and he knew not what I meant for it was unchristian-like, and without Example; and desired they would deal with him as he would deal with one of them; for it was his Cause today, and might be theirs Tomorrow." [71] For this and similar incidents Essex became known for his liberality and humanity. The Lord Treasurer, however, was subsequently found guilty, fined fifty thousand pounds, and imprisoned in the Tower.

Essex also defended his own parliamentary rights in the 1624 session. When his chaplain, William Hulbocke, was arrested by Francis Guill, Essex appealed to the Upper House for justice. [72] According to a long tradition recently publicized in the rules, a peer's freedom of arrest during the parliamentary session extended to the members of his entourage. The Earl merely laid claim to his right. His appeal was accepted; Guill was subsequently apprehended.

In April, while Parliament was still in session, the King appointed a new Council of War to advise him in military matters. [73] The conclave included Lord Carew, Lord Brooke, Sir Edward Conway, Cecil, and Vere, most of whom possessed military experience of some sort. Essex was not reappointed; in fact, all the aristocratic malcontents were excluded from this council. They had had their opportunity and failed. They had, moreover, obstructed the royal will in Parliament on several occasions.

[71] *Lords Journal*, 3: 381.
[72] *Ibid.*, p. 377.
[73] Gardiner, *History*, 5: 223.

Nevertheless, James used the Defenders of Old English Honour. If they wanted to fight, they would have their opportunity. If they wanted old honor, they could find it on the battlefield. He would send them to the Continent as commanders of his project to recover the Palatinate. This plan, as the perceptive Venetian ambassador noted, "will get rid of three of the greatest enemies they had, namely the Earls of Oxford, Southampton, and Essex." [74] Essex was ready to go to the Continent. He had already received two letters from Christian of Brunswick, with whom he had corresponded earlier, thanking him for previous service and inviting him to render further assistance to the Protestant cause. [75]

In May the military plans jelled. The English and the Dutch, now in a defensive league, planned for a joint force of 10,000 soldiers to fight Spinola and, if possible, to regain the Palatinate. Prince Maurice, although still sickly, would command the army. The English would underwrite the expedition to the extent of one hundred thousand pounds, which they expected the Dutch to repay. The Dutch would levy 4,000 troops, while the English would provide four regiments of 1,500 men each. Each regiment would be headed by an English colonel to be named by the King. James was quick to appoint the malcontents—Southampton, Essex, and Oxford. [76] Prince Charles backed Sir John Burlacy, an experienced soldier who had fought in Ireland, for the fourth slot. James favored the Earl of Morton, a Scot whose better judgment told him to refuse the honor. After much discussion, the King finally induced Lord Willoughby, who had once fought alongside Essex's father, to come out of retirement. This choice no doubt pleased Essex, for the two lords appear to have been friendly, at least friendly rivals, at this stage of their careers. Southampton was appointed the ranking officer.

The drums were soon beating for volunteers. In June, shortly after the dissolution of Parliament, the Privy Council requested the lord lieutenants to assist the colonels in levying men and granted the authorities in the seaport towns permission to recruit volunteers for the army. [77] Essex experienced little difficulty in filling his

[74] C. S. P. Ven., 1623–1625, p. 333.

[75] In 1624, in April and again in June, Essex received friendly communications from Christian. See British Museum, Additional MSS, 46,188.

[76] C. S. P. Dom., 1623–1625, pp. 248, 251, 267, 434; and H. M. C. Tenth Report, Appendix 6, p. 111.

[77] A. P. C. 1623–1625, pp. 251, 258, 283.

ranks, for his name still possessed magnetic qualities. "The soldiers willing to serve," wrote a contemporary, "surpass the requirements of the levy." [78] Arthur Wilson went along as the Earl's secretary and aide-de-camp. William Baille, a Scottish soldier who later became lieutenant general of Scotland, served as a captain and Sydenham Poyntz, a London apprentice, volunteered for service under Baille and subsequently wrote a short account of his experience,[79] but very little is known of Essex's other subordinates.

Gervase Markham, a popular writer, publicized the forthcoming campaign and emulated its aristocratic commanders in a short work entitled *Honour in His Perfection*. He extolled the virtues of the four colonels and alluded to the glory of their ancestors. He had special praise for the Devereux, especially the second Earl, and glossed over the conspiracy. "O looke now upon the Princely Soldiers," he wrote, "looke upon these four noblemen, Oxford, Southampton, Essex and Willoughby, who like the foure Seasons of the Yeare, joyne together to make thee a plentiful harvest of thine own hearts wishes." [80] In his allegorical booklet entitled *Robert Earle of Essex His Ghost*, Thomas Scott, royal chaplain, reflected upon the glorious days of Queen Elizabeth's reign.[81] Speaking as the ghost of the second Earl, he lauded the deeds of the Devereux and condemned their pro-Spanish enemies. He no doubt hoped that the third Earl would follow in the footsteps of his father and become the leader of the anti-Spanish element in England. Already, a legend about Elizabeth's Essex was prevalent in England; already those who subscribed to it were looking to the third Earl of Essex.

In August the English expeditionary force landed in Holland. Essex unloaded his retinue and troops at Flushing. Oxford disembarked at Rotterdam. After some delay, brought about by contrary winds and threats from the Dunkirk pirates, Southampton too landed. Once ashore, a commission headed by Philip Burlamachi found them quarters in the Dutch garrisons and made arrangements

[78] *C. S. P. Ven., 1623–1625*, p. 397.

[79] A. T. S. Goodrich, *The Relation of Sydenham Poyntz*, Camden Society (London: Royal Historical Society, 1908), pp. 1–17.

[80] Markham, *Honour in His Perfection*, p. 6.

[81] The full entry reads *Robert Earle of Essex His Ghost Sent from Elizion to the Nobility, Gentry and Commonaltie of England* (Paradise, 1624). Essex's motto, *Virtutum Comes Invidia*, appears on the title page.

for pay. "The troops are in good order and very fine," wrote the Venetian ambassador in the United Provinces, "expectation is on tip toe." [82] However, the plague, which was raging in several cities, soon began to take its toll. Lord Conway's son was among the first to succumb.

The four colonels, meanwhile, proceeded to The Hague for a formal reception and strategy sessions. [83] On 29 August they were introduced by the English ambassador, Sir Dudley Carleton, to the Assembly of the Estates General. In a solemn Sabbath-day ceremony they took the oath of fealty. A week later, in response to a request made by Sir Dudley, the English officers were granted fifty-seven thousand guilders by the Estates General to pay their troops. Essex received a sum amounting to eighty-seven pounds. Among his subordinates who drew pay were Sir Charles Rich, Capt. Henry Swinton, Sir Walter Devereux, Sir Robert Knollys, Capt. Richard Wenman, Sir John Meyrick, and several lesser known Englishmen. [84] In September the four regimental commanders returned to their troops and joined the campaign in the Low Countries.

Throughout the autumn months the English troops idly waited for action; but action never came, for Spinola never dropped his guard. Prince Maurice's objective was simple: to relieve Breda from the Spanish siege. [85] With a smaller army he could not risk a direct engagement with Spinola, so he attempted to interrupt the general's lines of communication, tried to intercept enemy convoys, and sent scouts to search out the enemy's weak spots. By the beginning of November, Maurice realized that Breda would probably not be able to hold out through the entire winter. Supplies were running short. There was little hope of sending reinforcements and provisions by land or sea. On 5 November, Maurice tried to force the siege by sending to Breda 4,000 troops and a long train of wagons loaded with soldiers and provisions, but they retreated before the fire from Spinola's musketeers. In December another attempt to relieve the city by water failed. Providence seemed to side with the Spanish. Maurice, a victim of the gout, daily became

---

[82] C. S. P. Ven., 1623–1625, p. 422.

[83] Stopes, Southampton, p. 457.

[84] British Museum, Additional MSS, 46,188. There are several documents in Essex's papers dealing with this matter.

[85] H. M. C. Thirteenth Report, Appendix 2, pp. 115–17.

more ill as the last hopes of relieving his ancestral barony faded before his eyes.

Such was the situation when Essex went into winter quarters nearby at Roosendaal.[86] There had been no dramatic battle. There had been little glory in watching Spinola dominate the field. Worse yet, the English troops succumbed to the traditional enemies of the camp: food was scarce; malnutrition was common; disease set in and began to decimate the ranks. At this point Essex sent a request to Lord Cromwell, his deputy in Staffordshire, for replacements.[87]

One of the first to die of the "burning fever" was Lord Wriothesley, son and heir of Southampton. Soon after, the Earl of Southampton also became ill while trying to bring the body of his son back to England for interment. He reached Bergen op Zoom but could go no farther. There, in mid-November, not very far from the place of Sir Philip Sidney's demise, Essex's fatherly friend and Shakespeare's patron died of distemper. Shortly thereafter both father and son were transported on a small bark to England for burial. Essex received a firsthand account of the death from his subordinate and friend William Beeston; he retained the document until his death.[88]

Essex left no record of his reaction to this tragedy but no doubt he shared the sentiments of the Electress of the Palatinate. "You very well conceive that the death of the worthy Earl of Southampton did trouble me," she wrote in late November, "which I cannot think of but with grief. I have lost in him a most true and faithfull friend, both in him and his sonne."[89] Essex too lost a "true and faithfull friend" as well as a political mentor.

Instead of either returning to England for the winter, as he had done in previous years, or retiring to more commodious quarters in the Low Countries, as some other leaders did, Essex remained in

[86] Wilson, *Autobiography*, p. 467. For more details on the troops see the Bagot MSS, Folger Shakespeare Library, especially G.b. 14, fol. 15.

[87] *C. S. P. Dom., 1623–1625*, p. 381.

[88] See British Museum, Additional MSS, 46,188, for a letter addressed to Essex describing the deplorable state of the English troops. The writer also complained about the Dutch refusal to employ the English soldiers, who were inexperienced. There are several letters addressed to Essex dealing with Southampton's demise. One, from Beeston, describes Southampton's last days under the care of Dr. Samuel Turner, while another, addressed to the Council of War from Sir Dudley Carleton, describes his final hours.

[89] *H. M. C. Bathurst Manuscripts*, 2: 73.

the vicinity of Breda with his troops throughout the siege.[90] Daily the soldiers within the town dwindled before the superior forces of Spinola. Several English captains, including Sir James Lindsay and Sir Edward Conway, died of the plague, and General Vere and Lord Cromwell fell ill. The untimely deaths of several other leaders had a demoralizing effect upon the English troops. Within a month the aged Prince Maurice, a weary and disillusioned soldier, died in The Hague. Shortly thereafter the youthful Earl of Oxford was wounded in a skirmish near Breda. He retired to The Hague for rest and medical treatment, but by the end of May succumbed after having a servant inform Essex of his last wishes.[91]

This left Colonels Essex and Willoughby in charge of the English troops. A contemporary artist captured the situation in an engraved portrait of the two men.[92] Both are mounted on horses, Essex, a truncheon in his left hand, in the foreground, Willoughby behind him, while in the distant background stands the besieged town. Together they fought; together they survived the horrors of the siege of Breda. One day they would battle each other in a civil war, but in the fields of Brabant they shared the same fate—life in the face of death.

The English sovereign who had sent these young nobles to war in Brabant, meanwhile, became fatally ill with a tertian ague. On 24 March, after a terrible convulsion, James received his last communion and committed his soul to God. He died three days later. On 7 May, after a stately procession, the late King James was honored with a costly and magnificent state funeral.

The Earl of Essex did not return to England to pay his last respects to the deceased, whose body lay in state at Denmark House for over a month, nor did he return to London for the funeral ceremonies. Rather, he followed his orders and remained near Breda. No doubt Essex's feelings were divided. He had received from the late monarch the Essex earldom, the family lands which had been forfeited to Queen Elizabeth, gifts, small honors, and a place close to the late

[90] This paragraph is based upon the letters Essex received while in Brabant during the siege. They are preserved in the British Museum, Additional MSS, 46,188.

[91] *Ibid.*

[92] This is reprinted in A. M. Hind, *History of Engraving in England in the Sixteenth and Seventeenth Centuries* (Cambridge: At the University Press, 1956), plate 241. The engraved portraits of Essex by Renold Elstrack and William van de Passe, also reprinted by Hind, probably date from the same period.

heir apparent: for these royal favors Essex must have been grateful. Yet, he must have resented James's role in the forced marriage and the humiliating divorce, disliked his cowardly behavior and strange personality, and disapproved of his foreign policy. If these sentiments evoked a sense of relief in Essex, as they well might have, that relief was very likely accompanied by fear and anxiety concerning his future in the England of Charles I.

CHAPTER 6

Vice Admiral

I

ON THE MORNING of 15 May 1625, Essex and his fellow soldiers launched a final but futile attempt to lift the siege of Breda.[1] They left their winter quarters and advanced to the nearby castle of Terheyden, hoping to divert the Spanish siegers, but to no avail. Spinola had been forewarned of their plans. Short of ammunition, the English troops were forced to retire under heavy enemy fire after much hand-to-hand fighting. This defeat convinced the new Dutch commander, Frederick Henry, that any further shedding of blood would be pointless. He fell back a short distance and took up a defensive position at Langestaat. Shortly thereafter he encouraged his brother Prince Justinius, the leader of the besieged troops, to capitulate.

On 5 June, after the final articles of surrender were signed, the Breda garrison marched, with drums beating and colors flying, to rejoin their respective units. Outside the city gate, Justinius surrendered his sword to Spinola, who embraced the persons of distinction and praised them for their courage. To the disappointment of many a Spaniard, the terms were exceedingly mild: the besieged troops were permitted to keep their baggage; the Prince was allowed to remove his furniture; the Spanish were deprived of their spoils by a decree forbidding all pillaging.

Essex was deeply disturbed about the Breda campaign. The English soldiers were not to be blamed for the sad state of affairs, he contended; the lukewarm support rendered by the Dutch and their factious government, which was split over religious differences, must be held accountable. Moreover, the combined armies were simply not large enough to defeat Spinola. Thus, in March 1625, when Essex learned of Buckingham's forthcoming naval expedition, he made himself available to King James for a command. "I have

[1] For a discussion of the capitulation of Breda see Wedgwood, *Thirty Years War*, pp. 177–80.

now a sute to [your] gracious Matie which I humbly lay at your feete to consider," he wrote, "the which is, since busness waxeth could in these parts, you will think mee worthie of some imploiment in this new sea voyage." [2] By the time this request arrived in England, James was dead.

When Charles I succeeded to the throne in late March, he was determined to triumph where his father had failed.[3] He pledged himself and his country to the recovery of the Palatinate. He promised to restore the English to a stronger position in international affairs—even if it meant war with Spain. To attain these national goals, the youthful monarch pursued a more aggressive foreign policy. He married the French princess, Henrietta Maria, and concluded a defensive alliance with Louis XIII. He sent military aid to the Elector and to his uncle the King of Denmark. In a more radical move he sounded out the Dutch about an offensive-defensive pact aimed at the Spanish Hapsburgs.

To make his aggressive anti-Spanish foreign policy effective, Charles looked to the past and borrowed from the Dutch. The greatness of Elizabethan England and the Dutch republic stemmed from their maritime strength. The Royal Navy must be enlarged. Herein was James I's failure: he had done little to build up England's naval power against the Dutch, French, and Spanish.[4] To put England back on the international chessboard, Charles I called for more ships and advocated maritime wars. Realizing the need for national support, he issued writs for a Parliament. He also began negotiating with the Dutch for a joint naval expedition against the Spanish.

The plans for an armada unfolded piece by piece. In April the Privy Council called for a general muster and a rendezvous of the fleet.[5] The next month it ordered the impressment of several

[2] British Museum, Additional MSS, 46,189.

[3] In the absence of a definitive biography of King Charles, one is compelled to use the standard works of William Sanderson, Samuel R. Gardiner, John R. Green, and John Forster.

[4] For the naval history of this period see Martin Oppenheim, *The Administration of the Royal Navy, 1509–1660* (London, 1896), especially pp. 184–301, and his *The Naval Tracts of Sir William Monson*, 3 vols. (London: Naval Record Society, 1913), especially vol. 3, which covers the period from 1613–36. See also C. D. Penn, *The Navy under the Early Stuarts and its Influence on English History* (Leighton Buzzard and Manchester: Faith Press, 1913).

[5] John Rushworth, *Historical Collections*, 8 vols. (London, 1721), 1: 168.

thousand soldiers. On 6 May, Essex's deputy lieutenants in Staffordshire were ordered to levy, arm, and provision one hundred men
and have them in Plymouth by 25 May.[6] Later in the month
Charles I commissioned Buckingham, the royal favorite, Lord
High Admiral and established a Council of War which included
"our right, trusty and well beloved cousin, the Earl of Essex, Vice-
Admiral, and Sir Francis Steward, Knight, Rear Admiral of our
fleet."[7] The new King wanted Essex to assume a leading role in,
or at least lend his legendary name to, the English armada. Very
likely Arthur Wilson's observation was close to the truth: "The
Earle of Essex was not employed out of affection to him, but,
being a man beloved of the people, and the people not likeing the
Duke's exorbitant power, in thrusting the King upon this war,
which tended only to revenge his private injustices; the said Earle
was put in to sweeten the business."[8]

However, Lord Admiral Buckingham had other plans. A courtier
with no fighting experience on land or sea, he could scarcely afford
to be away from the Court and gamble his political future on a
risky military enterprise. Neither did he cherish the thought of
relinquishing the command of the armada to Essex, the royally
designated vice admiral, a potential rival who enjoyed widespread
popularity. Fearing Essex, Buckingham turned to Sir Edward
Cecil, a political dependent whom he had unsuccessfully supported
for the Palatinate command in 1620, and named him commander
and promised him a title.[9] Thus Essex was eased out of the command.

In early July, Essex, who was still in the Low Countries, received
from Whitehall his formal recall and an invitation to command a
regiment in the English armada.[10] The Earl returned to England
in the middle of the month, only to discover that the plague was
raging in London and spreading to the suburbs. The bells tolled continuously. Trade was at a standstill. The law courts in Westminster
had closed their doors. Rather than risk exposure to the dreaded
disease, Essex bypassed London and proceeded westward to Oxford,
where Parliament, which he hoped to attend, had been adjourned.

[6] *A. P. C. 1625–1626*, pp. 39, 44.

[7] *H. M. C. Twelfth Report*, Appendix, p. 201.

[8] Wilson, *Autobiography*, p. 467.

[9] See Cecil's letters printed in *Cabala*, pp. 167–70.

[10] *C. S. P. Dom., 1625–1626*, p. 49. The document, dated 29 June 1625 from
Whitehall, was written by Secretary of State Conway.

While it met, through 12 August, Essex stayed at his alma mater, Merton College. So many members, fearful of contracting the plague, refused to attend the first few scheduled meetings that the formal opening was postponed until 4 August, and then only twenty-nine nobles appeared for the King's speech. The avowed purpose of the Oxford Parliament was to secure supplies for the extraordinary military needs of the nation, especially for the fleet, which was already gathering along the Devonshire coast. Charles promised to declare war, but he obstinately refused to reveal the enemy or to state the precise destination of the armada—these were "mysteries of state" which the Crown guarded jealously. This refusal irked many commoners who feared that Charles—or more likely, Lord High Admiral Buckingham—might employ the fleet against the Huguenots rather than against the Spanish dons, so Parliament granted him only two temporal subsidies and refused to approve the traditional tunnage and poundage for life.[11]

Essex's role in the Upper House differed little from that in earlier sessions. Due to his rank and seniority, he was now named one of the Triers of Petitions. He went to the formal opening ceremonies at Christ's Church, listened to the King's speech, and, as usual, attended the deliberations very regularly. He was present when Parliament began to debate the controversial petition which demanded a stricter enforcement of laws against Catholics and sat on the committee, headed by his old ally Archbishop Abbot, which revised the bill. Although no record remains of his opinions or vote, there is little doubt that he sided with those of Puritan proclivities. On 10 August, Essex was added to his cousin the Earl of Warwick's committee, which safeguarded the rights of the peers.

Essex also attended the debates on 9 August, when the Duke of Buckingham defended the royal foreign policy and gave an account of the King's finances. In answer to several questions about the purpose and destination of the armada, Buckingham reassured his critics that it would be used against Spain.[12] To those skeptical

---

[11] *Lords Journal*, 3: 434. Actually Charles called the Parliament for 17 May but then postponed it several times until 18 July. On the later date, still in Westminster, he delivered his speech to a poorly attended assemblage which commenced to do business. Because the plague was keeping even more members away, Charles prorogued the Parliament until early August and set the meeting in Oxford.

[12] See Frances Relf, *Notes of the Debates in the House of Lords*, Camden Society (London: Royal Historical Society, 1929); Harold P. Cooke, *Charles I and His*

members who wondered if the fleet was not only half-prepared to sail, Buckingham answered on behalf of his King, "It is better far, both for your honours and mine, that with hazard of half the fleet, it be set forth, than, with the assured loss of so much provision, it stayed at home."[13] Three days later, upon realizing that the men meeting in Oxford would not grant him more funds and fearing an attack upon his favorite, Charles dissolved Parliament.

After the national assembly was adjourned, Essex and his train proceeded to Tottenham, the rural residence of his sister Dorothy and her husband, the Earl of Hertford.[14] Located in Wiltshire near Amesbury, Tottenham had fallen into the hands of the Seymour family during the reign of Henry VIII, when the monasteries were dissolved. The stately building, idyllically situated along the green-banked Avon River, had been known as Amesbury Abbey throughout medieval times. At Tottenham, Essex hunted and awaited the next royal command.

The condition of the English armada, meanwhile, turned from bad to worse. Several ships arrived late for the rendezvous.[15] Many ships were unseaworthy. Others lacked surgeons. There was a shortage of bread, vinegar, and clothing. Some soldiers had fled after receiving their initial pay, while others had fallen sick because of rotten provisions and disease, including the plague. Conditions were so bad that the Privy Council sent forth another request for troops. Still vacationing, Essex commissioned his deputy, Sir Simon Weston, to levy one hundred more Staffordians and send them to Plymouth.[16]

Discontent and disagreements among the officers made the situation even more disturbing. Essex and some of his cohorts protested that the officers' pay was less than that provided by other European

Early Parliaments (London: Sheldon Press, 1939); Samuel Rawson Gardiner, Debates in the House of Commons in 1625, Camden Society (London, 1873); Margaret A. Judson, The Crisis of the Constitution (New Brunswick: Rutgers University Press, 1949); and Edward Montagu's diary in H. M. C. Buccleuch Manuscripts, 3: 248–51.

13 Lords Journal, 3: 467.

14 Wilson, Autobiography, p. 467.

15 See Daniel Magnussen, "The Cadiz Expedition of 1625" (M.A. thesis, Montana State University, 1964), pp. 29–46 for a discussion of the deplorable conditions of the fleet and the soldiers.

16 A. P. C. 1625–1626, p. 136.

monarchs.[17] Essex was, moreover, personally dissatisfied with the leadership and his own rank. He had little respect for Buckingham, the master strategist, and no love for his socially inferior rival, Sir Edward Cecil. Essex had originally hoped—with good reason—to be the generalissimo of the armada. Instead, Buckingham had named Cecil commander-in-chief and Sir John Ogle, an experienced soldier who had fought under Prince Maurice for several years, second-in-command.[18] Essex had been offered a mere colonelcy. At this point, sometime in August apparently, the Earl decided against participating in the venture, believing that he deserved a higher rank and more pay.

His Majesty's government was determined to have Essex on the expedition.[19] Essex's presence would help the morale of the troops, they reasoned, and give the English a psychological advantage over the Spaniards. Among others, Sir William St. Leger, one of the Councilors of War, advised Secretary of State Edward Conway, who in turn informed the King, that Essex's presence was essential to success. Buckingham finally gave in. On 12 September he invited Essex to take Ogle's place as colonel general. When Essex turned down the offer, the King, who wanted the fleet to duplicate the foray of 1596, took the matter into his own hands. He personally requested Essex to join the expedition and agreed to commission him vice admiral of the armada and commander of an entire squadron as well as a regimental commander. This personal command from the King could not be refused, so Essex accepted the commissions, albeit somewhat reluctantly. He left Tottenham in mid-September 1625 and proceeded to Plymouth to join the fleet.[20]

II

THE ENGLISH flotilla which Essex joined was larger than any previous armada put afloat by the English.[21] For many months the King,

[17] C. S. P. Dom., 1625–1626, p. 78.

[18] Ibid., pp. 99–101.

[19] British Museum, Additional MSS, 46,188.

[20] See Walter Younge, Diary, ed. George Roberts, Camden Society (London, 1843), p. 86. Essex passed through the Honiton area, where Younge lived, on 14 September 1626.

[21] In the following section I have relied heavily upon the unpublished "Journal of the Swiftsure," located in P. R. O., S. P. 16/11: 67 (hereafter cited as

his advisers, and the Council of War had labored to have the flotilla ready for a mid-summer sailing. The ninety-odd English vessels, with a total tonnage of more than fifty thousand pounds, were manned by 5,441 seamen. The land soldiers numbered 9,983, making a total of 15,424 men. The artillery included ten large brass guns and ten small pieces. The fleet was divided into three squadrons, commanded by Cecil, Essex, and William Feilding, the Earl of Denbigh. The commanders and several hundred seamen sailed in the larger and more commodious royal ships, while the impressed soldiers were transported in the smaller merchant vessels. All ships, particularly the colliers, were overcrowded and many needed repairs. Discipline was lacking. Conditions on shipboard were often terrifying.

Sir Edward Cecil, grandson of the great Lord Burghley, commanded the English fleet from aboard the *Anne Royal*. Though Cecil had gained much military experience on the Continent, this was his first command. He was forced to rely entirely upon his own judgment or upon the advice of the sea captains for all naval matters. Cecil was a man of character but possessed neither popularity nor proficiency in the art of commandeering. He lacked imagination and initiative. That such a figure was ill-equipped to command a large force from two nations on such a large-scale undertaking seems obvious.

All the top Dutch and English land commanders plus a few of the sea captains constituted Cecil's Council of War.[22] The unwieldy group, numbering twenty-five, was to meet periodically to discuss strategy and advise the admiral. This system of collective leadership may have worked on land, but the practice was obviously poorly suited for naval operations. The Dutch officers included both the

---

"*Swiftsure* Journal"). Essex was aboard this ship, as was his aide-de-camp, Arthur Wilson, who very likely wrote the "Journal." He intimates on p. 469 of his *Autobiography* that he did so. For other manuscripts relating to the expedition see S. P. 16/8, 16/9, and 16/12. The following published accounts have also been utilized: Sir William Monson's naval tracts in *Churchill's Voyages*, ed. John Churchill, 4 vols. (London, 1704), especially vol. 3; John Glanville, *The Voyage to Cadiz*, ed. Alexander B. Grosart, Camden Society (London, 1883); Charles Dalton, *Life and Times of General Edward Cecil, Viscount Wimbledon*, 2 vols. (London, 1885); Arthur Wilson, *Historie;* and Sir Julian S. Corbett, *England in the Mediterranean, A Study of the Rise and Influence of British Power within the Straits, 1603–1713*, 2 vols. (London: Longmans, Green and Company, 1904), 1: 115.

[22] British Museum, Egerton MSS, 2541, fol. 47a; and Glanville, *Voyage*, p. 36.

late Prince Maurice's illegitimate son, William of Nassau, who had secured much military experience in the fields of Flanders, and Laurence Revell, a high-ranking and able commander from Piedmont who had also fought on the Continent. Most of the English leaders likewise had little or no naval warfare to their credit. The sea captains and seamen who did possess naval experience had virtually no voice in the strategy of the operation. Though the success of the expedition probably rested to a great degree upon their knowledge and judgment—at least at the tactical level—they took orders rather than gave them.

Essex, who bore the titles of vice admiral and colonel general, commanded his squadron of thirty-one ships from aboard the *Swiftsure*, a fast and dependable bark weighing nine hundred tons, which was manned by two-hundred fifty sailors and captained by Sir Samuel Argall, a well-seasoned argonaut who had fought in the Mediterranean Sea. Essex's four regiments, totaling slightly over 3,000 soldiers and led by Viscount Valentia, Lord Delaware, and Lord Howard, were transported on twenty-odd small vessels, including three munition ships, two horse ships, and two ketches. To keep the record straight for his contemporaries and posterity, the Earl of Essex kept a journal of the military venture.[23]

On 3 October, Essex received orders to proceed to Falmouth with forty sail, while Cecil and the remainder of the flotilla awaited the arrival of their Dutch cofighters.[24] About three o'clock in the afternoon, after a twenty-one gun salute, the *Swiftsure* sailed forth. By noon the next day Essex and his squadron anchored in Falmouth Haven. When Essex set sail again on the afternoon of 5 October, after receiving word from Cecil, a sudden shift in wind and some stormy weather forced the English vessels back into the harbor.

Admiral Cecil, meanwhile, joined the Dutch contingent and, like Essex, awaited better sailing weather. While doing so, he wrote a series of instructions for the government of the fleet.[25] All men caught swearing, gaming, stealing, quarreling, or drunk would be punished accordingly. Landsmen, he insisted, should learn something about the ship, especially the ropes, while seamen were to be taught some of the elements of land fighting. No one was to disembark without

[23] See note 21 above.
[24] British Museum, Additional MSS 46,189.
[25] Glanville, *Voyage*, pp. 2–4.

leave. Upon landing, the sailors were forbidden to consume foreign wines, fish, and fresh fruit. Women were not to be forced. Every morning and evening, the commanders were to communicate with the admiral. In case any vessels of the armada became separated, Cecil warned, they were to proceed to the first rendezvous, off the South Cape at 37° latitude, or the second, at either Cádiz or Saint Lucar. Unfortunately, Cecil did not take so much care in distributing these instructions as he did in formulating them. Essex waited nearly a week before receiving his copy. Several ship captains received only the last two articles, dealing with the rendezvous, and some received no articles whatsoever.

On 8 October, with fair weather and northeasterly wind, Essex again departed from Falmouth Haven into the Channel, where the separated halves of the fleet rejoined early the following morning. In addition to his copy of the ordinances of war, Essex received some special instructions about naval combat and an admonitory letter from Cecil, instructing him not to divulge to the common man any information about the rendezvous or final destination of the armada.

For two days Neptune favored the English with a good sea. Then foul weather set in. From the evening of 12 October to the morning of 14 October the flotilla fought its first storm. The result was confusion. Most of the ships were widely dispersed. One ship lost a main mast. Virtually every ship suffered some damage. The *Robert*, a ship in Essex's squadron, capsized. Several smaller barks were lost. The long landing boats of many ships were destroyed. The storm meant a watery grave for several hundred men.

On 18 October the *Swiftsure* captain sighted South Cape, the first rendezvous of the English armada. Here, on 20 October, after most of the stragglers arrived, Cecil convened a Council of War aboard the *Anne Royal* and distributed further instructions about sea fighting.[26] Upon first contact with the Spanish fleet, which they hoped to intercept, the English vessels were to immediately fall into battle formation. Admiral Cecil's squadron would lead the way into naval combat, Essex would form his squadron along the leeward side, and the Dutch admiral would arrange his ships at the starboard side. The earl of Denbigh was to bring up the rear as a reserve and a source of additional munitions. None of the vessels

---

26 "*Swiftsure* Journal."

was to commence fighting until Cecil signaled. Even after the combat began, no man was to board an enemy ship without explicit instructions from the *Anne Royal.*

Consulting his sealed instructions, which represented the commands of Charles and Buckingham, Cecil also revealed to the Council of War the avowed purpose of the expedition. The three objectives of the English armada, according to these secret plans, were to destroy Spanish shipping, secure some place of importance in Spain, and seize the plate fleet. To best achieve these goals, His Majesty's government recommended the seizure of Lisbon, Cádiz, or Saint Lucar. Upon hearing these official objectives, the Council of War began debating the pros and cons of each port.[27] Lisbon, everyone agreed, was out, for the flotilla had already passed the Portuguese capital city. Saint Lucar and Cádiz both had strong advocates among the conferees, but the majority finally decided upon Saint Lucar. Control of that harbor would best enable them to intercept the plate fleet and conquer Cádiz and Seville.

The sea captains and shipmasters, however, balked at this decision. They raised serious objections to the entire proposal. Saint Lucar, they contended, was a barred haven, and as such was extremely dangerous for any ship at any time of the year. For a large foreign fleet to attempt to enter the port in the winter season, with the ever-present threat of storms and without the assistance of a pilot, was unthinkable to the seamen. "To that I could say no more to them," Cecil confessed, "being as I was not as great a seaman, and that I was strictly bound to their advice that did professe the sea."[28] The success of an amphibious operation like this, as Cecil soon learned, depended more upon naval tactics than upon army strategy.

Thwarted by this veto, the Council of War considered alternative proposals. Some commanders advocated an assault upon the wealthy and famed city of Malaga, claiming it was weaker and more accessible than Cádiz. Sir Henry Bruce, a well-seasoned army officer, spoke for the seizure of Gibraltar, then a small and unimportant town, pointing out that it would serve as an excellent base from which to harass Spanish shipping. But the Council of War, after turning down both counterproposals, finally decided to strike at Cádiz. The initial objective was Saint Mary's Port, a small harbor

[27] Magnussen, "Cadiz," pp. 53–54.
[28] See Cecil's account in P. R. O., S. P. 16/8.

along the northern coast of the Bay of Cádiz, which, because of a low shoreline, would afford the English troops a better landing than Cádiz proper. From here the English vessels could torment Spanish ships, lie out of gun range of Cádiz, replenish their depleted supplies of water, and when the opportunity presented itself, lay waste to Cádiz, as Essex had done in 1596. On to Cádiz!

III

Cádiz was distinguished by its beautiful harbor, its fishing and overseas shipping to both Asia and America, its great wealth, and its wine.[29] The city proper sat upon the low, sandy Isla de León, separated from the mainland proper by the San Pedro Channel, a narrow and swift-current arm of the sea about fifteen fathoms deep. At the head of the channel were the celebrated Pillars of Hercules. At the middle it was crossed by the Bridge of Suazo—the sole link between Cádiz and the mainland. The island itself was covered with vineyards and citrus-fruit trees. The significance of Cádiz lay in its strategic commercial location. Each year silver fleets from the New World, one from Vera Cruz and the other from Brazil, unloaded their precious cargo in its superb harbor. All Catholic Europe would feel the adverse effects of an English victory at Cádiz.

On 22 October, as the English armada approached the port, Cecil called another Council of War to plan the landing operation.[30] The Earl of Essex, it was decided, should lead the armada into the Bay of Cádiz and anchor his vessels as close to land as possible. Once anchored, the soldiers were to disembark, occupy Saint Mary's Port, and wait for further orders.

Essex promptly returned to the *Swiftsure* to prepare for the landing. Cecil's specific instructions arrived in a letter about 11:00 A.M. "My very good lord," Cecil wrote, "I sent a message onely to your lordship to make haste in accordance to the resolution wee took in Councell, your lordship then present. These are therefore to desire your lordship to make haste to gett in & to have such a birth for me, the Admiral of Holland & the Rear Admiral, that we may lie conveniently for the landing of our men & that it may please your lordship to give orders, that the ships wherein the souldiers

---

[29] See Geronimo de la Concepcion, *Cadiz Illustrada* (Amsterdam, 1690).
[30] "*Swiftsure* Journal."

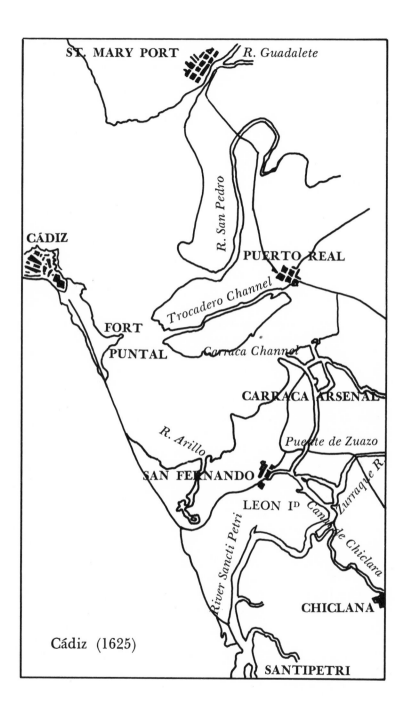

ST. MARY PORT   *R. Guadalete*

R. San Pedro

CÁDIZ

PUERTO REAL

Trocadero Channel

FORT

PUNTAL   *Carraca Channel*

CARRACA ARSENAL

R. Arillo

Puente de Zuazo

SAN FERNANDO

Zurraque R.

LEON I^D   *Caño de Chiclara*

River Sancti Petri

CHICLANA

Cádiz (1625)

SANTIPETRI

are may be next to the shore, as nigh St. Mary Port as may be."[31]

At 2 P.M., Essex led the English armada into the Cádiz Road. At this crucial juncture, Essex encountered seventeen Spanish galleons from the Brazil fleet and about twelve small galleys, all anchored in the harbor. Directly ahead of the *Swiftsure*, in the middle of the Road, were two huge galleons, one with fifty-two guns, another with forty-two, both of "Great burthen and force," blocking his entry to Saint Mary's Port. As Essex approached, the enemy opened fire with several salvos. Fortunately, he had enough room to slip through the enemy crossfire without exposing the *Swiftsure* to point-blank range. He held fire until he came closer to the galleys. Finally, at half-blank range, Essex ordered his cannoneers to fire. Their second salvo sank one galley. Fearful, outnumbered, and out-maneuvered, the remaining Spanish vessels scattered. The larger galleons on Essex's left cut their anchor cables and sped toward Puntal, a nearby fortress, hoping to receive protection from the land artillery. In their flight two ran aground.

Thus far the *Swiftsure* had confronted the enemy alone, for the rest of the fleet had lagged about one-half league astern. Cecil had made no provision for this turn of events, although he attempted to save the situation by sailing through Essex's reluctant squadron and shouting orders to the captains to follow closer to the vice admiral. He shouted in vain, for the merchant captains and crews, who had been pressed into the service, were reluctant to engage in a fight which might damage their vessels or endanger their lives. "Essex was left alone to his glory and his danger," S. R. Gardiner states, "as Cecil, who did not even know the names of the vessels under his command, was unable to call the laggards to account."[32]

Only toward the very end of the sea skirmish did the *Rainbow* move in and fire a few shots at long range. Essex hesitated to pursue his prey and follow up this initial surprise by capturing the Spanish ships, partly because the *Swiftsure*, a large and heavy hulk, could not risk pursuit into the shallow waters without a skilled pilot, especially after the tide began to ebb. He therefore commanded the crew to drop anchor and awaited further instructions. The orders to overtake the enemy never came, and smaller English vessels which might have safely captured the Spanish ships lagged behind.

[31] Glanville, *Voyage*, p. 42.
[32] Gardiner, *History*, 6: 15.

Thus the English allowed the Spanish galleons, possibly laden with bullion from Brazil, and the Neapolitan galleys to slip away. This proved to be a fatal mistake.

Once the initial fight was over, Admiral Cecil led the remainder. of the armada into the immense harbor and immediately convened a Council of War. The capture of Saint Mary's Port was now out of the question; the strategy needed to be revised to fit the realities of the moment. Some members wanted to attack Cádiz. Essex reportedly pressed for the seizure of the Spanish galleons at all costs. Cecil, however, favored a landing operation; he induced the council to proceed with his plan of action. The larger ships were to remain anchored in the deeper water, while the lighter ones were to advance upon Fort Puntal and batter it with their heaviest guns in preparation for landing.

That night a contingent of five Dutch and twenty small English colliers, under the command of William of Nassau, moved into the shallow waters and bombarded Fort Puntal until midnight. The fortress guarded the narrow entrance, about one-half mile wide, into the inner harbor, where the Spanish galleons had taken refuge, and at the same time protected Cádiz. Cecil's plan, however promising on paper, failed. Many Hollanders were killed and several English colliers ran aground.

At daybreak the following morning, 23 October, Essex was visited by William of Nassau, who came to report the results of the attack.[33] The Dutch leader was furious. His troops, he claimed, had been "sorely beaten" during the night. Two Dutch ships had sunk. The captains of the light English ships, he complained, were chiefly responsible for these losses, for again they moved slowly and refused to follow their orders. Essex and Cecil, both ashamed of the cowardly performance of the collier captains and their crews, promised William of Nassau that the English would avenge the deaths of their Dutch allies. Cecil decided that Essex would lead his squadron against Fort Puntal and give the Spanish their due.

No time was lost. Essex immediately sailed the *Swiftsure* within range of the fort, assumed a broadside position, anchored, and, before the Spanish had time to shift their guns, launched the cannon-ade.[34] For several hours the salvos rang forth. By 4:00 P.M. the fortress was "very much battered." The ramparts were beaten

[33] Glanville, *Voyage*, p. 43.
[34] See Sir William St. Leger to Buckingham, P. R. O., S. P. 16/8, fol. 59.

down and all but one of the enemy cannons had been damaged. English losses were minimal. The *Swiftsure* lost one man, one cannon, and one anchor.

Cecil then ordered Sir John Burrows, commander of one of Essex's regiments, to land his troops and obtain the surrender of Fort Puntal.[35] In the ensuing operation some of Burrows's men were killed by huge stones cast from the parapets of the fortress. Nevertheless, most of his regiment reached shore and prepared for the attack, but the Spanish general, Don Francisco Bustamente, capitulated to Burrows upon receiving honorable terms. The English soldiers took possession of the fortress while the Spanish troops marched out of the gate with their colors flying.

"As soon as the Captain of the fort came forth," wrote the author of the "*Swiftsure* Journal," "he asked what ship the *Swiftsure* was & what man of quality was in her, whereupon he was asked by a Capt. if he knew who it was had taken Cales [Cádiz] before; he answered, yes he did know, it was the Earl of Essex. The Capt. replyed to him again the Earl of Essex his sone was in that ship, then said he I think the devill is there as well, but he desired that he might have the honor granted him to goe aboard that he might see the Earl and the ship, which was granted."[36] This was one of Essex's finest hours.

On this strategic toehold, halfway between Cádiz and the Bridge of Suazo, Admiral Cecil landed his horses and soldiers, using the fire power of the fort to cover the landing operation. By nine o'clock the following morning the impressed troops were ashore, waiting near the fort for further instructions from Cecil. Still aboard the flagship, he remained undecided about the next move.

The Spaniards, meanwhile, reacted swiftly to the English invasion of their prized seaport.[37] Taking advantage of the tide and their shallower draught, the captains of the Spanish ships immediately sought safety in the upper reaches of the Cádiz harbor. Preparing for the worst, the Cádiz authorities then used a galley to remove many valuable public and personal items to the mainland, before the very

---

[35] "*Swiftsure* Journal."   [36] *Ibid.*

[37] See Concepcion's *Cadiz Illustrada; C. S. P. Ven., 1625–1626*, pp. 78, 119–21, 208–210; and Ruth Saunders Magurn, *The Letters of Peter Paul Rubens* (Cambridge: At the University Press, 1955), pp. 119–20. It is interesting to note that the Spanish knew of the English armada as early as June, though of course they did not know immediately of its departure and arrival.

eyes of the English sea captains, thereby hoping to forestall any attack motivated solely by the desire for pillage. Don Fernando Giron, the governor of Cádiz, sent forth numerous requests for succor. All the nearby coastal towns were alerted and entreated to send ships and troops. The Duke of Medina Sidonia, the principal magnate in the area, alerted a garrison of Moroccan troops. Reinforcements were soon on their way from every village along the southern coast of Spain. In short order Cádiz received 4,000 reinforcements. The all-important Bridge of Suazo was placed under the command of Don Luis Portocamero with two thousand foot and seven guns.

Among the perplexing problems confronting the Council of War which met aboard the *Swiftsure* on 24 October were how to have the flotilla inflict the greatest damage to Spanish shipping and whether the army should attempt to seize Cádiz, or as Essex recommended, first concentrate all its efforts upon capturing the Spanish galleons in the harbor and then, perhaps, cut off all reinforcements to the city.[38] It would be foolish, the majority concluded, to risk an assault upon Cádiz without first making the soldiers and fleet secure from enemy counterattacks. The Council of War, following Cecil's suggestions, therefore voted to seize the strategic Bridge of Suazo. Against Essex's advice, Cecil assumed personal command of this undertaking.

To maintain communications with the fleet and thus assure a steady flow of supplies, Cecil appointed Rear Admiral Denbigh in charge of the fleet.[39] As instructed on short notice, Denbigh landed his own men and dispersed the ships so that they could maintain complete control of the harbor but was unable to supply the army with seven days' rations of food and drink. Under these circumstances Essex landed his troops and prepared to advance upon the Bridge of Suazo.

Just before joining his troops, Cecil also ordered a contingent of English ships to seize, sink, or fire the Spanish vessels which had earlier eluded Essex. Though assigned to this seaman's task, Essex delegated it to one who was far better qualified, Capt. Samuel Argall.[40] The latter, taking the *Swiftsure* and several other ships in

[38] "*Swiftsure* Journal." Also see St. Leger's letter to Buckingham, see note 34 above.
[39] *Ibid.*, pp. 59–60.
[40] *Ibid.*

Essex's squadron, reconnoitered the Bay of Cádiz in search of his prey. This project, however, met with little success. The Spanish and Neapolitan sea captains, who knew the tidal patterns and shallow spots, had taken advantage of nature and combined it with their own ingenuity to outwit the English. Argall returned to Fort Puntal empty-handed.

Meanwhile, the English army, under Cecil's command, met blunder with blunder. Eager to seize the Bridge of Suazo before the enemy gathered more troops, Cecil tossed all caution to the four winds. He began marching the green troops, whose knapsacks were already empty, long before Denbigh could land the rations of meat, bread, cheese, and beer. Neglecting to guard the rear, Cecil needlessly exposed the last regiment of the marching army to an ambush by a small contingent of Spaniards who had come from Cádiz for that specific purpose. Only after he lost several men did he send Col. John Burgh to cover the rear and flank. Whether it was a result of poor intelligence or bad judgment is not recorded, but Cecil took a long, sandy route to his objective.

For these grave mistakes Cecil and his undisciplined troops paid dearly. The day was hot, and the food and water had not arrived. All the men were fatigued from the six-mile march, and a few fainted. Realizing that an attack under these conditions could hardly succeed, Cecil finally gave in to the desires of his men. He halted the march and permitted the troops to search the nearby homes for food and water, but food was not to be found and the local water was brackish. One soldier, however, discovered some wine cellars filled with five hundred casks of new Spanish wine. There was replenishment aplenty.

Although quite apprehensive, Cecil distributed the wine in limited quantities to his thirsty troops. This proved to be his undoing. One portion of Spanish wine produced the desire for more and more. Cecil then ordered the remaining tuns to be broken to prevent further intoxication, whereupon the angry troops cursed him and lapped the wine from the floors of the cellars. The whole army, reduced to a state of raving drunkenness, refused to march to the Bridge of Suazo. It was an unforgettable night for the English army —especially for its commanders.

By morning the English soldiers, all suffering from the lack of solid food, were more ready to sleep than fight. Realizing that they had been defeated by Spanish wine, Cecil and his staff decided to withdraw to Fort Puntal without fighting. The troops were not fit to attack, let alone hope to win, their strategic objective. To face the enemy under such disgraceful circumstances with such ignoble creatures would be more dishonorable than retreating.

Even the retreat failed. About 100 soldiers, many still inebriated, were left behind to face the Spaniards. Some of these men were later found with their throats slit and their ears and noses cut off. Many soldiers fainted during the withdrawal march; some stragglers were shot by Spanish ambushers. Some of those who returned alive to the landing site had to wait for their food and water. Few of the troops were prepared to assault Cádiz proper after such a harrowing experience.

After returning to Fort Puntal, Cecil called another Council of War meeting to determine the next course of action.[41] He asked if the armada leaders would be deemed dishonorable if they relinquished their original objective of capturing Cádiz. Obviously not, claimed the majority of the councilors; it was simply good judgment, military prudence, to leave at that time. If the English troops had approached Cádiz proper, broken ground, entrenched themselves, and *then* retreated, they might be considered dishonorable. Cádiz had not been, and could not then be, attempted, for it was too well armed to fall without a siege; and the English were scarcely prepared for that. The soldiers were hardly fit for action, and rain had rendered the musketeers next to useless. Besides, the Council of War argued, since the primary objective of the expedition was to seize the Spanish silver fleet, it would be far better to leave Cádiz entirely.

Cecil, who hoped to salvage some good from the fiasco, was not won over easily. He agreed that an assault upon Cádiz was untenable but did not wish to leave the harbor as long as the English held the advantage of Fort Puntal. This his subordinate members of the council would not agree to; the whole armada, they demanded, must prepare to embark and leave the Bay of Cádiz. Outnumbered and outranked by several noblemen, the admiral capitulated to the will of the majority.

On 27 October, Cecil dispatched the English soldiers to their respective troop ships. The wind was right, the tide perfect. While the troops loaded, Essex personally supervised a rear-guard action

41 Glanville, *Voyage*, p. 65.

against the Spanish, who finally advanced from Cádiz.[42] The Spaniards charged the retreating English so vigorously that Essex was forced to draw his troops into battle formation to prevent the enemy from cutting off their final retreat. Col. Edward Harwood, the youngest officer in the army, bore the brunt of this attack; he held his ground and kept the enemy busy during the whole operation. By nightfall all the English, except a small garrison in Fort Puntal under Colonel Burgh, were safely anchored beyond the range of the cannons of Cádiz. That night the citizens of the town celebrated their delivery from the enemy.

The next day, after razing and dismantling Fort Puntal, Colonel Burgh and his regiment rejoined the flotilla. Before leaving the Bay of Cádiz, Cecil convened another Council of War. Upon learning that two ships, the *Rainbow* and the *Dreadnought*, were too leaky to sail the open seas, the councilors ordered their captains to return directly to England.[43] They also decided to send all the sick and wounded back with those vessels. Ships that needed fresh water—as several did—were ordered to wait until the armada reached the Atlantic shoreline. The remaining ships were to rendezvous off South Cape and search for the Spanish plate fleet.

The following morning, somewhat less than one week after his arrival, Essex turned his back on Cádiz. No doubt his feelings were echoed in the words of his secretary, who later wrote: "The attempt upon the Isle of Cadiz was foolish, managed by a commander in chief who could not make the best use of the fair advantage he found."[44] The Cádiz failure, from Essex's viewpoint, must be laid directly at the feet of the commander. Cecil was to blame; he must bear the brunt of the criticism.

IV

AFTER AN uneventful passage the English fleet arrived at its prearranged rendezvous on 4 November.[45] There the commanders commenced their vigil for the Spanish plate fleet. Unbeknown to Cecil, this project was hopeless from the very beginning, for the forewarned captains of the Spanish treasure ships had swept far

[42] *Ibid.*, p. 71.
[43] *Ibid.*, p. 76.
[44] Arthur Wilson, *Autobiography*, p. 468.
[45] See Sir Thomas Love's account, quoted in *C. S. P. Dom., 1625–1626*, p. 175.

south of their usual route, crept along the coast of Africa, and then sailed into Cádiz Bay two days after Cecil's departure. Actually the two fleets had passed each other—at a distance, of course—shortly after 27 October.

The condition of the English fleet was deteriorating daily. The weather proved very uncongenial. More and more ships reported leaks and crusted bottoms. On some ships soldiers were dying of thirst, while on others they drank beer and wine. Much of the food, which had been supplied by fraudulent contractors, became rotten and malodorous. Conditions became so bad that Admiral Cecil called for a Council of War aboard the royal flagship. Each member told the same story: the plague was spreading to the sailors, and the ships were becoming more difficult to man. There was little debate and no disagreement. Since the enemy had not been sighted and since the men were hardly fit for an encounter, the councilors concurred that the flotilla should return to Plymouth. On 17 November, three days earlier than originally planned, the ships fixed their sails and pointed their prows northward toward England.

The Earl of Essex, still aboard the *Swiftsure*, was among the last commanders to leave South Cape.[46] Variable winds and stormy weather made his ship's progress northward extremely difficult. After ten days on unpredictable seas, the fleet encountered a treacherous winter storm.[47] Violent wind caused the *Swiftsure* to lose a foresail and break a tiller. During the voyage Essex had lost contact with all but six of his ships; on 28 November he lost contact with them. Land remained out of sight. One week later, after more violent winds and rain, the *Swiftsure* cast anchor in Falmouth Bay. The crew had been reduced from 250 to 40 men. "That night," the ship's journalist noted in his log, "the Earl of Essex went ashore."[48]

Essex discovered that he was not among the last—as he originally believed—but rather was the first to return from Cádiz. The next day he sailed to Plymouth, where he disembarked, and immediately proceeded to London. He must have gotten little or no sleep, for he arrived at Hampton Court the following evening and had the unpleasant task of breaking the first news of the fate of the English

[46] "*Swiftsure* Journal."

[47] See Cecil's letter to Sir John Coke dated 8 November 1625 from aboard the *Anne Royal;* it is reprinted in *H. M. C. Twelfth Report*, Appendix 1, p. 225.

[48] "*Swiftsure* Journal." Also see *C. S. P. Dom., 1625–1626*, pp. 171, 176; *C. S. P. Ven., 1625–1626*, p. 253; and *H. M. C. Eleventh Report*, Appendix 1, p. 40.

armada to the King and to Lord Admiral Buckingham.[49] The town of Cádiz, he contended, was too strongly fortified to warrant risking a direct assault, and the English army was ill-prepared for a lengthy siege. The expedition, in short, had failed to attain any of its stated objectives. In the course of his first hand report Essex depreciated Admiral Cecil and complained about the naval contractors.

Gradually more news of the fiasco trickled into England. By mid-December twenty-four ships of Essex's squadron had returned to Plymouth. Some vessels from the other two squadrons also straggled into the southern port towns.[50] All bore the same ill tidings. Most of the captains confirmed Essex's opinions. Many letters addressed to Buckingham and Secretary Coke substantiated the report of the vice admiral. Sir Michael Geere, a ship captain, complained about poor leadership, faulty tactics, the prevalency of the plague, lack of water, spoiled food, and the needless loss of life. Sir Thomas Love, another sea captain, wrote of the merciless storm, the leaky royal ships, and the rotten provisions.

Admiral Cecil, meanwhile, landed in Kinsale, Ireland, with several other ships.[51] The same storm that had battered down the foresail of the *Swiftsure* had scattered the vessels in Cecil's squadron in all directions. Some landed in Scilly, some in Portsmouth and Plymouth, others along the coast of Ireland. The *Anne Royal* needed so much repair that Cecil, who resolved to stay with the flagship, spent the Christmas season, January, and part of February in Ireland. He undoubtedly hoped that time and distance would diminish the ill effects of the Cádiz defeat and leave his reputation unscathed. The damage had already been done, however, for the oral and written accounts of Essex, Geere, St. Leger, Love, and others had implicated Cecil and the naval officials in England.

Upon returning to England late in February, Cecil nevertheless hoped to reconcile himself with Charles. The sovereign, however, denied Cecil his presence and flatly refused to grant him the promised title until after an inquiry. In late March the official investigation got under way. Nine colonels, led by Essex and seconded by Lords

[49] P. R. O., S. P. 16/11: 30, a letter from Sir James Bagg to Secretary of State Conway; also see Sir Michael Geere's letter to his son William in S. P. 16/12: 41–45.

[50] See P. R. O., S. P. 16/12: 1–45, for various accounts of the return passage.

[51] *C. S. P. Ven., 1625–1626*, pp. 312, 340, 353.

Conway, Cromwell, and Valentia, charged that Cecil was the principal cause of most miscarriages at Cádiz.[52] Cecil had not given them the proper authority to pursue the Spanish galleons, they contended, until it was much too late. Relying chiefly upon his connection with Buckingham to protect himself in this crisis, Cecil promptly denied the charges of his subordinates and issued a series of countercharges before the Privy Council. The army colonels, especially those who had let the Spanish ships sail into hiding without giving fight, were responsible for the defeat at Cádiz, rebutted Cecil. As the investigation progressed, the charges and counter charges grew hotter and hotter.[53] The verbal battle narrowed to a debate over the instructions which Cecil had written for his subordinates. Essex claimed that Cecil's orders had been distributed late and that they explicitly had forbidden any Englishman to give fight without a specific order from the commander in chief.

Cecil then set out to prove himself guiltless of the accusations.[54] Essex, he retorted, had first seen a copy of the instructions at Plymouth before sailing. Besides, Essex and his colonels had not read the written instructions carefully, Cecil continued, or they would not have refused to fight. He attempted to clear himself of all responsibility for supply shortages and rotten food. He even sought to exonerate himself of the bacchanalia near the Bridge of Suazo. Cecil refused to assume the blame for the errors, disorders, miscarriages, and retreats at Cádiz.

Information about the investigation, which was held behind closed doors, soon leaked out to the public. It was learned that the venture had cost about £313,000 and that the prize booty from three captured ships amounted to no more than £200,000.[55] The total loss of six English ships and considerable damage to many others merely made the financial losses more staggering. The loss of human life was worse. Of the 10,000 soldiers who left Plymouth in October, only 4,618 returned home in December—a mortality

[52] British Museum, Stowe MSS, 151, and Additional MSS, 46,188.

[53] For a discussion of the inquiry see Magnussen, "Cadiz," pp. 97–100. Also see Thomas Meuty's letter to Lady Cornwallis in Lord Braybrooke, ed., *The Private correspondence of Jane, Lady Cornwallis* (London, 1842), p. 152.

[54] When the Council Board demanded Cecil's account in writing, he wrote his *Journal*, which was based on the official account of Glanville. His account, published in 1626, was rebutted point by point by an anonymous critic whose views were reprinted in Oppenheim, *Naval Tracts*, 3: 150.

[55] See de Villiers, *Hastings Journal*, p. 40.

rate of over 50 percent—and few died while fighting. The bare facts did not lie: the Cádiz venture was clearly a failure. Who, if anyone, was responsible for the tragic loss of lives and property was not known. The charges revealed little more than sharp personal differences.

The evidence gathered by the secretary of state, Sir John Coke, however, bespoke more of the real truth about the expedition.[56] Between December and March this diligent civil servant questioned the returning captains and investigated the whole venture, probably at the request of the King. His notes reveal a slightly different story from the one at the examination. As the English flotilla had sailed around South Cape, he discovered, the English ships had been spotted by the Spanish, who had forwarded the news to all the coastal cities, Cádiz included. The element of surprise, then, had been virtually absent. Coke also found out: (1) that some captains possessed copies of Cecil's instructions, but others did not; (2) that the winter season prevented some ships from taking their best ordnance; (3) that the soldiers lacked adequate provisions; (4) that the English fleet lingered too long near the Spanish shoreline before attempting Cádiz; (5) that Cecil's decision to attack Cádiz during low tide represented very poor judgment; (6) that Essex, upon attacking, was neither properly instructed nor sufficiently supported; (7) that the English leaders exercised poor judgment in not firing upon the Spanish galleons and landing immediately; and (8) that all the soldiers were so discouraged and so deprived of water that they turned to the new wine. Coke's findings hardly exonerated Cecil of responsibility for the debacle.

Although most observant contemporaries either knew or suspected the truth revealed in the investigation, little came of the evidence or the whole inquiry. "Cecil accuses his colonels and they accuse him," the Venetian ambassador wrote to the Senate. "They propose to make a scapegoat of Captain Love, a dependent of the Duke . . . they expect that examination will blow over without being blamed."[57] The inquiry soon passed into oblivion. Despite the overwhelming evidence of poor leadership, the council cleared the commander. Lord High Admiral Buckingham succeeded in protecting Cecil and in reconciling him with the King. To Essex's chagrin Cecil

56 His correspondence and notes contain a wealth of information; see the Coke MSS, *H. M. C. Twelfth Report*, Appendix 1, pp. 225–65.

57 *C. S. P. Ven., 1625–1626*, p. 383.

assumed his place in the House of Lords before the year was half over.[58]

Some members in the House of Commons, however, did not dismiss the Cádiz defeat so quickly as the Privy Council had. The majority considered the venture a fiasco from its very inception, but they were not simply content to cast the blame at Cecil. Sir John Eliot, a popular member of the opposition, called for an investigation. "Our honour is ruined," he contended, "our ships are sunk, our men perished; not by the sword, not by the enemy, not by charges, but, as the strongest predictions discerned and made it apparent beforehand, by those we trust."[59] If anyone was to be blamed for the failure, many members of the Lower House argued, let it be the prime mover himself, Lord Admiral Buckingham.

Essex, meanwhile, resumed his political duties. Though failing at Cádiz to duplicate his father's feat, he retained the confidence of the Crown, for on the last day of the year he was reappointed lord lieutenant of Staffordshire.[60] With the renewed commission from Whitehall came an admonition to keep his regiment filled with good soldiers and to see that they were adequately provisioned. Essex could not easily forget the Cádiz voyage. What might have been a golden opportunity to win personal glory and public esteem had turned into a disgraceful experience. What might have become a worthwhile investigation of naval policy and administration had been obfuscated. Realizing that Buckingham and his dependents were behind this and the defeat, Essex resolved never again to serve under the Lord Admiral's leadership. If this resolution further alienated him from Charles I and the Court, Essex was prepared to face and to suffer the consequences.

[58] He was created Baron Cecil and Viscount Wimbledon on 9 November 1625. See Cokayne, *Complete Peerage*, 12: 740.

[59] For the complete speech and some critical comments see John Forster, *Sir John Eliot: A Biography, 1590–1632*, 2 vols. (London, 1865), 1: 517–18. In 1628, Eliot reiterated his demand for an inquiry.

[60] *A. P. C. 1625–1626*, pp. 486, 497.

CHAPTER 7

A Refractory Lord

I

IF ESSEX SUFFERED any loss of prestige or royal favor from the Cádiz disaster, there was no sign of it at Charles' coronation in Westminster Abbey on 2 February 1626. The colorful Candlemas Day ceremony brought out the dignitaries of state, the royal favorites, and all the peers.[1] To the chagrin of many nobles the Duke of Buckingham dominated the solemn affair. To the dismay of many clergy Dr. Laud, the new ecclesiastical favorite, assumed a significant role in the arrangement and conduct of the ceremony. As Earl Marshal, the Earl of Arundel supervised the processions and military ritual accompanying the coronation.

By virtue of his title and name, Essex had a place of honor in this, his second, coronation and occupied a prominent place in the processional from Westminster Hall to the Abbey.[2] Preceding him were the heralds, the aldermen of London, the newly created Knights of Bath, the Privy Councilors, barons, bishops, viscounts, and earls. Directly before him the Earl of Dorset carried the first sword. Essex himself, in his coronation robes and coroneted cap, bore the second sword.[3] Whereas in 1603 he had been assisted by his uncle the Earl of Northumberland, Essex now carried the symbolic emblem alone.

After taking his coronation oath, Charles called upon Essex to help him remove the heavy ceremonial robe. This done, Archbishop Abbot and Bishop Laud proceeded to annoint and crown the King, who sat in the coronation chair. Charles girdled himself with Edward the Confessor's sword and posed to receive homage from

---

[1] Frankland, *Annals*, pp. 114–19.

[2] William Sanderson, *A Compleat History* (London, 1658), pp. 24–28; and *H. M. C. Rutland Manuscripts*, 1: 475.

[3] Sanderson (*A Compleat History*, p. 24) wrote that Essex carried the second sword of state, while D'Ewes (*Autobiography*, 1: 174) claimed that he carried the long scepter.

the Duke of Buckingham on behalf of the lords. The lords laid their hands upon the crown and promised to give their lives, if necessary, to defend both King and kingdom. Then the bishops knelt before Charles and kissed him. After a prayer, communion, and Gloria Patri the newly crowned monarch retired briefly to King Edward's chapel to change his clothes. Essex had the honor of assisting him don a short red velvet, ermine-lined robe, after which the coronation procession left the Abbey and returned to Whitehall.

By giving Essex a conspicuous place in the ceremonies Charles revealed his intention to appease the opposition lords and to forget the past. Yet, in spite of these conciliatory public gestures, Charles I did not bring Essex into the inner circles of his government. He did not follow up with higher honors or one of the much-coveted offices. He did not create Essex a Knight of Bath or induct him into the Order of the Garter. Not long after his coronation Charles selected several new Privy Councilors and elevated several lords to earldoms. For Essex there was nothing. As long as royal favorites like Buckingham and prelates like Laud had the King's ear and the control of patronage, Essex could hold little hope of ever attaining the high places once held by his father. It became clearer and clearer that Essex's fate was to be political exclusion.

This fate Essex sensed by the summer of 1626, if not before, for thereafter he revealed himself as anything but a King's man. This is not to say that Essex and his parliamentary associates questioned the monarchical system, the legitimacy of the dynasty, or the sovereignty of their King. Rather, the aristocratic opposition questioned the nature and limits of that authority, criticized the use of the royal prerogative, and opposed royal policies. They concentrated their political attacks neither on the kingly office nor on Charles personally but on royal ministers and favorites. Parliament served as the principal battleground.

The stated purpose of the Parliament which Charles convened on 6 February was to solve the national crisis brought about by the Cádiz expedition.[4] This costly debacle had drained the royal treasury so drastically that there was talk of pawning the crown jewels to Dutch financiers. Counting on the capture of the Spanish silver fleet, both Charles and Buckingham had committed England to more foreign aid and additional expeditions on the Continent.

[4] Cobbett, *Parliamentary History*, 2: 44; Gardiner, *History*, 6: 56–62; and Rushworth, *Historical Collections*, 1: 199.

Deeply in debt and with little hope of extending his credit, Charles was obliged to call upon Parliament for economic assistance, even though it meant sacrificing some pride and risking an attack upon his policies.

Essex, who had recently passed his thirty-fifth birthday, was by now a seasoned member of the Upper House, having served in every Parliament since 1614.[5] Though lacking the dignity of a Privy Councilor and the parliamentary skill of the late Earl of Southampton, he demanded respect and enjoyed much popularity. Because of his experience and seniority he assumed an increasingly important role in the deliberations. He still refrained from delivering long and flowery speeches; instead, Essex called for action. Several times when the discussion strayed, Essex sponsored motions which brought the Upper House back to the business at hand. Sometimes he acted as an arbitrator between the conflicting viewpoints. Equally important were his connections with members of the House of Commons.

Essex's influence in the Lower House stemmed from his popularity and power in local affairs. In 1626 he was not only lord lieutenant and justice of the peace of Staffordshire but lord lieutenant of Essex and commissioner of the peace of Warwick, all of which gave him local prestige and opportunity for patronage. Essex exercised his influence by appointing Essex men to the various local offices. His deputy lieutenants included Sir Edward Littleton, who had participated in the 1601 *coup d'état;* Sir William Bowyer, a faithful follower of the Devereux family for two generations; Sir Simon Weston and Richard Dyott, both prominent men among the Staffordshire gentry; and James Quarrels, a London merchant and M.P.[6] No doubt Sir Walter Devereux owed his place on the Warwickshire Commission for Peace to his titled brother. The appointments of Thomas Parkes, Harvey Bagot, Bowyer, and John Bowes to the office of sheriff of Staffordshire also reflect the Earl's patronage. Some of the office holders had served under his father; several had served under the third Earl in the Continental campaigns.

Several Essex men secured seats in the House of Commons.[7] Bowyer and Weston sat for the county of Staffordshire, Sir Walter

5 *Lords Journal*, 3: 494–510.

6 Compiled from *A. P. C.* various volumes and pages; and British Museum Additional MSS, 46,188.

7 Wedgwood, *Historical Collections of Staffordshire*, various pages.

for Tamworth, and Dyott for Lichfield. In subsequent parliamentary sessions Bagot sat for Staffordshire, Dyott for Lichfield, and Sir Walter again for Tamworth. Essex, in short, converted his reputation and his military powers into political influence. This practice enabled members of the Upper House to exert some influence in the Commons. Although Essex did not control Staffordshire or Herefordshire, as was often the case in some English counties, or possess exclusive nominating power in the above-mentioned boroughs, it is clear that he had a voice in the selection of representatives to the Lower House.

On 15 February, after subscribing to the customary oath, Essex was named to the Committee for Petitions, the all-powerful steering committee empowered to determine which petitions should be acted upon in the Upper House.[8] He shared this honor with the Earls of Salisbury, Montgomery, Mulgrave, and Bridgewater, six bishops, and several barons. The driving force of the group, however, proved to be Lord Saye, the ambitious and able leader of the aristocratic opposition who had stepped into Southampton's shoes. This committee received from the parent body authority to obtain legal documents (deeds, records, or writings) from other courts and secured the power to formally reject any petition presented to it. Under Saye's vigorous leadership, Essex and his colleagues wielded noteworthy judicial and legislative powers.

The most pressing business concerned national defense. England found herself in a precarious international situation—as Charles I and his Privy Councilors had already indicated in their preliminary speeches to Parliament—for she was at odds with Europe's two most powerful nations, Spain and France. That the former might seek revenge for the recent Cádiz expedition was feared by many an Englishman; that France would soon attack La Rochelle, the Huguenot citadel, was taken for granted. To meet this double-pronged threat, Charles I demanded action. His critics, however, demanded explanations. In the Lower House, Sir John Eliot, the zealous parliamentarian, called for another post mortem investigation of the Cádiz debacle.[9] The Lords, acting in a more constructive manner, sought to put England into a posture of defense against Spain,[10] so they established a committee which was to meet

8 *Lords Journal*, 3: 500.
9 Gardiner, *History*, 6: 62.
10 *Lords Journal*, 3: 511–20.

regularly in the Painted Chamber. Essex and George Carew, the
newly created Earl of Totnes, and master of the ordnance, were the
most experienced and qualified members. Events forced them to work
fast. Within a matter of days, after the required three readings, they
presented the military-preparedness bill to Charles I for approval.

It came none too soon. On 6 March the Lords were confronted
with news of an advancing Spanish armada. Clearly, a national
emergency was at hand. A large committee, including Essex and
Totnes, was ordered to survey the defenses. The chairman soon
reported that England lacked powder, pikes, and arms. To meet
the crisis, the master of the ordnance requested a large offensive
fleet, a small flotilla to defend the coasts, a large army, and necessary
funds. Essex served on a small subcommittee which was empowered
to purchase the needed material. Before most of these measure were
adequately dealt with, however, the peers became involved in several
bitter domestic battles.

Essex's humanitarian interests found expression in this Parliament.
In early March he became chairman of a committee concerned
with Charterhouse Hospital.[11] In 1611, England's richest commoner, Thomas Sutton, purchased Charterhouse from the Earl of
Suffolk with the intention of using it for some humanitarian purpose.
Although Sutton secured letters patent, which empowered him to
fulfill his plan, he died before he could realize it. Nevertheless, his
will—contested soon after his death—provided for a hospital and a
school. After much legal bickering, the courts decided in 1614 that
the will was valid and that its terms should be fulfilled. A hospital
for the aged and a school were erected on the site, as planned, but
by the time of the accession of Charles there were so many unpaid
debts that its future was uncertain. At that juncture Essex presented
a bill designed to give parliamentary sanction to Charterhouse
Hospital. He read the bill in the Upper House and chaired the
sessions which ironed out all imperfections and answered the earlier
objections. The Earl's diligence paid off, for on 23 March the bill
passed on its third reading in the House of Lords. Because Charles
abruptly dissolved this Parliament without signing any bills,
however, the Charterhouse petition lay dormant until 1628, when
it was reintroduced, passed, and approved as a private act.

Essex and the other opposition members of the Lords also defended their political privileges. Sparked by such figures as Essex's

[11] *Ibid.*, pp. 503, 522.

brother-in-law the Earl of Hertford and Lord Saye, the peers reasserted their ancient rights and endeavored to broaden the base of their power. Their reform of the proxy system, in particular, reduced the royal influence in the Upper House.[12] The abuse in the proxy privilege was obvious to all lords, for it permitted an extraordinary concentration of power. Instead of "one lord, one vote" the system allowed Buckingham to have as many as fourteen votes and Arundel as many as six. That the Crown utilized the privilege to secure a clear majority in the Upper House was obvious; and that Buckingham should exercise such power was more than many peers could tolerate. Thus, on 25 February 1626, after some preliminary discussions, the Lords engaged in a lengthy and heated debate over a motion to limit each peer to two proxies. Lord Saye advocated the reform, pointing out that without some limitation the House of Lords was in danger of being dominated by two or three men. He was seconded by the Earls of Essex, Mulgrave, Pembroke, and Hertford, and Lord Russell. Although vehemently opposed by the Duke of Buckingham, the reformers won their way. Henceforth no peer could hold more than two proxies, and spiritual lords would be obligated to grant their proxies only to divines.

Having won the initial skirmish with Buckingham, the opposition peers retained the initiative by utilizing their judicial powers. Capitalizing on their pivotal place in the traditional trinity of King-Lords-Commons, they successfully mediated a bitter precedence dispute between Robert de Vere and Lord Willoughby. Exercising their appellate powers and following the recommendations of the Committee on Petitions, the Lords reviewed several cases from lower courts. Claiming original jurisdiction, they also entertained a grievance petition from a Ludgate prisoner who had been committed without cause. The peers also made liberal use both of their judicial powers to defend their right of freedom from arrest and of the *habeas corpus* writ to free their arrested dependents from prison. They declared several Englishmen in contempt of the House of Lords, served subpoenas with little hesitation, and challenged the decisions and jurisdiction not only of sheriffs and bailiffs but of the Court of Chancery and even the mighty Privy Council.

The Lords also steadfastly defended their right to attend Parliament. Regarding this as a birthright, they insisted upon receiving

[12] For a complete discussion of this see my "Arundel Case, 1626," *Historian* 26 (1964): 332–47.

a royal writ and upon attending the debates without fear of reprisal. The fact that the Crown had recently denied this right to two peers, the Bishop of Lincoln and the Earl of Bristol, only made the Upper House more sensitive and anxious to press the matter at the appropriate moment. The moment came on 4 March when Charles arrested the Earl of Arundel and removed him from the Privy Council. Arundel had allowed his eldest son, Henry, Lord Maltravers, clandestinely to marry Elizabeth Stuart, the King's cousin, without first securing the royal consent. Upon finding out, Charles I was so furious that he took action against all parties involved. He placed the couple under the watchful eye of Archbishop Abbot, ordered the Countess of Arundel to the house of her mother-in-law and forbade her to attend Court, and placed Arundel under the observation of four guards, who conducted the powerful lord to the Tower of London. The King rode roughshod over Arundel's parliamentary rights of attendance and freedom from arrest.

The Upper House, spearheaded by the disgruntled Bishop of Lincoln, who had only recently returned after similar treatment, proceeded to take up Arundel's cause. Some peers blindly defended the King, others held fast to their rights. The majority ordered the Committee on Privileges to investigate the matter and search the *Journal* for precedents. On 15 March the Lords debated the matter. The issue was clear and simple: could the Crown commit a lord without cause during Parliament? The Lord President defended Charles I on the basis of precedent. Lord Saye claimed that precedent was no excuse for such a violation of parliamentary rights—a violation to him so dangerous that he demanded a formal protestation. The majority, however, decided against a declaration; instead they disregarded the issue for the moment.

On 5 April, Essex's brother-in-law reintroduced the subject by pointing out that Charles I had not only deprived Arundel of his vote but also had deprived those peers whose proxies Arundel held. As chairman of the Committee on Privileges, Hertford also reported that a search of the *Journal* revealed that no peer had ever been committed during Parliament without judgment by the other nobles. Again Lord Saye tried to prod the peers into petitioning for Arundel's release. After criticizing those noblemen who cited histories instead of parliamentary records as evidence, he called upon his colleagues to petition Charles for the release. The majority now went with him, and a remonstrance was written, approved by the whole House, and presented to the King on 19 April. Charles ignored the protest or at least chose not to answer it promptly. A second "very select committee," which included Essex, was empowered to request that the King answer the earlier petition. Their document was framed in such demanding and presumptuous language, however, that Charles objected, so much so that he came to the Upper House and lectured the peers on the rights of the Crown in such matters. He promised to answer the initial petition at his royal pleasure.

On 17 May, after further delay, Essex demanded action. His motion that another petition be drawn and sent to Charles I was promptly passed. Charles answered on 20 May: Arundel would not be released. He had been committed for a cause—a cause which would be revealed at the proper time. His right had not been infringed upon, so there was no breach of privilege.

The royal refusal, of course, made the opposition peers only more determined to have their way on the matter. The privilege committee, which Essex called for, produced another document, which requested the cause of Arundel's arrest, and forwarded it to Charles. The ruler, upon receiving this third communication, promised that either the cause would soon be made public or Arundel would be released. Neither of these alternatives satisfied the petitioners, however, so on 25 May, after several acrimonious speeches, the peers voted to cease all legislative business until Arundel was restored to their midst. They deemed it "a high indignity that the House of Commons had the power to redeem two of their members in a few days, whereas their lordships cannot attain so much in some months." [13]

This tactic proved sufficient. By 5 June, Arundel had his release order and three days later rejoined his peers. Once back he protested his loyalty, thanked Charles I, and commended his fellow peers for their tireless efforts in freeing him. He also requested that because the Upper House was a court of record the *Journal* should state that his imprisonment should never be used as a precedent. He knew that the House of Lords was as precedent-conscious as the House of Commons.

Essex was rewarded on 9 June for his assistance in the Arundel case by being added to the Committee for Privileges. Although he had earned the appointment by his defense of aristocratic rights,

13 *Lords Journal*, 3: 641.

it should not be forgotten that his brother-in-law the Earl of Hertford headed the committee. This appointment drew Essex into the inner circles of the aristocratic opposition. He was thereafter regarded by Charles I as an opposition lord.

Essex played a similar role in the Bristol-Buckingham controversy.[14] The Earl of Bristol, an avowed enemy of Buckingham, had been confined to Sherburne Manor since 1624 and was denied all freedom of action. He had not been permitted to attend the 1625 sitting of Parliament; he had been denied a place at the coronation; and he had been refused admission to the 1626 session. He stubbornly denied his guilt and refused to admit to charges which he believed were devised to keep him silent; instead, he waited for an opportune moment to strike back at his principal adversary, Buckingham.

In March 1626, with the Arundel case already before the Upper House, the time was ripe for revenge. Bristol first demanded that he be either freed unconditionally or tried by his peers in an open court. Secondly, he demanded a writ which would allow him to attend Parliament. Charles, fearing the consequences of granting the demands and yet hoping to avert an open battle with the Lords, engaged in duplicity. He reluctantly sent the writ but at the same time made it clear in a covering letter that Bristol must stay away from the Upper House. Charles feared "the terrible Earl" and wanted to keep him silent. But Bristol would not be silenced. Disregarding Charles's covering letter, he went to London and prepared to join his colleagues. Although he could not secure his seat immediately, he placed himself at the mercy of his peers and petitioned for justice on 17 April.

At this point Essex took up Bristol's cause. Here was another opportunity to assert the power and privileges of aristocracy. Here was a chance to educate Charles and Buckingham about the political rights of English peers. Bristol's case offered Essex, who still smarted from Buckingham's blunders in the Cádiz expedition, some measure of political revenge. Therefore that Essex moved that the House of Lords entertain Bristol's petition is not surprising. The motion was promptly passed and the petition was assigned to a committee. The King reacted furiously to these political maneuvers. Of his personal feelings about Essex there remains no record, but he most certainly disapproved of Essex's role in the affair. Of his reaction

[14] For Essex's role in the case see Gardiner, *Notes of the Debates 1626*, pp. 142–44, 151, 157, 167, 182, 185–88.

to the motion which Essex made, however, there is abundant evidence: Charles accused Bristol of treason, thereby hoping to divert the attention of the Lords or prejudice the case.

Thus began one of the most complicated state trials ever to come before the Upper House. There were charges, countercharges, and counter-countercharges. In effect, two trials, each involving Buckingham and Bristol, were held. Each peer accused the other of treasonable activities. Each vied for the opportunity of being heard first. Each had a sympathetic and highly prejudiced following among the peerage. Early in May the opposing sides appeared for the legal battle. Attorney General Sir Robert Heath read the formal treason charge against Bristol, who responded with a formal charge against Buckingham. This brought up the procedural conundrum of which case should be heard first. Hoping for the initial advantage, both sides claimed priority and refused to compromise.

Justice demanded a compromise—a compromise provided by Essex: he moved that the two cases proceed simultaneously in the House of Lords. The majority of the Lords concurred. Thus, from the early days of May until the Middle of June the Upper House was the scene of a unique legal battle for which there was no precedent. Among the legal technicalities to be determined—if the trial was to be fair—were whether Bristol should be given a written copy of the charges and whether he should be allowed legal counsel. Even deciding whether the peers themselves—without legal training —or the Crown should determine those matters presented a problem. Because neither could achieve much impartiality, and hence neither could guarantee a fair trial, Essex argued that professional judges should be consulted to decide those procedural questions for which there were no precedents. Certainly their opinions would produce a more just trial, he believed; so he sponsored a motion to that effect. Again, on 9 May, the majority concurred.

Shortly thereafter, even though Charles was opposed to any concessions, Bristol won the right of counsel in a precedent-making decision, and the trial proceeded more rapidly. Bristol reiterated his loyalty to the Stuart sovereigns, denied any complicity with the Spanish negotiators, and commenced to answer the attorney general's charges. To prove his innocence, he read correspondence which incriminated Buckingham, implicated Lord Conway, and compromised the King. By the end of May the English sovereign realized that Bristol had established his innocence and that the House of Lords would clear him of the treason charge.

The case against Buckingham, meanwhile, changed from a trial by peers to an impeachment trial. At first the Lords wanted to examine the royal favorite by themselves. This the House of Commons would not permit. Bristol also did not want such an investigation, so he slipped incriminating evidence to the Lower House. Finally, after several demands, the Lords consented to share their case against Buckingham with the Commons. On 8 May the impeachment trial of the royal favorite began.[15]

Charles soon saw the danger signs. He realized that both Houses were determined to destroy Buckingham. If Parliament continued, his favorite would certainly be found guilty and then, like Bacon and Cranfield, stripped of his offices. It was either Parliament or Buckingham. Charles remained by his favorite and dissolved the assembly over the noisy protests of the Lords, who hoped to finish their legislative and judicial business. To demonstrate his obvious disgust with the parliamentary system of government, he promptly seized and imprisoned both Arundel and Bristol. This defiant act merely made the case of the aristocratic opposition stronger and future attacks upon the royal prerogative more certain. If an aristocrat could not freely exercise his political rights, there was little hope for a member of the House of Commons, or for that matter, any Englishman.

II

AFTER THE dissolution of Parliament the Earl of Essex turned from politics to soldiering. Because of an earlier contract he was obliged to serve the Dutch in a military capacity until 4 November.[16] As lord lieutenant he was still responsible for mustering and training troops in Staffordshire, a duty which he continued to delegate to his deputy lieutenants. He had his Cádiz soldiers to care for. In June, Essex was also asked to serve in an armada which aimed to attack Spanish shipping in the Bay of Biscay. Lord Admiral Buckingham was the titular head of the expedition, for which preliminary preparations were already in progress. Although some Englishmen

[15] *Lords Journal*, 3: 595–610; and Gardiner, *History*, 6: 98–119.

[16] Wilson, *Autobiography*, p. 123. Two years earlier Essex contracted to fight for the United Provinces for three summers. He had been granted a license for the same from James I and in 1625 had secured an exemption from his contract through the efforts of Charles.

may have considered it a high honor to secure a vice admiralty in such an undertaking, Essex thought otherwise and flatly rejected Buckingham's solicitation. In so refusing, Essex merely fulfilled his vow never to fight under the Duke.

When Charles learned of this peremptory rebuff, he demanded Essex's explanation. "The King asked him why he would not accept," a contemporary explained, "who answered, he would have accepted, and for a meaner office, to his majesty's service, if his majesty himself had offered it; but to receive it from another he thought not so fit, as for other reasons, so especially because he knew his majesty's pleasure. Whereupon the King, displeased, bade him go whither he would, and come again when he sent for him." [17] The King's displeasure did not seem to disturb Essex. Shortly after this verbal exchange Essex, taking Charles at his word, requested permission to return to the Low Countries. Charles reluctantly consented, whereupon Essex rejoined his regiment.

After the ill-fated Cádiz venture the troops had returned to English soil. The common soldiers were billeted in the southern counties, mainly in the port towns. Some of Essex's soldiers were quartered in Cornwall and Devonshire but most, including his personal guard, were stationed in Essex.[18] Here, while their commander attended Parliament, the defeated soldiers had gone through a rigorous training program in preparation for the next assignment. Charles brought back an experienced training cadre, including Edward Harcourt, a dependent of Essex, from the Continent to teach the English officers "the true modern use of arms and order of soldiers."[19] The English captains, in turn, trained their enlisted men in the art of war, thereby hoping to narrow the military gap between England and the nations on the Continent.

To fill his ranks, Essex was empowered by the Privy Council to raise more troops in Staffordshire.[20] In late July the English volunteers embarked for the Low Countries to fight for the Dutch government. Besides Essex, the contingent included Sir Walter

[17] R. F. Williams, *The Court and times of Charles the First*, 2 vols. (London, 1848), 1: 24.

[18] *A. P. C. 1625–1626*, pp. 75, 76, 326.

[19] *H. M. C. Thirteenth Report*, Appendix 4, pp. 446 ff.; and British Museum, Additional MSS, 46,188.

[20] H. M. MSS, William Salt Library, Stafford. A letter dated 10 July 1626 from the Privy Council required Essex to hold a general muster in Staffordshire; see Bagot MSS G.b. 14, fol. 18, Folger Shakespeare Library.

Devereux, Sir Charles Rich, and William Paulet.[21] Essex's cousin
Sir Charles, a brother of the Earl of Warwick, had fought and
hunted with Essex many times before. Paulet, who had served
under Essex at Cádiz, was a younger son of the Marquess of Winchester. Landing at the port Helvoetsluys on 21 July 1626, the
English soldiers proceeded to Cleves, where they joined the war-
weary army of Frederick Henry, Prince of Orange.[22] Now head
of the House of Orange, he had assumed the leadership of the Dutch
operations upon the death of his brother, Prince Maurice. He communicated with Essex on several occasions. Near a convent at
Mary-Bom the English troops entrenched themselves and awaited
the worst. Here they fought a losing war against the army of
Spinola, the hero of Breda, who controlled the Rhine River Valley.

The cause for which Essex had fought ebbed low in 1626.[23] All
the regiments had empty ranks. Some units lacked leaders. Most of
the men had gone three months without pay. Malnutrition and the
plague made matters worse. Such an army was not prepared to
take to the field and assume the offensive against Spinola.[24]

While the combined Dutch and English armies staged defensive
operations in Cleves, their allies unsuccessfully attempted aggressive
warfare in Germany proper. General Ernst von Mansfeld, foolishly
hoping to knock Albrecht von Wallenstein out of the war, suffered
a resounding defeat at the Bridge of Dessau in May; by the end of
the year, after a retreat into Silesia, he was dead. In June, youthful
Christian of Brunswick, with an army he recruited from peasants
and armed with sticks, launched an attack upon Tilly's outposts in
hopes of liberating the Protestants of Hesse. The twenty-eight-year-
old leader died soon after discovering that the Hessians did not wish
to be liberated. Two months later Christian IV of Denmark after a
series of successes in Saxony, decided to confront Tilly in a pitched
battle. The result was calamitous. Though courageous, the Danish
monarch went down to defeat in a bloody battle fought outside the
town of Lutter. After losing all his cannon and most of his men,
Christian luckily escaped with his life after having his horse shot
from under him. By summer's end the cause of Protestantism was
severely shattered.

21 See P. R. O., S. P. 16/32: 32 for a complete list of the troops.
22 Wilson, *Autobiography*, p. 468.
23 Gardiner, *History*, 6: 133–51; and Wedgwood, *Thirty Years War*, pp. 189–99.
24 Wilson, *Autobiography*, p. 468.

In the autumn Charles, realizing the gravity of the situation, renewed his efforts to give further aid to Denmark. He attended the meetings of the Privy Council more regularly and vowed to stake his life and Crown for Christian's cause. Promising more financial assistance, the English sovereign sold some of the royal plate and talked of sending 10,000 English and Scottish soldiers to Christian. To fulfill these commitments, Charles demanded more from his subjects than some were willing to give. Among other things, he ordered Archbishop Abbot to use his office to gain support for the Danish sovereign.[25] To make good his promises, the English sovereign decided to terminate his military contract with the Dutch and ship the seasoned volunteers to fight under Christian IV.

Consequently, on 5 November, one day after the expiration of the contract, Charles sent Essex and his fellow commanders new instructions. "Having intention to send our dear uncle, the King of Denmark, the regiments under your command," Charles wrote, "we require you not only to prepare yourselves for this employment, but also to give the present order to the captains of the several companies and their officers in each regiment to be in like readiness. having made their companies as complete as possible they are to hold themselves in readiness to embark, as at this season any delay may present and stop your passage."[26]

The command of the expeditionary force remained uncertain. Buckingham recommended one of his dependents Lord Willoughby for the position. Charles, however, favored Alexander Lindsey, brother of the Earl of Morton. Some Privy Councilors favored Essex; others supported Col. Charles Morgan, a seasoned and extremely able commander. After extensive discussion the monarch finally acceded to Buckingham and offered the command to Willoughby, who, because of pressing family matters, was compelled to decline. It seemed that Essex would be the obvious alternative.[27] Nevertheless, Charles offered the command to his nominee, Lindsey, who likewise rejected the honor. Certainly this refusal meant that Essex would receive the next nomination. But not so! Charles again passed up the popular Earl and named instead Colonel Morgan, who readily accepted the post.

[25] David Wilkins, *Concilia Magnae Britanniae et Hiberniae*, 4 vols. (London, 1731), 4: 473.

[26] *C. S. P. Dom.*, *1625–1649*, p. 168.

[27] *C. S. P. Ven.*, *1626–1628*, pp. 22, 43.

Essex was deeply offended by these decisions. He outranked all the nominees, especially commoner Morgan. The aristocrat had noteworthy military experience and was the senior colonel. Instead of remaining with his troops and serving under Morgan, the Earl of Essex promptly returned to England and proceeded to register his complaints. As the Venetian ambassador noted: "The Earl of Essex since his return from the Netherlands, had resigned the regiment he commanded in that service, being offended, *and not without reason,* at Colonel Morgan being preferred to him for the command in Denmark." [28]

III

THE ENGLAND to which Essex returned in November was more sharply divided than ever. After dissolving Parliament without securing the subsidies necessary to conduct the war, Charles attempted to raise a war purse through his own means. He trimmed the cost of the Queen's Court, crossed off several names from the pension roll, appealed to the nobles and bishops for a loan, put up for sale several royal estates, called for a special fast-day collection, and vainly appealed to the London authorities for a large loan. When these measures failed, he sold some plate and many of the crown jewels and used others for security on private loans. In July the King appealed to all his subjects for a "free gift." Parliament had in fact voted several subsidies, Charles rationalized, but they had not passed through the final stages because several incendiaries had worked against the common good. To collect the funds which he felt Parliament intended to levy, Charles applied pressure upon the judges and the justices of the peace. Rich and poor were expected to contribute the amount listed in the benevolence book. Many paid under duress, but others hung back. One group in Westminster rioted in protest against the irregular proceedings and shouted in unison: "A Parliament! A Parliament! or else no subsidies." [29]

Some coastal towns had additional obligations to meet. Each port designated by the Privy Council was required to outfit and victual two ships—or provide the equivalent ship money—for the navy. The officials of Truro in Cornwall offered to contribute one-twelfth of the amount to meet the expense, but they would not

[28] *Ibid.,* p. 62.
[29] Williams, *Court and times,* 1: 131.

provide the stated sum. The town fathers at King's Lynn, Wells, and Burnham flatly refused to assume such a heavy burden at a time when trade was poor.[30] Similar opposition came from Crediton, Chester, Dartmouth, Carlisle, and most of the other solicited towns. Hundreds of Englishmen, especially those in the southern counties, vocally protested and defied the royal request for benevolences and ships.

Charles also resorted to another extraparliamentary financial device, known as the forced loan. Although more successful with this expedient than any other, he soon encountered hostility from many quarters. Several London parishes, including the prosperous ones in the West End, denied the loan on grounds of poverty. In October, Saint Clement Danes, where Essex lived, was the scene of a riot to protest the measure.[31] The high and wealthy also vigorously opposed this new financial policy, for since the loans were graduated on a crude ability-to-pay schedule, the nobles and bishops were tapped for the greatest amounts. Most earls, including Essex, were expected to loan upwards of five hundred pounds. Naturally there were protests from the titled nobles, especially from those peers who placed their political faith in parliamentary rather than prerogative government.

Essex spearheaded this protest movement among the peers.[32] From August to November there is no record of aristocratic opposition, but in November, soon after his return from Cleves, Essex's name appeared at the head of a list of fifteen "refractory lords." Among these aristocratic "refusers," as they were called, were the Earls of Warwick, Lincoln, Bolingbroke, and Clare and Lord Saye, all avowed critics of royal policies. This resistance movement which Essex initiated was viewed with alarm by the King and his advisers. Any form of resistance constituted a clear and present danger, but such a movement headed by aristocrats, especially by some with military experience, was a serious threat to the nation's security. The Privy Council, obviously disturbed, was divided over how to handle the matter. The Earl of Dorset proposed that the refusing lords be promptly committed to prison. The majority of the councilors, however, felt that such an act might do more harm than good, chiefly because some of the judges entertained doubts about

[30] *H. M. C. Twelfth Report,* 1: 275–80; and P. R. O., S. P. 16/37, fols. 41, 50.
[31] Rushworth, *Historical Collections,* 1: 422.
[32] See *C. S. P. Dom., 1625–1626,* p. 485.

the legality of the forced loans. Although the refusing lords retained their freedom, their names were recorded in the Black Book, which was kept for such purposes.

IV

Soon after these events the Earl of Essex retreated to Chartley Manor. Here he remained in semiseclusion for more than a year. Here he could forget the horrors of the Thirty Years War and enjoy the pleasures of the rural countryside. He was kept informed about important affairs by his faithful subordinate and cousin Sir Charles Rich, who wrote of Mansfeld's death, the activities in Court, the movements of the English troops, the Scottish plans for a large army and flotilla, and his own continuous loyalty and devotion.[33] Several attempts were made to pry Essex from Chartley, but he refused to leave.[34] Early in 1627 he turned down Buckingham's offer to lead a regiment in the forthcoming expedition to the Isle of Rhé. Later he refused the Earl of Warwick's offer to man a privateer against the Portuguese, rejected another bid to fight under Colonel Morgan in northern Germany, and denied the Prince of Orange's plea for assistance. As long as Buckingham remained the King's master strategist, Essex dissociated himself from all military enterprises.

Essex remained sympathetic with the Protestant cause on the Continent, nevertheless, and continued to assist that cause in his own deliberate manner. He corresponded with several leaders and sympathized with the plight of the unpaid soldiers. Many of the volunteers who had fought at Cádiz a year earlier still had not been paid. Some soldiers begged or stole; others were forced to borrow money at excessive rates of interest. To alleviate their deplorable situation, some Cádiz captains took justice into their own hands and sent a strongly worded petition to the King, for which they received a sharp rebuke. In February, Essex's own troops, still stationed in the Low Countries, resorted to mutiny to secure their long-overdue wages.

When Essex heard about the rebellion, he lent his name to a petition which requested relief. There was need for immediate action lest the disgruntled men desert or, worse yet, sell their services to Spinola. Essex and his fellow petitioners demanded that

[33] British Museum, Additional MSS, 46,188.
[34] *Ibid.*

the troops be paid before being transported to Germany. This support undoubtedly enhanced Essex's popularity among the common fighting men. Charles paid dearly for not meeting the demands of the petitioners, for within a month Essex's fears became statistical facts. A contemporary reported that he saw "a letter from Holland, which saith that the Earl of Essex's company, consisting of 163 when they were come to shipside, and their colours lodged, all save 40 refused to go. The country soldiers here kept great disorder, and were very insolent."[35] Instead of 6,000 soldiers Sir Charles Morgan could only muster 2,472 disillusioned and unpaid men; well over 2,000 had deserted. To send such an army to Christian IV would amount to an insult.

To replenish the English regiments, Essex was ordered by the Privy Council, in a letter dated at Whitehall on 2 March and signed by Richard Weston, to equip, arm, and train a contingent of 100 troops, provide each soldier with four shillings for conduct money, and then send them to the rendezvous point along the east coast.[36] Shortly thereafter, in March, he held a muster in Lichfield green, selected the required number of able-bodied men, and commenced to train them in the art of war. On 30 March he shipped the inexperienced troops to Hull under the charge of a trusted aide Thomas Littleton. Because of slow posts and some undisclosed difficulties the Staffordshire recruits arrived late at their rendezvous and thus slowed down the operation. The Privy Council, distrusting Essex and construing the delay as defiance, sent him a pointed reprimand. Essex, who had by then sent the recruits, admitted delay but insisted that it was unintentional and merely due to the slowness of communications. To substantiate his claims and demonstrate his loyalty to His Majesty's government, the Lord of Chartley ordered a general muster of all able-bodied Staffordians.[37] As usual, it was held at Lichfield. The deputy lieutenants managed the details and Essex assumed responsibility for the facts submitted to the Privy Council. The county of Stafford, Essex reported, could boast 6,000 able-bodied men between sixteen and sixty. The trained forces were all physically fit; their arms were up to date and in working order. The captains were all "well affected" in religion. The entire

[35] Williams, *Court and times*, 1: 218.

[36] See British Museum, Additional MSS, 46,188; and P. R. O., S. P. 16/61: 57, 68.

[37] See *C. S. P. Dom., 1627–1628*, pp. 234–46.

county was, moreover, in a very good posture of defense, for it had adequate supplies of ammunition and all its beacons were operative. Stafford, Essex concluded in his appraisal, was not deficient; and Lord Lieutenant Essex, by implication, was fulfilling his responsibilities.

Meanwhile, the resistance movement which Essex had started became a nationwide protest.[38] In some counties the royal proclamations concerning the forced loans were not even read. Many men of substance refused to lend their money to the King under such conditions. The refusers were almost without exception taken into custody and committed to prison for resisting the royal command— even committed without hearing a stated charge—a clear violation of the rights of Englishmen. In February 1627 the Earl of Lincoln publicly agitated against the loan, whereupon he was seized and brought before the Star Chamber Court.[39] There, when questioned about his political activities, the recalcitrant Earl took refuge in his social position and its concomitant privileges. When asked by the Star Chamber judges to take the customary oath, he peremptorily refused on the grounds that nobles enjoyed immunity from oaths. Failing to extract an oath or a confession from Lincoln, the Star Chamber sent him to the Tower—again without stating a specific charge. The Earls of Bolingbroke, Kent, and Huntingdon were ousted from lord lieutenancies. Warwick was forced to surrender some of the arms stored in his London armory. The Earl of Northumberland received the same treatment.

Essex also paid a price for his opposition. In March he was instructed to attend the Privy Council for refusing to contribute to the forced loan, but he appears to have ignored the summons. In June he was removed from his two lord lieutenancies. The Earl of Monmouth, who replaced him in Staffordshire, sent him an apologetic letter, explaining his acceptance of the office which Essex had held continuously for nearly fifteen years.[40] Only after Monmouth had been pressured by the King, he claimed, had he reluctantly accepted the position, and he requested Essex's forgiveness. The latter's response was most congenial: "Seeing it hath pleased his Majesty so farr to declare his displeasure towards me as to remove

38 See M. C. Wren, "London and the Twenty Ships, 1627," *American Historical Review* 55 (1950): 321–35; and P. R. O., S. P. 16/61: 1, 6, 7.

39 Gardiner, *History*, 6: 156.

40 British Museum, Additional MSS, 46,188.

me from those commands I held in this County, I am glad that
you are designed to bee my successor in that lieutenancy, the place
I chiefly valued as a mark of his Maj. favor . . . it is my hope that
his Maty wilbe pleased in his owne tyme, and according to the
measure of his owne Royal hart, to remove this cloud which now
hangs over mee; and to receyve mee againe into his grace and favor,
which is the onely glorie I doe and ever shall value in this world." [41]
Whether this profession of constancy and loyalty would bring him
back into the good graces of the King remained to be seen. Meanwhile, he adamantly refused to contribute to the royal coffers.

V

By JANUARY 1628, Charles I found himself in a precarious political
position. He had suffered several diplomatic reverses and military
setbacks and was deep in debt and saddled with several international
commitments. Yet he stubbornly refused to change his foreign
policy or to oust his favorites. He continued to raise funds without
the consent of Parliament and to commit to prison those who
refused to contribute to their forced-loan quotas. He had by this
persistence alienated many of his subjects and united the opposition.
Having unsuccessfully tried to live without Parliament, he now
had no alternative but to call one, although he deeply feared the
consequences. Charles knew that he would have trouble obtaining
funds from the Lower House. He realized that the opposition in
both Houses would demand relief from accumulated grievances,
especially the forced loans, and he was apprehensive about another
attack upon Buckingham.

On 30 January the parliamentary writs were issued, and elections
soon got under way. [42] Letters calling for the nomination and
election of royally favored individuals were sent to several high
constables and lord lieutenants, but several "refusers" put themselves forward for election nevertheless. Throughout England the
contests were fought with unusual zeal and bitterness. In Cornwall
a "refuser" named William Coryton decided not to run after being
threatened. Soldiers had to be called to ensure order in some
elections. Not only did Charles fail to secure a safe majority but he

[41] *Ibid.*
[42] Williams, *Court and times*, 1: 321–30.

was obliged to face more than twenty-five "refusers" in the House of Commons.

Charles felt more secure with the Upper House.[43] He hoped through pressure and fear to keep away the Earls of Arundel, Bristol, and Lincoln, the Bishop of Lincoln, and Archbishop Abbot, all of whom were out of royal favor. By creating several new peers and elevating a few more to higher ranks before the beginning of Parliament, he managed to increase the size of his faithful faction, and by exerting pressure on the ecclesiastical hierarchy he secured an even greater backing. In addition, to protect Buckingham from being impeached, Charles reached a gentleman's agreement with his more moderate critics, who had enough influence in the Lower House to restrain would-be impeachers. The precise terms of this political understanding have not survived, but the existence of a truce concerning Buckingham was noted by several contemporaries. In all likelihood the moderate opposition agreed to let the royal favorite alone in exchange for the presence of the aforementioned peers whom Charles tried to exclude.

Essex again allied himself with the opposition faction, headed by Lord Saye.[44] The daily roll calls indicate that Essex was present at each deliberation. Since he held the proxy of his hunting crony Lord Cromwell, this assured at least two dependable votes for the opposition. Several incidents reveal his partisanship. He helped usher in the controversial Earl of Bristol, who had been excluded by the King, and he secured seats on most important committees. Rank and seniority confirmed his place on the powerful Committee for Petitions and the Committee for Privileges.[45] He appears to have been chairman of a committee empowered to give economic assistance to the wives and widows of those sailors recently captured by the Barbary pirates. Essex also served on committees dealing with military preparedness, the discovery of recusants, the licensing of alehouses, and sumptuary legislation. Thanks to the leadership of the Upper House several of these bills were enacted.

Essex and his fellow peers continued to assert their freedom from ar-

---

[43] See Relf, *Debates*, pp. 63–229 for the 1628 debates.

[44] *Lords Journal*, 3: 687–725.

[45] From external evidence we learn that Essex accepted and supported the private petitions of Richard Palmer and one Vaughan, both of which were in the nature of appeals, but there is no indication of how they fared in the Upper House; see *H. M. C. Fourth Report*, pp. 17, 19. It is also possible that Essex advanced the case of Sir Francis Coningsby, a subordinate officer; see *Lords Journal*, 3: 833.

rest. On 31 May, he successfully claimed the privilege for his chaplain, Dr. William Sherbourne, who had been arrested for riotous activity at Saint John's College, Oxford, during the session of Parliament.[46] Essex was also instrumental in extending this political privilege.[47] On May Day the Lords heard the case of Sir Andrew Gray, who had arrested one of the Earl of Warwick's privateering captains and impounded the cargo one day before the first meeting of Parliament. Warwick, of course, claimed breach of privilege and demanded the release of his ship and its cargo. After some discussion the Upper House concurred and issued a permanent order: the goods of privileged persons enjoyed the same immunity from arrest as the person himself. The question of whether to commit Sir Andrew to prison on a retroactive order then arose. Warwick himself said no. Westmorland said yes. Essex put forth a mediative proposal which prevailed, so Sir Andrew was merely reprehended verbally and warned against future infractions.

Essex also supported a move to reform the office of lord lieutenant.[48] Appointment to this local office, which the Crown depended upon for law, order, defense, elections, and some tax collections, was made by the King and his Privy Council. Most appointments were automatically renewed each year so that in some counties the office was regarded as a lifetime assignment or an ancestral inheritance. Although the office seldom provided monetary gain, it did offer the holder local power and prestige. It was, furthermore, one of the last refuges of the military-minded nobles. In ousting the refractory lords from this local office, Charles invited hostility from the victims. On 19 May the Earl of Huntingdon, who had been removed, demanded the restoration of the lord lieutenancies to their respective holders. Essex promptly arose and supported his colleague. Some of the individuals who made this complaint soon began to devise a bill which would make the lord lieutenants answerable to Parliament. Though never given a full hearing in open Parliament, the debates were advantageous, for within a year Essex was reappointed lord lieutenant of Staffordshire.

While the aristocrats in the Upper House asserted the rights of their class, the Lower House attended to the rights of all Englishmen. Abandoning their personal attack upon Buckingham, members of the Commons turned to such royal abuses as forced loans,

46 Relf, *Debates*, p. 211.
47 *Ibid.*, p. 140.
48 *Ibid.*, pp. 179, 219.

martial law in peacetime, the mandatory billeting of soldiers, extraparliamentary taxation, and imprisonment without trial or bail. The majority in the Commons agreed to keep the purse strings tied until Charles guaranteed relief from these abuses, but their leaders were divided over some of the details and the means to achieve their ends.

The Lords held a pivotal position during these debates on the liberty of English subjects.[49] They could refuse to confer with the Commons, turn down the bill, amend clauses, or postpone action. The King, of course, hoped to wield enough influence in the Upper House to prevent the royal prerogative from being trimmed, while the Commons hoped to convert the Lords to their position on the rights of Englishmen. With Buckingham's faction, the Privy Councilors, the clergy, and the eight new peerages created during the months of April and May, Charles hoped to counteract the opposition peers, who tended to side with the Commons. Since these two extremes could check and cancel each other, a centrist group led by Arundel and Bristol actually held the precarious balance of political power.

Try as he might, Charles could not control his Lords. On 7 April, ignoring his pleas for supplies, the Upper House conferred with the Lower about liberty of the subject. Two days later the peers themselves launched a debate on the proposals which eventually became the Petition of Right. The central issue concerned the discretionary power of the Crown to commit a person to prison. Charles and his advisers laid claim to broad discretionary powers to ensure internal security. The Commons demanded absolute guarantees against any arbitrary imprisonment. The Lords—divided among themselves —listened to both sides of the controversial issue, scoured parliamentary records, cited precedents, read statutes, and dissected the Magna Carta. While the Crown relied upon the Lord Keeper and the attorney general to carry the burden of the case, the commoners secured the services of Coke, Selden, and Littleton to present their arguments.

Essex sided with Lord Saye but he said little. He did, however,

49 Frances Helen Relf, "The Petition of Right," *University of Minnesota Studies in the Social Sciences*, study 8 (Minneapolis, 1917). While Miss Relf does not ignore the role of the Upper House in these debates, she concentrates on the House of Commons. I have relied heavily upon her monograph and edition of the *Debates* and upon the *Lords Journal* as primary sources.

engage in some significant parliamentary maneuvers. On 12 April, while the Upper House was engaged in a debate concerning *habeas corpus*, Essex shrewdly moved for a committee of the whole to discuss the matter.[50] Thus, the peers, instead of being limited to one speech per debate, could speak more frequently and more freely—a device which generally worked to the advantage of the opposition lords. Lord Saye then seconded the motion, the House passed it, and the debate continued. At a late hour, amidst a thin House, the Lords decided to call upon the judges for their opinions. In the course of delivering their opinions the justices were asked whether the Magna Carta was still in force. "The Great Charter of England," they declared, "and the six subsequent Statutes mentioned by commons do still stand in force." [51] This declaration merely augmented the peers' arguments. They continued to wonder why, if the Magna Carta was in force, it was not adhered to and how, in the light of the Great Charter and the six statutes, the King could commit a man without cause.

While the debate went back and forth, the ranks of the aristocratic opposition increased to over fifty. According to Rev. Joseph Mead: "The greater part of the Lords stand for the king's prerogative against the subjects' liberties; that my lord president made a speech in the upper house on the king's behalf, endeavouring to show the inconveniences which might follow in having our kings so tied. Against whom the earl of Arundel stood up, confuted him, and made a public protestation against him and the rest who were of the same opinion, concluding that those liberties which now they would betray, were those which had cost so much of their predecessors' blood to maintain them; and for his own part, he was resolved to lose his life, and spend his own blood, rather than he would ever give consent to the betraying of them. Of his part were fifty lords and earls; Shrewsbury, Essex, Sussex, Warwick, Lincoln, Devonshire, Bristol, Saye, Clare, Bolingbroke, Mulgrave, and the more ancient nobility." [52]

In an effort to terminate the bitter debate, Charles entered the House of Lords on 28 April and agreed to govern by the laws of the land, including the Magna Carta, and to maintain the liberties and estates of his subjects. This conciliatory move, however sensible,

---

50 Relf, *Debates*, p. 88.
51 *Lords Journal*, 3: 739.
52 Williams, *Court and times*, 1: 346.

did not pacify the commoners, who demanded a categorical confirmation of their recently violated rights. Verbal promises were not sufficient; they could be broken too easily. A written document like the Magna Carta was mandatory and should be in the form of a petition—a petition of right—to be signed by the King. The Lords could join if they wished.

On 9 May the Petition of Right was received in the Upper House, read twice, and sent to a special committee which, to the King's chagrin, accepted the general propositions in the document. About the same time, a large group of Scottish nobles and gentry informed Charles that they stood behind the Commons and called for immediate approval of the petition. This the King was not prepared to do, so sincerely believing that the royal prerogative would be trimmed too closely by the document as it stood, he outlined his position in a letter addressed to the Lords. He reaffirmed his absolute right to commit a person without cause but at the same time promised to use the power only in extraordinary circumstances.

The majority of Essex's fellow peers, including the middle group, regarded this as a genuine conciliatory move and sought to modify the petition so that Charles could sign it in good faith. Buckingham moved that the House promptly consider the matter. The opposition, realizing that they were outnumbered, reverted to stalling tactics. Westmorland insisted upon following the proposed agenda, while Essex moved that the House "do no other business that night." [53] Both diversionary measures passed, whereupon Essex and his partisan allies left the Parliament House, assuming that no business would follow.

That assumption proved wrong, however, for Buckingham and his followers held a rump session in which they voted a letter of thanks to Charles for his conciliatory move. The next day, upon hearing of Buckingham's maneuver, Essex was so furious that he protested the rump session and demanded an explanation. [54] He was seconded by Lords Saye and Grey. These efforts of the opposition proved futile, for the House of Lords decided that the late session, despite Essex's terminal motion, represented acceptable parliamentary procedure. The opposition had been outwitted by the Duke.

Two weeks passed before the Upper Chamber voted on the petition. During that time there were interminable speeches in each

[53] Relf, *Debates*, p. 119.
[54] *Ibid.*, pp. 53, 155.

House and many conferences between them. The Lords, acting as mediators, attempted to reach an accŏmmodation between King and Commons. The latter, led by Coke, reluctantly changed some words and phrases which did not alter the substance, and the majority in the Lords granted several concessions which they deemed consistent with the royal prerogative. In the end, Buckingham's faction conceded far more than they originally intended, so the petition emerged as a true victory for the libertarians.

During these deliberations Essex himself assumed a mediative role between Buckingham and Saye, who on 24 May had exchanged some harsh words after a clash over the petition.[55] This Essex deplored publicly in a speech delivered two days later. If any sharp differences arise in the course of heated debate, he declared, let the differences be settled inside Parliament. Such was a gentleman's way; such was the parliamentary way. Though he detested Buckingham personally, Essex brought about an agreement between the Duke and Lord Saye—an agreement which proved instrumental in the final passage of the Petition of Right.

In a joint session held on 27 May, Sir Edward Coke congratulated the Lords for their "noble and most happy concurrence."[56] He lauded them for their deeds as well as their words. He reminded them of their aristocratic ancestors who had struck the first blow for liberty by extracting the Great Charter from King John at Runnymede and claimed that the Petition of Right was true exposition of the earlier document. In each case the aristocracy was to be praised for its leadership in the cause of liberty. Shortly after this eulogy the Lords read the revised Petition of right three times so that it could be recorded in the Statute Book. Each time it passed unanimously.

Five days later, Charles met with both Houses to deliver his answer to the joint petition. He and the Lord Keeper both emphasized the necessity of preserving the royal prerogative and the people's liberties. The Petition of Right was then read in its entirety. It expressly forbade the Crown to (1) billet soldiers in private houses without consent, (2) imprison anyone without a specific charge, (3) levy a tax, gift, forced loan, or benevolence, and (4) declare martial law in peacetime. Though the document clearly circum-

---

55 *Ibid.*, p. 205.
56 *Lords Journal*, 3: 826.

scribed his power, Charles I answered, "The King willeth that Right be done according to the Laws and Customs of the Realm." [57] This answer, however, did not satisfy the petitioners. Instead of responding with the customary *"Soit Droit fait comme il est desire,"* Charles had merely expressed a willingness to abide by the law of the land. The petitioners construed this as a deliberate evasion or an ambiguous answer.

The members of the Lower House withheld the promised subsidies until they secured the appropriate reply to their petition.[58] Eliot began to discuss the general state of the kingdom and the recent defeats. A resumption of the Duke's impeachment was in the offing. Charles was so enraged when he heard of these occurrences that on 5 June he asked the Lords to adjourn for the day, stopped debate in the Lower House, and almost dissolved Parliament. At this point the Commons defended their right of free speech and their power of impeachment, while the Lords, sensing the serious consequences arising from a dissolution, intervened and asked the King to refrain from any termination—a request which was subsequently granted. The following day the peers, led by the opposition, began to discuss England's declining position in world affairs. The Earl of Bristol, ever critical of Charles's foreign policy, called for a subcommittee to deal with the state of the kingdom.

Within this context Essex delivered one of his few recorded speeches. He acknowledged that Charles's approval of the petition was a move in the right direction, but he also asserted the need for a complete reappraisal of England's position in world affairs. Such a reappraisal was fitting and proper. Parliament, he concurred with Eliot and Bristol, was better suited than the Privy Council for such a task. The precedent for such action was the Great Council, the *Magnum Concilium* of medieval times. "Wee are the great Counsell of the Kingdom," Essex contended, "and I think his Majesty cannot but take it well if wee humbly present the state of the Kingdome unto his Majesty a discharge of our Consciences and dutyes." [59] Bristol, of course, concurred with Essex's argument, as did Huntingdon. The Earl of Carlisle, a loyal supporter of the King, disagreed and refused to support the proposal, claiming that the King knew more about the state of the kingdom than any men

[57] *Ibid.*, p. 843.
[58] See Gardiner, *History*, 6: 289–309.
[59] Relf, *Debates*, p. 218.

in Parliament. When reduced to a vote, this thinly disguised criticism of Buckingham and his policies was defeated.

To extricate themselves from the deadlock between King and Parliament, the Lords then assumed the initiative and asked the Commons to confer with them about securing a more satisfactory answer to the Petition of Right. At the ensuing meeting both Houses agreed to appeal to the King; he consented to give a satisfactory reply that very afternoon. Thus, on 7 June, Charles went to the Upper House to reassure Parliament that his earlier approval of the Petition of Right was genuine. After denying any intentional ambiguity, Charles replied, *"Soit Droit fait comme il est desire."* The Commons applauded Charles and soon granted him the five subsidies. That evening Londoners celebrated the occasion with bonfires and ale.

VI

Essex also assumed a central role in the impeachment of Dr. Roger Manwaring.[60] A year earlier this divine had preached two controversial sermons in which he defended the King's right to raise taxes without parliamentary consent, castigated the "refusers" for denying the King's collection agents, and enunciated the doctrine of absolute obedience. Once published, Dr. Manwaring's elevated notions concerning monarchial government and his corresponding depreciation of Parliament soon came to the attention of several members of Parliament, not the least of whom was John Pym.

On 4 June, Pym presented to a joint conference of both Houses a declaration composed of five charges against Manwaring, which he explained in a long, flowery speech. Manwaring's actions represented a serious threat to parliamentary prestige, Pym reasoned, and his political ideas sounded more suited to an absolute than a parliamentary monarchy. Manwaring had committed a crime against all lovers of liberty; churchman or not, he must now pay the price for his publicly stated views. Because he was a member of His Majesty's ecclesiastical administration Manwaring would be tried in the High Court of Parliament. Pym invited both Houses to join in the impeachment.

On 9 June, Lord Keeper Thomas Coventry reported to the Upper House on the impeachment conference and asked for the

[60] *Ibid.*, p. 219.

Lords' wishes. Essex, one of the "refusers" attacked by Manwaring, promptly moved that the divine be sent for and confronted with the charges.[61] Two days later the churchman appeared before the bar of the House of Lords and categorically denied Pym's charges, whereupon two examinations from witnesses were read by the clerk. Again the divine refused to admit his guilt, an act which could only mean a lengthy trial to ascertain the truth of the matter. Manwaring insisted that he be granted time to prepare his case, a copy of the charges, recourse to his library, and the right to counsel. These requests, Essex agreed, were essential to justice and were granted.

The following day Essex and the Bishop of Lincoln examined Richard Badger, the printer of Manwaring's sermons, to determine why the King commanded the printing and why the Bishop of London approved. Upon interrogating Badger the two men discovered that William Laud, Charles's clerical favorite, had sent letters authorizing the printing of Manwaring's sermons. Essex and Lincoln then visited the Bishop of London, who confirmed the printer's interpretation. These facts, when presented to the whole House, were likewise confirmed by Buckingham, Dorset, Montgomery, and the bishops involved in the controversy. Although several powerful officials had approved of Dr. Manwaring's words a year earlier, no one now dared defend him.

Dr. Manwaring presented himself before the Upper House on 13 June.[62] He humbly begged for mercy and offered to submit himself to the Lords, who found him guilty and ordered him to be imprisoned in the Fleet, fined one thousand pounds, suspended from the ministry for three years, denied any future ecclesiastical dignity, and forbidden to ever again preach at Court. The harshness of the sentence undoubtedly resulted from the fact that many of Manwaring's judges had been the object of his sermonizing.

Toward the end of the session the Lords passed the subsidy bill. When Commons revived its impeachment case against Buckingham and began to talk of a remonstrance designed to curtail tonnage and poundage, Charles I suddenly called a halt to the proceedings on 26 June. Without even taking time to put on his formal robes, he entered the House of Lords, delivered a short admonitory speech, gave his assent to the various bills, and then prorogued Parliament.

61 *Ibid.*
62 Gardiner, *History*, 6: 312–15.

Soon after the prorogation Charles made several attempts to recapture the trust and support of England's leading families. In a conciliatory move the King invited all the opposition peers to the Presence Chamber at Whitehall.[63] There in symbolic gesture he asked his political enemies to forget the past. This Essex and several of his partisan allies, including Saye, Lincoln, and Warwick, willingly did. Charles also revamped his ministry and made several significant ecclesiastical appointments. The Earl of Manchester was named Lord Privy Seal; Lord Weston superseded the Earl of Marlborough as Lord Treasurer, while Marlborough became Lord President of the Privy Council; the Earl of Dorset was made the Queen's Lord Chamberlain; and Lord George Goring became Master of the Queen's Horse. Four lords, including the Earls of Lindsey and Darby, were added to the Privy Council, and William Laud, the Arminian adviser, was translated to the bishopric of London. To appease the opposition, Charles forced Buckingham to surrender his wardenship of the Cinque Ports. Among those considered for the surrendered post were Essex and his cousin the Earl of Warwick.[64] The office was, however, awarded to Essex's sworn enemy and onetime brother-in-law Henry Howard, now the Earl of Suffolk, who very likely paid a fancy price for it.

Essex, meanwhile, retired to his country estates in Staffordshire for the remainder of the year.[65] There he tended to his personal affairs, hunted the stag, and received reports of public events: the preparations for the relief of La Rochelle, the mutiny of unpaid sailors in Portsmouth, the assassination of the Duke of Buckingham by John Felton, the Duke's funeral and burial in Westminster Abbey, and Felton's trial and execution.

Although far removed from these happenings, Essex became implicated in Buckingham's death. In October, shortly before Felton was brought to trial, a man named Robert Savage accused the Earl and several of his fellow opposition peers of inspiring the plot and hiring Felton to carry out the details of the murder.[66] The accused peers, when confronted with Savage's words, demanded that the accuser be examined and the rumor smothered. Savage was summoned before the Star Chamber, where he quickly disclaimed

[63] Williams, *Court and times*, 1: 359.
[64] *C. S. P. Ven., 1628–1629*, p. 180.
[65] Wilson, *Autobiography*, p. 468.
[66] Williams, *Court and times*, 1: 430.

his accusation. The retraction did not save him from harsh treatment, however, for he was subsequently censured, pilloried, and whipped from the Fleet to Westminster Palace and back. The authorities also slit his nose, cut off one ear, and branded his cheek with the letters *F. A.*—the telltale stigma which signified to the world a false accuser.

Exactly how much Essex knew about these events is uncertain. He did hear of Buckingham's murder soon after the event, his secretary Arthur Wilson reports, and was so interested in learning all the facts that he immediately sent Wilson to Portsmouth to ferret out the details.

These events led Charles to postpone the calling of Parliament from October to January. During the interim he again reconstructed his administration, filled the offices vacated by Buckingham, and launched a new peace offensive toward France. He made the Marquess of Hamilton, a Scot, Master of the Horse—a post which Essex himself undoubtedly coveted. The sovereign named Viscount Dorchester secretary of state in place of Lord Conway, who was made Lord President of the Privy Council. He took the place of the Earl of Marlborough, now out of favor. In a more significant move, Charles secured a *rapprochement* with the Earl of Arundel by restoring his suite in Whitehall Palace and awarding him a lucrative position—the currant-importation monopoly. Similarly, Archbishop Abbot was invited to resume residence at Whitehall, asked to return to the Privy Council sessions, and allowed to kiss the King's hand. One rumor which proved to be false claimed that Charles would make Lord Saye and the Earl of Bedford Privy Councilors.

VII

THE PARLIAMENT which convened on 20 January 1629 proved to be a disappointment.[67] The session was exceptionally short, lasting less than seven weeks, and extremely stormy. Attendance was poor. Some days went by without any business being transacted. With these conditions, plus the season and the psychological letdown wrought by the Petition of Right, it is a wonder that Parliament

67 See Cobbett, *Parliamentary History*, 2: 442; and Wallace Notestein and Frances Helen Relf, *Commons Debates for 1629*, Research Publications for the University of Minnesota (Minneapolis, 1921).

passed the six measures that it did. The two Houses tended to pull in opposite directions, for there was no common political enemy like Buckingham to bring them together in a concurrent judicial process and there were fewer bills to be considered. Consequently, conferences between the Houses were scarce; close contacts between members of both Houses became a thing of the past; and common objectives and hopes were all but absent.

The House of Commons concerned itself mainly with the revenue problem and the religious situation. Specifically, the Commons hoped to make Parliament the exclusive grantor of tonnage and poundage revenues, thereby curtailing the Crown's control. When this matter bogged down over a complicated legal dispute involving the royal seizure of cargoes, the radical element in the Lower House launched an assault upon some Anglican clergy. Reaffirming their strong beliefs in the Elizabethan establishment, these Parliament members complained about the Catholic menace at home and abroad. There were too many papists in England, Sir Robert Philips contended, and too many English subjects taking orders in the Catholic nations. More alarming, according to another member of the Commons, was the spread of Catholic practices within the Anglican Church, an increase which was attributed to the sympathy of many churchmen and government officials in high places. The fact that Arminians like Laud and the late Montaigne enjoyed royal favor only made the evil more intolerable. This diversionary attack upon the ecclesiastical hierarchy brought the Puritan fringe to the fore. It put Sir Francis Rouse, a militant and outspoken Puritan, into the political limelight and brought an obscure member of Parliament from Huntingdon by the name of Oliver Cromwell to his feet for the first time. In his initial parliamentary utterance Cromwell denounced the existence of "popery" among the Anglican divines near his home.[68]

The Earl of Essex, who would one day feel the lash of Cromwell's tongue, was then fulfilling his duties in the House of Lords.[69] He attended all but one of the twenty-three meetings, resumed his places on the Committee for Petitions and the Committee for Privileges, served on a select committee empowered to deal with matters pertaining to national defense, and was a member of

[68] Wilbur Cortez Abbott, *The Writings and Speeches of Oliver Cromwell*, 4 vols. (Cambridge: Harvard University Press, 1937), 1: 61–62.
[69] *Lords Journal*, 4: 5–21.

Abbot's committee, which wrote a bill designed to improve the economic status of the lower clergy—one of the few bills which passed that session.

On 16 February, Essex and his fellow peers attempted to rehabilitate the historic earldom of Oxford, a title which dated back to the Norman Conquest. The honor, presently held by Aubrey de Vere, a minor, had in recent years dwindled to a mere fraction of its former size. Through no fault of his own the twentieth Earl of Oxford was, as Arundel put it, "denuded of any Estate to support this honour." [70] This was deemed a grave injustice, a travesty against the present holder and his class, a wrong which should be righted. Here was a peer "full of honour and worth," blessed with the best blood in England and the highest honors, but belittled by a small estate. The King, Arundel declared, should grant the Earl more land from the royal residue. This proposal, which had the support of the Defenders of Old English Honour, passed with no dissents, and a committee was selected to present the matter to Charles, who graciously took the matter under advisement. Both pieces of class legislation reflect the predominance of the Earl of Arundel in the Upper House. [71]

Arundel's leadership also prevailed throughout the debates on precedency. The King, according to a select committee established to investigate the grievances, was guilty of granting—more likely selling—Irish and Scottish titles to Englishmen. The recipients of these peerages generally remained in England and paid little attention to their new estates and less to their concomitant military obligations. The Lords' committee called these absentee landlords foreigners and considered intolerable the manner in which this "foreign nobility" claimed precedence privileges in England. It was one thing for the Stuart sovereigns to grant English titles to Scottish and Irish notables as a "courtesy," but it was another matter to treat an Irish or Scottish title on the same par as an English title.

After lengthy discussion, the Upper House petitioned the King for redress of their grievance. Although malcontents such as Essex and Spencer were appointed to help draw up the petition, moderates

70 *Ibid.*, p. 34.
71 See M. F. S. Hervey, *The Life, Correspondence and Collections of Thomas Howard, the Earl of Arundel* (Cambridge: At the University Press, 1921).

predominated. In very mild language the Lords complained to Charles about the excessive creations and the consequent abuse relating to precedence and asked him to return to the customs of his predecessors in granting peerages. "And as your majesty's honour is equally concerned in this with the interest of your kingdoms and subjects," they pleaded, "so toe doubt not that your majesty's gracious care is to reduce and maintain your nobility in their antient lustre; which shall equally tend to your majesty's service and happiness, and to our own contentment."[72] Few peers could object to either the tone or the terms of this document.

Three days later a small delegation, composed primarily of Privy Councilors, presented the paper to the King. Charles dodged an immediate and final answer, claiming that such a "weighty business" required more time. He also admitted that it was easier to prevent a grievance like this than to redress it after the precedent had been established. Before answering the document, Charles dissolved Parliament, leaving Essex and his fellow peers to be plagued with the problem of precedence.

What brought about the dissolution of Parliament was a radical remonstrance, offered by Sir John Eliot, in the House of Commons. Upon receiving word of the matter, which, if carried to its conclusion, would have stripped him of large amounts of revenue, Charles called upon the Commons to adjourn themselves. When the revolutionary leaders learned of their King's command, which they misunderstood to be a dissolution, they used bodily force to hold the speaker of the Commons in the chair. This defiant action provoked Charles into a fit of rage: he sent not only his Black Rod to formally dissolve Parliament but an armed guard to force the door if need be. Fortunately, just before the Black Rod arrived, the Commons had adjourned their meeting to 10 March. On that date the impatient and bitterly disillusioned monarch came to the House of Lords and personally prepared to dissolve both Houses in a joint session. Before putting his seal of approval to the bills passed, he delivered a diatribe against the "vipers" in the Lower House. Praising the peers for their temperate political behavior and excusing the innocent members in the Commons, he castigated those radical firebrands who put their own private grievances before the public good. "To conclude, my lords," he stated, "as those evil-affected persons

[72] *Lords Journal*, 4: 25–27.

must look for their rewards, so you that are here of the higher-house, may justly claim from me that protection and favor, that a good king oweth to his loyal and faithful nobility." [73]

Just as the Lords and the Commons parted ways during the session, so the King parted ways with parliamentary government during the years which followed. Filled with disgust at the obstructionist activities of the Commons, particularly its leaders, Charles resolved to live without Parliament, as his father-in-law Louis XIII had done since 1614, when he last called a national assembly. The English monarch was determined at least to wait—a long time, if necessary—for a more propitious time, even at the risk of making more enemies, rather than suffer the painful humiliation of another Petition of Right. Essex and his fellow peers waited for over ten long years before receiving another writ requesting them to attend the High Court of Parliament.

[73] *Ibid.*, p. 43.

CHAPTER 8

A Country Party Peer

I

IN THE EARLY MONTHS of 1629, shortly after the dissolution of Parliament, Essex turned his back upon London and resumed the mode of life which had been interrupted by the call to arms.[1] For a decade, except when special occasions demanded his presence in the City, he resided in the countryside. Still scornful of favorites, he found little in common with those nobles who fawned on the Queen. Ever hopeful of a parliamentary approach to national policy, he possessed little sympathy for advisers like Bishop Laud and Lord Chancellor Coventry who strongly upheld the royal prerogative.

At the time, Essex had just become thirty-eight and surely wondered about the future. He undoubtedly sensed personal as well as political failure. The facts that Frances had suffered with the Earl of Somerset in his many tribulations, bore him a beautiful daughter, and, though quite sickly, still lived with him in semiseclusion all tended to substantiate her contentions in the scandalous annulment proceedings and justify her drastic legal actions and remarriage. Also they weakened Essex's arguments and raised serious doubts about his claims. That Essex, who above all things needed an heir, did not court women or remarry seemed to confirm the suspicions of the doubters. Some individuals feared that his celibacy would mean the end of the House of Devereux and that the family estates possibly would revert to the monarch who excluded the owner from public place.

If Essex could do little to better his political career in Caroline England, he could do something about his personal fate: he could re-create his life in the countryside, accept personal failure, and attempt to resolve his conflicts and rebuild his life on a new foundation. In September 1629, Essex took the first step toward that reshaping. Since his former wife still lived and he might have

[1] Wilson, *Autobiography*, p. 468.

wondered about the morality of his remarrying, Essex turned to John Williams, Bishop of Lincoln, the Welsh-born cleric who had befriended the opposition leaders.[2] In hopes of securing the bishop's technical advice in the matter, Essex invited him to Chartley Manor.[3] After visiting Chartley the bishop, to whom Essex had granted several personal favors, agreed to investigate the matter thoroughly upon returning to his country estate near Lincoln. Finally in a letter dated 27 February 1630, Bishop Williams forwarded his conclusions in cautiously phrased terms. "Your lpp. may, in pointe of conscience," he advised Essex, "mary when you please, and where you please, provided that she be such a one, as the canons of the church doth allowe to cohabit."[4]

While waiting for the Bishop's decision Essex pursued a path that led to matrimony. He left Chartley in late autumn and traveled to Wiltshire, where he wintered with his favorite sister, Frances, and her husband, the Earl of Hertford, both of whom welcomed him as an integral part of their household. "These lines cannot tell you how much I long for a good conclusion of the parliament," Frances had written him many months before, "that I may have the hapiness to see you heare where theare is younge company that present theare service to you, and say much in the expectations of you heare."[5] The closely knit family relationship implicit in this invitation continued throughout the thirties. Frances's country houses were his to use. Her husband's chases and parks were Essex's to enjoy. Her friends became his friends.

Among those persons who enjoyed the Countess of Hertford's hospitality during the Yuletide festivities of 1629 was a young woman named Elizabeth Paulet, whose beauty drew comments from several contemporaries. To one she was "a young gentlewoman of a most sweet and bewitching countenance, and affiable and gentle conversation."[6] To another she was "pretty but poor."[7] Betty Paulet could take pride in her surname, to be sure, for the Paulets commanded respect throughout the South. She could claim John Paulet, the Marquess of Winchester as an uncle. This

2 *DNB*, 20: 414–20.
3 British Museum, Additional MSS, 46,189.
4 *Ibid.*
5 *Ibid.*
6 Devereux, *Lives of the Devereux*, 2: 300.
7 Sanderson, *A Compleat History*, p. 152.

connection enabled her to break into the aristocratic circles of her family, but everyone knew that her father, Sir William Paulet, was not merely a lowly knight, but an illegitimate offspring of the late Marquess of Winchester. Sir William resided at Edington, a small Wiltshire village about ten miles northwest of Tottenham, near Bratton Castle, and possessed very limited economic resources.[8]

Essex became enamored with Betty Paulet and she with him. These mutual sentiments did not escape the Countess of Hertford, who invited Betty to remain at Tottenham as a house guest during the entire Christmas season. By Twelfth Night, if not before, she had captured the heart of Robert Devereux, who promptly proposed marriage. He called upon lawyer John Selden to work out a marriage settlement. Frances, who thoroughly approved of the match, helped with the arrangements. The wedding, with clearance from the Bishop of London, took place during the Lenten season, on 11 March 1630, at Netley Castle, the Earl of Hertford's residence in Hampshire.[9]

The marriage precipitated a crisis in Essex's household which culminated in the dismissal of Arthur Wilson.[10] Having advised Essex against the match, he openly expressed his detestation of the new Countess. This attitude so aroused the hostility of the bride that she wanted her husband's confidant discharged. Believing that Wilson, who possessed a powerful influence over her husband, might well jeopardize their marriage, Betty harassed the secretary in every way she could. She deliberately audited Wilson's accounts in hopes of trapping him but found no irregularities. She tried to convince her husband that Wilson constituted an intolerable and expendable threat to their happiness. Finally, the jealous bride threatened to remain alone in her chamber until Wilson was dismissed.

Essex gradually surrendered to his wife's will. After employing Rowland Laugherne to handle his personal affairs, Essex dismissed Wilson from his household, thus terminating a long and intimate association. The two men parted on fairly amicable terms. The Earl awarded his former confidant an annual stipend sufficient for him to live on his own. Wilson moved to Trinity College, Oxford, where he studied theology and began writing plays and

[8] Codrington, *Life and Death*, p. 11.
[9] Roger Le Strange, *The Reign of King Charles* (London, 1656), p. 119.
[10] Wilson, *Autobiography*, pp. 468–71.

poetry. While at Trinity, Wilson also started working on his colorful *Autobiography* and the histories which bear his name. In 1635, Wilson finally married and then went into the service of the Earl of Warwick—a position which Essex helped him to secure.

Essex and his bride assumed a routine existence in the country. Only rarely did Essex go to London. Once a year, invariably during the summer months, he traveled to the Midlands to oversee his manors. Essex grew so fond of the southern climate, the terrain, and the company of Hertford's circle that he commenced to look for a desirable estate near Tottenham House. His sister Frances, in particular, was instrumental in persuading him to reside in the South; she did not hide her disapproval of Chartley Manor as a residence for a new bride. Essex himself agreed that, especially during the winter months, life could be miserable in the cold and damp rooms of the ancient manor house. When, after searching for several months, Essex still had not located a suitable country house in the vicinity of Amesbury, he received a generous offer from his brother-in-law. "I perceive you cannot fitt yourselfe with a house in these parts to your likinge," wrote Hertford. "I am gladd of it for I see noe reason you should put your selfe to soe unnecessary a charge, where you may soe free commande the house of a frende that so much desireth your company as myself." [11] Essex accepted this gracious invitation: thereafter he and his bride spent most of the year at Tottenham House. [12]

A different Essex emerged as a result of the remarriage. He was no longer the aloof, taciturn soldier but became more mellow and infinitely more sociable. Although he corresponded with his wartime cronies, several of whom were fighting on the Continent, he spent little time with them. Instead he enjoyed the good company of the Hertford circle. More important, the noble drew closer to his family—to the Countess of Leicester, to his mother and his step-father, and to his brothers and sisters, with whom he corresponded regularly—and devoted more time to family matters. He took a special interest in Frances's children, Frank and Robin (no doubt his namesake). He chased the stag with Hertford, bowled with his half brother, Ulrich Burke, Viscount Tunbridge, and spent many

[11] British Museum, Additional MSS, 46,189.

[12] "The Earl of Essex keeps house in the Earl of Hertford's House at Ames-bury," wrote John Nicholas to his son in November 1636, "and the Earl of Hertford is gone to Netley to Winter." See *C. S. P. Dom., 1636–1637*, p. 196.

an evening playing backgammon and cards with his family and
their friends. For the only time in his life Essex assumed the role of a
family-oriented aristocrat.

Essex also turned to literature for diversion. During his leisure
hours, according to Codrington, "he would employ that time in the
perusal of some labored poem, and having great judgment, especially in the English verse, it was his custom to applaud the professors
on that art, as high as their desert, and to reward them above it;
and he was in no way inclined to the sullen opinion of those men
who disclaim the muses, and esteem poems to be unlawful, as
unprofitable." [13] Codrington's statements can now be validated by
an inventory of Essex's library. [14] In addition to several copies of
the Bible and a harmony of the Gospels, Essex owned a goodly
number of quartos, pamphlets, sermons, and manuscripts covering
a variety of subjects. The titles reveal a rather lively interest in the
contemporary religious controversy, for he possessed the major
works of John Preston, Bishop Moreton, the Bishop of Armagh, and
Dr. John Lightfoot and the sermons of Gauden, Marshall, and Shute
to mention but a few. Editions of Tacitus's *History*, Caesar's *Com-
mentaries*, Plutarch's *Lives*, Eusebius's *Ecclesiastical History*, Herbert's
Description of the Persian Monarchy, Serres's *History of France*, Marcel-
linus's *Roman History*, Polybius's *History*, and John Foxe's *Martyrs*
betray a lively interest in the past. That he possessed a copy of
Amadis of Gaul, the bible of chivalry-conscious knights and nobles,
is important. It is equally interesting to note that he had copies of
legal writings of Sir Edward Coke, Robert Cotton, and William
Prynne.

Essex also succumbed to the relatively new fad of visiting the
watering places. [15] He sought recreation at Bath, along with several
members of the Hertford circle, and visited his mother and his
in-laws at Tunbridge Wells in Kent. It is not certain that he drank
the water or sweated in the bathhouse—as his sister Frances and his
mother did—but he seems to have associated with several members

[13] Codrington, *Life and Death*, pp. 11–12.

[14] This is from the Jessop family papers in the British Museum, Additional
MSS, 46,189. See my analysis of his holdings in "The Lord General's Library,
1646," pp. 115–23.

[15] Neither Wilson nor Codrington mentions these facts, but it is clear from
Essex's correspondence with his sister and stepbrother that he went to Tunbridge
Wells. See Additional MSS, 46,189.

of the so-called Country Party who congregated at such places. If nothing else, the spas provided England's leisure class with a convenient place to exchange views on the personal rule of Charles I.

These rustic recreations, however diverting, should not obscure the fact that Essex's responsibilities as head of the House of Devereux increased yearly. His duties included renewing manorial leases at Chartley, looking after his grandmother and his mother, and considering family marriages. He was also concerned about his will, complicated by the absence of an heir.

Essex frequently attended his aged grandmother, the Countess of Leicester, who still lived in semiseclusion at Drayton Basset, the northern Warwickshire estate which Leicester had settled upon her.[16] Though in her ninetieth year (in 1630), she took a walk each morning, wrote her own letters, and collected rents from her tenants. She had written her will nearly a decade earlier and had added several codicils.[17] The Countess appointed Essex to be executor and fulfill her last wishes. The lineal descendant of her first husband, Walter Devereux, Essex would inherit the lands which she had held for over a half-century by virtue of that marriage and the lands that Leicester had bestowed upon her. The Countess forewarned Essex, her favorite grandchild, of trouble that might arise from his cousin the Earl of Carlisle, who might contest the will and final settlement. In one of her last letters she granted Essex the power of attorney to fight for his potential inheritance against the claims of Carlisle, a courtier who enjoyed the King's company and influence.[18] Essex guarded his inheritance with care and patience. Whenever traveling to and from Chartley, he appears to have stopped at Drayton Basset. He also corresponded with his grandmother and she with him until her dying day.

During these years Essex also devoted more time to his mother, who was plagued with the gout and paralyzed in one arm, and to his stepfather.[19] Clanricarde had spent the early years of his married life in Connacht. In 1624, upon obtaining the barony of Somerhill, he turned the management of his Irish holdings over to a steward,

[16] Williams, *Court and times*, 2: 171.

[17] The authorities at Somerset House made a copy of her will available to me.

[18] This letter is among those transmitted by William Jessop to the British Museum; see Additional MSS, 46,189.

[19] *Ibid.*

returned to England, and settled at Somerhill Manor, a short distance from Tunbridge Wells. He conformed to the aristocratic customs and fads of the day and insisted that his children do likewise. He made his peace with Charles and proved himself a model English Catholic by paying his recusancy fines. In August 1628, he was elevated to the English earldom of Saint Albans.

Thereafter Essex developed closer ties with his mother's family. He corresponded with his stepfather and proffered advice on several matters. He became the confidant and spokesman of his half brother, Viscount Tunbridge, the only son and heir to the Clanricarde title and estates. They became bosom friends and political allies. Essex also helped rescue his half sister Lady Honora from spinsterhood.[20] The exact details remain obscure, but her name became linked with Essex's newly acquired relative John Paulet, Marquess of Winchester, a very eligible widower and distinguished aristocrat. Very likely Essex or Frances promoted the match. Lady Honora, highly pleased with the prospects of marrying the Marquess, requested that Essex approve the final terms, which he did in the summer of 1633. The marriage took place soon after.

Essex also assisted his younger sister, Lady Dorothy, whose marriage to Sir Henry Shirley had failed. In 1627, after twelve years of marriage, Sir Henry had been publicly disgraced before the Privy Council and subsequently imprisoned for disparaging the honor of the Earl of Huntingdon, one of Essex's political allies.[21] Not long after his release Shirley had been accused before the Court of High Commission of adultery.[22] Confronted with the charge and concerned for her two children, Lady Dorothy had sued for a divorce. She had been supported not only by her brother but by the aged primate who still heard such cases; she had been opposed by her husband, Buckingham, and the King. After a series of complicated legal maneuvers, Lady Dorothy was finally separated from her husband and awarded alimony. In 1632, when Sir Henry adamantly refused to make the required payment, Essex went to the aid of his sister and nephews by taking them into his household. Upon Sir Henry's death in 1635, Essex, as executor of the estate, disposed of Shirley's possessions and looked after the interests of Lady Dorothy. He reserved the right of guardianship over his

20 *Ibid.*
21 *A. P. C. 1627–1628*, pp. 134, 161, 197, 201.
22 Cobbett, *State Trials*, 2: 1456.

namesake, Robert, who remained in Essex's household until he reached his majority and received a Protestant education.[23]

Essex soon became involved in the remarriage of Lady Dorothy. Within a year the attractive widow married Anthony Stafford. "And here is also one Mr. Stafford," a contemporary gossip noted in March 1635, "who buried but two months since his wife, married in Queen's Chapel at Somerset-House to the Lady Dorothy Shirley, a sister to my Lord of Essex, and I hear they both repent it already."[24] This marriage helps explain why several of Stafford's manuscripts constitute part of Essex's literary holdings.

Essex's associations with his favorite sister, Frances, became more frequent and much closer.[25] The pair frequently played sham, a parlor game, and bowled on the greens at Tottenham. When apart they kept in touch with each other through messengers and personally penned letters. The extant communications from the Countess of Hertford reveal a close familial relationship between the correspondents. Essex learned of her visit to Blackfriar's in London, her associations with the Rich family and Lady Devonshire, her chronic ills, her trips to Somerhill, her watering at Tunbridge Wells, her monotony and boredom, her medical prescriptions, and her continuous concern for Essex's welfare. A few surviving letters written by the Earl of Hertford reveal that his political alliance with Essex was cemented by a close personal friendship. From these and other letters from nobles like Warwick one can infer that the members of the Country Party were united not merely by a common enemy but by kinship, intermarriage, mutual economic interests, and the diversions of a leisured class.

Essex's idyllic interlude was interrupted by a series of deaths, including that of his grandmother, which further increased his responsibilities. "The old Countess of Leicester died in the Beginning of Christmas [25 December 1631]," a Londoner noted, "which instantly put a great part of this Court and Town into Mourning. . . . Her Estate is fallen to my Lord of Essex."[26] Shortly after Christ-

23 Octavius Ogle, *Calendar of Clarendon State Papers*, 4 vols. (Oxford: Clarendon Press, 1869–76), 1: 81,221.

24 David Mathew, *The Social Structure of Caroline England* (Oxford: Clarendon Press, 1945), p. 130.

25 British Museum, Additional MSS, 46,189. The collection includes twenty-odd pieces of correspondence sent between them in the 1630s.

26 William Knowler, *The Earl of Strafford's Letters and Despatches*, 2 vols. (London, 1739), 1: 359.

mas, Essex journeyed to Drayton, where he arranged for and then attended the funeral, held in February. The burial spot was in Beauchamp Chapel, Warwick, next to that of her second husband. During the extended mourning period many demands were made of Essex, for as the administrator of the Countess's estate he had to execute the terms of the will. As principal inheritor, he fell heir to a multitude of problems relating to leases, rents, heriots, and the like. This inheritance, nonetheless, increased his total worth and added appreciably to his annual income.

Before he had time to assume the additional duties thrust upon him, the Earl of Essex received word that his mother had died in Somerhill, presumably of natural causes, at sixty-four. "On Friday [20 February 1632]," wrote Sir John Pory to a friend, "my Lord of Essex accompanied by my Lord Warwick and the Earl of Holland, was present at the solemnization of his mother's funeral in the chancel at Tonbridge; her corps in a chariot, covered with black velvet (attended by eight coaches and a great troup of horse) being brought thither by torches at midnight." [27]

Later that year Essex learned of the death of his former wife, Frances, the Countess of Somerset, who left a devoted but ostracized husband and a teen-age daughter. Had she lived five years longer she would have seen her daughter, Anne, married to William Lord Russell at Saint Benet's Church, London. Had she lived ten years longer she would have witnessed a close political alliance between her son-in-law and her former husband. There is no record of Essex's reaction to her death, on 22 August at Chiswick House. He seems to have taken an extraordinary interest in it, though, for among his few surviving papers is a postmortem examination, giving a detailed description of the deceased woman. Signed by four doctors, it reveals that she died of uterine cancer.[28] What satisfaction, if any, Essex received from this morbid information, whether he requested it, and why he preserved it all remain enshrouded in mystery.

[27] Pory to Sir Thomas Puckering in Sir Henry Ellis, *Original letters illustrative of English History*, 11 vols. (London, 1825–46), 2d ser., 3: 266. See Collins, *Letters and Memorials*, 1: 69, for her epitaph.

[28] British Museum, Additional MSS, 46,189. In his recently published biography entitled *The Notorious Lady Essex* (New York: Dial Press, 1969), Edward Le Comte reaches the tentative conclusion that Frances died of this disease after he speculates on this possibility throughout the work. Unfortunately he did not use the examination located in Essex's papers.

Concurrently Essex was beset by a crisis of considerable magnitude in his own household. When, after approximately a year of marriage, the new Countess of Essex did not produce an heir, some tongues began to compare the second marriage to the first. After two years there were rumblings about separation and annulment. The marriage, nonetheless, remained intact but was still childless. During the sixth year of their marriage, the Countess became implicated in an adultery case which scandalized the Hertford circle.[29] In March 1636, Essex went to Chartley, as was his custom, leaving his wife with her relatives and friends at Netley Castle, one of Hertford's holdings. During Essex's absence the Countess became intimate with Sir William Uvedale, described by Edmund Verney as "a most accomplished man, handsome, and knowing as much as learning, long travels and great observation could make him."[30] Sir William appears to have been friendly with the Seymours and on the periphery of their social circle. So faithfully had he served the Stuarts in all the Parliaments since 1623 that he was named treasurer of His Majesty's Chamber.

The intimacy soon blossomed into an *affaire*, and the *affaire* rapidly came to the attention of Sir Walter Devereux, who promptly set in motion a plot to entrap the guilty pair. He went to Netley Castle and conspired with Essex's servants to secure incriminating evidence against the supposed adulterer. First he forced one of the chambermaids to reveal her knowledge of their relationship. Next he set up a ladder outside the Countess's suite to use in securing first hand information. Finally, convinced of his sister-in-law's guilt, he forced her chamber door one evening and confronted the couple personally with the charge of adultery. Sir William, seated on the edge of the bed, promptly denied the charge, claiming that he was really interested in the Countess's unmarried sister, and then quickly left the scene. Sir Walter, refusing to take Uvedale's denial at face value, proceeded to lecture Betty concerning the evils of illicit love and unladylike behavior. After threatening to inform Essex of the entire incident, he left the Countess, who was furious at the invasion of her privacy and afraid of the possible consequences. News of the scandal soon leaked out to the public.

Essex, still at Chartley, was informed of the episode in a letter

[29] John Bruce, *Letters and Papers of the Verney Family down to the end of 1639* (Camden Society, 1853), p. 168.
[30] *Ibid.*

from his brother. Upon receipt of the letter Essex is reputed to have ordered the Countess out of Netlêy Castle. It is possible that he had suspected his wife's indiscreet relationship with Uvedale, and as some contemporaries insisted, had deliberately left for Chartley and assigned his brother the task of obtaining information about the principals. Whatever the case, the Devereux name again became tainted by scandal. Essex himself was accused of setting a trap. Sir Walter was condemned for playing the role of informer.

Upon returning after the scandal died down, Essex commenced negotiations through a lawyer, very likely John Selden, for a separation from his wife.[31] The propositions which mediators drew up on the last day of March proved to be premature, for in the midst of the negotiations the Countess of Essex astounded her contemporaries with the announcement that she was pregnant.[32] This news immediately caused people to wonder who the father was and when the child had been conceived. The Countess's condition, which undoubtedly caused many a smile, forced Essex to drop the separation proposals and reconsider the entire matter. If it was his child, perhaps the Uvedale *affaire* had been fabricated. Perhaps Sir Walter, detesting Betty and fearing the birth of a son, had concocted the story to foster his own interests as a potential heir to the Essex title and estates. How could Essex be certain of the truth? If he claimed the child and it looked more like Uvedale, he would be the cuckold again. If Essex refused to recognize the child as his own and it proved to be his, he would appear the jealous fool. Finally Essex made a Solomon-like decision: if the child was born by Guy Fawkes Day, he would claim it as his progeny and remain married to Betty Paulet, but if it was born after 5 November, he vowed to denounce the child as Uvedale's bastard and divorce his wife. If there was a chance that the child was conceived before he left for Chartley, Essex evidently reasoned, it was a Devereux not a Uvedale.

From early April until early November the Earl must have experienced much anxiety. How he spent his time during these summer months cannot be ascertained, but he appears to have remained at Tottenham House and to have reached an agreement with his wife. As the weeks passed into months, the situation became

31 Williams, *Court and times*, 2: 239–40.
32 Bruce, *Verney Papers*, pp. 169 ff.

more and more tense until, finally, on the deadline day the Countess gave birth to a son. Essex promptly claimed his paternity, named the youth after himself, and passed to him the title of Viscount Hereford.[33] At last, after two marriages, at the age of forty-five Essex had an heir.

The joy engendered by this event soon gave way to mourning. Viscount Hereford died of an undisclosed cause,[34] very likely the plague, slightly more than a month later. After the funeral, Essex buried the infant on the Countess of Leicester's estate at Drayton. This death only made the infant's paternity more difficult to determine. His life probably would have changed the course of his father's career and very likely altered the path of English history.

The demise of his only son and heir marked another turning point in Essex's life. Some, if not the Earl himself, undoubtedly regarded the death as a divine judgment against him and, particularly, his spouse, and as a confirmation of the adultery incrimination. Essex kept his word and remained married. Thereafter, however, he shunned women and put aside all hopes of a successful marriage and an heir. He relegated the Countess to a small and inconspicuous place in his life. The possibility that Uvedale may have fathered his late son and heir must have preyed on Essex's mind. The fact that Uvedale was a sycophant and place holder in the Court of Charles I must have irked him.[35] Very likely he carried deep in his heart a bitter resentment against the Stuart monarchs whose decisions not only barred his path to greatness and glory but added misery to life's tragedies.

II

To understand Essex's place in the Caroline social structure, it is necessary to analyze his estates, ascertain his worth, and describe his household administration. The deaths of his grandmother and his mother increased the total landholdings and broadened the geographic and economic base of Essex's manorial complex. The increase spelled not only a larger income but twice as many tenants

[33] Tenison, *Elizabethan England*, 12: 534.

[34] Collins, *Letters and Memorials*, 2: 454.

[35] It is interesting to note that Uvedale, one of Somerset's dependents in his earlier years, became the King's paymaster in the King's army. An undercurrent of intense personal rivalry between Essex and Uvedale must have persisted throughout the 1630s and 1640s.

and an enlarged staff. The geographic distribution alone posed managerial problems, for the original nucleus of Devereux properties was dwarfed by holdings in several more English counties, Wales, and Ireland. In the evolution of the aggregation the Devereux had moved their residence from Herefordshire to Staffordshire and then, with the second Earl of Essex, to Essex House in London, farther from their lands. The diversity of tenure, resulting from marriages, new purchases, jointures, and moieties, demanded increasing time and professional advice. Chartley Manor itself required a great deal of attention. The personal fortunes of Essex titleholders and their wives had further complicated matters. The early deaths of both the first and second Earls of Essex had placed the administration of some lands under the jurisdiction of the exploitive Court of Wards on two occasions. The longevity of the widows, furthermore, had tied up large portions of the estate for extended periods of time.

Any analysis of Essex's holdings is of necessity incomplete because the bulk of the Devereux papers did not survive the Civil Wars. Nevertheless, the wills of the principals provide a skeletal outline.[36] A survey of Essex House and a court-leet record from Chartley, both resulting from Essex's demise in 1646, give some microscopic detail.[37] Scattered references in public records, local histories, and private papers furnish some additional information. By the continuous enlargement of the Devereux lands through inheritance, purchase, gifts, and repayment for debts, the Earl of Essex was a moderately wealthy nobleman on the eve of his second marriage. His income of about four thousand pounds a year compared favorably with that of other nobles: he occupied a median position among his fellow peers.[38] This simplified picture is, however, obscured by other considerations. Many of his peers were mortgaged

[36] The first Earl's will is printed in Devereux, *Lives of the Devereux*, 2: 483–85, and the second Earl's is in Tenison, *Elizabethan England*, 12: 149. The third Earl's will, after a lengthy legal battle, was proven in Probate Court in 1663.

[37] According to a provision in the Statute of Uses, a survey of Essex's possessions was made at the time of his death. The Essex House inventory became part of Jessop's papers and is in the British Museum, Additional MSS, 46,189. The court-leet record of Chartley is part of the uncatalogued portion of the Stowe MSS, Huntington Library.

[38] For a complete analysis of the wealth of the peerage see Stone, *The Crisis of the Aristocracy, 1558–1641* (Oxford: Clarendon Press, 1965), pp. 760–61. It would appear that Professor Stone underestimated Essex's annual income by nearly half.

beyond reasonable limits. Others were heavily indebted to fellow noblemen or London merchants and financiers for luxuries, offices, and titles. Essex appears to have been solvent, living within his annual income.

Between 1630 and 1637 his income was nearly doubled through the lands he inherited and purchased. From his grandmother he received Bennington in Hertford, Dimmock in Gloucester, Monkton in Pembroke, Llanthomas in Brecknock, Oldhall in Essex, and Drayton in Staffordshire plus several tenements scattered about southern England. From his mother he inherited Teinton and Bicknor in Gloucester, Merevale in Warwick (including the deer park), Hay in Brecknock, and several holdings in Ireland. By 1637, Essex's income amounted to about eight thousand pounds a year. The increase came not from tax farming, as in the case of the Earl of Arundel, or from privateering, as in the case of the Earl of Warwick, but from simple inheritance and sound estate management.

Essex House, onetime official residence of the second Earl of Essex, had been held by the Countess of Leicester who, preferring the countryside of Warwickshire, rented the London mansion in turn to her relatives, the second Earl of Essex; his widow; the third Earl, who appears to have forfeited the right to sublet the house; her granddaughter the Countess of Carlisle; her grandson Robert Sidney; and Walter Devereux.[39] The multistoried mansion, with its forty-odd rooms and turreted tower, was situated a short distance from the old wall near Temple Bar in the exclusive parish of Saint Clement Danes. The third Earl, upon inheriting Essex House in 1632, seems to have rented it to his brother-in-law Hertford for several years, reserving the right of hospitality for himself and his wife. In March 1639, however, for eleven hundred pounds cash and an undisclosed annual rent, Essex and the Countess of Hertford agreed upon a moiety, whereby she and her husband would occupy part of the mansion for the remainder of their lives.[40]

[39] According to Leicester's will, which was probated 6 September 1588, his widow had use of the house as long as she lived. The third Earl, who inherited it through his father, did not move into the house until after her death in 1632. See Collins, *Letters and Memorials*, 1: 74; and Tenison, *Elizabethan England*, 12: 428.

[40] This moiety, apparently drawn up by John Selden, is printed in the appendix to Charles Lethbridge Kingsford, "Essex House," *Archaeologia*, 2d ser. 23 (1922–23): 13.

Thereafter Frances and Hertford, holding a ninety-nine-year lease, resided in the eastern half of the house, while Essex lived in the western portion. They shared the chapel, great hall, pump room, and gardens and split the costs of maintenance. A year after making this agreement Essex stipulated in his will that his portion should descend to the heirs of his other sister, Dorothy. This arrangement, which Essex considered fair and equitable, provoked a bitter legal battle when, after his death, each sister claimed the other's moiety.

All totalled, Chartley comprised three thousand acres of land under the plow, two thousand acres of pasture, one thousand acres of forage land, and about one thousand acres of woodland. Essex's buildings included, in addition to the manor house and parish churches, 140 messauges, 100 cottages, 100 tofts, 10 dovecotes, and 6 mills; there were also 140 gardens, 100 orchards, a fishery, and two parks reserved for hunting. Gayton was known for its fertile, well-watered soil; Frodswall for its gravel; Weston for its saltworks; Shugborough Park for its bountiful woods and beautiful streams; and nearby Cannock Chase for its fallow deer. More than anything else, however, Chartley was widely recognized for being one of the few places in all England that still had a herd of wild ox.

Chartley Manor supported 144 tenants, including 33 freeholders, 80 indentured leaseholders of the common land, 15 leaseholders of the demesne lands, and 16 who rented cottages. A few tenants held both common and demesne lands. Most of Essex's tenants held their land for three lives, but a few had twenty-one year leases and one had a thirty-six year lease. Like a medieval magnate Essex still exacted from his tenants one of the most aggravating obligations of serfdom, the heriot, or death tax. Sometimes Essex still demanded "the best beast"; in other cases he required a monetary sum averaging about three pounds; occasionally he reserved the right to take either. Essex's annual intake from his Chartley lands amounted to over six hundred pounds a year.

In the southeastern corner of Staffordshire, about two miles west of Tamworth, lay Drayton Basset.[41] In addition to several

[41] See John A. Langford, *Staffordshire and Warwickshire*, 2 vols. (London, n.d.), 2: 254ff.; Wedgwood, *Historical Collections of Staffordshire*, N. S. 4: 17ff.; Thomas Harwood, *A Survey of Staffordshire* (London, 1844), pp. 55–57; William Pitt, *A Topographical History of Staffordshire* (Newcastle under Lyme, 1817); and Frederick Calvert, *Staffordshire* (Birmingham, 1830).

hundred acres of tillable land Drayton comprised a formal garden, a banqueting house, wooded areas, and a beautiful manor house. Here in the great hall Essex supposedly had once carved his initials and coronet.

Merevale also descended to Essex.[42] Nearby lay the town of Sutton Colfield, which Essex governed as steward and from which he received a large portion of his income. Although these Warwickshire holdings did not give Essex much power in county politics, he seems to have possessed some influence in the Tamworth elections.

Soon after his accession James I had let it be known that the Devereux lands in Wales and the West Country—which had been forfeited by the attainder of Elizabeth's Essex—were for sale and that the widowed Countess of Essex would have the first opportunity to buy them, for seven thousand pounds. The Countess repurchased the lands for her son with the money she had received from her mother's estate. The Herefordshire lands included several choice manors located in the Wye drainage basin: Ross Borough, Ross Foreign, and Fawnhope in Greytree Hundred; Byford, Lyonshall, and Moorcourt in Webtree Hundred; Eardsland in Huntington Hundred; Wobbley and Pembridge in Stretford Hundred; and Walfrod in Wigmore Hundred.[43] Shortly after making the purchase, the Countess established a trust, assigning to herself income from the estates during her lifetime, thereby preserving the lands from grasping courts and courtiers, and designating the remainder for her son and his heirs. In the event of default, the estates would be divided between her two daughters. The trustees included the Earl of Northumberland and Lord Rich, both Essex's uncles; Lord Norris; and Sir Henry Lindley. In 1632, Essex fell heir to these lands, which apparently had been managed, at the Countess's request, by a steward, Sir Walter Pye. Clanricarde requested that Pye be retained.[44]

Essex also possessed several properties in the home counties and Wales.[45] He purchased Enfield, a Middlesex manor valued at six hundred pounds a year, from Sir William Langley sometime

---

[42] See P. R. O., Index to Patent Rolls for Essex's holdings in Warwickshire.

[43] William H. Cooke, *Collections Toward the History and Antiquities of the County of Hereford*, 3 vols. (London, 1882), 3: 105–10.

[44] British Museum, Additional MSS, 46,189.

[45] *Ibid.*

in the 1630s. Little Raine, a manor which Essex visited only rarely, gave him a political toehold in the county of Essex. He repurchased Bennington in Hertfordshire, a manor which he had been forced to sell to Sir Julius Caesar in order to repay his dowry, in 1630. From his Cardigan estates in Wales he received three hundred pounds a year.

Essex increased his income through nonagricultural means. From his tenants in Newcastle under Lyme, where he owned Talbot House, several tenements, and some valuable acreage within the borough limits, the Earl received a small but dependable income. More important, these properties gave him a voice in borough politics.[46] Though he never became mayor—as did his father—he utilized his influence in the nomination of members to the House of Commons on several occasions. From several tenements adjacent to Essex House along Milford Lane, one of which John Pym occupied, Essex received additional revenue.[47] He collected fifty pounds a year from a mill at Lichfield and annually received thirty-four pounds from the tithers at Stowe. From cutting and selling trees on his heavily wooded estates in Herefordshire he netted many an additional pound sterling; each year he carried on logging operations at Bodenham, Wobbley, and Fawnhope.

Essex's largest single source of income, however, came from the coal mines which he owned and managed in connection with Merevale.[48] From the coal and the soil he netted about one thousand pounds a year—a tidy sum in any nobleman's ledger. Unfortunately the number of colliers, the type of extractions, the retailing methods, or the market cannot be determined. Essex also increased his income from the sale of timber on enclosed land. Taking advantage of his rights as guardian over some undisclosed ward, he applied to his cousin the Earl of Holland for a license to fell trees and enclose land in the Forest of Whittlewood in Northamptonshire. Holland, who had charge of such business, sent a nine-year license with a caution to Essex to leave some trees standing.[49] It is most interesting,

[46] See Thomas Pape, *Newcastle-under-Lyme in Tudor and Early Stuart Times* (Manchester: At the University Press, 1938), pp. 143–45.

[47] See Kingsford, "Essex House," plates I and II, pp. 16–17. It is clear from several illustrations dating from the seventeenth century that there were several tenements along Milford Lane and the Strand.

[48] British Museum, Additional MSS, 46,189.

[49] *C. S. P. Dom., 1639–1640*, p. 154.

nevertheless, that Essex willingly utilized his land for both extractive and nonagrarian purposes.

The total income from Essex's Irish landholdings amounted to about three thousand pounds a year.[50] These lands, scattered throughout Wexford, Meath, Louth, and Monaghan, represented the fruits of his forebears' military service there, for both his grandfather and his father had participated in the Elizabethan conquest of Ireland and received large amounts of land. His Irish inheritance also included Carew Castle, Carrick Mac Ross, and over twenty towns located in the Pale, plus the barony of Donnemayne. Holding the lands directly from the King, he possessed broad palatinate powers; but, like his ancestors, Essex governed them as an absentee landlord and delegated the normal managerial responsibilities to a steward.

In the spring of 1633, Essex crossed to Ireland and spent several months visiting his estates there. The specific purpose of his visit remains unknown, but he had problems with his tenants and his Irish holdings had been enlarged by his inheritance. Perhaps he merely wished to survey his holdings, both old and new, so that he could secure firsthand knowledge of his properties and their values and deal directly with the new Lord Deputy. Very likely he had to collect heriots, renew leases, and discuss managerial matters with his steward.

In July, before returning to England, the Earl traveled to Dublin to make his peace with the new lord deputy, Sir Thomas Wentworth, who had arrived only recently.[51] Apparently Essex asked Wentworth to look after his interests on the island. It is evident from a letter written several months after his return that Essex appreciated the lord deputy's hospitality. "At my being in Dublin I received so noble usage from you," he wrote from Essex House, "that it hath encouraged me to render you all Thanks for your

50 For the following information see Devereux, *Lives of the Devereux*, 2: 307; *C. S. P. Carew Papers, 1603–1624*, p. 313; *A. P. C. 1616–1617*, pp. 251, 307; British Museum, Additional MSS, 46,189, for letters between Essex, Strafford and Clanricarde about their respective lands in Ireland; and various references in M. A. E. Green, ed., *Calendar of the Proceedings of the Committee for Compounding*, 5 vols. (London, 1889–1902).

51 For Strafford's Irish administration see Hugh F. Kearney, *Strafford in Ireland* (Manchester: At the University Press, 1959), and C. V. Wedgwood's reinterpretation, *Thomas Wentworth: A Reevaluation* (London: Jonathan Cape, 1961), especially the introduction.

favours, and to desire the Continuance of them."[52] In answer to this communication Wentworth promised to look after Essex's affairs. The next year the lord deputy assumed the role of mediator in a complicated land dispute between Essex and John Dillon, a tenant who broke a contract, and put forward a proposal designed to pacify both parties. However, when Essex discovered that the proposal demanded more of him than of Dillon, he refused to accept the compromise and registered his complaint in a lengthy letter addressed to the lord deputy.[53] The final disposition of the matter is uncertain, but it is clear that Essex was very displeased with Wentworth in September 1634.

Essex's stepfather openly clashed with the new lord deputy.[54] The Earl of Clanricarde correctly feared that the proposed colonization of Connacht would lessen his autonomous control over Galway, the largest county in Ireland. For a few years he succeeded in forestalling Wentworth's plantation scheme. He opposed it in the Irish Parliament of 1634; he employed agents who fought it in England; and he secured the assistance of relatives, including Essex, to oppose it—all to no avail. In 1635 the lord deputy proceeded to claim Galway for the King and initiated defective title proceedings against Clanricarde. These actions proved more than Essex's stepfather could physically withstand, for he died in November, shortly after hearing of Wentworth's designs.[55] During the last week of the year Clanricarde was buried at Somerhill near Essex's mother.

Clanricarde's son and heir, Ulrich Burke, Viscount Tunbridge, sought to avenge his father's death and still retain power in Connacht. In 1636 he traveled to Ireland and talked to his tenants and many Irish landowners, who empowered him to mediate a solution between them and the Crown.[56] He then presented a

[52] Knowler, *Strafford's Letters*, 2: 205, 232.

[53] How this letter, which bears Essex's signature and seal, became deposited in the local museum at Stow-on-the-Wold, where it is presently located, is somewhat mystifying to the local authorities. It is entirely possible that Essex lost the letter while on one of his several stops there during the Civil Wars.

[54] A running conflict between Strafford and both father and son lasted until Strafford's death. See Knowler, *Strafford's Letters*, 2: 6, 36, 367, 381; Kearney, *Strafford*, pp. 68, 93; and Aidan Clarke, *The Old English in Ireland* (Ithaca: Cornell University Press, 1966), pp. 90–110.

[55] John Lodge, *The Peerage of Ireland*, 7 vols. (London, 1789), 1: 130–35.

[56] Knowler, *Strafford's Letters*, 2: 6, 36.

submission to Lord Deputy Wentworth, who refused to accept it on technical grounds, and finally appealed to Charles, who awaited the decision of his judges. In March 1638 the judges declared that Clanricarde's patents were not merely defective but void of any legal protection. This decision struck so much fear in the Irish magnate that he all but capitulated to the lord deputy.

The new Earl of Clanricarde was saved from utter destruction, however, by earthshaking events in Scotland, which demanded not only the attention of Wentworth but the loyalty of the Irish. In 1639, Charles I, fearing an uprising in Connacht, reversed Wentworth's policy and granted Clanricarde clear title to all his Irish estates in exchange for his loyalty. By this reversal Clanricarde was able to free his lands from the proposed plantation, retain his revenue of over sixty-five hundred pounds a year, and keep most of his palatine powers. Charles virtually undid Wentworth's work, for thereafter the rest of the Irish magnates clamored for similar treatment and begged for concessions.

These bitter conflicts cemented the ties between Essex and his half brother.[57] For several years the two shared a common enemy in the King's minister. Their religious differences seemed inconsequential in their struggle against Wentworth.

III

THROUGHOUT the 1630s, Essex was much concerned with the acquisition and preservation of his inheritance. Whereas before 1629 he spent his energy upon military service overseas, the recruitment of troops, and parliamentary affairs, he now directed his attention to the management of his estates. During the summer months he generally resided at Chartley and personally supervised his Staffordshire holdings. En route he seems usually to have stopped at Drayton and Merevale to view his lands. Also he made the special trip to Ireland to care for pressing matters.

Nevertheless, like almost all other aristocratic landowners, Essex delegated most of the routine responsibilities of manorial management to subordinates.[58] His household staff amounted to more

[57] British Museum, Additional MSS, 46,189.

[58] Most of the information in the ensuing pages has been culled from the British Museum, Additional MSS, 46,188–91; Wilson, *Autobiography*, pp. 457–72; *A. P. C.;* and *C. S. P. Dom.*

than fifty persons. He also relied upon several "favorites" for advice, including his secretary, Rowland Laugherne, and Sir John Meyrick. When Essex needed special legal work he seems to have employed the best lawyers in England—Selden, Sir Philip Stapleton, and Oliver St. John. When he demanded medical care he called upon Dr. John Clarke, author of *Pharmacopoeia* and one of England's best physicians. When the Earl had a particular religious problem he consulted the Bishop of Lincoln rather than the several chaplains and divines he patronized.

Essex delegated his provincial responsibilities to stewards, bailiffs, and deputies. He relied upon Richard and Harvey Bagot, sons of his father's steward Walter Bagot, to oversee his Staffordshire estates. Sir Walter Pye, barrister and attorney for the Court of Wards, remained the steward for his lands in Gloucester and Herefordshire. Essex depended upon William Wingfield, son of the conspirator and apparently a political dependent, to manage his properties in Warwickshire and seems to have employed his cousin Sir Nathaniel Rich to look after his Irish land holdings. In addition to alloting these men the traditional duties and remunerations Essex gave several of them and their relatives vested interests in his lands. He awarded Harvey Bagot part interest in some Staffordshire lands and sold half interest in Drayton to Wingfield, who had sat for Lichfield in several Parliaments and served for Staffordshire in 1628.

Essex continued to exercise his political influence in local government. Despite his opposition in Parliament, he was reappointed lord lieutenant of Staffordshire in 1629, a post which he retained for a decade. Since the nation remained at peace during most of these years, the demands of the office were not so great as in the twenties; nevertheless, Essex was responsible for keeping the trained bands prepared and the county in a posture of defense. In 1629, in response to Charles's expressed displeasure over the fighting force, Essex and his fellow lord lieutenants were ordered to muster the trained bands, to review both horse and foot, and "to see the same and to see compleate according to the moderne fashion." [59] Some years Essex appears to have personally carried out orders from the Privy Council; other years he delegated them to his

[59] *A. P. C. 1628–1629*, p. 421. Essex delegated some of his military obligations to deputy lieutenants, according to the official correspondence in the Bagot MSS, Folger Shakespeare Library.

deputies. One of the principal problems Essex confronted was negligence. Sometimes "gentlemen of worth" refused to respond to the muster. One time, in 1631, the foot soldiers were described as "ablemen, well armed," while the horses were labeled "very defective." [60] Essex forwarded the names of the defaulters to the Privy Council. Another problem concerned obsolescence: many soldiers were armed with inferior weapons, some with bows and arrows. Essex and his deputies solved this by contracting with a local mercer to supply the trained bands with the latest guns, matches, and powder. They also contracted with Staffordshire lead miners for supplies of bullets. The Earl's wartime experience on the Continent gave him a distinct advantage in fulfilling the demands of the post.

From 1628 to 1637, Essex also served on the Warwickshire Commission of Peace, an office which offered him some prestige and influence. Shortly after receiving his inheritance, which included several manors in Cardiganshire, Essex also assumed a larger voice in Welsh politics. On 12 May 1633 he was named to the Council for Wales and the Marches, which, under the leadership of the Earl of Bridgewater, constituted the principal administrative and judicial agency there.[61] This appointment gave Essex opportunity to meet with Coventry, Portland, Manchester, Arundel, Pembroke, and several others. The council also included Essex's brother, Sir Richard Leveson, and Sir Robert Harley, all favorably disposed to the Earl.

Despite his increased prestige in local politics, Essex remained outside the inner orbits of Caroline society and government. He was still denied a place on the Privy Council. He remained excluded from the Court festivities. He did not attend the christening of Prince Charles in 1630. He did not frequent the Court masques and plays. He did not attend Parliament—there were no assemblies to attend. Five years passed without a Parliament. Six years passed and still Charles I gave no sign of convening one. Without Parliament there was little organized opposition. Without Parliament the peers could not check the Crown by trying ministers impeached by the Commons, nor could they protect their class privileges. In short, parliamentary peers like Essex, Saye, Warwick, Brook, and

[60] C. S. P. Dom., 1631–1633, p. 165.

[61] See Thomas Rymer's Foedera, 20 vols. (London: 1704–32), 19: 350.

Spencer were impotent in national politics, however powerful they remained in the counties and towns.

Their grievances, meanwhile, accrued at a compound rate.[62] They complained of the King's reliance upon ecclesiastics such as Laud and Juxon for advice. They murmured against the grasping Court of Wards and the high handed Star Chamber court. They contested the royal claims to the forests and tidal wastelands. Southampton was furious when fined twenty thousand pounds in the Court of the Forest. Lord Berkeley grumbled at the royal claims to his foreshore lands in Gloucester. The Earl of Clanricarde protested when Wentworth tried to force him to reside in Galway, and he reacted violently when the lord deputy tried to strip him of his land and palatine powers. Warwick became quite "troubled" when notified that he would have to share his lord lieutenancy with Lord Maynard, a courtesan. Lord Morley registered a bitter complaint when the Star Chamber imprisoned him in the Tower and fined him twenty thousand pounds for creating a courtroom scene in a fit of passion. Lord Digby protested when called before the Star Chamber and accused of being a troublemaker. The peers, especially those who had opposed Charles in Parliament, also rankled under some financial expedients which made mockery of honor and chivalry. All knightworthy men, Charles ordered, should be dubbed and then compelled to pay their knighting fees or be fined. Likewise, all knights who had not paid their coronation fees should do so or suffer the consequences. This extortive device, which prolonged unparliamentary government, met with resistance on all sides. The Earl of Newcastle encountered refusers in the Midlands. The Earl of Manchester met with opposition in Northampton. In February 1632 the Earl of Kingston flatly refused to pay his fees, whereupon he was fined two thousand pounds. And he was not alone, for about twenty-five peers stood with him.

Essex assumed the leadership of the aristocratic protestation. In July 1632, according to a contemporary, "my Lord of Essex and divers others of the nobility appeared before the lords of the privy council at Whitehall, about the compounding for their knighthoods. His lordship said, he was not only present at the coronation, but employed also in services very near his majesty's person, as bearing the sword before him, and helping him put on and off his robes;

62 See Gardiner, *History*, 7: 299–390 and 8: 67–221.

and was there ready to have received knighthood, or any other honour his majesty should have pleased to vouchsafe on him. So, my lord treasurer asked his lordship whether he would stand to that plea. He said he would; and so said all the rest."[63] Although Essex and many other worthy Englishmen refused to participate in this perversion of a chivalrous rite, the Crown collected upwards of one hundred thousand pounds over a period of five years. It proved to be a shortlived victory, however, for within a decade Essex and his fellow recalcitrants succeeded in abolishing obligatory knighthood forever.

In 1633, Essex's Puritan chaplain, Thomas Pestell, became a victim of Archbishop Laud's policy of conformity.[64] Pestell refused adamantly to comply with the new ceremonials that Laud demanded of all churchmen, whereupon he was summoned to Lambeth Palace. Here, before the Court of High Commission, he was charged with, and declared guilty of, abuse of his patron's trust and insubordination to ecclesiastical superiors. Pestell capitulated to the powers that were. Without a Parliament and the power to exercise the parliamentary privileges which he had earlier used to protect another chaplain, Essex could not save Pestell from reprisal.

IV

THROUGHOUT the 1630s Essex retained his reputation as a soldier and continued to make contacts with some of the leading military figures of his day. He received letters from Frederick, Prince of Orange, the Duke of Brunswick, Count Mansfeld; and Constantijn Huygens.[65] His services were sought by many heads of state. In 1629 the Queen of Bohemia, with whom Essex corresponded for several years, tried unsuccessfully to induce him to take up arms and once again lend assistance to her cause.[66] That same year the Prince of Orange vainly attempted to secure his services. The next year the Venetian authorities, searching for an experienced com-

[63] Sir John Pory to Sir Thomas Puckering in Williams, *Court and times*, 2: 163. Also see Firth, *House of Lords*, p. 56; and Rushworth, *Historical Collections*, 2: 71. For a discussion of this subject see H. S. Grazebrook, "Obligatory Knighthood," *Historical Collections of Staffordshire* (Birmingham, 1881), 2: 1–11.

[64] *DNB*, 15: 931–32.

[65] British Museum, Additional MSS, 46,189.

[66] L. M. Baker, *The Letters of Elizabeth Queen of Bohemia* (London: Bodley Head, 1953), p. 77.

mander, approached Essex and his cousin Warwick.[67] Essex was honored in 1631 by a bid for his services from the leading warrior statesman of his day, Gustavus Adolphus, who was planning the military conquest of the Catholic powers of Europe.[68] In each instance Essex turned down the offer.

These refusals did not dampen Essex's interest in the Continental situation. He received from Col. Edward Harwood, a faithful dependent, several firsthand accounts describing the fighting in the Low Countries and the terrible condition of the troops.[69] He also secured from Sir Jacob Astley, one of England's most renowned professional soldiers, much information about affairs in Germany, including a description of the capitulation of Frankfurt in 1633. He was informed by Sir Charles Rich of developments in London. Likewise, he received numerous anonymous news letters—some directed to him, some merely forwarded—recounting events on the Continent. Essex was regarded by these correspondents as a military authority.

Essex also continued to befriend soldiers and represent the interests of war veterans. In 1630 he used his influence to obtain a pension for Edward Taylor, a maimed soldier, who had one time served under him on the Continent.[70] The following year Essex rendered assistance to Capt., Robert Smith, a displaced soldier who had fought with him at Cádiz, who applied to the Council of War for relief.[71] Essex also employed some of the retiring veterans in his personal household and on his estates. He used Captain Wenman, who had served under him in several campaigns on the Continent, as a confidential messenger. He used his patronage as lord lieutenant to find places for veterans. His genuine and enduring interest in the welfare of England's soldiers became well known. His efforts on behalf of veterans gave him an acknowledged popularity among the masses. It is not surprising, then, that Clarendon called him a "darling of the sword-men."

The Earl also endeared himself to the chivalrous. He still chased the stag with great vigor and was fond of hounds and horses. He attended the Court of Chivalry—the last of its kind—in April

[67] C. S. P. Ven., 1629–1632, p. 386.

[68] British Museum, Additional MSS, 46,189.

[69] Ibid.

[70] C. S. P. Dom., 1629–1631, p. 267.

[71] Ibid., p. 495.

1634.[72] A household inventory reveals that he purchased several swords in addition to the ones he already owned. To decorate Essex House, he hung tapestries depicting forest scenes and stag hunts and thus revealing his preferences. Titles in his library indicate an interest in the military heroes of the ancient and medieval past.

In 1636, Essex became the idol of Charles I's nephew, Charles Louis, Prince Elector of Palatine, who came to England for a state visit. Throughout the official tour, which had been approved by Charles I and acclaimed by men of Essex's stripe, Elizabeth, the Electress of Palatine, had hopes of securing assistance for the recovery of her son's kingdom, Bohemia. The Prince, warmly welcomed by both Charles and Henrietta Maria, was well received by most Englishmen. In early 1636 he held court for "the Protestant interest" and on 3 February invited some gentlemen, including Sir Simonds D'Ewes, to visit him. D'Ewes wrote in his *Autobiography:* "I went to Newmarket in my coach, carrying my wife, my brother Richard D'Ewes, and my youngest sister Elizabeth D'Ewes, with me thither; where having dined in the afternoon, we were all admitted into the Prince Elector's bedchamber, who saluted my wife and my sister, and gave my brother his hand to kiss. He was marvellously pleased with the ancient Roman coins I gave him, and then, leaving the Earl of Essex and divers other noblemen at the fire, he retired with me to a window, where I gave him such a solid and faithful advice for the recovery of his lost country and dominions as he highly approved." [73]

In the summer Essex and the Prince Elector were again together, at Oxford University.[74] On 29 August, after being introduced to the Convocation, the Prince was granted the power to nominate several favorites for honorary degrees. In addition to naming his younger brother, Prince Rupert, he nominated the Earl of Essex and eleven other prominent Englishmen. Thus, two days later Oxford University conferred upon Essex a second Master of Arts degree. The ceremony was followed by a tour of the Bodleian Library, a sumptuous banquet given by Archbishop Laud, and a

[72] See G. D. Squibb, *The High Court of Chivalry* (Oxford: Clarendon Press, 1959), p. 54, for the details of this case.

[73] D'Ewes, *Autobiography*, 2: 138–39.

[74] See Sir Charles E. Mallet, *History of the University of Oxford*, 3 vols. (London: Longmans, Green, 1924), 2: 341.

dramatic production. The following morning the royal family and their distinguished guests proceeded to Woodstock to hunt. In the procession Essex was called upon to carry the sword of state before the King.

Six months transpired before the Prince Elector returned to Holland. Although he secured little financial assistance, he did not return empty handed. He endeared himself to countless Englishmen, won moral support for his cause, and, more important, obtained from his uncle the loan of fourteen English vessels, which were to be employed to regain Bohemia. Just before departing the Prince appealed to Charles I for experienced military leaders to assist him in his forthcoming campaign. He seems to have personally solicited Essex's services, and the Earl apparently agreed to render his assistance.[75] But the Prince sought in vain: Charles stubbornly vetoed the request.

Essex, again rebuffed by his King, resumed his semiretired existence in the countryside.

[75] Collins, *Letters and Memorials*, 2: 472.

CHAPTER 9

Essex and the Covenanters

I

IN THE CLOSING weeks of 1638 the Earl of Essex came out of retirement to serve his King and country.[1] Armed conflict with the Scottish Covenanters seemed inevitable. Charles refused to set aside his religious policy of anglicanizing the Kirk, while the Covenanters, now well organized and up in arms, refused to concede to the uncompromising demands of their King. Persuasion had failed. Threats had proved useless. Negotiations had broken down. Both sides commenced to prepare for war in the summer and autumn months.

That the Covenanters intended to fight unto death for their "true religion" seemed certain. Col. Alexander Leslie, Scotland's leading professional soldier, returned to Edinburgh from the Continent, where he had been fighting against the Hapsburgs, and proceeded to organize a national army. The powerful nobles, especially John Leslie, Earl of Rothes; Archibald Campbell, Earl of Argyll; and James Graham, Earl of Montrose, assumed the leadership of the national resistance movement and prepared for

[1] The principal sources for this chapter are: Gardiner, *History;* C. V. Wedgwood, *The King's Peace* (London: Collins, 1955); Jane Lane, *The Reign of King Covenant* (London: R. Hale, 1956); David Mathew, *Scotland Under Charles I* (London: Eyre and Spottiswoode, 1955); Charles S. Terry, *The Life and Campaigns of Alexander Leslie First Earl of Leven* (London, 1899); John Buchan, *Montrose, a History* (Boston: Houghton Mifflin Company, 1928); Leopold Von Ranke, *A History of England*, 6 vols. (Oxford: 1875), vol. 2; William Chambers, *The Scottish Church From Earliest Times to 1881* (Edinburgh, 1881); G. D. Henderson, *Religious Life in Seventeenth Century Scotland* (Cambridge: At the University Press, 1937); George M. Paul, *Diary of Sir Archibald Johnston of Wariston 1632–1639* (Edinburgh: Scottish Historical Society, 1911); Robert Baillie, *The Letters and Journals of Robert Baillie* ed. David Laing (Edinburgh, 1841); the Earl of Rutland's diary in *H. M. C. Rutland Manuscripts;* Samuel Rawson Gardiner, *The Hamilton Papers* (Camden Society Publications, 1880); and John Nalson, *An Impartial Collection of Great Affairs of State from the Beginning of the Scottish Rebellion to the Year 1649* (London, 1682).

the forthcoming conflict. They drew up military instructions, circulated them throughout the countryside, and delegated the responsibility for recruiting, training, and mustering an army to other covenanting nobles. Some Covenanters sought allies in France and military assistance on the Continent, while others established contacts with disgruntled English nobles. By the Christmas season 1638, Scotland was ready and poised for war: a peaceful solution seemed remote, if not impossible.

In England counterpreparations proceeded more slowly. During the summer months the Privy Council had remained divided over whether England should assume a military posture. Arundel, Francis Cottington, and Sir Francis Windebank favored war, while Northumberland, Vane, and Coke preferred to wait and find some peaceful solution. The English nation was ill-prepared for an armed conflict. The King's coffers were nearly empty and credit was hard to obtain. The royal magazines lacked both arms and ammunition. "The people through all England are generally so discontented," wrote the Earl of Northumberland, "by reason of the Multitude of Projects daily imposed upon them as I think there is reason to fear that a great Part of them will be readier to join with the Scots than to draw their Swords in the King's Service."[2]

These distasteful realities did not dissuade the King from preparing for a war against the Covenanters. Arundel called upon the people of the northern counties to provide themselves with arms and ammunition—bows and spears, if nothing else. He also sent cannon and muskets to the garrisons at Berwick, Carlisle, and Newcastle to check any sudden invasion from the north. The Privy Council ordered the lord lieutenants to recruit troops and hold musters. It reappointed Essex lord lieutenant of Staffordshire.[3] It ordered arms from the Netherlands. It drew up plans for an army of over twelve thousand foot soldiers and devised a grand strategy for defensive operations against the rebels. How the English monarch intended to finance the forthcoming conflict without calling a Parliament remained something of a mystery even to those closest to him.

At this crucial juncture Charles turned to Essex and other experienced military figures for assistance. With no standing army and no permanent minister of war, military preparations proceeded

2 Knowler, *Stafford's Letters*, 2: 186.
3 *A. P. C.*, MSS P. C. 2/49.

on an *ad hoc* basis. The King first established a committee of the Privy Council to supervise the operations against the Scots.[4] This special Council of War met in consultation with the King at White-hall, then appointed commanders, discussed logistics, and deter-mined the over-all military strategy. Since custom dictated that the commander be from the nobility (preferably a peer from an ancient family), they concurred that the Earl of Arundel, then Earl Marshal of England, should be named the lord general. This appointment proved most unfortunate: while Arundel could claim precedence over all other peers in England, he had no military experience.

The Council of War then nominated Essex as second-in-command, with the title General of the Horse.[5] The choice was in many respects a natural one, for he was popular among the soldiers and could point to military experience. He had good birth and a title that brought back memories of Elizabethan glory. Moreover, he was anti-Scottish. According to Clarendon, Essex was the "most popular man of the Kingdom and . . . , between a hatred and contempt of the Scots had nothing like an affection for any one man of the nation; and therefore was so pleased with this promotion that he began to love the King better for conferring it upon him, and entered upon the province with great fidelity and alacrity, and was capable from that hour of any impression the King would have fixed upon him."[6]

Mountjoy Blount, Earl of Newport, the bastard son of Essex's aunt Penelope, was named general of artillery. His military exper-ience in the Low Countries had given him many ideas about mili-tary reform. Sir Jacob Astley, Essex's friend and correspondent, was appointed the sergeant-major general. A professional soldier with much experience on the Continent, he had been busy forti-fying Hull, Berwick, and Newcastle for several months. Henry Wilmot, who had recently returned from the Netherlands, was named commissary general. The unit commanders included the Earls of Newcastle and Pembroke, Viscount Grandison, and Lord Clifford.

---

[4] Wedgwood, *The King's Peace*, p. 234.

[5] *C. S. P. Ven., 1638–1639*, p. 479.

[6] Edward Hyde, Earl of Clarendon, *The history of the rebellion and civil wars in England*, ed. W. D. Macray, 6 vols. (Oxford, 1888), 2: 48. For a similar appraisal of Essex see Philip Warwick, *Memoires of the Reigne of Charles I* (London, 1701), p. 29.

On 25 November 1638, Essex, Newport, and Astley received orders from the Council of War to appraise the state of military preparedness and recommend any changes they deemed essential.[7] Their inquiry revealed that the trained bands were poorly equipped; that the foot soldiers were inadequately clothed, ill-disciplined, and unpaid; that most of the troops had little or no training; and that many units, including the horse, were plagued with absenteeism. To remedy this deplorable situation, the commanders, led by Newport, recommended a series of reforms.[8] They advocated greater uniformity in dress and arms, urged the lord lieutenants to better enforce the laws against absenteeism, and prescribed a national mustering system of both foot and horse. Most of these recommendations, however, were disregarded.

Essex was devoting himself to equipping the English troops.[9] To modernize a locally trained army was no simple task. Since Leslie and other Scottish leaders would undoubtedly have the more advanced arms used on the Continent, Essex and Newport thought it advisable for the English leaders to do the same. Therefore they imported the most modern arms available from the Low Countries. Essex soon discovered, however, that some of that equipment was defective. The bandoleers were made of paper instead of leather. The swords needed repair. The pikes were almost useless. To rectify this confused situation, by direct command the King prohibited all armorers from working on any projects but those relating to the defense of England against the Scots. He then ordered all saddlery suppliers to attend Essex and consult with him about Continental saddles and other modern appurtenances. The recommendations made by Essex, who had experience with the Continental cavalry tactics and saddlery styles, were to be committed to paper and returned to the council for final approval. In response to a plea from Essex, the Elector of the Palatinate sent military personnel who had fought for the Protestant cause on the Continent.[10] In introducing Continental techniques and personnel, Essex must be considered a precursor of Cromwell.

[7] C. S. P. Dom., 1638–1639, p. 120.

[8] H. M. C. Twelfth Report, Appendix 2, p. 208.

[9] P. R. O., S. P. 16/448: 42; and C. S. P. Dom., 1638–1639, p. 315.

[10] H. M. C. Twelfth Report, Appendix 9, p. 174. In a letter dated 8 March 1639, the Elector recommended the bearer to Essex as one "who hath followed me this last summer, and hath some yeares served under the States and Swedes; therefor

The King also added Essex and Newport to the Council of War.[11] On 18 January 1639 the reconstructed council met at Whitehall with Charles to consider ways of expediting war preparations. The council first ordered Arundel, Essex, and Newport to meet with the ordnance officers and auditors to determine the matériel and monetary needs of an army of 24,000 foot and 6,000 horse plus a train of artillery. Having agreed that the cavalry units were to be raised in those counties most remote from the Border, the council commissioned Arundel and Essex to consider the most efficient means of transporting them to the rendezvous at York and to estimate the cost of the same "with all speed." By the last week of January the King had sent letters to all his nobles, commanding them to attend his standard at York. He also ordered the mayor of Newcastle to fortify the port and prepare for war.

The effectiveness of these measures was soon undone by Charles's decision to reshuffle the commands—at Essex's expense. In late January the King announced that the Earl of Holland would supplant Essex as General of the Horse in the forthcoming campaign and that Essex would serve under Arundel as lieutenant general.[12] The precise cause of this untimely shift in commands remains somewhat obscure. In December, Holland had placed his services at Essex's disposal, but the latter, presumably, did nothing about the offer. Holland, like his half brother, the Earl of Newport, was the son of Penelope Devereux, Essex's aunt. His father was Robert Rich, the Earl of Warwick. An obsequious courtier who had been with the Queen's coterie for more than a decade, Holland was reputed to be inexperienced, indeed incompetent, in military matters. Having failed to secure either the office of Lord Admiral, which went to the Earl of Northumberland, or a generalship for the Scottish expedition, he turned to the Queen, who begged her husband to make Holland the general of the cavalry. Whatever the cause, the reshuffle was a tragic blunder. Both Arundel and Essex were insulted by the move. Arundel, who could trace his ancestry to the Norman Conquest, had no use for the illegitimate upstart

---

I make noe doubt, but he will fitt to doe his Majesty some service that way, though I hope it will not be needful within his dominions." In all likelihood this messenger was Philbert Du Bois, an artillery expert who served in the Scottish expedition.

11 *Ibid.*, p. 323.

12 Knowler, *Strafford's Letters*, 2: 276.

whose title lacked the luster of age and service. Essex was indignant because the new order took away the most important part of his command. Although Charles attempted to appease Essex by giving him the higher rank of lieutenant general, the damage was done, for the greater dignity meant less opportunity for military glory and patronage.

Final preparations for the campaign now went forward without delay. After much discussion, the King decided to appear at the York rendezvous and, if feasible, deal directly with his rebellious Scottish subjects. To finance the campaign, Charles appealed to the nobles, the bureaucracy, the members of the Court, the bishops, and the city of London for "free benevolences."[13] The clergy contributed liberally to the cause, but many lords balked and protested; in fact, Lords Saye and Brooke refused to contribute to the war chest, claiming that the King should call a Parliament to raise funds. The aldermen of London rejected the King's request for one hundred thousand pounds and 3,000 men. Thus the English sovereign was forced to raise money by selling some offices, confiscating property, and resorting to other extraparliamentary devices, all of which irritated his critics.

Before departing for the North the Earl of Essex attended to some private matters.[14] It was at this time that he leased half of Essex House to the Countess of Hertford and her husband. The motive behind this arrangement remains obscure. Perhaps Essex wished to separate himself from his second spouse, or perhaps he merely wanted the company of his sister and his brother-in-law. He may have made the agreement because he needed ready cash to equip himself for the forthcoming campaign or had some premonition of death. Whatever the cause, the effects were far-reaching. Henceforth Essex and the Earl of Hertford lived under the same roof, worshipped together at Saint Clement Danes, frequented the same places in London, acted in concert, and fought for similar causes.

On 20 March Essex was ordered to proceed to York immediately, direct the vice-president of the Council of the North to muster the troops of Yorkshire and Durham, and then lead them all to

[13] See *H. M. C. Twelfth Report*, Appendix 2, p. 216; and *Ninth Report*, Appendix 2, p. 498.

[14] Kingsford, "Essex House," pp. 1–54. Also see Norman G. Brett-James, *The Growth of Stuart London* (London: G. Allen and Unwin, 1935), p. 148.

Newcastle, where he was to meet Sir Jacob Astley.[15] After joining
Astley, Essex was supposed to arrange for the reinforcement of Berwick
and Carlisle. If the Scottish army moved toward the Border, he was
to assemble all the troops in the northern counties and act in the
best interests of his King and the English nation. To prepare the
way for Essex, the Earl of Arundel wrote Henry Clifford, the Earl
of Cumberland, to this effect: "My Lord Essex is coming swifter
than I can. If your Lordship see him at Newcastle, I am sure that
your Lordship will use him as the King's General, and I hope to
see you soon after him."[16] Until his superiors arrived, then, Essex
was the "King's General."

Upon reaching York on 22 March, Essex consulted with Sir
Edward Osborne and Sir Arthur Ingram about the condition of
the army and informed them that the paymaster would soon arrive
with money for the troops. The following day Essex hastened toward
the Border. He met Astley at Newcastle and began to ferret out
intelligence regarding the troop movements of the Covenanters.[17]
He no doubt learned that on 21 March they had won Edinburgh
"without a stroke" and seized the King's arsenal at Dalkeith, where
they had carried off the crown jewels, arms, and powder. He probably heard that the Scots had occupied Dumbarton. The tidings
from Berwick gave cause for alarm; intelligence reports indicated
that a Scottish contingent was on the move. "We are informed the
Covenanters intend to take this town," the mayor of Berwick warned
Essex, "and we have called on the Scotsmen in this town of all
degrees before us this morning, who have taken the oath of supremacy and allegiance willingly."[18]

Essex seized control of this situation, which called for prompt
action. Using the rather broad authority in his instructions, he
ordered Lord Clifford to secure Carlisle. He and Astley then
mustered together 1,000 foot and 100 horse soldiers and hastened
toward Berwick to ensure English control of the bridgehead across
the Tweed. They arrived on 1 April and secured the bridge. Essex
encountered no Scottish opposition and was warmly welcomed by
the citizens. "And that Noble Earl by his resolution, good conduct

[15] Devereux, *Lives of the Devereux*, 2: 309–12.

[16] *H. M. C. Third Report*, Appendix 2, p. 40.

[17] Knowler, *Strafford's Letters*, 2: 317.

[18] This letter from Mayor William Nemo et al. is printed in *H. M. C. Twelfth
Report*, Appendix 2, p. 217.

and celerity," wrote Secretary Coke to Windebank, "hath both
done this good service to His Majesty; and won himself much honour
and gotten the soldiers' hearts." [19]

On 5 April, having attained his objective, Essex deputed a governor to command the troops in Berwick and then returned to
York to participate in some strategy discussions.[20] The need for
such deliberations was legion. Charles found himself with little
money and insufficient troops for a long campaign. The English
nobles had not responded so enthusiastically as Charles and his
advisers had hoped. Those deputy lieutenants charged with
recruiting troops in their counties had not raised the designated
quotas. The ranks of the trained bands which had arrived on
schedule were filled with many undesirables who committed
robberies and resorted to violence while passing through the
countryside. The worst news, however, came from Scotland, where
George Gordon Lord Huntley had capitulated to the Covenanters,
thus giving them a more solid front. Especially important was the
fact that the Covenanters could then concentrate additional
troops along the Border. One rumor estimated Leslie's army at
30,000 men. Faced with these stark realities, the English sovereign
and his advisers changed their plans. They also proclaimed a free
and general pardon to all but nineteen covenanting lords, thereby
hoping to divide the people from their leaders. Thus, instead of
launching an invasion, the King and his advisers decided to hold
fast to their positions, bid for time, and avoid any direct confrontation with the Covenanters.

As instructed, Essex returned to Berwick and retained his command over that town until the arrival of Robert Bertie, the Earl of
Lindsey. One week later he wrote Windebank, the King's secretary
in London: "I promise you we will not be cozened of the town,
and if we should, as I fear it not, it would be sold so dear, the
victors shall have no occasion to bray, although all our men and
officers know not what discipline means. The Scots hath stopped all
comers from us; this town being fed from thence, puts us to a little
strait, still we can be provided out of England. But I have stopped
all transport of coals into Scotland, which they cannot well want." [21]

[19] Devereux, *Lives of the Devereux*, 2: 310.

[20] *C. S. P. Dom., 1639*, p. 37.

[21] Devereux, *Lives of the Devereux*, 2: 313. Also see *Miscellaneous State Papers*,
ed. Philip Yorke, Earl of Hardwicke, 2 vols. (London, 1778), 2: 127 (hereafter
cited as *Hardwicke State Papers*).

Essex remained in Berwick for three weeks, during which time he
was joined by Clanricarde and the Earl of Newcastle.

In the King's camp, meanwhile, dissension ruled. Lord General
Arundel and the Earl of Newport quarreled over military strategy.[22]
Charles discovered that some English peers dared to defend the
Scottish National Covenant. Worse yet, he discovered that Lord
Saye and Lord Brooke, while agreeing to defend England, categorically refused to commit themselves and their troops to an armed
invasion of Scotland. There were no English laws or customs, they
contended, that called upon Englishmen to commit aggression
against their Scottish compatriots. To prevent this political heresy
from spreading, the English sovereign called together all his
peers on 21 April and required them to take an oath of loyalty and
obedience. All but two lords subscribed. Lord Saye, shrewdly
requesting time to consider the matter, doubted the legality of an
oath which required him to kill a fellow subject. Lord Brooke
refused to sign on similar grounds. Both peers were promptly
placed under arrest and held in custody, but several days later, after
receiving some legal advice from Attorney General Banks, the
King released them. Taking his soldiers with him, Lord Saye
left York, contending that, according to feudal custom, the attendant men belonged to him not the King.

The Covenanters soon provided Essex with an opportunity to
prove his loyalty. On 19 April, Montrose, Rothes, Argyll, and
eleven other Covenanters wrote Essex a letter of appeal and accommodation. Portraying themselves as law-abiding subjects whose
actions were continually misunderstood, they cast the blame upon
those "of greatest place and credit, whose private bias runs wide
and clean contrary to the publick good."[23] Denying their desire
for war, the Covenanters appealed to Essex to mediate between
them and the King. "God is our witness," they wrote, "that we
desire no National quarrel to arise betwixt us, or to taste the bitter
fruit which may set ours and childrens teeth on edge, but rather
hold our selves obliged in conscience of our duty to God, our Prince
and all our Nations, and our Brethern, to try all just and lawful
means for the removal of all causes of difference betwixt the two
Nations, who are yet linked together, and should be still in all the
strongest bonds of affection and common interests, and to be always

22 From the Rutland diary in *H. M. C. Rutland Manuscripts*, 1: 507.

23 Sloane MSS 650, fol. 93. This letter, dated 19 April 1639, is printed in
Bibliotheca Regia (London, 1659), pp. 363–66.

ready to offer the occasion of greater satisfaction in this kinde, of clearing our Loyal intentions to our Prince, and to all whom it may concern, as namely to your Lordship in regard to your place and command at this time, by means whatsoever shall be thought expedient on both sides."

On 21 April the Earl of Essex, still in command at Berwick, received word that a messenger wanted safe-conduct guarantees so he could present Essex with the aforementioned letter from the Covenanters.[24] Essex, obviously hoping to avoid any compromise gestures which might be misconstrued by his rivals and the King, was so "troubled" and uncertain about handling the matter that at first he refused to grant the safe-conduct. He confided in Clanricarde, and they decided to consult the Earl of Newcastle, one of the King's most trusted lords, before taking any action. The peers agreed to grant the safe-conduct and receive the messenger, William Cunningham, who then proceeded south to Berwick, where he read a copy of the controversial letter to the three earls. Upon hearing the contents, Essex promptly refused to break the seal and read the original. When Cunningham attempted to discuss the document at greater length, Essex would not listen but did agree to forward the sealed letter to His Majesty.

To forestall any attacks upon his integrity and remove all doubts about his honorable intentions, Essex immediately forwarded the Covenanters' letter to Charles, along with a covering letter in his own hand.[25] He explained to the King the nature of the overture made to him at Berwick and, denouncing the authors as ungrateful, emphasized that he was very disturbed about being sought by the Scots as a mediator. Anticipating the aspersions of his enemies, Essex disclaimed any separate negotiations with the covenanting lords. To demonstrate his loyalty, Essex asked the King to exclude him from any pacification negotiations which might result from these or other gestures.

The damage, however, had been done: thereafter Essex was suspect. The King read the Covenanters' letter and returned it to Essex without comment.[26] The Earl of Holland, who learned of the contents, took advantage of the opportunity to besmirch his rival's

[24] *C. S. P. Dom., 1639*, pp. 38, 99, 137; and Baillie, *Letters*, 1: 204.

[25] His letter, describing the whole episode, is in *H. M. C. Ninth Report*, Appendix 2, p. 439. Posted from Berwick, it bears the date 22 April 1639. I have seen no reference to it in any secondary accounts.

[26] Wedgwood, *The King's Peace*, p. 265.

reputation by labeling him a traitor. Lord General Arundel was affronted because the Covenanters had directed their accommodation gestures toward Essex, an inferior officer, rather than himself. Before long both Arundel and Holland received similar communications from the Scots, as did the Earl of Newcastle in May.[27] Charles answered the Covenanters by leading his army toward the Border.

While the royal retinue was entertained at Raby Castle, the country seat of Sir Henry Vane, comptroller of the household,[28] Essex appeared on 2 May to reaffirm his loyalty to the Crown. Three days later the army arrived at Durham, where, in the ancient cathedral, Charles, Arundel, Essex, and several other nobles listened to Bishop John Cosin denounce the evils of rebellion and the virtues of obedience to the King. This homily, later printed and widely distributed by royal command, was based on the familiar biblical injunction "Let every soul be subject unto the higher powers." Although Essex later repudiated the substance of Bishop Cosin's views on the subject, he appears to have adhered to the doctrine of obedience on the eve of the Puritan upheaval.

The King's army marched into Newcastle on 9 May. Arundel rode at the head of the army, "gallantly mounted and vested *a la soldado* with scarf and panache." [29] The troops were welcomed with chiming bells and cannons. The King remained in the port town for a fortnight. On the day of his arrival he issued a proclamation which contained a general pardon for all the Scottish rebels. It was promulgated in church in the presence of the army commanders, Essex included, and the following day Charles reviewed his troops. If the King was unhappy about the size and condition of his army, he did not show it by his actions, for he continued his march toward the Border. The last stage of the journey further weakened the troops. The soldiers were plagued with unseasonably hot weather, inadequte supplies of water and food, a smallpox epidemic, and an ominous eclipse of the sun. Berwick, moreover, offered little relief to a discomforted and disorderly army. The town was too small to contain the English troops; consequently, they camped in an open area southwest of the port.

Essex remained with his soldiers and close to his sovereign during those unsettling days. Doubtless he wanted to disprove his detractors

[27] *Bibliotheca Regia*, pp. 366–68.
[28] *H. M. C. Rutland Manuscripts*, 1: 510.
[29] Devereux, *Lives of the Devereux*, 2: 319.

with outward demonstrations of devotion and loyalty. If he hoped to regain his sovereign's complete confidence and receive the assignment to lead a contingent against the Scots, he did not succeed, for Charles appointed others to perform the task.

On 1 June the Earl of Arundel led a small group across the Tweed, ceremoniously read a royal proclamation calling upon the people of Scotland to be obedient and loyal subjects, and then marched back the same day without a skirmish. Two days later, in response to intelligence reports that the Scottish army under Leslie was near Kelso, the King sent the Earls of Holland and Newcastle with 300 horse and 3,000 foot soldiers to confront the enemy. When Holland encountered a superior Scottish army in the vicinity of the town, he halted his advance, exchanged threats with Leslie, and then decided to withdraw to the Border. Pursued by the Covenanters, Holland returned to Berwick, where he became the butt of ridicule for his cowardly actions. He blamed the retreat on Arundel's scoutmaster. By the middle of June the English field commanders were fighting among themselves more vigorously than against the Covenanters. Essex remained on the sidelines.

In the midst of these reverses the English monarch decided to initiate negotiations with the Scots. In early June he received word that the aldermen of London had turned down his request for a loan. About the same time he was advised by his wife, his Privy Councilors, and Sir Thomas Wentworth, the lord deputy of Ireland, to temporarily abandon his plans to invade Scotland, lest he suffer a military defeat at the hands of the rebellious Covenanters.[30] When Charles saw the size and condition of the Scottish army as they encamped across the Tweed and compared it with his own demoralized soldiers and divided command, he decided to follow the suggestions of those who recommended pacification. The Scots responded favorably to the preliminary gestures. According to Thomas Harrison, the covenanting lords expressed their preference for Essex over Arundel as the principal negotiator.[31]

Peace negotiations began on 11 June in the lord general's tent, situated outside Berwick. The English delegation included Essex, Arundel, Holland, Salisbury, and Berkshire, and the Scottish delegation was composed of Rothes, Dunfermline, Loudon, Alexander Henderson, and Warriston. For a week the negotiators met

[30] Ogle, *Clarendon State Papers*, 1: 180.
[31] *C. S. P. Dom., 1639*, p. 264.

daily to discuss alternatives to war. Essex, the only English commissioner who was not a Privy Councilor, appears to have attended
the sessions, but he was overshadowed by others in higher places.
The passive role he played may well have been deliberate, for
according to Clarendon, "the Earl of Essex, still preserving his
grandeur and punctuality, positively refused to meddle in the treaty,
or to be communicated with." [32] Charles dominated the meetings. [33]
Arundel foolishly rebuked the Covenanters for following the path
of rebellion and war to achieve their selfish ends. Warriston and
Henderson endangered the negotiations with intemperate language
and harsh demands. Argyll was courteous and moderate but firm in
presenting the Covenanters' case. Despite many heated words and
serious reservations on both sides, a compromise was achieved.
Charles promised the Covenanters another Parliament and a
General Assembly to resolve the religious differences. The armies
would be withdrawn from the Border and then disbanded.

The Pacification of Berwick was signed on 19 June in Arundel's
tent. [34] Peace, though tenuous, prevailed along the Tweed. Many of
the English lords remained behind for a pacification feast hosted
by General Leslie. There the English sovereign played a game
of ninepins with his erstwhile enemies. Abraham Cowley commemorated the pacification with a short poem, which captured the
optimism of the moment:

> This happy concord in no blood is writ,
>   None can grudge Heaven full thanks for it:
> No mothers here lament their children's fate,
> And like the peace, but think, it comes too late.
>   No widows hear the jocund bells,
>   And take them for their husbands' knells:
> No drop of blood is spilt, which might be said
> To mark our joyful holiday with red. [35]

If Essex disapproved of the conduct of the English field commanders in the first Bishops' War, as he very likely did, he left no
record of his sentiments. He probably resented the King's reliance
upon Holland rather than himself. The King further abused Essex
when, in public, he summarily dismissed the Earl from his command,
causing a great loss of dignity. "The earl of Essex, who had merited

32 Clarendon, *History*, 2: 48.
33 *Hardwicke State Papers*, 2: 139.
34 *H. M. C. Rutland Manuscripts*, 1: 513.
35 Abraham Cowley, *Works* (London, 1684), p. 7.

very well throughout the whole affair," wrote Clarendon, "was discharged in the crowd, without ordinary ceremony."[36]

II

ESSEX returned to London after the Bishops' War and remained aloof from public affairs for many months. He did not participate in Charles's triumphal return to London in early August. He did not attend the round of festivities in honor of the Queen Mother. He did not partake in the Feast of Saint George, held at Windsor in October, for he was not named to fill one of the three vacancies in the Order of the Garter. He was, seemingly, piqued because Charles questioned his loyalty, neglected to honor him for services rendered, and turned to others for military advice and service.

It was Essex's rivals and enemies who reaped the honors, rewards, and places in the following months. Not the least of these was the lord deputy of Ireland, Viscount Wentworth, who was summoned by Charles to return to England. Once back in Westminster, Wentworth became the King's principal adviser.[37] The lord deputy dominated the new ruling junta within the Privy Council. He had established a strong and efficient government in Ireland; he would now duplicate his feat in Scotland. Wentworth wanted war. Wentworth wanted to summon the Irish Parliament. Wentworth wanted to manage the English Parliament. Wentworth wanted a new Council of War. Wentworth wanted different generals. Wentworth got what he wanted. Charles named the Earl of Northumberland as commander in chief and Lord Conway as General of the Horse, replacing Arundel and Holland respectively, and then proceeded to reconstruct the Council of War along different lines. He not only passed over Essex in each instance but elevated Wentworth to the earldom of Strafford and eventually appointed him to fill Essex's place as lieutenant general.[38]

These changes galled Essex, an envious lord, and caused resentment among the other officers who had been shoved aside. "For I am sure, at that time no Man was more forward in His Majesty's Service than the Earl of Essex," observed Sir Edward Walker, "and had His Majesty been pleased the succeeding Year to have

[36] Clarendon, *History*, 2: 52.

[37] Collins, *Letters and Memorials*, 2: 623; and C. V. Wedgwood, *Strafford* (London: Collins, 1966), pp. 270–84.

[38] *C. S. P. Dom., 1639–1640*, p. 321.

made him General instead of the Earl of Northumberland, in probability the Success of that Undertaking had been more fortunate, and that Earl not so much discontent as he was."[39] Clarendon reached a similar conclusion: "I am persuaded if this war had been left to the managery of the same officers, or rather if the earl of Essex had been made general . . . the earl of Essex would have discharged his trust with courage and fidelity, and therefore probably with success."[40] Charles and Wentworth committed a serious blunder from which neither fully recovered.

Rebuffed and resentful, Essex now cast his lot with those disgruntled peers and commoners who looked to Lord Saye and John Pym for leadership. This opposition faction, involved in a dangerous game that bordered on treason, began to communicate with some Covenanters who had come to London to plead their cause before the English sovereign. "The earls of Essex, Bedford, Holland, and Lord Saye, Hampden and Pym and diverse other lords and gentlemen of great interest and quality were deep in with them," Bulstrode Whitelocke noted.[41] The significance of this connection between the opposition groups of the two nations can hardly be overemphasized. It gave the Covenanters a voice, however weak, and an ear in England. More important, it gave to the English opposition religious and political creeds and rationalizations to justify reform in the church and rebellion in the state. This marriage of convenience produced a revival of the doctrine of resistance and rebellion, a Committee of Both Kingdoms, a Solemn League and Covenant, and a Westminster Confession. Through this union the dynamic, even revolutionary, Calvinism which had made possible the Scottish Kirk in the sixteenth century was transmitted to England. Without this fusion of Scottish Calvinism and English Puritanism the Great Rebellion might well have been abortive.[42]

[39] Sir Edward Walker, *Historical Discourses upon Several Occasions* (London, 1705), p. 347.

[40] Clarendon, *History*, 2: 80.

[41] Bulstrode Whitelocke, *Memorials of English Affairs*, 4 vols. (Oxford, 1853), 1: 94. The Devereux papers in the British Museum include some letters which Pym forwarded to Essex in 1639, evidence that the two men corresponded. See Additional MSS, 46,189.

[42] On this thesis see my article, "Essex and the Aristocratic Opposition to the Early Stuarts," *Journal of Modern History* 32 (1960): 224–33; and Leo Solt, "Revolutionary Calvinist Parties in England under Elizabeth and Charles I," *Church History* 27 (1958): 234–39.

A ground swell of popular discontent during the early months of 1640 strengthened the hand of the · opposition. The sheriff of Yorkshire encouraged the local gentry to refuse to pay the hated ship money, while a grand jury in Northamptonshire declared the collection of ship money illegal. Puritanism caused even greater unrest. In Huntingdon the vicar of Saint Ives complained that his whole parish refused to receive the sacrament at the altar rail. In Lewes a group of justices protested against the Laudian alterations made in the Sussex churches. In Northumberland the Puritan meetings prospered while half the church pews were reputed to be empty.

The elections to the Short Parliament took place in this restless environment. The Privy Council made every effort to secure the return of commoners who would support the policies of the Crown or what was called the Court Party, while the leaders of the opposition Country Party hoped to elect enough commoners to constitute a majority in the Lower House. Some royal and pocket boroughs witnessed no contests, for their representatives were hand-picked. However, many borough and county elections degenerated into contests between rival families or factions. In some cases the elections were so close that cautious sheriffs issued double returns, thus allowing the House of Commons to decide which candidate was duly elected. For over a century the Crown had managed to secure places for the royal officials and advisers, and for a quarter of a century the opposition leaders, including nobles in the Upper House, had secured seats for men of their persuasion. The election techniques of both groups were similar. While the Earl of Lindsey lined up seats for his son Sir Peregrine Bertie, Lord Saye found safe places for his two sons. While Edward Nicholas, a Court nominee, lost his election in Sandwich, the opposition candidate from Hastings lost his to a Court nominee. Nevertheless, when all the returns were in, the opposition appeared to have the edge.

The Earl of Essex strongly influenced the nomination and election of several M.P.'s to the Short Parliament.[43] The recipients of his patronage included Sir Walter Devereux, who sat for Lichfield; Sir Walter's son-in-law Sir Edward Littleton, who sat for Staffordshire; Sir John Meyrick, who represented Newcastle; and Sir

---

[43] In *Newcastle-under-Lyme*, p. 143, Pape writes: "The Earl of Essex strongly influenced the election of the Staffordshire borough members, as four of his nominees were returned, two for Tamworth and one each for Lichfield and Newcastle."

Simon Archer and George Abbott, both of whom sat for Tamworth. Sir Walter had assisted his brother in a duel in 1613, served under him in the Palatinate, and helped him in Ireland. Significantly, shortly before the Parliament convened, Essex conveyed his estates in Hereford, Middlesex, and Wales to Sir Walter, Meyrick, and three others, under the condition that he receive the income from the properties as long as he lived.[44] That these men were dependent upon their benefactor during the session and after seems obvious. Two of these nominees were sons of Elizabethans who had been Essexians. Littleton, whose father had participated in the Essex conspiracy of 1601, had served faithfully in several local offices. Reputed to have been a nonconformist, he remained committed to Parliament for the first two years of the Civil Wars. Welsh-born Sir John Meyrick, son of conspirator Sir Gelly, had served under the third Earl of Essex on the Continent and in Scotland. Abbott, known as "the Puritan," later won a seat in the Long Parliament as a recruiter. It is of course impossible to determine how the men in Essex's faction stood on particular issues or how they voted in the Short Parliament, but in all likelihood they took their cues from Essex in the Upper House and from Pym in the Lower House.

Parliament convened on 13 April 1640 in Westminster. The King, dressed in his regal robes, occupied the throne on an elevated platform at one end of the hall, while ten-year-old Prince Charles, elegantly appareled, sat at his left hand. The peers, in richly colored parliamentary robes, assumed their rightful places according to the customs of precedence; and then the Commoners were summoned to attend the King and listen to his speech announcing the purpose of their gathering. Charles turned to Lord Keeper Sir John Finch, who explained that the primary purpose of calling Parliament was to provide the King with monies to fight the Covenanters. The Commoners, therefore, should be generous and grant liberal subsidies, pass a retroactive bill giving Charles tonnage and poundage for the entire reign, and confirm the customs duties the King had levied. Then, and only then, would the English sovereign entertain grievance petitions.

The Earl of Essex attended all eighteen daily sessions of the Short Parliament.[45] On 16 April he won appointments to the Grand

44 This information is incorporated into Essex's will, which was probated 17 February 1663.
45 Lords Journal, 4: 45–92.

Committee for Privileges and the subcommittee empowered to deal with the customs and orders of the Upper House. He also served on the Committee for Petitions. Essex and his fellow peers accomplished little in this Parliament but did change the procedure for handling petitions; initiate several new peers, including the Earl of Strafford; listen to several privilege cases involving freedom from arrest; and concern themselves with a few minor bills.

Under the leadership of John Pym, M.P. for Tavistock, the opposition in the Lower House seized the initiative and proceeded to deal with grievances before, rather than after, supplies.[46] They brought their complaints into the open and debated them during the first week. They received petitions against the religious policies of Laud and the tax measures of the Crown. They launched legislative inquiries into the Hampden ship-money case and the arrest of several M.P.'s. Neither the speaker of the house nor the King's nominees possessed enough persuasive power or votes to prevail. The King's request for supplies to finance another campaign in Scotland hardly received a hearing.

To reverse this trend and to prevent collusion between the two Houses, the King attended the House of Lords, somewhat unexpectedly, on 21 April, at which time he delivered a short but pointed speech. He castigated the Commons for inverting the order of business. He then reaffirmed his desperate need for money, defended his religious and ship-money policies, and promised that he would consider grievances, but only after the summer campaign in Scotland. "I conjure your lordships to consider your own honour and mine," he pleaded in conclusion, "and the preposterous course of the commons; and desire that your lordships will not join with them, but will leave them to themselves. I desire you to be careful in this point, else, if the Supply come not at this time, I will not say what mischief may and must follow."[47] After this thinly veiled threat, Charles left the House and turned matters over to the Lord Keeper. The Upper House then went into a committee of the whole and freely discussed the King's speech. After a lengthy debate the peers resolved: (1) that supplies should take precedence over all other matters and (2) that the Upper House should confer with the

[46] For Pym's role see Goodwin F. Berquist, "Revolution Through Persuasion: John Pym's Appeal to the Moderates in 1640," *Quarterly Journal of Speech* 49 (1963): 23–30.

[47] *Lords Journal*, 4: 63.

Lower House and persuade the Commons to put aside their grievances and vote to grant the money. Sixty-one Lords followed the leadership of Strafford in passing these resolutions, while twenty-five Lords who sided with the Commons' position voted against them. The nucleus of this dissenting group, which included Essex, was composed of those Defenders of Old English Honour who had earlier opposed the King and his father.

By the last week of April the two Houses were at loggerheads over the supply issue. The Commons refused to budge on the matter. Attempts to break the deadlock failed. Strafford, who hoped to split the Commons' majority, suggested that the King reduce his monetary demands and promise to discontinue the ship-money levy. This compromise did not placate the Commons. Thus, after some discussion of the matter in Privy Council on 5 May, the King dissolved Parliament.

Shortly thereafter the King struck back with vengeance at several leaders who had dared to oppose him. He arrested and imprisoned Saye, Brooke, Pym, Hampden, and Sir Walter Earle, and had their lodgings searched for evidence of complicity with the Covenanters. Essex was not implicated. Essex House was not touched. Though some contemporaries believed him guilty of traitorous contacts with the Covenanters, there is no evidence of any in Essex's extant papers. He remained a loyal, though embittered, lord in the wake of the Short Parliament. On the last day of May he was reappointed lord lieutenant of Staffordshire.[48]

III

REBUFFED BY THE House of Commons, the king turned to other sources for funds to use in warring against the Scottish rebels. From Convocation he secured a sizable benevolence.[49] From Strafford he received money and the promise of 8,000 Irish troops. From the Spanish, with whom Strafford had been negotiating, he obtained the promise of a large sum to be used in providing warships that would convoy troops to the Low Countries. From his trusted advisers and courtiers he received grants and loans. He even tricked the merchants of London into lending him two hundred thousand

48 *C. S. P. Dom., 1640*, p. 249.
49 Whitelocke, *Memorials*, 1: 101.

pounds after seizing their bullion that had been deposited in the mint.

Meanwhile, military preparations for the forthcoming campaign went forward. Strafford, committed to a vigorous offensive war, made plans to take an Irish army to Scotland. He called for a blockade of Scottish shipping. He also began tampering with the Tudor system of recruiting and mustering, which relied upon the lord lieutenants and their deputies. This system, which had worked quite effectively during the sixteenth century, was no more dependable than the lord lieutenant in each county. Since most of the opposition lords served as lord lieutenants, Strafford was reluctant to entrust them with military authority. And yet, because these lords were popular leaders in their localities and were needed to maintain law and order, it was dangerous to abandon the whole system. Some changes were essential, for in many counties there was large-scale discontent in the ranks.[50] Throughout East Anglia the recruits broke into the local churches and removed the communion rails. In Wiltshire, the pressed soldiers protested against the northern expedition. In Derbyshire the mustered levies set fire to a mill and killed the deer in the Earl of Huntingdon's park. In Wakefield they released the prisoners in the house of correction. In Hereford, Oxford, Marlborough, and Leominster the troops resorted to violence of various types. Such was the army that Strafford hoped to put on the battlefield against the Scots.

Although some lord lieutenants were replaced as a result of these disturbances, Essex retained his position in Staffordshire. He delegated the responsibilities to deputies—Sir Henry Bagot, William Wrotlesley, and Thomas Compton—who mustered the levies and then marched them into Uttoxeter.[51] On 1 July while the deputy lieutenants were dining, some unruly soldiers left the billets and leveled the fences in the forest lands recently enclosed by the King. Essex, who had remained in London, was ordered by the Privy Council to apprehend those men who defied law and order. He appears to have handled the matter successfully through his deputy lieutenants.

Several members of the aristocratic opposition, extremely unhappy over the dissolution of the Short Parliament, had in the

[50] For a discussion of the dissatisfaction see John Bruce, *Notes on the Treaty carried on at Ripon*, Camden Society Publications (London, 1869), p. xi.

[51] *C. S. P. Dom., 1640*, p. 374.

meantime befriended the Covenanters. Hoping to force Charles to call another Parliament, they urged the Covenanters to invade England and promised them financial assistance.[52] The initial invitation, probably verbal, came as no surprise to the leading Covenanters, for they had communicated with the Earl of Bedford, Lord Russell, Lord Saye, and Lord Brooke since the outbreak of the rebellion in Scotland. Yet, before launching an invasion of England, they demanded a written invitation, an engagement or agreement, from their English sympathizers. In midsummer they received what they wanted, a letter signed by seven peers—Essex, Bedford, Brooke, Warwick, Saye, Mandeville, and Savile—which in the guise of a refusal really invited the Covenanters and wished them well.

Essex's role in this treasonous enterprise was obscured by the subsequent statement of Lord Savile, an ambitious rival of Strafford, that the letter was a forgery. If a forgery, it exonerates Essex of any direct collusion with the Covenanters; if authentic, it is clear evidence of complicity in the invitation. Whatever the case, Essex was closely associated with the other six peers; he was sympathetic with their political ends; the Scots did invade England as a result of the letter; and Essex's actions later in the summer served to raise doubts about his loyalty.

On 20 August the Covenanters crossed the Tweed at Coldstream and, according to plans known to the English conspirators, pushed southward to Newcastle. One week later, after inadequate preparations, Charles led his army north from York to confront the enemy. His foot soldiers proved to be exceedingly disorderly and prone to violence; the northern gentry, especially those in Yorkshire who opposed an offensive war, only gave half-hearted co-operation; and the illness of the lord general necessitated a reshuffling of commands. Northumberland's place was filled by his subordinate, Lord Conway, an experienced but indecisive general; Conway's placed was filled by Strafford, a decisive but inexperienced leader. Essex and the other generals excluded from the previous campaign were again ignored.

[52] I am deeply indebted to Prof. Glenn Gray for the information dealing with the English invitation to the Covenanters in the summer of 1640. Besides making available to me his notes from both published and manuscript sources too numerous to mention, he gave me the benefit of his interpretation of these events. For the traditional, but somewhat outdated version, see Gardiner, *History*, 9: 179.

The Covenanters took full advantage of the English weaknesses. In short order, under Leslie's command, they took Wooler and then Newburn, thus outflanking Berwick and the English contingent stationed there. On 30 August the Scots took Newcastle without even firing a shot; Lord Conway had evacuated the town and retreated to Durham rather than risk defeat. The King and Strafford, meanwhile, fell back to York with their troops. Faced with a superior military force, all that Charles could hope to salvage from the situation was an armistice; and an armistice there would be.

During these humiliating events Essex remained at his mansion on the Strand. He and the Earl of Bedford, another excluded and embittered peer, joined Warwick, Saye, Brooke, Pym, and Hampden in discussions the ostensible purpose of which concerned the colonization of Providence Island; the real reason concerned a request by the Scottish Covenanters for assistance from the disgruntled nobles and gentry of England. It is evident that there were communications between some of the Covenanters and these peers. These English nobles met in Warwick's London house to discuss the Scottish request and the possibility of extending the National Covenant to England. They refused to assist the Scots with money and man power or to support the National Covenant, but they did launch a concerted drive for another English Parliament.

The King, who was kept abreast of these developments by the Queen, commanded his Privy Councilors in London to break up the clandestine meetings of the opposition peers. He ordered Cottington, who had been named lieutenant of the Tower, to maintain law and order in the City at all costs. He then named the Earl of Arundel the captain general of all forces south of the Trent and commissioned him to protect Queen Henrietta Maria and his two young sons. Arundel ordered the Earl of Bedford to return to the country and personally assume his duties as lord lieutenant of Devonshire. The Privy Council and the Queen hinted that Essex should leave London and offer his services to the King, which would have required him to serve under Strafford.

Essex ignored the suggestions: he was too deeply committed to the opposition to retreat. Instead, he remained in London with his embittered colleagues and assisted them in preparing a petition addressed to the King.[53] Joining him and Bedford, whose names

---

[53] For Essex's role in these meetings and the events which followed see Windebank's correspondence with Charles in Ogle, *Clarendon State Papers*, 2: 94–115.

appeared at the head of the signatured section of the document, were the Earls of Warwick, Bristol, Bolingbroke, Hertford, and Mulgrave, Viscounts Saye and Mandeville, and Lords Brooke, Howard, and Paget.[54] The petitioners enumerated their grievances and called for a new Parliament and a treaty with the Scots. In particular, they deplored the continued collection of ship money, the persistence of Laudian innovations in religion, the billeting of soldiers in violation of the Petition of Right, the favors shown to Roman Catholics in and out of the government, and the moves on the part of Strafford to transport Irish troops to fight the Scots in northern England. They felt that Parliament should redress these wrongs with new laws and punish those persons who had given the King evil counsel.

Essex's role in this petition remains somewhat obscure. He took part in the private discussions which produced the document. Windebank, the King's secretary in London, regarded him as something of the ringleader. Yet the document appears to have been drafted by Pym and Oliver St. John. Pym lodged in one of Essex's tenements along Milford Lane and St. John, a well-known London barrister, was later named an executor of Essex's estate. Essex's relationship with these men appears to have been professional and political rather than social. In all likelihood he was instrumental in securing the support and signature of his brother-in-law the Earl of Hertford for their document.

Shortly after the petition became public Henrietta Maria concluded that the King should be informed of Essex's actions and that efforts should be made to remove him from London. She wrote her husband and recommended that Essex be employed to fight against the Scots. Because Essex was quite sensitive about protocol, she cautioned, he should be personally invited by the King "in the most obliging way; that it will be of great importance to call him from the ill-affected lords here, and a great contentment to all kinds of people."[55] The council, which also took the matter under advisement, reached the same conclusion: Essex should be induced by the King to serve against the Covenanters. On 31 August, Winde-

---

[54] P. R. O., S. P. 16/465: 16. Essex's signature is on all three copies of this petition at the P. R. O. Folio 17, which includes six more signatures, was probably that of 9 September, alluded to in M. A. E. Green, ed., *Diary of John Rous*, Camden Society Publications (London, 1856), p. 93.

[55] *C. S. P. Dom., 1640*, p. 652.

bank wrote Charles of the council's deliberations and suggestions.[56] On the following day, after learning that Essex, Warwick, Bedford, and Saye had held another conference, Windebank again urged the King to send for Essex.

The King took the advice of his councilors and ignored the demands of the petitioners. On 2 September he commanded "all unattached Lord Lieutenants to return at once to their own counties," a move designed to disperse the opposition peers who had been meeting in London. All Englishmen, Charles lectured, should be "serving the King, every one upon his charge for the defence of the realm, which is taken as canonical in Yorkshire, and may be so in London."[57]

But Charles dealt separately with Essex, sending for him early in September, according to Sir Henry Vane.[58] Before Essex left London, however, he met with Privy Councilors Cottington and Dorset at Essex House.[59] What transpired at the meeting remains something of a mystery. The King either invited or commanded Essex to attend him in Yorkshire and to resume his military command. Essex almost certainly regarded this as a disingenuous gesture and refused, for the following day he appeared at the Council Board with Hertford to answer questions about his role in the August petition and his connections with the Covenanters. The councilors listened to Essex's answers and to his arguments for a new Parliament. After the meeting, Windebank wrote Charles that all was not well in the capital. The council was divided over whether a Parliament should be called. The opposition, continuing to meet in secret, encouraged apprentices to rise in protest. It seemed certain that the city fathers would soon petition for a Parliament.[60]

Meanwhile, Essex prepared to attend Charles at York,[60] leaving London on 15 September with his brother-in-law and Sir Francis Seymour. It is not clear whether this journey was a response to the King's personal request for Essex's presence or whether it was a

56 Bruce, *Treaty at Ripon*, p. 78.

57 This response comes from a notation dated 2 September in York and made by Charles on a letter he received from Windebank about Essex. Ogle, *Clarendon State Papers*, 1: 205.

58 *Ibid.*, p. 204. "I have already invited him and mean to do it more effectively," Charles claimed, "to come along with the forces of his country."

59 P. R. O., S. P. 16/464: fol. 45. This is from Windebank's notes about the meeting.

60 *C. S. P. Dom., 1640–1641*, p. 46.

response to the royal writ, issued on 7 September, demanding that he attend a meeting of the Great Council, which was to convene at York on 24 September.

The Great Council assembled at 9 A.M. on 24 September in the Hall of Deans near Yorkminster.[61] The King, speaking from a canopied seat at the upper end of the hall, opened the meeting with a conciliatory welcome designed to secure unanimous support. He invited the attendant lords, who numbered between seventy and eighty, to speak without fear of reprisal. Bristol criticized the royal policies advocated by Strafford. Lord Saye pleaded for a Parliament. Finally, after much debate Charles decided to concede to the wishes of his critics. He promised to call a Parliament as soon as possible. He promptly appointed sixteen English commissioners, including opposition peers, to negotiate a treaty with the Covenanters. Before concluding the first meeting he appointed six lords, led by Lord Privy Seal, the Earl of Manchester and Lord Chamberlain Pembroke, to secure a loan of two hundred thousand pounds from the city of London.

In subsequent deliberations Charles proved to be equally conciliatory. He yielded to the Scottish commanders' demand that truce negotiations be held at Ripon rather than York. When the opposition peers recommended some military reforms to the Great Council, Charles granted their suggestions. When the Earl of Clanricarde demanded that Strafford's administrative decision regarding his Irish lands be reversed, the King agreed, even though he undercut the position of his favorite minister. No doubt he hoped to win friends and divide his enemies through these numerous concessions.

Essex attended the meetings of the Great Council with his usual regularity. He said little, however, for Bristol and Savile dominated the debates; but his presence was obvious and his prestige fully recognized by the King. On 25 September he signed the letter the deputed lords sent in hopes of borrowing money from the City. He was one of the sixteen commissioners named to treat with the Scots.[62] Among those clergy who preached to the Great Council was Thomas Pestell, who had been Essex's chaplain during the reign of the late King and was now a royal chaplain in ordinary. That the King selected Pestell out of deference to Essex seems very

---

61 Nalson, *An Impartial Collection*, 1: 443.
62 *Hardwicke State Papers*, 2: 227.

likely. The King's reversal of Strafford's decision concerning Clanricarde's lands was also intended to appease Essex, since he too possessed much land in Ireland.[63]

The Treaty of Ripon, which Essex helped negotiate, was signed on 20 October.[64] It was, in truth, merely a truce. Both sides concurred that the final settlement should be postponed until after the forthcoming Parliament convened. The Scots were to occupy Northumberland and Durham as security and receive as maintenance for their army eight hundred and fifty pounds a day. Without a decisive battle the English sovereign lost the Bishops' Wars and the ensuing peace. In conceding to the Covenanters, Charles was also capitulating to the aristocratic opposition who negotiated the treaty and at the same time won their demand for a Parliament. Thus on the eve of the Long Parliament, Essex and his fellow peers held the balance of power in Great Britain. They stood as mediators between their King and his rebellious Scottish subjects and between the Crown and the commonalty. They had captured the initiative from the Crown during the Scottish crisis. That they would combine with their cohorts in the Lower House and impeach the King's evil councilors, particularly the Earl of Strafford, was a foredrawn conclusion.

Essex played a significant role, though a silent one, during these epoch-making events. His name, which brought back memories of his father; his reputation as a loyal but much maligned and excluded peer; his continuous interest in and devotion to the Protestant cause on the Continent; his faithful attendance and useful experience in the House of Lords; and his good birth, high honor and prestige all stood in sharp contrast to Strafford. If anyone should have received a high command in the 1640 campaign against the Scots, it should have been Essex. To appoint Strafford was a gross mistake and a personal insult to Essex. To bestow upon Strafford one of the highest and most envied honors in the land, the Order of the Garter, as Charles did in mid-September, and to exclude Essex, whose forebears had been members of the exclusive military order, was an invitation to trouble.

[63] *Ibid.*, p. 207.

[64] Bruce, *Treaty at Ripon*, p. 2. Essex attended all but one session, but he assumed a more passive role than Bristol and Saye, who dominated the negotiations. Also see Martin D. Needels, "The Treaty of Ripon" (M.A. thesis, University of Nebraska, 1966).

Shortly after the signing of the Treaty of Ripon, Essex's suppressed animosity toward Strafford manifested itself in public. "My Lord of Essex and the Deputy lately fell out," noted one contemporary, "because that Deputy advised the King for present war without delay; My Lord of Essex told him that advice argued him to be a traitor, and all others that should give the King such counsel. But now [Strafford] begins to comply with the nobles, and desires the King not to answer any objections that shall be made against him in Parliament."[65]

During the last week of October the Earl of Essex and his fellow commissioners proceeded southward to prepare for the forthcoming session of Parliament. Essex apparently returned via Chartley and Tamworth to transact some private business. In Tamworth he secured from the Earl of Chesterfield a proxy, which he soon put to use in the House of Lords. He then traveled to Woburn Abbey, the country estate of his political ally the Earl of Bedford, where he rejoined the commissioners.[66] There the whole party was entertained before returning to Westminster, where Strafford would get his due, with Essex one of the peers dispensing justice.

[65] J. P. Collier, *Trevelyan Papers*, Camden Society (London, 1872), p. 194.
[66] Gladys Scott Thomson, *Life in a Noble Household* (London: Jonathan Cape, 1950), p. 32.

CHAPTER 10

Essex and Strafford

I

THE LONDON WHICH Essex reentered on the eve of the Long Parliament seethed with anxious and angry people.[1] The rabble, incited by the opposition leaders, began to turn against the clergy, particularly the Archbishop of Canterbury, who had imprudently introduced new rites into the liturgy, and against the judges who sat on the Court of High Commission. More respectable Londoners defiantly rejected the King's men in several local elections and voted down the royally preferred nominee for Lord Mayor. While the government of London passed into the hands of the opposition, the rest of England, though less volatile, simmered with grievances and pent-up discontent. Most Englishmen in the countryside deeply resented the extraparliamentary taxes, especially the ship-money levies, and the consequent drain of wealth into the coffers of the King.

The widespread distrust and dissatisfaction manifested itself openly in the elections to the forthcoming Parliament.[2] Numerous grievance petitions were circulated and forwarded to the House of Commons. Heated contests developed in many county and borough elections. There was much shuffling for places, solicitation of votes, and management of elections. Many elections ended in dispute or near riot. Forty irregular election cases were turned over to the Lower House for final determination. Upsets were common. Some boroughs hitherto considered safe seats for the Court returned anti-Court members. In the final analysis the anti-Court party emerged victorious and thus controlled a majority of the seats in the House of Commons.

Essex used his patronage and popularity to make that victory

[1] See Valerie Pearl, *London and the Outbreak of the Puritan Revolution* (Oxford: Clarendon Press, 1961), especially pp. 107–160.

[2] See R. N. Kershaw, "The Elections for the Long Parliament, 1640," *English Historical Review* 38 (1923): 496–508.

possible. Although he did not control any pocket borough, as did the King and some peers, including Pembroke, he exerted influence in several local elections. "Certainly the power of the earls of Essex, Warwick, Bedford, and Pembroke," writes Mary Frear Keeler, "and of the lords Montague, Say and Sele, and Brooke is reflected in the return of members of their families and of strong Puritan groups from the areas where their estates lay."[3] The returns from Staffordshire, as usual, reflected Essex's personal power and prestige. County members Sir William Bowyer and Sir Edward Littleton, both elected at Stafford on 8 October, were sympathetic with the opposition's demands for reform. The same can be said of Lichfield's representatives, Sir Walter Devereux and Michael Noble. Devereux played only a minor role in the Lower House, but he was always ready to act in his brother's behalf. Noble, town clerk of Lichfield and a newcomer to Parliament, had grievances against the Court of High Commission and appears to have advocated ecclesiastical reform. The hundred-odd electors of Newcastle under Lyme returned Sir Richard Leveson, a man of Royalist sentiments who was later expelled, and Sir John Meyrick, a devoted dependent of Essex. It is probable that the electors selected Meyrick out of deference to his patron's rising popularity in national affairs. In Stafford, the borough closest to Chartley, Essex's influence was nil, for both of the elected gentry proved to be antiparliamentarians. In Tamworth, however, Essex made his influence felt in the election of Ferdinando Stanhope, a son of the Earl of Chesterfield, whose proxy he held, and William Strode, the outspoken critic of the Crown who favored radical religious reforms. When Strode preferred to serve for a Devonshire borough, Henry Wilmot, a professional army man who had fought with Essex on the Continent and had criticized Strafford, was selected to fill the vacated spot. Although wielding more influence than any other Staffordian, Essex did not have the complete backing of the local landowners.[4]

Because he held lands there Essex also exercised some influence in Herefordshire. In the county election held at Hereford Castle on 24 October the leading contestants, Sir Robert Harley and Fitz-william Coningsby, were Essexians. "Both were local men who seemed to have the general support of the country party," according

[3] Mary Frear Keeler, *The Long Parliament, 1640–41: A Biographical Study of Its Members* (Philadelphia: American Philosophical Society, 1954), pp. 9–12.

[4] *Ibid.*, pp. 62, 156, 254, 113, 250, 285, 348, 386, and 395 for the M.P.'s mentioned in this paragraph.

The Earl of Essex and Henry, Prince of Wales

The Earl of Essex, 1612

A miniature attributed to Isaac Oliver, reproduced by courtesy of the owner.

Frances Howard, Countess of Essex

Reproduced from the painting (artist unknown) in the National Portrait Gallery.

BASIS
VIRTVTVM
CONSTAN:
TIA.

VICO: HEREFORD

NOBILISSIMUS D.º

ROBERTUS DEVEREVX

COMES ESSEXIÆ:

The right Honourable and most noble ROBERT
DEVEREVX Earle of Essex and Ewe Visco: Here:
forde, Lord Bourchier & Louaine, Ba: Ferrers of Chart:
ley.

The Earl of Essex

From an engraving by Renold Elstrack, reproduced by the courtesy of the Trustees of the British Museum.

The Earl of Essex

From a painting by Daniel Mytens on loan to the National Portrait Gallery from the Duke of Portland.

The Earl of Essex and Soldiers Engaged in Military Exercises

From an engraving by William van de Passe, reproduced by the courtesy of the Trustees of the British Museum.

Chartley House in Staffordshire

The Illustrious Lord, Robert Deureux Earle of Essex and E.w. Viscount
Hereford Baron of Ferrers of Chartley. Lo: Bourchier & Louain, &c.

VIRTVTIS COMES. INVIDIA.

If Bounty, Courage, Curtesye Desert
Of noblest choice, could haue beē shew by Art
This one PIECE had exprest, Them ALL in THIS
Liues what perfection can or BEE or Is.
Essex; heyre to his FATHER: by his blood.
His birth, his honours GREAT his virtues GOOD.
What Time can add to Meritt for approu'd,
In ESSEX must last happy, that's BE
LOV'D.

The Earl of Essex in Armor

From an anonymous engraving in the National Portrait Gallery.

The Earl of Essex in Armor

From the painting by Robert Walker, reproduced by permission of the National Portrait Gallery.

An°. Dom̃: 1643

VERA EFFIGIES ROBERTI DEVEREVX COMITIS. ESSEX.

Robert Earle of Essex, his Excellence. Generall of ỹ Army,
Jmployed for ỹ defence of the Protestant Religion. ỹ safety of his
Ma:ᵗⁱᵉˢ Person. & of ỹ Parliament. ỹ preseruation of ỹ Lawes. Liberties. & Peace
of ỹ Kingdome. & protection of his Ma:ᵗⁱᵉˢ subiects from violence & oppression.

The Earl of Essex in Sash and Armor

Reproduced by courtesy of the Trustees of the British Museum
from a 1643 print, possibly engraved by William Faithorne.

The House of Lords (above) and the House of Commons (below)

From the frontispiece of Edward Husband's A Collection of all the publicke Orders *(1646).*

My lo:

Theare hath been a long and strict
obligation betwixt the famelise of my
lo: of Bedfourds and mine, Yeat in
this generall cause that wee are myn-
gaged in, which is for the maintenance
of religion, and the liberte and just
fredom of the subject of England, the
plotters againgt all theause growing
evrie day more maliciously bent to the
ruine of theam all, would have made
mee layed aside all perticulers ends
of my owne, But hearing by an intimat
frend of his, his desier to returne, really
to searue the perlement with his lyfe
and fortune, being very sensible of
his fault in deserting the pelement,
and beijng an eie widnes of theare
ill intentions to the distruction of this
kingdom, desired a pass to returne,
and my reception to this side, which
I deed by that great favor and trust
the perlement pleased to intrust mee
with, Which by the hazard of my lyfe use for your safetie
being this 30 of
Decr 1643   your lo: most humble
           servant   Essex

The Earl of Essex's Handwriting and Signature

*This letter from Essex to the Speaker of the House of Lords,
dated December, 1643, is reproduced from the original, which is
in the House of Lords Record Office.*

Essex on Horseback, 1643

Contemporary Broadside Showing Lord General Essex and a List
of His Victories

A Funerall Monument: or the manner of the Herse of the

most Renowned *Robert Devereux,* Earl of *Essex* and Ewe, Viscount *Hereford,* L. *Ferrers of Chartley, Bourchier* and *Lovaine, Englands* late Lord Generall, who deceased Septemb. 14. 1646. With a briefe Recirement of his valour and fidelity in the Kingdomes just Cause, against the Enemies of Religion, Parliament and Kingdome, whose Funerall is to be solemnized on Tuesday the 13. of October, 1646.

Broadside portraying the Funeral Cortege of the Earl of Essex

Reproduced by courtesy of the Trustees of the British Museum.

The Funeral Effigy of Essex, 1646

Reproduced from a contemporary broadside by courtesy of the Trustees of the British Museum.

to Miss Keeler, "but to safeguard their election they solicited the backing of the Earl of Essex." [5] The precise nature and extent of Essex's influence is not clear. He did not appear in person but perhaps rendered financial assistance or sent a letter of nomination. Both Essexians were returned to the Lower House after much politicking and the expenditure of over £150 for wine and lodging.

Essex also enjoyed the support of many friends and relatives who were elected to the Long Parliament through the influence of others. Sir Francis Knollys, a descendant on his father's side of the family, and Sir Thomas Walsingham, a cousin on his mother's side were elected, as was Sir Thomas Roe, diplomat and councilor, who corresponded with Essex on several occasions and resided at Essex House in the late 1630s. Antiquarian John Selden and solicitor Oliver St. John, both of whom had had legal dealings with Essex, were among the leading spirits of the opposition in the Lower House.

The opposition peers were preparing for the oncoming test of strength. The leaders of the so-called Country Party descended upon London, and several, especially Warwick, Brooke, and Holland, used their homes as meeting places for the anti-Court leaders in the forthcoming sessions. Essex occupied a central place in the inter-locking web of kinship and friendship that united the aristocratic opposition. In addition to being related to the Earl of Warwick, the Earl of Holland, and the Earl of Newport, he was, through his late aunt Dorothy Devereux, a cousin of the Earl of Northumberland and the Countess of Carlisle. Through his sisters and brothers he had connections with the Seymours, the Shirleys, and the Burkes of Ireland: Francis Seymour, a critic in the Lower House, was his brother-in-law, and the Irish Earl of Clanricarde, who held the English earldom of Saint Albans, was his half brother. Although some of these magnates did not share Essex's bitter resentment toward the King, most of them held Essex in high esteem and followed his leadership in the initial assaults upon the House of Stuart.

The proxy registrations for the Long Parliament reflect some of these interconnecting links. [6] Essex held the proxies of the Earl of

[5] *Ibid.*, p. 50. Also see Harley's letter to Essex in *H. M. C. Fourteenth Report*, Appendix 2, p. 65.

[6] From the House of Lords' MSS Proxy Books of 2 and 3 Charles I, which are not deposited in Victoria Tower but in the P. R. O. For the importance of the proxies, which are completely ignored by Firth, see my article, "The Arundel Case."

Chesterfield and the Earl of Kent. Later in the session, after Kent began to attend the Upper House, Essex secured Clanricarde's proxy. The Earl of Northumberland held the proxies of two cousins, the Earl of Leicester and the Earl of Danby, while the Earl of Warwick held those of the Earl of Sussex and Lord Robartes. Opposition leaders Bedford, Clare, Holland, Saye, and Mandeville each accumulated the maximum of two proxies. Thus, the anti-Court group controlled a fair-sized and cohesive bloc of votes: this explains how only about twenty peers obtained and maintained the initiative, or at least the balance of power, in the Upper House in the Long Parliament. Obviously, it was out of desperation that Charles created fourteen new barons during the first session of the Long Parliament.

The Upper House in 1640 was composed of 124 temporal lords and 26 spiritual lords.[7] The number who personally attended Parliament was considerably less. Two lords Lionel Cranfield, the Earl of Middlesex, and the Bishop of Lincoln, were excluded—the former by an impeachment sentence rendered in 1624, the latter by royal prohibition. Those who were summoned included 1 duke, 1 marquess, 63 earls, 5 viscounts, 54 barons, 2 archbishops and 24 bishops. However, during the first session of the Long Parliament, 38 temporal peers and 5 spiritual peers absented themselves and exercised the proxy privilege, thus giving the attendant peers additional voting power in the plenary sessions.

The King formally opened Parliament on 3 November.[8] To forestall criticism of unnecessary expenditure, he eliminated the customary processional. Instead, he appeared at the Upper House in his regal robes and ascended the elevated chair of state with little fanfare. To his left sat Prince Charles, a dark-complexioned youth, and the Earl of Bath, who bore the symbolic sword of state. To his right, bearing the cap of state, were the Earl of Essex and Robert Bertie, the Earl of Lindsey. Lindsey, who had fought with the second earl in the 1590s and with Essex himself in the Low Countries in 1624, possessed many of the honors that Essex lacked and envied. Within two years these friendly rivals would be at sword points—one fighting for the King, the other for Parliament.

After the King's speech, which emphasized the need for money

---

[7] See John Langton Sanford, *Studies and Illustrations of the Great Rebellion* (London, 1858), p. 285; and Firth, *House of Lords*, p. 24.

[8] *Lords Journal*, 4: 80.

and harmony, the peers commenced to organize themselves along traditional lines. They listened to the Clerk of the Parliaments read the Roll of Remembrances, received from the Lord Chancellor their assignments of committees, and conferred with a committee from the Lower House about arrangements for a fast day.

Essex secured places on the most important committees. He was appointed one of the Triers, was named to the Grand Committee for Privileges and to the smaller subcommittee which dealt with the customs and orders of the Upper House, and received a place on the influential Committee for Petitions, which then played a more central role in House business. Subsequently Essex was also appointed to several select committees which the Upper House established to deal with the disbanding of the armies, legal abuses, and the decay of trade. He was later named to a select committee concerned with religious grievances.

Essex assumed these parliamentary responsibilities with the eagerness of a zealot. He diligently attended the plenary sessions: not once did he miss a roll call. Because of his dependability and high sense of duty and because of his contacts with Pym, Hampden, and St. John, he frequently served as a conferee in discussions with leaders of the Lower House. In the eyes of Clarendon, "he was not a good speaker in public, yet having sat long in Parliament, and so acquainted with the order of it in very active times, was a better speaker there than anywhere else, and, being always heard with attention and respect, had much authority in debates."[9]

In Clarendon's judgment Essex was one of the leaders of the aristocratic opposition. Another one was the Earl of Bedford, a moderate man who, like Essex, had been excluded from high office and the Court and had a special detestation for the Court of Star Chamber, which had harassed him on several occasions. Lord Saye, the disgruntled peer who toyed with the idea of migrating to the New World along with his coreligionists, had several long-standing grudges against the Stuarts. He was most bitter over the religious policies of the King and Archbishop Laud. Because of his advanced religious views and daring espousal of popular causes, Saye was widely acclaimed in the Lower House and among the Puritans in and around London. Edward Montagu, Viscount Mandeville, the pious son of the Earl of Manchester, associated with the Puritan-dominated Providence Island Company and was

9 Clarendon, *History*, 3: 28.

Pym's closest connection among the peers. John Digby, the Earl of Bristol, very moderate and independent-minded, frequently supported some of the opposition leaders. In the early days of the Long Parliament these peers along with Warwick, Brooke, Bridgewater, Bolingbroke, and Hertford succeeded in capturing the political initiative from the King's adherents.

The return of Essex's longtime friend and ally John Williams, Bishop of Lincoln, the erstwhile critic of Charles who had been removed from office, harassed by the Star Chamber, and excluded from Parliament, constituted an early success of the opposition.[10] His assignments to the Committee for Privileges and the Committee for Petitions and his subsequent chairmanship of the Committee for Religion underscored the weakness of the King's party among the peers. His subsequent translation to the archbishopric of York in 1641 marked a clear victory for the reforming element among the peerage. In all likelihood Essex was instrumental in bringing about the return and elevation of Williams to preferment.

The opposition lords were individuals, first and foremost, indebted to no borough or county for their parliamentary actions. Their inherent differences and conflicting interests sometimes made unified action difficult to achieve. Yet, the existence of a common cause and a common enemy served to counteract the otherwise independent and centrifugal tendencies among them. The cause was the removal of "evil councilors" from high places; the enemy was the Earl of Strafford—Essex's bête noire—whose impeachment overshadowed all other business for the first six months of the Long Parliament.

II

THOMAS WENTWORTH, the Earl of Strafford, began his career in the Lower House as a critic of the Crown but later reversed himself and became a staunch supporter of Charles I.[11] He had the con-

10 *Lords Journal*, 4: 92. The significance of his return and his close relationship with Essex has been overlooked by scholars.

11 Throughout this chapter I have relied upon C. V. Wedgwood's revised biography of Strafford, *Thomas Wentworth: A Reevaluation*. Also see William L. Fish, "The Straffordians—A Cross Section of Conservative Political Thought," *Historian* 12 (1959): 341–55; Clayton Roberts, *The Growth of Responsible Government in Stuart England* (Cambridge: At the University Press, 1966), pp. 77–105; and Conrad Russell, "The Theory of Treason in the Trial of Strafford," *English Historical Review* 80 (1965): 30–49.

fidence of his King and enjoyed some support from relatives like the Earl of Cumberland and the Earl of Clare, but his enemies were numerous in both Houses of Parliament. He had alienated members of Parliament such as Selden when he switched from being a defender of the liberties of the subject to being a proponent of the royal prerogative. He had antagonized many gentry and aristocrats with his tough economic measures in England and Ireland and then made himself repugnant to the Scots and Puritans in England by advocating an armed invasion of Scotland and increased subsidies.

The Scottish Covenanters first had suggested that Strafford be removed from high office by impeachment—a suggestion which was considered by some opposition peers who gathered at York. Essex had intimated that Strafford would be punished in that manner.[12] Strafford sensed his vulnerability, so he remained in the North with the army. This Charles refused to permit: he commanded Strafford to attend the House of Lords. During Strafford's absence the opposition leaders carefully prepared for the forthcoming impeachment trial. They listened to the complaints of Irishmen who possessed either firsthand experience or secondhand knowledge of his hardfisted rule in Ireland and established a select committee to deal with all matters relating to that country. On 7 November, Pym hinted at misrule there, even suggesting that the Irish army had been brought to Britain expressly to reduce, not the Scots, but the English. On the same day Sir John Clotworthy, a disgruntled Irishman who had secured a seat in the Lower House through the influence of the opposition, openly attacked Strafford.

The frontal assault commenced on 11 November, the very day that Strafford assumed his seat in the Upper House. "My Lords," Pym charged in a full House, "in the name of the Commons of Parliament and the country I impeach Thomas, Earl of Strafford, Lord Lieutenant of Ireland of high treason. I am commissioned to request that he be removed from Parliament and committed to prison."[13] The Earl of Manchester, then Lord Privy Seal, commanded Strafford to kneel before the bar and listen to the formal accusation. Pym promised to deliver more complete charges later in the session. Meanwhile, the accused was deprived of his seat and taken into custody.

[12] Devereux, *Lives of the Devereux*, 2: 324.
[13] Rushworth, *Historical Collections*, 8: 3.

From that day until May the Earl of Essex strove to remove Strafford from office. Sometimes he worked in the open; often he labored behind the scenes; at all times he sought vengeance against his foe. On 12 November 1640 he was selected along with Bedford, Bristol, and three other peers to persuade the King to commit Strafford to prison. Charles I agreed to expedite the matter. On the following day, as the clerk noted in the *Journal*, "upon the Motion of the Earl of Essex, it was agreed by their Lordships, that the rest of their Lordships that have any occasion to go to him [Strafford] should in like manner acquaint the House first with it." [14] Essex's motion passed: thereafter Strafford's visitors became a matter of public knowledge and record.

On 25 November, Essex and his compeers listened to Pym read the original articles of impeachment, seven in number, which had been approved by the Commons the day before. Strafford, who was brought to the Upper House to face his accusers, refused to give direct answers to the charges. Instead, he bid for time and asked permission to consult with counsel and to examine witnesses. He also requested the names of those witnesses whom the prosecution planned to examine and two days later petitioned the Upper House for the right to cross-examine them. In effect, he appealed to his peers and judges for a fair trial.

The Lords did not decide rashly against Strafford on these procedural matters. It was in their own interests to guard their judicial power jealously: what happened to Strafford could set a precedent for what might happen to them. They balked at some demands from the House of Commons. They consulted their judicial assistants in the Upper House and searched for precedents. They then appointed a committee, which included Essex and most of the opposition peers, to confer with the Lower House about impeachment procedures. [15] This conference produced a compromise between the demands of the respective Houses. Strafford would have counsel and be permitted to cross-examine witnesses at the actual trial. A committee of the Upper House would be appointed to conduct the preliminary examinations of witnesses and take depositions, but a delegation from the Lower House would be present at the examinations.

[14] *Lords Journal*, 4: 91.
[15] *Ibid.*, p. 99.

Essex and his fellow anti-Court peers dominated this committee. The ten examiners, plus the five commoners who had drawn up the impeachment articles, were empowered to interrogate the witnesses behind closed doors and cautioned to keep the depositions secret. Later they were permitted to examine any member of the Lower House and any peer or judge sitting in the House of Lords. When Strafford learned that his impeachers would be present at the examinations, he first protested on grounds of precedent and fairness; he then asked that he might attend the examinations with counsel to confront his accusers and cross-examine the witnesses. He was politely ignored in both instances. Through the remainder of December, even through the Christmas season recess, Essex and the questioners accumulated evidence and substantiated the charges against Strafford.

Parliament also launched impeachment proceedings against other "evil counsilors." In early December the leaders in the Lower House set their sights upon Windebank, who was suspected of using his power in the Privy Council to protect recusants. Rather than confront his enemies, the King's secretary went into hiding briefly and then fled to France.[16] On 18 December the Archbishop of Canterbury, William Laud, was impeached for high treason, deprived of his seat in the Upper House, and taken into custody. The same fate awaited Lord Keeper Finch and the Bishop of Bath and Wells. A few days after Christmas, Sir George Radcliffe, Strafford's aide, and several judges were impeached by the Lower House.[17] These additional impeachments made Strafford's *cause célèbre* more complex and confusing, for they eliminated several Straffordians from the Upper House and at the same time prejudiced any testimony that they might give against Strafford.

In the midst of the concurrent impeachment proceedings the Upper House belatedly established a committee to consider the "manner of proceeding in judgements against peers."[18] Opposition lords like Essex, Warwick, Saye, and the Bishop of Lincoln predominated. On their recommendations the Upper House concurred that all material witnesses were disqualified from sitting as judges in the Strafford trial. This eliminated moderates such as Bristol and

16 Gardiner, *History*, 9: 247.
17 *Lords Journal*, 4: 119.
18 *Ibid.*, p. 115.

Northumberland, who had already testified, and cut many of Strafford's supporters in the Upper Chamber. Black Tom could expect little justice and less mercy from his enemies in the months that followed.

The events of the next month bear this out only too well. On 16 January in response to Pym's demand for speedier justice, the Lords turned over the depositions of the examination committee to the Lower House. This new evidence was then preempted by the prosecution in the Lower House to expand and augment the seven original impeachment articles. As a result of these rather irregular proceedings twenty-eight charges were produced and formally approved by the Commons on 30 January. Later that day Strafford, looking very pale, was brought before the bar in the Upper House to hear the prosecution's expanded indictment against him. The accused man asked for three months—about the same length of time consumed by his impeachers—to prepare his formal defense. His request was promptly denied. The Commons wanted to allow him merely a week end. The Lords, after some discussion, granted him two weeks, but they insisted that he answer the charges formally in writing.

The two weeks passed. On 13 February the defendant petitioned the Lords for more time to secure records and information from Ireland. His appeal was refused. Three days later he renewed his petition. It too was rejected. "On the Monday the Earle of Strafford sent this petition to the High House for some longer tyme," wrote Covenanter Robert Baillie, "my Lord Saye spoke somewhat for the petition; but Essex against it. On Tuesday the Lower House sent up a message by Mr. Pym, requireing that no more tyme might be granted."[19] In a rare instance the opposition peers were divided over Strafford, for Lord Saye followed a moderate course of action. Later in the week, after appearing personally before the Lords, Strafford benefited from this breach in the ranks when he was granted another week to perfect his case and redraft his two-hundred-page manuscript. In the interim the Lords, under constant pressure from the Lower House, produced several decisions regarding the forthcoming trial. They agreed that the bishops would not sit as judges because it was an *agitatione causae sanguinis;* they excused from the ranks of the judges those recently elevated peers who had acted as accusers in the House of Commons; they also granted

19 Baillie, *Letters*, 1: 301.

Strafford the right to counsel in his trial, but he was to have "no more use of counsel than the needs of just defence requires."[20]

On 24 February, Strafford was supposed to present his answer to the Upper House. The bishops and disqualified peers withdrew. The King called the accused to his side and talked at length before Strafford's counsel, Richard Lane, read the document. Item by item for three hours he repudiated the charges of the impeachers and defended Strafford on grounds of law, custom, and royal prerogative. At the end of the long session he requested that the Lords give him permission to cross-examine the witnesses. Permission was denied until the trial.

Preparations went forward very slowly. The Lords commenced to consider details for the trial, but they were continually confronted with questions about procedures from the Lower House. The Commons wanted to know where the trial would be held, whether some designated members of the Lower House or a specially appointed legal counsel would prosecute, and whether members of the Lower House would be examined at the trial. Time after time the peers conferred with the Commons about these and other matters relating to the forthcoming spectacle. The judges consulted precedents. The Lords searched their *Journal* for records of earlier impeachments.

By mid-March the two Houses finally agreed upon most of the details. The celebrated trial would begin on 22 March in Westminster Hall, which had been the scene of several state trials in medieval times and could accommodate all members of Parliament plus some spectators. After a great amount of disagreement over the right of counsel, the Lords compromised and agreed to allow it in matters of law but not in matters of fact. Under pressure from the Lower House, which had begun debate on a bill to strip the bishops of their temporal powers, the Upper House reaffirmed its earlier stand: the bishops could not attend the trial as judges.

Essex participated in most of these conferences and deliberations. On 12 March he came to the assistance of Lord Brooke, the popular Puritan peer, who made a speech which antagonized the Court party, especially the Earl of Bath. "The Lord Brooke was called to the bar yesterday by the Earl of Bath," a contemporary reported, "but excused by the Earl of Essex. The exception that Bath took was

[20] Rushworth, *Historical Collections*, 8: 20.

that in a speech he mentioned these heads, viz., God, the Parliament and the King, putting the King after the Parliament."[21] Essex, who undoubtedly shared Lord Brooke's views on the relationship between the King and Parliament, managed to protect his ally from a politically inspired counterattack.

Essex also took exception to Strafford's answer to the twenty-seventh article of the charge, which accused Strafford of imposing and collecting a tax in Yorkshire without lawful warrant. Strafford contended that the King's Great Council had consented to the tax —a contention which Essex contested. His compeers concurred, issued a protestation, and placed Essex on a conference committee to discuss the matter with the prosecution. At Essex's request the protestation was appended to the charges against Strafford.[22] Three days later the controversial petition of August 1640 was brought to the Upper House, read aloud, and recorded verbatim in the *Journal*. To remove all doubts regarding the loyalty and intentions of Essex and his fellow petitioners, the Lords passed a series of resolutions applauding the actions which Strafford had aspersed. One resolution praised the petitioners for their leadership in the matter. Another thanked Lord Mandeville and Lord Howard for delivering the document to the King. Finally, the Lords "Re-solved, upon the Question, *nemine contradicente*, That this House doth approve of the Substance and Contents of this petition, and do make it an Act of this House."[23]

Throughout the pretrial preparations the King gradually turned toward the opposition leaders to fill various government posts vacated by the impeached. More often than not the appointments were preceded by rumors—some true, some false—and followed by much criticism. In December 1640 it was rumored in London that Essex had been appointed to succeed Northumberland as General of the Army.[24] It is possible, though very unlikely, that the King offered Essex this post to remove him from London and that Essex refused to accept the honor. In January another false rumor had Essex appointed lord lieutenant of Ireland in Strafford's place.[25] In early February it was rumored that Bedford would be named

[21] *H. M. C. Twelfth Report*, Appendix 2, p. 273.
[22] *Commons Journal*, 2: 105.
[23] *Lords Journal*, 4: 189.
[24] *C.S.P. Ven.*, *1640–41*, p. 102.
[25] *C.S.P. Dom.*, *1640–41*, p. 439.

Lord Treasurer, Saye would be appointed master of the Court of Wards, Pym would be named Chancellor of the Exchequer, and Holles would become secretary of state. All these men, according to one contemporary, had private conversations with the Queen about the reshuffling. Another claimed that Charles, hoping to save Strafford, was on the verge of making these new appointments but changed his mind at the last moment.

On 19 February, just four days after the Upper House passed the Triennial Bill and a subsidy bill, the King actually named seven of his severest critics to the Privy Council: Essex, Bedford, Bristol, Hertford, Saye, Mandeville, and Savile. Some time later he bestowed the same honor upon Warwick. This concession to the opposition, generally believed to have been the Marquess of Hamilton's doings, "the king did cheerfully, but the calling and admitting men to that board is not a work that can be indifferent; the reputation, if not the government, of the state so much depending on it." [26] The King's attempt to win over these popular peers who might carry the Lower House with them, Clarendon went on to note, was not only hazardous but a serious mistake. Charles's government appeared popular, but in fact it gave rise to an inner group of loyal councilors, a cabinet-council or junta, to whom Charles turned for most advice.

III

Essex and his fellow opposition peers were not content with impeaching and removing those councilors who had rendered advice or made decisions for Charles I. They contended, as their medieval predecessors had on many occasions, that the monarchical system needed to be reformed. The Stuart sovereigns should be stripped of their excessive prerogative powers and made more dependent upon Parliament. The monarch should rely more upon parliamentary selected councilors for advice and decision making and less upon Privy Councilors or the Queen's courtiers. Parliaments should meet frequently—in fact, regularly—and they rather than the King should reform the body politic. The various courts and councils which the Tudor monarchs had used and abused to enhance the power of the Crown should be abolished. The peers, in short,

[26] Clarendon, *History* (1849 ed.), 1: 274.

should revert to pre-Tudor times, back to the days of the Lancastrian monarchs, when the power and privileges of their class were
greater. They should reassert themselves and recover their lost
rights and privileges.[27]

The need for change was obvious. The English sovereign could
not even defeat the Scots. The financial and military policies of his
government had, in effect, proved sorely inadequate. The profusion
of grievance petitions which poured into both Houses underscored
widespread dissatisfaction. Never in the history of parliamentary
government had the House of Lords received so many petitions
protesting abuses in the various judicatories of both church and
state. Never had so many commoners sought relief from injustice
and irregularities in the prerogative councils and courts by appealing
to the Upper House. To handle the flood of petitions, the House of
Lords established a select committee to examine abuses in the
courts of justice.[28] This committee, which Essex sat on, received
cases involving ship money, false arrests, violations of habeas
corpus, excessive bail and fines, and cruelty. The committee
generally listened to the grievance, consulted with the attendant
judges, and then recommended action to the whole House. Many
cases from lower courts were reversed; some were vacated; others
were transferred to common-law courts for retrial.

Before long both Houses began to consider the abolition of those
prerogative courts and councils which had been the mainstays of
Tudor and Stuart despotism. In late November the Lower House
also empowered a committee, which included John Selden and
Edward Hyde, to investigate the High Court of Chivalry, a civil-law
court that had been the center of graft and influence for several
decades. On 4 January 1641, Essex, Hertford, Warwick, Bristol,
Saye, and several other peers were appointed to inquire into the
Court of Star Chamber. One week later two larger committees, both
of which included Essex, began to draft legislation designed to
eliminate the abuses in the prerogative courts. One bill aimed to
prevent the disposal of judicial places to those persons receiving

[27] For a more complete statement of the reactionary nature of the nobility's
resistance see my "Essex and the Aristocratic Opposition to the Early Stuarts,"
pp. 224–33.

[28] Virtually all of the material in this section has been garnered from the
Lords Journal, 4: 80–290. Goldwin Smith's treatment of this subject, "The Reform
of the Laws in England, 1640–1660," *University of Toronto Quarterly* 10 (1941):
469–81 is weak in its discussion of the early years of the Long Parliament.

pensions from a foreign power. According to the second and more important bill, henceforth judges would hold their places not by the King's pleasure but on the basis of good behavior. The King, upon learning of this measure, agreed to introduce the reform which ensured a more independent judiciary without further ado—a clear victory for those who adhered to the principles of Sir Edward Coke.

The proposal of the Lower House to make the calling of Parliament independent of the Crown moved more slowly, for it encountered resistance. The Commons wanted Parliament to meet regularly, preferably annually, according to statutes passed during the reign of Edward III, while the King and many peers, upholding the royal prerogative, stood for the *status quo*. To counteract this known resistance, the leaders in the Lower House trimmed their demands in the Triennial Bill, which set up machinery for summoning a Parliament at least every three years. The Lords received the bill on 20 January. Two days later, on a motion introduced by the Earl of Essex, the measure passed its first reading in a thin House.[29]

Charles was disturbed by these and other changes. To clarify his position, on 25 January he delivered to the peers a speech describing the state of the kingdom. England's pressing needs, he contended, were the payment of the two armies stationed along the Border and the defense of the realm. He acknowledged the necessity for some reforms and agreed to assent to several bills then pending in Parliament. "I shall willingly concur with you to find out and reform all Innovations in Church and Commonwealth," he promised, "that all Courts of Justice shall be regulated according to Law; my intention being to reduce all Matters of Religion and Government to what they were in the purest Times of Queen Elizabeth's days." Regarding the Triennial Bill, he announced, "I cannot give way."[30]

Yet he did give way. Within a week the Triennial Bill was submitted to a committee dominated by Essex and like-minded peers. On 5 February, upon this committee's recommendations, the measure passed its third reading in the Upper Chamber. It now awaited the concurrence of the King, who balked and stalled for ten days. Finally, on 15 February, Charles agreed to assent to the

[29] *H.M.C. Buccleuch Manuscripts*, 3: 410.
[30] *Lords Journal*, 4: 142.

bill in exchange for a subsidy bill. The following day Essex and several opposition leaders were delegated to thank the King for his concurrence in the matter. It was clearly a victory for those Englishmen who cherished parliamentary government.

Ecclesiastical reform threatened to fragment the ranks of the opposition.[31] On one end of the religious spectrum were a few Catholic peers, including the Earl of Clanricarde, who defended the *status quo;* at the other extreme were a few commoners, like Oliver Cromwell and William Strode, who favored root-and-branch changes in the direction of independency. Religious opinion was hopelessly divided between these extremes. Many anti-Laudians advocated moderate reforms within the existing episcopal framework, while some antiepiscopal Puritans advocated a national church along Presbyterian lines. Some, like John Selden, wished to retain the episcopal hierarchy but curtail the temporal powers of the bishops; others, like Nathaniel Fiennes, would have abolished the episcopate and substituted a system modeled after that of the Scottish Covenanters; still others, like Cromwell, favored the autonomy of the individual congregation. Time accentuated these divisions.

Most lords favored the preservation of the existing establishment. Approximately twenty prelates comprised a hard-core nucleus opposed to any and all change in the constitutional structure of the church. The majority of the temporal peers concurred with the bishops on most ecclesiastical issues. Only a small minority advocated reformation; a few preferred a weakened episcopal system in which the bishops played little or no part in temporal affairs; a few advocated a national church similar to that of Scotland; and only Lord Saye and Lord Brooke appear to have advocated separatist doctrines. The radical Puritans in the Upper House had little or no hope of realizing their ends short of war, for they were outnumbered.[32]

The Earl of Essex realized these facts only too well. He and concurring peers reacted unfavorably to most ecclesiastical innovations that emanated from the Lower House. They feared the political consequences of reformation. They supported the Commons' demands for stricter enforcement of the laws against recusants and

31 In March, Essex pointed out that the Scottish commissioners' demands for religious unity might well "breed distractions among the two Houses." See Gardiner, *History*, 9: 299.

32 Baillie, *Letters*, 1: 275.

for eliminating the Catholics from the English army. They concurred on the impeachment of ecclesiastical leaders like Archbishop Laud and Bishop Wren. But they took a dim view of the rising tide of antiepiscopal opinion in the Lower House and the City. Yet they were not completely unresponsive to religious change. In late January, under pressure from Puritans in the Lower House, the Lords took under consideration a complaint concerning the lax enforcement of laws by the Jesuits and the Catholic priests. Under Essex's leadership they conferred with the Commons about the matter and, after some discussion, decided to join them in a petition. The King, upon receiving that petition, announced his concern over the increase of papists and promised to enforce the laws against them. To pacify the revolutionary Puritans, the Lords ordered the bishops to restore the communion table to its pre-laudian position in the chancel and established a committee, which included Essex and a large number of opposition peers, to consider innovations in the church. This committee, after meeting for several months and considering several proposals for reform, could reach no agreement. It turned down Archbishop James Ussher's synodical system modeled after the primitive church; it flatly rejected the Covenanters' plans for a national church along prebyterial lines; and it declined a compromise proposal for a more representative episcopate, advocated by its chairman, Bishop Williams.

Essex's personal religious views remain extremely difficult to ascertain. He maintained cordial relationships with Archbishop Abbot until the churchman's death in 1633. Essex's connection with the Bishop of Lincoln, however, was closer and more confidential. Essex appears to have conformed to the teachings and practices of the established church throughout the pre–Civil War period. Yet, he disliked Archbishop Laud and some of the appointments to the episcopal bench. "The earl of Essex," Clarendon wrote, "was rather displeased with the person of the archbishop and some other bishops than indevoted to the function; and towards some of them he had great reverence and kindness, as bishop Mourton, bishop Hall, and some other less formal and more popular prelates: and he was as much devoted as any man to the Book of Common Prayer, and obliged all his servants to be constantly present with him at it, his household chaplain always be a most conformable man and a good scholar."[33]

Nevertheless, other evidence indicates his dissatisfaction with the

[33] Clarendon, *History* (1849 ed.), 1: 328.

religious situation in England. Like his father, Essex was a militant Protestant, a staunch antipapist who favored strong ties with the Protestant nations on the Continent. He also preferred the Calvinistic to the Arminian variety of Protestantism; of this there is no doubt. That he associated with Puritan divines is also evident. A shelf list of his library reflects an interest in Puritanism and in religious controversy, especially after the succession of Laud, although he also possessed writings of the orthodox divines. It is exceedingly difficult to learn much from his choice of chaplains. Attached to his household were William Hulbocke in 1621, William Sherbourne in 1628, and George Wall in 1642, none of whom attained any national attention as preachers or scholars. Essex's nomination of Josias Shute, a renowned Hebrew scholar and preacher who later sat in the Westminster Assembly of Divines as a Presbyterian, to deliver a Fast Day sermon to Parliament on 26 March 1628 reflects a preference for the Puritan wing of the church. Yet, socially speaking, Essex mixed freely with Catholics and Protestants of many proclivities. He retained close ties with his half brother, the Earl of Clanricarde; his brother-in-law Anthony Stafford, who lived in his household; and his sister the Marchioness of Winchester, all of whom were Catholics. These conflicting facts, when placed side by side, bespeak a broad-minded attitude toward the religious differences of his day.

Essex did favor the Bishops' Bill, which called for the removal of bishops from courts and councils and the House of Lords. This proposal, according to Clarendon, "was contrived with great deliberation and preparation, to dispose men to consent to it; and to this many of the house of peers were much disposed; and amongst them, none more than the Earl of Essex, and all of the popular Lords." [34] This bill, which passed the House of Commons during Strafford's impeachment trial, was forwarded to the House of Lords on 1 May. There, after some long and bitter debates, it was quashed on 8 June. What the opposition failed to accomplish by legislation, however, it then achieved during the summer months when the Lower House commenced impeachment proceedings against most of the remaining bishops whose votes stood in their paths.

Throughout these religious disputations the Upper House broadened its jurisdiction in the diplomatic and military areas.[35]

[34] *Ibid.*, p. 329.
[35] See *Lords Journal*, 4: 101–270.

Responding to the demands of the opposition, particularly those leaders in the Commons, Charles permitted Parliament to work out the treaty arrangements with the Scottish Covenanters. Common sense rather than abstract principles dictated this course of action. Only Parliament possessed the financial wherewithal to disband and maintain the two armies in the northern counties, thus giving the opposition leaders in the House of Commons and in London a noteworthy voice in the negotiations. Pym and his lieutenants hoped to secure enough funds to keep the Covenanters in arms until the King made several concessions. This stratagem had the practical effect of prolonging the treaty negotiations.

Essex participated in these drawn-out negotiations with the Scots. He served on the Lords' select committee, established on 14 November, to deal with "the Northern Business." This committee, with Bristol its chairman, dealt with the maintenance of the two armies in the North and the disbanding plans as well as the treaty terms. It met frequently, conferrred with the leaders of the Lower House, and reported periodically to the parent body about its deliberations. Several members of this committee, including Essex, Bedford, Holland, and Warwick, also served as royally appointed and parliamentary approved commissioners, whose purpose it was to carry out the formal negotiations between the two nations. It is difficult at times to differentiate between the actions of the two groups. Evidence shows, however, that Essex assumed an increasingly larger role in the Scottish negotiations.

Essex gradually became the parliamentary military expert in matters relating to Scotland. In February he was named to the committee empowered to provide funds for the English troops. A month later he was appointed to confer with members of the Lower House about dismantling the English fortresses at Berwick and Carlisle. In early March, Essex was singled out by the King to inform the Lords of disorders in the English army. Essex's report on 12 March led to a joint conference with the leaders of the Commons. Henceforth, he was the principal liaison between the King, the Lords, and the Commons in matters relating to the disbanding of the two armies. Hardly a week passed without his conferring with the Commons about the armies. On 25 March he was one of eight Lords and sixteen commoners selected by the Committee of Both Houses to arrange for a loan from the city of London to pay the troops. Essex, Bedford, and Holland were authorized to collect relief contributions for the English army at Berwick. A month later Essex was instrumental in raising £4,366 from his fellow peers for the cause.

Meanwhile, Essex and his compeers also directed their attention to the impeachment trial of the Earl of Strafford.

IV

LONDONERS had a memorable day on 22 March. Many shops were closed. Most government business came to a halt. Large numbers of citizens crowded the area around Westminster Hall to secure seats on public benches or to catch a glimpse of the principal actors in the forthcoming political drama. A special guard was selected to maintain law and order. Never before had so much time, so much expense and attention, been devoted to the trial of a public official.

Essex and his fellow peers assembled quite early in the Upper Chamber on that eventful day.[36] After conducting some pressing business they proceeded two by two to Westminster Hall. Within the specially prepared building, which was filled to overflowing, rank and precedence prevailed. On both sides of the rectangularly shaped hall were ascending bleachers reserved for the members of Parliament, the Scottish Commissions, and other persons of influence. Strafford, enclosed in a small box with the lieutenant of the Tower, occupied the center of the stage. To his right were those commoners selected to manage the prosecution; to his left were witnesses and spectators; and behind him were his legal advisers. Directly in front of Strafford sat the Lords and the officers of the court. In the very center of the crowded hall were the clerks, the masters of the chancery, the judges of the high courts, and the Earl of Arundel, the Lord High Steward of the court—all of whom enjoyed the luxury of cushionlike woolsacks.

Essex, one of the eighty peers who attended the daily sessions of the trial, was seated to Strafford's left with the other Privy Councilors. Not once did he miss a roll call. His principal responsibility as a judge was to listen to the speeches of the prosecution managers, evaluate the evidence, weigh the rebuttals of the defendant's

[36] For a narrative account of the trial see Wedgwood's revised biography, *Strafford*, pp. 337–52.

counsel, and then determine whether the councilor was innocent or guilty of high treason.

The first day was taken up with dull preliminaries. Strafford was ushered into the hall by the lieutenant of the Tower and forced to kneel at the bar, thus submitting himself to the High Court of Parliament. The trial began with the clerk of Parliament's reading the charges and then Strafford's answers. It was so late when the clerk finished the tedious task that court was adjourned until the following morning. Strafford was taken back to the Tower for security.

The next day the prosecution began its case with great gusto. Pym began with an attack upon Strafford's illegal and oftimes cruel actions as an administrator. He appealed to the Lords to judge Strafford by his actions—many of which were inhumane, ignoble, and unbefitting of his rank and title—and disregard the written defense. Pym then called upon new witnesses, who gave fresh testimony on several matters omitted from the articles. To the dismay of Pym and his fellow managers Strafford won several procedural skirmishes. Strafford challenged and successfully excluded one witness on grounds of prejudice. For every assertion, he had a denial; for every denial, he had a counterdenial. The weaknesses of the charges and of the prosecution's case soon became evident.

On the following morning lawyer John Maynard spoke about the law of treason. In his written defense Strafford had admitted many of the charges but protested that they were not treasonable; he contended that he was merely abiding by the law and carrying out the King's command. Maynard took exception to this legalistic view of treason. Although none of Strafford's acts may have been individually illegal, he maintained, collectively they constituted treason and were therefore punishable by the law of treason. "It is a habit," Maynard charged, "a trade, a mystery of treason exercised by this great lord." [37] After this legal homily Maynard proceeded to the second article, which dealt with Strafford's tenure as president of the Council of the North. Again Strafford succeeded in undercutting the testimony of the witnesses with questions, inferences, doubts, and defenses of his actions.

And thus the trial went forward, hour upon hour, day after day, for several weeks. By the first week of April the pattern was set.

[37] *Ibid.*, p. 341. Also see Conrad Russell, "The Theory of Treason," pp. 30–50.

Strafford claimed that the impeachment trial was a conspiracy against him and that many procedural decisions were unfair and prejudicial. His claim, of course, rang true. Most of the attendant commoners and a bloc of opposition peers had already made up their minds about Strafford's guilt. The proceedings were repeatedly irregular and unfair. The victim's requests for equal time and equitable treatment were more often than not denied. His objections to witnesses and evidence were frequently overruled.

Yet, despite these adversities, Strafford convinced some Lords of his innocence. By appealing to fair play he convinced some moderate peers, like Bedford, that most of the Commons' charges were either groundless or exaggerated; and by appealing to law and custom he convinced some vacillating peers, like Bristol, that his actions were not treasonable and that the Commons' arguments of constructive treason did not stand the test of logic and precedence. Strafford won the sympathy of those peers who held the balance of power in the Upper House. By early April, when called upon to make his summary defense, Strafford's fate was by no means settled. A majority of the peers put aside the Commons' request for immediate action and voted in a plenary session to grant the defendant additional time to prepare his final statements.

On 10 April, Strafford began his summation.[38] It was an unforgettable occasion. The spectators crowded into Westminster Hall earlier than usual and the benches were filled to overflowing. All hoped to hear Black Tom speak in his own defense. They were denied their pleasure, however, for shortly after Arundel opened the session, manager John Glynn requested that he be allowed to call upon two new witnesses. Strafford vigorously protested against this irregular gambit and argued on grounds of equity that he be allowed the same privilege. The Lords, confounded by these unanticipated maneuvers, withdrew for an hour and appointed a committee, which included Essex, to consult with the judges. The judges concurred with Strafford, and a majority of the peers concurred with the judges. The tide was turning.

Strafford took immediate advantage of his procedural victory by pressing the question further, asking whether he could call witnesses on all the charges or only those which the Commons reopened. Again the Lords withdrew and decided in Strafford's favor. Pym and his managers were now faced with a difficult choice. They could con-

38 *Lords Journal,* 4: 211.

tinue the trial and allow Strafford new opportunities to answer the charges and undermine their case or they could forego the new witnesses and force Strafford into an immediate summation. Believing that the defendant was bluffing, they decided on the former course of action, whereupon Strafford announced that he had new evidence to submit on several of the charges. This produced an immediate uproar. The attendant members of the Commons called upon Glynn to withdraw the request. The Lords shouted for adjournment. Before Arundel could rule, the crowd departed amidst much noise, while the confused managers attempted to fasten the blame for the tactical blunder on each other. Strafford and the King, one observant contemporary noted, looked at each other and laughed before going their separate ways.

For anti-Straffordians like Essex this occurrence constituted a serious setback because they had risked their future careers on dishonoring this arrogant councilor, who seemed to wriggle out of every charge. Throughout the trial Essex continued to serve on, and act as reporter for, the examination committee.[39] On 26 March he participated in the examination of the Archbishop of Armagh, and on 4 April he and three other peers deputed by the Upper House examined the Earl of Northumberland at Syon House.[40] It was a week later that Essex rebutted Strafford's contentions regarding Article 27 (which tested the loyalty of the opposition peers) by directing a series of questions to John Burroughs, a witness for the defense. In these and other actions which are hidden by silence and time Essex labored in vain. For all practical purposes the impeachment trial terminated in mid-April when the opposition virtually gave up their attempt to use due processes of law to find Strafford guilty of treason. Instead, they reverted to a more certain method of achieving the same end—an attainder.

The decision to use the attainder was made in the Lower House by Pym and his cohorts on 10 April, shortly after they had been outmaneuvered by Strafford. The idea was not new. St. John had considered this alternative earlier in the session; antiquarian D'Ewes had made a study of earlier attainders. The anti-Straffordians in the Lower House were convinced that the defendant was guilty of

[39] British Museum, Additional MSS, 46,189. This collection also contains several papers relating to Strafford's misrule in the Council of the North.

[40] *Lords Journal*, 4: 119, 207. Essex also served on a committee to examine Cottington; see *H. M. C. House of Lords Manuscripts*, 11: 239.

high treason and were determined to bring him to the execution block without waiting for formality. The attainder, which had been prepared in advance, was read for the first time and passed that day before adjournment. Four days later, after a conference with the Lords, the bill of attainder passed its second reading in the Lower House. The following day the opposition leaders, responding to angry Straffordians, defended their actions. In a plenary session they then rationalized their position by passing a resolution to this effect: "That the evidence of Fact being given, it was in Proposition, from the Beginning, to go by way of Bill: And that a Bill exhibited here for his Attainder . . . That the Proceeding by way of Bill stands in no way of Opposition to those Proceedings that have already been in this business."[41] Thus did Pym justify his new course of action.

On 16 April the bill of attainder took final form in the Lower House. "That it is sufficiently proved," the House further resolved, "that Thomas Earl of Strafford hath endeavored to subvert the ancient and fundamental Laws of these Realms of England and Ireland; and to introduce an arbitrary and tyrannical Government against Law." For several days the Commons discussed the resolution. Lord Digby opposed it in eloquent terms. So did Essex's friend Selden, a staunch defender of Parliament against the Court, who could not convince himself that Strafford had committed high treason. In the end Pym and Lucius Cary, Lord Falkland, had their way. The bill of attainder passed its third reading on 21 April by a vote of 204 to 59. It was promptly forwarded to the Upper House for passage.[42]

The bill was coolly received in the Upper Chamber. It made mockery of due process. It denigrated much that the peers and their legal assistants stood for. To many peers, especially the King's closest supporters, Pym's attainder strategy represented a travesty of justice. To others, like Bedford and Bristol, it smacked of extreme partisanship and political vengeance at its worst. That the Lords let the bill sit for several days and that many Englishmen, including the King, believed that it would die a natural death in the Upper House is not surprising.

Strafford and his sovereign, meanwhile, utilized the brief

41 *Commons Journal*, 2: 121.

42 I have used Prof. Glenn Gray's transcripts of the "D'Ewes Diary" (Harleian 163) and the "Bishops Diary" (Harleian 6424) in my account of the attainder. The originals are located in the British Museum.

breathing space to muster support to quash the attainder in the Upper House. Charles sought the support of Bristol and Bedford to prevent the bill from passing. Strafford asked Hamilton to intervene in his behalf. None of these measures proved potent enough to prevent the bill from passing its first reading on 26 April, after many Londoners mobbed Parliament with a petition (reputedly signed by twenty thousand Englishmen) demanding Strafford's life.

Strafford's fate became the talk of the town.[43] That night Essex ventured forth with his brother-in-law Hertford to Piccadilly, a fashionable spot where well-to-do Londoners went to walk and to talk about the events of the day. While the two men conversed about Strafford's destiny, Edward Hyde was talking with the Earl of Bedford, who had been recently persuaded by the King to save Strafford. Bedford rationalized his position on grounds that valuable concessions could be wrought from the Crown if the Earl of Strafford were imprisoned for life or perhaps banished from England but not put to death by means of an attainder. To accomplish this, Bedford claimed that he needed the support of Essex; so he assigned Hyde to persuade Essex to reconsider the matter.

This was no simple task. Hyde approached Essex later that same evening at Piccadilly and was praised for his forthright opposition to the prerogative courts and for reviving Parliament's indignation against Strafford. After denying that he had intended to attack Strafford in a recent speech, Hyde stressed the need to proceed by trial rather than by the bill of attainder. Although Strafford was certainly guilty of crime and misdemeanors, Hyde explained, there was not enough evidence to find him guilty of high treason and therefore he did not deserve to die.

Essex shook his head and replied, "Stone-dead hath no fellow." [44]

Strafford must pay with his life. If he were permitted to live, Essex argued, "the King would presently grant him his pardon and his estate, release all fines, and would likewise give him his liberty, as soon as he had a mind to receive his service; which would be as soon as the parliament should be ended." Essex contended that the King could not be trusted in this matter, and therefore there could be no compromise. Shortly after this exchange Essex excused himself and left Hyde with his task unfinished.

But Hyde did not give up very easily. He soon approached

---

[43] For these discussions see Clarendon, *History* (1849 ed.), 1: 340.
[44] *Ibid.*, pp. 341–43.

Essex again about the same subject. Essex apparently listened very patiently to Hyde's arguments but resolutely refused to change his position. When asked how he could in clear conscience advise the King to vote for the attainder when he knew it was contrary to the King's conscience, Essex is reputed to have replied, "The King was obliged in conscience to conform himself and his own understanding to the advice and conscience of his Parliament." [45] Such was the novel doctrine of parliamentary supremacy which Essex and his allies espoused. Although Hyde held Essex in great esteem and made him the marred hero of his *History of the Great Rebellion*, he took exception to those arguments which subordinated the King to Parliament. [46]

Since Essex's anti-Straffordian faction had lost the support of Bedford and Bristol and their coteries, it looked as though Strafford might win the battle for his life. Under normal circumstances the majority would have won their way and quashed the attainder. But the political situation in the spring of 1641 was not normal; Pym and his lieutenants in the Lower House saw to that. Pym rejected some overtures from the King that might have made him Chancellor of the Exchequer. He refused to believe that the King's conciliatory gestures toward the opposition were made in good faith. He knew of intrigues in the Queen's Court and the army, and he had every reason to believe that the King was playing a double game with moderates like Bedford.

In rumor-ridden London, on 27 April the bill passed its second reading in the Upper House. Two days later the peers listened to Oliver St. John argue the Commons' case for death by attainder. Both Strafford and the King attended. The argument was long; the tone was retaliatory. Contending that the impeachment charges had been proved in the trial, St. John asked the Lords to put aside their scruples about the statutory method of justice and to pass the bill before Strafford escaped. "He that would not have had others to have a law," St. John asked rhetorically, "why should he have any himself?" [47] At the end of this speech, one of the most vicious yet delivered, Strafford remained mute and appealed to heaven with his hands and eyes.

[45] *Ibid.*
[46] For an excellent discussion of this theme see Irene Coltman's *Private Men and Public Causes* (London: Faher and Faher, 1962), pp. 124–27.
[47] Wedgwood, *Strafford*, p. 370.

On May Day, after discussing the situation with Bedford and Bristol, the King tried to save Strafford's life by appealing to the Upper House. In a poor, ill-timed speech Charles restated his opposition to the attainder and reiterated his threat to reject it—if it passed the Lords. "My Lords," the King pleaded, "I hope you know what a tender thing conscience is: yet I must declare unto you that to satisfy my people I would do great matters; but this of conscience, no fear or respect whatsoever shall make me go against it." [48] This weak defense helped Strafford less than it did Essex.

Time now played into Essex's hands. The King lost the valuable moderative services of Bedford, who contracted a case of smallpox which confined him to his London mansion and soon led to his death. The Puritan preachers of London clamored from their pulpits for Strafford's death. On 2 May restless apprentices and sailors raised havoc with those resident ambassadors from Catholic countries. The following day Pym played another trump card. In the fear-ridden Lower House, which was surrounded by restless throngs of Londoners, he revealed what he knew about a recent conspiracy. Certain members of the Queen's Court, in conjunction with some officers in the army, Pym dramatically announced, conspired to save Strafford and dissolve Parliament by force. The Commons demanded an immediate investigation of the entire matter.

In this atmosphere rumors increased by geometric progression. There were plots and counterplots: England was to be invaded; Parliament would be blown up in Guy Fawkes fashion; the Tower would be seized; English recusants, or worse yet, the Catholics in Ireland were preparing to rise in revolt and deliver Britain into the hands of the pope. Somehow all these fear-fostered fabrications were related to the Earl of Strafford. As the rumors generated mass hysteria, so the hysteria generated violence—some undoubtedly expected or perhaps even planned, but a great deal of it spontaneous. Many shops closed. Numerous shopkeepers formed mobs in London. Soon they were armed and ready for action. They marched to Westminster crying for justice. Some of the unruly multitude toppled the carriages of the peers going to Parliament. Others threatened the life of Straffordians like Lord Digby.

Mob rule tipped the scales of justice against Strafford. In the violent conditions surrounding Parliament the peers feared the

48 Rushworth, *Historical Collections*, 8: 166.

consequences of rejecting the bill of attainder. Edward Montagu realized this only too well when, on 8 May, he wrote to his father, Viscount Mandeville, who was absent from the Upper House: "Since my coming to London, there hath been great tumults and disorders, especially about Westminster, by reason, as the common people say, that they have not justice against my lord Strafford . . . The Lords have been sitting all this day about the Earl of Strafford's bill. I hear there is no question but it will pass them. We fear there is a desire to convey him away, which makes the city watch the Tower every night."[49] Events proved these predictions correct. Many cowardly peers were absent from the Upper House. The bishops could not vote because the matter involved the shedding of blood. The moderates lost control of the Upper House. By the time the bill of attainder came up for its third and last reading only forty-eight peers attended the House. Thirty-seven consented to its passage. It was a political victory for the opposition groups in both Houses. For Essex it was also a personal victory with overtones of vengeance—a vengeance fostered by envy and hatred.

Shortly after high noon on 12 May the Earl of Strafford was ushered from his room in the Tower to the same courtyard that had been the death site for Essex's father forty years earlier. The victim mounted the scaffold, which was surrounded by dense crowds, and spoke his last words as he knelt before the block:

I am at the door going out, and my next step must be from time to eternity; to clear myself to you all, I do solemnly protest before God I am not guilty of that crime laid to my charge, nor have ever had the least inclination or intention to damnify or prejudice the King, the state, the laws or religion of this Kingdom, but with my best endeavors to serve all, and to support all.[50]

Essex's enemy was now stone dead and but a memory to his fellow Englishmen.

[49] *H. M. C. Montagu Manuscripts*, p. 129.

[50] Wedgwood, *Strafford*, p. 33. For a contemporary justification of the execution see *A Declaration shewing the Necessity of the Earl of Strafford's Suffering* (London, 1641), reprinted in Sir Walter Scott, *Somers Tracts*, 13 vols. (London, 1809–15), 4: 223–27.

CHAPTER 11

Lord Chamberlain

I

IN THE MONTHS following Strafford's execution the King was politically paralyzed. He could no longer dissolve Parliament without the concurrence of Lords and Commons. He could not disband the army of his enemy, the Scottish Covenanters, nor could he pay the arrears of his own English troops: he was bankrupt and consequently at the mercy of the Lower House. He could— and did—bid for time in hopes of extricating himself from this financial bind and securing support either from his subjects or from foreign allies. Time, he hoped, would bring some assistance from the French, engender a Royalist party in Scotland, and weaken the alliance between the Lords and the Commons in Parliament.

The Lower House, conscious of the King's helplessness, retained the political initiative in the months following Strafford's death. Pym persistently exploited the fears of both M.P.'s and Londoners, capitalized on rumors of plots and invasions, continued to pressure Charles by demanding the removal of more "evil councilors," and kept alive the issue of ecclesiastical reform. Periodically, he regrouped his forces and outlined the attainments and the unattained objectives in a petition or a protestation. Yet, despite this power, Pym and his radical compatriots were not invited by the King to participate in the government as officeholders or councilors, several rumors to the contrary notwithstanding.

The Upper House maintained the balance of power between the King and the commonalty.[1] The Lords could quash bills and delay impeachment proceedings. They could exert personal influence over the King. The opposition peers were courted by the King, who needed their power and popularity. Several opposition lords responded to the royal bid for their support: they put aside all

[1] For a complete treatment of this subject see Corinne Comstock Weston, "Beginnings of the Classical Theory of the English Constitution," *Proceedings of the American Philosophical Society*, 100 (1956): 133–44.

private bills and labored on the pressing public matters before the House.

The air of crisis which prevailed before and shortly after Strafford's execution enabled Essex and his allies to enhance Parliament's authority in military matters. To prevent Strafford from fleeing the country, to prevent a rumored *coup d'état* on the part of some over-zealous army officers, to protect themselves from the rabble, and to provide for the disbanding of the armies along the Border: for these reasons and others—some real, some fabricated—opposition leaders in both Houses concerned themselves with military measures. They took advantage of rumors to make demands of the King, to ensure the defense of the realm, and to forestall an armed over-throw of the Long Parliament. Against his better judgment and because his hands were tied, the English sovereign conceded much to his political adversaries. He followed Parliament's suggestions regarding the defense of the Channel Islands and Portsmouth. He also permitted Parliament to deliberate on matters pertaining to the disbanding of the two armies in the North.

Yet, Charles continued to exclude Essex. He ignored Essex's plan for a permanent military command under the supervision of Parliament. In early May, shortly before Strafford's death, Charles appointed the Earl of Holland and the Earl of Newport, both of whom had been set aside a year earlier, General of the Army and constable of the Tower, respectively. That he could not bring himself to name Essex to a military or political position was, according to Clarendon, a foolish mistake. "It was wondered at by many," he wrote in his *History*, "and sure was a great misfortune to the King, that he chose not rather at that time (though the business was only to disband) to constitute the earl of Essex general of his army, than the earl of Holland . . . for his [Essex's] pride and ambition, which were not accompanied with any habit of ill nature, were very capable of obligations; and he had a faithfulness and constancy in his nature, which had kept him always religious in matters of trust." [2]

A majority in the Commons agreed with Clarendon's opinion. On 7 May they requested the House of Lords to persuade the King to appoint Essex the lord lieutenant of Yorkshire—an obvious move to counterbalance Holland's influence in the North—and on the following day both Houses petitioned the King to name Essex

[2] Clarendon, *History* (1849 ed.), 1: 382.

to that post.[3] The King ignored their joint request until on 19 May the House of Commons sought an answer to their petition. Although Charles had already promised the place to Lord Savile, he reluctantly responded to the demands of Parliament: "His Majesty hath taken into Consideration the Desire of both Houses, concerning the conferring of the Lord Lieutenancy of Yorkshire upon the Earl of Essex; and the Cause why his Majesty did not give Answer before now was, a Grant was made under the Great Seal of the Same to the Lord Savile, who is become Suitor to His Majesty to give him leave (seeing it is at the Insistance of both Houses) to surrender up his Patent to His Majesty; who hath accepted of that Surrender, and is willing to bestow it upon the Earl of Essex."[4] That same day Essex received the appointment, which afforded him a greater voice in the disbanding operations along the Border.

During the summer months Essex exercised his military authority in several instances. He used his patronage to appoint Protestants fully committed to the cause of Parliament. In late June, for example, he commissioned Lord Ferdinando Fairfax, whose father had fought at Rouen with the second Earl of Essex in 1591, to command a regiment of troops in West Riding.[5] In early July, Essex named Robert Strickland, an M.P. sitting for Aldborough, to serve as his deputy lieutenant in Yorkshire. Essex also remained the principal liaison between the Earl of Holland and Parliament in matters relating to the armies along the Border. Throughout the summer, until the armies were finally disbanded, he received Holland's reports on their dismissal, communicated the information to the Upper Chamber, and conferred with Commons' leaders when occasion demanded.

In the meantime, Charles attempted to broaden the basis of his support among the aristocracy. He created several new barons and elevated some peers to higher ranks.[6] He forced several of his office-holding Privy Councilors to step aside, and gradually turned their places over to opposition peers. Soon after Strafford's death, Lord Saye, otherwise known as Old Subility, was named master of the Court of Wards in Cottington's place. On 17 May, shortly

[3] Professor Gray's transcript of the "D'Ewes Diary" (Harleian 163), p. 417.

[4] *Lords Journal*, 4: 254.

[5] *H. M. C. Ninth Report*, Appendix 2, p. 432.

[6] Wedgwood, *The King's Peace*, pp. 435–45; and Rushworth, *Historical Collections*, 4: 279.

after the Earl of Newcastle resigned as the governor of the Prince of Wales, the Earl of Hertford was named to fill the post. To take the place of the late lord deputy of Ireland, the King selected Robert Sidney the Earl of Leicester, a descendant of Sir Henry Sidney. In June the Earl of Pembroke was honored with the chancellorship of Oxford, an office which Laud vacated. Rumors of more reshufflings circulated all summer—of Pym being named Chancellor of the Exchequer, of Holles becoming secretary of state, of Lord Saye being Lord Treasurer, of Hampden assuming control of the duchy of Lancaster, and several others.[7]

In July, Essex finally became a high officer of state. A sharp controversy in the House of Lords precipitated the appointment. The Earl of Pembroke, then Lord Chamberlain, was involved in a legal dispute with Lord Maltravers, son of the Earl of Arundel, about their respective rights to Sutton Marsh. Having failed to resolve their differences, they took their case to the Upper House for mediation. There on 19 July the controversy produced a verbal duel between the disputants.[8] Tempers flared and insults were exchanged. Lord Chamberlain Pembroke struck Lord Maltravers on the floor of the Upper House, thus desecrating the High Court of Parliament. When Charles learned of the fracas, he took the two nobles into custody and placed them in the Tower.

Essex benefited from this squabble. Charles stripped Pembroke of his position and bestowed it upon Essex.[9] One account claims Charles acted on the advice of the Queen, who detested Pembroke; another attributed the action to Bishop Williams, who now advised the King in many matters. According to Clarendon, Charles removed Pembroke because the latter had voted against Strafford. Whatever the case, Essex secured a high official place in the King's government. The office was worth about fifty thousand crowns a year. The Lord Chamberlain was expected to remain close to the King and oversee his household. While the Court was in Westminster he resided in a special suite in Whitehall Palace. More important, he controlled the King's private purse and the selection of

7 Gardiner, *History*, 9: 409–13.

8 For the best account of this incident see *H.M.C. Tenth Report*, Appendix 6, pp. 111, 143–44.

9 Gardiner, *History*, 9: 412. Also see the Elector Palatine's comments in a letter to the Queen of Bohemia dated 28 July 1641 in the Forster MSS, Victoria and Albert Museum.

chaplains and tutors of the heir apparent. Although the Venetian ambassador held serious reservations about Essex's religious views, he recognized the tactical significance of the appointment: "His Majesty has conferred the appointment on the Earl of Essex, a leading man among the Puritans. Although in the past he has shown himself utterly opposed to the King's interests, His Majesty hopes that the stimulus of ambition as well as of profit will suffice to secure his devotion, and if he succeeds in winning over the earl he will have achieved a great gain, since that nobleman possesses the strongest party in parliament." [10]

Whatever elation Essex may have experienced from elevation to this office was soon overshadowed by tragedy. Sometime in July his only brother, Sir Walter Devereux, then in his late forties, died in London, probably in Essex House. Very likely he succumbed to the plague. Essex lost a faithful political dependent as well as a beloved brother, and the Lower House lost a member dedicated to the "good old cause." On many occasions Sir Walter had come to his brother's aid and served him in both private and public matters.

Essex received another honor when he was named Captain General of this Side Trent, a post which made him responsible for the defense of the southern half of England during the forthcoming trip of the King to Scotland.[11] When Charles submitted his measure to Parliament it received prompt approval by both Houses. The actual commission from Charles bore the date of 9 August.[12] On the eve of the King's departure for Scotland, then, the Earl of Essex possessed considerable authority by virtue of his military and civil offices.

These appointments did not pacify the King's critics in the Lower House. Those men remained excluded from the inner circles of decision making. They persisted in their demand for reforms in both church and state and continued to deplore the existence of "evil councilors" in high places. In June the leaders in the Lower House proceeded to impeach Archbishop Laud. In July they impeached six judges and all thirteen bishops who had approved of the Laudian canons passed in the recent Convocation, although

10 C. S. P. Ven., 1640–1641, p. 195.

11 The parliamentary or constitutional history of England from the earliest times to the restoration of Charles II, 24 vols. (London, 1751–62), 9: 461–62 (hereafter cited as Old Parliamentary History).

12 See Rymer, Foedera, 20: 479.

Charles contested the claim that these men were "evil councilors." The Lords showed little interest in the proceedings.

Essex and his colleagues, meanwhile, strengthened their pivotal position in the body politic. They approved some measures dealing with class privileges and concurred with their allies in the Lower House on several constitutional changes. At the same time they quashed several proposals which they judged inimical to the interests of the aristocracy and the nation. Most of the legislation they passed remained on the statute book long after the Puritan Revolution. Several bills cut back the prerogative power of the King. In early July the Lords abolished the hated Court of High Commission and the Court of Star Chamber. A further bill declared all ship-money devices illegal; another took away the power of the Crown to determine and regulate forest boundaries; a third prevented the King from exacting the detested fees connected with forced knighthood. Essex was also behind the proposal, which eventually ended in legislation, to petition the King against the selling of honors—a move sparked by Charles's sale of titles to several barons and baronets. All in all, Essex and his fellow peers were more successful than the Commons in their efforts to reshape the constitution by limiting the power of the Crown and making the King more dependent upon Parliament.

During the summer months Parliament devoted more time and energy to the Scottish treaty than to any other matter of business. The high cost of maintaining two armies along the Border produced a great amount of concern. When the King announced in June that he would visit Scotland both Houses worked diligently to complete the treaty negotiations before he departed. Day after day the commissioners of the two nations met and debated the treaty article by article. Then the matter was deliberated in Parliament. Although the terms of the treaty were, for all practical purposes, agreed upon by the end of June, the formal approval by the King in Parliament had to wait until the Lower House raised nearly eight hundred thousand pounds to pay the arrears of the two armies. This was no simple matter, for the financial situation in England was deplorable.

As the time for his departure for Scotland drew nigh the English sovereign received several requests from the opposition leaders to continue to delay his trip. In mid-June he had deferred his journey for several weeks, and on 29 June, out of deference to the opposition leaders of both Houses, he had agreed to postpone his departure until 10 August. On 7 August, Denzil Holles suggested that the Lower House petition the King to defer his departure a fortnight. Parliament needed more time, he contended, to approve the treaty and establish an interim government. In this state of semiemergency Parliament agreed to conduct business on the Sabbath—an unheard-of practice—to persuade the King to stay and work on unfinished business.

Parliament also pressed the King to establish some executive authority to act in his absence. The King, fully aware of the need, informed the Upper House that he planned to empower some of his Privy Councilors to carry out the necessary functions of government. For several days the matter was debated. The Lords appear to have agreed with Charles; the Commons, however, advocated "a *Custos Regni* or *Locum tenens* during his Absence out of the Kingdom." [13] Selden searched the past for precedents, the judges were consulted, and the two Houses conferred. Eventually the King won. There was a method in the Commons' recommendation, however, for as historian John Nalson noted, "had the King consented, the Earl of Essex, then their Darling, had been the Man, and how far Ambition and Revenge armed with such power and supported with such a prevailing Faction might have transported him his future Actions do most evidently demonstrate." [14] Essex was, nevertheless, appointed by Charles to serve on the fourteen-man interim group called the Lords Commissioners.

On Sunday, 8 August, the Commons gathered at 6 A.M. at Saint Margaret's to hear prayers and listen to Edmund Calamy's sermon. Both Houses then convened at 9 A.M. to transact business. They first resolved that the Sabbath meeting did not constitute a precedent and then concurred in sending a committee to the King to dissuade him from leaving. Essex, who was selected to head the delegation, reported back that the mission was unsuccessful: Charles flatly refused to change his plans again. Instead the King invited all members of Parliament to the banqueting room in Whitehall to hear his departing speech. At the appointed hour of 4 P.M. Charles informed his petitioners that necessity demanded his presence in Edinburgh and that he could not possibly postpone his journey another day. No one, not even his newly appointed Lord Chamberlain, could dissuade him from his duty in this matter.

[13] Nalson, *An Impartial Collection*, 2: 412.
[14] *Ibid.*, p. 425. Also see *Old Parliamentary History*, 9: 463.

Finally, at 2 P.M. on 10 August, Charles Stuart and his cousin the Duke of Lennox departed for the land of their nativity.

II

In the King's absence the Queen, remaining at Richmond, had few instructions and no real authority. Except for a very few more or less *ad hoc* meetings, the Privy Council ceased to function as a body. The King's secretary, Edward Nicholas, had limited authority to forward information and act upon specific instructions that he received from the King or the Queen.[15] Both Houses, thinned somewhat by plague, postponed all private business. In this political vacuum Parliament fully utilized its power to carry England through several crises which developed. It made liberal use of orders and resorted to ordinances and proclamations—temporary lawmaking powers that had been the monopoly of the Crown for centuries—to achieve its ends.[16] The Upper Chamber even elected its own speaker without royal approval.

The opposition leaders, most apprehensive about the situation, feared—with good reason—that Charles might win the support of the Scots, march on England, and then forcefully dissolve Parliament. They so mistrusted their sovereign that a few days after his departure they selected a watchdog committee composed of two peers (Bedford and Howard) and four commoners (Fiennes, William Armyn, Sir Philip Stapleton, and Hampden) to observe the King's activities in Scotland.[17] Both Houses voted more money and kept pressure on Lord General Holland about speedy disbanding. On 11 August the speaker of the Upper House ordered Holland to disband the Scottish troops "with all possible speed."[18] To expedite matters, the two Houses passed an ordinance on 24 August calling for faster collection and immediate transportation of the poll tax to York. These actions soon bore fruit, for the House of Lords learned that Holland was faithfully following his instructions and that the Scots were evacuating the northern counties of England. By 7 September, the day set aside by Parlia-

15 Nicholas's correspondence constitutes the best primary source for these months. See G. F. Warner, *Correspondence of Sir Edward Nicholas*, 4 vols., Camden Society (London, 1886–1920), especially vol. 1.

16 Gardiner, *History*, 10: 4–10.

17 *Lords Journal*, 4: 372.

18 *Ibid.*, p. 360.

ment as a Fast Day, England was seemingly free from the Scottish menace.

Essex figured largely in these affairs.[19] As a principal liaison between Holland and other leaders and Parliament, on 11 August he revealed to the Lords the King's wishes regarding the payment of arrears to Sir John Conyers, the governor of Berwick. Several days later Essex was named along with three other peers to draw up a disbanding order, which was subsequently sent to the Earl of Holland in York. On 20 August, Lord Essex complained to a group of conferees that one of his communications to the Lower House concerning disbanding had been printed without his consent and demanded an investigation of the matter. On 28 August, he revealed a letter to the Upper House from Lord Howard of Escrick, announcing that the disbanding would be completed as soon as the money arrived from London. The following week he reported twice about the progress of disbanding; in both instances he read to the Upper House letters received from Holland.

Essex also spearheaded a move in the Upper House to prevent the recruitment and transportation of Irishmen to foreign ports. On 14 August, two days after he reported about a captain who wanted leave to do that, Essex and three other peers were appointed to confer with the Commons' leaders about the matter. Much discussion ensued. The leadership of the Lower House came out strongly against the practice, and Essex and his compeers concurred. On 9 September the two Houses issued an ordinance prohibiting the transportation of any troops, Irishmen included, out of the realm without "the Consent and Advice of the Lords and Commons in Parliament."[20] Essex worked closely with the Commons' leaders in passing this measure.

Defense of the realm gave the opposition even greater opportunities to enlarge Parliament's authority in military matters. Leaders of the Lower House were quick to seize the initiative; shortly after the King departed, they appointed a committee to consider putting England into a posture of defense and requested the Lords to do likewise. Their concern, though genuine, stemmed from fear—fear of invasion from abroad, fear of another army plot, and fear of a papist uprising. On 15 August they conferred

[19] See *C. S. P. Dom., 1641–1643*, p. 64; and Nalson, *An Impartial Collection*, 2: 457.

[20] *Lords Journal*, 4: 365.

with delegates from the Upper House about the necessity of making secure the Tower of London and the Channel Islands. On the following day Sir Walter Earle recommended "that some Authority shall be given to some Person in the Absence of the King to put the Kingdom into a posture of Defence. And to do all things necessary for the Defence of the Kingdom." [21] This person, Earle further contended, should make a man-power survey and restore arms to the counties.

Rumors of a military coup provoked the Lords into taking immediate action on Earle's proposal: they appointed a committee under Essex's leadership and proceeded to confer with the Commons. On 16 August the Lords ordered Holland to prevent the removal of any artillery and munitions from Hull except by the consent of both Houses. On the following day Essex spoke to the master of defense. "The Lord Chamberlain desired," reported the clerk of Parliament, "That, seeing the King had been pleased to bestow favour upon him as to make him, in His Majesty's absence in Scotland, Captain General of the South by Commissioner, that there be some Course taken how the said Commission may take Effect, and be enabled to perform what is required from him when Occasion serves, both for levying Men and raising Monies, and resisting of Invasion if any should be; therefor he made it his humble request, that some Order and Rule may be given herein, that he might execute the Commision for the Good of the Kingdom." [22] Essex's commission contained the means whereby Parliament could defend itself and the nation in case of emergency.

Fresh rumors of a "gunpowder plot" to blow up Parliament moved the peers into action the next morning. Peter Heywood, justice of the peace, was authorized to make a search of all those dwellings, taverns, and cellars underneath the Upper Chamber for gunpowder or any other materials which might endanger the lives of the peers. Later in the day the Earl of Newport, constable of the Tower, under pressure from both Houses, agreed to personally reside in the Tower of London to prevent any *coup d'état*. He was also ordered to reinforce his garrison. The Commons reacted quickly to this situation by passing the following resolution: "That the Clerk of the Crown shall be required to send a true and authen-

21 *Commons Journal*, 2: 249.

22 *Lords Journal*, 4: 368. Also see Helen Barber, "The Journal of Sir Simonds D'Ewes" (Ph.D. diss., Cornell University, 1927), 2: 88.

tic copy of the Commission granted to the Lord Chamberlain for being his Majesty's Lieutenant General on this Side Trent."[23] They hoped to use Essex's emergency powers to protect themselves and the kingdom from potential enemies.

Essex himself took several precautions. On about 23 August he ordered all officers residing in Whitehall to remove their belongings and deliver their keys to him.[24] That same day he recommended to Parliament that more gunpowder was needed to ensure the adequate defense of London. A few days later the two Houses ordered the Earl of Holland to ship all ordnance and munitions from the garrisons at Berwick and Carlisle to the Tower of London. Two days later Essex, Warwick, and Bishop Williams were appointed by their colleagues to consult with the Commons about these and other matters relating to the defense and security of London and the nation.

The appearance and spread of the plague intensified the political atmosphere. Mounting deaths in August and September produced fear, uncertainty, and near hysteria. Families with means of escape left London for the countryside. The judges of Westminster closed their courts. Attendance in Parliament declined sharply. The Lower House issued a special order designed to prevent the spread of the plague in Westminster, and a few days later extended it to cover the counties of Middlesex and Surrey. On 9 September, after a joint conference, the two Houses issued special orders—modeled after those issued by the King in council—to meet the emergency. That same day both Lords and Commons granted a long-overdue adjournment. Both Houses had met continuously for over ten months and members were tired and impatient. So, despite the business at hand, the opposition relented and agreed to recess from 9 September to 20 October.

Yet the opposition leaders were not prepared to set everything aside and thus risk losing the political initiative and their recently acquired power. They did not trust the King and his coterie in Scotland. To ensure victories already won, they made provision for an interim government of a select committee appointed from each House; the Lords named seventeen peers, including three Privy Councilors, and the Lower House named forty-five, including

23 *Commons Journal*, 2: 262.
24 *Diurnal Occurrences* (London), 1641, p. 343.

Pym and his cohorts.[25] The two groups were required to meet regularly throughout the recess to handle matters specially designated by each House; when necessity demanded, they were instructed to meet conjointly. Nothing was said of emergency power in case of a national crisis.

Essex was selected to serve on this interim committee along with Lord Keeper Littleton, Lord Privy Seal Manchester, Clare, Denbigh, and eleven others.[26] Despite the increase of the plague Essex remained in his official suite at Whitehall. He attended the Tuesday and Saturday meetings of the Lords' recess committee and some joint conferences with the Commons' group. He also met secretly with the opposition leaders on several equally significant occasions.[27] Once he joined the Earl of Newport, Lord Saye, Lord Mandeville, and Lord Wharton at Holland's suburban mansion at Kensington. On another occasion these and other peers met at Mandeville's lodging at Chelsea. Sometimes they were joined by Pym, Hampden, and other politicians from the Lower House.[28] In addition to handling routine matters relating to disbanding and Scottish affairs they plotted strategy for the postrecess session of Parliament, worked on the Grand Remonstrance, and discussed the Scottish system of selecting Privy Councilors from Parliament.

On 9 October, Essex and a handful of Privy Councilors convened in Whitehall Palace to face a potentially explosive situation. The King planned to permit the disbanded soldiers to sell their services to both Spanish and French ambassadors. The members of Parliament, however, had opposed these preparations by passing the ordinance which prohibited the recruitment and transportation of soldiers to foreign soil. The soldiers, restless and looking for employment, threatened the peace and security of the infected city. The Privy Councilors instructed Secretary Nicholas to write the King immediately and then act according to his instructions, but by the

25 *Old Parliamentary History*, 9: 537.

26 *Lords Journal*, 4: 392.

27 See *C. S. P. Ven., 1640–42*, p. 215; Sir Edward Nicholas's correspondence appended to *The Diary and Correspondence of John Evelyn*, ed. William Bray (London: George Routledge and Sons, 1906), pp. 765–90; and Willson Coates, *The Journal of Sir Simonds D'Ewes* (New Haven: Yale University Press, 1942), p. 353 (hereafter cited as *D'Ewes's Journal*).

28 On these matters see the sources cited in the previous note plus Wedgwood, *The King's Peace*, p. 451.

time the Privy Councilors received Charles's permission to use "anie means" they had already acted. At a second Privy Council meeting, held in Whitehall on 12 October, they ordered the justices of the peace in and around London "to take course, that a more effectual and strict order be taken for present sending away all the disbanded souldiers."[29]

The King, still in Edinburgh, was kept abreast of these happenings by his wife and his secretary. From the latter he heard of the infection, the increase of schismatics, and the unrest. He learned of the opposition's designs to remove more councilors and introduce the Scottish system of conciliar selection. He also was informed about the meetings of the opposition leaders and the moves of Parliament's interim groups to extend the recess period and postpone the resumption of business until November. Charles suggested that Nicholas search out the most faithful public servants and discuss all these matters with them and follow their advice until the sovereign returned.

One day before the reconvening of Parliament, on 19 October, Essex and the fellow committeemen were shocked to learn in a letter from Lord Howard of Escrick, writing from Scotland, of a royal conspiracy, known in part by the King, to seize and murder Argyll and Hamilton.[30] The plot—called the Incident—was poorly planned and executed. The committee members concluded that the papists were behind it and that the conspirators very likely had connections with the English recusants. For these reasons they decided to act quickly to forestall similar happenings in London or Westminster.

The Earl of Essex, captain general south of Trent, was put in charge of this emergency operation.[31] The extent to which he participated in the recess committee's decision to establish a guard remains obscure. Nevertheless, he promptly responded to the orders and assumed command of the situation. He mustered the trained bands of Westminster and assigned the various units to their respective duties. He placed four units, a total of five hundred men, in the palace yard to protect the members of both Houses. The soldiers, armed at all times, were to render around-the-clock

[29] Bray, *Diary of John Evelyn*, p. 771.

[30] There is a complete discussion of the Incident in Wedgwood, *The King's Peace*, pp. 460–66.

[31] Coates, *D'Ewes's Journal*, p. 18n.

protection to prevent tumults from breaking out in the vicinity of Westminster Palace. When the members of Parliament returned to their respective Houses the following day, 20 October, they confronted this *fait accompli*. Questions were immediately raised and explanations demanded.

In the Upper House, Essex explained that he had "received a Desire from the Committee of the House of Commons, which sat during the Time of the late Recess, that there might be a Guard of Soldiers around the Parliament to prevent the insolencies and affronts of Soldiers at this time about the Town, and to secure the Houses against other Designs which they have Reason to suspect until Parliament meets and gives further Order therein." This explanation satisfied the suspicious, apparently, for the Lords then concurred with the Commons on the matter. "Hereupon it was Ordered," Nalson noted, "That the Lord Chamberlain by virtue of this Order continue a Guard of Souldiers, to guard the Parliament Houses until the further Pleasure of the Parliament be known; and that the Number of the said Soldiers shall be wholly left unto the discretion and management of the said Lord Chamberlain, Captain General."[32] Some peers, if not all, were disturbed about the Incident and concerned about their own safety.

During the succeeding weeks both Houses devoted increasing amounts of time to the security of Parliament and the defense of the nation against plots. All private petitions and bills were put aside indefinitely. On 21 October, after a conference with leaders from the Commons, the Lords decided to form a "strong guard" in London and Westminster. The following day the Lords' commissioners issued a proclamation against disturbances and ordered the dispersal of all unemployed soldiers.[33] These precautions came none too soon, for that night trouble erupted near the palace yard. Some of the disbanded troops caused a disturbance in a nearby tavern. Essex called out the guard to quiet them. The troublemakers were apprehended and taken into custody. The Lords called the culprits to the bar of justice, found them in contempt, and then incarcerated them in Gatehouse Prison. The Commons went even further: they reversed their stand on the transportation of soldiers overseas. Henceforth foreign-born troops could be sent anywhere.

32 Nalson, *An Impartial Collection*, 2: 487.
33 *Lords Journal*, 4: 401.

The Lord Chamberlain also became involved in a move to secure Prince Charles. On 29 October several members of the Lower House complained that the eleven-year-old heir apparent was spending too much time at Oatlands with his Catholic mother instead of remaining at Richmond Palace with his Anglican tutors and aristocratic playmates. The next day, after representatives of both Houses discussed the matter in a joint conference, Parliament decided to act within the framework of Essex's commission, which empowered the Lord Chamberlain to provide for the security of the Prince.[34] As instructed, Essex handled the matter and reported to Parliament as soon as possible. He requested Hertford, the Prince's governor, to remove the youth from Oatlands and provide for his safety. Secondly, he requested his cousin Holland to attend the Queen and inform her of the reasons for Parliament's actions.

Essex played a major role in the events which followed. On 2 November he reported to the House of Commons that, after some resistance from the Queen, arrangements for the return of Prince Charles had been completed by Hertford. Essex also informed the House, D'Ewes reported in his diary, "that hee had acquainted Marquesse Hartford that hee should suffer no persons to come about the Prince but such as hee would answeare for."[35] That same day Essex also participated in a conference with Commons' leaders concerning a guard for Parliament. He informed the conferees, D'Ewes noted, that some of the officers guarding Parliament refused to obey his command. The Lower House, after hearing of this insubordination, proceeded to punish the guilty officers. They also engaged in a long debate about the necessity for a larger permanent guard for Parliament; they did not, however, reach any agreement on the details, for there remained many questions, such as which soldiers should be employed for the protection of Parliament, how they would be paid, and where they would be stationed. In the absence of complete agreement the entire matter was turned over to a committee headed by Sir Gilbert Gerrard. Meanwhile, the temporary guard, under Essex's command, continued to provide protection for the members of Parliament.

Two days later the Lords took up the matter. They quite rightly feared that the forthcoming Guy Fawkes Day celebrations might

[34] Coates, *D'Ewes's Journal*, p. 60.
[35] *Ibid.*, p. 70.

precipitate a riot. After some discussion they voted "that the Lord Chamberlain of His Majesty's Household, Captain General of the South Parts of this Kingdom shall give Order to the Lord Mayor of the City of London, to safe guard the said City, as there shall be cause, against all Tumults and Disorders that shall happen in or about the said City and the Liberties of the same, upon any occasion whatever." [36] Recognizing that the trained bands from Middlesex could not provide the needed protection, the Lords turned to the City for assistance. However, the Commons postponed action on the matter until they had an opportunity to reexamine Essex's commission.

On 6 November, during a debate in the Commons about the state of the kingdom, Oliver Cromwell, the radical Puritan who sat for Cambridge, moved that the Lower House "should desire the Lords that an ordinance of Parliament might passe to give the Earle of Essex power to assemble at all times the trained bands of the kingdome on this side Trent for the defence thereof till further order were taken by Parliament." [37] Cromwell's motion, sparked by ominous news of the Irish Rebellion, passed the Lower House in the following form: "That the Earl of Essex may have power from both Houses of Parliament to Command the Trained Bands on this Side Trent, upon all Occasions, for the Defence of the Kingdom; and that this Power may continue until the Parliament shall further order." [38] This measure, which came up for a long debate in a joint conference, met some opposition from the Lords, who deferred action for an indefinite period of time. No doubt some peers mistrusted the move and the prime mover. Some may have mistrusted Essex at this juncture, for after the conference the Upper House voted "That the Lord Chamberlain, Captain General of the South do discharge the Trained bands from their Night Watchings." [39]

That same day Essex was also asked to provide Parliament with a complete list of Queen Henrietta Maria's priests and servants— a request which he as Lord Chamberlain had no trouble honoring. [40] Two days later, acting upon orders from the Upper House, he supervised a search of the parish of Saint Katherine's for papist plotters rumored to be in the area, and reported that forty potential

36 Nalson, *An Impartial Collection*, 2: 603.
37 Coates, *D'Ewes's Journal*, p. 97.
38 *Lords Journal*, 4: 426.
39 *Ibid.*
40 *Ibid.*, pp. 426–37.

conspirators, all armed with pistols, were lodged near the Tower. These men, Essex further revealed, were being paid fourteen pence a day by John Bourke of Lincoln's Inn. They had been recruited by a Capt. Robert More, an Irish Catholic, whose recruitment funds came from Spain. The soldiers were promptly disarmed and Bourke was taken into custody by Essex under the authority of his commission.

The worsening Irish situation enabled Parliament to enlarge its military jurisdiction on grounds of public necessity. The Lower House set up a Council of War—a body which included several Essexians—and proceeded to make arrangements for the raising and transporting of 8,000 troops to suppress the Irish rebels. Both Houses approved an ordinance authorizing the lord deputy, the Earl of Leicester, to levy troops. On 10 November the Upper House passed an order preventing Irishmen from embarking for Ireland and another one recalling all English Catholics from Ireland "except the Earl of St. Albans and such other persons as have their ancient Estates and Habitation there."[41] Parliament's exemption of Essex's brother, Saint Albans, who had gone to Ireland in September, bespeaks of his influence in the matter.

Parliament also took several security precautions in England. The House of Commons provided poll-tax monies for Essex's parliamentary guard, appointed a pay clerk, and set up a pay schedule for the guard. A few days later the Upper House ordered the Earl of Newport to transfer all arms from Kingston-upon-Hull to the Tower of London for safekeeping. And on 13 November, Essex was named chairman of a committee to oversee the enforcement of all statutes and orders against recusants. Two days later a London tailor Thomas Beale reported to the Upper House on the details of a plot to murder Pym and at least 108 Puritans in the Lower House. Each was a marked man with a price on his head.

This plot produced another long debate concerning the defense of the kingdom and the security of Parliament. Again, Essex figured in an ordinance designed to increase Parliament's control over the police powers of the nation. "Mr. Hollis brought in the ordinance drawn by the Committee to putt the trained bands in a posture of defence and to give the command to the Earle of Essex," D'Ewes noted.[42] This measure, like that introduced earlier by

41 *Ibid.*, p. 433.
42 Coates, *D'Ewes's Journal*, p. 147.

Cromwell, passed the Lower House and was submitted to a joint conference for further consideration. At the conference managed by Pym the following day, the draft ordinance was discussed at length and modified to eliminate some objectionable phrases. The revised draft empowered the Earl of Essex "to have the trained bands of several counties in readiness, and do hereby give him power to command them whensoever these shall be needed to march and gather themselves in a body, and to oppose and set upon those who shall attempt, or do anything which may be prejudicial to the public peace."[43] At an extended debate in the Upper House the following day, serious objections to the proposal were voiced by several peers—so serious that the measure was again revised and returned to the Lower House. The revision, in effect, changed the measure from an ordinance to a full-fledged bill, for upon the instructions of Parliament the attorney general took it to Nicholas, who forwarded it to Charles for approval.

The two Houses, while concurring in matters of defense and security, disagreed about religious reform. Upon the reopening of Parliament on 20 October the opposition in the Commons renewed its attack upon the established church.[44] The leaders demanded a more rigorous enforcement of recusancy laws. They pressed the Lords to speed up the proceedings against the impeached bishops. They were backed in the Upper House by Essex, Mandeville, and Brooke but were checked by a majority of the Lords, who voted to postpone action. On 3 November the Lower Chamber passed the Bishops' Exclusion Bill, which stripped the clergy of their temporal jurisdiction, and forwarded it to the House of Lords for passage. The Lords allowed the bill to pass its first reading but then buried it in a committee. This did not quell the opposition, however, for they kept up the attack. On the suggestion of Bishop Williams they sequestered all Laud's inferior offices and stripped him of his appointive authority. Essex's position in these matters remained somewhat ambivalent: he supported the Commons' demand for speedier impeachment of the thirteen bishops, yet seems to have opposed the Bishops' Exclusion Bill.

Next to religion, the Grand Remonstrance drove the widest

43 From the original order in the House of Lords Record Office, Main Papers, dated 16 November 1641.

44 W. A. Shaw, *A History of the English Church during the Civil Wars and under the Commonwealth*, 2 vols. (London: Longmans and Company, 1900), 1: 101–18.

wedge between Lords and Commons.[45] For many months a select committee of the Lower House had worked halfheartedly toward a summary statement of the nation's grievances. More recently, especially during the recess, the radical leaders had prepared a lengthy document for approval by the Lower House. In early November it was introduced to the parent body and discussed for several days. Finally on 22 November, after nearly a year's preparation, the Grand Remonstrance received final approval. Royal prerogativists like Edward Hyde, Viscount Falkland, and John Culpeper opposed the entire document, especially those provisions which had the effect of changing the constitution, but their efforts were in vain; the Grand Remonstrance passed the Lower House, after an extended debate which lasted into the morning hours, by vote of 159 to 148. The victorious majority then demanded that the document be printed and distributed.

Most of the peers, including Essex and his fellow opposition lords, objected to the method, as well as to many of the provisions, of the Grand Remonstrance. The Commons in effect brushed aside the Upper House. They did not seek the advice of the Lords in a conference and did not strive for concurrence. Instead, they ignored the peers, passed the measure unilaterally, and then appealed to the people of England by publishing it without the consent of the King or the peers. Nor was this all. Pym's verbal assault on "evil councilors" raised several questions in the Upper House.[46] The Lords began to wonder whom he had in mind—those councilors who were already impeached or some of the newly appointed ones like Essex and Hertford.

III

THE ENGLISH SOVEREIGN was then preparing for his return to London. For many weeks Nicholas had urged him to leave Scotland before events got too far out of hand. Finally, in mid-November, Charles adjourned the Estates and celebrated with the Scottish leaders at Holyrood House, distributing honors to his friends and his former enemies.

[45] See Willson H. Coates, "Some Observations on the Grand Remonstrance," *Journal of Modern History* 4 (1932): 1–17; Gardiner, *History*, 10: 64–75; and Abbott, *Cromwell*, 1: 143.

[46] Gardiner, *History*, 10: 55.

Lord Chamberlain Essex helped complete the arrangements for the ruler's return to Whitehall. Charles received the warmest welcome since his coronation.[47] It was modeled after the triumphal reentry of a Roman general to the capital. On 24 November the reception party, including the Queen, the two princes, and the Marquess of Hamilton, gathered at Theobalds. Essex joined them that evening. The next day the royal retinue was met at Stanford Hill by a host of dignitaries. Here, after an exchange of short speeches, the King knighted both the Lord Mayor and the recorder of London with the sword of the City and then permitted the attendant aldermen and councilors to kiss his hands. All the welcomers then proceeded to conduct His Majesty in a long, formal processional to the heart of London. The cavalcade included one hundred of England's most distinguished citizens: the Privy Councilors, the aldermen, the city marshal, the sheriff of Middlesex and his trumpeters, the King's trumpeters, several heralds, the Queen and her coterie, the two princes and their Courts, and scores of other ladies and gentlemen of quality.[48]

Late in the afternoon Charles led his party through the City to Whitehall Palace, which Essex had prepared for his return. The footmen lighted the way with flambeaux. The trumpeters announced the coming of the King to Westminster. According to one observer, "the Conduits of Cheapside and Fleet-Street all the while running with Wine. In the passage by the South door of St. Paul's Cathedral, the Quire, with Sackbuts and Cornets, sung an Anthem of Praise to God, with Prayers for their Majesties long Lives, that his Majesty was extremely pleased with it, and gave them very particular Thanks, as all the way of his Passage . . . The Citizens blessing and praying for their Majesties and their Royal issue, and their Majesties returning the same Blessings upon the Heads of the Citizens."[49] The King was visibly touched by this display of loyalty.

However, within hours of the King's return to London, Essex was forced to surrender his military commission. The need for captain general was over now. The following day, 26 November, he reported to Parliament. "The Lord Chamberlain signified to this House,"

[47] For facts about Charles's return see Rushworth, *Historical Collections*, 4: 429–35.

[48] Nalson, *An Impartial Collection*, 2: 675–79.

[49] See *Ovatio Carolina* (London, 1641), reprinted in *Harleian Miscellany*, 5: 95.

the clerk recorded, "That the King being returned home, his Lordship hath delivered up his Commission of Captain General of the South Parts of this Kingdom, into his Majesties Hands, so that his Lordship cannot now take any Order for the Guarding of the Parliament, as was Ordered by the Parliament; therefore he desired their Lordships to consider of what Course is fit to be taken herein, he having now no Power to obey their Commands. Hereupon, it was Resolved to communicate the matter to the House of Commons at a Conference which was done accordingly."[50]

The leaders of the Lower House took exception to Essex's dismissal. In fact, the Commons' leadership requested that both Houses petition the King to continue the guard under Essex's command. A majority in the Upper House, however, voted down the proposal; instead, they agreed to merely ask the King to consider retaining the guard. Warwick and Digby secured from Charles a message explaining his actions and a compromise regarding a guard. "I did command the Guards to be dismissed," Charles explained, "because I knew no Cause the Parliament had of Fears; but I perceived the Molestation that the keeping of them would bring upon those Subjects of mine which were to perform that Service; besides the General Apprehensions and Jealousies which thereby might disquiet all My People: and I do Expect that when the Parliament shall desire of Me any thing like this Extraordinary, and that which appears of ill consequence, that they will give me such particular Reasons as may satisfie My Judgment, if they expect I should grant their Desire."[51] It is clear from this reprimand that the King disapproved of the guard and distrusted the motives of those leaders, especially Essex, who had taken the extraordinary action. But to pacify those who claimed otherwise Charles compromised by appointing the Earl of Dorset to command the trained bands for a few days to determine whether or not there was still a need. This incident, especially the appointment of Dorset, must have irked Essex, for it appeared that he had been cashiered and then replaced by the Queen's favorite.

The radicals in the Lower House reacted to these insults with drastic countermeasures. William Strode, the M.P. Essex had supported for election to the Long Parliament, called for a bill

[50] *Lords Journal*, 4: 453.

[51] Nalson, *An Impartial Collection*, 2: 685. Also see *H. M. C. Buccleuch Manuscripts*, 1: 286–88.

putting the entire kingdom in a posture of defense—a proposal which Gardiner called the germ of the Militia Bill. The following day Sir Arthur Haselrig, after reviving the matter, pointed out the precedents for maintaining a guard and questioned the King's dismissal. The King's guard under Dorset, he contended, was illegal.[52] The Commons then established a select committee to deal with the problem.

That same day violence over keeping the guard was narrowly averted.[53] Hundreds of apprentices congregated outside Parliament House to bait the clergymen by crying for no bishops. The situation because extremely tense. To break up a brawl between the Westminster Bands and the London apprentices, Dorset's troops dealt harshly with the protesting apprentices. Fortunately, no blood was shed. But Dorset had shown his colors: henceforth he was detested by political enemies. The following day, 30 November, King Pym capitalized on this affair and kept the guard issue alive. Parliament needed a guard, he contended, and should appoint the commander. If Pym could choose, the commander would be Essex.

But Pym did not have his way. Essex was out—displaced by Dorset, the Queen's favorite—although he retained his places as Lord Chamberlain, Privy Councilor, and lord lieutenant of Yorkshire. His prestige and popularity were still useful to the King. In the succeeding weeks Essex was also utilized by Parliament as a go-between on numerous occasions. In early December, at the request of the House of Lords, he informed the King of the need for guards to protect the transportation of arms from London to Chester,[54] and then reported on the matter to his colleagues. On 17 December, two days after the Lower House published the Grand Remonstrance, Essex helped arrange for a meeting between the King and a joint delegation from Parliament; it was, in fact, Lord Chamberlain Essex who presented the delegation to the King at Whitehall.[55]

The King, too, used Essex to act on his behalf. On 20 December Charles had him inform the Upper House that the recently received privilege petition would soon be returned.[56] The answer, an

[52] Coates, *D'Ewes's Journal*, pp. 202–8.

[53] John Forster, *The Debates on the Grand Remonstrance* (London, 1860), pp. 358, 373.

[54] *Lords Journal*, 4: 463–65.

[55] Coates, *D'Ewes's Journal*, p. 305.

[56] *Lords Journal*, 4: 481.

apology to both houses, may well have been Essex's doing. Yet it is clear from the extant evidence that Essex was not a member of Charles's inner cabinet that governed England during these crucial months. He resided in Whitehall and participated in the sporadic meetings of the Privy Council. He rendered advice when the King called upon him and he acted as a liaison between the opposition and the sovereign, but he appears to have had little voice in the making of decisions. He was too committed to Parliament and too closely associated with the opposition leaders to be completely trusted as a royal confidant.

Meanwhile, Essex figured in several partisan skirmishes relating to military and police powers. On 7 December, Sir Arthur Haselrig presented to the Lower House his radical Militia Bill. All of the horse and foot, it provided, would be centralized and placed under two generals who would be responsible to Parliament. "In this Act there is such unlimited and independent power given to these persons that whatsoever hath been usurped by any prince is here to be settled by Act of Parliament upon these men," wrote a contemporary.[57] Although the bill did not name the two generals, Essex, Holland, and Northumberland were mentioned as the most likely candidates. The first reading of Haselrig's proposal was rejected by a vote of 158 to 125.

Three weeks later, after several demonstrations, the Lower House renewed its demand for a parliamentary guard under Essex's command. The King had dismissed Essex, and the troops had been disbanded by Essex's successor, Dorset, on the premise that Parliament had no pressing need for protection. But the Lord Mayor had not preserved the peace. The bishops had been assaulted on their way to the House of Lords.[58] People thronged around the doors of both Houses. When asked to leave, the crowds refused, saying that they feared reprisal. Something had to be done to protect those Englishmen who attended Parliament.

On 27 December, while the Puritan apprentices continued to demonstrate outside the Upper House, the peers acted to preserve the parliamentary processes. They empowered a committee composed of Essex and several of his colleagues to examine the warrants of the soldiers, investigate the cause and continuance of the demonstrations against the bishops, and recommend some preventive measures. The committee suggested that Parliament

57 *H. M. C. Twelfth Report*, 2: 296.
58 *Lords Journal*, 4: 492.

petition the King for an armed guard. Even Lord Digby, one of the King's most faithful supporters, concurred with the recommendation. After much discussion the House of Commons "resolved upon the Question, That this shall be the answeare to the Lords, That wee shall joine with their Lordships in petitioning his Majestie to have a guard soe as the Earl of Essex may command it and that it may be approved by both houses of Parliament."[59]

The revised proposal trenched upon the royal prerogative so heavily that the Lords turned it down the following day. It is not clear whether the majority also objected to Essex—but whether they did or not the result was the same. Finally, the Lords issued antiriot writs on the basis of a statute passed in 1412. The Lord Keeper distributed the writs to the sheriffs and the justices of the peace and commanded them to establish watches and protect members of Parliament from the mob; in choosing this device the peers rejected Essex. The political consequences of this exclusion were fatal to the King's party in the Upper House.[60]

On the last day of December the commoners, ignoring the Lords, who refused to join them, renewed their demands for a parliamentary guard by petitioning the King. They did not want the trained bands of Westminster or the soldiers in the Tower. Nor did they desire the Earl of Dorset as the commander. Rather, they demanded that the trained bands of the City be "commanded by the Earl of Essex, Lord Chamberlain of your Majesties Household, of whose fidelities to your Majestie and the Commonwealth have had long experience."[61]

It is easy to discern why the commonalty clamored for Essex. A Londoner by birth and residence, he enjoyed an unequalled popularity among the masses of London, particularly after his role in Strafford's trial and attainder. An experienced horseman and commander who had fought for the cause of international Protestantism on several occasions, he had a good reputation among the soldiers of both London and the country at large. A staunch supporter of Parliament and the defender of the rights of Englishmen, he had many devotees in the Lower House. His surname and title brought back memories of Elizabethan greatness. He was the living

[59] Coates, *D'Ewes's Journal*, p. 356.

[60] *Lords Journal*, 4: 496.

[61] See *A proposition or Message Sent the 31 of December 1641 To His Majestie By the House of Commons for a Guard* (London, 1641).

beneficiary of a popular legend which had appeared during his father's lifetime and blossomed after his father's execution in the Tower courtyard.

Yet, it is difficult to appraise Essex's performance as Lord Chamberlain. His tenure was brief—about nine months—and the times were abnormal. He had little opportunity to advise the King, who was in Scotland most of the time, and he never gained the complete confidence of those who comprised the ruling clique. When he took up residence in Whitehall, the hub of politics and diplomacy, he rubbed elbows with many of the King's friends, but he exercised little patronage and less power. There is no reason to believe that he exerted any influence over the appointment of royal chaplains, as the Earl of Pembroke had, although he may well have had some voice in the translation of his old friend Joseph Hall from the bishopric of Exeter to Norwich, a larger and more lucrative see, and in the elevation of John Williams, Bishop of Lincoln, to the archepiscopal see of York. There is no evidence that Essex influenced the heir apparent or his brother through the appointment of tutors. He performed such routine duties as granting funds from the King's private purse to the Duke of York's barber, Thomas Walpoole, and signing warrants for the payment of book purchases made by Prince Charles's tutor, Brian Duppa, the Bishop of Salisbury. He also received and acted upon many private petitions submitted by commoners, several of whom came from Staffordshire; in each instance, Essex presented the petition to the Upper House and used his influence and prestige to secure justice in the High Court of Parliament.[62]

John Cragg, a minor poet who lived through the Puritan upheaval, incorporated this theme into a short poem entitled *A Prophecy Concerning the Earl of Essex now is*, published in booklet form in late December 1641. The frontispiece depicts Essex and several of his colleagues seated at a table, attempting to resolve their differences by persuasion, and on the second page Essex appears in the garb of peace. The poem begins:

> Prepare your self, brave Robert Essex Earl,
> In Britain Great, you are a pretious pearle:
> God hath ordained you for some other end:

[62] For these cases see *H.M.C. Fourth Report*, p. 98; *H.M.C. House of Lords Manuscripts*, n.s., 11: 316, 320; *Lords Journal*, 4: 479, 645; and Miscellaneous Collections, HM 374, Huntington Library.

> Then in Great Britain all your days to spend.
> Your fathers fame, and good report I heare,
> It made all Irish rebels stand in feare,
> He was of valour and courage stout,
> And whilst he liv'd he plagu'd the Romish Rout
> His name was feared in Ireland, France and Spaine;
> Because the truth of Christ he did maintaine.
> He made a vow, which made proud Rome to storme,
> You are his Son, you must his vow performe.[63]

IV

IN 1642 the rift between Essex and Charles widened so greatly that it became virtually impossible to bridge the gap between them. Throughout the first three months Essex continued to dwell in his suite at Whitehall. He retained his several offices and even used his prestige and popularity to attempt an accommodation between the King and the disgruntled populace. Still, the issues that separated the two men became more numerous, and in the final analysis, Essex placed his devotion to Parliament above his loyalty to Charles.

The monarch commenced the new year with a counterattack upon the opposition leaders. He added to the Privy Council several members of the constitutional moderates—the Earl of Southampton, Viscount Falkland, and Sir John Culpeper—all of whom were rewarded with places.[64] Charles then carried the political war into the enemy camp. On 3 January, after hasty preparations, the Lord Keeper informed the Upper House that Lord Mandeville, Pym, Hampden, William Strode, Holles, and Haselrig were charged with high treason. Kymbolton denied the charge, of course, and demanded the right to be heard. The opposition peers, reacting with deliberate speed to protect their colleague, empowered a committee including Essex, Bath, and Warwick, to consider the charge and investigate precedents.[65]

In the meantime the five commoners, known as the Five Members, learned of the charges against them and prepared for the worst. They were not taken into custody immediately; instead Charles used the time to secure evidence and gain political support for his counterblow against John Pym. The King kept his guard

---

[63] From the British Museum, Thomason Collection.
[64] *H. M. C. Twelfth Report*, 2: 302–4.
[65] *Old Parliamentary History*, 10: 158.

intact to prevent any bloodshed. He informed some lawyers at the Inns of Court of the charges against the Five Members and appealed to them to stand by in case he needed their support. He also searched the houses of the accused for incriminating evidence. During the night of 4 January, Charles made plans for the arrest of the Five Members. He decided to march with attendants into the Lower Chamber the afternoon of the following day and seize his adversaries before they could escape. It was a daring plan with manifold risks. It required perfect timing and secrecy to succeed.

Essex entered the action at this point, however, and foiled the King's stratagem. During the dinner hour Lord Essex learned the details of the plan from his cousin the Countess of Carlisle and immediately tipped off the accused commoners before the afternoon session began. When Charles approached the House of Commons the Five Members fled through a back door to a barge which was waiting for them. After leaving his troops in the lobby Charles boldly entered the Lower House, thus violating a long and cherished tradition, and proceeded to the speaker's chair, greeting some commoners along the way. Seeing that the Five Members were not present, he then realized that he had been betrayed and had fallen into a trap set by King Pym. Just before leaving the Lower Chamber, Charles is reputed to have remarked, "All my birds have flown." [66]

In the succeeding days the breach between the King and his political antagonists increased. Parliament obstinately refused to conduct any business in Westminster. The Lower House, however, met in committee at Guildhall and complained about the lack of a guard and denounced those who assisted the King in his foolhardy schemes. The members of the Common Council, turning against the King and defying the Lord Mayor, petitioned against the presence of dangerous recusants in the kingdom. On 8 January they formed an *ad hoc* body called the Committee for Safety to deal with the emergency and advocated a guard under the command of Philip Skippon, a popular professional soldier who frequented the Artillery Yard. The City, quite clearly, sided with the Five Members against the King.

The English sovereign, realizing too late the magnitude of his miscalculation, decided to solicit support in the counties. He remained at Whitehall Palace long enough to see the apprentices and

---

[66] John Forster, *The Arrest of the Five Members* (London, 1860), p. 175.

sailors protest his actions, to learn that the trained bands of London
were mobilized and placed under Skippon's command, and to hear
the movement of cannon and the drilling of soldiers. By 10 January,
Charles was convinced that the members of the royal family,
including himself, were in jeopardy. Under cover of darkness he
departed to Hampton Court with his spouse and their three children.
He never returned of his own free will.

Essex played an ambivalent role in the events leading to the
King's flight from London: he betrayed his sovereign by revealing
to Pym information which allowed the Five Members to escape,
but he permitted his reputation and popularity to be exploited by
the King in an attempt to reach an accommodation with the City
authorities. He then "moved that the House of Peers, as a work
very proper for them, would interpose between the King and his
people, and mediate to his Majesty on behalf of the persons accused,
for which he was reprehended by his friends and afterwards laughed
at himself when he found how much stronger defence they had
than the best mediation could prove on their behalf."[67] The
Commons cared little about the doctrine of interposition or the
mechanics of mediation. Essex also sought to persuade the King to
remain in Westminster near Parliament rather than flee to the
countryside with his family. On 10 January, shortly before the
royal family departed, he, Holland, and Lady Carlisle visited
Charles and tried to convince him to remain near the City. The
King, taking the advice of the Queen and her courtiers, refused to
change his plans. Essex's efforts to mediate came to nought.

Shortly before leaving London, however, the King ordered Essex
and Holland to follow him to Hampton Court. "The earl of Essex
resolved to go," wrote Clarendon, "and to that purpose was making
himself ready when the earl of Holland came to him and privately
dissuaded him, assuring him that if they two went they should be
murdered at Hampton Court; whereupon they left the King to his
small retinue and in a most disconsolate, perplexed condition,
in more need of comfort and counsel than they had every known
him; and instead of attending their master in that exigent, they
went together into the city where the committee sat, and where they
were not the less welcome for being known to have been invited to
have waited upon their majesties."[68] The appeal from his cousin

[67] Clarendon, *History* (Macray ed.), bk. 4, sects. 31 and 196.
[68] *Ibid.*

Holland on grounds of self-preservation diverted Essex from following his inclination to obey the King's command.

The next day Essex presented to the Upper House his dilemma
regarding that command. The Lords agreed with him rather than
with the King, "whereupon the House Commanded the Lord
Chamberlain and the Earl of Holland to attend this House, and
would not dispense with their Absence, in regard of the many
great and urgent business depending in this House." [69] Thus
Parliament legalized what the recalcitrant Lords had previously
decided on their own.

Parliament, meanwhile, moved to establish a national militia
under its jurisdiction. The House of Lords approved a weakened
version of the Militia Bill which retained several features of the
traditional system. Written by the King's solicitor general, Oliver
St. John, a follower of Essex in the Lower House, it called for the
retention of the lord lieutenant system at the county level and
implied that the aristocrats would continue to dominate those
offices. The lord lieutenants would be appointed by and be responsible to Parliament rather than the King—an innovation
which trod on the royal prerogative. The Lords had hoped that
this bill, in contrast to the more radical measure emanating from
the Commons, might gain the King's consent, for it preserved some
measure of aristocratic control over the military. The Commons
apparently accepted the general features of this measure, for they
recommended that the members of the respective counties begin
naming persons to fill the places. They altered some phrases and
added a rather sharp preface to the bill, however, and the amended
bill, when returned to the House of Lords, caused quite a stir. The
preface infuriated all the King's men and most of the moderates.
More important, a majority disapproved of the moves of the Commons to nominate particular persons before the measure passed
Parliament. Thus the two Houses reached an impasse on St. John's
Militia Bill.

Essex and his opposition colleagues then proposed a conference
with the Lower House to compose their differences. When this
proposal failed, a minority of thirty-two Lords drew up a formal
protest. Essex, now the high-ranking peer among the opposition,
was the first to sign. [70] Two days later his name again headed a

69 Nalson, *An Impartial Collection*, 2: 836.
70 *Old Parliamentary History*, 10: 233.

protestation.[71] The Lords were asked to join the Lower House in a petition calling for parliamentary control over the forts and castles of England. In the midst of the debate the Duke of Richmond, the King's chief spokesman in the Upper House, had the audacity to propose that Parliament adjourn for a six-months' cooling-off period. For this impolitic statement he was castigated, shamed, and forced to make a public apology. His apology, presented later in the day, was accepted by a majority of the peers, but fourteen Lords registered a formal protest in the belief that Richmond's punishment was too mild.[72]

The King's supporters in the Upper House still included a small number of bishops who had escaped earlier assaults by the Lower House. Most bishops, however, were in prison awaiting trial. Meanwhile, anticlerical sentiment was increasing in the City and the countryside. Finally, on 5 February, after a prolonged debate, the Lords passed the Bishops' Exclusion Bill by a vote of thirty-six to twenty-three. The Earl of Essex, who had originally opposed disabling the bishops in this manner, evidently switched and voted for exclusion.[73] The following week, hopeful that this concession might forestall more radical attacks upon the established church, Charles approved the measure.

This political compromise further weakened the King's cause in the Upper House. In the weeks and months that followed, more and more peers were absent from the daily sittings of the House of Lords. Some joined the King; others returned to their country estates; still others claimed sickness. Charles attempted to bolster the dwindling cause in various ways. He offered a general pardon to all his subjects, including Lord Mandeville, and ordered the absentee lords to attend the debates. He required the Lord Keeper to call the roll. But, try as he did, the King failed to muster a stable majority in the House of Lords.

This failure played into the hands of Essex and the hard-core opposition leaders, who, now working hand in glove with the Commons' leadership, assumed more military powers as they prepared the nation for armed conflict.[74] They reconfirmed Skippon's appointment as commander of the guard for Parliament;

---

[71] Sanford, *Studies*, pp. 477–81.
[72] *Old Parliamentary History*, 10: 252.
[73] *Lords Journal*, 4: 529, 564, 568, 583.
[74] *Ibid.*, pp. 508, 511, 521.

they wrested from Charles the dismissal of Sir John Byron and the appointment of Sir John Conyers, an Essexian, as lieutenant of the Tower; and they joined the Commons in several orders aimed at securing arms and ammunition. The aristocratic opposition then joined the Lower House and petitioned the King for the establishment of a parliamentary controlled militia.

The King's rejection of the petition was debated in Parliament for several days.[75] Leaders of both Houses conferred on naming the lord lieutenants of the respective counties and amended some phrases but refused to alter the substance of the bill to meet the royal objections. They then returned it to the King, hoping that the deplorable situation in Ireland would more or less compel him to approve it. On 28 February the King expressed a willingness to accept the bill if certain conditions were met. He agreed to approve the men nominated in the bill if he, rather than Parliament, would possess the power to issue and terminate the commissions and if the inflammatory preface were eliminated or amended.

Upon learning of the King's rejection of the Militia Bill, the leaders of Parliament proceeded to put the kingdom in a posture of defense without securing royal approval of their actions. On 2 March they ordered the Earl of Northumberland, the Lord Admiral, to put the navy in a state of readiness. Three days later, both Houses passed the Militia Ordinance.[76] (The leaders of both Houses, realizing that the King would not sign the bill, finally resorted to this expedient legislative form, which did not require the royal signature. They had used the ordinance during the King's stay in Scotland and they were informed by legal antiquarians of sound precedents for such procedure.) The provisions of the Militia Ordinance were similar to those in the bill which had been approved by the Lords three weeks earlier. The purpose of the measure was simply stated: to provide for the safety "of His Majesty's person, the Parliament and kingdom in this time of imminent danger."[77] It then listed the new parliamentary designated lord lieutenants by counties. All the appointees except for Sir John Bankes, Sir Henry Vane, and Denzil Holles were noblemen. Those earls who had been opposed to the King predominated. Most of them were assigned one county, but a few lords were assigned two or more.

[75] *Ibid.*, pp. 558 ff.
[76] *Ibid.*, p. 625.
[77] Rushworth, *Historical Collections*, 4: 520.

Essex was appointed to three counties—Staffordshire, Yorkshire, and Montgomeryshire. His powers were almost identical to those previously granted by the King. He was empowered to recruit, arm, muster, and train troops within the designated counties. He was to be assisted, moreover, by deputy lieutenants of his own choosing. Upon receiving from Parliament their instructions, he was required to suppress all rebellions, insurrections, and invasions that occurred, either within the respective county or in any other part of England or Wales.

The Earl of Essex dutifully complied with these terms. On the appointed day, 7 March, he was the first peer to submit his old commissions, covering Staffordshire and Yorkshire.[78] Essex transferred his allegiance in military matters from the King to Parliament by these actions, but he and his compeers retained those powers for the aristocracy, not the commonalty, and in so doing hoped to ensure aristocratic leadership. They, the natural aristocracy who had led the nation in peace and war, were prepared to follow in the footsteps of their medieval predecessors—even if it meant civil war.

Both sides now prepared for a trial by battle. Parliament reiterated its demand that all lord lieutenants surrender their old commissions. The Lords called for the suppression of all armed forces levied without the advice and consent of Parliament. They proceeded to consult with the Commons in the nomination of deputy lieutenants for the respective counties and filled those lord lieutenancies turned down by Lords Hertford, Cumberland, Strange, and Wharton. They then established the exact form of the commission. They also joined with the Lower House in a petition asking Charles to appoint the Earl of Warwick as the vice admiral in place of Sir John Pennington. When the King refused, they issued the order to the Earl of Northumberland, still Lord Admiral, who promptly complied.

V

THE KING had arrived at York on 19 March and had begun to put into effect plans which he hoped would split the ranks of the aristocratic opposition. He commanded Holland and Pembroke to

[78] *Lords Journal*, 4: 629.

attend him to celebrate the Feast of Saint George, which fell on 23 April. The two peers, upon the receipt of their letters on 21 March, reported the matter to the House of Lords. That body defiantly countermanded the King and ordered them to remain in Westminster and attend "the affairs of the Kingdom now discussed in Parliament." [79] If Charles had intended to attract them by appealing to their loyalty to the exclusive Order of Saint George, he did not succeed. Several days later it was rumored in London that the King would make Hertford and Southampton Knights of the Garter during the forthcoming festivities in order to draw them from the City and divide the opposition.

On 28 March, Essex also received a personal communication from Charles, summoning him to York. "Our will and command therefor is," wrote the King, "that you repair hitherto to our Court, as soon as you may conveniently, to give your attendance in the place and charge which you hold under us as a private officer of our house and councillor of state . . . we shall expect your present answer thereunto." [80] He could not appeal to Essex's loyalty to the Order of Saint George, for the Lord was not a member, so Charles appealed to his sense of duty.

Essex promptly brought the matter before the House of Lords. "Next, the Lord Chamberlain acquainted this House," the clerk of Parliament wrote, "That he hath received a Letter from His Majesty, to give his Attendance at Yorke; but, before he took any Resolution therein, he thought it his Duty to acquaint this House therewith, and to receive their Lordships Directions." [81] The Earl of Salisbury and Lord Savile subsequently reported that they had received similar communications. After considerable discussion, the Lords approved the following resolution: "That the Lord Chamberlain of His Majesty's Household, the Earl of Salisbury, the Earl of Holland and the Lord Savile and all other Lords have not the Leave of this House to be absent, shall give their attendance on this House, in regard of the great and weighty affairs of the Kingdom now in Agitation." [82]

Soon thereafter Essex received a second letter from the King, commanding him to ignore the Lord's resolution and come to

[79] *Ibid.*, p. 658.
[80] *Ibid.*, p. 673.
[81] *Ibid.*
[82] *Ibid.*

York. "Wee doe hereby lett you know," the communication, dated 2 April, read, "that Wee are pleased to dispense with your absence from Our said Parliament, Our said Writt, or any thing therein conteined to the contrary notwithstanding." [83] If the King could demand attendance at Parliament, he could also dispense with it, if he so desired, and issue a higher command: such was the essence of the King's argument. Charles's personal letter, when received by Essex, constituted a royal warrant; from the explicit command there was no way of escape short of disobedience, and disobedience bordered on treason.

Still Essex refused to attend the King in York; instead he remained in London. The next week he received a third letter, dated 9 April and personally delivered by Lord Falkland. "We are so much unsatisfied with the Excuse you made for not obeying our Command for your Attendance on us here, according to the Duty of your place in our Household," the King wrote, "that we thought good, by these our letters, to second our former Command; and that you may be the more inexcusable, we have accompanied our said Command with our Licence and Dispensation inclosed for your Absence from Parliament . . . in case you shall persist in your Disobedience, we then require and command you to deliver up into the Hands of the Lord Falkland, one of our principal Secretaries of State, for our use, the Ensigns of your office." [84]

As before, Essex refused to respond personally to obey the royal injunction; rather he presented Charles's letter to the Upper House and asked whether he should obey or defy the King's explicit command, whether he should surrender his office, and whether he should answer the King's letter. As before, the Upper House directed him to defy the royal instructions and comply with the earlier order of Parliament. In fact, the previous order was reread in the Upper House. The Earl of Holland, who received a similar missive, was treated in like fashion. "The Lords went into a Debate on this Matter," writes Clarendon, "and, afterward, resolved to command the two Earls attendance on this House, on the great and urgent Affairs now depending in Parliament; notwithstanding his Majesty's letters and dispensations." [85]

Essex had no alternative but to resign his position as Lord

---

[83] *H.M.C. House of Lords Manuscripts*, n.s., 12: 317.

[84] *Old Parliamentary History*, 10: 429.

[85] Clarendon, *History* (Macray ed.), bk. 5, sect. 33.

Chamberlain. He and Holland stepped outside the House of Lords and turned over the insignias of their offices to the King's personal representative, Lord Falkland. Their forced resignation led to a debate in the Upper House about the honor and privileges of Parliament. The Lords, obviously disgusted by the King's disregard of their authority, passed three resolutions. The Commons went even further: they denounced the King's dismissal of Essex and Holland as "an Injury to the Parliament and the Whole Kingdom."[86]

The dismissal of Essex, according to Clarendon, was a tragic blunder. "And there is great reason to believe that if that resolution the King had taken had not been too obstinately pursued at that time," he wrote, "many of the mischieves which afterward fell out would have been prevented; and without doubt, if the staff had remained still in the hands of the earl of Essex, by which he was charged with the defence and security of the King's person, he would never have been prevailed with to have taken upon him the command of that army which was afterwards raised against the King's, and with which so many battles were fought. And there can be as little doubt, in any man who knew the nature and temper of that time, that it had been utterly impossible for the two Houses of Parliament to have raised an army then if the earl of Essex had not consented to be general of that army."[87]

While the Royalist peers departed for York to participate in the festivities of the Order of Saint George, the Earl of Essex remained in the City and labored for the cause of Parliament.

[86] *Lords Journal*, 4: 713–19.
[87] Clarendon, *History* (Macray ed.), bk. 5, sect. 33.

CHAPTER 12

Captain General

I

AT THE TIME OF HIS resignation as Lord Chamberlain, the Earl of Essex was an unhappily married nobleman of fifty-two. He was not welcome at Court. He remained outside the inner circles which governed England. In surrendering his staff to Lord Falkland, Essex relinquished little power, for Charles had never entrusted him with much authority. Nevertheless, the forced resignation must have infuriated Essex. And it must have been humiliating for him, ever envious of those in high places, to be discarded, after having filled the office less than one year. This ouster, after the public cashiering during the Scottish war, made a personal *rapprochement* between Charles and Essex virtually impossible. Henceforth they were antagonists in a prolonged struggle which culminated in bloodshed.

Essex remained committed to the parliamentary monarchy which the Long Parliament had established, however. He stood for monarchy, the aristocracy, and the episcopacy; he opposed republicans, levellers, and sectarian radicals. He favored a Lancastrian type of kingship in which the aristocracy held the balance of the political power between a weak monarch dependent upon Parliament for advice and a prosperous commonalty. His objectives remained reactionary. His opposition to the King followed the traditional forms of medieval noblemen and Lancastrian parliaments. He would, in short, foster the removal of those councilors who surrounded the King and prevented further reformation. He would retaliate against his enemies through parliamentary means. He would not lift his sword against his sovereign—as his father had unwisely done—without a command from Parliament.

Within hours of his ouster Parliament evinced its loyalty to Essex through several official acts. On 13 April both Houses resolved that the forced resignation was a great disservice to the whole kingdom; that Essex was not guilty of disobedience in attending Parliament in Westminster rather than the King in York; and that those who

300

accepted the offices vacated by Essex and Holland were guilty of ignoble acts against Parliament.[1] Essex's dismissal, the House of Lords contended, stemmed from the influence of "evil councilors" around the King.

Essex resumed his old place in the Upper House between the Earls of Bedford and Lincoln. He lost his claim to higher precedence. In the eyes of the clerk of Parliament he was no longer "*camerar hospiti*," but simply "*comes* Essex." The removal also compelled him to relinquish his official suite in Whitehall and resume his residence in Essex House on the Strand. These demotions did not deter Essex's political activity in the Upper House. He continued to sit on the most important committees, often serving as chairman, and he played a larger role in joint conferences with opposition leaders in the Lower House. Equally important, he remained the Lords' principal authority in military matters.

In the weeks following his ouster Essex relegated much time and energy to the proposed expedition to Ireland.[2] He served with Lords Mandeville and Robartes as an auditor of the poll tax collected for the suppression of the Irish rebellion. He also helped draft detailed instructions for the lord lieutenant of Ireland and assisted in the recruitment of 10,000 volunteers. One unfounded rumor claimed that he would be named commander of the Irish venture. "They do not relax their energy over the levies of the English for that campaign," the Venetian envoy noted, "and it is said that those will be commanded by the Earl of Essex, one who made himself known more than any other as the declared enemy of his Majesty's interests and also as an inexorable persecutor of the Catholic faith." [3]

The efforts of Essex and his colleagues produced immediate results. Thousands of Londoners enlisted during the first week. By 10 May the trained bands were ready for their first review, which took place in Finsbury Field. About 8,000 volunteers, led by their newly appointed officers, paraded before those members of Parliament who had been invited to observe the affair. At the appointed hour the Earl of Essex appeared at Finsbury Field in a newly purchased gilt coach.[4] He, Holland, Northumberland, and several

1 *Lords Journal*, 4: 719.
2 *Ibid.*, 5: 1–33.
3 *C. S. P. Ven., 1641–1642*, p. 46.
4 *H. M. C. Fifth Report*, p. 178.

other peers were honored with specially prepared tents and entertainment. The following day Essex was appointed to a special committee authorized to secure additional supplies of saltpeter and gunpowder for the militia.

Meanwhile, the King established a broader-based party outside of Parliament. Through the efforts of Queen Henrietta Maria he secured some promises of man power and material from the Netherlands. He made a special appeal to the Scots for assistance, but their leaders promptly rejected his propositions. Charles witnessed greater success in rallying support in the northern counties, particularly Yorkshire. In mid-May he invited all the noblemen and gentry to attend him in York for the ostensible purpose of launching a move against Sir John Hotham, governor of Hull, who had defied royal orders.[5] Except for a small minority, whose protests were overridden, most of the Yorkshire landholders stood with the King rather than Parliament in the showdown over Hull. This bid was so heartening that on 3 June, Charles appealed to several thousand Yorkshire residents, who had been summoned to a meeting at Heyworth Moor near York, and announced his intention to establish a personal guard.[6] The response to his appeals was most gratifying: within one week he had a praetorian guard of 600 troopers to protect his person and assist him in the maintenance of law and order. Prince Charles was awarded the command of a troop of horse. The soldiers were paid from the royal coffers every Saturday. Here was the nucleus of an army which the King could use against Hull—and perhaps against Parliament.

The opposition leaders in Westminster viewed these developments with alarm. Both Houses petitioned the King to reverse his plans. "Therefore we do humbly beseech your Majesty to disband all such Forces, as by your Command are assembled," they requested, "and relying upon your Security (as your predecessors have done) upon the Laws and Affections of your People, you will be pleased to desist from any further Designs of this nature, contenting yourself with the usual and ordinary Guards; otherwise we shall hold ourselves bound in Duty towards God, and the Trust reposed in us by the People, and the Fundamental Laws and Constitution of this Kingdom, to employ our Care and utmost Power to secure the Parliament, and Preserve the Peace and Quiet of the Kingdom."[7]

5 Rushworth, *Historical Collections*, 4: 616–21.
6 *Ibid.*, p. 616.
7 *Ibid.*, p. 721.

These strong words meant war—civil war—if the King did not back down. Charles did not concede.

During the latter part of May a few peers called for accommodations to prevent a civil war. The Earl of Bristol made a courageous attempt on 20 May to reconcile differences when he called for the formation of a joint committee to negotiate with Charles, but his appeals were ignored by the majority. Three days later the Earl of Northumberland moved that the Upper House take the initiative, draw up articles of accommodation, and commence negotiations with the King—with or without the Commons—to avert bloodshed.[8] The Lords took up this suggestion and established a committee, which included Essex, Northumberland, Saye, and five other peers, to discuss ways of preventing war. The following day they presented fourteen propositions which, they hoped, might form the basis for negotiation. After lengthy debate, during which the proposal was enlarged by five additional provisions and called the Nineteen Propositions, both Houses agreed to them on 1 June.[9] The propositions demanded parliamentary control of the high offices of state, the enforcement of the recusancy laws, reform of the church, and support of the Protestants on the Continent, to mention the most important. Subsequently forwarded to York, they were regarded by the King as more of an ultimatum than a basis for negotiation. Charles accepted nine of the provisions, but his rejection of the others, most of which reduced the royal prerogative, precluded any dealings with Essex and like-minded peers.

Despite his strong commitment to Parliament, Essex used his prestige for intercessory purposes. Representing the interests of Lord Willoughby of Parnham, who had received a summons from the King to attend him at York, Essex persuaded Parliament to thank Willoughby for his continuing adherence to its cause.[10] In mid-May he interceded on behalf of Robert Pierrepont, the Earl of Kingston, then absent from the Upper House because of sickness, and secured for him a leave of absence.[11] Two weeks later Essex received from Lord Paget, who was busy carrying out the Militia Ordinance in Buckinghamshire, a letter opposing the bill calling for an ecclesiastical assembly. Essex dutifully reported the matter to the Upper House. Paget's opposition meant little, however, for

[8] *Old Parliamentary History*, 11: 56.

[9] See Weston, "The Beginnings of the Classical Theory," pp. 133–41.

[10] *Lords Journal*, 5: 102.

[11] *H. M. C. Fifth Report*, p. 23.

Parliament soon passed the measure which called into existence the Westminster Assembly of Divines.[12] Willoughby, Kingston, and Paget appealed to Essex for intercessory purposes in the mounting struggle between King and Parliament; in each case Essex, not wishing to be compromised by vacillating or hostile peers, treated the request as a public matter and laid it before Parliament.

Neither the public moves toward an accommodation nor the private gestures by peers proved sufficient to turn back the tide of internecine strife. After the presentation of the Nineteen Propositions and the King's rejection of the same, both sides turned their attention from the suppression of the Irish Rebellion to preparation for civil war. Parliament raised troops for its own defense and for the protection of the King's person, and the King recruited volunteers to protect the royal prerogative and preserve Parliament and the liberties of the subject. Parliament also began to tap the large financial resources of the commercial groups in the southeastern counties, especially in London. On 1 June, the very day Parliament approved the Nineteen Propositions, Essex and six fellow peers were empowered by the Upper Chamber to borrow money from the City; they presented their case before the council, which promptly complied with a loan of one hundred thousand pounds.[13] The following week Parliament appealed to all Englishmen to support its cause with gifts of money, plate, and horse. The response among the members of Parliament was very satisfying. In a semipublic display of generosity the Lords on 10 June announced their contributions: Northumberland, a high-ranking opposition lord, subscribed for two thousand pounds plus twenty horses; Essex agreed to contribute one thousand pounds plus twenty horses; Holland, ever short of cash because of debt, gave thirty horses; Pembroke agreed to one thousand pounds and fifty horses; Saye promised one thousand pounds. All those peers committed to the cause of Parliament contributed something, however small. The Commons did likewise.

The Earl of Essex, meanwhile, put into effect Parliament's Militia Ordinance. The need to replace lord lieutenants led Parliament to stipulate that deputy lieutenants should be permitted to carry out the terms of the ordinance in those counties which lacked a lord lieutenant. In most cases, however, the specified lord lieuten-

12 *Commons Journal*, 2: 591.
13 *Lords Journal*, 5: 97–123.

ant put the controversial ordinance into working operation: Willoughby in Lincolnshire, Holland in Middlesex, Stamford in Leicestershire, Brooke in Warwickshire, and Warwick in Essex, to mention but a few. Because of the burdensome duties in the metropolitan area the Earl of Essex appears to have relied upon deputy lieutenants in his three counties.

The King, still in the North, labored under distinct disadvantages to counteract these measures. He was deep in debt—in fact, nearly bankrupt—and a poor credit risk, with the City against him. His broad appeals to all Englishmen produced only a limited response. His French in-laws were slow to produce money and material. His Dutch allies were more loyal, but their bankers balked at the Queen's move to pawn her royal jewels. The King also lacked control over the two largest magazines in England: the Tower of London and the port town of Hull. With no chance of securing the Tower, since it had been taken over by Parliament, he concentrated his efforts on Hull. His efforts fared badly. His appeals to Sir John Hotham and the people of Hull came to nought. A feeble attempt to take the port by surprise proved abortive. Charles might have been successful if he could have maintained control of the sea, but with the navy loyal to the pro-Parliament Earl of Warwick, Charles stood little chance of regaining the magazine at Hull. To compensate for these losses, Charles launched several moves in mid-June to secure the magazines in the counties. Through well–co-ordinated efforts he gained the magazines and port facilities of Newcastle and Portsmouth, but elsewhere he met with only limited success.

Charles also found himself in an awkward constitutional position regarding the raising and training of troops. Neither he nor his father, nor their Tudor predecessors for that matter, had relied upon a standing army to maintain their authority. To conduct their wars on foreign soil, or in Ireland and Scotland, they had depended upon Parliament to raise the funds through special levies. To maintain law and order within England, they counted upon the lord lieutenants and their deputies, all of whom received their instructions from the Privy Council, and upon their trained bands in the respective counties.[14] With Parliament now opposed to him, the King could

[14] G. Scott Thomson, *Lords-Lieutenant in the Sixteenth Century* (London: Longmans Green and Company, 1923); and by the same author, "The Origin and Growth of the Office of Deputy-Lieutenant," *Transactions of the Royal Historical Society*, 4th ser. 5 (1922): 150–67.

not count upon funds from special levies or upon mercenaries. With the lord lieutenants and their deputies now accountable to Parliament by virtue of the Militia Ordinance, he could hardly rely upon that system without creating great confusion. His efforts to establish a bodyguard, though successful, had been discredited by Parliament. At this juncture the King resorted to the almost defunct commission of array.[15]

The first such commission, dated 11 June, was granted to the Earls of Huntingdon and Devonshire, who were authorized to muster troops in the county of Leicester.[16] Ten days later Henry Hasting, Huntingdon's son, proceeded to carry out the terms of the commission in the town of Leicester, where he encountered many supporters of Parliament and followers of Henry Grey, the Earl of Stamford. There ensued a local furor which culminated in blows, but no blood was shed. This open hostility did not deter Charles from his plan to raise an army. He issued commissions of array to several trustworthy peers committed to his cause, but within a few weeks the House of Commons declared them illegal. Charles countered by issuing a series of proclamations designed to undermine parliamentary authority.

Essex and his compeers reacted with increased bitterness and resorted to several warlike gestures. They backed those lord lieutenants, like Willoughby and Stamford, who were recruiting under the terms of the Militia Ordinance, but on 11 June they declared nine Royalist peers in contempt of the House. Six days later a small committee, which included Essex and Northumberland, was designated to appoint the training and field officers for the militia being raised in London.[17] On 21 June both Houses justified their actions and pronounced the principles for which they would, if necessary, fight.

Parliament next began to name commanders for the various military units. Actually, the King's dismissal of Northumberland as Lord Admiral during the last week of June precipitated this move. When the Lords learned of the ouster, they informed the Commons, whereupon both Houses conferred and passed an ordinance naming

[15] Arthur H. Noyes, *The Military Obligation in Medieval England*, Ohio State University Studies, no. 11 (Columbus, 1930), pp. 56–67.

[16] E. B. G. Warburton, *Memoirs of Prince Rupert and the Cavaliers*, 3 vols. (London, 1849), 1: 294. According to Clarendon, even some Royalists disapproved of the commission of array; see his *History* (1849 ed.), 1: 246.

[17] *Commons Journal*, 2: 632.

the Earl of Warwick, then the parliamentary designated vice admiral, to command the fleet. On the following day Warwick, who had commanded the fleet for several months in fact, though not in name, pressured his subordinates into accepting him as their Lord Admiral. All the captains except five and most of the crews placed themselves under Warwick's banner, thus assuring Parliament's control of the navy—and command of the seas.

Several days later Parliament turned to Essex. On 6 July both Houses, finding the trained bands insufficient for a war, passed an ordinance calling for an army of 10,000 soldiers to be raised in London and its environs.[18] This measure, very likely precipitated by news of the King's march toward Hull and a rumor of Hotham's defeat, said nothing about a commanding general. No mention was made until the following week. On 12 July, after no recorded debate, the following resolutions were introduced in the Lower House:

Resolved, "That an Army shall be forthwith raised for the Safety of the King's Person, the Defence of both Houses of Parliament, and of those who have obeyed their Orders and Commands; and for the Preservation of the true Religion, the Laws, Liberties, and Peace of the Kingdom."

Resolved, "That the Earl of Essex be named General thereof.

Resolved, "That a Petition shall be forthwith prepared, to move the King to good Accord with the Parliament, and to prevent a Civil War."

Resolved, "That this House doth declare, That, in this Cause, for the Safety of the King's Person, and the Defence of both Houses of Parliament, and of those who have obeyed their Orders and Commands, &c. they will live and die with the Earl of Essex, whom they have nominated General in this Cause."[19]

These measures, after passing the Lower House with no dissent, were immediately forwarded to the Upper House for concurrence. The Lords likewise passed them without any recorded protest. "Hereupon the Earl gave their Lordships Thanks," the clerk noted in the *Journal*, "professing his Integrity and Loyalty to the King to be as much as any; and that he would live and die with their Lordships in this Cause."

Three days later Parliament approved Essex's commission. After a wordy preface, which rationalized the appointment, it named him

18 See C. H. Firth and R. S. Rait, *Acts and Ordinances of the Interregnum*, 3 vols. (London: His Majesty's Stationers Office, 1911), 1: 14.

19 *Old Parliamentary History*, 11: 288.

"Captain-General and Chief Commander of the Army to be raised."
The commission gave Essex authority to raise both horse and foot
throughout England and Wales; to employ them in any type of
military action he considered essential to protect Parliament and
preserve the King's person; to appoint and remove subordinate
commanders of both horse and foot units; to command forts and
castles; to establish and publish a body of rules for the conduct of
the army; and to discipline those soldiers who violated the rules of
war. Parliament also promised to defend Essex and his subordinates
against the King: "That the Said Earl, the Commanders and Officers
of the said Army, and all his Majesty's Officers and Subjects whatsoever, in the Execution of this Premises, shall be saved harmless, and
defended by the Power and Authority of both Houses of Parliament."[20]

The appointment of Essex to the captain generalcy came as no
surprise to most Englishmen. He was acceptable to the various
groups that comprised the opposition: the residue of the peerage
in the Upper House, the majority of those in the Lower House, and
the populace of the City. Of Essex's commitment to the cause of
Parliament there was no doubt, for throughout his life he had upheld
parliamentary government. He had worked closely with members
of the Lower House for several years and with those peers now in
the majority. No member of the Upper House was so highly
esteemed and popular among those who now dominated the House
of Commons as the Earl of Essex. If the army was to be commanded
by a nobleman—and most Englishmen accepted that premise—no
other peer was more preferable. Essex was also acceptable to London.
Although dubbed a member of the Country Party, he was in fact
deeply committed to the City.[21] He was, after all, London born and
bred and had maintained ties with Londoners throughout his adult
life. In sharp contrast to many noblemen, he spent much of his
income in the City and employed Londoners at Essex House.

That Essex was generally popular and held prestige is certain.

[20] Firth and Rait, *Acts and Ordinances*, 1: 14–16.

[21] Historians have all but ignored most strong ties that many of the Country
Party peers had with London and Westminster. Most of them had London man-
sions. Most of them spent much time and money there. Many of them had business
and professional ties with Londoners. For a discussion of the attraction of London
to aristocrats see Stone, *The Crisis of the Aristocracy*, pp. 385–98; also see Pearl,
London and the Puritan Revolution, pp. 107–59.

He possessed a Norman name, a string of military-minded ancestors whose names figured in the medieval chronicles, and a title that brought back memories of Tudor glory in Ireland, Holland, France, Portugal, and Spain. Everyone knew that he was the son of Elizabeth's Essex. By now his late father's reputation had changed from that of a traitor to that of a legendary hero with martyrlike qualities. The third Earl of Essex was also blessed with some of his father's attributes. He was aristocratic in bearing, liberal with his wealth, and motivated by those chivalrous ideals which Englishmen cherished. Like his father, he appealed to those martially-minded contemporaries who were stirred by past military glory. He had befriended many Englishmen with military experience and employed many of his father's retainers and/or their sons. Both in and out of Parliament he spoke for the military interests.[22]

Essex's military experience is more difficult to appraise. He had fought on the Continent during the first decade of the Thirty Years War. He had fought in Scotland. Except for the fateful Cádiz expedition, his experience was limited to defensive operations. Without doubt, many other English soldiers, especially professional soldiers like Sir Jacob Astley, possessed more military experience. Yet, Essex had long served as a lord lieutenant; had corresponded with several of the Continental leaders, including Christian of Brunswick and Gustavus Adolphus; and recognized the value of those who possessed wartime experience, and employed them whenever possible. Essex could point to as much military experience as any nobleman of equal rank. He lacked recent experience on the battlefield, but other qualities and assets compensated for this deficiency. He could attract, recruit, and train troops. He knew something of military administration. Most important, he commanded the confidence and respect of countless Englishmen committed to Parliament.

Several contemporaries alluded to the lord general's military experience and leadership qualities. According to Thomas Hobbes, "The Earl of Essex had been in the wars abroad, and wanted neither experience, judgment, nor courage, to perform such an undertaking. And besides that, you have heard, I believe, how

22 It is interesting to note in this connection that Donald Lupton dedicated his book entitled *A Warre-like Treatise of the Pike* (London, 1642) to Essex. See M. J. D. Cockle, *A Bibliography of English Military books up to 1642* (London: Simpkin, Marshall, Hamilton, Kent and Company, 1900), p. 123.

great a darling of the people his father had been before him, and
what honour he had gotten by the success of his enterprise upon
Calais, and in some other military actions." [23] "If the Earl of Essex
had refused that command [to serve as captain general]," William
Lilly contended, "our cause in all likelihood had sunk, we having
never a nobleman either willing or capable of it." [24] It mattered
little to many Englishmen that Essex's military experience was
limited to defensive warfare; what mattered most were those
traits in his character and personality which stirred men to support
the cause of Parliament.

II

THROUGHOUT the summer Lord General Essex prepared himself
and his army for the oncoming trial by battle. He spent less time
in the Upper Chamber and more time in London recruiting men
and training troops in the artillery garden and in Finsbury Field.
He appeared in Parliament only when absolutely necessary; consequently, he was assigned to few committees and conferences between the Houses. When in Westminster, he spent most of his time
with the Committee of Safety, Parliament's wartime junta which
handled many of the major decisions relating to logistics and
strategy, and attended to several pressing matters relating to the
oncoming conflict. He had to supervise the mustering and instruction
of trained bands in those counties wherein he was lord lieutenant.
He had to provide himself with the proper insignia, the best armor,
and the latest equipment for waging war, and the paraphernalia
and dress befitting a soldier of his rank and station. Within a week
of his appointment he enclosed some of his inherited lands in
Herefordshire, no doubt to defray the cost of these items. [25]

Essex's associations with his relatives deteriorated in the wake of
these preparations. He went through the motions of maintaining
cordial relations with the Earl of Clanricarde, who had gone to
Ireland shortly before the Rebellion, but found it increasingly
difficult to do so. [26] He corresponded more or less regularly with

[23] Thomas Hobbes, *Behemoth* (London, 1890 ed.), p. 111.

[24] William Lilly, *Several Observations on the Life and Death of King Charles I* (London,
1651), p. 239.

[25] *H.M.C. Fifth Report*, p. 38.

[26] Marquis of Clanricarde, *Memoirs and Letters* (London, 1757), pp. 14, 29, 39,
49, 60, 62, 77, 145, 147, 181.

Clanricarde through mid-July, but the letters betray a strained relationship.[27] Essex continued to receive letters from his brother during the summer months, even after the outbreak of hostilities, but does not appear to have replied to them. In mid-November the Earl of Clanricarde's servant Richard Brewer, who had previously benefitted from Essex's protection, was seized in Maidstone and subsequently incarcerated for recusancy by the House of Lords. Essex made no effort to intercede as he had done before.[28] By then Clanricarde gave every indication of being a staunch Royalist.

Essex's close relationship with his sister the Countess of Hertford and her family, the Seymours, terminated about the same time. The Countess appears to have left London for her favorite manor in Wiltshire. Her husband joined the King and soon assumed command of a Royalist army. Likewise their eldest son enlisted in that army and fought under the King's colors throughout the Civil War. Essex's ties with his in-laws, the Paulets, and his stepsister, Honora, suffered the same fate. For the remainder of his days the lord general remained alienated from those who had been closest to him only five years earlier. Thus did the conflict pit family against family and brother against brother.

During the summer months Essex prepared for the eventuality of death. If Gardiner, who does not cite his source, is reliable, Essex provided himself with a coffin and a winding sheet.[29] He also composed his last will and testament, committed himself first to God, as was the custom, and then disposed of his possessions. It is highly significant that he selected the following as executors of his estate: the Earl of Northumberland, the Earl of Warwick, John Hampden, and Oliver St. John, all dedicated leaders of the parliamentary cause. The will itself, dated 5 August, included a repudiation of all earlier wills, references to those previously transacted conveyances and commitments still in force, and a series of bequests to relatives and friends.[30] He bequeathed to the Countess of Hertford his lands in Herefordshire and all those lands previously deeded to Sir Walter Devereux, and to his nephew Sir Charles Shirley,

27 *Ibid.*, p. 270.

28 *Lords Journal*, 5: 453.

29 S. R. Gardiner, *History of the Great Civil War*, 4 vols. (London, 1893), 1: 21 (hereafter cited as *Civil War*).

30 I am indebted to the authorities at Somerset House for making a copy of Essex's will available to me.

Essex House and the surrounding tenements. Essex also provided that two thousand pounds of the income from his estate should be set aside for monetary bequests to his many servants. He awarded to the Earl of Northumberland the guardianship of Sir Charles. He also bequeathed the sum of two hundred pounds to the poor people living in the parish of Saint Clement Danes and on his manors in Staffordshire. Lastly, he awarded one hundred pounds to each of his executors. The document was signed by Essex and attested by two household servants, Thomas Pudsey and William Wren.

III

During the remainder of the summer the lord general devoted himself to Parliament's army. Although the terms of his commission were rather broad, Essex was narrowly limited by the very authority that had named him commander; the Lower House, in particular, did not care to entrust too much power to one man, not even the popular man of their choice. What Parliament gave, moreover, it could take away. When Parliament delegated its authority, it expected reports so that the people of England could be properly informed. When Parliament granted funds for a particular project, it demanded an accounting of the expenditures. Parliament supervised the war effort; of this there was little doubt.

Essex accepted this dictum: it could be no other way. Yet, it made his tasks exceedingly difficult, hampering his many activities and prolonging his military preparations. In several instances Parliament exercized its authority and appointed officers without consulting Essex. On 14 July, the day before Essex received his commission, Parliament passed a resolution naming the Earl of Bedford General of the Horse.[31] Although there is reason to believe that Essex and Bedford were on the best of terms—the two men sat next to each other in the House of Lords—this appointment circumscribed Essex's power. Sir Gilbert Gerrard received his commission as treasurer of war, not from Essex, but from Parliament, after the Lower House selected him for the post. Time after time Essex found himself undercut and his authority narrowed by his new sovereign: Parliament.

[31] *Lords Journals,* 5: 211.

Despite the handicaps stemming from a collective authority, Essex managed to put an army on the field during the summer of 1642.[32] He employed a retinue of aides consistent with his station. For his personal medical officer he chose one Mr. Langley, very likely Timothy Langley, who rendered valuable assistance to John Thurloe during the Protectorate. His personal servants included Thomas Pudsey and Richard Mitchell. His chaplain was none other than Cornelius Burgess, the Oxford-educated Presbyterian lecturer, who along with Stephen Marshall and Edmund Calamy championed reformation along Presbyterian lines. Essex's closest advisers appear to have been Meyrick, Hampden, Stapleton, and Robartes.

Essex drew his bodyguard, a select group of 100 mounted troopers, from those gentlemen registered in the Inns of Court.[33] He named Sir Philip Stapleton, a faithful political ally, commander of the elite group. The troopers appealed to those would-be lawyers who possessed military experience, especially those who trained weekly in the Artillery Garden. The guard included Charles Fleetwood, an ambitious student in his twenty-fourth year, who later served under the Earl of Manchester and Oliver Cromwell; Thomas Harrison, a devout Puritan from Nottingham, best known for his recent service as a major general under Cromwell; Henry Ireton, student at Middle Temple, who later became Cromwell's ally and understudy; Nathaniel Rich, a member of Gray's Inn, who later secured a colonelcy in Cromwell's New Model Army; Richard Fiennes, the fourth son of Lord Saye; Francis Russell, student at Gray's Inn and subsequently elected to the Long Parliament; and Edmund Ludlow, the republican chronicler of the "good old cause," then reading law at Inner Temple. Essex armed these men of substance with cuirasses and swords and then trained them in the

[32] The best account of these preparations is found in Alfred H. Burne and Peter Young, *The Great Civil War* (London: Eyre and Spottiswoode, 1959), pp. 3–16. Also see C. H. Firth, *Cromwell's Army*, ed. P. H. Hardacre (New York: Barnes and Noble, 1962), especially the preface and the introductory chapter; J. W. Fortescue, *A History of the British Army*, 13 vols. (London, 1899), vol. 1; Francis Grose, *Military Antiquities*, 2 vols. (London, 1812); J. S. Omond, *Parliament and the Army* (Cambridge: At the University Press, 1933); and Charles Ffoulkes, *The Gun-Founders of England* (Cambridge: At the University Press, 1937). For the personnel in the respective armies in 1642 see Edward Peacock, *The Army Lists of the Roundheads and Cavaliers* (London, 1863).

[33] There is no comprehensive study of Essex's life guard, despite its significance, but the best account is in *Ludlow's Memoirs*, ed. C. H. Firth, 2 vols. (Oxford: 1894), 1: 38–41.

art of horsemanship. He also provided them with a colorful banner —an orange field with a white border—and a motto which read "God with us."

Essex next selected staff officers to carry out the details of military administration and specialized functions. They generally traveled in his train. In addition to Gerrard this group included Lionell Copley, the mustermaster general; Dr. Isaac Dorislaus, John Selden's friend who served Essex as judge advocate; Henry Parker, barrister and member of Lincoln's Inn, who bore the title of secretary of the army; and Robert Chambers, auditor. The field officers, who were expected to carry out Essex's command on the field of battle, included Sir John Meyrick, Essex's faithful ally and beneficiary, as sergeant major; Capt. James Seigneur, provost marshal general; and Thomas Richardson, carriage master general. Never before in English history had an English army been so thoroughly organized and structured—thanks to Essex and his experienced advisers who introduced practices from the Continent.

For purposes of command and administration Essex's army was divided into three man-power groupings: horse, foot, and artillery.[34] At the head of each division was a general plus a small staff of assistants, all of whom, except for the Earl of Bedford, were appointed by and responsible to Essex. Bedford, General of the Horse, was assisted by a five-man staff, the most important figures being his lieutenant general, Sir William Balfour, a Scottish soldier who had fought in several campaigns on the Continent, and Sir John Dalbier, quartermaster general, who had served under Count Mansfeld and Gustavus Adolphus during the Thirty Years War. By 19 August the horse units under these and other officers totaled 59 troops, each troop composed of 60 horse. Also attached to Bedford's command were four troops of dragoons, each troop composed of 100 mounted infantry soldiers. The combined strength of the horse and dragoons, when the ranks were filled, was about 4,000.

Essex's foot regiments, fixed at 1,200 soldiers, were commanded by colonels.[35] Each of the colonels was responsible for recruiting his own men; each was paid "levy money" as soon as a minimum number of men enlisted. The commanders Essex selected for his

---

[34] From *The List of the Army Raised Under the Command of his Excellency Robert Earl of Essex* (London, 1642). It is from this and subsequent published lists that Peacock composed his nineteenth-century list of personnel.

[35] See Davies, "Parliamentary Army," pp. 47–48. Also see Julian Corbett, "The Colonel and His Command," *American Historical Review* 2 (1896): 1–11.

foot regiments included several peers, namely, the Earls of Peterborough and Stamford, Lord Brooke, Lord Mandeville, Lord Saye,
Lord Rockford, and Lord St. John, and several well-known commoners, such as Denzil Holles and John Hampden. The problems
relating to the recruitment, equipping, and training of the foot
(most of whom lacked experience) were prodigious.

Essex appointed John Mordaunt, the Earl of Peterborough, to be
general of the ordnance and lead the artillery unit.[36] It included a
lieutenant general, his assistant, a surveyor, an engineer, several
commissaries and purveyors, pioneers, a master gunner, a petardeer,
and several other specialists. The selection of Peterborough for this
post is difficult to comprehend, for he lacked experience and was
also responsible for raising a regiment of foot. None of the officers in
this unit achieved national fame; they were, in fact, treated as
inferior, auxiliary soldiers. The exact nature of the relationship
between this unit and the Artillery Company of London remains
obscure, but it would appear that the leaders of the Artillery Company sided with the King rather than Parliament.

To co-ordinate the efforts of thousands of Englishmen, Essex
relied upon the time-tested Council of War. He appointed Meyrick
as president, Balfour to represent the horse, Sir William Constable
and two other colonels to represent the foot regiments, Lt. Gen.
Philip Emanuel de Boyse to represent the artillery unit, and Dr.
Dorislaus. This advisory and decision-making body was convened at
the captain general's behest. Essex dominated the council by virtue
of his title, rank, and prestige. No other peer and no influential
member of the Commons were included in that body. That Parliament did not possess complete confidence in Essex and his cohorts
is evident in the watchdog committee which they soon appointed
to check the council.[37]

Both Houses of Parliament, meanwhile, called for action. On
23 July the Upper House "ordered, That the Lord General shall
pursue his Levies with all Vigor and Speed he can, for the Safety
of the King, Kingdom, and Defence of the Parliament."[38] This
pressure paid off. The recruiters beat the drums more enthusiastically.

---

[36] See Burne and Young, *Civil War*, pp. 11–12; and G. A. Raikes, *The Ancient
Vellum Book of the Honourable Artillery Company* (London, 1890). For a discussion of
the Artillery Garden, where the artillery trained, see Brett-James, *Stuart London*,
pp. 42, 50, 360, 458, and 481.

[37] Rushworth, *Historical Collections*, 5: 17.

[38] *Lords Journal*, 5: 234.

"The Earl of Essex is attending diligently to the enlistment of cavalry," wrote the Venetian ambassador, "[and] many of the parliamentarians who are committed have undertaken to collect regiments and they contemplate adjourning the sittings of parliament for some days for the purpose of sending those who belong to this party into the country so that they may the more easily carry their offers into effect."[39] The response was gratifying indeed, for volunteers enlisted by the thousands and came to the Artillery Garden on 26 July for a general muster. "At the first appearance in the artillery garden, where the volunteers were to be listed," Codrington noted, "there came no less than four-thousand of them, in one day, who declared their resolutions to live and die with the Earl of Essex."[40]

Essex personally participated in the general muster by delivering a short speech of encouragement. "The Earl of Essex coming into the Artillery Garden one Tuesday late being the 26 of July in his Coach caused the people greatly to rejoyce and fling up their hats for joye," an enterprising observer reported, "and gathering great multitudes about his Coach he spake to them with great respect."[41] The composition of the army reflected the open-door recruitment policies of the lord general. The ranks included several non-English officers—Scots like Balfour and Sir James Ramsey, both of whom had fought with the Swedish army, and experienced Dutch soldiers like Dalbier and de Boyse. Capt. Carlo Fantom, a Croatian soldier capable of speaking thirteen languages, volunteered to fight in Sir Robert Pye's regiment. "Robert Earl of Essex, General for the Parliament," Aubrey wrote, "had this Captain Fantom in high esteem; for he was an admirable horse officer, and taught the cavalry of the army the way of fighting with horse."[42]

Essex's army, if judged by the chaplains attached to each unit, contained Puritans of many leanings.[43] Some chaplains favored

[39] *C.S.P. Ven.*, *1641–1642*, p. 123.

[40] Codrington, *Life and Death*, p. 13.

[41] *The Earl of Essex His Speech in the Artillerie Garden to the soldiers on Tuesday last* (London, 1642), published anonymously on 28 July.

[42] John Aubrey, *Brief Lives*, ed. Oliver Lawson Dick (Ann Arbor: Michigan University Press, 1962), p. 105.

[43] See Leo Solt, *Saints in Arms* (Stanford: Stanford University Press, 1959), p. 106; Sanford, *Studies*, p. 517; and Mark Noble, *The History of King Killers*, 2 vols. (London, 1720), 1: 55.

CAPTAIN GENERAL 317

moderate reforms along Presbyterian lines, while others spoke for root-and-branch innovations along Independent and Baptist lines. Marshall, Richard Vines, and Burgess, all of whom participated in the Westminster Assembly, were inclined toward Presbyterianism; Calybute Downing, the chaplain attached to Robartes's regiment, was an Independent; William Erbury, a chaplain in Skippon's regiment, was a free-thinking Puritan, variously dubbed an antinomian and a Seeker; and William Sedgwick, who served in Constable's regiment, was a mystic. That Essex's army was a seedbed of Puritan nonconformity there can be little doubt.

Parliament, recognizing the problems stemming from the indiscriminate and hasty recruitment of soldiers, attempted to solve the problem rather than prevent it. On 1 August both Houses decided that Essex's soldiers, particularly the officers, should be required to demonstrate their loyalty by subscription to an oath. "I will defend, maintain, and obey the two Houses of Parliament," the oath read, "and in pursuance of their Direction and Command, the Right Honourable Robert Earl of Essex, as Captain General of all the forces raised, and to be raised, for the Defence of the Protestant Religion, the King's person, Honours, and State, the Power and Privileges of Parliament, and the just Rights and liberties of the Subject, and the Security and Peace of the Kingdom."[44] When Sir Sidney Montagu spoke against this oath in the House of Commons, he was forthrightly expelled from his seat and replaced by a more dedicated crusader for the "good old cause."[45]

As more soldiers enlisted in his army Lord General Essex was confronted with discipline problems. Reports of excessive drinking, robbery, and other forms of disorderly conduct committed by soldiers stationed in London found their way into Parliament. On 16 August the Upper House, disturbed by these reports, ordered Lord Saye to draw up orders calling upon Essex to take proper precautionary and punitive measures to prevent such crimes. Over a week later, after Lord Saye's draft had been approved by the present body, Essex was ordered to establish a system of military discipline.

On 8 September 1642, Essex issued his military code under the title *Lawes and Ordinances of War Established for the better conduct of the*

[44] *Old Parliamentary History*, 11: 364.
[45] Warwick, *Memoires*, p. 22.

Army.[46] Copies were promptly distributed to each unit commander, who was told to read them all at the next muster and, thereafter, one instruction each week. The *Lawes and Ordinances* contained a long list of military duties with corresponding penalties. Blasphemy was to be punished by boring the culprit's tongue with a red-hot iron; cursing by "losse of Pay"; neglect of divine worship by a severe censure; intelligence with the enemy by death; drunkenness by loss of rank; rape, ravishment, and murder by death; seizure of a dead man's goods by a double restoration; and absence without leave and false alarm by death. The soldier who used "words leading to the death of the Lord General" was likewise to be punished by death. Some crimes called for death with "no mercy." The severity of these military regulations reflected both the traditions of the past and the temper of the times.

Essex also encountered numerous difficulties relating to arms and supply. The munitions brought to London in mid-July from Hull were stored in several different warehouses, some private, some public. By a parliamentary command dated 20 July some were allotted to Sir William Balfour. Through its control of the purse and its doctrine of supremacy, Parliament made policies and issued specific orders which sometimes complicated rather than simplified the logistical matters in Essex's army. Conflicts and delays were common. Only with great difficulty did the lord general prepare Parliament's army for the field.

IV

THE KING also was preparing for the oncoming trial by battle. On 9 August, after consulting his advisers, he put forth a rather lengthy proclamation calling for the suppression of the "Rebellion under the Command of Robert Earl of Essex."[47] It began with a

46 For earlier codes see Cockle, *Bibliography*, p. 95. The third Earl of Essex's code, which went through several editions, remained the military code for Parliament's army throughout the two Civil Wars. Shortly before it was published, an anonymous editor republished the second Earl of Essex's military instructions in conjunction with Sir Edward Harwood's *Advice* and dedicated them both to the third Earl of Essex, the late Earl of Bedford, and the Earl of Southampton; see the reprinted version in *Harleian Miscellany*, 5: 195.

47 Rushworth, *Historical Collections*, 4: 769–72.

recitation of Parliament's many preparations for war without royal consent and ended with a condemnation of the rebel in chief by name. It alluded to the illegal mustering and training of "great numbers of Horse and Foot" by Parliament, to the appointment of Essex as captain general of those forces, to Essex's "Traiterous and Rebellious Designs" in accepting the commission, and to his warlike actions against the King in Portsmouth and countless castles and magazines throughout the land. Charles was convinced that these actions made Essex guilty of high treason. The rebellion must cease. Essex must be seized, tried, and judged for his crimes.

In an effort short of war to break the ring of rebellion, Charles offered "Grace and Clemency towards such of our Subjects as have been abused and misled to the said Earl." He refused to pardon the ringleader, but to all Essex's supporters he offered a general amnesty extending for six days, after which he threatened to use force to suppress the rebellion. Charles then commanded all local officials to resist and subdue everyone who raised troops or offered battle in the name of Essex or Parliament. Charles made special reference to the fact that Essex's brother-in-law Hertford possessed a royal commission appointing him lieutenant general of the King's forces in the West and Wales and that Hertford rather than Essex should be supported in this crisis.

When this proclamation and a covering letter from the King were received and then read in the House of Lords on 11 August, Essex rose and reminded his peers that he had been made lord general "at the Desire, Command and Authority, of both Houses of Parliament, and not of his own seeking, and he professed his actions should show him as a dutiful Subject as any the King hath." The Lords of course supported Essex. They informed the Commons of the King's communication and held a joint conference about the matter. Parliament's leaders were, for the most part, highly offended by the King's proclamation. Parliament had ordered Essex to raise an army; Essex had dutifully responded. Many members, especially those who held commands in the army, were insulted by references to them and at the King's attempt to separate them by the use of pardon. Essex himself spoke at the conference and reiterated his loyalty and devotion to the law, claiming that "he was as ready to adventure his Life for Defence of the Law."[48]

[48] *Lords Journal*, 5: 282–83.

Essex's compeers answered the King's accusation with a parliamentary declaration denouncing the proclamation against Essex and condemning, not the King, but "those Traitorous Counsellors about his Majesty."[49] They also defended their appointment of Essex. "The said Lords and Commons do declare," the document read, "That they will maintain and assist him, and adhere to the said Earl with their Lives and Estates in the same Cause, as in Conscience and Duty to God, the King and their Country." The members of Parliament refused to capitulate. Essex's cause was their cause. He would remain their generalissimo.

Plots and rumors of plots against Essex's life became commonplace. A man named Abel Winckefield was accused by two informants of saying, "This was for the Earl of Essex, he might be killed or hanged, his father was beheaded and none of them died in their beds."[50] Edward Sandeford, a London tailor, apparently was hired to assassinate Essex. At the demand of the Upper House the accused was taken into custody and brought to justice. Witnesses left their depositions with the chief justice of the King's Bench. Sandeford, according to one witness, was supposed to have said that he hoped to see the Earl of Essex's head "taken off." Another witness gave a similar testimony. For his statements Sandeford was brought before the bar of the House of Lords, pronounced guilty, and then sentenced to a series of stiff penalties, including a large fine, a period in the Cheapside pillory, and a cattail whipping to Bridewell, where he was to work during the remainder of his days. To speak derogatively of Parliament's appointed leader was a high crime akin to treason in Civil War England.

On 12 August, Charles issued his call to arms. The royal standard would be raised at Nottingham on 22 August, he announced, and all subjects loyal to the "true Protestant Religion" were invited to answer the summons. They should bring with them horse, arms, ammunition, and other necessities. All volunteers would be paid for their services. All gifts of produce or cash would be welcome. Yet, even before actual hostilities broke out, the King's cause suffered greatly. Money was still scarce, especially in the North, and credit was difficult to obtain. The rich economic resources were in the south, where Parliament dominated, and most of the large

49 Rushworth, *Historical Collections*, 4: 772.

50 For information about Winckefield see *H. M. C. Thirteenth Report*, Appendix 1, p. 54; for Sandeford see Rushworth, *Historical Collections*, 4: 559.

ports—Bristol, Plymouth, and Hull—were in Parliament's hands. The wealth and man power of London were behind Parliament. Charles's cause was not hopeless, however. He could appeal to his people in high-principled terms—on the basis of personal loyalty, obedience to God and the powers that be, and dedication to English law and traditions. He counted on the countryside to respond favorably to his call to arms. He expected support from cathedral cities like York, Exeter, Durham, and Chester, from the university communities of Oxford and Cambridge, and from the towns in the northern and western counties. He relied upon many noblemen and gentry who possessed castles, private armories, and large stables to support him. Translated into strategic and tactical terms, Charles could expect the North and the West to remain Royalist and could depend on the cavalry to win him victories.

Another advantage that Charles possessed over Parliament was the unity of his high command.[51] There was one supreme commander, the King, not the diffused or confused diversity that plagued the parliamentary army. The King had a Council of War, over which he personally presided; he did not have to contend with any committees or ambitious Puritans like Cromwell, as did Essex. The King's staff was composed mainly of peers. The Earl of Lindsey, who had served with Essex on the Continent, was named commander in chief. His subordinate was a Scot, Lt. Gen. Patrick Ruthven, the Earl of Forth, who had fought on the Continent under Swedish colors. Prince Rupert of the Palatinate, an eager and experienced soldier who had fought in the Thirty Years War, was given command of the horse upon his arrival in England in mid-August; since he was the King's nephew, he had direct access to Charles and possessed a certain independence that other officers did not enjoy. He brought with him a staff of professional soldiers and his younger brother, Prince Maurice. Sir Jacob Astley, the professional soldier who had served Essex in Scotland, became major general of the foot. Sir William Uvedale, who had made a cuckold of Essex in 1632, was named the King's treasurer at war. Charles also appointed several peers to command various sections of England. He named Essex's brother-in-law the Marquess of Hertford captain general over all troops in the West and in Wales; he gave the Earl of Newcastle a

[51] See Burne and Young, *Civil War*, pp. 8–9; and Ian Roy, "The Royalist Council of War, 1642–1646," *Bulletin of the Institute of Historical Research* 35 (1962): 150–68.

special appointment in the northern counties. Thus, though the King possessed greater unity of command than did Parliament, he too had to contend with some centrifugal forces in his army.

In the early evening hours of 22 August, in inclement weather, the King removed the royal standard from Nottingham Castle and erected it in a field behind the ancient fortress.[52] Sir Edmund Verney, the knight marshall, performed the symbolic rite to the beating of drums and the blaring of trumpets. On the flag at the top of the standard were the King's arms with a hand pointed to the royal crown and a motto reading Give Caesar his Due. The herald at arms then read a royal proclamation calling upon all loyal Englishmen to suppress the rebellion led by the Earl of Essex. That night, while the King slept, a tempest blew down the standard.

At a meeting held shortly after the standard-raising ceremonies, some Royalist peers proposed a peace overture to Parliament, whereupon the King, Clarendon noted, was deeply offended and refused to consider it. The following day the Earl of Southampton reintroduced the same proposal; a peace overture could do little harm, he claimed, and it might accomplish much good. Furthermore, he warned, the King was in deep trouble if he could not muster more support than he had at York and Nottingham. Charles finally relented and reluctantly agreed to a short, simple statement asking Parliament to appoint several peace commissioners for purposes of negotiating a settlement. Should the overture fail, he concluded, "we have done our Duty so amply, that God will absolve Us from the Guilt of any of that Blood which must be spilt."[53]

When Parliament promptly rejected this overture, Charles accelerated his preparations for war. On 29 August he sent instructions to his commissioners of array and all those local officials loyal to him. England was in a state of rebellion, he announced, and the rebels must be suppressed. Parliament's ordinances must be disobeyed, its army stopped. "I do declare that the Army now under the Command of the Earl of Essex," he announced to his local magistrates, "and raised in any part of the Kingdom by his Direction, or by the Direction of any pretended Ordinance, is raised against us and to take away our Life from Us; and that he, and all who adhere to him, are traitors by the known and established Laws of

52 Clarendon, *History* (1849 ed.), 2: 317–20.
53 Rushworth, *Historical Collections*, 4: 785.

this Kingdom." [54] He also made plans to march westward, hoping to enlarge his force with volunteers from Wales and the western counties.

While traveling through Staffordshire on his way to Shrewsbury, the King passed near Chartley in an obvious move to undermine support for Essex in the area. The Royalists, it is reported, would have razed Chartley Manor and destroyed the entire grounds if the King had not personally restrained them. Instead, Charles moved on to Stafford, the county town, and issued his commission of array to counteract the local influence of Essex. [55] The King continued to confuse this conflict with the Essex conspiracy of 1601. He considered it a rebellion—not a revolution or a civil war—and in all his official pronouncements singled out Essex as the rebel in chief. This personal dimension prevailed before, during, and after the Puritan upheaval, to be sure; but Charles erred in overemphasizing that dimension, for in so doing he oversimplified the nature and extent of the struggle at hand. Such oversimplification proved fateful to his cause. Essex had behind him thousands—tens of thousands—of Englishmen committed not to a man but to a cause: parliamentary government.

[54] *Ibid.*, pp. 681–83.

[55] See D. R. Guttery, *The Great Civil War in Midland Parish* (Birmingham: Cornish Brothers, 1950), pp. 18–20; and Sanderson, *A Compleat History*, p. 575.

CHAPTER 13

The Edgehill Campaign (1642): Draw

I

IN LATE SUMMER, shortly before leaving London for the field, the Earl of Essex contended with Parliament over his command. "He is anxious to induce parliament to declare him Grand Constable of England first," wrote the Venetian envoy, "and to grant him despotic powers for conducting the war as well as to negotiate and conclude the adjustment with the king in the way that may seem best to him. The parliamentarians have not as yet consented to make him this grant owing to the important consequences involved."[1] Essex's bid for peace-making authority was promptly rejected by Parliament. This rejection did not hamper his spirit, outwardly at least, although it caused some hard feelings between him and the leaders in the Lower House. It may account for his recurring reluctance to make a major move without word from Parliament. Both Houses made certain that Essex would remain a mere general responsible to their collective authority and not become a Roman-like dictator or medieval protector. Parliament retained jurisdiction over peace and grand strategy. Essex would exercise authority in matters relating to tactics and logistics, but even this circumscribed power would be subject to Parliament's supervision.

In the morning hours of 9 September, Essex appeared in the House of Lords and asked his peers to give him leave. His *pro forma* request was granted, of course, and he left Parliament amidst "great solemnity."[2] He proceeded by coach to his mansion on the Strand, where he stopped off briefly, and then through Temple Bar and the Moorfields to the new Artillery Yard, and on to Highgate. From the masses of London he received a send-off befitting a king. He was hailed by "an infinite number of people" who lined themselves along the streets and shouted "God Bless my

[1] *C. S. P. Ven., 1641–1642*, p. 154.
[2] *Lords Journal*, 5: 345.

Lord General." [3] Some uttered prayers for him and his army. Others sent forth volleys. No rebel had received such a royal farewell before.

At Highgate the lord general paused for some solemnities. John Martin delivered a departing sermon and offered prayers for Essex and his subordinates, and Lord Robartes eulogized Essex in a grandiloquent speech. [4] He alluded to Essex's "worthy father," still remembered by many Englishmen for his noble actions, and spoke in glowing terms of Essex's honorable name, noble spirit, magnanimity, and devotion to the King and Parliament. The cause of Parliament and the cause of Essex were one and the same. Parliament was the hope of three kingdoms, he contended, the hope of the Protestant religion, and all liberty-loving Englishmen. The lord general, as heroic a general as England ever had, would rid the country of the malignants, the papists, and those "evil councilors" around the King. Essex was in the great tradition of military statesmen. "Some sacred charm dwells in the name of Essex," Robartes went on, "that so sweet a violence attracts the iron-hearted souldiers to follow your Excellence." [5]

The ceremonies over, the lord general progressed northward by coach to Saint Albans, where he spent the night. He appears to have accepted the hospitality of the Countess of Sussex, who, though kindly disposed toward the lord general and his life guard, which she described as "very fine and very well-horsed," snubbed the rank-and-file soldiers and expressed hope that they would leave soon without incident. [6]

Essex then moved northwestward, along Watling Street. Upon reaching Northampton, he was warmly welcomed by 300 officers of the trained bands and a host of well-wishers from the neighboring communities. His arrival, a contemporary observed, "was great joy and comfort to us all, but in the night there was a Pistoll Bullet shot in at his chamber window, which mist him narrowly, that

[3] Codrington, *Life and Death*, p. 13.

[4] See *The Resolution of the Right Honourable the Earl of Essex his Excellencie* (London, 1642), which printed Robartes's speech. The title page contained a woodcut portrayal of Essex, mounted on a charger, with his general's staff in his hand.

[5] The title "His Excellency" was usually reserved for military leaders who came from the ranks of royalty or the aristocracy. In 1586 the Earl of Leicester and in 1624 the Prince of Orange were honored with the title. See British Museum, Additional MSS, 46,188; and Collins, *Letters and Memorials*, 1 : 52.

[6] *H. M. C. Seventh Report*, p. 441.

caused the Towne to be up in arms on a sudden, but who it was that did it, we cannot find as yet."[7] Despite this incident, which caused much concern, the lord general remained in the town for over one week. He raised his standard, established temporary headquarters, prepared for a general muster, and conducted a formal review of his army, now about 15,000 strong.[8] Most of the soldiers were billeted in surrounding communities or encamped in nearby fields. "On Wednesday the 14th," wrote Nehemiah Wharton, "our forces marched into the field, and the Lord General viewed us, both front, rear, and flanks, when the drums beating and the trumpets sounding, it made a harmony delectable to our friends but terrible to our enemies."[9] Wiser men than Wharton depicted the army in less-glowing terms. Some of the horse lacked saddles. Many of the rank and file wanted to pillage, although Essex's orders forbade it. All the soldiers lacked pay. Not without reason did Essex request of Parliament one hundred thousand pounds. "He protests that if their daily pay is not supplied to the troops it is to be feared that they will desert their banners," wrote the Venetian ambassador about Essex, "and if this should happen it will prove a difficult task subsequently to collect a new body of troops equally numerous."[10]

On 15 September, Essex appealed to the Lord Mayor and the aldermen of London for funds. "I am confident that we may bring the business to a quicke and happy conclusion," he wrote, ". . . yet are we in one great straight . . . [for] our treasure, which must maintaine our Army grows neare an end; and you will know our Army be kept one day together without pay: what ruin it would bring unto us all, if a disbanding should happen."[11] The city

[7] From a pamphlet entitled *Exceeding Joyful Newes from His Excellencie The Earl of Essex* (London, 1642), which forms part of the Thomason Collection in the British Museum. For a secondary account see Alfred Kingston, *East Anglia and the Great Civil War* (London, 1897), p. 71.

[8] *The True Relation of the Entertainment of My Lord of Essex at Northampton* (London, 1642).

[9] Devereux, *Lives and Letters*, 2: 347. Wharton's letters were edited by Sir Henry Ellis and published as "The Letters from a subaltern officer of the Earl of Essex's Army," in *Archaeologia* 35 (1853): 310–30.

[10] *C. S. P. Ven., 1641–1642*, p. 165.

[11] There are several printed editions of this letter in the Thomason Collection. I have used the broadside edition entitled *A Letter sent from his Excellency Robert Earl of Essex to the Lord Mayor of London* (London, 1642).

Edgehill (1642)

March of Essex - - - - -
March of the King -·-·-·-

fathers ordered this plea for money published in broadside form; two days later they provided Essex with funds to pay his army. In Northampton on the following day, while waiting for the money to arrive, the soldiers celebrated the Sabbath in Puritan style, with sermons delivered by army chaplains. "Sabbath day we peaceably enjoyed with Mr. Obadiah Sedgwick," wrote subaltern Wharton, "who gave us two heavenly sermons." [12] Essex no doubt listened to Burgess or Marshall, while other units listened to Simeon Ash and John Sedgwick—all nonconformist chaplains who had volunteered for service in Essex's army. These preachers, imbued with the teachings of Christ as interpreted by John Calvin, gave Parliament's cause a religious fervor that was absent in the King's camp.

On Monday the lord general and his troops, rested and paid, departed from the ancient town of Northampton in pursuit of the King. Marching westward they passed through West Haddon and Crick and encamped along the Avon near Rugby that night. On 20 September they progressed through Dunsmore Heath and Riton, where they crossed the Avon, and on to Baggington, a short distance south of Coventry. Here they were joined by the Earl of Stamford, Col. John Hampden, Col. Hugh Cholmley, and their troops plus the eighteen-piece artillery unit. The following day the enlarged army pressed westward through Warwick toward Worcester. "This night we marched two miles farther unto Barford," wrote Wharton, "where our quarter, as constantly it is since his Excellency's coming, was very poor, many of our soldiers having neither beds, bread, nor water, which makes them grieve very strong, for backbiters have been seen to march upon some of them, six on breast, and eight deep at their open order." [13]

II

As Essex advanced toward the King, his colleagues in Westminster expanded the war effort. They empowered the Committee of Safety to issue warrants for the military supplies and pay. On 13 September they set the wages of the volunteers at eight pence per day. Ten days later, on the recommendation of the Committee for Safety, they tried to solve the problem of undermanned units still

12 Devereux, *Lives and Letters*, 2: 347.

13 See *Ibid.*, p. 348, for a description of the march to Worcester and the quote from Wharton's letter.

in the London area. All foot regiments with 400 or more soldiers and all horse with 40 or more were ordered to rendezvous within forty-eight hours and prepare to join the lord general's army near Worcester.

The most pressing business before Parliament in mid-September concerned special instructions for Essex and a petition addressed to the King. Finally, after extended debate and some disagreement, on 21 September both Houses concurred. The resulting eight instructions comprised several strategic objectives and military regulations which Essex was commanded to follow. He was instructed to engage the King in battle as soon as possible; to secure the King's person; to punish all those who aspersed Parliament; to apprehend all those Royalist peers impeached by Parliament; to prevent violence and plundering where possible; to collect money, plate, and horse from willing contributors; and to protect the lives and property of those committed to Parliament. "You shall observe such further Directions and Instructions," it concluded, "as you shall, from Time to Time, receive from both Houses of Parliament." [14]

Parliament directed Essex to present to Charles a petition which contained a condemnation of the Laudian religious practices and a denouncement of those councilors responsible for enforcing them; a justification of Paliament's establishment of any army; a defense of their appointment of Essex as lord general; a request that the King withdraw himself from his "wicked" councilors and lay down his arms; and a promise that they would "serve your Majesty with all Honour, yeeld all due Obedience and Subjection, and dutifully endeavour to secure your Person and Estate from all Dangers, and to the betterment of our power, to procure and establish to your self, and your People, all the Blessings of a glorious and happy Reign." By the time Essex received this "Humble Petition," blood had been shed near Worcester.

The King's strategy was quite transparent. His decision to move away from Essex and London into the Severn valley was dictated by military necessity: he needed more foot and horse before engaging Essex in battle, and he counted on those troops recently raised in Wales and the western counties. Shrewsbury would be his headquarters. Prince Rupert, meanwhile, received orders to protect Worcester and Sir John Byron, who was stationed there.

[14] The manuscript is in the British Museum, Egerton MSS, 2541. It is printed in *Old Parliamentary History*, 11: 429–31.

Essex was determind to expel the Royalists from Worcester and gain control of that city. On 23 September he ordered Col. Edwin Sandys to take a regiment of foot and five troops of horse and capture Powicke Bridge, a short distance south of Worcester—a move designed to cut off Byron's retreat. This action led to a direct encounter between Prince Rupert, who was covering the retreat, and the advancing units under Sandys. The two forces clashed near the bridge in the afternoon. The Parliamentarians, surprised by an unexpected regiment under Rupert, broke field and fled before charging cavalry. Colonel Sandys was mortally wounded, and his horse were forced to retreat. Rupert won the skirmish without question, yet he did not prevent Essex from gaining control of Worcester.

Just before entering the town on the rainy morning of 24 September the lord general delivered a speech—his longest recorded speech—to his unit commanders. The need for encouragement and admonition was great. The soldiers were complaining about the weather, the lack of shelter, and the paucity of food and drink. "I do promise, in the sight of Almighty God," he began, "that I shall undertake nothing but what shall tend to the advancement of the Protestant religion, the securing of His Majesty's royal person, the maintenence of the just privilege of Parliament, and the liberty and property of the subject. . . . Likewise I do promise that my ear shall be open to hear the complaint of the poorest of my soldiers, though against the chiefest of my officers; neither shall his greatness, if justly taxed, gain any privilege; but I shall be ready to execute justice against all, from the greatest to the least." [15]

Essex demanded of his subordinate officers a similar standard of conduct. "I shall desire all and every officer to endeavor by love and affable carriage to command his soldiers," he advised them, "since what is done for fear is done unwillingly, and what is unwillingly attempted can never prosper. Likewise it is my request, that you be careful in exercising your men, and bring them to use their arms readily and expertly, and not to busy them in practising the ceremonious forms of military discipline." The lord general then reread the *Lawes and Ordinances* and demanded strict adherence to them. "And lastly," he concluded his speech, "that you avoid cruelty; for it is my desire rather to save the lives of thousands than

[15] The printed version of the lord general's discourse was entitled *A Worthy Speech Spoken by His Excellence The Earl of Essex* (London, 1642).

to kill one, so that it may be done without prejudice." There was little Prussian severity and much aristocratic gentility in Essex's code of conduct.

Essex remained in Worcester for three weeks.[16] One of his first acts was to dispatch a detachment under the command of the Earl of Stamford to secure Hereford; this move forestalled any surprise attack from the west and enabled him to obtain some provisions and reinforcements. He then attended to the pressing needs of his army. The response to his plea to London for fresh troops and lighter artillery was apparently good, for by 19 October he was reputed to have sixteen regiments, well armed and recently paid.

Essex also attempted to present Parliament's "Humble Petition" to the King. He sent Charles Fleetwood, a member of his life guard, to the Royalist headquarters in Shrewsbury with a message to the Earl of Dorset, whom he used as an intermediary. "I am command-ed by the Parliament to present their humble desires in a Petition to his Majesty," he wrote, "which I desire your Lordship to ac-quaint him with; that I may know his Majesty's pleasure in what manner he will have it presented to him." [17] Dorset placed the matter before the King, who in turn answered Essex through Dorset. Charles agreed to receive the petition but demanded that it be presented by someone not "accused of Treason," thus excluding Essex and a host of other parliamentarians. Essex's private reaction to this rebuff has not survived, but his public response appeared in the form of a letter addressed to the Committee of Safety. "I cannot send such who have been already accused by Name," he explained, "without exposing them to the uttermost Hazard; and to send others, who are not personally named might upon this Restriction, allow that Exception; and thereby deeply wound the Parliament, who never admitted any such Restriction. This causeth me to suspend the sending of the Petition, and to make this Address to the Committee." [18] The lord general had followed his instructions: the next step was up to Parliament.

Both Houses moved on 3 October. The speaker of the Upper House presented the issue, including copies of Essex's and Charles's letters, to the peers. The Lower House, informed by the Committee of Safety, likewise dealt with the business. A conference between

[16] Warburton, *Rupert*, 1: 410.
[17] *Old Parliamentary History*, 11: 439.
[18] *Ibid.*, p. 440.

the leaders of both Houses ensued and the parent bodies soon approved the resultant recommendations. The lord general need not deliver the Humble Petition; nevertheless, they resolved that "the Lord General shall signify unto His Majesty, by such Means as he shall think fit, the Resolution of both Houses concerning the Delivery of the Petition." [19]

The King arrived in Shrewsbury to prepare for his major military stroke against Parliament—a march upon London.[20] During his stay in Shropshire, events had taken a decided turn for the better. The size of his array increased daily. From Wales and Lancashire and Cheshire came volunteers by the hundreds. He secured some plate—enough to set up a mint at Shrewsbury—and promises of more money poured in. Rumors of the King's proposed march on the City preceded him by several days. As early as 7 October, perhaps even before, Viscount Mandeville, in Worcester with Essex, knew of that possibility. "We are still at Worcester, watching what the King will do," he wrote John Pym. "It is rumoured that he will march towards London on Monday next. Others think that he will advance towards us, which may be probable, because he sent 2,000 foot into Bridgnorth. I pray haste down the Scotch commanders." [21] Parliament now reversed itself, resolving instead that "the Lord General by himself or sure hands as he shall think fit, shall with all convenient speed, deliver the Petition unto his Majestie." [22]

From Worcester the lord general again wrote Dorset about presenting Parliament's petition to the King. He included in his communication the votes of Parliament and a request for safe-conduct guarantees. Dorset presented the message and the enclosures to Charles, who again refused to deal with Essex. "His Majesty would not receive any petition," Dorset wrote back, "by the hands as such as he had, by name, proclaimed a traitor." [23] Upon the receipt of this second rebuff, on 18 October, the lord general wrote the Committee of Safety about his fruitless efforts to present the petition to Charles: [24] "My Lords, this Answer did not take me

19 *Lords Journal*, 5: 385.
20 Warburton, *Rupert*, 2: 1–13.
21 *H. M. C. Tenth Report*, Appendix 6, p. 87.
22 *Ibid.*, *Fifth Report*, p. 52.
23 *Lords Journal*, 5: 412.
24 *Ibid.*

unprovided, for, since the first Answer I sent up to the Parliament, I expected no better. And for my Head, which is so much sought after, if God please, I intend to sell it at such a Rate that the Buyers shall be no great Purchasers." That same day the parliamentary watchdog committee forwarded a similar account to the same body. "This we humbly conceive to be a 'most high indignity' and scorn cast upon the authority of the Parliament in the person of his Excellency," they wrote, "and a final and utter rejection of the submissive, dutiful and earnest desire of peace so often laid at his feat." [25]

Charles's strategy upon leaving Shrewsbury was to move quickly toward the City, the center of Parliament's influence, and force London to capitulate before Essex could return.[26] He counted on many Londoners to come to his side once he appeared, and hoped for support from the nearby counties and abroad. He calculated that Essex, though closer to London than he, would depart later and move more slowly because of larger numbers. Charles did not intend to engage Essex while en route.

The King's plan, however well conceived, soon went awry. Surprise and speed were essential to its success. He lacked both. Essex knew of the plan at least five days before the Royalist army departed; Parliament was aware of it on the eve of the ruler's departure. It took the King ten days to march from Shrewsbury to southern Warwickshire. When it became apparent that Essex might well beat him to the City or force him to battle in the London area, Charles revised his strategy. Instead of racing Parliament's army to London at the risk of losing all, the King decided to engage Essex in the Midlands, where circumstances would be more conducive to his securing a battlefield victory. Thus did Charles on 22 October swing abruptly from his London-bound course toward Stratford-on-Avon in hopes of taking the Parliamentary army by surprise.

Essex's primary objective—next to capturing the King—was to prevent the Royalist army from reaching London.[27] Therefore he

25 *H. M. C. Tenth Report*, Appendix 6, p. 88.

26 See Warburton, *Rupert*, 2: 5–13 for his moves toward Edgehill.

27 Devereux, *Lives and Letters*, 2: 354–57, and Gardiner, *Civil War*, 1: 40–43. For information concerning the battle of Edgehill see Godfrey Davies, "The Battle of Edgehill," *English Historical Review* 36 (1921): 30–44; and A. H. Burnes, *The Battlefields of England* (London: B. T. Batsford, 1950), pp. 200–220.

sought to keep his army between London and Charles. Essex allowed his artillery unit, invariably much slower than the others, to lag behind, and he pressed his horse and foot ahead with forced marches. The miles between the two armies narrowed hourly as they converged on Banbury in northern Oxfordshire. By 22 October they were within a few hours' march of each other. The King was at Edgcott, four miles north of Banbury, while Essex was at Kineton, a small village located two miles north of Edgehill.

That evening the King convened a Council of War to decide the best course of action for the following day. In agreeing to move southward and, if possible, take Banbury, then in the hands of Parliament, the King and his advisers seem to have disregarded the fact that Essex was fast on their heels and might intercept them at the town. However, some Royalist scouts discovered that Essex was at Kineton and that some of his foot and artillery had not yet come up. At a second Council of War, held later that night, it was decided to take Essex by surprise and give battle. The King called for a rendezvous of all his troops along the crest of Edgehill. This decision gave the Royalists the initiative, the element of surprise, the tactical advantage of elevation, and the possibility of superior numbers. Equally important, it placed the Royalists between Essex and the center of his military strength. A clear-cut victory for the King would delay Essex and open the road to London.

Essex had little inkling of the King's revised strategy. It was the lord general's intention to spend the day in the Kineton area to give his soldiers, who had been marching rather steadily for forty-eight hours, a well-earned Sunday rest and to allow his straggling artillery and foot units to catch up with the main body of the army. The possibility of an engagement at Edgehill on the Sabbath did not seem to have occurred to Essex and his closest advisers.

Intelligence of the King's rendezvous along the brow of Edgehill arrived at the lord general's headquarters about 9 A.M., as Essex left for church. He reportedly began immediately to organize his men for the oncoming battle. He commanded his straggling troops to arrive as rapidly as possible. He took full advantage of the King's slowness and carefully watched the maneuvers of the Royalists through a "perspective glass." By noon Essex was marching his troops in a battle-line arrangement toward the Vale of the Red Horse, a point two miles south of town where he waited for the King.

The Royalists had marched the four-mile distance from Edgcott and occupied the ridge of Edgehill during the morning hours. From his elevated position the King had a commanding view of the slope leading down to the Vale of the Red Horse, of the brook running northward toward Kineton, of the town itself, and of the several hedges and copses that lay between him and Essex's army. About noon the King's army advanced from this superior tactical position along the crest down the slopes toward Parliament's army.

By one o'clock the two armies were drawn up a few hundred yards apart at the foot of Edgehill. The rival forces were quite evenly matched in man power. If anything, the King had a slight edge, with about 10,000 foot, approximately 2,500 horse, and 1,000 dragoons, totaling about 13,500 soldiers; Essex's army numbered about 10,500 foot and 2,500 horse, giving him about 13,000 soldiers. Each army had small artillery units. Each commander placed his infantry in the center, according to the practice of the day, and the cavalry units on the flanks. Essex employed experienced officers at the head of his brigade: Sir John Meldrum to the right, backed by two regiments of horse under the command of Balfour and Stapleton, and Charles Essex to the left, backed by a reserve unit of foot commanded by Thomas Ballard. The lord general placed Sir James Ramsey's regiment on the left flank, Basil Fielding's on the right flank, the light artillery between the various units, and the heavier to the rear. His own life guard remained in reserve as part of Ballard's regiment. The Cavaliers, following the Swedish system, had greater infantry strength in the center front lines and no reserve. Never before had so many soldiers gathered in battle on English soil.

The battle commenced with an artillery barrage between the hours of three and four. Because the Royalist artillery were forced to fire from their hillside position, their shots were ineffective. The cannonade, which lasted about one hour, was followed by two cavalry charges, one led by Prince Rupert against Ramsey, the other by Wilmot against Fielding. Rupert lived up to his reputation that day: he succeeded in breaking the ranks of his enemy and forcing the whole left side of Parliament's army, including the units under the command of Charles Essex and Ramsey, into a disorderly retreat toward Kineton. The Royalist troops pursued their adversaries so fast and blindly that Rupert lost effective control over them; they were only checked by a confrontation with John

Hampden's regiment, which was advancing to the battle from the north. The left wing under Wilmot also met with initial success, routing many of Fielding's horse. If the battle had terminated with these first charges, it would have been a victory for the King and his cause, for both wings of the Parliamentary forces had given way.

The center of Essex's army held fast, however, and reserves of foot and horse came forward. The Royalist wave began to ebb; the tide of battle began to turn. Balfour and Stapleton counter-charged against the flank and rear of the Royalist battleline with considerable success. From this point on, the foot exchanged musket fire and engaged in hand-to-hand combat. Gradually the Royalist foot began to give way. The mortally wounded Earl of Lindsey and his son, Lord Willoughby, were captured. Lindsey's regiment was cut to pieces. The King's personal guard was crushed as the Parliamentarians captured the royal standard and fatally wounded the standard-bearer, Sir Edmund Verney. Only the oncoming darkness and the heroism of two Royalists on the right wing saved the King from defeat. The lord general claimed, according to Stephen Marshall, "that he never saw less of man in anything than this battle, nor more of God."[28]

Essex remained on the field at the head of his own unit during the early stages of the battle. From his vantage point, located to the left and in the rear of Charles Essex's brigade, he planned his countermoves and issued his orders. William Sanderson, the Royalist biographer of Charles I, gave Essex credit for taking advantage of Rupert's charge to personally lead the countercharge against the opposition.[29] Only after some of his advisers pressed him to "retire from danger" did the lord general withdraw to the rear, where he was safe from enemy gunfire. That night Essex slept on the battle-field with his men. It was the honorable thing to do. The wounded had to be cared for. The arms and provisions lost in battle must be recovered. Thus, in the words of Clarendon, "the earl of Essex, wisely, never suffered them to stir all that night; presuming reasonably, that if they were drawn off never so little from that place, their numbers would lessen, and that many would run away; and therefore he caused all manner of provisions, which the country supplied him plentifully, to be brought thither to them for their repast, and reposed himself with them in the place."[30] The arrival

---

[28] Codrington, *Life and Death*, p. 117.
[29] Sanderson, *A Compleat History*, p. 585.
[30] Clarendon, *History* (1849 ed.), 2: 387.

of 2,000 fresh troops that night must have raised his spirits. The following morning Essex gave orders for the burial of the dead, regrouped his troops, and secured meat and drink for them.

Both sides claimed victory at the battle of Edgehill, but in truth neither side won. Edgehill ended in a draw. It did not end the conflict. It decided little. The King did not achieve his twofold objective of defeating Parliament's army and marching into London. He did not terminate what he hoped would be a short war. He did shake the enemy and clear his path to Oxford, but he did not prevent Essex from returning to the City. Lord General Essex neither defeated the King soundly nor forced him to come to terms. He did delay the King's army enough to forestall a Royalist seizure of London. This, in the final analysis, proved to be the decisive factor in the outcome of the campaign.

III

PROTECTED BY darkness the opposing armies, neither willing to concede victory, remained on the field of battle in the Vale of the Red Horse. The King drew his forces back toward the foot of the slope and remained with them through the night, while Essex, falling back three-quarters of a mile, did the same. The Cavaliers, believing that their antagonists had retreated, built fires to combat the cold autumn air. The Roundheads, Ludlow wrote, suffered even more from the cold, for Essex prohibited them from building fires. To those Englishmen fortunate enough to survive, it was an unforgettable experience.

The following morning the King visited the battlefield to view the dead and the damage to his army. He was appalled at the sight and at the dejected spirit of the troops. Remaining near Edgehill that day, the Royalists mustered, calculated their losses, and gave decent burial to the dead. At the Council of War, Rupert's suggestion of another encounter against Parliament's army was turned down in favor of a decision, backed by Lord Forth, to advance upon London. Rupert then proposed that the King's forces march rapidly to London and dissolve Parliament before Essex and his army could return. Again Rupert was overruled in favor of Bristol and men of moderation. Out of deference to the fuming Prince, however, the King permitted him to attack Essex's rear guard and roam about the countryside.

The King issued a "free pardon" proclamation which had been intended for the preceding day.[31] "His Majesty, verily believing that many of his Subjects who are now in actual Rebellion against him are ignorant against whom they fight," the promulgation read, "is graciously pleased to promise free Pardon to both Officers and Soldiers (except those that are, by Name, proclaimed Traitors) who shall lay down their Arms and submit themselves to his Majesty." The pardon, of course, excepted Essex and a host of others Copies of this proclamation, antedated 23 October, were subsequently sent to London and distributed throughout the countryside in anticipation of undermining the fighting spirit of those weakhearted supporters of Parliament.

In the aftermath of Edgehill the lord general faced several momentous decisions regarding military strategy. One alternative was to continue the battle in hopes of turning a draw into a decisive victory. Backed by the professional advice of Dalbier, among others, he rejected this proposal on several grounds. The troops were weary and, more important, Parliament's battlefield position was poor, for the King still possessed the tactical advantage of height and the strategic edge of being between Essex and London. Should Essex be defeated in a second encounter or even be forced to retreat, the way to London would be open to the Royalists, and it would be difficult to prevent or forestall a Royalist march upon the City. The risks of a follow-up engagement at Edgehill were simply too great.

An alternative proposal, to pursue the King, harass the rear of his army, and wait for a more opportune time and place to give battle, was also rejected as too risky. The King might well beat Essex to London and force a capitulation of the City and a dissolution of Parliament in advance of the lord general's return. Instead, Essex decided to rest his army briefly at Warwick, a Parliamentary stronghold, and then proceed as rapidly as possible toward London along the faster road, which skirted the Chilterns, on the east. The wisdom of this decision, though frustrating to those who clamored for immediate victory, soon became apparent to men of sound judgment. Thus did Essex leave Kineton on 25 October for Warwick, approximately eight miles to the north.[32]

Essex remained near Warwick for several days. He established

[31] *Old Parliamentary History*, 11: 471.
[32] *H. M. C. Seventh Report*, p. 441.

quarters in Warwick Castle, the country seat of his political ally Lord Brooke, and stationed his soldiers in and around the town. "The earl of Essex continued still at Warwick repairing his broken troops," Clarendon wrote, "which everyday lessened and impaired; for the number of his slain was greater than it was reported to be, there being very many killed in the chase, and many who died of their wounds after they were carried off." [33] He made no attempt to pursue the King or prevent the surrender of Banbury, a Puritan center, to the Royalists. Instead he readied his troops for the march toward London.

The King, too, began to march to London. He appointed as his new commander Lord Forth, the experienced Scot who had fought on the Continent, and decided to capture county houses, castles, and towns while advancing. [34] He seized Lord Saye's estate at Broughton and marched into Banbury, the center of Saye's influence, where he forced the inhabitants to surrender and enlist in his army. Charles then named Lord Saye's local rival, the Earl of Northampton, governor of Banbury. On 27 October, Charles was warmly received at Oxford by the university officials and most of the students. A few days later Rupert attacked Windsor Castle, which he failed to win, and then ravaged the countryside around Aylesbury before rejoining the King. During the first week of November the King proceeded down the Thames toward London. On Tuesday he took Benson; on Wednesday, Reading; on Guy Fawkes Day, Colebrook, where he received a firm peace overture. Each day the Londoners became more apprehensive about their fate.

The lord general would come to their aid—but in his own deliberate and cautious manner. After leaving Warwick he crossed the Chilterns at the easternmost point and proceeded via Daventry, Towcaster, Woburn, and Saint Albans, driving his army by forced marches. Along the way he reinforced his troops wherever possible and encouraged the fainthearted. On his return, according to Clarendon, "a great fame came before him of the strength and courage of his army; though in truth it was not answerable to the report." [35] But Essex's man-power problems increased as he approached London. He feared that many soldiers would desert as soon as they

[33] Clarendon, *History* (1849 ed.), 2: 398.

[34] See William D. Macray, *Letters and Papers of Patrick Ruthven, Earl of Forth and Brentford* (London, 1868).

[35] Clarendon, *History* (1849 ed.), 2: 417.

passed through the gates of the City. He was deeply concerned lest his army, upon arriving in London before the King, would not be large enough to meet Charles in a pitched battle. Thus he sent forth appeals in several directions. On 1 November he sent a direct and somewhat desperate plea to the deputy lieutenants and "well-affected Gentry of Lincolnshire" for equipment of all types.[36] Three days later, while at the Earl of Bedford's Woburn Abbey, he made a similar plea to the deputy lieutenants of Buckingham-shire. On 5 November he wrote his political ally John Pym about desertion in the ranks of his regiments: "If thear bee a search made in London and Essex, I beleeve many will return; the Army is marching; thearfore I end with this desier, that wee may have spare arms of picks and muskets. I have often wrote for them."[37] The situation was grave, Essex admitted, but all was not lost.

Essex spent the following day, Sunday, in Saint Albans, deploying his tired troops and assigning newly recruited ones to various stations on the periphery of the metropolitan area. He had beaten Charles to London, as he had planned, but his depleted army felt the effects of Edgehill and the forced marches. "The army of Essex consists of 5,000 infantry and 1,000 cavalry," wrote the Venetian ambassador. "With the greatest energy and application he is endeavouring to increase it with fresh men from this city, with others from the country and with sailors, with the idea of leading it out later on to try conclusions once more with that of his Majesty. The interested parliamentarians assert persistently that within a very short space they will have got together under their banners a force of 12,000 men on foot and 3,000 horse and that they will march very soon to confront the king."[38] It was these experienced but wearied soldiers whom Essex stationed at Kingston, Staines, Colebrook, and Brentford.

The people of London and Westminster were preparing for the worst. The members of Parliament, fearing that Essex might not return in time, raised more troops and placed them under the command of the Earl of Warwick. Parliament also moved the King's

[36] Essex to Sir Thomas Trollope et al. in *H. M. C. Fifteenth Report*, Appendix 4, p. 141; and Warburton, *Rupert*, 2: 53.

[37] British Museum, Additional MSS, 11,692, fol. 27. That same day Essex sent a similar message to the Committee of Safety (see fol. 29).

[38] *C. S. P. Ven., 1641–1642*, p. 198.

young children to a safe place, passed a measure designed to maintain the wives and children of those soldiers killed or maimed in the service of Parliament, and pressed horses. Early in November both Houses concurred on legislation guaranteeing all London apprentices who volunteered for service in Parliament's army their seniority rights and privileges.

Some parliamentary leaders also began to talk about the possibility of a negotiated settlement. The first concrete proposal emanated from the Upper House, where it was initiated by the Earls of Northumberland and Holland, but within a few days a peace party emerged in the Lower House as well.[39] On 2 November both Houses agreed to sound out the King. That some members were genuine in their desire for negotiation cannot be denied, but it is also true that many viewed talks as a tactical maneuver to delay the King until Essex arrived with his army. On the following day Sir Peter Killegrew was dispatched to secure from Charles the promise of safe-conduct for Parliament's commissioners. Instead of giving Killegrew an immediate and direct answer, the King, who was ready to leave Reading for London, procrastinated for several days and declared that one of Parliament's commissioners, Sir John Evelyn, was unacceptable because he had been declared a traitor. Meanwhile, the Committee of Safety, under Northumberland's leadership, began to discuss several propositions which aimed at the prevention of further bloodshed and the establishment of a firm and acceptable peace. Before making these proposals public, however, Northumberland insised that Essex should be consulted.

Essex learned of these peace feelers by means of a letter he received from the Committee of Safety.[40] He seems to have regarded the peace gestures as genuine, but he sensed that they stemmed from the weakness of Parliament's military position. He was so sensitive about the matter that he wrote two letters putting forward his views on the subject. In the first one, addressed to Pym, he asserted that his army would arrive before the King's and that it would hold together after arriving in London. In the second, addressed to Northumberland, he pointed out the incompatability

[39] Codrington, *Life and Death*, p. 18. Also see John Vicars, *God in the Mount* (London, 1643), p. 208.

[40] Devereux, *Lives and Letters*, 2: 359.

of Parliament's suing for peace while Rupert plundered the area
west of London. Essex refused to commit himself firmly for or
against a peace treaty at that time. He simply advised caution.

Upon his arrival in London two days later, on 7 November,
Essex received a hero's welcome. He was, according to the *Perfect
Diurnal*, "joyfully received by the Parliament, and thousands of
those that were well affected did flock to see him."[41] He came not
only as a victor—the victor of Edgehill—but as a savior, for he had
outdistanced the King and thus saved Londoners from Prince
Rupert and the Royalists. Later that day Essex informed a joint
conference of the status of his troops. "The Army hath had a long
March," he related, "and as soon as they are fit, we will quarter
them in such places as shall be most convenient for the preservation
of these parts."[42] The following day a deputation from Parliament
appealed to the masses of London at Guildhall. In a haranguing
speech the chairman of the delegation, Lord Brooke, defended
Parliament against some adverse criticism and praised the Parliamentary army. "We are no Rebels," he replied to the King's charges,
and then eulogized the Earl of Essex's performance at Edgehill.[43]

On 11 November, Parliament approved a resolution granting
Essex five thousand pounds as a token of its appreciation.[44] William
Dugdale, Royalist antiquarian, described this gesture as a move "to
puff up their General with such vain apprehensions as might hearten
... further employment."[45] The Venetian envoy, ever an astute
observer, noted an undercurrent of hostility to the generosity of
Parliament. Several publishers used the occasion to capitalize on
Essex's newsworthiness. One printed a panegyric entitled *The Earl
of Essex His Loyalty and Love*. Another came out with *London's
Joyful Gratulation and Thankful Remembrance for their Safties*, which
included a short doggerel in honor of Essex's victory at Edgehill:

> Illustrious Essex, who so truly good,
> His vertue dignifies his name and stood:
> Which being deduced from ancient stem,
> With Chartlyes barronie even had on him.
> To whom by right inheritance did arrive

---

41 *Ibid.*, p. 360.

42 *Lords Journal*, 5: 437.

43 Robert E. L. Strider, *Lord Brooke* (Cambridge: Harvard University Press,
1958), p. 62.

44 Rushworth, *Historical Collections*, 5: 55.

45 See his *A Short View of the late troubles in England* (London, 1681), p. 111.

The stile of Earl of Essex and of Ewe,
Whose father, that same darling and delight
Of manhood vanquished in victorious fight.[46]

The lord general also became fair game for personal ridicule. At the outbreak of hostilities the Countess of Essex departed from London and joined the Royalists in Oxford, where she consorted with Sir Thomas Higgons. When the Countess gave birth to a son in late December 1642, the lord general became the butt of more sarcasm and derision. "When his Majesty read the first news of it," wrote one contemporary, "In Truth, said his Majesty, I think he is no more the father of it than I am, and Gentlemen here I clear myself of it before you all."[47] For years thereafter Essex was dubbed "his Oxcellency" by many Royalist lampooners.

IV

THE LORD GENERAL, in the meantime, was faced with several exigencies. His soldiers proved to be exceedingly unruly. Some had killed deer in Hyde Park; others had done the same in Marylebone Park. Complaints of disorderly conduct abounded. The lord general's *Lawes and Ordinances* were flouted so profusely that Parliament intervened with a declaration that set aside the guarantees of the Petition of Right and put into effect martial law. "That from henceforth the Officers and Soldiers of the said Army may not expect any further Forbearance of such Punishment to be inflicted on them," the ordinance read, "for any Offence, as shall be due to them by the said Laws and Ordinances; but that the Lord General may and ought to punish them, by death or otherwise, according to their demerits."[48] Thereafter Essex had the power of life and death over the soldiers in Parliament's army.

That same day Essex was ordered by Parliament to take the field and call a general muster.[49] Under "pain of death" all previously

[46] From the British Museum, Thomason Collection.

[47] *H. M. C. Thirteenth Report*, Appendix 1, p. 86. Also see Devereux, *Lives and Letters*, 2: 306; and Warburton, *Rupert*, 1: 420. For the Countess of Essex's subsequent career see *A Funeral Oration Spoken over the Grave of the Lady Eliz: Countess of Essex by her Husband, Sir Thomas Higgons att her Interment at the Cathedral Church at Winchester. Sept. 16th 1656*, in the British Museum, Additional MSS, 5830.

[48] Published on 10 November 1642 as *A Declaration of the Lords and Commons in Parliament Concerning the Regulating of great Inconveniences in His Excellencies Army*.

[49] *Lords Journal*, 5: 439.

enlisted soldiers were ordered by both Houses to repair to their colors in the palace yard. The new volunteers, mostly apprentices from London, assembled in Finsbury Field, where they were formally enlisted and reviewed by Essex and several other peers. Two days later, on 11 November, the lord general and his reinforced army marched out of London toward the King. Essex was soon joined by Philip Skippon and his trained bands.

In the early morning hours of 12 November, as a heavy mist hovered over the town of Brentford, Prince Rupert attacked, presumably with the tacit consent of the King, and took the Parliamentary forces there completely by surprise.[50] He encountered some opposition from experienced soldiers in Holles's regiment, most of whom had fought at Edgehill, but none from Lord Brooke's; in fact, the soldiers in the latter's unit fled for their lives. One fearless captain, John Lilburne, assumed command of the situation in the absence of his superiors and attempted to persuade his fellow soldiers to remain and fight, but his valiant efforts were in vain. He was captured and imprisoned by Rupert and the Cavaliers. Rupert took about 500 prisoners and won a moral victory. Among those killed at Brentford was Sgt. Maj. James Quarrels, who had served Essex for many years.[51]

Parliament regarded the Brentford incident as a breach of good faith on the part of the Royalists. Many members considered Rupert's actions outrageous. The Parliamentarians were acting with honor: Essex had abstained from all acts that might be construed as hostile and had personally returned to London to engage in the peace discussions, and both Houses accepted most of the King's conditions.

The lord general was in the House of Lords when news of the Brentford defeat broke in Westminster. He was promptly ordered by Parliament to "pursue the enemy with all advantage whatsoever."[52] In the words of Robert Codrington, "Immediately his Excellency, the Earl of Essex departed from London, and marched against the enemy."[53] The enemy had to be stopped at Brentford at all costs. There was little time. The strategy was simple: there must be a grand show of force to delay the King's entry into

[50] Sanderson has a thorough coverage of these events in *A Compleat History*, pp. 591–95; also see Davies, "Documents," pp. 64–67.

[51] Vicars, *God in the Mount*, p. 216.

[52] Devereux, *Lives and Letters*, 2: 362.

[53] Codrington, *Life and Death*, p. 18.

London, so Essex issued a general order for all troops in the London area to proceed to Turnham Green as soon as possible. That night soldiers from Essex's army came from the several stations to Turnham Green. The trained bands of the City, joined by many able-bodied citizens, did the same.

On the morning of 13 November the King found his way to London blocked by a mass of 24,000 human beings.[54] The sheer magnitude of the force—twice that of the King's—was sobering to the Royalists, Rupert included. It would be folly for them to risk a full-fledged battle against such odds. Essex had the numerical edge. He also had the advantage of being close to his base of supplies. Equally important, he occupied an excellent defensive position, with the City at his back. If the King had fought at this juncture, Clarendon conjectured, he might have forfeited his crown on the spot.

Essex's army, despite its heterogeneous composition, stood fast at Turnham Green that Sabbath day. Although several members of Parliament advocated a general engagement, the professional soldiers in the army advised against this strategy. At a Council of War called by Essex the soldiers won. It was decided to wait for the King to move before committing the army to a pitched battle. Most of the peers came to the field. The Earls of Holland and Northumberland helped Essex organize the hastily assembled array. "The General Essex likewise took great pains in the field," wrote Whitelocke, "and accompanied with the Lords and Commons with him, rode from Regiment to Regiment, encouraging of them; and where he had spoken to them, the Souldiers would throw up their Caps and shout, crying 'Hey for old Robin.'"[55]

"Old Robin" outsmarted the King at Turnham Green. He held his ground and forced the Royalists to retreat: in so doing he saved London and its suburbs from Royalist domination and the ravages of war. In the battle of Turnham Green—a battle which was never fought—Essex emerged the victor.

V

As THE KING withdrew to Oxford, Essex gave a slow, cautious pursuit as far as Windsor. The lord general stationed one contingent

[54] See Austin Woolrych, *Battles of the English Civil War* (London: B. T. Batsford, 1961), pp. 15–20.

[55] Whitelocke, *Memorials* (1682 ed.), p. 62.

in Aylesbury and sent some troops southward to prevent the Royalists from sweeping around him, but he refused to follow up with a direct engagement—a refusal which caused widespread apprehension and evoked criticism among the zealots in the House of Commons. Instead, he gradually permitted the trained bands to return to London. With the help of a fresh loan from the City he paid his soldiers and prepared for the winter season.

After Turnham Green the lord general was again honored for his devotion to the cause of Parliament. In mid-November he was eulogized in *An Exact Relation of the Battle Fought on Saturday last at Aston between the Kings Army and the Earl of Essex his Forces*.[56] About this time several engravers struck medals featuring the Earl of Essex. One medalion depicted him as the victorious hero of Edgehill, the obverse side showing him in an equestrian pose with the legend *Robertus Comes Essexiae*,[57] and the reverse side including his coat of arms in an oval shield with his motto *Basis Virtutum Constantia* on the band. Another medal, with the legend "The sword of the Lord and of Gideon," depicted over Essex's head a hand brandishing a sword. These medalions, issued in gold and silver, were furnished with hooks for suspension around the neck of the purchaser.

Meanwhile, Parliament further prepared for war. Two days after Turnham Green the members accepted an offer of the London citizens to raise an auxiliary force of 1,000 light horse and 3,000 dragoons. The offer was generous, but the conditions had an ominous overtone of City dictation. The new troops were to be commanded by the lord general—"none but Essex"—but Skippon was singled out as major general. On 26 November the two Houses passed an ordinance making mandatory the assessment of all those who had not previously contributed to the cause. Three days later Parliament established county-level commissaries and commanded them to supply the army with provisions. That same day they authorized John Pickering to open formal negotiations with the Scots in hopeful anticipation of an alliance.

Lord General Essex then put his army into a defensive posture designed to protect London during the winter months. He selected

56 This was published on 14 November 1642 and is in the British Museum, Thomason Collection.

57 See Edward Hawkins, *Medallic Illustrations of the History of Great Britain*, 2 vols. (London, 1885), 1: 295–300. For a complete discussion of these medals see Ernst H. Kantorowicz, *The King's Two Bodies* (Princeton: Princeton University Press, 1957), p. 507.

Windsor, which had fallen to Parliament in October, for his army headquarters. It was a natural choice: Windsor was close enough to the City to allow maintenance of steady lines of supply and yet distant enough to forestall a Royalist advance upon London or Westminster from the west. The castle afforded Essex a commanding and defensible position with commodious quarters. The surrounding grounds, particularly the park and the forest, provided him with adequate space for his foot soldiers and plenty of recreational facilities for his staff. The roads radiating from Windsor enabled him to obtain intelligence concerning the King's actions in Oxford and the Royalist army's moves in the South and the West.

Essex remained there throughout December and was pressed by some members of Parliament "to advance to attack the King's quarters, before he can take any advantage from the junction of other forces which he expects. But the unsuitable season, the new fortifications erected by his Majesty, and more than all the desire of the commanders to fill their own purses, have so far prevented anything being done." [58] Essex did not, however, lay aside his sword or drop his guard. He garrisoned those cities and towns loyal to Parliament: Gloucester, Bristol, Exeter, Dover, Southampton, Plymouth, and Marlborough. He also appealed to the newly established county committees to forward him supplies and equipment.

During the second week of December the lord general received from Treasurer Gerrard ten thousand pounds to pay his soldiers. Essex immediately thanked the Commitee of Safety and gave them a full report of the military situation. A contingent under Sir William Waller was in Sussex attempting to win part of that county to Parliament's side. Another force was in Marlborough in an effort to control the eastern portion of Wiltshire. A third contingent would soon be sent to Devonshire. The week after Essex paid his troops he revealed that Parliamentary forces had taken Winchester. The lord general won praise for this victory, of course, and Parliament ordered a day of thanksgiving to celebrate it.

About this time Essex faced several dilemmas concerning prisoners of war. He received a request from the former Lord Willoughby, now the new Earl of Lindsey, who had been captured at Edgehill, to be removed from Lord Brooke's custody in Warwick Castle to London. When Essex presented this matter to Parliament,

[58] *C. S. P. Ven., 1641–1642,* p. 216.

he was empowered to act as "he shall think fit" in such matters.[59]
The King, meanwhile, began to treat prisoners as he chose. On
6 December, Capt. John Lilburne, that indefatigable critic of
Stuart government who had been captured at Brentford, was
found guilty of treason by the Royalists in Oxford and sentenced
to death by Chief Justice Robert Heath.[60] Before Lilburne was
executed, however, Parliament threatened to retaliate in kind if
the Royalists carried through with the sentence. This warning
apparently was sufficient to forestall the execution, for Charles
backed down, no doubt fearing the loss of Lindsey. There ensued
a series of complicated negotiations and prisoner exchanges involving Lindsey, Lilburne, and five other captains captured at Brentford. Before long, as a result of Essex's endeavors, Parliament's
officers were freed.

The lord general also confronted one of the most disconcerting
problems of his military career—the divisiveness of provincialism.[61]
Such a force was, of course, latent in the structure and composition
of the Lower House. Moreover, the Militia Ordinance fostered
localism, for it gave considerable power to the local gentry. Throughout the Civil War the problem would recur many times. During the
summer of 1642, Parliament had permitted the several communities
to supplement the Militia Ordinance by providing for their own
defense. In theory these local measures were subject to Parliament
and the lord general; in practice the locally raised troops could not
be counted upon to serve outside the county. Sometimes the
community raised troops on the condition that they fight under a
particular commander. Parliament and its officers could scarcely
turn down these proposals, although the conditions placed on them
handicapped the high command.

Separate sectional commanders with rather broad powers created
similar difficulties. In September, Parliament had authorized
Lord Fairfax to raise an army in Yorkshire. Essex was compelled by Parliament to issue him a commission, yet he retained
little authority over Fairfax after it was granted. In December, the
two Houses recommended Lord Robartes to Essex as commander
of troops in the West. That same month several members of Essex's

[59] *Lords Journal*, 5: 463.

[60] *Ibid.*, p. 515. Also see Gardiner, *Civil War*, 1: 73; Rushworth, *Historical
Collections*, 5: 93; and Andrew Clark, *The Life and Times of Anthony Wood*, anti-
quary, of Oxford, 1632-1695, described by himself, 5 vols. (Oxford, 1891-1900), 1: 72.

[61] See Abbott, *Cromwell*, 1: 207; and Dugdale, *Short View*, p. 113.

life guard succumbed to local pressures and returned to their native counties, where they raised troops to defend those districts during the winter months.[62] Ireton returned to Nottingham, Ludlow recruited a force in Wiltshire, and Capt. Oliver Cromwell, after having been paid £204 by Essex on 17 December, returned home for the same purpose.

Before long these county-level military organizations coalesced into sectional associations.[63] In November, to illustrate, several Midland counties formally banded together for defense during the winter months. In December associations sprang up all over England: the Eastern Association, the Western Association, the Northern Association, and an association which included Wales and several western counties. Parliament formally sanctioned these groups by appointing commanders and ordering the lord general to issue them commissions. These measures must have had a demoralizing effect upon Parliament's high command. They increased the complexity of the whole military structure, threatened the unity of command, and encouraged further proliferation of the war effort to the point that many participants thought and fought along local and sectional lines.

From the viewpoint of the lord general, whose authority was diluted, these measures made defensive operations in the winter and offensive maneuvers in the summer immeasurably complicated. Essex in all likelihood disapproved of the diffusion and decentralization of the war effort. In December one contemporary noted that he had "grown into great jealousies with his great masters; and with him most of the best commanders of that party,"[64] but there is little concrete information of outright disagreement and no evidence of open opposition of any sort. On the other hand, the lord general became the butt of some criticism for his refusal to take the war into the enemy's camp during the winter months. The war party in the Lower House and London disapproved of Essex's reluctance to take the initiative and give battle. Radical Henry Marten disparaged Essex when he asserted, "It is summer in Devonshire, summer in Yorkshire and cold winter in Windsor."[65]

[62] See Ludlow, *Memoirs*, 1: 49.

[63] See Firth and Rait, *Acts and Ordinances*, 1: 51, 52, 54.

[64] Arthur Trevor to the Marquis of Ormonde, in Thomas Carte, *Ormonde Papers*, 2 vols. (London, 1739), 1: 17.

[65] J. H. Hexter, *The Reign of King Pym* (Cambridge: Harvard University Press, 1941), p. 110.

In mid-December the King attempted to take advantage of whatever disillusionment Essex may have experienced with Parliament by offering him a "free pardon" if he would but "forbear to proceed any further in this destructive war."[66] Essex may have been disappointed at the recent turn of events, but he was not prepared to defect or take himself out of the war, pardon or not. Rather, he took refuge in Parliament. "But having such a great trust reposed in me, and committed to my charge by both Houses of Parliament," he responded to Charles, "I cannot conceive but that I am bound in conscience, according to the law of God, to discharge that trust which is reposed in me by your great and honorable council, being for the defence of your Majesty's person, God's true religion, the privileges of both Houses of Parliament, the liberties of your good subjects, and the good of the Commonwealth."[67] Essex refused to yield in his constancy to Parliament. If Englishmen would live and die for Essex, he would live and die for Parliament.

The lord general spent the Christmas season at Windsor Castle, where in 1601, as a child, he had been taken from nearby Eton College and placed under the supervision of the dean of Saint George's Chapel for security. It was at Windsor that he had learned his late father's fate in the Tower courtyard. One wonders what thoughts about the past—both the dark distant past of bygone decades and the vivid past of recent months—went through his mind as he worshiped in the chapel or hunted the stag in Windsor Park during the yuletide season.

VI

AFTER THE Edgehill campaign His Excellency spent most of his time dealing with military matters. His defense strategy was simple: to maintain the territory presently held by Parliament and, in particular, defend the home counties from Royalist incursions. He did not launch a winter assault on Reading or Oxford nor did he devise plans for winter operations elsewhere. His army, impoverished and extremely short of horse, was ill-suited for an effective winter campaign. Instead of there being a general cessation of

66 See *His Majesties' Gracious Message* (London, 1642), published on 19 December.
67 Devereux, *Life and Letters*, 1: 364.

hostilities during the winter months, the conflicts were localized to a great extent. In some counties there were sporadic raids and skirmishes between the opposing sides. In many areas the antagonists fought for control of local magazines, market towns, ports, and castles.

Essex found it increasingly difficult to preserve the unity of his command. In theory he was commander in chief, with broad authority over Parliament's manifold military operations; in practice he found himself limited—by localism, by personal and partisan rivalries, by distance and poor communications, and by Parliament. Fortunately, he enjoyed the backing of majorities in both Houses although as the winter wore on he was subjected to an increasing amount of criticism by a handful of outspoken radicals in the Commons.[68] Because he remained with his army at Windsor, he was compelled to rely upon his colleagues in the Upper House and his political allies in the Lower House to defend him. He was frequently visited by members of Parliament. He set up a messenger service which informed him about new ordinances and orders passed in the two Houses and kept him in touch with events in the East and the North.

Within the framework of Parliament's supervisory authority the lord general exercised limited appointive powers.[69] He secured the services of a new secretary, John Baldwin, who wrote many of the warrants and messages that bear Essex's name. On 14 January 1643, Essex commissioned Sir Samuel Luke as scoutmaster general and authorized him to establish and maintain an intelligence office on the premises of Eton College. Thereafter twenty scouts kept Luke well informed about the comings and goings of Royalists; Luke, in turn, forwarded periodic reports, oftimes daily, to the lord general. Essex also granted commissions to colonels like William Purefoy of Warwickshire to raise regiments in their native counties.[70] He also named governors, including Rowland Laugherne, to those garrisoned towns and castles under the sway of

[68] See Hexter, *King Pym* for a thorough treatment of this subject.

[69] See Sir Samuel Luke, *Journal of Sir Samuel Luke*, ed. I. G. Philip, 3 vols., Oxford Record Society (Oxford, 1950–52), 1: i–vi, for these appointments and Essex's life at Windsor.

[70] See P. R. O., S. P. 16/497: 44, for Purefoy's commission; and Rushworth, *Historical Collections*, 5: 303 for Laugherne's appointment.

Parliament, and appears to have exercised some influence in the selection of chaplains serving the various regiments in his army.

Essex also exercised certain "prerogative powers."[71] In early winter, for example, he signed a formal document granting protection against plundering to the Earl of Sussex's home at Gorhambury. In early February, Essex granted protection to his brother-in-law, the Royalist Marquess of Hertford. Likewise, matters relating to the imprisonment and exchange of captives came within the jurisdiction of Essex's commission.[72] On 4 February, Parliament, conceding to the City authorities, passed an order calling for the removal of all incarcerated Royalists in London to Windsor. They were committed to the custody of the lord general, who placed them in the keep. Henceforth Royalist prisoners were taken to London for interrogation by members of Parliament and then transferred to Windsor for further questioning and safekeeping. Essex appears to have treated his captured adversaries humanely, entertaining and supporting their petitions for release and helping to arrange for their exchange. His handling of passes was equally liberal: he frequently permitted avowed Royalists, even potential troublemakers, to pass between enemy camps, a practice which drew criticism from militants in the Lower House.

Many and varied difficulties that winter at Windsor made administration exceedingly complex. Keeping his army, now one-third its original size,[73] intact to adequately protect London proved to be an impossible and unrewarding task for the lord general. The soldiers killed in the Edgehill campaign had not been replaced. Desertion and defection increased at an alarming rate. When their commanders retired to their respective counties, several units of horse disappeared. Many other soldiers simply returned to London, without leave or pay, to secure employment and food through the winter season. Some deserters eventually defected. Luke reported that four German soldiers who had fought under Essex left Windsor and joined the Royalists in Oxford, where, it was rumored, Charles received them with kisses. That officers, too, defected, had a demoralizing effect. Early in the year Essex's colleague the Earl of Bedford laid aside his commission with no explanation; later he joined the King at Oxford.

71 See *H. M. C. Seventh Report*, p. 442; and Clanricarde, *Memoirs*, p. 340.

72 See *Lords Journal*, 5: 589–91; Luke, *Journal*, 1: 4; and *H. M. C. Thirteenth Report*, Appendix 1, p. 104.

73 See Davies, "Parliamentary Army," pp. 36–39.

During the winter, Parliament issued several orders demanding that the soldiers in London return to their proper units. Essex himself held several musters and issued two proclamations—at least the printers gave them that distinction—designed to keep the army together.[74] All the officers were commanded to fill their units. All enlisted men were to report to duty immediately.[75] Those men who followed these orders would be granted their allowances; those who did not would be cashiered. Apparently the measures were not successful, for when Essex entered the campaign in April he was still understrength.

The crux of the problem was finances: Essex did not have enough money to pay his soldiers.[76] The three hundred thousand pounds Parliament appropriated did not meet the actual costs of keeping the army—even in its reduced state—on the field. By February there was not a penny in the accounts of Sir Gilbert Gerrard to pay the remaining soldiers. By the middle of the month 400 soldiers who were two months in arrears fled to London, whereupon the City authorities, fearful of mutinous activities, complained to Parliament.[77] That body sent a delegation, which included Lord Saye and Sir Philip Stapleton, to Windsor to discuss the matter with Essex. He sided with the unpaid common soldiers and demanded of Parliament enough funds—at least forty thousand pounds—to pay arrears. Some of those soldiers remaining in Windsor took the law into their own hands and expropriated the natural provisions they found in Windsor Forest, killing and consuming more than five hundred deer, and plundering Saint George's Chapel, where they seized most of the plate belonging to the Order of the Garter. Until Parliament devised a better means of financing a large army on an annual basis the situation would be increasingly troublesome for Essex.

At Westminster, meanwhile, Parliament gravitated between peace and war.[78] The peace movement was stronger in the Upper House, where it encompassed a majority of the peers, than in the

[74] *Two Proclamations by His Excellency Robert Earl of Essex*, printed on 8 March 1643 by "his Excellency's command." A reprinting of the *Lawes and Ordinances* soon followed.

[75] See Gardiner, *Civil War*, 1: 91; Davies, "Documents," 68–71; and *Mercurius Aulicus* (Oxford), 1643, pp. 49, 162.

[76] *Mercurius Aulicus* (Oxford), 1643, pp. 77, 126, 149, 200.

[77] *Lords Journal*, 6: 21.

[78] For a full discussion of these talks see Gardiner, *Civil War*, 1: 74–84, 89–109.

Commons, where it was opposed by radicals who clamored for victory on the battlefield. For three months the combatants negotiated in an atmosphere of apprehension and mistrust. Parliament put forth propositions which, though rejected, were answered point by point by the King; his proposals for settlement likewise were rebutted and turned down. Scores of messages were exchanged and safe-conducts were granted by both sides, but with no success.

Essex assumed an ambivalent role in these negotiations. He remained in Windsor with his army throughout the bargaining period and took no role in the formation of Parliament's overture or in the rejection of the King's. His compeers, however, deemed his judgment so essential to an acceptable settlement that they requested his opinion. "My Lord, if I had known of it before it had been voted," he wrote the speaker of the Upper House in mid-February, "I should clearly have delivered my Opinion, and then submitted myself and it to your Lordships greater Wisdoms; but, my Lord, now I know my duty: the Armies you have raised are so dispersed, and so many Difficulties in it, that it is too great a Burthen for me to undertake to deliver my Opinion. . . . My Lord, if I knew how to give a clearer Answer to a Business I am so great a Stranger to, having been at none of the Debates, I should shew my Obedience to their Commands." [79] The lord general possessed some misgivings about a cessation yet refused to take a stand for or against it after Parliament had spoken.

Upon learning of Essex's misgivings the Upper House sent Lord Saye and Lord Howard of Escrick to Windsor to discuss the matter at length. Essex convened the Council of War for the occasion, and there ensued long deliberations over the details of the proposed cessation. These consultations at Windsor gave birth to a very detailed paper with precise terms regarding booty, safe-conducts, prisoner exchanges, siege warfare, provisions for violations of the same, and instructions concerning how the lord general would enforce the terms. The finished document, which bore Essex's imprint, was approved by the Lords the following day, 24 February, after several alterations, and by the House of Commons a few days later.

Charles took exception to several sections in the propositions and sent Parliament a rather involved answer explaining his position. On 8 March, after a conference between the leaders of

[79] *Lords Journal*, 5: 614.

both Houses about the King's answer, Parliament dispatched a
delegation, headed by Lord Newnham, to discuss the controversy
with Essex and the Council of War. Lord General Essex propounded
his objections to the King's answer:[80] the first article, which pertained to the provisioning of the troops during the cessation,
contained several ambiguous statements; the second article did
not give a suitable definition of a soldier; the third article, concerning communication during the cessation, was phrased so
generally that the Royalist armies could easily subvert the truce;
and the seventh article, which pertained to the exchange of prisoners,
contained a clause which contradicted the second. These objections
were reduced to writing and presented to Parliament by the delegation. A revised version of the cessation, which eliminated most
of the lord general's objections, was finally approved by Parliament
and forwarded to Charles, who still could not accept the whole
proposal. Charles demanded custody of the fleet and those garrisons
then under control of Parliament and took exception to Parliament's
terms concerning trade during the cessation period. On these
points the parliamentary leaders refused to give way. The negotiations reached an impasse.

During the bargaining both King and Commons frequently
acted in bad faith: the members of the Lower House kept their
demands so high that the King could not accept them, and the
King offered counterproposals which the Commons could not
accept. The Lords, caught in the middle, became more sharply
divided than ever over the issue of peace. At first a majority of the
peers gave wholehearted support to Northumberland, the principal
spokesman for a negotiated settlement, while a minority under
Lord Saye sided with the Commons.

Essex himself reflected the split in the Upper House. He wanted
peace, but peace on terms similar to those in the Nineteen Propositions. He desired a cessation, but one embodying his own rather
stringent conditions. When the Upper House accepted Essex's
conditions, they assumed such an uncompromising position that
they ended up closer to the majority in the Lower House than to
Northumberland. The Earl of Northumberland attempted to
keep the negotiations alive and Lord Falkland renewed his appeals
to Parliament, but the King's pronouncement of 12 April so

[80] *Ibid.*, pp. 642–43.

insulted Parliament that the following day it recalled its negotiators from Oxford and increased the war preparations.

Elsewhere in England the combatants resorted to the sword. "Whilst these overtures and discourses were made of peace," Clarendon observed, "the Kingdom in all parts felt the sad effects of war, the King nor the parliament using any slackness in pursuing their business by the sword; and the persons of honour and quality in most counties more vigourously declaring themselves what they had done." [81] Throughout the countryside there were skirmishes, sieges, plunderings, and encounters of various types. In January, Sir Ralph Hopton routed a strong party of Parliamentarians near Bodmin. In February, the Royalists under Rupert carried out a successful assault upon Cirencester and captured over 1,000 prisoners—a victory which threatened Parliament's garrisons at Bristol and Gloucester. In mid-March they gained control of Staffordshire by defeating the Parliamentarians at Hopton Heath and at Heywood. Shortly thereafter Prince Rupert took the town of Birmingham, the sword-manufacturing center of England, and the life of its volunteer defender, the Earl of Denbigh. To all these actions the King gave tacit—if not active—consent. If the peace negotiations failed for lack of good faith the King and Prince Rupert were by no means blameless.

Essex himself did not leave Windsor during the peace negotiations. He did not deem it advisable to move toward Oxford on his own, especially since his cavalry was weak, nor did he receive orders from Parliament to advance. Yet, Parliament intended to meet force with force and thus counter the successes of the Royalists in the western and Midland counties. [82] To do that, on 11 February, shortly after the news of Rupert's designs upon Bristol and Gloucester, both Houses passed an ordinance naming Sir William Waller sergeant-major general of Gloucestershire, Wiltshire, Somersetshire, Worcestershire, and Shropshire and empowered him to raise troops and collect funds. In reality, Sir William, the darling of the City, commanded his army semi-independently of Essex. He had direct access to the authorities in London and the leadership in the Commons. He received a good press. Thus, with broad support, he inaugurated a campaign into the western counties in an effort

[81] See Clarendon, *History* (1849 ed.), 2: 483 for a treatment of these skirmishes.

[82] See *Lords Journal*, 5: 602; Firth and Rait, *Acts and Ordinances*, 1: 80–85; and Ludlow, *Memoirs*, 1: 49.

to counter both the inactivity of Essex and the gains of the Royalists. He was successful in Chichester, Malmesbury, Hereford, Tewksbury, and Gloucester. He darted from town to town and struck like lightning. Yet, despite these daring and newsworthy exploits, Waller's over-all effectiveness was deficient, for he left no permanent garrisons and won few friends among the country gentry.

By early April the lord general was prepared to take to the field, but whether his soldiers would march without their pay remained to be seen. Most Parliamentarians put their trust in him. Majorities in both Houses desired that Essex continue as their commander. However, pockets of opposition became more vocal as the war dragged on. Most of the criticism came from impatient and frustrated Londoners who wanted a quick, decisive victory over the King. Some came from militants in the Lower House. Derogatory remarks at times took the form of popular verse and song:

> Farewell, my Lord of Essex, with hey,
> Farewell, my Lord of Essex, with ho,
>   He sleeps till eleven,
>   And leaves the cause to six or seven,
>   But 'tis no matter—their hope's in heaven!
>   With a hey, trolly, lolly, ho![83]

Undertones of dissatisfaction persisted through the winter months. Some Londoners even talked about establishing a new army and appointing a different general responsible to London's Common Council.[84]

Waller's stunning success on the field gave some substance to the criticism. It appeared as though the lord general consumed large quantities of money and wasted time while Waller was winning the war. "Whilst Waller fights," wrote Royalist Sanderson, "their General Essex solicits the Parliament with Letters inclining to petition for a Peace."[85] Also, rumors reported that the lord general would resign his commission. "We hear that the two Houses have sent to the Earl of Essex to deliver up his commission," Secretary Nicholas wrote to Rupert in early April, "and they will give him an honourable recompence, and that they intend to make Mr. Hampden their

---

[83] Warburton, *Rupert*, 2: 222.

[84] See Pearl, *London and the Puritan Revolution*, p. 259; and Luke, *Journal*, 1: 21.

[85] Sanderson, *A Compleat History*, p. 625.

general, but of this we have no other certainty than that they are very discontented at the delays of the Earl of Essex."[86] Delays or not, Essex himself had no intention of surrendering his command, and Parliament did not ask him to resign. By the time Rupert received the above communication from the King's secretary, the lord general was moving with his army from Windsor toward the King's garrison at Reading.

[86] Donald Nicholas, *Mr. Secretary Nicholas* (London: Bodley Head, 1955), p. 179.

CHAPTER 14

The Oxford Campaign (1643):
Stalemate

I

On 13 April, Lord General Essex started his spring campaign by advancing from Windsor in a westward direction along the south bank of the Thames.[1] His objective was a direct confrontation with the King in the vicinity of Oxford. His immediate plans called for the seizure of Reading, Wallingford, and Abingdon, Royalist-controlled towns between Windsor and Oxford which had been garrisoned through the winter months. His army, reduced by desertion and sickness, was to be reinforced by that of Lord Grey of Warke's force, then over 5,000 strong. London was to keep Essex well supplied with victuals and arms. Parliament was to provide him with funds.

In a well-executed maneuver on 15 April, Essex swept around the south side of Reading, feinted a direct march toward Oxford, and then wheeled around for an assault upon Reading from the west. Here he was joined by Lord Grey. Together the two armies encircled the town and secured the nearby bridge of Caversham, thereby cutting off all lines of communication between the Royalists in the garrison and the King at Oxford. Before starting the assault Essex sent a trumpet to the governor, Sir Arthur Aston, an avowed Catholic, and demanded the immediate surrender of the garrison. Although vastly outnumbered, Aston stubbornly refused to capitulate, vowing instead to remain in the encircled town until death if need be. "Thereupon his Excellency," wrote Codrington, "taking compassion on the women and children, which were to undergo the common danger, he sent unto the governor, that they might be suffered to come forth, but this also was refused by the colonel."[2]

[1] See Luke, *Journal*, 1: 39–75 for the Reading campaign. Also see the pamphlet *Good and True Newes from Reading* in the British Museum, Thomason Collection.
[2] Codrington, *Life and Death*, p. 20.

Aston persevered for several more days, and the lord general ordered his men to prepare for battle.

At this point Essex convened the Council of War. A minority of the members, mainly those who commanded the regiments of horse, wanted to storm the garrison; the majority, following the leadership of Essex and the foot commanders, decided upon the slower and surer "approach" method, which entailed artillery bombardments and progressively smaller encirclements. To ensure the success of the siege, the lord general first forced the enemy from Caversham Hill and planted his army firmly on the northeastern edge of Reading, while Lord Grey secured the bridge located on the southeastern perimeter of the town. From the heights of Caversham Hill the artillery let loose a series of cannonades to weaken the enemy and, perhaps, force a capitulation before Parliamentarian blood was shed. Essex's soldiers kept up the barrage for several days. They shot down a church steeple, which had been used by the Royalists for observation, and they caused Governor Aston, who was wounded by flying bricks, to turn his command over to his subordinate, Col. Basil Fielding.

The King, still in Oxford, viewed these developments with alarm, for if Reading fell to Parliament's army and if Essex pressed ahead, the city of Oxford would be endangered. Charles immediately ordered Prince Rupert to hasten to Reading before the besieged Royalists surrendered to Essex. According to Sir Edward Nicholas, the Royalists had "news that the Lord Grey's forces have joined with the Earl of Essex's, that they have begirt Redding so as no man can come forth or go in; that Sir Arthur Aston is dangerously hurt, and that if Prince Rupert come not instantly Redding will be lost."[3] He concluded, "Wherefore I pray hasten his Highness with as many dragoons and foot as may be possible spared." Three days later Charles himself headed toward Reading to free the encircled Royalists from Essex's clutches.

On 24 April the lord general sent the House of Lords a full account of his military operations and most pressing needs. "I assure you, it is a very strongly fortified Town, all palisaded, and strong in Outworks," he wrote. "I am very loath to venture the Soldiers upon such Works, being probable that many may be lost in Storming; and now especially it were our great Hazard, the

3 H. M. C. Hastings Manuscripts, 2: 98.

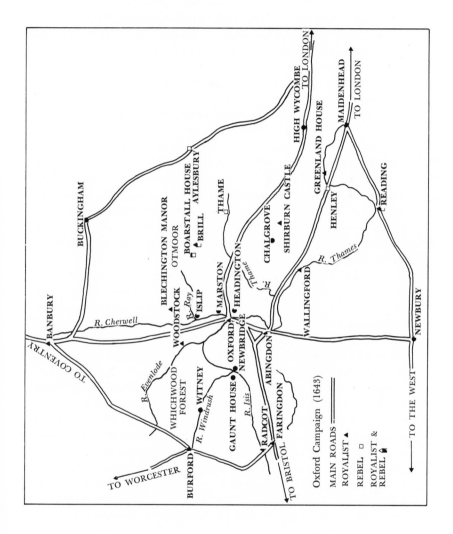

TO WORCESTER
BURFORD
TO COVENTRY
BANBURY
BUCKINGHAM
R. Cherwell
R. Evenlode
WHICHWOOD FOREST
R. Windrush
WITNEY
GAUNT HOUSE
R. Isis
RADCOT
FARINGDON
TO BRISTOL
ABINGDON
NEWBRIDGE
OXFORD
WOODSTOCK
R. Ray
ISLIP
BLECHINGTON MANOR
OTMOOR
BOARSTALL HOUSE
BRILL
AYLESBURY
MARSTON
THAME
HEADINGTON
R. Thame
CHALGROVE
SHIRBURN CASTLE
HIGH WYCOMBE
TO LONDON
GREENLAND HOUSE
MAIDENHEAD
TO LONDON
HENLEY
READING
R. Thames
WALLINGFORD
NEWBURY
TO THE WEST

Oxford Campaign (1643)
MAIN ROADS ═══
ROYALIST ▲
REBEL □
ROYALIST &
REBEL ◧

Enemy being so near, and we must be in a Posture to fight; but I doubt not but GOD'S Blessings, I shall give you a good account of this great Business. Sir Wm. Waller doth not come to me, according to my Expectation and Order, though Prince Maurice become from him, and turned upon me, so that I have now all the King's forces to deal with, both without and within the Town, without the Assistance which I had Reason to look for."[4] Despite the gloomy tone of the communication Essex soon fulfilled his promise.

Two days later he forced the Royalists in Reading to surrender and to sign a treaty. Charles and Rupert had arrived too late and with insufficient reinforcements to lift the siege. They had failed to recapture Caversham Bridge. Nor had Maurice and Rupert joined forces, as Essex had feared, and given him battle. To the besieged Royalists a negotiated surrender seemed the only feasible alternative to certain defeat. The surrender terms offered by Essex were mild and the King was quite satisfied. The following day the defenders of Reading began to leave the beleaguered town. Everything went well until the Royalists marched out toward Oxford with the honors of war. As they passed the rank and file of Essex's troopers, who stood guard to oversee the withdrawal, the Royalists were "not only reviled, and reproachfully used, but many of them disarmed, and most of the wagons plundered, in the presence of the Earl of Essex himself and the chief officers; who seemed offended at it, and not able to prevent it; the unruliness of their common men being so great."[5]

Essex regarded the fall of Reading as a godsend—a glorious beginning to a campaign which he hoped would terminate the war. Several pro-Parliament pamphleteers applauded Essex and his army in their accounts of the siege and the surrender. Parliament approved a resolution thanking him for his victory over the Royalists. The Commons thought so highly of their generalissimo that on 26 May, exactly one month after the capitulation, they passed an ordinance establishing Essex's salary at ten thousand pounds per year, a large sum which was to be paid by the sequestration of delinquents' estates.[6]

[4] *Lords Journal*, 6: 16.
[5] Clarendon, *History* (1849 ed.), 2: 30.
[6] British Museum, Additional MSS, 40,630.

II

ELSEWHERE THE FORTUNES of war were mixed. In the counties of the Eastern Association, Lord Grey of Groby and Col. Cromwell succeeded in stamping out Royalism, but on 16 May the Earl of Stamford was soundly defeated at Stratton in the West by Sir Ralph Hopton. Four days later, after a series of reverses, Sir Thomas Fairfax defeated Goring at Wakefield in West Riding; in the Midlands, however, the Cavaliers took the battle honors as the campaign got under way. Rupert captured Lichfield, while the Earl of Northampton beat the Parliamentarians at Middleton Cheyney. News from Bristol revealed defections and plots to surrender the city to the Cavaliers. Even "William the Conqueror" Waller, compelled to abandon Hereford after a brief occupation, failed to regain Worcester. The year of hoped-for victory was fast becoming also a year of defeats and reverses for Parliament.

Meanwhile, the lord general's soldiers paid dearly for their victory at Reading. The siege warfare trimmed the size of Essex's army. The biting frost and rain and the paucity of provisions lowered the resistance of the troops and rendered them susceptible to disease. "Not long after this it pleased Almighty God," wrote Codrington, "to visit the army of the Parliament with sickness, by which many of our young men perished, and the rest by reason of their weakness were disabled from doing any great service in the field. His excellency omitted nothing that might give redress unto them." [7] The epidemic, very likely influenza or typhus, soon decimated the ranks of the army, particularly the poorly paid foot soldiers. By July, according to the estimates of Godfrey Davies, Essex had only 5,500 men on the field—3,000 foot and 2,500 horse—of the original 16,000 he had recruited the previous year. [8] Worse yet, the high mortality produced increased desertion and defection. "The Earl of Essex his soldiers run away daily by great numbers from him," wrote Sir Edward Nicholas in May, "and money is very hardly gotten and slowly at London by the two Houses which troubles them much." [9] Disheartened, Essex remained at Reading and thereabouts until some of these conditions were alleviated.

To continue an effective campaign against Oxford, Essex needed

[7] Codrington, *Life and Death*, p. 22.

[8] Davies, "Parliamentary Army," p. 41.

[9] *H. M. C. Hastings Manuscripts*, 2: 99.

more horses, more foot, and most of all, more funds. To secure the horses, he appealed to the law of war and used the powers granted to him by Parliament's commission.[10] He encouraged his subordinates to seize horses wherever they could and issued warrants for that purpose. He empowered Cornet Corbett to appropriate four horses from the stable of Thomas Southal. However, when their owner protested to Parliament, the lord general was gently reprimanded by Pym and Pembroke and compelled to restore the animals. This and similar cases soon provoked such an adverse reaction in London that the victims of horse stealing demanded that Parliament pass legislation to protect them from Essex's preemptive seizures. On 10 May both Houses concurred on an ordinance which ensured the owner a fair value for his horse plus a receipt for the same. Two weeks later Parliament empowered the lords' lieutenants and their deputies to apply this method in the counties.

Essex encountered similar difficulties in recruiting troops to replenish his reduced ranks. More and more officers like Cromwell and Ireton went to their counties and sectional associations. Often they took with them experienced enlistees, leaving Essex with raw recruits, and sometimes they competed with Essex by offering potential deserters better enlistment terms. If Essex could have relied upon the various associations to recognize him as the unquestioned commander in chief of Parliament's army, and if he could have depended upon them to respond immediately to his commands, some of the difficulties arising from the diffusion of the military operations would have been lessened. Frequently, however, his subordinates questioned his authority, procrastinated, or appealed directly to Parliament.

In the final analysis Essex's army depended upon Parliament for its sustenance: without that body, especially the Commons, the lord general could accomplish nothing. Essex realized this fundamental proposition only too well. He remained in constant communication with both Houses. Sometimes he sent verbal messages with Philip Stapleton. Oftimes he relied upon an official letter or report; as time wore on these were addressed less frequently to the speaker of the House of Lords and more frequently to the speaker

[10] For the crisis over the supply of horses see *H. M. C. Thirteenth Report*, Appendix 1, pp. 106, 705–708; *Lords Journal*, 6: 28, 90; Firth and Rait, *Acts and Ordinances*, 1: 156, 162; and *C. S. P. Dom., 1641–1643*, pp. 459–66.

of the House of Commons. In a few rare instances he came to Parliament and personally pleaded his cause. One such occasion occurred during the second week of May, when Essex delivered to his peers a very sobering report concerning the military situation. He recounted the taking of Reading, for which he was formally commended, and then rendered a realistic appraisal of the state of the army. "The Lord General represented to this House," wrote the clerk of Parliament in the *Journal*, "and the great want of Provisions of Money, which is the Reason why the Army cannot march, and take Advantages which occur to them."[11]

Parliament attempted to resolve some of these perplexing problems through legislation. It increased the number of sequestrations to provide funds for Essex's army and Warwick's navy; it passed an order permitting Colonel Cromwell to expropriate provisions from the Royalist delinquents of Cambridge; and it sent detailed instructions to the county officials for collecting the weekly assessments and levied a tax on all those Englishmen who had not yet contributed to the war effort. To meet the crisis which Essex outlined in his recent speech, Parliament secured from the City loans based on anticipated revenues. Before long Essex's paymaster received funds for arrears and provisions.

Parliament hoped that these interrelated measures would enable the lord general to refurbish his army and continue his march upon Oxford. On 18 May, Essex issued a proclamation, which was subsequently printed in broadside form and distributed in London, calling upon all soldiers in the metropolitan area to repair to the fields. "It is my expresse will and pleasure," it began, "and I do hereby declare, that if any the said Officers or Souldiers whatsoever, shall not forthwith upon publication hereof made, repair to their severall Quarters in the Army . . . that every such Officer and Souldier, not having after this Proclamation made a particular license from Me, shall be forthwith casheered, and also proceeded against by the Councell of Warre, according to the Rules of Martiall Discipline."[12] Essex concluded this strong-worded edict with a warning to all citizens who harbored deserters, and a request that local authorities help him enforce it.

[11] *Lords Journal*, 6: 43.

[12] This proclamation appeared in broadside form under the title of *Robert Earl of Essex, To all those whom it may concern.*

The lord general continued to encounter some opposition to his conduct of war.[13] To reinforce his army after the siege of Reading, he had remained in Berkshire until some replacements and supplies arrived. To provision their men, some of Essex's subordinates had solicited funds from the local landowners. To keep body and soul together, some of the rank-and-file soldiers had resorted to plundering and pilfering in the Reading vicinity. These practices irked the Berkshire gentry so much that the men drafted a protest and submitted it to Parliament, hoping to secure some relief. Parliament in turn confronted the lord general with the matter. Always very sensitive about any disparagement that reflected upon his military reputation, Essex admitted the existence of the practices, apologized for his subordinates, and then promised to alleviate the situation. But the damage was already done. Essex's detractors in the City and the Commons used this and similar signs of dissatisfaction to criticize him. Essex's defenders in the Lower House, however, promptly came to his defense and gave him a vote of confidence, which is reflected in the speaker's letter of 2 June: "That the great care and good affection, with which your Excellency hath constantly proceeded in the management of this weighty and public affair, doth so far supercede all vain reports with vulgar censures, that with them they can make no impression to impute the least unto your Excellency."[14] Essex still had the majority in the Lower House behind him.

III

ON 6 JUNE, after spending six weeks in the Reading area, the lord general finally renewed his advance toward Oxford.[15] He crossed the Thames at Caversham Bridge and progressed northward in a zigzag manner, passing through the towns of Henley, Nettlebed, Stokenchurch, and Tame, keeping the river between his army and the King's, and marching his troops between Oxford and London. He hoped to beleaguer Oxford, as he had Reading, but it soon became evident that his army was totally unprepared for a siege or a direct engagement with the Royalists. Essex realized his sorry plight only too well. On 7 June he sent an urgent plea to Sir

[13] *Mercurius Aulicus* (Oxford), 1643, pp. 277–78, 286, 306.

[14] *H. M. C. Thirteenth Report*, Appendix 1, p. 709.

[15] Devereux, *Lives and Letters*, 2: 367.

Thomas Barrington, a local landowner in Essex, for all the troops the county could spare, especially units of horse and dragoons.[16] Two days later he addressed a similar appeal, which was subsequently published in London, to the "Gentlemen, Freeholders and other Well-affected people in the County of Essex."[17] Essex's friend and subordinate Col. John Hampden made a similar request to Barrington.[18] On 24 June the lord general reiterated his appeal to Barrington, but the response was disappointing indeed.

The Royalists, meanwhile, made every effort to prevent Essex from advancing upon Oxford and other garrisons along the Thames.[19] They bid for time and refused to offer battle until conditions were in their favor. Charles ordered the Queen to send more reinforcements to Oxford. He gave Prince Rupert free rein to harass Parliament's garrisons and troops in the Midlands, and he called upon the citizens of Oxford to bear arms in case Essex made an attempt upon the university town. He amassed vast stores of provisions and ammunition for use in the event of a siege. The King also reinforced the Royalist garrisons at Wallingford, Abingdon, and Oxford. He brought in additional troops from surrounding counties and ordered the foot soldiers to dig deep trenches. When Essex's army advanced northward, several miles east of Tame, Charles set up a strong fortification at Culham Hill, a high point equidistant between Abingdon and Oxford. In Oxford the students helped build magazines and dig earthworks in and around their colleges. Around-the-clock watches were set up; guards were stationed at all the bridgeheads across the Thames; the horses were kept saddled in case there was a surprise attack. Some of the royal advisers wanted the King to move to Wallingford Castle, which was the most defensible garrison in the area, but Charles rejected their advice. Instead, he anxiously awaited the hour that the lord general's troops would arrive.

Essex did not attack, however, for his army was still too impoverished for a full-fledged offensive against the reinforced Royalists.

[16] British Museum, Egerton MSS, 2646, fol. 258.

[17] *Ibid.*

[18] *Ibid.*, 2643, fol. 7. This was Hampden's last letter.

[19] See Frederick J. Varley, *The Siege of Oxford* (Oxford: Clarendon Press, 1932), pp, 121–26; Peter Young, "King Charles I's Army of 1643–1645," *Journal of the Society for Army Historical Research* 18 (1939: 27–31); and Clark, *Life and Times of Anthony Wood,* 1: 99–105.

He moved his army northward, parallel to the Thames, and then sat down a short distance east of Oxford. "The Earl of Essex is now approached to a town within ten miles of this place," wrote Nicholas to Henry Hastings, "but we hear he hath not above 1,000 men more in his army than we have."[20] From Sir Samuel Luke the commander learned of the Royalists' antisiege measures at Wallingford and Abingdon, of the King's fortifications at Culham Hill with troops from Woodstock and the surrounding towns, of the arrival of Irish officers, of the coming of the Queen with reinforcements, of Rupert's fearsome cavalry stationed at Islip, and of the King's plans for a counteroffensive. One intelligence report claimed that the King had an army 20,000 strong in the Oxford area. Against these odds the cautious lord general refused to commit his troops to either a siege or a pitched battle.

Essex's antagonists, however, did not wait when they realized that Parliament's army was too weakened and ill-prepared for a direct confrontation. Even before the King's mid-June decision to strike against the Parliamentary forces, Prince Rupert, having obtained information about Essex's plans from renegade Col. John Hurey, a Scottish mercenary, initiated a series of daring cavalry forays upon Parliament's army. With nearly 2,000 troops, mostly horse and dragoons, Rupert left Oxford on 7 June, crossed the River Thames, overwhelmed Colonel Morley's regiment at Postcombe, and then pushed on to Chinnor, where he fired the town and defeated Luke's dragoons.[21] The Prince then drove ahead to seize a Parliamentary convoy which, he learned from Hurey, contained supplies and pay money totaling about twenty-one thousand pounds; but failing to locate the convoy, he began to draw back toward his own lines. Upon discovering that Essex's horse, now in hot pursuit, might cut off his retreat, Rupert drew up his own horse and faced his pursuers at Chalgrove Field. The ensuing battle was hard fought. The Prince led a cavalry charge which routed many Parliamentary dragoons, while Gen. Henry Percy struck at the flank of Parliament's horse and put them into confusion. Prince Rupert then rallied his horse and fell back to the west side of the Thames, claiming victory for the King. He captured about 100 prisoners, left about 45 Parliamentarians dead in Chalgrove Field, and wounded many more.

20 *H. M. C. Hastings Manuscripts*, 2: 103.
21 See Gardiner, *Civil War*, 1: 151.

The wounded included the lord general's friend and ally John Hampden, who, after receiving two bullets in the shoulder, rode off early in the fight to return to Essex's headquarters at Tame.[22] There, after suffering for six days, Hampden expired on 24 June. Although not remembered for his words or spectacular deeds, he possessed sober judgment and an indomitable spirit. His death constituted a serious loss to Parliament's cause and to Essex. The reticent gentleman from Buckinghamshire had been at Essex's side as the Parliamentary observer for nearly one year and had served him loyally in several capacities. Essex had held Hampden in such esteem that he had named him an executor to his estate.

The intelligence reports which Essex received at Tame were alarming. One spy reported on 20 June that the King was planning to advance, fire the town of Tame, and drive Essex from the area. The following day another report related how Charles had called upon all Oxonians to take up arms and prepare to advance upon Tame. Luke received word of a general muster held by Charles at Oxford and learned that the Queen was en route to Oxford with a force rumored at 10,000. Some of this information was farfetched, to be sure, but the King did commence to move toward Essex's army in the last days of June. While the bulk of the Royalists edged toward Essex, Rupert led a cavalry contingent, reputedly 5,000 strong, into Buckinghamshire to strike at the rear of Parliament's army and perhaps cut off the supply lines with London.

The news from other sectors was even more disheartening to the lord general. In mid-June he learned from Col. Nathaniel Fiennes, governor of Bristol, of the shortage of arms and the lack of money and provisions in that city; the situation was so dire, in fact, that Fiennes was advised by his brother to resign.[23] About the same time bad news came from Hull: the Hothams, who had been in communication with the Royalists, now openly defected. From Oxford came a royal proclamation which called upon all Englishmen to repudiate the authority of Parliament and disobey its orders.[24] The proclamation also extended a general pardon to all Englishmen who laid down their arms, except Essex, Warwick, Stamford, Manchester, Saye, and several leaders in the Commons.

[22] Lord George Nugent, *Some Memorials of John Hampden*, 2 vols. (London, 1831), 2: 428–39.

[23] Ogle, *Clarendon State Papers*, 1: 242.

[24] Rushworth, *Historical Collections*, 5: 334.

Essex attempted to change this disturbing trend of events by importuning the House of Commons and Lord Saye to make every effort to save Bristol. The least that Parliament could do, he contended, was to send Colonel Fiennes two additional troops of horse and the money to pay arrears: "This I think little enough both in respect of the importance of that place as being the Key of the West of England."[25] The lord general also renewed his appeal to the people of Essex. "I desire you to raise sixty able horse in yor County," he wrote to Barrington, "according to the terms of a late ordinance of Parliament, and to send them unto me for the recruiting of my owne Regiment. The speedy effecting whereof wilbe of much advantage to the service in home."[26] The response to this request was no different from previous ones—too little, too late.

The lord general and his fellow officers on the field received the blame for these reversals. They were criticized in the counties for not putting up stronger resistance against the Royalists. They were attacked in Parliament for not launching an offensive against the King. When Essex heard of the mounting criticism, he answered his detractors with explanations and then threatened to resign. On 29 June he wrote to the speaker of the Lower House:

The displeasure that the officers of this army are fallen into in general and I in particular came unexpected to me. I am sorry it should be conceived that through our neglect the counties should be discouraged from sending more men or money for the relief of the army. Sir, hitherto, it is but the cries of poor people that suffer which have grieved me; but the last, that our neglect should bring dishonour to the Parliament in making men believe that the subjects are much safer in protection of the King's army than of the Parliament's wounds us so deeply that I must be forced to say, that never army served with more fidelity than this. . . . I shall take all the care I can that the army may secure these parts from the ranging of the King's horse and secure the counties between London and the army. My only suit is, that my imperfections may not be a means the army should disband for want of supply; but rather that the army may be paid, and there may be somebody placed in the head of it, in whom they may put confidence in.[27]

Before long this ill-disguised offer to resign became a threat; in the meantime, the lord general, very apologetic and extremely sensitive

25 House of Lords Record Office, Main Papers.
26 British Museum, Egerton MSS, 2646, fol. 289.
27 *H. M. C. Thirteenth Report*, Appendix 1, p. 715.

to the mounting dissatisfaction over his leadership, recommended parliamentary solutions to the difficulties.

On the last day of June he suggested that a select committee visit the field quarters of the soldiers and report their findings to Parliament. "I very much desire that some of the Lords of your House might be sent down," he suggested to the speaker of Upper House, "that, together with some of the House of Commons we may confer and debate of Things of great Necessity to be considered of, which I most desire may be done with all possible Speed."[28] Parliament, reacting promptly and favorably to this suggestion, appointed a committee composed of the Earl of Holland, Lord Howard of Escrick, and four commoners, all of whom met with Essex on 2 July at Tame. There they viewed the deteriorated army. There they witnessed the effects of the "new disease." There they heard Essex describe the military situation: how the King was pressing from the west, how Prince Rupert harassed Parliament's troops in Buckinghamshire, and how the Earl of Newcastle threatened Hull and parts south.

Two days later, after the parliamentary delegation returned to Westminster, Essex abandoned Tame and marched northward, keeping his army between London and Prince Rupert. As he advanced slowly through the heart of Buckinghamshire, his army dwindled even more. By the time he arrived in Great Brickhill, a small town several miles north of Aylesbury, Lord General Essex was extremely despondent. His army was too weak to fight. His importunities seemed to fall upon deaf ears. "But about this time, the Earl of Essex," noted William Dugdale, "made complaint to them by Letters, for want of Horse, Arms, and proposed to them a treaty of peace."[29]

A treaty of peace. Essex became so low in spirits and so disillusioned that he sent to Parliament an ultimatum which included a proposal for a negotiated settlement. "If it were thought fit to send to his Majesty to have peace," he wrote the speaker of the House of Commons, "with the settling of religion, the laws and liberties of the subject, and to bring unto just trials those chief delinquents that have brought all this mischief to both kingdoms . . . or else, if His Majesty shall please to absent himself, there may be a day set down to give a period to all these unhappy distractions by a battle,

[28] *Lords Journal*, 6: 116.
[29] *Short View*, p. 122.

in which, when and where they shall choose that may be thought any way indifferent, I shall be ready to perform that duty I owe you and the proposition to be agreed upon between His Majesty and the Parliament, may be sent to such an indifferent place that both armies may be drawn near the one to the other, that if peace be not concluded, it may be ended by the sword."[30] This missive, read in the Lower House on 10 July and in the Upper House the following day, precipitated a political stir beyond expectation.

For John Pym and his middle group Essex's talk about peace and the proposal of a massive trial by battle were exceedingly embarrassing and risky.[31] They had supported the lord general from the beginning of the war, stood by him through several crises, and countered earlier opposition to his leadership. Now he seemed to ignore their political authority and side with those who clamored for accommodation. Now he appeared to betray his backers in Parliament and jeopardize the moderate position. His propositions were completely unrealistic, being predicated on an insurmountable "if." Would the King "absent himself?" Would he agree to a showdown "trial by battle?" Could a neutral place be agreed upon? To a practical politician like Pym the lord general's peace proposal was implausible.

In a second letter addressed to Speaker William Lenthall three days later, the lord general omitted all mention of peace. He did, however, reiterate his pressing needs and make several recommendations for furthering the war effort. He suggested that another parliamentary committee visit his army and investigate its grave problems. He even issued a personal invitation to Sir Henry Vane, one of his sharpest critics in the Lower House, to review the military situation. "I shall go hand in hand with him to the walls of Oxford," Essex promised with a touch of irony. "If any supplies come down, they would be both welcome and needful; however, God willing the army shall be led on to the most advantage our judgment shall guide us to. It is in God's hands to give the victory."[32] This communication was, needless to say, pleasant news to Pym's party in the Commons.

Pym's proposal for an excise tax finally passed its third reading

[30] Devereux, *Lives and Letters*, 2: 367. J. H. Hexter claims that the "trial by battle" suggestion came from Stapleton.

[31] Hexter, *King Pym*, p. 104.

[32] Devereux, *Lives and Letters*, 2: 369.

in both Houses on 2 July. That same day the following resolution was approved: "That his Excellency my Lord General be desired to dispose of, or move with his Army or any Part thereof, in such Manner as he shall think most fitting for the Safety and Defence of the Kingdom, and every Part thereof."[33] Essex was still master of the field. He still enjoyed the confidence of Parliament. In retrospect, it would seem that his peace gesture was a political tactic to secure money and material. And secure them he did, for on 13 July, Essex received a vote of confidence in Parliament and had several of his military requests approved. Both Houses agreed to send him twenty thousand pounds to pay his troops and five hundred horses to fill his empty ranks. In addition the Lower House ordered Vane to observe the army and report on His Excellency's handling of affairs.

The situation in other parts of England turned from bad to worse.[34] In mid-July when the Queen came down from the North with several thousand soldiers the Royalists under the command of the Earl of Newcastle had already gained control of all Yorkshire but Hull and its immediate environs, and had started to advance up the Vale of Trent into Lincolnshire. Except for a few pockets of resistance the northern counties were in Royalist hands. News from the West was equally sobering for Parliament. On 5 July, Waller suffered a humiliating defeat at the hands of Lord Hopton at Lansdown in Wiltshire, and on 13 July was soundly beaten by Lord Wilmot at Roundway Down. Sir William, who was fortunate to escape with his life, hastened to London to recruit more soldiers. "This caused dimunition of the former Fame of Waller," Bulstrode Whitelocke noted, "which raised up near a competition or emulation with Essex himself, and caused some slackning of mutual Succours and Assistance, to the prejudice of their common cause."[35]

These reverses were topped by the capitulation of Bristol.[36] After the forces of King and Queen joined with those of Rupert in mid-July, the Royalists initiated a well-conceived plan to expel Parliament's forces from the Severn Basin. The King and the

[33] *Lords Journal*, 6: 145.

[34] Gardiner, *Civil War*, 1: 166 ff.

[35] Whitelocke, *Memorials* (1682 ed.), p. 67.

[36] There is a good account of the fall of Bristol in C. V. Wedgwood, *The King's War* (London: Collins, 1958), pp. 232–35. Also see Warburton, *Rupert*, 1: 236–41; and Luke, *Journal*, 2: 126.

Queen remained in Oxford with a guard to hold off Essex, while Prince Rupert and the Marquess of Hertford converged upon Bristol with their armies. Several weeks earlier Essex had called upon Parliament to provide Governor Fiennes with more men and provisions to forestall a Royalist drive. In mid-July his intelligence reports indicated that the Royalists would strike at either Gloucester or Bristol—perhaps both—before advancing upon London. Subsequent information all pointed to the same conclusion: Bristol would be attacked by a large Royalist force—an army much larger than either Fiennes or Essex could put on the field—and Gloucester would be next.

The siege of Bristol commenced on 23 July, a Sunday, when Rupert joined Hertford and Maurice two miles outside the city. After some deliberation Rupert took a position north of the town, while Hertford assumed a position to the south. Rupert summoned the enemy to capitulate, but he was turned down by Fiennes, who hoped that his defenses would hold until relief arrived. In the early morning hours of 26 July the Royalists began to storm the nearly impregnable defenses of the port. They were met with such deadly counterfire that some Royalist officers wanted to withdraw to prevent unnecessary bloodshed. Rupert refused to draw back and the Royalists fought their way to the ancient castle where Fiennes had his headquarters. Toward the end of the day Governor Fiennes, realizing that he could not hold out much longer because of dwindling supplies of ammunition and the lack of reinforcements, sent out a truce trumpet and called for a parley. That night he signed the surrender terms. The following morning Fiennes and his troops gave up the city to their adversaries. It was a humiliating hour for the Parliamentarians. The second-largest urban center in England, and one of the nation's largest outports, Bristol had fallen into Royalist hands. The Severn Basin was now open to the Royalists. Governor Fiennes returned to London deeply humiliated. He was subsequently subjected to bitter attacks in Parliament and eventually court-martialed.

The lord general remained powerless in the midst of these adversities. Twice he had warned Parliament of Bristol's strategic significance. He had recommended that Governor Fiennes be provided with more ammunition and provisions. He had sent Waller into the area to check the Royalists. From his position near Aylesbury, where he was still stationed, he could not forestall the collapse of

Bristol without risking the security of London. His army was too decimated to be divided. His soldiers, still lacking pay and clothes, were incapable of either relieving Bristol or engaging the King's force near Oxford. Parliament's cause reached its nadir during the last days of July.

IV

Essex's political enemies reaped full advantage of these defeats and reverses. They used the lord general as a convenient scapegoat for Parliament's troubles. They had criticized him before for being slow and overcautious. They had opposed his proposals for peace. Throughout July the lord general was lampooned in the press and censured from the pulpit. The Lord Mayor's chaplain preached against him. Several newspapers and pamphlets castigated him for a do-nothing military policy and appeasement proclivities. He was caricatured "sitting in an easy chair, a glass of wine in one hand, a pipe in the other, an English Nero bibbing while London burned, or at least might burn any minute."[37] Very proud and sensitive, His Excellency stomached the abuse with a stoic forbearance and did not lash back in the same manner.

The motives of Essex's detractors were quite simple: his enemies hoped to oust him as Parliament's generalissimo and replace him with a commoner more to their liking. The war party in the Commons wanted a more militant battlefield stalwart who would inspire Englishmen to greater enthusiasm. Some of them resented Essex's aristocratic background and bearing. Most of them preferred a general from their own class—a Waller, a Skippon, or a Cromwell—to His Excellency. Even before Essex had expressed his peace proposals, some disgruntled Londoners had devised a plan to raise an army of 10,000 "godly" volunteers. Later in the month they renewed their efforts with increased vigor. Some dissatisfied Londoners petitioned Parliament for an ordinance which would place all the soldiers recruited in London and its liberties under the sole command of the Committee for the Militia of the City, which was directed by both Houses of Parliament.[38] Two days later a second petition, submitted by another group of citizens,

---

[37] Quoted in Hexter, *King Pym*, p. 119.
[38] Pearl, *London and the Puritan Revolution*, p. 271.

proposed a levy en masse. Both of these measures struck deeply at the reputation and authority of the lord general.

At this critical juncture Waller returned to London from the West.[39] On 27 July, despite his recent drubbing at Roundway Down, he was given a hero's welcome. At a meeting initiated by Marten he was voted commander in chief of the London militia. Sir William accepted the honor, of course, and his advocates waxed eloquent about the glorious future of the cause. His devotees then attempted to win their way in Parliament, purveying rumors about the lord general, predicting the fall of Bristol and the collapse of Gloucester, and, in short, blaming Essex for the defeats and reverses which had befallen the parliamentary cause.

Sir William Waller became the man of the hour. He had proven himself an able commander earlier in the conflict. He had professional skill. He was, in the eyes of D'Ewes, "a man of extraordinary valour and integrity."[40] He had demonstrated his competence many times against the Royalists, especially in the West, and he was beyond doubt an excellent tactician. He had struck fear into the hearts of the enemy soldiers. Waller himself was party to the removal of Essex; in fact, he used every opportunity to disparage his commander. He lent his name to the anti-Essex factions in the City and the Commons, permitted his supporters to put him forward against Essex, and even had the audacity to blame Essex for his recent defeat at Roundway Down.

Throughout the struggle, however, the majorities in both Houses continued to follow the leadership of Pym rather than radicals like Marten and Rigby. They passed Pym's excise measure. They passed an ordinance for raising 7,000 foot and 1,100 horse from London and the nearby counties; ignoring the radicals, they followed Pym's recommendations and appointed the Earl of Manchester to command it. On Saturday, 29 July, in an effort to head off the moves of the radicals, Pym went along with the bill naming Waller a unit commander. However, to preserve the unity of command and prevent an independent army from being formed under radical control, Waller was to receive his commission from Lord General Essex. This compromise—and a compromise it was—evoked criticism and caused consternation in several political circles. It did not pacify the radicals, who wanted a separate army and a

39 Whitelocke, *Memorials* (1682 ed.), p. 67.
40 Devereux, *Lives and Letters*, 2: 374.

different commander, nor did it quiet Waller, who disliked serving under Essex; but it did enable Pym and Essex to weather the political storm brewing in London.

Lord General Essex, then ill with a case of consumption, was furious with Waller and London. "It is reported that Lord Essex is much incensed with the City," wrote a contemporary pamphleteer, "for Saturday's business, for making Sir William Waller a general, and for their neglect and slight of him. He sent Sir Philip Stapleton the last night to the houses with a letter, shewing how much he is undervalued and abused, together with some propositions to them, and some resolutions of his own. Some of the lords are also discontented: if not prevented, they are likely to be of the Earl of Essex's opinion, and be ready to side with him in that course which he intends ere long. God direct him and them!" [41]

In his formal report, which was read before Parliament on the last day of July, the lord general did not mention peace or negotiation. He presented a straightforward analysis of the army's condition and its needs:

1. The Number of Foot Three Thousand marching Men, at least Three Thousand sick, occasioned by the Want of Pay, ill Cloathing, and all other Miseries which attend an unpaid, sickly Army.

2. The Number of the Horse Two Thousand Five Hundred (Three Thousand last Muster) occasioned by Loss of Horses upon hard Duty and Service, Recruite of Horse though often desire not performed; besides, by reason of a new Army, the present Regiments much lessened, listing themselves elsewhere for the new Army, expecting better Pay and Cloathing, and, upon their going hence, are entertained and protected; and great Discouragements and Scandals put upon his Excellency, the Officers, and Army, either through false Suggestions of some amongst us, or the Misunderstanding of others, poisoning the Affections of the People, which hinder Recruits and Contributions. [42]

Here indeed was a sorry picture of the "good old cause."

The remedies which Essex recommended in the same communication were sixfold:

1. A speedy Pay of the Arrears, and a constant Pay settled for the future, which will draw on Recruits, and give way to more strict Discipline: and that Cloaths may be provided, according to a Thousand for every Regiment, to which Purpose an Ordinance for a Press be immediately passed.

[41] Quoted in Warburton, *Rupert*, 2: 265.
[42] *Lords Journal*, 6: 160.

2. That Eight Hundred Horses be sent, and Two Hundred Monthly provided for Recruits.

3. That the Forces be raised may not be put into a new Army, until the old Regiments be recruited; no Officer or Soldier to be entertained into any other Employment, and that severe Punishment be executed upon such, and those that entertain them.

4. That such as shall be found guilty of any Scandals laid upon his Excellency, any of his Officers, or Army, may be severely punished whereby the like Offences may be no more committed; and a Declaration of both Houses passed, for the Vindication of his Excellency and them.

5. That, full Power having been given to his Excellency, by an Ordinance of Both Houses, for the granting of all Commissions, for the raising or commanding of any Forces, Towns, or Garrisons, it is conceived most requisite for the better Ordering of the Army, that no Commission be granted whatsoever, but from his Excellency; the Want of which breeds Disobedience to his Excellency's Commands, to the Prejudice of the Kingdom.

6. That the Loss of the West if rumoured to be occasioned by his Excellency; desired, it may be thoroughly examined what the Loss was, and the Occasions of it.

The lord general was demanding a showdown with his detractors and Parliament over the conduct of the war. His recommendations were reasonable: he wished to preserve a uniform strategy and a unity of command.

The Lords debated these points one at a time that very day. In each instance they stood squarely behind Essex. The vacancies in the army should be replaced by recruits immediately, and if necessary, Parliament should pass an impressment ordinance. To vindicate the lord general from false aspersions circulating about England, the recent defeat should be investigated. There should be only one commander, namely, Essex, and all subordinates should receive their commands from him. The troops should be paid their arrears with funds raised by the Commons. That the lord general still had the confidence of the Upper House is crystal clear.

In the Lower House, though the going was slower, Pym managed to gain support for several of Essex's recommendations. The day the report was read Pym pushed through the Commons a resolution enabling Essex to recruit 4,000 volunteers to replenish his army. On 1 August he induced the Lower House to order the Committee of Safety to arrange for the payment of arrears and the provision of clothing.[43] The Lower House concurred that Essex and his

43 *Commons Journal*, 3: 190.

officers who had been disparaged by rumors and aspersions should be vindicated by a public declaration. By 2 August all Essex's demands save one—the one calling for an inquiry into the defeat at Roundway Down—were granted by the Lower House.

Meanwhile, the peace faction in the Upper House, taking advantage of Essex's displeasure and the confused political situation, reintroduced the issue of cessation.[44] On 2 August the Upper House, at the Earl of Holland's suggestion, authorized a small committee to prepare some preliminary propositions to offer to the King. Two days later their proposals were approved by the whole House. But, instead of forwarding them to the Lower House for concurrence, as was customary, the Lords sent Holland to solicit Essex's support. However, Essex could not accept Holland's proposals, for they smacked of capitulation rather than compromise. They gave the King his revenues, the navy, the magazines and the forts, and the Tower of London, all with no enforceable guarantees. Both armies were to be disbanded. Parliament was to have its privileges, but all expelled members were to be readmitted, thus giving the Royalists a majority in the Upper House. If Essex had accepted these terms, Clarendon surmised, "before an independent army was raised, which was shortly after done, it could not probably have failed of the success desired. But the earl was too scrupulous and too punctual to that which he called a trust; and this was too barefaced a separation for him to engage in."[45]

John Pym then persuaded Essex not only to repudiate the proposals but to grant Waller a limited commission. The details of what transpired at the Aylesbury meeting between the two political allies are not known, but it would appear that Pym convinced the lord general of the wisdom of his position, which preserved the unity of command and at the same time pacified some of the members of the war party who clamored for Waller's appointment. Thus did Essex on 6 August issue Waller a limited commission to lead London's militia.[46]

In late July the lord general decided to quit Aylesbury. His

[44] *Lords Journal*, 6: 163–80.

[45] Clarendon, *History* (1849 ed.), 3: 159.

[46] *Lords Journal*, 6: 172. On 7 August the clerk recorded that the lord general "hath sent a Commission for Sir Wm. Waller to be Commander of all the Forces of the City of London; offering to their Lordships' consideration; that Serjeant Major Skippon is, by an Act of Common Council, made Commander of the Forces of London."

army was greatly diminished. "Unless present order be taken for the supplying the army with money," he wrote William Lenthall, speaker of the Lower House, "their necessities are so great, it will be impossible for me to keep them together. For besides their former arrears, they are now three weeks without pay; many sick men recover, but finding no money they have small comfort. I am now marching to a fresh quarter, where, if they may have pay, recruits, and clothing, most of them being almost naked, and our soldiers not drawn away with new levies, I doubt not but in a short time to have a considerable army." [47] Small wonder that Essex was withdrawing toward London!

The majority in the Lower House now resorted to experimentation. To tighten the management of the conflict, the Commons called into being a Council of War to supplant the slow and disputatious Committee of Safety (which had been discredited by Northumberland's peace offensive anyway) and to breathe new life into the war effort.[48] The Commons also passed a series of ordinances which increased monies and provided more man power for the armies on the field. Consequently, a money bill for the maintenance of Essex's army passed both Houses on 3 August. A week later Parliament agreed to support a new army 10,000 strong; this figure included the 4,000 troops which had been designated for the lord general earlier in the month. The funds were to come from the recent assessment. To facilitate the recruitment of a new army, Parliament empowered the county committees to impress soldiers.

Parliament also passed legislation which reunited the counties of the Eastern Association. In effect, Lord Grey of Warke, who had been recalcitrant of late, was superseded by the Earl of Manchester, and new instructions were issued to the local leaders. Several members of the Westminster Assembly of Divines who hailed from those counties were ordered to return to their respective parishes and "stir up the People in those Counties to rise for their defence." [49] To preserve the unity of command and strategy—a constant ingredient in Pym's formula for victory—Parliament insisted that Manchester be named sergeant-major general and that he receive

[47] Devereux, *Lives and Letters*, 2: 370.
[48] For these measures see Wedgwood, *The King's War*, pp. 236–39.
[49] *Lords Journal*, 6: 174.

his commission from Essex. On 12 August, Essex signed the formal document and forwarded it to his colleague. On that same day Parliament passed an ordinance calling for the levy of 1,000 dragoons from the county of Essex, known for its excellent horse and man-power reserves, and the following week they called for a speedy press of 2,000 gunners, trumpeters, and surgeons to be raised in the counties of the Eastern Association.

During the course of these preparations, while the army regrouped near Uxbridge, the lord general was visited by a special parliamentary delegation. The representatives were authorized to explain the reforms and their implications to Essex and his staff, to iron out difficulties relative to Waller and the command controversy, and to secure Essex's complete backing for the forthcoming push against the King. In the words of Clarendon: "They sent a formal committee of both Houses to him, to use all imaginable art, and application to him, to recover him to his former vigour and zeal in their cause. They told him the high value the houses had of the service he had done, and the hazards, dangers, and losses he had for their sakes undergone: that he would receive as ample a vindication for the calumnies and aspersions raised on him as he could desire, from the full testimony and confidence of the two houses; and if the infamous authors of them could be found, their punishment should be as notorious as their libels."[50]

Parliament also made good its promise regarding a declaration vindicating the lord general from the false accusations bruited about London. On 17 August, *A Remonstrance to Vindicate His Excellencie Robert Earle of Essex from Some False Aspersions* came off the printing presses in London.[51] "The faithful nobleman," the *Remonstrance* began, "had been falsely maligned in public speeches and printed words" although he was "as true a Patriot to all interests of England." He had served his sovereign well in the Palatinate, Spain, Holland, and Scotland—so well that Parliament had given him a broad commission not unlike that of a "Roman dictator"—and he had served Parliament just as faithfully. His army, to be sure, had faltered of late because of adversities beyond his control. And, to make matters worse, some of his subordinates (meaning Waller) had been insubordinate. Yet, despite these

[50] Clarendon, *History* (1849 ed.), 3: 146.
[51] British Museum, Thomason Collection.

discouragements, Essex remained as devoted to Parliament and the Kingdom as ever.

Parliament offered the vindicated commander more support in the days which followed. It authorized him to impress 2,000 men in London and provided him with funds for that purpose.[52] On 18 August it ordered all Essex's soldiers—the deserters, the absent without leave, and the new volunteers—to repair to their colors for new clothes and supplies. All violators would be punished according to the *Lawes and Ordinances*. On the following day, after a joint conference, Parliament instructed a special committee to visit the lord general and discuss with him problems relating to security, recruitment, payment of arrears, provisions, musters, and interarmy co-operation.

Thus did Essex survive the worst political storm of his career. He secured a reinforced and refurbished army. He retained his support in Parliament. He kept his command. He outflanked Waller and the radicals of the City. Without the leadership of Pym and the support of the middle group in the Commons he might well have been shoved aside or compelled to resign. Without the lord general, on the other hand, Pym might have been forced to give in to those on his Left. Together Essex and Pym labored to put a better army on the field.

The Oxford campaign, meanwhile, turned into a stalemate. Essex secured the town of Reading for Parliament and he checked the Royalists from advancing upon London. But his offensive actions in the Thames River valley came to nought. He failed to take Abingdon and Wallingford. He did not assault and secure Oxford, as he originally intended, nor did he engage his adversary in a pitched battle. He could not even hold his original positions in the Thames valley against Royalist incursions and was ultimately forced to draw back into a defensive position near Uxbridge.

Whether his renovated army could turn the tide remained to be seen.

[52] *Lords Journal*, 6: 190.

CHAPTER 15

The Gloucester Campaign (1643): Victory

I

THE RENDEZVOUS which the lord general set for 22 August at Hounslow Heath took place as scheduled.[1] There, at noon, an army of 10,000 soldiers assembled for an inspection by Parliament's liaison committee. It marked the first time that such a conglomeration of Englishmen had gathered together for war: there were upwards of 5,000 experienced volunteers, many sick and some wounded, who had fought for Essex during the previous year; about 2,000 willing, but inexperienced, volunteers, who had only recently enlisted in the army; and approximately 2,000 conscripts, unwilling and inexperienced Londoners, who had been impressed. Added to this motley mass of man power were the trained bands— the blue and the red regiments of Skippon—who had never fought outside Middlesex. Essex thanked them for responding to the call to arms, issued marching orders, and proceeded along the road to Oxford. His objective was the besieged city of Gloucester.

It took Essex a week to progress through Buckinghamshire. To keep his army intact, he marched en masse, moving slowly in a zigzag pattern to confuse the Royalists, who watched him very closely. Leaving Uxbridge, he dipped southward to Colebrooke and then westward to Maidenhead, as if to take the southern road which bypassed Oxford on the south; instead, he recrosssed the Thames and followed the northern route toward Oxford, moving through Beaconsfield; Bearton, where he obtained clothes for his soldiers; and Aylesbury, where he was joined by Lord Grey. On 29 August, after resting one day at Aylesbury, Essex progressed into the western part of Buckinghamshire.

The following day, after proceeding to Brackley Heath, the lord general was joined by newly levied troops from Bedfordshire and

1 See Codrington, *Life and Death*, pp. 22–24 for these events.

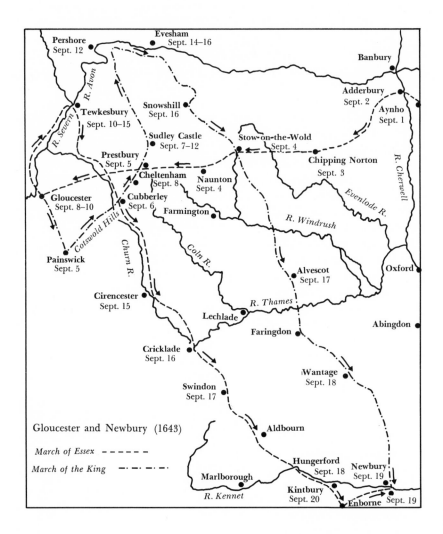

Pershore
Sept. 12

Evesham
Sept. 14–16

Banbury

R. Avon

Adderbury
Sept. 2

Aynho
Sept. 1

Snowshill
Sept. 16

Tewkesbury
Sept. 10–15

R. Severn

Sudley Castle
Sept. 7–12

Stow-on-the-Wold
Sept. 4

Chipping Norton
Sept. 3

Prestbury
Sept. 5

R. Cherwell

Cheltenham
Sept. 8

Naunton
Sept. 4

Evenlode R.

Gloucester
Sept. 8–10

Cubberley
Sept. 6

Farmington

R. Windrush

Cotswold Hills

Churn R.

Coln R.

Painswick
Sept. 5

Alvescot
Sept. 17

Oxford

Cirencester
Sept. 15

R. Thames

Lechlade

Abingdon

Faringdon

Cricklade
Sept. 16

Wantage
Sept. 18

Swindon
Sept. 17

Gloucester and Newbury (1643)

March of Essex – – – – –

March of the King —·—·—·—·

Aldbourn

Marlborough

Hungerford
Sept. 18

Newbury
Sept. 19

Kintbury
Sept. 20

Enborne Sept. 19

R. Kennet

Leicestershire. By now his renovated army had burgeoned to more than 20,000 soldiers, many of whom were still so poorly armed and provisioned that Essex again importuned Barrington and the people of Essex. "Gentlemen," he began, "When the army quartered at Tame I desired some officers there to send to Lieutenant Colonel Fennicke three hundred pounds for the use of Sir Thomas Barrington's regiment upon the promise of repayment thereof suddenly; but it being not done, the money is expected from me, therefore I desire you will be pleased to send the same to me forthwith that they may be satisfied." [2] The logistical problems attending an army of such proportions were prodigious.

Throughout these hectic August days the Royalists dominated the military scene. Robert Dormer, the Earl of Carnavon gained control of Dorset, except for Lyme and Poole, while Prince Maurice's forces secured Devonshire, except for Exeter and Plymouth. The Royalist army under Rupert, pausing briefly to deliberate after the taking of Bristol, pressed on to Gloucester.[3] In the first week of August, Sir Samuel Luke knew of Prince Rupert's plans to storm Gloucester with 10,000 troops and then proceed to London. Rupert was soon joined by his uncle Charles, who personally directed the preliminaries of the siege, and the two men then summoned the city to surrender and offered a pardon to all who would give up their arms. The summons was turned down by Governor Edward Massey. Thomas Pudsey, a native of Staffordshire who later served Essex, actually delivered the refusal message to Charles.

Governor Massey's work was now cut out for him. His troops numbered fewer than 1,500 and his provisions were scanty. Furthermore, he did not have the backing of the local officials or citizens. In a letter addressed to Lenthall he bemoaned the fact that the Royalists outnumbered the Roundheads ten to one. He had every reason to negotiate or capitulate. Only after the Puritan minority gained control of the Gloucester government did he begin to prepare his defenses and appeal for succor. Massey's means of defense were limited; his artillery pieces were small and he possessed fewer than fifty barrels of gunpowder.

[2] British Museum, Egerton MSS, 2646.

[3] For the siege of Gloucester see Warburton, *Rupert*, 2: 279–95; Rushworth, *Historical Colllections*, 5: 287 ff.; and Sanderson, *A Compleat History*, pp. 630–35. *Bibliotheca Gloucestrensis* (Gloucester, 1825), contains reprints of many contemporary pamphlets dealing with the siege.

The Royalists seemed to have a distinct edge over Governor Massey. Rupert had over 6,000 soldiers—enough to keep the city encircled—and superior artillery power. As the siege progressed the King drew troops from Wallingford, Abingdon, and even Aylesbury, and brought supplies from Bristol and Oxford. He ordered all spare horses in Oxford to be sent to the besiegers at Gloucester. Yet, despite the advantages of superior man power and material, the King's forces could not force Massey to surrender. The siege endured into September, with no conclusive results. "The siege of Gloucester occupies the attention of all," observed the Venetian envoy early that month, "although success would not indemnify the king for his last opportunities, yet it will give his army considerable advantage." [4] Not even a large contingent of reinforcements from Exeter, which swelled the Royalist army to 12,000 men, was sufficient to break through.

Essex, meanwhile, pressed forward to end the siege before Massey's supplies ran out. The lord general did not encounter any Royalists until he reached Oxfordshire, and then Lord Wilmot offered only token resistance. In early September, Essex marched slowly through the Cotswolds via Chipping Norton to Stow-on-the Wold. On 5 September he advanced to the Presbury Hills and drew up his entire army to view Gloucester and the rear guard of the retreating army of the King. The following day Essex entered the city of Gloucester. He received a savior's welcome, for he had succeeded in lifting the siege with a minimum amount of bloodshed. His superior force had compelled the Royalists to withdraw. Several days later, as was his custom, Essex informed Parliament about his recent success. "Upon Tuesday, in the evening," he wrote the speaker of the Lower House, "the King's forces seeing us approach, raised their siege from before Gloucester, whither it pleased God we came very seasonably, for the Governor had not above two or three barrels of powder left; yet he managed his business with so much judgment and courage, that the enemy not knowing of such want, had but small hope of obtaining their desires." [5] The lord general then requested of Parliament funds to pay the liberated soldiers who had fought under Massey, 1,000 more soldiers for his own army, and the troops of Sir William Waller.

When the details of the Gloucester siege and its timely relief were

[4] *C. S. P. Ven., 1643–1647*, p. 58.
[5] Devereux, *Lives and Letters*, 2: 379–80.

publicized in London, the lord general and Massey were widely acclaimed.[6] Both were featured as heroes in several newsbook accounts of the event and won plaudits from the pulpit. Parliament commended Massey with a resolution and bestowed upon him a gift of one thousand pounds.[7] On returning to London some time after the passage of this resolution, Essex received a warm welcome and similar honors. An anonymously published poem hailed the lord general as a hero:

> For formidable Essex from afar
> Upon the mountains (like a blazing-star)
> Appears to the malignants, and portends
> Ruin and death; but his distressed friends
> With animating vigour he inspires,
> And warms at distance by auspicious fires;
> As when the sun with his ascent doth cleer
> The winter tempests, and recruit the year.[8]

In retrospect, Essex's relief of Gloucester marked the turning point in the Civil War. In the words of Thomas May, historian of the war: "Gloucester not only stopt the career of the King's Victories; but made a great change in the Conditions of the sides. The City was gallantly defended against a great and flourishing Army; wherein Massey, the Governour, justly gained a wonderful re-known; so long did he defend the City, until General Essex could be recruited with an Army great enough to raise the Siege, and march thither, from London, eighty miles."[9] The King's decision to besiege Gloucester, rather than engage Essex or march upon London, had consequences from which the Royalists never completely recovered. The prolonged siege gave the Parliamentary forces time to recuperate from several losses and enabled Parliament to finance and raise another army. Governor Massey's heroic stand against tremendous odds provided Parliamentarians everywhere with a rallying point. Essex's well-conceived and carefully executed relief served to counteract the demoralizing effects of a

[6] These events were publicized in several anonymously published accounts plus Ralph Rounthwaite's *A True Relation of the Late Expedition of His Excellency, Robert Earl of Essex, for the Relief of Gloucester* (London, 1643), which was approved by Parliament. For a discussion of these sources see *Bibliotheca Gloucestrensis.*

[7] Rushworth, *Historical Collections*, 5: 295.

[8] Published in 1643 and reprinted in Scott, *Somers' Tracts*, 5: 299.

[9] Thomas May, *The History of Parliament* (London, 1647), p. 61.

long series of defeats and reversed the trend of events in Parliament's favor.

II

ESSEX remained in the Severn Valley for ten days, resting his weary troops and helping Governor Massey strengthen his defenses at Gloucester. Also he planned his next move. He could not remain in Gloucester, where there was a severe shortage of food.[10] There was a danger, moreover, that the Royalist force under Prince Maurice, which had taken Exeter in early September, would join Rupert's soldiers to bottle up Essex's army a considerable distance from his base of supplies. The lord general, fully aware of these possibilities, remained near Gloucester for only two nights and then moved north to Tewkesbury, where he reprovisioned his army. Neither he nor the King, who had fallen back to Worcester, sought a general engagement.

In Westminster the members of Parliament sought ways to ensure the continued success of the Gloucester campaign.[11] On 6 September they passed an ordinance authorizing the Militia Committee of London to raise an army under Waller's command. Sir William was to receive his commission from Essex, according to the previously arranged compromise, and the army, once formed, was to join Essex as soon as possible. Together the combined forces would engage the Royalists. The recruitment of troops was, however, not simple. News that Sir William had been routed earlier in the month made the task difficult indeed for recruiters. Essex had replenished his ranks with many of those who might have signed up with Waller. The response was so poor that Parliament—again under pressure from the City—passed an ordinance permitting Waller to impress 5,000 men and enlist the apprentice watermen.

On 15 September, after a feint toward Worcester, the lord general struck out toward the road which led from Bath to London.[12] After marching in the dark he arrived at Royalist-held Cirencester at an early morning hour and took the town completely by surprise. Most of the soldiers in the vicinity were captured, and a large quantity of provisions bound for Oxford was seized. Codrington observed: "This good service was performed about two of the

---

[10] Davies, "Parliamentary Army," p. 41.

[11] *Lords Journal*, 5: 203–21.

[12] Rushworth, *Historical Collections*, 5: 293.

clock in the morning, the enemy, for the most part, being taken
prisoners in their beds, and their horses feeding in the stables: there
was also a magazine of victuals seized on, which was welcome booty
to our soldiers. There were taken, in all, four-hundred prisoners,
and as many soldiers." [13] After feeding his hungry troops, Essex
hastened toward Wiltshire. That night he was at Crickdale; by
17 September he reached Swindon. If all went well, he would
reach the Bristol Road the following day and return to the London
area without mishap before the Royalists could get there.

Charles had other plans for his antagonist. He was now determined to intercept Parliament's army and give Essex battle before
the lord general could return to his base of supplies. As soon as the
King learned of Essex's march southward from Tewkesbury he
put his army in pursuit. Sending Prince Rupert and his cavalry
ahead to harass and retard the enemy, Charles and Lord Forth
followed with the foot and artillery. Though slowed up by rain
and muddy roads, the Royalists pursued Essex at a good pace. By
17 September the King was within a day's reach of Essex, and
Rupert was within striking distance.

In the early morning hours of 18 September, as Parliament's
army marched through Aldborne Chase, Prince Rupert moved in
swiftly to cut off Essex's cavalry from the rest of the army. A time-
consuming and costly skirmish ensued. "Rupert's cavalry came in
large numbers," in Codrington's words, "and were so marshalled
to charge our enemy of foot, being then on their march in several
divisions; which caused our foot to unite themselves into one gross,
our horse perpetually skirmishing with them, to keep them off from
the foot. In the meantime, the dragoons on both sides gave fire
in full bodies on one another, on the side of the hill, that the woods
above, and the vallies below, did echo with the thunder of the
charge. There were about fourscore slain upon the place and more
than as many more were sorely wounded." [14]

The skirmish at Aldborne Chase slowed Essex's army down just
enough so that it reached Hungerford instead of Newbury late that
night. [15] The following day both armies converged on Newbury:

[13] Codrington, *Life and Death*, p. 23. Codrington appears to have been with
Essex on this campaign.

[14] *Ibid.*, p. 24. Also see *Mercurius Britannicus* (London), 1643, no. 5, p. 38.

[15] See Burne and Young, *Civil War*, pp. 99–100, for the battle of Newbury and
the preceding events. Walter Money's *First and Second Battles of Newbury* (London,
1884), pp. 1–59, is still the best single source.

the Royalists came from Wantage, where they had spent the night, while Parliament's army marched the nine miles from Hungerford. In the late afternoon Essex's advanced quartermaster unit moved into the town and began to make arrangements for billeting his soldiers. Before they completed their task, however, they were dispersed by Prince Rupert's cavalry, and before the main body of Essex's army arrived, the Royalists assumed control of the town. The King, having won the race to Newbury, lost no time in securing a superior position in preparation for a full battle. He planted his army between Essex and London along the road which lead from Hungerford to Reading. His troops held an elevated position overlooking the River Kennet to the north and the road to Reading. His cavalry had fresh reinforcements from Oxford and the western counties.

As the lord general approached Newbury from the west with his wet and wearied soldiers, he learned from his scouts that the advanced billeting contingent had been bested by Rupert, that the King had taken possession of the town and the surrounding heights, and that the Royalists had fresh troops. He rightly assumed that the King would not let him pass to London without doing battle. Since the hour was too late for an engagement that day, Essex halted his troops at Enborne, a village about two miles west of the King's camp, and prepared for the morrow. "All that night our army lay in the fields, impatient of the sloth of darkness, and wishing for the morning's light, to exercise their valour; and the rather, because the King had sent a challenge over night to the Lord General to give battle the next morning," wrote Codrington. "A great part of the enemy's army continued also in the field, incapable of sleep, their enemy being so nigh." [16]

Essex commenced the battle of Newbury with little tactical advantage. His army, reduced by the recent forced marches and by disease, was slightly smaller than that of the King. The lord general's artillery and horse were clearly inferior. His foot were tired and lacked food. His position was less desirable than that of his adversary. Charles may have had the tactical edge, but he lacked one essential ingredient for a prolonged pitched battle: a large supply of ammunition. His supplies were so dangerously low that even Prince Rupert—usually overanxious to fight—advised against an encounter until additional supplies could be brought from

[16] Codrington, *Life and Death*, pp. 24–25.

Oxford. Rupert did not carry the Council of War on this matter, however, so the Royalists went into the battle short of ammunition. It proved to be a fatal mistake.

Essex assumed the offensive early in the morning. He ordered the main body of his infantry to advance eastward along the slightly elevated ground, parallel to the road. Protected from the King's cavalry by hedgerows and enclosed gardens, they managed to advance and infiltrate the enemy's center before the Royalists realized what was happening. Once the King's musketeers began to run out of ammunition their fire slackened and they started to give up ground. The lord general, meanwhile, sent Hampden's well-seasoned regiment forward to secure Round Hill, a vantage point to the right, in hopes of using it to check any Royalist flanking maneuvers. This gambit did not bear immediate results, for Prince Rupert, perceiving Essex's intention, brought up his cavalry, outflanked Hampden's regiment, and fell upon the rear of Parliament's army.

Gradually the tide of battle turned. Essex secured Round Hill, from whence he launched an artillery barrage against the Royalists, and his foot then pressed to the crest of the hill and began to push their opponents back toward Newbury. As the day wore on, the Royalists relinquished more ground. By nightfall Essex's army had succeeded in gaining control of the elevated position originally held by the King's troops. They had outfought the Royalists. After dark the King's army left Newbury and retreated toward Oxford.

Essex claimed the victory at Newbury. He kept the field and forced the King to retreat. He sustained fewer losses than did his adversary. His army had outmaneuvered and outfought the enemy. Lord Robartes's initial cavalry charge contributed much to the success. Sir Philip Stapleton's five charges at the head of the life guard also made a great difference between defeat and victory. But the lord general himself deserved the highest honors, Codrington contended, "for, before the battle was begun, he did ride from one regiment to another, and did inflame them with courage, and perceiving in them all an eager desire to battle with their enemies, he collected to himself a sure presage of victory to come. I have heard that when in the heat and tempest of the fight, some friends did advise him to leave off his white hat, because it rendered an object too remarkable to the enemy No, replied the earl, it is not the hat but the heart, the hat is not capable of either fear or honour. He himself, being foremost in person, did lead up the city regiment, and when a vast body of the enemy's horse had given so violent a charge that they had broken quite through it, he quickly rallied his men together, and, with undaunted courage, did lead them up the hill." [17]

If judged by the numbers of killed and wounded in the Newbury action, Parliament's army unquestionably won the battle. Several dedicated and well-known Royalist figures lost their lives there. Lord Falkland, the King's high-minded secretary of state, was killed by a musket ball. With the King at his side, the Earl of Carnarvon, a hot-blooded supporter of the Crown, died that night in a nearby inn from a wound sustained in the battle. Other notables who met with death were the Earl of Sunderland; Col. Thomas Morgan; and Colonel Fielding. The wounded included the Earl of Carlisle; Lord Andover; Sir Charles Lucas; Col. Charles Gherrard; Sir John Russell; Sir Edward Sackville; and Henry Howard. On Parliament's side, the few men of quality who died included Col. Thomas Tucker, Lt. Col. Charles Essex, Capt. Thomas Hunt, and several lesser-known officers. Many members of the trained bands fell at Newbury. Whitelocke claimed that Parliament lost about 500 soldiers, whereas the Royalists lost about 2,000.

News of the engagement traveled far and fast. Rumors and exaggerated accounts appeared in Oxford and London. At Saint Clement Danes, Master Daniel Evans honored the dead at Newbury with a fast-day sermon and appealed to his parishioners for contributions to help the widows and the maimed. "O Beloved can you forget the Soulders," he importuned, "I say the Soulders, who have spent their bloud for Christ, as Christ did for them, even their own precious bloud in God's cause at Newbury. But what the Lord hath done for us at that place I shall now be silent of." [18] The editor of *Mercurius Aulicus*, the Royalist newsbook printed at Oxford, after first refusing to believe the information about Newbury, finally accepted the fact of Parliament's victory, and the other Royalist authors soon followed suit. [19] Several years later Royalist historian William Sanderson concluded in his biography of Charles I

[17] *Ibid.*, p. 26.
[18] Dugdale, *Short View*, p. 568.
[19] See pp. 535–45.

that the success of the battle "gave much grace to the General Essex and repute to the London Trained bands."[20]

On 22 September, Lord General Essex entered Reading and rested his army for several days. That same day he drafted a letter to the House of Commons giving a full account of his recent victory and listing his most pressing needs. The members of the Lower House, jubilant over the news, gave immediate attention to the matter. They set aside 26 September, a Sunday, as a day of thanksgiving to celebrate the "good Successes of the Lord General's army."[21] They also voted that a joint parliamentary committee be appointed to "acquaint his Excellency what Value and Esteem the Houses set upon the great Service done by the Blessing of GOD upon the Conduct of his Excellency and the Valour of the Army."[22] The committee was also instructed to assure Essex that soldiers, supplies, and money for arrears would be forthcoming.

His Excellency welcomed the joint committee and then returned with its members to London via Windsor. He again received a hero's welcome. Leaders of Parliament paid him their respects. In the Upper House, according to the *Lords Journal*, "it was moved, 'That the Lord General being now at his House in London, that this House may go with their Speaker, to give his Lordship Thanks for this House, for his great Service done to this Kingdom.'"[23] The Lower House passed a similar resolution. On 26 September, His Excellency held court at Essex House as a host of parliamentary leaders attended him. "The House of Commons with their Speaker went to Essex-house to congratulate the General his safe return to them," noted Bulstrode Whitelocke, "The Lord Mayor and Aldermen of London waited in their Scarlet Gowns upon the General, and highly complemented him, as the Protector and Defender of their lives and Fortunes, and of their Wives and Children."[24] Londoners had never before received a rebel general so warmly.

Two days later the trained bands and auxiliaries returned to the London area and marched triumphantly through the City's

[20] Sanderson, *A Compleat History*, p. 649.
[21] *Lords Journal*, 6: 230.
[22] *Ibid.*, p. 231.
[23] *Ibid.*, p. 232.
[24] Whitelocke, *Memorials* (1682 ed.), p. 70.

streets.[25] Each man wore a green bough in his hat in memory of the battle of Newbury. Essex met them at Finsbury Field and conducted a formal review before dismissing them. Later that day he staged a dramatic reappearance in the House of Lords. He presented to Parliament several Royalist cornets which he had captured at Cirencester and Newbury and gave a brief account of their seizure.

In the eyes of most members of Parliament, Lord General Essex had turned the tide. He had succeeded in reversing the trend of defeats into a series of battlefield victories. He had saved not only the cities of Gloucester and London but the whole cause. He also recovered his prestige and redeemed his reputation at Waller's expense. "General Essex has given permission for Waller to take any men of his army that he wishes for such enterprises as he may decide upon," the Venetian ambassador reported. "Meanwhile he moves in a halo of glory here, having recovered his reputation by the relief of Gloucester, and vindicated himself with the citizens of London, who had reviled him."[26] The Gloucester campaign was Essex's crowning military achievement, his finest demonstration on the field of battle. Clarendon realized this only too well when he composed his *History*. "Without doubt, the action was performed by him with incomparable conduct and courage," he wrote, "in every part whereof very much was to be imputed to his own personal virtue; and it may well be reckoned amongst the most soldierly actions of this unhappy war."[27]

III

THE HOUSE OF LORDS to which Essex returned was much diminished.[28] Earlier in the year Parliament had excluded those peers who were at war against it. During the late summer months, when several peers were in the field, attendance averaged about ten lords per meeting. The faithful few included: the speaker, Lord Grey of Warke; the Earls of Bolingbroke, Lincoln, Stamford, Denbigh, Salisbury, Northumberland, Rutland, Pembroke, and Nottingham; Viscount Saye; and Lords Dacres, Wharton, Hunsden, Howard, and Bruce. In November the Earl of Carnarvon and the

25 *Mercurius Britannicus*, no. 6, p. 46.
26 *C. S. P. Ven.*, *1643–1647*, p. 29.
27 Clarendon, *History* (1849 ed.), 3: 183.
28 See *Lords Journal*, 6: 224–83.

Earl of Kent, both of whom had recently succeeded to their late fathers' titles and estates, made their political debuts in the Upper House. In December the vacillating Earl of Holland returned to his place after having been ostracized by the Royalists in Oxford. The return of other neutral and wavering peers during the winter season also served to improve the attendance and to make for a more respectable assembly.

Nevertheless, the Upper House became more dependent upon the Commons as the war wore on. Its principal function was concurrence. It initiated certain measures relating to class and personal privilege and retained control of its judicial powers, but it conceded to the Commons in matters relating to the conduct of the war and domestic legislation. Several of Essex's actions reflect this political trend. He corresponded less with the speaker of the House of Lords and more with Lenthall. In his quest for funds Essex was forced to appeal to the Commons rather than the Lords. In his conflict with Waller and the City he became more dependent upon Pym and the moderates in the Commons. The lord general's increased reliance upon the Lower House to win the war signified the progressive impotence of the Lords.

Shortly after returning to London, the lord general became involved in another political squabble with Sir William Waller, who harbored a deep antipathy against Essex and Pym. Waller still blamed the lord general for his defeat at Roundway Down. He detested Pym for backing Essex in the earlier struggle over the command and the issuance of a commission. More recent developments had piqued Waller increasingly and made him thirsty for revenge. He had been slurred by Essex in Parliament. He had been completely overshadowed by Essex in the recent Gloucester campaign. During that campaign, he had refused to assist Essex at Newbury—as Parliament had ordered—and had remained immobile at Windsor. This refusal infuriated Pym and precipitated a showdown over the army command.

The showdown between Essex and Waller came during the first week of October. Waller charged that his unpaid army, which never reached full strength, was deserting him for lack of wages and that many of his troops were enlisting in Essex's victorious army, which had recently received its arrears. Essex countered with a suggestion that Waller's semi-independent army be disbanded as soon as possible. A majority in the Upper House, however, resolved to keep Waller's army intact but place it under Essex. "Hereupon this House thought fit," the resolution was worded, "that, according to the former Resolution of both Houses, that the Forces under Sir Wm. Waller be put under the Command of the Lord General, and all Commissions to be given by him." [29]

Waller and his faction were furious. The Lower House, fearful of alienating those in the City who backed Sir William, balked at the Lords' resolution. The lord general, however, would not settle for anything less than Waller's resignation and the dismantling of his newly recruited army. On 7 October, Essex gave Parliament the alternative of supporting him and the principle of a unified command or Waller and a divided command. "The Lord General desired of this House, and the House of Commons," as the clerk of Parliament recorded it, "Leave to deliver up his Commission, and to go beyond the Seas, in regard of the Commission to Sir Wm. Waller, which is inconsistent with his, and in regard of the many Discouragements he hath received in being General." [30] Through this thinly veiled threat, now backed by battlefield victories and increased popularity in London, Essex attained his political objective. His peers reversed themselves and demanded that Waller deliver his commission, thus confirming the unity of command principle.

The Lords' action brought immediate results in the Lower Chamber. The majority in the Commons would not hear of Essex's resignation. When faced with the threatening alternative, they came to Essex's side in such numbers that Waller, who was in the Lower House at the time, offered to surrender the controversial commission. Later in the day, after a joint delegation from both Houses discussed the whole matter with the lord general, they passed a resolution designed to end the wrangling. "Sir Wm. Waller is under the Command of the Lord General," they resolved, "and ought to receive his Instructions from my Lord General and is bound to obey him, notwithstanding any Thing contained in his Commission." [31] Two days later, on 9 October, Sir William formally yielded his earlier commission to Parliament. The accommodation, in fact, turned out to be a compromise, for Essex agreed to grant Waller a new commission to command the trained bands.

[29] *Ibid.*, p. 242.
[30] *Ibid.*, p. 246.
[31] *Ibid.*, p. 247.

Meanwhile, the lord general prepared to take the Oath of the Covenant.[32] In July the Covenanters had sent a delegation to Westminster to broach the subject of an offensive alliance to Pym and the moderates. In August, when the cause of Parliament reached its nadir, Parliament responded by sending a delegation, headed by Sir Henry Vane, to negotiate a military alliance. The Covenanters, fearful of a Royalist uprising and distrustful of the King's moves in Ireland, were very congenial to the idea, but they wanted more than the conventional military pact. The two nations, they insisted, should combine in a formal religious association—a covenant—and swear common allegiance to God. The Covenanters won their way, after ten days of intense bargaining, and the terms of the Solemn League and Covenant were agreed upon within a fortnight. Each nation would support the other in both offensive and defensive military operations against their common enemy—the King. The English were to render monetary assistance to the Covenanters, who were to send an army south across the Border to defeat the Royalists in the northern counties. The leaders of both nations, moreover, were to take the Oath of the Covenant.

On 25 September the treaty commissioners from Scotland, many commoners, and a handful of peers signed the Solemn League and Covenant at Margaret's Westminster, thus sealing the pact between the rebels of both nations. On 15 October those absentee peers who had not signed the original pact went to Westminster Abbey and heard a sermon preached by Dr. Thomas Temple, a member of the Westminster Assembly of Divines, based on Nehemiah 10:29: "They clave to their brethren, their nobles, and entered into a curse, and into an oath, to walk in God's law which was given by Moses the servant of God, and to observe and do all the commandments of the Lord our Lord, and his judgment and his statutes." After the sermon the Earls of Essex, Warwick, Pembroke, Salisbury, Suffolk, Denbigh, Bolingbroke, and Stamford subscribed to the Covenant.[33]

Shortly after the battle at Newbury the King recaptured Reading, which he had lost to Parliament earlier in the year, and garrisoned Abingdon, Wallingford, and several other towns between Oxford and Parliament's forces. The presence of many Royalist soldiers in these garrisons gave rise to rumors that the King intended a

[32] See Wedgwood, *The King's War*, pp. 239–41.
[33] *Mercurius Civicus* (London) 1643, no. 21.

general muster of all his troops in preparation for a march upon London. The King also sent contingents into Buckinghamshire and Bedfordshire to protect the northern and eastern approaches to Oxford. Sir Lewis Dives and Prince Rupert took and fortified Newport Pagnell and Bedford, respectively.

Parliament's army, meanwhile, sought to counter these Royalist operations.[34] It was Parliament's hope to regain control of Reading before winter set in. So that this might be accomplished the lord general stationed a fairly large garrison of troops under Waller's command at Windsor. A few days later, in mid-October, Essex himself prepared to move to Windsor and lead the attack. He ordered all his soldiers in the London area to repair to their colors and arrange to march toward Reading. He wrote Sir Thomas Barrington to ready his troops for the assault. He also insisted, as before, that Parliament appoint a joint committee to advise him about matters of supply and strategy.

Before leaving London for the field, however, Essex was plagued with several urgent administrative decisions. Under constant pressure to investigate the case of Nathaniel Fiennes, Lord Saye's son, who had been accused of cowardice for his surrender of Bristol,[35] Essex summoned a Council of War to consider the matter. On 18 October, one day before Essex's departure for Windsor, the Upper House received from Lord Willoughby of Parham, the lord lieutenant of Lincolnshire and a staunch supporter of Parliament, a request that he be granted a higher rank.[36] By a recent ordinance of Parliament, Willoughby complained, his county had been added to the Eastern Association and his authority had been eclipsed by the Earl of Manchester. Through a subordinate, Sir Anthony Erby, he petitioned the House of Commons for a higher rank, commensurate with his social position. The Lower House recommended that the lord general appoint the disgruntled peer to "some Honourable Command under him." The Lords concurred that same day.

The lord general was compelled to drop these matters and return to the field. News of a Royalist rendezvous at Banbury, of Rupert's march into Bedford, and of Dives's seizure of Newport Pagnell induced the Parliamentary leaders to modify their plans. On

34 Luke, *Journal*, 2: 163; and Rushworth, *Historical Collections*, 5: 281–83.
35 *Lords Journal*, 6: 260.
36 *Ibid.*, p. 261.

18 October they reversed their previous order about the recovery of Reading and authorized the lord general to march the trained bands to wherever he saw fit.[37] Essex abandoned his plan to assault that town and decided to repulse the Royalists from Bedfordshire. That same day he directed Barrington to send reinforcements into Hertfordshire as soon as possible. He left London the following day and marched his army to Windsor and then northward into Hertfordshire. His first act was to establish Saint Albans as his headquarters.[38] Like Windsor, it was of strategic importance: it guarded the Watling Street entrance to London. Essex immediately took measures to fortify the place.[39]

To contain the advance of the enemy, Essex also called forth the trained bands of Hertfordshire. The response was heart-warming, for between 3,000 and 4,000 men answered the call to arms and mustered at Hitchin, from which they marched westward to repulse the enemy. The combined forces soon recaptured Bedford from Prince Rupert, drove Dives from Newport Pagnell, and caused the Royalists to retreat toward Oxford.[40] Essex then garrisoned the town of Newport Pagnell and stationed a sizable contingent there under the command of Philip Skippon.[41]

On 30 October, Essex sent two communications to the speaker of the House of Lords. The first dealt with Lord Willoughby's difficulties in Lincolnshire. It appears that he had been ordered by Parliament to march his troops into Hertfordshire to assist Essex, had refused to obey the orders, and had sent Essex an explanation of his insubordination. His troops were forty weeks in arrears, he complained, while Cromwell's soldiers were well paid. If Parliament would permit him, he would pay the troops out of the estates taken from delinquents; if not, Parliament should find other means. Without money he would not march. The lord general's second communication contained an account of his own army and its needs. "Without a present considerable supply of money to pay the army, it will quickly be consumed," he contended, ". . . And,

[37] *Ibid.*, p. 262; and *Mercurius Civicus*, 1643, no. 21.

[38] See Luke, *Journal*, 3: 188–93.

[39] Alfred Kingston, *Hertfordshire during the civil war and long parliament* (London, 1894), p. 38.

[40] H. G. Tibbutt, *The Life and Letters of Sir Lewis Dyve*, Bedfordshire Record Society (Luton, 1948), pp. 43–45.

[41] *H. M. C. Thirteenth Report*, Appendix 1, p. 144.

my Lord, soldiers that have done so good service will expect duly their pay if not reward."[42] This plea evoked immediate results: Parliament voted three thousand pounds for the lord general himself and twenty thousand pounds for his army, both to be paid out of excise taxes. The heads of Parliament and the City seemed satisfied with His Excellency's leadership.

The funds which Essex received from Parliament to pay his army did not, however, satisfy the needs of troops on the field. It took so long for the money to filter down to the rank-and-file soldiers that many deserted. The desertions in turn jeopardized Parliament's defenses. "If I had a competent strength," Skippon complained to Essex from Newport Pagnell, "I would have a bout with them, but as I am, and this place being yet so very open, it is not counselable, for the enemy hath 12 regiments of horse, 3,000 foot at least, six pieces, one a demi-culverin, and many commanded foot out of Oxford being come unto them, if our intelligence be true. I beseech your Excellency cause four scouts to stay here with me, for I have none but by chance, and be pleased to call upon the Committee of Hertfordshire, and let Sir Samuel Luke do the like to those in Bedfordshire that we may have money to pay our soldiers on Saturday next, or we shall be but in an ill condition with them."[43] To alleviate this situation, the lord general reverted to several drastic measures. He commissioned Thomas Taylor, a London citizen, to raise a company of archers to assist in the defense of London.[44] He also recommended to the Upper House that the cost of maintaining the garrison at Newport Pagnell be distributed among all the counties of the Eastern Association. These measures accomplished little, apparently, for His Excellency soon returned to Westminster to plead his case.

On 10 November, after resuming his place in the Upper House between the Earl of Rutland and Suffolk, Essex personally presented arguments for increased funds to keep the army on the field during the winter months.[45] The request was sent to the Committee of Safety for immediate consideration. That same day he also laid before the Lords an unopened message from the Royalists, which he had received from a trumpet the day before. The letter, written

42 *Ibid.*, p. 145.
43 *Ibid.*, pp. 148–49.
44 Rushworth, *Historical Collections*, 5: 371.
45 *Lords Journal*, 6: 301.

by the Earl of Forth and addressed to Essex, was read by the clerk
of the Parliaments. It contained a threat that the King intended to
bring Irish troops to England. The Upper House, after lengthy
discussion, forwarded the correspondence to the Commons. Three
days later the King went through with his plans. He sent the Marquess of Ormonde to Ireland with specific orders to return with
Irish troops. Soon contingents of Irish soldiers began landing along
the coastal towns of Wales and England.

This disturbing news was followed by more. In mid-November
the lord general learned that Plymouth, then in dire straits, was
about to fall to the Royalists. Many reinforcements recently sent to
relieve the situation were already dead, wounded, or sick. The
besieged Parliamentarians were twenty-one weeks in arrears.
There was a severe shortage of arms and provisions. Many soldiers
threatened to desert. Sir William Brereton's report to Parliament
contained equally disheartening news from Bristol and Chester:
several thousand Irish soldiers were on their way to England and
eleven Royalist ships laden with provisions had recently landed at
Bristol. The King's supporters were preparing for a major thrust
against Parliament. If help was not soon forthcoming, the whole
West would be lost and the rest of the kingdom would be in great
danger.

A few days later Essex hastily returned to the field to cope with a
mutiny within the ranks of his army. An early snowfall made
conditions intolerable. The troops were poorly clad, cold, hungry,
and discontented for want of pay. "The winter is already come,"
wrote Charles Rich to Barrington, "and our lying in the field hath
lost us more men than have been taken away either by the sword
or bullet, notwithstanding which we are ready to persist, and
unwilling to wait any opportunity of doing God honour and our
country service." [46] The sick needed attention. The horses needed
shoes. All needed food. When several hundred of the discontented
soldiers assembled and threatened to pillage Saint Albans in late
November, Essex promptly returned and somehow quelled the
gathering storm.

Essex was back in London by 22 November to secure more funds
from Parliament. He was soon besieged by more bad news and
additional demands for money. On 25 November he received from

[46] Kingston, *Hertfordshire*, p. 147.

Sir William Waller, whose troops were deserting him outside
Basing House, an urgent request for able officers.[47] A few days
later Col. Thomas May, then in Cheshire, asked for dragoons,
pistols, muskets, and gunpowder. Because of the circumstances it
was natural for Essex to spend considerable time in London and
Westminster. "Essex remains here, pressing for money," noticed
the Venetian ambassador. "His army, divided between St. Albans
and Newport, is already much enfeebled and dwindles daily. . . .
There are difficulties not only in the matter of money but of soldiers
also, and they are touting every day for volunteers under specious
pretexts, without result, while the citizens are prevented from going
out by the demands of the city and their own inclination."[48]

The crowning blow to these disturbing developments struck on
8 December,[49] when John Pym, the formidable parliamentary
leader passed away at Derby House after a lingering illness. Five
days later, after thousands of Londoners viewed his body, he was
honored with a large state funeral attended by most members of
Parliament. He was buried in Westminster Abbey, a short distance
from Essex's final resting place.

Pym's death was a great loss to Parliament.[50] He had embodied
the heart and soul of the parliamentary cause, which he had held
together for several years. From his earliest days in Parliament
until his final utterance he had persistently opposed the Stuart
sovereigns and their arbitrary policies. He had helped manage the
impeachment of Buckingham, helped draft the Petition of Right,
led the attack upon Strafford, and inspired the Grand Remonstrance.
More important, Pym had formed a powerful political bloc in the
House of Commons—the moderates, or the middle group—and an
alliance with the Earl of Essex's faction in the House of Lords. For
over two years the leaders of this political union had labored
against common enemies in Parliament and on the field of battle.
They had limited the authority of the monarch and his ministers,
abolished the instruments of prerogative government, and secured
a greater voice for Parliament in the affairs of state. They were
not, however, doctrinaires. They had no dream of utopia. They

---

47 H. M. C. Thirteenth Report, Appendix 1, p. 159.

48 C. S. P. Ven., 1643–1647, p. 48.

49 Rushworth, Historical Collections, 5: 377.

50 For these statements on Pym, especially his relationship with Essex, see
Hexter, King Pym, pp. 91–93, 113, 115–16.

had no vision of a cabinet system of government. They were not driven by a compelling desire to establish a New Jerusalem in Stuart England. If anything, they looked backward and emulated those periods in English history when Parliament had exercised a greater control over the Crown. While Pym lived, the middle group was committed to the preservation of the basic institutions of English society: the hereditary monarchy, the hierarchical social structure, the bicameral legislature, the established religion and a state church, the common law and its courts, and private property. Although Pym may have at times resorted to some revolutionary means to accomplish his ends, he was at heart a conservative reformer devoted to the extension of liberty and the preservation of property.

Essex lost his most important political ally in the House of Commons with Pym's death. Between the two men had existed an understanding based, not so much on personal friendship or class interests, but on common enemies and similar ends. Pym and Essex had opposed the same men and favored the same constitutional reforms. Pym and Essex had combined against the King in the crisis over the militia. Pym had backed Essex for the command and secured funds to operate the army. Pym had stood for aristocratic leadership in the army and the navy—the traditional, medieval view toward military command—and for unity of command and strategy as long as he lived. He had shielded Essex from the radicals in the Commons and the City. He had defended Essex against those who would have deserted him and established a separate army. He had, in short, remained faithful to the lord general through the doldrums, the defeats, and the crises. Pym had depended upon Essex to defeat the King on the field of battle; Essex had counted upon Pym to provide the political wherewithal for that victory.

CHAPTER 16

The War in Westminster: Rivalries and Reversals

I

ON 9 DECEMBER, the day after John Pym died, Essex rejoined his troops in Hertfordshire. In all likelihood he timed his return to forestall excessive desertions and prevent demonstrations resulting from the demise of the parliamentary leader. Several pressing matters also demanded his attention in Saint Albans. There were knotty jurisdictional disputes awaiting mediation, winter defenses to be supervised, troop movements and new assignments to be determined, a series of courts-martial scheduled for mid-December, and sick and unpaid soldiers to be provided for. Strategic and logistic matters relating to the coming of the Scots and the forthcoming campaign in the north also needed consideration. To meet these demands, the lord general kept away from Parliament for the remainder of December.

Shortly after arriving in Saint Albans he convened a Council of War to hear the case of Col. Nathaniel Fiennes.[1] Fiennes's commission, signed by Essex on 1 May 1643, had ordered him to take Bristol and the forces there into his charge as governor and "by all possible ways and means (except in point of civil government) to provide for the defence and security of the same, and to maintain the same against the enemies and opposition whatsoever."[2] When he capitulated on 26 July, after resisting the Royalist assaulters only three days and after signing terms which required him to give up his army, Fiennes was severely castigated by the Waller faction in the House of Commons, many of whom were at odds with his father. Fiennes had defended himself against his accusers. He had justified his actions in a speech delivered before the Lower House and had published an apologetic narrative explaining his surrender. But his

[1] See above, p. 398.
[2] Cobbett, *State Trials*, 4: 278–79.

political enemies refused to ignore the matter. Clement Walker, a Presbyterian leader from Somerset, had responded to Fiennes in *An Answer;* and in his book entitled *Rome's Masterpiece,* William Prynne, the caustic controversialist, had attacked Fiennes and alluded to "the most cowardly and unworthy Surrender of Bristol." [3]

Essex stood behind Fiennes throughout the whole affair. In October he had summoned Prynne and Walker to a Council of War and ordered them to make good their allegations. The two critics then had petitioned Essex to convene a court-martial in London or Westminster to try Fiennes. When Essex refused to grant their petition, they drafted articles of impeachment against Fiennes and appealed to the House of Commons for justice. On 15 November that body ordered the lord general to handle the matter on his own; but Essex flatly refused to hold a court-martial in London, where King Mob might rule against his subordinate. Instead, he instructed Dr. Isaac Dorislaus, his judge advocate, to convene the Council of War at Saint Albans in mid-December.

On 14 December the lord general and his Council of War assembled in the room adjoining Moot Hall in Saint Albans. Lord Robartes presided over the hearings, and Dorislaus handled the legal technicalities. Just before Dorislaus started to read the charges which the critics hoped to prove, Prynne moved that the public be allowed to hear the trial. Fiennes objected on grounds of precedents regarding courts-martial. A verbal duel ensued between Dorislaus and Prynne, the former standing for a closed-door trial, the latter defending a public trial. After several exchanges Lord Robartes called a recess and consulted Essex. Essex claimed that "he would not infringe on the Privileges of the Council, whom he thought the prosecutors seemed to distrust by demanding a public trial." [4] The court-martial was held behind closed doors.

For nine days the Council of War listened to the arguments. On the first day the prosecution led off with its ten charges against Fiennes, and the defense replied to them one at a time. The second day was devoted to the proof and the defense of the first three articles. The following week was taken up with article four: the capital charge which accused the defender of cowardly and treasonous acts. Fiennes lost a procedural move to suppress all paper depositions. His objection to the deposition of Sir William Waller, an

[3] *Ibid.*, p. 185.

[4] See *Ibid.*, pp. 185–298, for a full account of the trial.

openly hostile witness, was overruled. Having won these procedural gambits, the prosecutors then pressed home their charges, introducing dozens of depositions plus Fiennes's commission and his correspondence with Essex into the record, and quoting from the published accounts. To clinch their case, Prynne and Walker appealed to Essex's *Lawes and Ordinances*: "That whosoever yieldeth up any town, fort, magazine, victuals, ammunition, arms, or that moveth any such thing upon Extremity, and that to the Governor, or in Council, shall be executed as a traitor."[5]

Upon extremity: this was the crucial phrase. If Fiennes produced witnesses to testify that he had surrendered under "extremity," he would be innocent of the charge; if not, he would be found guilty of treason and condemned to death by the laws promulgated by the lord general himself. Fiennes did not produce the witnesses. From this rather harsh law of war there was no way of escape. He had voluntarily surrendered Bristol before having been reduced to "utter extremity" and had, moreover, permitted the enemy to secure some of Parliament's arms, thereby clearly violating the martial laws laid down by the lord general. The proofs pointed to his guilt under the *Lawes and Ordinances*: this much seemed certain when the trial ended two days before Christmas.

On 29 December, after a holiday recess, Essex reconvened the Council of War for the verdict and the sentence. The council found Fiennes guilty of the charges, reported Dr. Dorislaus, and sentenced him to death.[6] It was reported that the defendant was "astonished" at the sentence, for he had expected his station and his connection with Essex to save him. When he demanded to know the basis of the decision, he was told that it was not customary for a court to reveal its reasons. When he sought to appeal his case to Parliament, he was turned down because the House of Commons had already spoken by delegating the matter to the Council of War. Fiennes did not pay the supreme price for his crime, however; rather he was kept in custody for several weeks and eventually pardoned by Lord General Essex.

Essex extended the same mercy toward Capt. Carlo Fantom, a notorious Croatian mercenary who, according to Aubrey, "was very quarrelsome and a great Ravisher."[7] Captain Fantom, the son

[5] *Ibid.*, p. 267.
[6] *Ibid.*, p. 297.
[7] Aubrey, *Brief Lives*, pp. 105–6.

of a Catholic, took pleasure in baiting his fellow troopers and boasting of his exploits. He also claimed to have a secret formula which made his body impervious to musket bullets, thus making him a "Hard-man." Although many thought him a devil, he was highly regarded in Parliament's army headquarters. "Robert Earl of Essex, General for the Parliament had this Capt. Fantom in high esteeme: for he was an admirable Horse-officer, and taught the Cavalry of the army the way of fighting with Horse; the General saved him from hanging twice for Ravishing; once at Winchester, and at St. Albans." Neither of these reprieves wore well with Essex's political enemies.

The lord general's treatment of Royalists was, in the eyes of his critics at least, dangerously lenient.[8] Throughout the war he made liberal use of his authority to release and exchange prisoners. In June 1643 he released Edmund Sheffield, the son of the Earl of Mulgrave, and Thomas Howard, Lord Berkshire's son, in exchange for Mr. Edwards, a relatively unknown soldier, at the behest of Prince Rupert.[9] That same month he pardoned Edmund Waller, who had been condemned to die and fined ten thousand pounds, and later granted him his complete freedom. Later in the summer he released the Earl of Lindsey, the son of his late rival, who had been captured at Edgehill. Essex was equally magnanimous in granting safe-conducts to the friends and relatives of Royalist peers.[10] He issued a pass to Lady Elizabeth Capell, an avowed Royalist, and her household, which allowed them to travel unmolested from Saint Albans to Oxford. He discharged from prison one Capt. Edward Longvil, an officer in the King's army, offered him protection, and then permitted him to return to his home. He even granted some potentially dangerous Royalists licenses to travel to the Continent. These humane concessions to the enemy reflected Essex's aristocratic breeding and his chivalrous code of conduct.

His policy toward enemy spies proved more stringent. On 18 October 1643, Parliament demanded that all suspects be "pro-

[8] Concerning these cases see *Lords Journal*, 6: 63, 65, 90, 153; Ludlow, *Memoirs*, 1: 88; Warburton, *Rupert*, 2: 211; and Green, *Calendar for Compounding*, 2: 846, 897, 1389.

[9] Essex's letter to Prince Rupert about this matter is located in the William Salt Library.

[10] See British Museum, Additional MSS, 40,630, fol. 131a; Ellis, *Original letters*, 2d ser., 3: 223; *H. M. C. House of Lords Manuscripts*, 6: 3, 147; and the Newbattle Manuscripts, pt. 2, vol. 2, fol. 9, Register House, Edinburgh.

ceeded against according to the Rules and Grounds of War."[11] This law, in effect, gave the lord general the power to bring a suspect to trial before the Council of War. On 24 November at a Council of War held at Essex House two men were found guilty of spying and were sentenced to death. The following week Daniel Kniverton, who was apprehended and imprisoned in the Fleet for distributing the King's proclamation in London, was publicly executed on a gibbet at the Royal Exchange after the traditional speech and prayer. Richard Carpenter, who was found guilty of delivering royal writs to the judges, was more fortunate, for his execution was stayed by Essex and he was committed to Bridewell.

Essex's conduct of the war during the winter season exposed him to much criticism and several political attacks. The war party in the House of Commons demanded offensive warfare throughout the entire year. Essex did not. He used the winter season for recuperation, training, and preparation for the forthcoming campaign, and believed in keeping his forces intact and in assuming defensive positions along the perimeter of London. His traditionalist views on the subject—akin to those of the King—ran counter to those of Waller and Cromwell, both of whom committed their troops to battle, whether it was winter or not.

The lord general intended to retain Saint Albans as his headquarters and Newport Pagnell as his garrison outpost throughout the winter season. But the militants in the Lower House, now that Pym was dead, took a different view of this strategy. They detested the fact that Essex had given up Reading, after having taken it earlier in the year; that he had only a token force at Windsor; and that he showed no indication of rendering assistance to Waller in the South. Moreover, they soon made their influence felt in Parliament and the Committee of Safety. Just two days after Pym's interment the Committee of Safety ordered Essex to send Waller reinforcements and to consider moving his headquarters from Saint Albans to Farnham to be closer to Waller.

Essex found it extremely difficult to comply with these orders. He reluctantly arranged to send Waller 500 horse, as the Committee requested, but he also reiterated his own need for money and reinforcements. "I hope, now I have spared so great a Strength of Horse from these Parts," he wrote the committee on 14 December,

[11] Rushworth, *Historical Collections*, 5: 367–70; and Whitelocke, *Memorials* (1682 ed.), p. 74.

"there will be a care taken for the Supply of Horse and Arms, most of the Horsemen being on Foot, the strongest Troops sent away, and divers of the Counties having not sent in the numbers of Horse they promised." [12] In the same letter the lord general refused to move his headquarters south, "unless the Parliament commands it," on grounds that his army was sorely needed in Hertfordshire and Buckinghamshire. The House of Lords, supporting Essex in the matter, passed a resolution calling for the defense of Newport Pagnell and authorizing the collection of money for the same.

Three days later the Committee of Safety ordered Essex to march his army southward as soon as possible. Waller was in trouble. Prince Rupert was marching toward him with an army 6,000 strong. From his headquarters in Saint Albans the lord general again adjured to his peers, hoping to convince the rest of Parliament and the committee to allow him to remain at Newport. The surrounding area would be rendered defenseless and lost if he withdrew southward, Essex contended; the whole cause would be jeopardized. The envious commander concluded his argument with several biting gibes. "And likewise I conceive Sir Wm. Waller cannot be in any great Danger," he wrote the speaker of the Upper House, "having the Benefit of so safe a Place as Farnham (now fortified) that the Enemy (especially in this Season of the Year) will not do him Harm; besides, the Addition of Strength I send him is so considerable, that I hold them able to encounter with a Thousand of the Enemy's." [13] This sarcastic communication convinced few in Westminster.

Parliament rejected Essex's request to remain at Newport Pagnell for the winter. The lord general should "pursue the Advice given him in these Letters by the Committee of Safety," the resolution of 20 December read, "So soon as Forces shall be put into Newport Pagnell for the Safety thereof, whereby he may draw up his own Forces to himself to march." [14] The lord general had no option: Parliament had spoken. Its resolution, which amounted to a capitulation to Waller's demands, did not please Essex, for, as Whitelocke noticed, "a little discontent began to kindle betwixt him and the House of Commons, and the Committee of Safety." [15]

12 *Lords Journal*, 6: 347.
13 *Ibid.*, p. 347.
14 *Ibid.*, p. 346.
15 Whitelocke, *Memorials* (1682 ed.), p. 75.

Several of His Excellency's political activities in the weeks after Pym's death aroused suspicion and provoked criticism. Two private conferences with le Comte d'Harcourt, who came from France to London to mediate the Civil War, and early January discussions with a delegation of Dutch mediators gave the leaders of the war party cause to grumble.[16] His associations with defectors and former defectors had similar effects. Essex was the principal spokesman for the Earl of Holland, who, after returning to Parliament from Oxford, petitioned the Upper House for his liberty and relief from sequestration. Holland's petition, dated 16 December, was referred to Essex, and in mid-January, on his recommendation, the Lords made moves to readmit their vacillating compeer.[17]

Essex also interceded for the Earl of Bedford, who had defected to the King's side the previous August. Bedford had second thoughts about his defection and considered returning to Parliament. During the last week of December he left Oxford, appeared at Essex's headquarters in Saint Albans two days after Christmas, and put himself at the mercy of Parliament. Essex received him warmly and then took him into custody on a temporary basis until receiving instructions from Parliament. While at Saint Albans, the Earl of Bedford compounded with Essex to give the army a week's pay— an act obviously designed to dispel doubts about his intentions and loyalty. The lord general, who had assured Bedford a pass, made arrangements to conduct the double-defector to Westminster and wrote an intercessory letter on his behalf.[18] Two days later the speaker, Lord Grey of Warke, read Essex's letter and placed Bedford, who had been conducted to Westminster, under the custody of the gentleman-usher of the House. The next day he was committed to the custody of Lord Brooke.

The Earl of Essex returned to the City on 1 January.[19] He had completed the defenses of Newport Pagnell, paid his troops some of their arrears, and ordered the Earl of Manchester to send several hundred foot and horse to reinforce the town of Bedford. Just before departing from Saint Albans, he had received word from

[16] C. S. P. Ven., 1643–1647, p. 67. According to the Venetian envoy, Essex received the ambassadors at the Tower of London.

[17] Lords Journal, 6: 340, 377.

[18] The original of this letter, written in Essex's own hand, is located in the Main Papers, House of Lords Record Office, under the date 30 December 1643.

[19] Lords Journal, 6: 353, 361.

Manchester that the reinforcements were on their way. But before marching his army southward, as Parliament had twice demanded, Essex returned to that body to personally confront his political rivals.

II

UPON RESUMING his place in the House of Lords on 2 January, the lord general and his followers set out to restore public confidence in the Westminster Parliament—thus counteracting the rival Parliament which the King summoned to meet in Oxford later in the month—and to recapture the political initiative from the Independents in the Lower House. For men of Essex's persuasion the situation was indeed critical. The House of Peers had dwindled to a mere handful of faithfuls. The English sovereign had more peers in his retinue than Parliament had in Westminster. Moreover, after the King's newly summoned Parliament convened at Oxford, the Lords in Westminster would look ridiculously small in contrast. As the Upper House became smaller, furthermore, the Lower House assumed a larger role in all matters before Parliament; in fact, the Lower House so completely dominated the legislative process that the Upper House offered little check or effective opposition. The Peers concurred, they conferred and consulted, but they were helplessly dependent upon the Lower House. During the three years that Pym had managed the Commons the moderates like the lord general had little to fear, for Pym had worked closely with the Essex faction on most matters.

Pym's successors in the Lower House attempted to keep the moderates united but failed. Sir Henry Vane and Oliver St. John simply could not keep all the moderates together and they soon lost control of the powerful middle group. Divisiveness along politico-religious lines set in. Personal and factional rivalries came to the fore. All these augured ill for Essex. It was an open secret that Sir Harry Vane, a militant Independent who demanded immediate victory in a full war against the King, disapproved of Essex's conduct of the fighting.

The running conflict between the lord general and Sir William Waller broke into the open again on 2 January. Waller had been quite active on the field during recent months: he had beleaguered Basing House, started a siege of Arundel, and fought Royalists throughout the counties of Kent, Surrey, Sussex, and Hampshire. Yet he lacked a full commission, apparently simply because Essex refused to issue one. Waller appealed to his friends in the Commons, and on 1 January that body ordered the lord general to send him a bona fide commission. Essex reluctantly issued another commission and then sent a detailed explanation to the speaker of the Lower House. The original commission to Waller was different, limited in scope, in fact. "For the reasons of my limitations in the former commission," he continued, "I forbear to give them; but whensoever the Houses shall command me, I shall be ready to make it appear I did no more than I ought to do, having received so great a trust from the Parliament, in the discharge of my duty, and then to submit to their further pleasure." Essex concluded his defense by professing complete dedication to the cause. "And for my own part," he wrote, "I am every day so confirmed in the justness of the cause, that let the strength I have be never so weak, I shall never desert the cause as long as I have any blood in my veins, until this kingdom may be made happy by a blessed peace— which is all honest men's prayer—or to have an end by the sword, which is the intention of your assured friends." [20]

The following day Essex was honored by his fellow peers with an appointment to the Westminster Assembly of Divines. "The Lord General shall be added to the Assembly," the resolution read, "and to send to the House of Commons to desire their concurrence therein." [21] The Lower House concurred three days later. Through this move, and others like it, the more conservative elements hoped to counterbalance the power of the Independents, especially the Vane faction, in both Parliament and the Westminster Assembly. Apparently the Lords believed that the lord general, now inclined toward a Presbyterian settlement, would be able to put his prestige and popularity to some advantage in the assembly.

Essex House served as the headquarters of Parliament's army while the lord general was in London. Messengers took regular intelligence reports to him from Luke in Newport Pagnell, and carried orders and warrants Essex issued to subordinates. Messengers from Saint Albans, Newport Pagnell, and Windsor kept him in touch with his army. When occasion demanded, he took correspondence before Parliament and made reports on the military

[20] Devereux, *Lives and Letters*, 2: 385–87.
[21] *Lords Journal*, 6: 364. Also see Baillie, *Letters*, 2: 30.

situation. Officers who went to London brought him news from the field. Only rarely was he absent from the House of Lords. He maintained a large staff of servants at Essex House and kept a large table. He attended divine services at Saint Clement Danes; in fact, he was very likely instrumental in securing the appointment of Richard Vines, a Puritan divine of the Westminster Assembly, as rector of that church in the early weeks of 1644.

In mid-January, shortly after Waller's return to the City, Essex took advantage of an opportunity to strike back at his critics. During the first part of January, it seems, Sir Harry Vane and Oliver St. John received from King Charles through Lord Lovelace a peace overture, which included a promise of liberty of conscience.[22] The recipients kept the matter secret for fear of being politically embarrassed. But the lord general heard about the letter and its contents, probably through his intelligence agents at Newport, and exposed the subject to Parliament on 16 January. He first revealed the Lovelace-Vane correspondence. He then complained (probably tongue in cheek) that he could not very well discharge his duty as Parliament's general with treacherous plotting going on behind his back. He demanded an investigation of the matter.

Two days later Essex participated in the City-sponsored celebration timed to correspond with the Covenanters' march into England. On the morning of 18 January both Houses convened at Saint Margaret's, where they listened to a sermon delivered by Stephen Marshall, and then marched in formal procession along the crowded street guarded by trained bands. "First went the Lord Mayor and Aldermen in the Scarlet Gowns, and the Common Council," Whitelocke reported, "then the Lord General, Lord Admiral, Earl of Manchester, and other Lords attended with divers Colonels and military officers. After the Lords came the Members of the House of Commons, and the Commissioners of Scotland, then the Assembly of Divines, and as they went through Cheapside, on a Scaffold, many Popish pictures, Crucifixes, and Superstitious Relicks were burnt before them."[23] The dignitaries proceeded to Merchant Taylor's Hall for a sumptuous banquet.

---

[22] See Bertha M. Gardiner, "A Secret Negotiation with Charles the First, 1643–1644," *Camden Society Miscellany*, no. 8 (London, 1883), pp. 1–19; and Abbott, *Cromwell*, 1: 274. The proposal was also described in an anonymously published pamphlet entitled *A Cunning Plot* (London, 1644).

[23] Whitelocke, *Memorials* (1682 ed.), p. 76. Also see Baillie, *Letters*, 2: 133.

The following day the Scottish army of the Solemn League and Covenant entered England.

III

On 22 January 1644, the House of Lords in Westminster, reacting to the King's convening a new Parliament at Oxford, held its preannounced roll call.[24] Twenty-two peers, or about 15 per cent of the total, were present in the Upper Chamber. The faithful few were: Northumberland; Warwick; Essex; Pembroke; Rutland; Kent; Lincoln; Bolingbroke; Stamford; Manchester; Salisbury; Nottingham; Denbigh; Suffolk; Saye; Grey; Howard; Bruce; Willoughby; North; Wharton; and Hunsdon. In due course a handful of neutralist and vacillating Lords showed their colors for Parliament: the Earl of Clare returned in March, the Earls of Kingston and Westmorland and Lord Conway in April. Yet, the total number of Lords committed to Parliament stood at about 30 out of 120 in prewar Parliaments. It was hardly a representative group that remained in Westminster to continue fighting for the cause of Parliament.

On that same day the Oxford Parliament convened in the Great Hall at Christ Church for the King's speech.[25] About one hundred Royalist peers attended or sent their proxies, but the response of the commoners was disappointing, for only slightly over the same number appeared at the first meeting. If Charles hoped to attract a large group of Parliament members from Westminster to Oxford, he failed, for they defected in only small numbers. If he hoped to force the Westminster Parliament out of business, he also failed, for his rival Parliament only sharpened the bitterness and increased the competition between the warring sides. Nevertheless, for nearly three months the Mongrel Parliament transacted business in Oxford.

On 27 January the Oxford Parliament, after much debate, gave formal approval to a peace overture addressed to the Earl of Essex.[26] The discussion centered on the best means to initiate

---

[24] Lords Journal, 6: 387.

[25] See Rushworth, Historical Collections, 5: 560; and Sanderson, A Compleat History, pp. 665–70.

[26] Whitelocke, Memorials (1682 ed.), p. 77; and Clarendon, History (1849 ed.), 3: 304.

negotiations with those whom the King regarded as rebels. Because they contended that the Westminster Parliament was an unauthorized assembly without any legal footing, they refused to bargain with it as a Parliament. For the same reason, they decided against addressing their peace proposals to the speakers of either House. Instead, they selected Lord General Essex, whether he approved or not, as the principal object of their peace offensive. To Charles he was still the ringleader of the rebels. In the eyes of Royalist advisers Edward Hyde and Sir John Culpeper he was an honorable man whose word could be trusted and whose prestige and popularity could be exploited. He was addressed personally, not as lord general, but by his title. The appeal, subscribed to by the Prince of Wales and the Duke of York, both very young, and by 43 Lords and 118 commoners, was forwarded to Essex by a trumpeter. Printed copies of the letter were published and subsequently distributed throughout the kingdom.

The Royalists implored Essex to interpose in the bloody Civil War. The subscribers, it claimed, were meeting in Oxford in obedience to the King's command and writing with the King's consent. They wanted to restore England "to its former peace and security." The King, they contended, was gracious and sincere in his intention; he would, moreover, make concessions to bring about a lasting settlement. They also played on Essex's known hatred of the Scots. The Covenanters would cause endless destruction and much misery in England if they were not repulsed, the Royalists warned, "and we being desirous to beleeve your lordship (however engaged) a person likely to be sensibly touched with these considerations, have thought fit to invite you that part in this blessed work, which is onely capable to repaire all our misfortunes, and boye up the Kingdome from ruine." [27] This promise of a military plum was accompanied by a general pardon to all defectors.

The lord general received the King's trumpeter at Essex House three days later.[28] He apparently guessed the contents of the packet and shrewdly refused to open it in private. Instead, he took the sealed package to Parliament, reported the matter to the Upper House, and waited for instructions of how to treat it. A select committee, which included Essex, Northumberland, Warwick,

[27] See *A Copy of a Letter from the Members of Both Houses Assembled at Oxford to the Earl of Essex*, printed at Oxford on 27 January 1644.

[28] *Lords Journal*, 6: 399–401.

and Manchester, was then appointed to make its contents known to Parliament. Later that day Northumberland revealed that it contained a parchment addressed to Essex and signed by many Lords and commoners and a letter directed to Essex from the Earl of Forth. The contents of the latter were read by the clerk of Parliament. The Lords then directed Essex to treat it as a private matter and answer the letters as he saw fit.

Later that day he replied to the Earl of Forth. "My Lord, the maintenance of the Parliament of England, and of the privileges thereof," he wrote, "is that for which we are all resolved to spend our blood, as being the foundation whereon all our laws and liberties are built." [29] It was as simple as that. Although Essex did not formally present the overture to Parliament, in all likelihood he revealed its contents to some of his compeers, if not all, and to the Scottish commissioners in London. His curt reply disappointed those Royalists most desirous of an accommodation. In the words of Clarendon, one of the dejected Royalists, "he never, after taking the covenant and writing this letter, did one brave thing; but proved unfortunate in all he went about, even to his death." [30]

Two weeks passed. In mid-February the lord general received from the Earl of Forth a second packet, which he likewise placed before his peers. The Lords, as before, referred the matter to the newly formed Committee of Both Kingdoms, which instructed Essex to reply and grant safe-conducts only if the Royalists recognized Parliament. "You shew your nobleness in declaring your willingness to write to me in any business," he answered on 19 February, "as in that of peace, and I joyne with you in the same opinion that it ought to be a principall duty of those who are trusted in places of our commands, and therefore whensoever I shall receive any directions to those who have intrusted me I shall use my best endeavors." [31] When this message was returned to the Earl of Forth by Essex's personal trumpeter, the Royalists held a conference in Oxford to consider their next move. The participants, including several loyalist Scots, finally agreed that the next overture should be directed to Parliament rather than Essex.

[29] Devereux, *Lives and Letters*, 2: 390. Also see the broadside version of Essex's reply, published in London on 8 February 1644.

[30] Clarendon, *History* (1849 ed.), 3: 312.

[31] The original of Essex's answer is located in the British Museum, Sloan MSS, 18,797.

On 3 March, the King backed down, followed Essex's suggestion, and directed a conciliatory letter to the *Lords and Commons at Westminster*.[32] He proposed that each of the rival assemblies nominate a delegation and instruct it to find means of meeting "in a full and free Convention of Parliament." The convention, he suggested, would treat for peace and determine a settlement acceptable to all parties. This proposal, subscribed by the Lords and the Commons attending the Oxford Parliament, was given to the Earl of Forth, who forwarded it to Essex with a short covering letter. As before, the lord general dutifully reported the matter to the Upper House, and that body once again referred it to a committee, which opened the packet and appraised the contents.

The following day the King's letter was read to the House of Lords and sent to a conference committee. Essex managed the conference. After speaking with a delegation from the Commons, Essex reported that the joint conference rejected the King's proposal because it derogated the good name of the Westminster Parliament. They insisted that the King dissolve the Oxford Parliament and return to Westminster. The formal statement of this uncompromising rejection, signed by the speaker of both Houses, was forwarded to Essex for delivery to Forth. The enclosed message addressed to the King denied the authority of the Oxford Parliament, defended the legality of the Westminster Parliament, and rejected the whole idea of a convention. The continuance of the Parliament in Westminster, they reminded Charles, "is settled by a Law (which as other Laws of your Kingdom) your Majesty hath sworn to maintain, as we are sworn to our allegiance to your Majesty, (these obligations being reciprocal), we must in Duty, and accordingly are resolved with our Lives and Fortunes, to defend and preserve the just Rights and full Power of this Parliament."[33] The Westminster Parliament had spoken.

IV

THROUGHOUT these winter months Essex struggled to retain his full command and to maintain his army on the field. In late January, it will be recalled, he had reported to the Lords that he had received intelligence of certain members in the Lower House

[32] Rushworth, *Historical Collections*, 5: 569.
[33] *Lords Journal*, 6: 451.

who were secretly corresponding with some Royalists at Oxford.[34] To clinch his thinly veiled counterattack upon Sir Harry Vane, he then presented to the Upper House several pieces of evidence. That the lord general hoped to embarrass and discredit his enemy in the Lower House and to undermine Vane's position in parliamentary circles by this exposure seems certain. If he suggested that Sir Harry was guilty of treason, as Baillie claims he did, Essex made little headway in the matter, for Vane cleared himself of the implicating charge and the issue was soon dropped.

Five days after Essex submitted his evidence of Vane's complicity, on 29 January, the City authorities began grumbling about the commander's army.[35] The regiment stationed at Windsor was in arrears, complained the sheriff of London and some aldermen in a petition submitted to Parliament, and something should be done to remedy the situation. A second petition, presented to the Upper House by the Lord Mayor and the Common Council, called for a new system of assessment. In all likelihood Sir Harry stimulated these flank attacks upon the lord general. Regardless, Vane was the instigator of the move to supplant the Committee of Safety with a new executive junta, thus enabling the war party to secure a larger voice.[36] It was an opportune time for such a change: Pym was dead; his followers were sharply divided; and the Scottish alliance, moreover, made some type of revision mandatory to give the Covenanters a voice in the conduct of the war.

The ordinance creating the Committee of Both Kingdoms encountered opposition from its inception. To check some resistance in the Upper House, Vane managed to have the bill drawn up and passed by the House of Lords, where it had the support of Northumberland, and then forwarded to the Lower House for concurrence. The original bill, which called for fourteen Englishmen and three Scottish commissioners (but excluded Holles, Essex's most open and avowed defender in the Lower House), was rejected by the Commons. Most commoners believed that the bill should have originated in their House. Some also objected to the composition of the committee. Others entertained doubts about the extensive power

[34] *Ibid.*, p. 391.

[35] *Ibid.*, p. 395.

[36] See Wallace Notestein, "The Establishment of the Committee of Both Kingdoms," *American Historical Review* 17 (1912): 477–95 for facts on the following pages.

granted to the junta. To answer these objections, Vane and St. John introduced a new bill, very similar to the original one, into the Lower House and increased the size of the committee.

The Earl of Essex, although named a member in both bills, launched a move to quash the new version. He realized that members of the Commons and the Covenanters would outnumber the peers and that the Independents might well hold the balance of power, especially when he, Robartes, and Wharton were on the battlefield. He realized too that he would be outnumbered in the deliberations, that his political influence would be limited and belittled, and that his military authority would be undermined. "His friends recognized that the new committee was directed against him and his opponents virtually admitted as much," wrote Notestein. "There is some evidence that the Lord General had been so far angered by the efforts to limit his power that he had threatened to resign. . . . His friends urged and with some force that to put over him a committee was to bind his hands in such a way as to prevent the best results, and that it would utterly discourage him." [37]

Essex made a last-ditch effort to scuttle the measure. On 14 February he proposed that Parliament strike certain crucial words from the new bill. He also recommended that the committee's life be shortened from three months to six weeks, or as the Lords stated, "untill the Lord General's army were recruited and . . . then the power of ordering and directing would be resumed to the LORD General alone." The Commons still refused to yield, however; they supported their form of the bill and insisted that the Lords pass the measure in its revised form. Finally, after two weeks of bickering and endless discussion, the Lords reluctantly approved it. Essex had lost the most crucial political battle of the war in Westminster. His authority was further limited and circumscribed.

The newly constituted Committee of Both Kingdoms held its first meeting on 17 February at Worcester House.[38] John Thurloe, who later served as Cromwell's right-hand man, was named its secretary. The committee consisted of twenty-five members: seven

[37] *Ibid.*, p. 493.

[38] From the *Register of the Committee of Both Kingdoms*, located in the Register House, Edinburgh. This official record of the transactions was written by either a member of the Scottish delegation or a specially designated clerk. (Hereafter it is cited as *Register of C. B. K.*)

English peers, fourteen English commoners, and four Scottish commissioners. Those who held commissions in Parliament's army included Essex, Manchester, Robartes, Wharton, Waller, Stapleton, Gerrard, Haselrig, Richard Browne, and Cromwell. When these men were on the field, the power devolved upon the remaining members: Northumberland, Warwick, Saye, Glynn, William Armyn, St. John, the two Vanes, Henry Pierrepont, and Henry Wallop, a majority of whom were inclined toward Independency, and the four Scottish commissioners. The group met once a day, sometimes twice, and worked closely with the House of Commons. It acted as a steering committee of Parliament in all matters relating to the conduct of the war.

Essex attended the initial deliberations of the committee with his usual diligence. During the first three months of its existence he rarely missed a session and then only when pressing military business demanded his presence elsewhere. It must have been frustrating and humiliating, for he was outvoted and outmaneuvered time after time by his political rivals. The commoners and the Scottish commissioners dominated the peers. One of their first moves was to establish committee control over the army—over the recruitment of soldiers, the provisioning of troops, and the determination of strategy. They demanded that the lord general act only upon their instructions and never without their express consent. "They hope that these indications of lack of confidence may force Essex to resign," the Venetian envoy observed, "to gratify the other generals who do not like obeying him, although it was from him that they received their commissions." [39]

The committee's actions the following month annoyed Essex even more. In March the members appointed Waller commander of all the forces of the West. That same month they granted Sir Thomas Fairfax, a commander in the northern counties, authority to select his own subordinate officers—a power which Essex had exercised since the beginning of the war. When in late March the committee ordered Sir William Balfour, Essex's able Commander of the Horse, to join Waller's westward marching army, Essex was furious. [40] Yet he was helpless to reverse the tide of events. He had all he could do to retain his command and the remainder of his officers.

[39] *C. S. P. Ven., 1643–1647,* p. 77.
[40] *Register of C. B. K.*

The situation in the lord general's own army was worsening. Bitter personality clashes and contentions between commanders persisted. Essex collided with Waller and Manchester. Manchester carried on a running fight with Willoughby. The Earl of Denbigh protested against the local committees. Instead of one Parliamentary army under the command of Lord General Essex there were now several armies with varying degrees of independence. The Scottish army, under the command of Alexander Leslie, Earl of Leven, took orders from the Scottish commissioners. In the North, Lord Fairfax and his son, although in communication with Essex, had secured a large measure of control over their troops. Waller in the South and West continued to enjoy a semi-independence because of strong support in the City; he frequently challenged the decisions and undercut the authority of Essex by appealing directly to his backers. In between were the armies of Essex and Manchester. The local forces in Wales under John Middleton, those in Cheshire under Brereton, those in Shropshire under Denbigh, and several others all dealt unilaterally with the House of Commons or the Committee of Both Kingdoms. On the eve of the 1644 campaign, then, the unity of command and strategy which Pym had struggled so hard to preserve no longer existed. In reality there were several armies, each competing against the others for money, matériel, and man power.

Despite these adversities, Essex managed to keep his army on the field.[41] Only a skeleton force remained, however, for the total strength of his infantry shrank to less than 2,000 soldiers. Some of the vacancies resulted from casualties, but more were caused by desertion. A heavy snowfall in January and the severe temperatures of February made life in the field intolerable. Among other problems the troops and officers had to contend with were crowded and filthy quarters, lack of food and clothing, and disease. Some succumbed to "pestilential fevers." The officers were reduced to half pay, and most soldiers were still in arrears, although those led by Manchester and Waller fared somewhat better. Many of the soldiers commenced to live off the land.

Essex's critics in the Lower House and the City complained about the composition of the army.[42] Far too many officers were

[41] See C. S. P. Dom., 1644, p. 77; and Davies, "Parliamentary Army," pp. 42–45.

[42] Whitelocke, Memorials (1682 ed.), pp. 76–81.

drawing high pay, they contended, and too many common soldiers had not taken the Solemn League and Covenant. In February the lord general was ordered by Parliament to meet with a select committee to determine which officers should continue in their commands and which should be dropped from the pay rosters. After a month's time the lord general and Parliament finally agreed. Essex was compelled to diminish the number of his colonels to seven and to eliminate several officers of lower ranks. An ordinance which passed on 11 March permitted Fairfax, who was short of experienced officers, to absorb those whom Essex relieved of their commands.

The lord general also attempted to refill his depleted ranks. He importuned Parliament for funds to pay his troops. He successfully pushed through Parliament a bill which allowed him to recruit 7,500 foot and 3,000 horse, plus an artillery unit. This bill, which passed the Lords on 24 January and the Lower House on 1 February, did not make adequate provision for financing the new recruits, so Essex turned to other means. In a proclamation issued in late February he threatened the deserters and defectors with death.[43] About the same time, he resorted to impressment to fill his ranks. These measures, however, fell short of the goal, and Essex was compelled to recruit and train another army before taking the field.

During the last week of March, after much debate, Parliament passed an ordinance designed to bring Essex's army up to its full strength.[44] It called for the recruitment of the same amount and type of personnel as the ordinance passed by the Commons on 1 February, but unlike that measure, it made provision for constant pay of the troops and spelled out the new lines of authority. The lord general would receive the sum of £30,504 per month from a meal tax; he would give account to Parliament for his administration of the army; he would be subject to orders of Parliament and the Committee of Both Kingdoms; and he would be supervised by four commissioners on the field.

Parliament passed a similar ordinance empowering Sir William Waller to raise an army of 3,000 foot, 1,200 horse, and 500 dragoons in the counties of Kent, Sussex, Surrey, and Hampshire. The original

43 From a broadside published in London and preserved in the British Museum, King Collection.
44 Firth and Rait, *Acts and Ordinances*, 1: 401–3.

draft of this proposal, initiated in the Lower House, mentioned
nothing of his relationship with the lord general. The House of
Lords, refusing to grant Waller an independent command, demanded that he take orders from the lord general; hence in the final
draft they inserted the phrase "under his Excellencie the E. of
Essex Lord General."[45] No doubt Essex, who was in the Upper
House at the time, was responsible for the restrictive insertion.
The fact that Sir William had just won a very significant battle
at Alresford did not alter Essex's opinion of his rival.

The strategy of the forthcoming campaign had already been
discussed and determined. In February, not long after the formation
of the Committee of Both Kingdoms, Parliament's political and
military leaders had met secretly in London and planned their
strategy.[46] The Earl of Warwick would maintain command of the
sea and, if possible, prevent the landing of French troops along the
southern coast and Irish soldiers along the western shores of England
and Wales. The Scottish army would march southward, secure the
Border counties and Yorkshire, and repulse the Royalists who
were grouped under the Earl of Newcastle. Sir William Brereton
(and Manchester, if necessary) would lead his forces northward
into Yorkshire to assist the Scots. Waller would maintain control
of the southeastern counties and secure the West, presumably the
southwestern counties included, for Parliament. Lord General
Essex would assume the defense of the metropolitan area against
a Royalist attack and then move against the King at Oxford at the
opportune time. He would be joined by Manchester's army and
assisted by auxiliaries from London. In theory, Essex remained
responsible for the attainment of these objectives; in reality the
Committee of Both Kingdoms assumed control and limited his
role in the major decisions.

These campaign plans became known to the King through the
untimely defection of Sir Richard Grenville, a professional soldier
well acquainted with the western parts of England. In autumn of
the previous year he had been commissioned a Lieutenant General
of the Horse by Essex and assigned to Waller's army in the South.
He had fought through the winter months and seemed devoted to
the cause of Parliament. In late February he had attended the
strategy sessions held in London and obtained secret information

[45] Gardiner, *Civil War*, 1: 339.
[46] *Ibid.*, p. 319.

about the upcoming campaign. In early March, not long after these
sessions, with no advance warning he reversed his loyalty and
joined the King at Oxford.[47] Grenville took with him about thirty-
five troopers, including his quartermaster, a coach with six horses,
and six hundred pounds of Parliament's pay money. More important, he divulged to the King information about the size of Parliament's armies and plans for the offensive. For doing so he naturally
was castigated by the Roundhead press and hung in effigy by
Londoners.[48]

Knowledge of Grenville's disclosures did not, however, bring
about any basic changes in Parliament's strategy: the Committee
of Both Kingdoms pressed ahead with its plans. On 22 February
the committee ordered Essex to send 300 soldiers to Gloucester,
again in distress, and to appoint a commander of the operation.
Shortly after Grenville's defection, the committee ordered Essex to
reassign Sir William Balfour, one of his best officers, to Sir William
Waller as a replacement for Grenville; only after considerable
procrastination and grumbling did Essex make the reassignment.
During the following weeks the committee concerned itself with the
recruitment, transportation of supplies, and a host of details relating
to the conduct of the war. In early April it ordered Waller to march
westward and give battle to Prince Maurice and Sir Ralph Hopton
and commanded Essex and Manchester to rendezvous their
respective forces at Aylesbury.[49] On 8 April, Parliament approved
a circular letter which demanded all the counties of England to
forward supplies to Aylesbury as soon as possible.

The lord general, still in London, continued to encounter
much trouble in preparing his army for the field. The response to
the new meal tax was disappointing. There simply was not enough
money to pay arrears and recruit new troops at the same time. The
artillery unit could not take the field for lack of arms. Despite these
inadequacies, the Committee of Both Kingdoms ordered the troops
to assemble at Aylesbury for the scheduled rendezvous, whereupon
Essex protested and adamantly refused to march unless additional
money and man power were forthcoming.[50] Instead, he remained in

47 See Luke, *Journal*, 3: 261; and Rushworth, *Historical Collections*, 5: 384.
48 *C. S. P. Ven., 1643–1647*, p. 86.
49 *Register of C. B. K.*
50 *Ibid.*

London for several more weeks to fill his vacated ranks and beg for funds. He met with some success. On 18 April, Parliament voted five hundred pounds for Essex's artillery unit; two weeks later the appropriation was increased by one thousand pounds. On 22 April, Parliament agreed to advance Essex ten thousand pounds from the excise commissioners' account, but this sum still fell short of the required amount. Essex stubbornly remained in the City.

While recruiting, Essex became embroiled in several political quarrels. On 22 April the Earl of Holland requested permission to accompany Essex on the field during the approaching campaign.[51] In all likelihood Essex, who had backed his cousin's return to Parliament, was privy to the request. The measure passed the Upper House that same day. The majority in the Commons took a completely different view of the subject, however, and flatly rejected Holland's petition. In the eyes of Vane and St. John, the Earl of Holland was an opportunistic and vacillating peer who could not be trusted with important military matters. He was something of an appeaser, moreover, and might have too great an influence over the lord general.

His Excellency also drew criticism for his prolonged delay. One speaker at Cooper's Hall bemoaned the size and heavy cost of Essex's immobile army. Other critics in the Common Council, complaining of Essex's procrastination, suggested that the army should be remodeled before taking the field. Still others accused the lord general of making speeches against the Scottish Covenanters. Amidst these political bickerings the House of Commons ordered the Committee of Both Kingdoms to consult the lord general about the delay and assure him that money would be forthcoming. They conferred later that day and reached an understanding. Essex promised to march within a week; his superiors agreed to supply him with funds. The committee in turn passed the following resolution: "That all of the forces under the immediate command of his Excellency and those under Sir William Waller shall march against the enemy wheresoever they shall appear in a body *in the south and west.*"[52] Although this pacified critics in the City, members on the committee would soon regret the latitude and ambiguity of the order.

[51] *Lords Journal*, 6: 526; and Whitelocke, *Memorials* (1682 ed.), p. 83.
[52] *Register of C. B. K.* Emphasis added.

During the following week the lord general sent his pressed and recruited soldiers ahead to a rendezvous point near Beaconsfield, probably to be fitted with clothing, and ordered the remnants of his old army to march south from Aylesbury and Saint Albans and join his new regiments. In early May, Parliament ordered Essex and the auxiliary forces of London to march to the rendezvous.[53] Meanwhile, Essex became involved in a political dispute connected with his command. The Upper House opposed the renewal of the ordinance which regulated the Eastern Association. In so doing, the Lords surely hoped to undermine the more or less independent command of Manchester and strike a blow at his ambitious subordinate, Lieutenant General Cromwell. For thirteen days the Upper House held out against renewing the measure.[54] Essex evidently was the principal obstructor in the matter, for only after he left London did the Lords relent and renew the ordinance.

Shortly before entering the campaign Essex lost another political skirmish.[55] On 7 May, Parliament began debating the renewal of the ordinance establishing the Committee of Both Kingdoms. Essex had opposed the original bill, which remained in force through 16 May, for several reasons. He had objected to the proportions of Lords and commoners. He had unsuccessfully opposed the broad powers granted to the committee. He had succeeded in limiting the duration of the committee's existence and no doubt hoped that Parliament would not allow the measure to lapse or modify it to include more peers. "There is another serious difference between the Houses about the confirmation of the Council of State for another three months, as the first three are about to expire," one contemporary wrote. "The Upper House wishes to increase the number, but the Lower strongly objects and would rather reduce them. Various conferences have been held, the Lords persisting in their negative, but they will have to give way in the end, as they always have done, through fear."[56] On 8 May the House of Lords was beseeched by the Commons to renew the ordinance. After a conference and some sharp words between the leaders of the respective

[53] C. S. P. Ven., 1643–1647, p. 100.
[54] Lords Journal, 6: 537–42.
[55] Whitelocke, Memorials (1682 ed.), p. 83.
[56] C. S. P. Ven., 1643–1647, p. 100.

Houses the Lords approved the renewal. Essex's efforts to protect his political flanks failed.

On 13 May he made final arrangements for his departure. He sent his personal baggage and carriages ahead to Beaconsfield.[57] He paid a visit to the Westminster Assembly and importuned the divines to remember him with fasting and prayer. The delegates stopped their deliberations on ecclesiastical reform and devoted the remainder of that day to divine services.[58]

Essex left London for the field the following day.

[57] Codrington, *Life and Death*, p. 28. For details of Essex's marches see Charles E. Long, *Diary of the Marches of the Royal Army during the Great Civil War, kept by Richard Symonds*, Camden Society (London, 1859), pp. 97–98.

[58] Baillie, *Letters*, 2: 184.

CHAPTER 17

The Western Campaign (1644):
Disaster

I

IN THE MORNING hours of 14 May 1644, Lord General Essex and Sir William Waller departed from London to rejoin their armies and commence their respective military operations.[1] Essex headed to Beaconsfield via Windsor; Waller struck southward to Farnham. The two commanders agreed to march their separate forces westward toward Oxford and battle the King at the most advantageous time. Essex was to move up the Thames River valley and approach Oxford from the east while Waller checked the Royalists at Newbury and then approached Oxford from the south. The two armies were to converge upon Oxford and encircle the Royalists before reinforcements and provisions arrived. This well-conceived pincer offensive required complete co-operation between Parliament's commanders for success.

Essex took the field the following day and led his army westward, parallel to the Thames.[2] On 19 May he took Reading without firing a shot. There he consulted with Waller, who had led his army northward toward the Thames from Newbury, and the two commanders planned their next series of moves. One week later the combined armies moved into evacuated Abingdon and occupied the town. To protect the property of the innocent inhabitants and the surrounding area, the lord general promulgated a proclamation against plundering.[3] The next week he attempted to close the ring around the King. He stationed a contingent at Abingdon to guard

---

[1] Clarendon, *History* (1849 ed.), 3: 359; and *Perfect Diurnal* (London) 1644, no. 42, p. 334.

[2] *H. M. C. Thirteenth Report*, 1: 172–78; and Whitelocke, *Memorials* (1682 ed.), p. 84.

[3] Rushworth, *Historical Collections*, 5: 670.

the southern approach to Oxford and sent Waller to Newbridge
to forestall a Royalist withdrawal to the west. Waller seized that
town and the roads leading westward out of Oxford. On 28 May,
Essex led his army across the Thames at Sandford Ferry and marched
northward to Bullington Green, where he displayed his army in
full view of Oxford as though he intended to attack, and then
proceeded along the eastern bank of the Cherwell toward Islip.
His troops came within cannon shot of the Royalists.

Essex made no concerted effort to engage the King in battle,
seeking instead to complete the encirclement operation.[4] By the end
of May the Royalist army, now deployed on the northern edge of
Oxford, was nearly surrounded by Parliament's forces. Essex was
at Islip with the bulk of his army, but he had detachments stationed
along the east banks of the Thames and the Cherwell to prevent a
Royalist breakthrough to the east. Waller, still at Newbridge, had
troops stationed at Eynsham and Woodstock. Essex now strove to
close the gap between Woodstock and Islip by gaining control of
the bridges over the Cherwell at Gosford and Enslow. If all went
well the Royalists would be completely encircled within a few days.

Charles was not intent upon extricating himself and his troops
from Parliament's trap. He convened the Council of War several
times to discuss the military situation. He gave up all ideas of a
direct confrontation with either Essex or Waller. Instead, he waited
for an opportune moment to withdraw from the area. One thing
was certain: he would not surrender. "I may be found in the hands
of the Earl of Essex," he averred, "but I shall be dead first."[5]
The English sovereign did not surrender, as Essex hoped, although
rumors to that effect reached Westminster. From some unrevealed
source the Committee for Both Kingdoms heard that the King
intended to give himself up and negotiate a peace settlement.
"We are credibly informed that his majesty intends to come for
London," the committee warned the lord general by letter. "We
desire you, that you will do your endeavor to inform yourself of the
same; and if you think that his majesty intends at all to come to

[4] Charles noted this near encirclement in his letter of 28 May to Prince Rupert,
which is reprinted in Ellis's *Original Letters*, 2d ser., 3: 316. For more facts about
the attempt to win Oxford see Varley, *The Siege of Oxford* (Oxford: Clarendon
Press, 1932), pp. 126–31.

[5] Gardiner, *Civil War*, 1: 352.

the armies, that you acquaint us with the same; and do nothing therein until the houses shall give direction."[6] If nothing else, this letter betrayed the faulty lines of communication and deep distrust between the committee and the lord general.

The committee's actions on 30 May added confusion to this deteriorating relationship. On that day it received word that the port town of Lyme, which had been besieged by Prince Maurice for many weeks, was desperately in need of succor. The matter was discussed at length and they agreed, in the words of their secretary Thurloe, "to send some *considerable forces* for the releafe of Lyme and acquaint them with the news from the Scottish army of Prince Ruperts march northward."[7] The Committee of Both Kingdoms did not specify what constituted "*considerable forces.*" The ambiguous letter sent to the lord general was open to even broader interpretation: "The Committee are clearly of the opinion that it is necessary to send presently such a strength as may relieve Lyme; which will not only preserve that town, that deserves so well, but be a means to prevent their levies of men and money now raising by a new association in those parts, and *to recover the whole West.*"[8] The committee soon realized that sending this open-ended order to Essex was a mistake.

On 2 June the lord general led his army toward Enslow Bridge, a Royalist-controlled structure located north of Islip across the Cherwell, with the object of crossing over to Woodstock and joining up with Waller, thus completing the cordon around the King.[9] The Royalists, about 2,000 strong, put up stiff resistance and fought valiantly to save the breastworks and the bridge, but they failed to stop Essex's vanguard from securing the bridgehead. Royalist losses were extensive. Essex lost only 40 men. This victory gave Essex a distinct advantage over the King and he now prepared to close the circle.

Charles was in imminent danger of being captured if Essex and Waller tightened their cordon about him. That night he withdrew his army to Oxford. The following morning he feigned an advance toward Abingdon. As the King hoped, Waller then drew back his army, thus opening the net which had been so carefully constructed.

6 Clarendon, *History* (1849 ed.), 3: 363.

7 *Register of C. B. K.* Emphasis added.

8 Gardiner, *Civil War*, 1: 355. Emphasis added.

9 *C. S. P. Dom., 1644*, pp. 181–96.

Late that night, rather than chance a battle or risk capture, the English sovereign fled from his wartime capital and marched his army of 3,000 horse and 2,500 foot along Banbury Road. By the evening of 4 June the Royalist army had progressed past Burford.

That morning Lord General Essex had led his army across the Cherwell and marched toward Woodstock, only to find that the King had eluded him by slipping through the gap created by Waller's withdrawal.[10] To make matters worse, Essex's army encountered a violent storm near Woodstock. Some of the London auxiliaries became so discouraged that they deserted and returned to London. Others turned to plundering. Essex himself appears to have borne his disappointment and pressed on after his prey. On 5 June he marched into Chipping Norton, nearly two days behind the King, then at Evesham. Waller, realizing that he had been duped by Charles's well-executed feint, had recovered his posture and was pursuing the Royalists via Witney and Burford. Not hindered by a heavy artillery train, as was Essex, he made greater progress and marched into Stow-on-the-Wold in the Cotswolds about the time that Essex arrived at Chipping Norton. Though closer to the King than Essex, Waller remained one day's march behind.

At this critical time Essex convened a Council of War to discuss the next move against the enemy.[11] The council, composed of the two generals, the commissioned officers of both armies, and Parliament's advisers, assembled at Chipping Norton on 6 June. Essex directed the council's attention to the multiple needs of the hour: the King must be pursued and forced to fight; the recently received orders from the Committee of Both Kingdoms regarding the relief of Lyme and the recovery of the West would have to be followed; and the Royalists remaining in the Thames valley, especially those about Oxford and Greenland House, must be subdued. The Council of War eventually decided to separate the two armies and have them seek different military objectives. Waller would continue his pursuit of the King and join Col. Edward Massey, who was still in Gloucester, and together they would engage the Royalists in battle. Because Sir William's army was lighter and faster, the

[10] H. G. Tibbutt, *The Letter Books of Sir Samuel Luke* (London: Her Majesty's Stationery Office, 1963), p. 20.

[11] See Sanderson, *A Compleat History*, p. 707; and Sir Edward Walker, *Historical Discourses* (London, 1705), p. 25.

argument went, he was better suited to King-chasing than were the lord general and his army.

Essex's troops would fulfill the Committee of Both Kingdoms's command regarding the relief of Lyme and the recovery of the West. Essex was farther from the King and closer to Lyme. He possessed greater experience in siege and countersiege warfare. He had the heavy guns and carriages of the artillery unit attached to the army. Other factors—most of which have been ignored by historians—also entered into this fateful decision. The Earl of Warwick had pressed upon the committee the need for land forces to assist him in the relief of the besieged port.[12] The possibility of combining with Warwick in an amphibious recovery of the West was most alluring. The chance to perhaps capture the Queen, then at Exeter, and to invade Waller's military sphere made the proposal even more attractive.

Sir William, failing to sway the council or change Essex's mind, reluctantly accepted the majority's decision and commenced his pursuit of the King. "Waller opposed this resolution all he could," Clarendon observed, "and urged some order and determination of the committee of both kingdoms in the point; and, that the west was assigned to him as his province, when the two armies should think fit to sever from each other. However, Essex gave him positive orders, as his general, to march according to the advice of the council of war; which he durst not disobey, but sent grievous complaints to the parliament of the usage he was forced to submit to."[13]

II

His Excellency, upon returning to his quarters at Chipping Norton later that day, informed the Committee of Both Kingdoms of the Council of War's decisions. "The King is now fled rather than gone with an army," he wrote, "having left his many and weighty carriages at Oxford, and is so much made up of lighthorsemen, as an army with carriages must come much behind him. I have therefore applied myself to the relief of Lyme, which, seeing you so recommend it to me, I durst not undertake with less than an army."[14] To the committee members this revelation, which did

12 See *C. S. P. Dom., 1644*, pp. 181–83 and 190 for the Warwick letters.
13 Clarendon, *History* (1849 ed.), 3: 368.
14 Devereux, *Lives and Letters*, 2: 400. The committee did not receive this

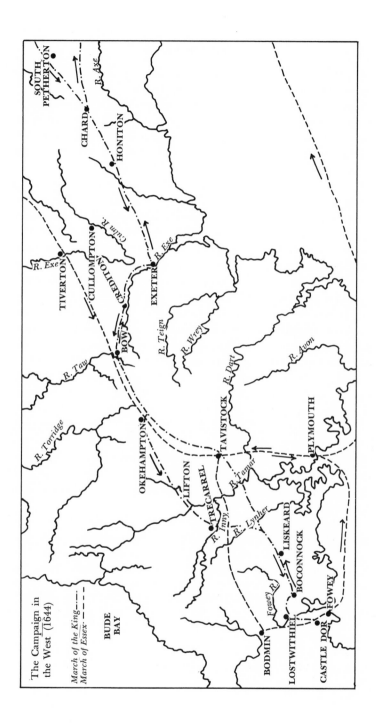

The Campaign in
the West (1644)

March of the King ·—·—·—
March of Essex ·— — — —

BUDE
BAY

SOUTH
PETHERTON

R. Axe

CHARD

HONITON

Culm R.

CULLOMPTON

R. Exe

TIVERTON

CREDITON

R. Exe

EXETER

BOW

R. Teign

R. Wrey

R. Taw

R. Avon

R. Torridge

OKEHAMPTON

TAVISTOCK

R. Dart

LIFTON

R. Tamar

TRECARREL

PLYMOUTH

R. Inny

R. Lynher

LISKEARD

BOCONNOCK

Fowey R.

BODMIN

LOSTWITHIEL

CASTLE DOR

FOWEY

not even mention Sir William Waller by name, was disconcerting indeed. They did not intend for Essex to march his whole army to Lyme. They did not anticipate a separation of Parliament's forces or a major shift in strategy. They did not expect their ambiguous messages regarding Lyme to produce a diversion of this magnitude. The committee registered its opposition to the decision of the Council of War and supported Waller.

Essex's decision to relieve Lyme with his entire army also precipitated a bitter triangular dispute between the Lords, the Commons, and the Committee of Both Kingdoms. The committee, taking the advice of the Lower House and ignoring the Upper House, directed that Essex dispatch only a contingent to Lyme and immediately return to the Oxford area with the bulk of his army.[15] To this order the Lords took exception; on 13 June they requested that the committee inform them of the original instructions which the lord general had received. The committee refused to honor this request, on grounds that it represented the wishes of only one House. The lord general's supporters in the Upper House, treated rather contemptuously, were helpless.

This resolution to reverse the decision of the Council of War was initiated by the lord general's enemies on Waller's behalf. According to Denzil Holles, a majority in the Commons wanted to sacrifice Essex's army in the Cotswolds to the King. "This, they knew," Holles contended, "would absolutely break my Lord of Essex who must harass his Army to follow a light moving body." [16] Sir Arthur Haselrig, who was singled out by Holles as the principal perpetrator of these moves, was reputed to have said that he would "ruin" the Lord General "or be ruined himself."

The central figure in this controversy, meantime, advanced toward Lyme. Essex left Chipping Norton soon after the Council

---

communication for several days. "We have sent this special messenger to you," the committee informed Essex, "by whom we desire to be informed of the condition of your affairs and what your designs for the present are, as also your opinion of the designs of the enemies. We are very much in the dark by want of intelligence, and therefore desire to have daily advertisements from you. You may rely on the discretion and fidelity of this messenger."

15 See the *Register of C. B. K.*; *Commons Journal*, 3: 528; and *Lords Journal*, 6: 588.

16 Denzil Holles, *Memoirs*, reprinted in *Maseres Select Tracts*, 2 vols. (London, 1815), 1: 203.

of War broke up, without waiting for further orders from the Committee of Both Kingdoms, and followed a direct route southward through Faringdon, Marlborough, Amesbury, and Salisbury to Cranborn, and then cut westward toward the besieged town. The march was fast and uneventful. On 10 June he stopped at Totenham, his brother-in-law's house near Amesbury, and enjoyed the hospitality of his sister. That evening he quartered at Cranborn, where he first received word of the committee's disapproval of the revised strategy. His reply contained a rationalization of his decision and an explanation of his recent moves. "I conceived that you were not displeased with my march, because you were silent for eight days together," he later explained, "and your silence seemed to me no less than an approbation; but now I am marched as far as Blandford in Dorsetshire, you direct me to make a stand, and send away a considerable party of horse for the relief of Lyme. Give me liberty to believe you are uninformed of late, or else I had not received such an unexpected countermand, after my unwearied endeavors in the pursuance of such instructions as I received from your own hands."[17] Instead of halting his march and returning to Oxfordshire, as the Committee of Both Kingdoms desired, Essex followed his earlier instructions and, bolstered by the actions of his peers, pressed toward Lyme.

During the night of 13 June, while quartered at Blandford, the Earl of Essex received further strictures regarding his march. The next morning he composed a detailed justification of the Council of War's decision and of his subsequent course of action and forwarded it to the Committee of Both Kingdoms. He concluded with a plea for support of his strategy. "If you encourage me to advance farther into the West," he wrote, "I hope in a reasonable time to relieve Lyme and distress Weymouth; but if you call back Sir Wm. Waller from pursuing the King, and stop me in my march to the West, we are like to lose the benefit of both armies this summer; because we are put upon cross services, which lie far out of our way, and are denied the benefit of those fair opportunities which God hath put into our hands. Consider what I have said, and if, by following your advice, the West be not reduced, Hopton's army be recruited, and Lyme lost, let not the blame be laid upon

[17] Devereux, *Lives and Letters*, 2: 406–7.

your Lordship's innocent, though suspected servant." [18] Whether the committee would back down upon the receipt of this bold reply was uncertain.

The committee's criticisms did not deter Essex. [19] The people of Lyme were in great difficulty. The 3,000 citizens of the port and the garrison of several hundred had withstood the siege of Prince Maurice for over six weeks. They had valiantly resisted several assaults by Maurice's army of 6,000 soldiers; they had refused to surrender despite several bombardments and severe shortages of food. During the first weeks of the heroic stand, the Earl of Warwick had been able to replenish the supplies of the besieged, but when the lord admiral was compelled to divert his ships to other projects, the plight of the defenders worsened daily. By the second week of June sickness had broken out among the populace and only a few days' supplies remained.

The arrival of Essex in Dorsetshire, however, changed the whole military picture. [20] Maurice did not relish a battlefield engagement with Parliament's army. Upon learning that Essex was in Dorchester, the Prince raised the siege and drew back to Exeter, where he offered protection to the Queen. The citizens of Lyme were jubilant, of course, and many gentlemen from the area came to Dorchester to pay their respects to the lord general and encourage him to press still farther westward along the coast toward Plymouth, which was threatened by a siege. "Although I have just grounds to conceive that what benefit soever is received by me or this army would be but little valued," he wrote his superiors in Westminster, "yet nothing shall make me neglect my duty, which makes me acquaint your Lordships that the town of Lyme, which shewed great constancy and valor in maintaining obedience to the Parliament, is now relieved." [21] Henceforth similar statements reflecting futility appeared in Essex's correspondence with the Committee of Both Kingdoms. Essex also felt compelled to justify his strategy against that of his rivals. "Your Lordships by this time know," he concluded the above letter, "that from whence

18 *Ibid.*, pp. 403–5.

19 *C. S. P. Dom., 1644*, p. 309.

20 Warburton, *Rupert*, 2: 423–30. For the adverse reaction of the local landowners to Essex's appearance in the southwest see the letters of Sir Richard Sydenham to the Earl of Bath in the Sackville MSS, Kent Archives Office.

21 Devereux, *Lives and Letters*, 2: 408.

Sir. Wm. Waller is, that notwithstanding your directions to him, both Lyme would have been lost and an army raised before he would have come for the relief of the one or the prevention of the other. And, for my sending a party of horse for the relief of Lyme, whosoever gave your Lordships that information were in great error, it being an impossible thing to have done." [22]

III

MEANWHILE, the Earl of Essex solicited support from the people of Dorset and seized several Royalist-controlled towns near Lyme. Sir William Balfour, now reattached to Essex, summoned Weymouth, the seaport from which the Royalists had secured valuable supplies from France. [23] Essex's own regiment forced Melcombe Regis and Sarfoote Castle to surrender, thus cutting off Portland. Having achieved these objectives with a minimum of bloodshed, the lord general resolved to advance along the coast. Before doing so, however, he and Warwick convened a Council of War to discuss the feasibility of an amphibious operation and to solve logistical problems. [24] Any doubts that Essex may have had about the advisability of such an operation were soon dispelled by the Earl of Warwick, Hugh Peters, and Lord Robartes, all of whom favored it.

This Council of War produced a bold and imaginative strategy. Essex would move, parallel to the seacoast, through Dorset, Devonshire, and Cornwall and summon the Royalist towns to surrender to Parliament. Local citizens would flock to his colors and his troops would be fed by well-wishers along the way. Warwick would sail his ships parallel to the coast, drive out enemy vessels, and keep Essex's army supplied with ammunition and provisions. The reduction of the West, the Council of War hoped, would cut off the King's supplies of money, man power, and ammunition. Moreover, the seizure of the Queen would also serve the interests of Parliament.

[22] *Ibid.*

[23] Whitelocke, *Memorials* (1682 ed.), p. 87; and Codrington, *Life and Death*, p. 30. That Essex captured a large amount of Royalist provisions at Weymouth is evident from *C. S. P. Dom., 1644*, p. 261.

[24] See J. R. Powell, *The Navy in the English Civil War* (London: Bailey Brothers, 1962), p. 72; and Whitelocke, *Memorials* (1682 ed.), p. 92. For Warwick's appraisal of the council see *C. S. P. Dom., 1644*, p. 251.

Without waiting for further instructions, the lord general proceeded to put the revised strategy into effect, although he did write the Committee of Both Kingdoms of his plans and sent Peters to Parliament with an account of the relief of Lyme.[25] He pressed farther toward Devonshire in pursuit of the Royalists. From the town of Bridport he importuned Parliament for both money and supplies. "I desire the Month's pay which we have so long expected," Essex wrote on 24 June, "that the Ammunition and Shoes which were heretofore promised to the Soldiers, may be speedily sent; otherwise the Service which I am desirous to do for the Kingdom and Parliament will suffer a great measure."[26] That same day he requested the deputy lieutenant of Essex to recruit and forward him 60 able horse as soon as possible. Essex did not know it at the time, but two days earlier Parliament had passed an ordinance granting the armies of Essex and Waller ten thousand pounds each for the payment of arrears.

The fortunes of Sir William Waller, in the meantime, worsened. He had pursued the Royalists through the Cotswolds and into the Severn Basin with little success.[27] He had captured Sudely Castle and gained some support from Massey, as had been planned, but his efforts to engage the King under favorable circumstances had been fruitless. After three weeks of cat-and-mouse maneuvers, Charles decided to put Waller to the test. The date was 29 June, the place Cropedy Bridge near Banbury. The results were disastrous for Sir William. His army, hungry and tired, put up a poor fight and retreated before the charge of the Earl of Cleveland. Shaken by defeat, many of the soldiers in the city brigade began to mutiny and shout to go home. A few days later Waller complained to Parliament that his army was falling apart. Waller himself soon returned to the City to obtain more money and recruit more troops. Blaming his defeat upon the lord general, of course, Waller claimed that he had been sacrificed to the King and vowed to avenge himself.

Upon leaving Bridport, Essex advanced in a zigzag pattern that took him through Chard, Axminster, Honiton, and Colhampton to Tiverton, where he quartered on 3 July. "The Earl of Warwick with his fleet sailed along the Coast as the Lord General marched,"

[25] C. S. P. Dom., 1644, p. 262.
[26] Lords Journal, 6: 607.
[27] Clarendon, History (1849 ed.), 3: 414.

reported Whitelocke, "and carried his Ammunition, and sent ships to keep the Enemy, and some to assist the Parliament Forces who besieged Guernsey Castle." [28] Their immediate objectives were to prevent the Queen and her retinue from fleeing to France and to cut off Prince Maurice's retreat. To this end the lord general bypassed some Royalist strongholds and left pockets of resistance to his rear. Sometimes he delegated subordinates to remain behind and reduce the avoided town or garrison. In late June he appointed Col. William Sydenham to remain at Weymouth and at Melcombe Regis as governor.[29] In the following weeks he ordered Sydenham to fortify the garrisons, recruit soldiers from the surrounding area, secure horses for the army, and forward captured provisions to the advancing regiments.

As Essex's army moved farther from its source of supply the soldiers began to live off the land. Both town and country dwellers were compelled to billet and feed them.[30] Captured Royalists were often forced to surrender their money and relinquish their horse to the advancing troops. The Civil War became increasingly uncivil and vindictive. When the Parliamentary troops executed seven Irish soldiers in Dorchester, the Royalists retaliated by hanging twelve Roundhead prisoners. When Essex executed a captured officer who had violated the *Lawes and Ordinances* and deserted, Prince Maurice responded by hanging a pro-Parliament sea captain, who had been captured near Lyme.

His Excellency's arrival in Devonshire caused much consternation in the Royalist camp. His army was reputed to be twice as large as that of Prince Maurice, who withdrew from Exeter and retreated northward toward Barnstaple. This Royalist withdrawal left the Queen and her household with little or no protection. "Upon the General's advance towards Exeter, the Queen sent a Trumpeter to desire him to forbear any Acts of hostility against the Town, for that she was weak and ill, being lately brought to bed there," Whitelocke wrote.[31] The Queen requested of Essex a safe-conduct which would permit her to travel to Bath for medical

[28] Whitelocke, *Memorials* (1682 ed.), p. 88. Also see *Perfect Diurnal*, 1644, no. 48, p. 379.

[29] See Essex's letters to Sydenham, British Museum, Egerton MSS, 2,126.

[30] See Green, *Calendar for Compounding*, 2: 873, 1123, 1173, and 1385 and 3: 1980, 2048.

[31] Whitelocke, *Memorials* (1682 ed.), p. 88.

attention and recuperation. The lord general, who had a very low opinion of the Queen, rejected her supplication and then, in a facetious vein, offered instead to personally conduct her to London, where she would obtain the best medical advice in England. Henrietta Maria declined her archenemy's obliging offer and chose instead the risk of flight. She soon departed from Exeter, leaving her newborn child in the hands of a governess, and headed westward toward Falmouth. Two weeks later she landed in France.

Rather than pursue the Queen westward, Essex remained in Devonshire to "raise the country" and fill the empty ranks of his army. He set up headquarters at Tiverton, a centrally located town, and billeted his troops in the surrounding hamlets. There he remained for several weeks, trying to secure money to pay the soldiers and recruiting among the local populace. He sent several requests to subordinates for reinforcements and provisions.[32]

The feeble response to the lord general's appeals must have been disheartening. "But the Westerne men come not in so fast to the Earle of Essex, as the Welchmen to Colonel Gerrard," gibed the editor of the Oxford-printed Royalist newspaper, *Mercurius Aulicus*, "for his Lordship tasted all the Western counties, findes his journey not to answer expectation."[33] Essex, fully aware of the mild response to his call to arms, explained the situation to the Committee of Both Kingdoms: "Although the counties of Somerset and Devon shew great affection for the Parliament, and to be rid of the Egyptian slavery, yet there are two things great hindrances to the aid we have of the country. The first is their desire to serve under their own countrymen, and not to be listed in my army, and those few country gentlemen that are wanting arms to arm them; so that although there be multitudes of bodies of men appear, yet little use can be made of them for the present, till arms and the gentlemen who have the power over them become down. The second is, the garrisons for the enemy keep the country greatly in awe."[34] Thus did Essex apologize for his self-imposed predicament.

The lord general's superiors in Westminster, to whom the above apology was addressed, lent only token support to the war in the western counties. The members of the Upper House stood by their

---

[32] See British Museum, Additional MSS, 29,137, fol. 7 for these unpublished letters.

[33] *Mercurius Aulicus*, 11 July 1644, p. 1081.

[34] Devereux, *Lives and Letters*, 2: 416.

peer, but majorities in the Lower House and the Committee of Both Kingdoms took a dim view of the lord general's expedition, especially after Waller's defeat at Cropedy Bridge and Cromwell's victory at Marston Moor in Yorkshire. The House of Commons, while giving reluctant approval to the formation of a Western Association, threw its weight behind the army of the Eastern Association under Manchester's leadership and demonstrated a willingness to expend money for the new army which Sir William Waller was recruiting in London.

IV

THE ENGLISH SOVEREIGN, having rid himself of Waller, was directing his attention toward Essex's army in the West.[35] On 7 July a Royalist Council of War convened at Evesham recommended that the King march to the West and save the Queen, who was then still in Cornwall, and crush Essex before his reinforcements arrived. Charles, realizing the golden opportunity at hand, soon advanced southwestward. It took the King nearly three weeks to reach Exeter. He wasted several precious days in Evesham before leaving on 12 July and traveled by carriage in almost leisurely style. He was joined at Bristol by Hopton's army. Although the Queen had embarked from Falmouth by the time he reached Somerset, Charles pressed ahead with his plan, hoping to entrap Essex in the West Country. Throughout the march he attempted to arouse the people and enlist them in his army, but the results were disappointing.

When, on 17 July, Essex learned that the Royalists were approaching with a large army, he was confronted with an *embarras du choix*. To his west lay Plymouth, needful of assistance, but beyond Plymouth were the hostile Cornish, the rocky-ridged landscape of Cornwall with limited supplies of food and forage, and the ever-narrowing coastlines which came to a point at Land's End. To his east, separating him from London and reinforcements by land, was the advancing army of the King, with forces twice as large as his own. To remain stationary was foolhardy. To escape was cowardly. To advance farther westward involved heavy risks and the

---

[35] For these Royalist moves see Gardiner, *Civil War*, 3: 7–24; Whitelocke, *Memorials* (1682 ed.), pp. 87–93; and Walker, *Historical Discourses*, especially pp. 45–63.

likelihood of an engagement on hostile soil. To win a battlefield victory against the combined armies of the Royalists, the lord general needed the assistance of another Parliamentary army— either Waller's or Manchester's—and until that additional force arrived he had to remain close to the sea and the Earl of Warwick.

The Council of War which Essex convened soon after learning of the King's advance debated at length the above alternatives and appraised their possible consequences. Upon reaching no unanimous agreement after deliberating most of the night, the council met the following day and finally reached a decision, which Essex immediately communicated to the Committee of Both Kingdoms. "It seemed a business of so great consequence," he wrote, "that we staid here this day to take it into consideration, and for further intelligence; but having little more of the last to ground upon, we have taken resolution to continue our former purposes, having had several messages from Plymouth of the great distress they are likely to be in if not suddenly relieved, being in great want of money to pay their soldiers and forage for their horses, which are kept in by the enemy from going abroad; hoping that Sir Wm. Waller with his army and additional forces will take care of the King's army." [36] If Essex expected Waller to check the King's army, he expected in vain.

During the following weeks Essex and Parliament grew more estranged than ever before. In mid-July the House of Commons angrily recalled Sir Philip Stapleton and Sir John Meyrick, both of whom had been appointed by the Lower House to advise and oversee the lord general, to render an account of themselves, the state of the army, and the over-all conduct of the campaign in the West. That an inquiry and political attack upon Essex would follow seemed certain. According to a statement in *Mercurius Aulicus*, some members were contemplating the impeachment of their colleagues, both of whom were very pro-Essex. [37] Both members were slow to respond to the demands of their adversaries in the Lower House.

The Committee of Both Kingdoms, though dominated by commoners, was less vindictive in its treatment of the lord general. As soon as it learned on 16 July of the King's decision at Evesham to march westward after Essex, the committee sent a messenger

36 Devereux, *Lives and Letters*, 2: 420.
37 *Mercurius Aulicus*, 16 July 1644, pp. 1,088–89.

to warn the lord general. At the same time, realizing Essex's need for military assistance, they instructed Waller to follow the King and send reinforcements to Dorchester.[38] Upon the receipt of this order, Waller went through the motions of preparing to march and sent a letter to the Lower House stating his intention to advance toward Charles, but he did not move immediately. After Waller's communication, which was probably a ruse to deceive Essexians, was received and read in the Commons, a majority in that House overruled the Committee of Both Kingdoms and ordered Waller to ignore the committee's earlier order and remain where he was. This politically inspired reversal, no doubt the work of Essex's enemies, was to have fateful consequences for Parliament's army in the West. Holles considered it an undisguised move to sacrifice the lord general to the Royalists.

Lord General Essex had left Tiverton on 18 July.[39] He hastened toward Crediton in hopes of surprising Prince Maurice, who had been quartered there; but the elusive Prince, skillfully avoiding an engagement until his uncle arrived in the area, managed to frustrate his adversary's designs by swiftly marching his army northward toward the Bristol Channel coast. Instead of dropping south to Exeter and advancing along the southern route to Plymouth, the lord general skirted along the north side of Dartmoor toward Tavistock. As he approached the last-named town he encountered Sir Richard Grenville's army, which numbered upwards of 2,000 men, and engaged them in several skirmishes in the vicinity.[40] One of Essex's regiments took possession of Mount Stamford and captured several pieces of ordnance. Another stormed Grenville's house in Tavistock and forced its defenders, who begged for a parley, to surrender. Reports indicated that the English were taken prisoners, but the Irish slain on the spot. From Grenville's magazine Essex secured two cannon, a large quantity of provisions, and money and plate valued at three thousand pounds. His vanguard secured the strategic bridgehead of Newbridge leading across the

[38] For at least a week before this decision the committee debated the disposition of Waller's army. See *Register of C. B. K.;* and Devereux, *Lives and Letters*, 2: 425. The orders commanded Waller to march west with two thousand horse and dragoons.

[39] Richard Symonds, *Diary of the marches of the royal army during the civil war*, ed. C. E. Long, Camden Society (London, 1859), pp. 39–42.

[40] See *The True Informer*, no. 41; and Whitelocke, *Memorials* (1682 ed.), pp. 93–95.

Tamar and forced Sir Richard Grenville to abandon his siege of Plymouth.

Essex then committed the most fatal mistake in his military career. On 27 July he crossed over the Tamar into Cornwall at Newbridge in pursuit of Sir Richard. Perhaps he hoped to engage Grenville's troops before they combined with the King's; perhaps he hoped to secure the all-important mines and cut off the King's supply of tin; perhaps he hoped to enlist the "Western men" he had been assured would respond to his call to arms; or perhaps he merely wished to "clear that country," as he claimed in his letter written from Tavistock. Whatever the precipitant motive, the advance was ill-advised, for it drew him away from Devonshire, which was pro-Parliament and blessed with provisions, into a hostile peninsular land which was strongly committed to the King and noted for its poverty. In terms of logistics as well as military strategy and tactics, it was a fatal blunder: this fact was soon manifest to both friend and foe alike. "The Earl of Essex marched with his army into Cornwall," Ludlow later commented, "yet to what publick end I could never understand, for the enemy there had already dispersed themselves. Some said he was perswaded to march thither by the Lord Robartes, to give him an opportunity to collect rents in those parts."[41]

Once in Cornwall the Parliamentary troops pursued Grenville and proceeded to "clear that country."[42] One contingent secured the bridge at Launceston and forced Grenville to retreat. The bulk of the army, however, pressed to Bodmin, which the lord general made his headquarters. At this town, noted for its weekly market (the largest in Cornwall) and semiannual fairs, he hoped to secure both enough provisions for his hungry soldiers and more recruits for his dwindling regiments. Moreover, he could easily move either northward along the Padstow estuary or southward along the Foy, thus enabling him to keep in touch with Warwick's fleet. There on 2 August the lord general learned that the King, fast on his heels, had already reached Liskeard, only twenty miles away. That same day, quite alarmed at the worsening situation, Essex issued marching orders and moved south to Lostwithiel.

From this market town Essex was enabled to retain his lines of communication with Warwick and access to the sea. The towns-

41 Ludlow, *Memoirs*, 1: 100.
42 See Whitelocke, *Memorials* (1682 ed.), pp. 95–101.

people, incensed with Essex's occupation, withheld their provisions and frequently harassed the soldiers. In his next letter to the Committee of Both Kingdoms the lord general, now pessimistic in tone, recounted these and other hardships confronting him at Lostwithiel. He wrote of the convergence of the three Royalist armies, of the opposition from the Cornish people, of the lack of victuals, and of the possibility of defeat if reinforcements were not soon forthcoming. Essex seems to have sensed by then, if not before, that Parliament had let him down. "There is some flying report in the country that Sir Wm. Waller should be advancing into these parts," he noted in conclusion, "but understanding by your last letters of the 17th of last month, that your Lordships had appointed him to send only a party, and that to advance no further than Dorchester, makes us that we can trust in nothing at present but God's blessing, the courage of our officers and our faithfulness to the cause." [43] Essex had been bested by his political enemies, and he knew it.

V

A few days later Charles initiated another peace overture.[44] He had Essex at a distinct military disadvantage. The sovereign's army lay to the east of Lostwithiel. Grenville's force checked Essex on the north and west. From prisoners captured at Lord Mohun's manor he probably learned that Essex was short of bread and other supplies. The English ruler no doubt hoped to avoid further bloodshed by forcing his weakened antagonist to defect or negotiate. The delegation making the overture consisted of William Seymour, Lord Beauchamp (Essex's young nephew); Richard Harding; Lord Wilmot; and several others. Beauchamp was commissioned to present to his uncle a personal communication from the King. Harding, a relatively unknown member of Charles's household, was to secure a free and private conference with Essex and then discuss peace. He was to assure Essex of the King's intentions for the public good and then persuade Essex to unite his army with the King's in a common war against the Scots.

Essex received his nephew "very kindly," Clarendon relates, and read the King's letter immediately. However, when asked by

43 Devereux, *Lives and Letters*, 2: 425.

44 See *H. M. C. House of Lords Manuscripts*, 6: 21; and Walker, *Historical Discourses*, pp. 55–58.

Beauchamp to receive Harding, who "had many good things to offer," Essex would proceed no further.[45] "The earl answered in short, that he would not permit Mr. Harding to come to him," Clarendon continued in his book, "nor would he have any treaty with the king, having received no warrant for it from the parliament upon which . . . Mr. Harding was to have urged, of the king's desire of peace, of the concurrence of all the lords, as well as those at Oxford as in the army, in the same desire of preserving the kingdom from a conquest by the Scots; and other discourse to that purpose; and of the king's readiness to give him security for the performance of all he had promised. To all which the earl answered sullenly, that, according to the commission he had received, he would defend the King's person and posterity, and that the best counsel he could give him was to get to his parliament." The lord general, faithful to the cause even when near defeat, refused to deal separately with the Royalists.

Essex also received a similar appeal from the principal officers in the Royalist army.[46] The document, signed by eighty-six field officers, was accompanied by a covering letter of explanation, written by Prince Maurice and the Earl of Brentford. They likewise alluded to the Scottish threat and reiterated the compelling need for negotiations to end the "unnatural war" between Englishmen. They suggested that the lord general and six of his officers meet with their general and an equal number of Royalist officers to work out some grounds for a truce. Essex, as adamant as ever, curtly rejected the proposal. "In the beginning of your letter," he wrote on 10 August, "you express by what authority you send it. I, having no power from Parliament, who employed me, to treat, cannot give way to it without breach of trust."[47] Had the lord general been less dedicated to Parliament and less candid in his dealing with the enemy he might well have changed the course of events and turned the tables on his detractors in Westminster.

News of these Royalist peace gestures caused grave concern in the City. Essex's political enemies were afraid that he might treat with the King. His friends, fearful of defeat, sought ways to render

[45] Clarendon, *History* (1849 ed.), 3: 407.

[46] Main Papers, House of Lords Record Office, under the date 9 August 1644. This request was read before the Upper House and incorporated into the official record a week later.

[47] Walker, *Historical Discourses*, p. 57.

assistance, but their efforts met with little success. Waller's army was unprepared. Browne's troops near Oxford were mutinous. The Earl of Manchester, who was instructed to march west in late July, disregarded the Committee of Both Kingdoms's order because he was preoccupied near Peterborough and Huntingdon. Finally, during the first week of August, the Commons commanded Waller's subordinate Lieutenant General Middleton to march his army of 2,000 horse and dragoons westward to divert the Royalists from Essex. They also ordered the sum of twenty thousand pounds for arrears and provisions to be forwarded to Plymouth. Acting upon a suggestion of the Westminster Assembly of Divines, they set aside a day of "publick humiliation, to implore the assistance of God, for the prosperous undertaking of the Lord General."[48] Most of these emergency measures came to nought. To Denzil Holles they were blatantly hypocritical moves to cover up the real intention of the majority in the House of Commons to ruin Essex.[49]

Meanwhile, the Royalists closed their net about the Parliamentary army. On 11 August, Grenville moved into Bodmin with more than 2,000 soldiers. The following day he seized Respryn Bridge, over the Fowey River, located a few miles north of Lostwithiel, and Lord Robartes's manor house, situated between Bodmin and Lostwithiel at Landydrock.[50] Three days later Sir Jacob Astley and Lord Goring gained control of the east bank of the Fowey down to the seacoast. They moved into Saint Viepe, stationed a detachment and cannon at Polruan, and occupied Lord Mohun's residence near Bodinnick Ferry. By mid-August Essex was encircled.

The lord general became more distressed with each passing day. He vainly hoped that somehow Parliamentary forces from the east would divert the Royalists and break their ring about him. Middleton's force, which penetrated into Somersetshire, was repulsed by Sir Francis Doddington on 14 August. Two days later the lord general, still holed up in Lostwithiel, again beseeched the Committee of Both Kingdoms to send reinforcements and bemoaned his plight. "If any forces had followed the King, as we expected when we came into these parts," he wrote with keen hindsight, "by human reason this war would have had a quick

---

48 Baillie, *Letters*, 2: 220; and Rushworth, *Historical Collections*, 5: 697.
49 Holles, *Memoirs*, p. 204.
50 Symonds, *Diary*, p. 54.

end, but since we are left to the providence of God I cannot despair
His Mercy, having found so much of it in our greatest straits."[51]
Surely Essex sensed the disaster that would soon overtake him in
Cornwall.

At sea, the Earl of Warwick strove in several ways to assist his
cousin. He continued to guard the Cornish coast in the event that
Essex decided to escape by sea. In a sudden raid on Fowey he
captured five Royalist ships and attempted to land provisions for
Essex's army. He appealed to the authorities at Plymouth for
money, victuals, and reinforcements to relieve Essex. "If Essex were
defeated," he warned, "Plymouth would be in great danger."[52]
The people of Plymouth, who had only 800 men to hold a line
four miles long, could spare no soldiers. They had little money.
They refused to send food which they might later need to survive
another Royalist siege.

In Westminster the Lords sought to assist their compeer. On
19 August they passed an ordinance associating the western counties. That same day they ordered Sir William Waller to march
west with his dragoons. Later they passed a resolution granting Sir
William ten thousand pounds from the excise tax so that he could
pay his soldiers and hasten his travels. These measures did not pass
the Commons, however. The Lower House went along with a day
of "solemn fast for Essex's army," and with a measure naming
Waller commander "under Essex" of all the horse in the kingdom.[53]
They even agreed to write Essex a letter of thanks and assurance,
but only after it was too late did they command Manchester to
advance and assist him.

On 21 August the King launched a concerted attack against his
adversary.[54] At seven o'clock in the morning, despite inclement
weather, the Royalists drew into battle formation and launched a
well-planned advance upon Lostwithiel along a four-mile front.
From the north Grenville stormed Restormal Castle, then occupied
by Col. John Were's regiment, and compelled Parliament's troops
to retreat. The combined force of Prince Maurice and the Earl of

---

[51] Devereux, *Lives and Letters*, 2: 431–32.

[52] Powell, *Navy*, pp. 74–75; and *C. S. P. Dom., 1644*, p. 436.

[53] *Lords Journal*, 6: 675–91.

[54] Whitelocke, *Memorials* (1682 ed.), p. 96. For a good secondary treatment see
Burne and Young, *Civil War*, pp. 172–75.

Brentford, meanwhile, took possession of the several hills surrounding Lostwithiel, including Beacon's Hill, and gained control of the road which led to Liskeard.

Essex, taken somewhat by surprise, offered little resistance. In the afternoon he sent forth some detachments to contain Grenville's advance, but he refused to allow his vastly outnumbered army to be drawn into an open battle. That night he remained on the field while the Royalists labored to raise a redoubt on Beacon's Hill. For two tense days sporadic fighting took place. Essex explained his desperate plight to the Committee of Both Kingdoms. "The time I have now will not permit me to write long lines," he related on 23 August, "but because I know not what reports may be made, I have thought fit to despatch the messenger to your Lordships with this only . . . If there not come forces, this army will be in much hazard, for besides the powerful enemy we have to deal withal, we are to keep Fowey and the passage of the river. The ways in this country being so strait, and no turnings for an army, that they who are first in them must either beat the other and make their way through or be starved." [55]

With no relief in sight the lord general resorted to the alternative of flight, hoping to save as many troops as possible.[56] The foot were to draw back to Fowey and then embark in Warwick's ships, while the horse, under Balfour's direction, were to break out of the cordon and rush full speed for the Devonshire border. The plan went forward as scheduled. In the pre-dawn hours of 31 August, Sir William Balfour skillfully led the Parliamentary cavalry, numbering about 2,000, through the enemy lines and down the road to Liskeard. Although chased by some Cavaliers as far as Saltash, Balfour managed to subdue his few pursuers and transport his troops across the Tamar into Devonshire. He arrived in Plymouth with losses of about 100 troopers. Essex's foot, meanwhile, carried out their withdrawal plans. Major General Skippon, in command of the rear guard, covered the retreat from a hill located south of Lostwithiel.[57] The bulk of the army marched down a narrow lane toward Fowey. Because of heavy rain several demi-culverins bogged down in ruts and were eventually abandoned.

[55] Devereux, *Lives and Letters*, 2: 433–34.
[56] Burne and Young, *Civil War*, pp. 176–79; and Gardiner, *Civil War*, 2: 15–19.
[57] Devereux, *Lives and Letters*, 2: 436.

The foot soldiers were so tired, Essex reported, that they could barely keep to their colors. They marched as far as Castle Dore, an ancient fortress, where they encamped for the night.

The Earl of Essex then decided to leave his troops and seek his own safety. His dwindling army, now without its cavalry and short on artillery, could not hope to turn the tide or even hold their present position. Morale was down. Even harder to cope with was the fact that Warwick's ships, which were to have transported the soldiers to safety, had not arrived; the contrary winds prevented a landing on the Fowey Peninsula, thus thwarting Essex's plans for salvaging his foot regiments.[58] Essex had his fill of Cornwall. He advised Skippon, a well-seasoned commander who wanted to continue fighting, to fall back to Menabilly and then surrender on the best terms he could obtain. Early the next morning Lord General Essex boarded a small fishing boat and sailed to Plymouth. He was accompanied by Sir John Meyrick and Lord Robartes, the author of the western design. "I thought it fit to look to myself," he later wrote, "it being a greater terror to me to be a slave to their contempts than a thousand deaths."[59]

VI

SKIPPON, now in charge of Essex's army, called a Council of War and proposed that the remaining foot, still totalling about 6,000, make a break for freedom as the cavalry had done, but he was overruled by a majority of the officers.[60] Instead, the Council of War ordered Skippon to request a parley and arrange for a surrender. The terms that Skippon secured for Parliament were remarkably lenient.[61] The Royalists, who sorely needed ordnance, demanded all arms, ammunition, and cannon. Not wishing to be burdened with hungry and poorly clad prisoners, the King permitted Skippon to lead his army eastward with the understanding that they would not fight against the King's troops until after they reached Southampton; Charles even offered them his protection in

[58] Symonds, *Diary*, pp. 62–63.
[59] Rushworth, *Historical Collections*, 5: 703.
[60] Whitelocke, *Memorials* (1682 ed.), pp. 97–99.
[61] See British Museum, Egerton MSS, 2,126, fol. 140, for the original document. See Additional MSS, 28,093, fol. 142 for a copy.

Cornwall and promised to supply them with a guard through the counties of Devonshire and Dorsetshire.

The next day, 2 September, the Parliamentary troops laid down their arms—over five thousand muskets and pistols, hundreds of swords, forty-two guns, and several carriages and wagons loaded with powder and match—and passed through the enemy lines. Jeered and harassed by the local townspeople, who held many grudges against the soldiers, the remnants of Essex's army proceeded east under Skippon's guidance and, with the protection of a guard through the western counties, eventually arrived in Portsmouth.

The Earl of Essex arrived safely in Plymouth on 2 September. Here, after rejoining Sir William Balfour, he learned that most of the horse, including his own life guard, had escaped their pursuers after breaking through the Royalist lines and were safe at the port. From here, soon after disembarking, he wrote Sir Philip Skippon, rationalizing his flight from Cornwall. "Sir, if you live," he promised, "I shall take as great care of you as of my father, if alive; if God otherwise dispose of you, as long as I have a drop of blood, I shall strive to revenge yours on the causers of it. The horse are come safe; nothing but fear of slavery and to be triumphed on, should have made us gone." [62]

The lord general did not send a full account of the disaster to the Committee of Both Kingdoms, which he now thoroughly distrusted, although he did lament their lack of concern and support. Instead he gave Sir Philip Stapleton, his trusted confidant and subordinate who was going to London, a full account of the defeat, written in Plymouth on 3 September. "It is the greatest blow that ever befell our Party," he concluded. "I desire nothing more than to come to the Tryal, such Losses as these must not be smothered up. I shall take the best care for the present security of this Town, I intend to lend them Money, and if the Parliament will provide Arms for their Relief, and Ships to transport them to Portsmouth . . . I intend to stay at Portsmouth until I know the Parliament's pleasure, whither I shall presently come up to give an Account, or tarry there 'till the Foot come up." [63]

The ill tidings of Essex's defeat produced diverse reactions in

[62] Devereux, *Lives and Letters*, 2: 436.
[63] Rushworth, *Historical Collections*, 5: 703–5.

the City. The Presbyterian divines in the Westminster Assembly, who had been critical of the Independents throughout August, now redoubled their denunciations.[64] The catastrophe was divine punishment for the self-interested activities of radicals like John Goodwin, John Milton, and Roger Williams. How else could their fasting and unanswered prayers for Essex and his army be explained? Baillie blamed the political Independents in the House of Commons. To counteract the derogatory reports of Essex's detractors, the author of *An Apologie and Vindication from all false and Malignant Aspersions for His Excellencie* likewise defended him.[65] Essex was a frequenter of Parliament, the anonymous pamphlet claimed, he cared for his soldiers on the field and looked after their everyday needs. He had served superbly at Edgehill, Brentford, Gloucester, and Newbury. He cared for the lives of his men so much that far fewer Parliamentarians perished in action than Royalists. For these and other marks of greatness Lord General Essex was to be commended, not castigated.

But castigated he was. He was attacked by John Goodwin, the Independent preacher, who used his pulpit in Coleman Street to pronounce that the Cornish disaster represented God's divine judgment against the Presbyterians. He was slurred by Oliver Cromwell: "We have some amongst us much slow in action: if we could all attend our own ends less, and our ease too, our business in the Army would go on wheels for expedition." The Independent soldiers in Cromwell's regiment apparently were jubilant, "as though it had been a victory new gained to themselves."[66]

Fortunately, Essex had many loyal friends and followers in Westminster who came to his defense. Not the least of these was Bulstrode Whitelocke. "Diverse who were no friends to Essex inveighed against him," he wrote with conviction, "as one that had quitted his Command and deserted his Army in the greatest danger, others excused and commended him for his actions, by which onely he could reserve himself, his Officers and Souldiers to doe the Parliament further service. Others condemned Waller, Manchester and Middleton, for not hastening more to the assis-

64 William Haller, *Liberty and Reformation in the Puritan Revolution* (New York: Columbia University Press, 1955), pp. 130–32.

65 The British Museum's copy of this pamphlet lists John Vicars as the probable author.

66 Haller, *Liberty and Reformation*, p. 146.

tance of the General, every one vented his own fancy and censure, but doubtless, he was a person of as much integrity, courage and honour, as any in his age; he was brought into this noose, by the wilfulness of others, and though his enemies took advantage against him upon it, yet many thought others to be more in fault then the General." [67]

[67] Whitelocke, *Memorials* (1682 ed.), p. 98.

CHAPTER 18

The Eclipse

I

IN THE WAKE of his capitulation Essex endeavored to recoup his losses. He established a temporary headquarters in Plymouth, where he remained for several days, and tried to regroup his demoralized soldiers. He instructed Lord Robartes to remain behind to defend that port against the King and Grenville and sent his own horse, under Balfour's command, toward Tavistock so it also might render some protection to the town. He made arrangements with the Earl of Warwick to sail eastward along the coast to Weymouth and Portsmouth, where Essex planned to rejoin his troops. Shortly before leaving Plymouth he rendered Parliament an account of his activities and his plans: "I have taken the best care I can to secure this Town, but without a present supply of men and money it will be in great danger unless there be strong forces coming this way. . . . I am this day taking shipping with my Lord Admiral, and intend to put in at Weymouth to see how that is strengthened, and from thence to Portsmouth, where I intend to tarry until I know Parliament's pleasure." [1]

Essex's troops proceeded toward Hampshire. [2] The foot, reduced to less than 6,000, marched across Devonshire and Dorsetshire to Portsmouth. The horse, still under Balfour's command, left a few days after Essex departed and followed a similar route toward Dorchester, where they expected to join Waller, who was moving westward. Not bound by the terms of Skippon's treaty with Charles, as were the foot, they skirmished with the Royalist foot near Crediton.

The bulk of the King's army remained in the Tamar valley for several days. On 10 September, Charles approached Plymouth and summoned the seaport to surrender under the threat of a sustained siege, but Robartes rejected the summons. Thus rebuffed the

[1] *H. M. C. House of Lords Manuscripts*, 6: 25.

[2] David Masson, *The Quarrel Between the Earl of Manchester and Cromwell*, Camden Society (London, 1875), p. 26; and *Perfect Diurnal*, 9 September 1644, p. 467.

King commissioned Grenville to block Plymouth by land and harass the townspeople, while he pressed eastward toward Chard and Salisbury. His object, now that summer was nearly spent, was to push back his adversaries toward London and strengthen his garrisons at Reading, Basingstoke, and Donnington Castle near Newbury.

The City reacted to this Royalist thrust with trepidation.[3] The Committee of Both Kingdoms ordered Essex to take measures to ensure the defense of Plymouth and made arrangements for the shipment of victuals and arms to that port. On 12 September the people of London, at the behest of the Westminster Assembly of Divines, put aside their work and solemnized the defeat of Essex with a day of humiliation and prayer. The following Sunday the Puritan preachers, especially Daniel Evans in Essex's own parish, thundered away at the Royalists. The political realists in Parliament and the Committee of Both Kingdoms, meanwhile, labored to reverse the King's successes and forestall his march upon the City. They prodded Waller to march toward Dorchester, again commanded Manchester to proceed westward toward Waller, and voted money for the defense of Plymouth.

The lord general spent over a month along the Hampshire coast refitting his army for the field. He set up his own headquarters in Portsmouth and took measures for the protection of Plymouth. He appointed Lord Robartes governor of that port, sent him a commission, and forwarded some supplies. On 13 September, Essex's defeated foot soldiers arrived in Hampshire. "Our poor naked foot came the last night to Southampton and thereabout," Essex reported to the Committee of Both Kingdoms, "the foot have been for the most part plundered, both officers and soldiers, by a treacherous enemy, though I hear many of their officers took a great deal of pains to prevent it."[4] The foot soldiers, disarmed and wearied, had been harassed by Royalists along the way from Lostwithiel to Hampshire.

During the next week Essex received several intelligence reports concerning the King's activities, which he dutifully forwarded to his masters in Westminster.[5] From Dalbier, still in the West, he learned that Charles was advancing eastward. From Waller, who

[3] *Register of C. B. K.*, fols. 67–71.
[4] *C. S. P. Dom., 1644*, p. 503.
[5] See *H. M. C. Thirteenth Report*, 1: 185–87.

was in Shaftesbury, he received confirmatory information.[6] His next communication, written three days later, was in the nature of a demand. "Receiving now this fresh intelligence from Sir William Waller, and Quarter-Master-General Dalbier," he wrote, "I desire that those things which were promised this army both for horse and foot may be sent, any delay from taking the field being most prejudicial at this present. In the meantime I have done what is in my power and that upon any summons from Sir William Waller I shall join my horse with his to make any impediment to the enemy if they march this way."[7] This promise of co-operation with his archrival, who was now retreating before the King, made Essex's political enemies appear petty.

The authorities in Westminster were at that time launching plans to halt the Royalist advance and reverse the course of the campaign. They secured from the city fathers the promise of five regiments of trained bands. They obtained from Manchester a promise to march more speedily toward Newbury. They ordered Essex to send his engineer, a Swedish expert named Jacob Cullenberg, to survey and fortify Reading.[8] On 28 September the Committee of Both Kingdoms ordered Essex and Manchester to send their horse ahead toward Marborough or Shaftesbury to join those of Waller and to march their foot to Newbury. The combined forces of Waller, Manchester, and Essex, they hoped, would be formidable enough to turn back the Royalists and, perhaps, defeat them in a general engagement.

The proposed conjunction of the three armies, however desirable from the military viewpoint, precipitated a prolonged controversy about the nature of the command.[9] The House of Lords held out for Essex. The House of Commons was divided between Waller and Manchester. The intense rivalries between the commanders and the controversies within the ranks further complicated the issue. The Earl of Manchester, though meek and slow to anger, refused to fight under commoner Waller and was reluctant to accept Essex's leadership. Lord General Essex would not take orders from Waller. Waller did not relish the thought of serving under either peer: Manchester was too slow and methodical for his liking, and Essex was stigmatized by defeat. Lieutenant General Cromwell's open

[6] *C. S. P. Dom., 1644*, p. 530.
[7] *H. M. C. Thirteenth Report*, 1: 185.
[8] *Register of C. B. K.*, fols. 72–75.
[9] Masson, *Quarrel*, pp. 25–35.

controversy with Manchester, his superior, intensified the struggle. These divisive rivalries, moreover, served the political ends of the Independents in Parliament and hurt the Presbyterian cause. "Our greatest feare," wrote Baillie, "is that the forces we have to oppose the King are full of jealousies and malice one against another."[10]

Essex now became the object of several underhanded designs. In mid-September the House of Commons voted that Waller and Manchester join forces against Charles. Despite the earlier efforts of Holles, it was only after Manchester protested that the Lower House relented and included Essex in their strategy. That the Independents in the Commons and the Committee of Both Kingdoms hoped to undermine Essex's authority and besmirch his reputation was obvious to most contemporary commentators. According to Royalist Sir Richard Bulstrode, it was "generally known, that there were great Designs against Essex, many being very desirous to remove him from his Station of General, upon their Jealousy that he was too much inclined to Peace, tho' we found no such thing from him."[11] Dr. Robert Baillie, who was in London at the time, made a similar observation: "The Independent party lying allwayes at the watch, finding us so low, and the Generall in the west shamefullie disgraced, began to lustilie to play their game. There first assay was on Manchester's army; there they had cast their strength, under Cromwell. . . . Their next assay was to have laid aside the Generall, and the remnant of his forces that Cromwell and their forces might be the more considerable."[12]

Lest these ulterior motives and the bitter feelings between the generals enable the King to defeat the combined armies and march upon London, Parliament reached a temporary compromise on 1 October. On that day they devised an ordinance designed to bring together the three armies in a common endeavor against the Royalists.[13] The lord general's troops would fight against the Royalists, as they had in the past, but Essex would no longer possess the sole military authority as commander in chief over his rival generals on the field. Parliament bestowed that authority upon the omnipotent Committee of Both Kingdoms.

[10] Baillie, *Letters*, 2: 229.
[11] Sir Richard Bulstrode, *Memoirs* (London, 1721), pp. 112–13.
[12] Baillie, *Letters*, 2: 234.
[13] Firth and Rait, *Acts and Ordinances*, 1: 515.

The committee then tried to unify the three armies.[14] Its members ordered Essex and Manchester to join Waller as soon as possible. Both generals procrastinated. On 5 October, Essex informed the committee that he could not possibly advance until he had more money and arms. The Earl of Manchester, still at Reading, also ignored subsequent instructions which commanded him to proceed toward Waller, who was drawing back to Newbury. Only after the committee allowed him to arrange for a separate rendezvous with Essex did Manchester consider mobilizing his troops for the oncoming venture against the King. Only after receiving assurance from Essex that the lord general, too, would join Waller did he start marching toward Newbury. Manchester won his point with the Committee of Both Kingdoms, but he antagonized many members of Parliament.

On 14 October the committee agreed upon a series of seventeen instructions designed to guide the three generals after their armies joined.[15] Instead of three separate commanders or one commander in chief they created a Council of War which included the three generals; Lord Robartes, who was still at Plymouth; Lt. Gen. Oliver Cromwell and Sir Arthur Haselrig, both Independents; and two members from the Commons. This collective command, packed to protect Waller, was empowered to make tactical decisions before and during each battle. No general could conduct a maneuver without the consent of the Council of War. All differences of opinion and deadlocks were to be referred to the Committee of Both Kingdoms. Essex was authorized to give verbal commands and his troops were supposed to assume the vanguard position at all times, but the committee refused to grant the lord general any decision-making authority. These instructions undercut Essex's power on the field and ensured the predominance of the Commons in military judgments.

II

WHILE THESE preparations were being made, Lord General Essex reassembled his shattered forces and planned for the forthcoming stand. He reopened direct lines of communication with Luke, his

[14] *Register of C. B. K.* under dates of 1–6 October 1644; and *C. S. P. Dom.*, *1644–1645*, pp. 5–11.

[15] For a discussion of these instructions see Burne and Young, *Civil War*, p. 182.

scoutmaster general, who was still in Newport Pagnell, and relied heavily upon his intelligence reports for news of Royalist activity.[16] Slowly and painfully Essex attempted to refurbish his army. He sorely needed more horse. He lacked sufficient artillery to confront the Royalists in pitched battle. He needed a new commissariat. All these shortages, plus the insufficiency of money and arms, detained him in Southampton. To secure more horse, he crossed over to the Isle of Wight and personally begged the townspeople and landowners. He entreated Parliament and the Committee of Both Kingdoms for money, medical supplies, and cannon but received very little assistance from his superiors. When a week passed and the situation had not changed, he wrote: "We have as yet neither drums, partisans, nor halberds. It will not only be difficult to call the soldiers together without drums, but the enemy, now that we are to march from them without sound of drums, will say that we are run away, they being more valiant in voice than in action. If our speed in marching does not answer your expectation, the commissioners here can best account for the reasons of the delay." [17] The lord general was thoroughly disgusted.

Nevertheless, after communicating with the Earl of Manchester about the date and place of their proposed rendezvous, Essex announced his plans: he would march from Southampton on 16 October and join Manchester the next day near Basingstoke. On the appointed day of departure, however, the southern coast was hit by such a severe storm that the lord general, who was raising horse on the Isle of Wight, postponed his marching orders two days. When the impatient members of the Committee of Both Kingdoms learned of this delay they immediately sent a messenger to order Essex to strike out for Basingstoke. By the time Essex received this directive from the committee he had already taken the field with his half-refurbished army.

The English sovereign, too, proceeded toward Newbury with all deliberate speed.[18] On 18 October his army, now 10,000 strong, arrived in Andover and forced a Parliamentary detachment to draw back to Basingstoke. Thus encouraged, he pressed on to Kinclerc in hopes of relieving Basingstoke before the Earl of Essex arrived with his reactivated army. But, upon finding himself outnumbered by the combined

16 British Museum, Stowe MSS, 190, fol. 8.
17 C. S. P. Dom., 1644–1645, p. 26.
18 Burne and Young, Civil War, pp. 180–83.

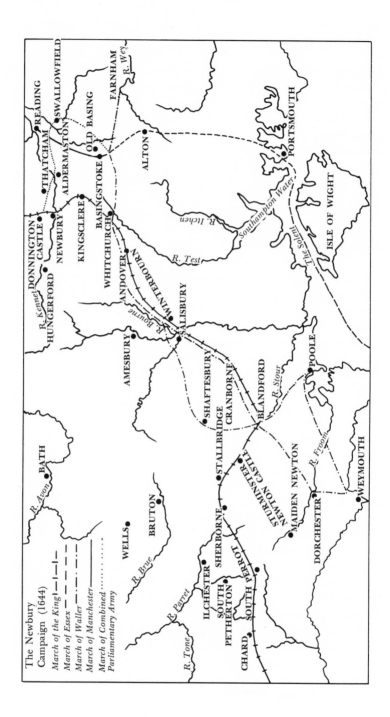

The Newbury
Campaign (1644)
March of the King ·—|—·—|—·
March of the Essex — — —
March of Waller —·—·—·—
March of Manchester ————
March of Combined ············
Parliamentary Army

forces of Essex, Waller, and Manchester, Charles abandoned his original objective, wheeled around and marched to Newbury the following day, and assumed a defensive posture north of the town.

The Parliamentary armies proceeded with their plans to assault Basing House, the fortresslike mansion of the Marquess of Winchester, which the Royalists still controlled. The armies launched a joint attack soon after their union. The assault was unsuccessful, however, so the Council of War decided to forsake the project and engage the King at Newbury before Prince Rupert's troops arrived there. A battle of major proportions was shaping up. On 22 October, in expectation of an engagement, Parliament called for a day of prayer and humiliation.

In preparation for the battle the Earl of Essex, following the instructions of the council, advanced toward the recaptured town of Reading, where he established his headquarters, so he could approach Newbury from the northeast.[19] His army, encamped midway between there and Newbury, was hardly prepared to lead the attack: the horse promised by Parliamentarians on the Isle of Wight had not yet arrived, the new train of artillery lacked the light cannon necessary for rapid movements, and the new commissaries assigned to Essex's forces were still in London.

Matters became further complicated by the lord general's sickness. Sometime during the third week of October he became ill with "excessive flux and vomiting."[20] Instead of resting he led his troops to Bucklebery Heath—located about four miles east of Newbury, within view of the enemy's horse—where a Council of War was scheduled to be held. At this critical point he contracted a fever. "My Lord General hath had upon him some indisposition for divers dayes," wrote the commissioners of the army to Parliament, "which hath ben much increased by his striving with it. He would not be persuaded from marching yesterday, and was resolved to have marched to-day, but not taking his rest last night he is growne feverish, and was forced to goe back to Reading on a feather bed layd in his coach; here will be much want of his presence. We shall conceal his absence as much as we can, and hope that those which are here will make all the supply that they can by extraordinary dilligence."[21]

19 *H. M. C. Thirteenth Report*, 1: 189.
20 *Ibid.*
21 *H. M. C. Tenth Report*, Appendix 6, p. 155.

The authorities in Westminster, responding immediately to the news of Essex's sickness, sent a surgeon to treat him. The Committee of Both Kingdoms, now worried about the effects which the lord general's sickness might have upon the morale of the soldiers and the outcome of the battle, sent a message wishing him well.[22] "We are very sorry to hear of your Lordship's indisposition, and that you have by so long striving against it, so much increased it," the message read. "We are sensible of the want of your presence at the army, yet desire your Lordship, however, to take special care of your health, that you may preserve yourself both to your friends and the public." That same day Parliament sent a delegation—one peer and two commoners—to express their concern and affection. Some cynics deemed this gesture "a bit of Courtship," observed Bulstrode Whitelocke, "but I think real, and there was cause enough that it should be so, the general having so highly reserved from them." [23]

While his men fought valiantly at Newbury the lord general remained bedridden in Reading under the care of his doctors. Appreciative of the attention shown him, he dictated a letter to his secretary and forwarded it to the Committee of Both Kingdoms. "It is a comfort to me in this time of mine affliction in mind and body, to see that I am continued in your care, being at this present so useless a servant to the State," he wrote on 28 October. "The particulars of my disease I shall crave pardon that I defer the account of till Doctor St. John, old Mr. Bowden of Reading and Langley mine own chiurgeon, shall set down the true state . . . but it is God's doing and I must with all humility submit to his pleasure." [24] From his sickbed Essex no doubt learned of the events of that day— of the courageous performances of his foot under the command of Skippon against Prince Maurice, of Manchester's poorly executed feint, of the recapture of his guns lost in Cornwall, of Oliver Cromwell's performance, of Manchester's failure to secure Shaw House before darkness set in, and of the Royalist flight to Wallingford while the Parliamentary troops were asleep.[25]

22 Devereux, *Lives and Letters*, 2: 443–44.

23 Whitelocke, *Memorials* (1682 ed.), p. 103.

24 Devereux, *Lives and Letters*, 2: 444.

25 Burne and Young, *Civil War*, pp. 183–90. Also see Simeon Ash, *A True Relation of the Most Chief Occurences at and since the late Battell at Newbury* (London, 1644); and Money, *Newbury*, pp. 107–87.

Newbury was a victory for Parliament: the united armies forced their adversary to retreat without gaining his objective. Yet, it was a hollow victory, for Parliament did not deliver the death blow or reap its advantage over the Royalist army. Both Royalist and Roundhead commentators had nothing but praise for Essex's soldiers. "Among the foot, the General's regiment, especially, did eminently well," Whitelocke reported, "and among all of the whole army, there was not one man, or party, horse or foot, seen either to desert their duty or dishearten their fellows." [26] According to Royalist Dugdale, "it was observed, that none of the Rebels fought more fiercely, than those, who delivering up their Arms in Cornwall . . . did engage never more to fight against the King." [27]

Lord General Essex remained confined to his quarters in Reading for two weeks. Separated from his troops, who encamped in the vicinity of Newbury, he had no voice in the Council of War deliberations following the engagement. He took no part in the fateful decision to summon Donnington Castle near Newbury. He was not present at the controversial session at Harwell, where a majority of the Council of War resolved not to engage the King, or at the meeting at Shaw Field, where the Earl of Manchester was castigated by both Cromwell and Haselrig. He tended to several routine matters while recuperating from his infirmity, however. He perused Luke's intelligence reports and forwarded them to his subordinates on the field, arranged for the shipment of supplies to his troops, attempted to stop stragglers from deserting, and corresponded regularly with Luke and the Committee of Both Kingdoms. On 7 November he left Reading by carriage and returned to London. [28]

Essex must have been exceedingly disappointed and disillusioned upon his return to London. Victory was nowhere in sight. The Royalist army remained intact on the field. The King had not capitulated. The prospects of a negotiated peace along the lines of the Nineteen Propositions were dim. Moreover, Essex's personal reputation as a general had suffered greatly during the recent campaign. His military authority had been circumscribed. His decisions had been criticized and questioned. His well-conceived plan to encircle the Royalist army had been foiled—in part by Waller's actions—and his ambitious expedition into the western

[26] Whitelocke, *Memorials* (1682 ed.), p. 104.
[27] Dugdale, *Short View*, p. 197; and Rushworth, *Historical Collections*, 5: 723.
[28] Tibbutt, *Luke*, p. 50; and British Museum, Stowe MSS, 190, fol. 130a.

counties had ended in defeat. Some of these reverses resulted from Essex's personal judgment, to be sure, but many stemmed from the machinations of his rival military subordinates and political enemies in the Committee of Both Kingdoms and the House of Commons. Whether Essex could recover his receding prestige and popularity was questionable.

III

Upon returning to London the lord general stayed in Essex House to recuperate from his illness. He remained under a doctor's care, apparently, and avoided most public gatherings. He handled the routine duties of his military office throughout the weeks of his recovery: he corresponded with Luke about the movements of enemy troops and with Major General Skippon about the disposition of his army on the field; he issued both warrants for pay and safe-conducts; and he gave orders for the release and exchange of prisoners.[29] Yet he attended the Committee of Both Kingdoms deliberations only three times during his recovery period and did not reappear in Parliament until the last week of November.

Morale in Parliament's army, meanwhile, reached a new low. The defeat of Essex's army in Cornwall could not be easily dismissed or forgotten. The recent battle of Newbury—which did not give Parliament a clean victory and thus end the war, as some members of Parliament had hoped it would—was disheartening. The return of the Royalists to Oxford with a substantial force meant a prolongation of the struggle through the winter season and into the next year. The King's cause had been weakened during the 1644 campaign, but the end of the war was not in sight. Something was wrong. Someone must be blamed. Scapegoats must be found.

The members of Parliament and the Committee of Both Kingdoms refused to accept the blame. The field commanders held their rivals responsible for the military reverses.[30] For his failure to capture the King, Waller blamed Essex. For his defeat in the West at the hands of the Royalists, the lord general blamed Waller.

---

[29] Essex granted a warrant on 25 November to release Lt. Col. William Paulet—the father of his estranged wife—who was a prisoner at Lambeth House. The original of the warrant is in HM 373, Huntington Library.

[30] Masson, *Quarrel*, pp. 58–75.

Cromwell charged his superior, the Earl of Manchester, with cowardice and incompetence in the Newbury campaign. Manchester countercharged that Cromwell was at fault for allowing the King to relieve Donnington Castle and return to Oxford. Some leaders, including Essex, hoped that these recriminations would provoke parliamentary investigations.

The rank-and-file soldiers became very restive. The small amount of money which Parliament appropriated for back pay proved insufficient. The food and clothing which the army commissaries ordered did not suffice. Some troops resorted to pilfering to keep body and soul together. Others deserted and sought employment in London. Still others turned to mutiny. Parliament, upon learning of these conditions from Essex and other returning members of Parliament, called for an investigation and renewed the Martial Law Ordinance. These deplorable conditions, plus the approaching winter, precluded further offensive operations. Nevertheless, Essex attempted to keep Parliament's forces intact. He tried to curb desertion. He appealed to Parliament for funds to pay those soldiers in arrears. In assigning the various armies winter quarters, he stationed his own foot regiments, still under Skippon's command, in Reading and the surrounding countryside and quartered his horse at Swallowfield in Berkshire. He placed Manchester's troops in the area about Abingdon and Waller's army south of the Thames near Farnham. He also stationed several contingents in Aylesbury and Bedford. The prime purpose of this cordon, as before, was to protect London and its environs from a Royalist incursion during the winter season.

Meanwhile, those members of Parliament who held commissions in the army went back to Westminster for the winter season.[31] In advance of their return several members put their cases before Parliament in anticipation of inquiries into the defeat in Cornwall and the draw at Newbury. Waller defended himself in a letter addressed to Parliament. Balfour and Manchester followed suit. These communications were read before the House of Lords and sparked a prolonged and vitriolic controversy between the respective individuals and their backers in Parliament.

On 12 November the Committee of Both Kingdoms, accepting the views of Waller and Cromwell, reprimanded Manchester for not preventing the Royalist relief of Donnington Castle and the

[31] Abbott, *Cromwell*, 1: 301.

escape of the King to Oxford.[32] The following day the House of Commons initiated an inquiry into Manchester's dilatory conduct after the battle of Newbury. Parliament received word on 18 November that the counties of the Eastern Association would no longer bear the charges of maintaining Manchester's army on the field. In an effort to deal with all these interrelated problems Parliament ordered the Committee of Both Kingdoms to appraise the condition of the armies on the field and consider a "new model" of military administration. Thus began a series of changes which would eventually divest Essex of his command.

Throughout the rest of the year the Earl of Manchester, vulnerable on several accounts, remained the main target of the Independent attack. He had little experience to justify his high command. He had ignored—even defied—the directives of the Committee of Both Kingdoms. He had moved slowly toward Newbury and refused to join Waller, and had not kept his army alert and intact after the action there, thus allowing the King to relieve Donnington Castle and escape unscathed. Therefore the Earl of Manchester was severely attacked by Oliver Cromwell in Parliament on 25 November. He was charged with cowardice and breach of trust. His loyalty to Parliament was questioned, his integrity impugned. "This recrimination was well accepted by the House of Commons," wrote astrologer Lilly, "who thereupon, and from that time, thought there was none of the House of Lords very fit to be entrusted with their future armies, but had then thoughts *of making a commoner their general.*"[33]

On 28 November, the day that Essex returned to Parliament, the Earl of Manchester rebutted these charges in a narrative account of the Newbury campaign.[34] He defended his actions and decisions and denied the accusations of his rival subordinate, even aspersing Cromwell's motives in the whole affair. Soon the dispute between the two commanders broadened into a controversy between the two Houses. Essex's majority in the Upper House supported Manchester in the quarrel. The Independent majority in the Lower House stood behind Cromwell. Class antagonisms became more manifest. Each House established a committee to inquire into the matter.

[32] Masson, *Quarrel*, pp. 54–58.

[33] William Lilly, *History of His Life and Times* (London, 1715), p. 118. Emphasis added.

[34] *Lords Journal*, 7: 77.

The lord general became involved in the Manchester-Cromwell dispute soon after his return to the House of Lords.[35] Although not directly implicated by Cromwell's charges, he had a vested interest in the outcome of the controversy. He undoubtedly feared that the attack upon his compeer might well be a prelude to an attack upon himself—or a general onslaught upon the aristocracy. Moreover, his name cropped up in the Commons committee investigating Manchester. One of his letters calling for the removal of some troops from Basing House was cited as evidence of his complicity with Manchester. About the same time, significantly, the finances of his army came under the scrutiny of the leadership of the Lower House.

On 3 December the Earl of Essex, now bitter about Cromwell's recriminations, invited to Essex House the Scots' commissioners and Whitelocke, Maynard, Meyrick, Holles, and Stapleton for a conference. They assembled secretly late in the night to consider the possibility of charging Cromwell with being an "incendiary." Whitelocke recorded the conversation.[36]

"I have sent for you upon a special occasion," Essex informed lawyers Maynard and Whitelocke, "to have your Advice and Counsel, and that in a matter of very great importance concerning both Kingdoms, in which, my Lords, the Commissioners of Scotland are concerned for their State, and we for ours; and they as well as we knowing your abilities and integrity, are very desirous of your counsel in this great business."

"We are come to obey your Excellencie's Command," responded Maynard, "and shall be ready to give our faithful advice in what shall be required of us."

"Your Excellence I am assured is fully satisfied of our affections and duty to your self," Whitelocke went on to say, "and to that cause in which we are all engaged, and my Lords, the Commissioners of Scotland will likewise, I hope, entertain no ill thoughts of us."

"My Lord Chancellor of Scotland," Essex then proceeded to explain, "and the rest of the Commissioners of that Kingdom, desired that you two by name might be consulted with upon this occasion, and I shall desire my Lord Chancellor who is a much better Oratour than I am to acquaint you what the business is."

35 C. S. P. Dom., 1644–1645, pp. 47, 168–70.

36 For this conference I have followed Whitelocke very closely. All the quotations are from the detailed account in his Memorials, pp. 111–14.

The Lord Chancellor of Scotland then spoke directly to the point: "You ken vary welle that General Lieutenant Cromwel is no friend of ours, and since the advance of our Army into England, he hath used all underhand and cunning means to take off from our honour and merit of this Kingdom; an evil requital of all our hazards and services: but so it is, and we are nevertheless fully satisfied of the affections and gratitude of the gude people of this Nation in the general. . . .

"He not onely is no friend to us, and to the Government of our Church, but he is also no well willer to his Excellency, whom you and we all have cause to love and honour; and if he be permitted to go on in his ways, it may, I fear, indanger the whole business; therefore we are to advise of some course to be taken for prevention of that mischief.

"You ken very weele the accord 'twist the twa Kingdoms, and the union by the Solemn League and Covenant, and if any be an Incendiary between the twa Nations, how is he to be proceeded against: now the matter is, wherein we desire your opinions, what you take the meaning of this word Incendiary to be, and whether Lieutenant General Cromwel be not an Incendiary, as is meant thereby, and whilke way wud be best to tak to proceed against him, if he be proved to be sike an Incendiary, and that will clepe his wings from soaring to the prejudice of our cause."

Upon the conclusion of this speech Essex requested the others in attendance to express their views. Whitelocke deemed it unwise to proceed against Cromwell. He was supported by Maynard. Both lawyers believed that the accusation against Cromwell, though true in substance, would be very difficult to prove in any court of law and that it would be doubly difficult, if not impossible, to prove it in Parliament. It would be foolhardy, if not very dangerous, they agreed, to risk an attack upon Cromwell without concrete evidence of incendiary activities.

Cromwell's political enemies then proceeded to cite some of their evidence. "Mr. Hollis, and Sir Philip Stapleton, and some other, spake smartly to the business," Whitelocke reported, "and mentioned some particular passages, and words of Cromwell tending to prove him to be an Incendiary, and they did not apprehend his interest in the House of Commons to be so much as was supposed; and they would willingly have been upon the accusation of him." The cautious Scots' commissioners, however, took the advice of the English lawyers and decided to wait until the case against Cromwell was more conclusive.

When Oliver Cromwell learned of these moves against him from some undisclosed attendant at the Essex House meeting, he reacted with alacrity. In the Lower House on 4 December he delivered another speech in defense of himself,[37] denying the accusations. That same day, before the special committee of inquiry, he testified that the Earl of Manchester had threatened to hang anyone who advised him to leave the counties of the Eastern Association for the West—an obvious move to implicate Manchester of insubordination. Cromwell's views were supported by the testimonies of several other officers.

Five days passed. The Independent majority in the Commons then launched a series of maneuvers which took their political opponents by surprise.[38] Zouch Tate, chairman of the committee of inquiry, reported that Parliament's inability to defeat the King and achieve final victory stemmed from the pride and covetousness of the field commanders of the various armies. Cromwell denounced those English peers who rendered only indifferent support to the war effort and those Covenanters who favored a negotiated settlement. He also called for new ways to achieve victory. Taking his cue, Tate presented to the House of Commons a revolutionary proposal since known as the Self-Denying Ordinance. Seconded by Vane, it won approval with little opposition.

The ostensible intention of the prime movers behind the proposal was to eliminate rivalries and bickering among the commanders of the army and to take politics out of the military decisions. "The House of Commons, in one hour, has ended all the quarrels which was betwixt Manchester, all the obloquies against the General, the grumblings against the proceedings of many members of their House," wrote Covenanter Baillie, "this done on a sudden, in one session, with great unanimitie, is still more and more admired by some, as a most wise, necessary, and heroick action." [39] But the real motives behind this measure, in the eyes of many other contemporaries, were not so high-minded. The wife of Col. John Hutchinson, a Roundhead, admitted that the move was designed by those who were unhappy with Essex's conduct of the war. "It was too

---

[37] Abbott, *Cromwell*, 1: 313.

[38] *Ibid.*, pp. 313–18.

[39] Baillie, *Letters*, 1: 247.

apparent how much the whole Parliament cause had been often hazarded, how many opportunities of finishing the war had been overslipped by the Earl of Essex's army," Lucy Hutchinson wrote, "and it was believed that he himself, with his commanders, rather endeavored to become arbiters of war and peace, than conquerors for the parliament; for it was known that he had given out such expressions. Wherefore those in the parliament who were grieved at the prejudice of the public interest, and loath to bring those men to public shame who had once merited it of them, devised to new model the army."[40]

Most Royalist commentators also viewed the Self-Denying Ordinance as a devious move on the part of the Independent leadership in the House of Commons to oust Lord General Essex. Clarendon put forth this view in his *History*. "They had been long unsatisfied with the earl of Essex," he wrote, "and he as much with them; both being more solicitous to suppress the other than to destroy the king. They bore the loss and dishonour he had sustained in Cornwall very well; and would have been glad that both he and his army had been quite cut off, instead of being dissolved; for all his officers and soldiers were corrupted in their affections toward them, and desired nothing but peace; so that they resolved never to trust or employ them."[41] Several other Royalist authors, including Edward Bulstrode and Thomas Hobbes, subscribed to similar explanations.

Some contemporaries regarded the proposal as a radical move, not directed specifically at either Essex or Manchester, but at the aristocracy and its privileged place in the social structure. Republican Edmund Ludlow confessed that the ordinance was put forward to rid the army of nobles in high places and replace them with commoners.[42] It is clear that the main force himself, Oliver Cromwell, cared little for aristocratic leadership: "I had rather have a plain russet-coated captain that knows what he fights for and loves what he knows, than that which you call a gentleman, and is nothing else."[43] On another occasion he was reputed to have

[40] Lucy Hutchinson, *Memoirs of the Life of Colonel John Hutchinson*, ed. Sir Charles H. Firth (London: Dent and Sons, 1906), p. 183.

[41] Clarendon, *History* (1849 ed.), 3: 467.

[42] Ludlow, *Memoirs*, 1: 358.

[43] Ernest Barker, *Traditions of Civility* (Cambridge: At the University Press, 1948), p. 187n.

openly declared his hatred of the aristocracy and the House of Lords, "wishing there was never a lord in England, and saying he loved such and such because they loved not lords." [44]

For several months the Self-Denying Ordinance cast its long shadow over those members of Parliament who held commissions. On 14 December the Lower House fully debated the ordinance in a committee of the whole. Some members opposed the measure. Others raised questions about the possible consequences, wondering such things as whether nonmembers like Skippon and Fairfax would replace the ousted commanders, whether some members of the Lower House would give up their seats in the Commons and keep their military commissions, whether Parliament could dispense with the law and exempt anyone, and whether the ordinance applied to the lord lieutenants and the justices of the peace. Answers to these and other questions were by no means clear and forth-coming. Three days later a faction of the House of Commons made a bid to amend the Self-Denying Ordinance by exempting Lord General Essex. [45] The voice vote was so inconclusive that the speaker called for a division. The amendment lost, but by a close vote of 93 to 100. Two days later in a thin House, the ordinance itself passed without a division and was subsequently sent up to the House of Lords for concurrence.

Essex and his compeers reacted negatively to the measure. Most Lords at first expressed surprise at this stratagem. They apparently had expected formal impeachment proceedings instead. They had not anticipated commoners like Cromwell and Waller voluntarily relinquishing their commands in Parliament's army. The leaders in the Upper House opposed the measure in every way possible. In the words of historian Thomas May, "the Lords were against that change, alledging that there was no need for new Commanders, where the old ones could be accused of no fault; that men of the noblest rank were fittest to command Armies, the contrary whereof might breed confusion in the Commonwealth." [46] Only after several promptings from the Lower House did the Lords give consideration to the Self-Denying Ordinance. Not until 30 December did they debate the matter fully and then they referred it to an eight-man committee, no doubt hoping to bury it.

[44] Holles, *Memoirs*, p. 201.
[45] Rushworth, *Historical Collections*, 6: 5.
[46] May, *History*, p. 65.

The Committee of Both Kingdoms, in the meantime, considered the remodeling of Parliament's military system. The members had been instructed to do so in mid-November, but they had not devoted much time to the matter until after the introduction of the Self-Denying Ordinance.[47] Throughout the rest of December members of the committee discussed possible ways to put a more effective army on the field during the following year. There was need for a single national army to replace the rival armies of Waller, Essex, and Manchester; for a more equitable system of financing the war effort; and for some reorganization of the command structure and the size of the various regiments. By early January the Committee of Both Kingdoms had a concrete proposal which they transmitted to the House of Commons.

On 6 January the Lower House asked the Upper House to expedite the passage of the Self-Denying Ordinance. The lords came out against it. "The putting every Member of either House of Parliament into an Incapacity of holding Military or Civil Offices during this War, may be of very dangerous Consequence," they explained in a written rejection, "because, how emergent soever the Occasion may be, it cannot be altered with deserting of a positive Rule imposed upon ourselves."[48] The statement, probably initiated by Essex, then specified the objections to the Self-Denying Ordinance:

First, it deprives the Peers of that Honour which in all Ages hath been given unto them, as may appear by many Writers; whose Part was, in being employed to Military Commands. It also crosses the constant Practice of the Peers of England; for our Stories make Mention, that in all Ages they have been principally active, to the Effusion of their Blood, and the Hazard of their Estates and Fortunes, in regaining and maintaining the fundamental Laws of the Land, the Rights and Liberties of the Subject; nor was there ever any Battle fought for those Ends, wherein the Nobility have not been employed in Places of chiefest Trust and Command; and it doth not only deprive them of their due Honour, but it lays a Blot upon them, by the Incapacity, which is a Punishment usually inflicted upon Delinquents, and such as have highly demerited from the Parliament . . .

The passing this Ordinance, as to the Military Part, will produce such an Alteration in all the Armies, as in apparent Probability must be of very dangerous Consequence to the Cause in Hand, especially in this Conjunc-

47 C. S. P. Dom., 1644–1645, pp. 182–85.
48 Lords Journal, 7: 129.

ture of Time; and therefore, until a new Model be propounded to succeed, they cannot but think this present Frame better than such a Confusion which is like to follow. Nor can we tarry long in the Expectation of what new Model, because the Preparation of it is already referred to the Consideration of the Committee of the Two Kingdoms, where the Commissioners of Scotland will contribute their Advice, and receive their Satisfaction in it; for, since the whole Scottish Nation are united with us in this great Cause, and cannot but extremely suffer in the Miscarriage of our Armies, and that we have engaged ourselves to them, that the Affairs of both Kingdoms, in Pursuance of our Covenant, shall be managed by the joint Advice and Direction of both Nations, it is very considerable how far we shall adventure upon so dangerous an Attempt, as is the introducing of so great a Change in the whole Management of our War, without our advising or consulting with them.

These reasons did not satisfy the leaders in the Lower House, who soon renewed their demand for passage. The Lords responded by rejecting the Self-Denying Ordinance by a vote of 15 to 4.

Meanwhile, the New Model Ordinance encountered less resistance in Parliament.[49] Without a division the House of Commons approved it on 11 January and began to choose officers of the New Model. Fairfax was named commander in chief by a vote of 101 to 69, Skippon was appointed major general, but the post of lieutenant general was left open for the moment. On 28 January the proposal was sent to the Lords. The New Model Army was to be underwritten by an assessment of fifty-six thousand pounds a month on those districts under Parliament's control. It was to be composed of twelve regiments of foot, ten of horse, and one of dragoons—a total of 21,400 soldiers.

To secure the passage of this measure in the Upper House, the Independents resorted to several machinations involving Essex. A Commons committee under the chairmanship of John Lisle began investigating the lord general's account books for evidence of malfeasance.[50] That same day Zouch Tate suggested that the House of Commons "consider of and present to the House some mark of honour to set upon the Lord General, the Earl of Essex, besides some other recompense which may remain as a testimony to posterity and an acknowledgment from the Parliament of England

[49] See Abbott, *Cromwell*, 1: 327–29.

[50] Whitelocke, *Memorials*, p. 120. There had been a move in this direction in late November, while Essex was recuperating at Essex House.

of the great and faithful services he had done to the Parliament and kingdom."[51] The following week the Committee of Both Kingdoms asked Essex to provide it with a complete report of the distribution of his troops quartered in Reading, Henley, and Aylesbury. By whatever means necessary the lord general's enemies were determined to remove him from office.

The situation in Parliament's army became more critical with each passing week.[52] Many soldiers lived by plundering. Morale was low. The officers, fearful of losing their commands if the New Model measure passed Parliament, became restive. One group of commissioned officers in Manchester's army protested against the Self-Denying Ordinance. Some of Essex's officers who had been assigned to Waller made a declaration: "We will rather go under any the Lord General should appoint, than with Sir William Waller, with all the money in England."[53] From Leatherhead, Waller reported that there was danger of a mutiny. From Newport Pagnell, Luke related that many troops, including some officers, were discontent. Most of the trouble stemmed from Parliament's recent action, Whitelocke contended. "Those who had been so well paid by the Parliament," he said, "now dispute their Commands, occasioned by the unsettledness of the Parliament's business, and the discontents among the Souldiery, because their General Essex was laid aside. And here began their first unruliness."[54]

On 4 February, after much debate, Essex's majority in the House of Lords approved a modified version of the ordinance.[55] They concurred with the internal reorganization of the army and the new system of finances, but they balked at that part of the ordinance which gave to Sir Thomas Fairfax sole authority to appoint his subordinates. They quite rightly feared that Fairfax would be partial to Independents and exclude those officers who had fought under Essex and Manchester. They demanded that all those officers above the rank of lieutenant should be selected by both Houses, thus giving the Lords a voice and a veto, and they insisted that all the officers in the New Model should take the Oath of the Covenant.

[51] *C. S. P. Dom., 1644–1645*, p. 265.
[52] See Whitelocke, *Memorials*, p. 126.
[53] Gardiner, *Civil War*, 2: 129.
[54] Whitelocke, *Memorials*, p. 126.
[55] *Lords Journal*, 7: 174–77.

To these provisos Oliver Cromwell took vigorous exception. He believed that the New Model's commander in chief rather than Parliament should have the appointive authority. On this particular matter Cromwell was outflanked by a majority in the Commons which resolved the differences with an acceptable compromise. The New Model's commander would nominate the officers, and the two Houses would approve or reject his choices. The Commons conceded that the officers in the New Model should take the Oath of the Covenant, providing that this did not mean a blind submission to a particular form of ecclesiastical government.

Essex and his colleagues then approved the New Model Ordinance. Some peers disliked the appointment of Fairfax, of course, and some objected to the Commons' provisions. But with the threat of mutinous troops hanging over their heads the Lords passed the measure on 15 February without further revisions.[56] In so doing, the lord general capitulated to Fairfax and the Independents in the House of Commons.

IV

THREE DAYS LATER Fairfax arrived in London, established quarters in Queen Street, where he was welcomed by a committee from the Lower House, and prepared for a formal reception in Parliament. The following day, appearing before the Commons with his wounded arm in a sling, he was acclaimed by Speaker Lenthall as a new Agamemnon. At the conclusion of his oration, while Fairfax stood bareheaded, Lenthall announced that "the House out of the great experience and confidence they had of the calour, conduct and fidelity of Sir Thomas Fairfax, had thought fit to confer the great trust of commanding their armies in chief upon him."[57]

That Essex's soldiers should dislike these events was a foregone conclusion. His troops stationed at Henley staged a mutiny in protest against the New Model Army and its commander. Essex's cavalry, which had been recently ordered to march toward Weymouth under Waller's command, continued to complain and to cry out for their displaced leader. Others deserted their posts and began pilfering. Not even a fortnight's pay quieted them down. For many weeks the officers in Essex's army remained very apprehensive

[56] *Ibid.*, p. 204.
[57] Clements R. Markham, *A Life of the Great Lord Fairfax* (London, 1870), p. 191.

about their future. Some petitioned Parliament and the Committee of Both Kingdoms. Others, worried about being demoted or ousted, sought Essex's help and advice.[58]

On 25 February the Lower House empowered a select committee to draw up a new Self-Denying Ordinance.[59] Four weeks passed before the committee brought the matter forward. In the interim Parliament proceeded to reorganize its military establishment along the lines of the New Model Ordinance. The House of Lords received Fairfax's list of officers proposed for the New Model Army.[60] The Upper House, ignoring a request for celerity, waited for over a week before giving the matter full consideration. The Lords were split over Fairfax's nominations. One group of peers, under Lord Saye's direction, wanted to approve the list as amended by the Commons. Another bloc of peers, led by Essex, wanted to reject the two colonels plus forty captains and call upon Fairfax to nominate more acceptable officers. The two factions were so evenly balanced that the final outcome, if the matter was put to a vote, was by no means certain. For several days the leading peers sought a compromise, but their efforts were fruitless.

The initial roll call vote to decide upon Fairfax's nominations took place on 17 March. Both Saye and Essex mustered ten votes,[61] deadlocking the House of Lords. Lord Saye temporarily had the majority support when he cast the proxy of the Earl of Mulgrave, but Essex countered by casting Clanricarde's proxy. This second deadlock brought the whole issue of proctorial voting to a head. The clerk of Parliament searched the precedents and found no order prohibiting the use of proxies to break a tie. Saye then injected the religious question into the dispute: on grounds that Clanricarde was a Catholic, Saye successfully challenged his voting powers and deemed the proxy vote which Essex had cast invalid. Essex was unsuccessful in attempting to invalidate Mulgrave's proxy and went down to defeat: the names of those officers rejected by his party were restored to the list and approved.

The next week the Independents, now triumphant in both Houses, pressed home their political advantage. They awarded the

---

[58] Tibbutt, *Luke*, p. 154; and *H. M. C. Thirteenth Report*, Appendix 1, p. 212.

[59] Gardiner, *Civil War*, 2: 186.

[60] *Lords Journal*, 7: 266.

[61] *Ibid.*, p. 276. Also see Firth, *House of Lords*, p. 148; and Carte, *Original Letters*, 1: 79.

Earl of Mulgrave financial compensation for losses that he and his son Lord Sheffield had sustained as a result of the war.[62] Two days later Parliament invited the Westminster Assembly of Divines to nominate chaplains to accompany the New Model Army. On 24 March the Lower House called for the report of its select committee and began debating the new Self-Denying Ordinance. These debates opened the old sores of contention. In the ensuing deliberations Essex was attacked in many speeches, and the House of Lords was criticized for its obstructionist tactics. In the words of Whitelocke: "Some imprudent speeches had been given out by some Members of the House of Commons, and others, upon the Lords rejecting the Ordinances of Self-Denying, and not concurring in other matters with the Commons; and as the Earl of Essex his party was strongest in the Lords House, so the party of his Enemies was most prevalent in the House of Commons."[63]

Meanwhile, Essex's military authority dwindled daily. His soldiers, according to an ordinance passed on 11 March, were permitted to reenlist in the New Model Army. Many did. Some were attracted to Fairfax's army by promises of higher and more regular pay; others saw opportunity for advancement. "This brought in almost all Essex his Foot to Fairfax," Whitelocke noted, "they being such Creatures as will be carried anywhere for money."[64] Essex could not keep his regiments intact; he was powerless to prevent the dissolution of his army. Some of his crack units were transferred to the New Model Army by direct orders from the Committee of Both Kingdoms. Two companies of dragoons stationed in Bedfordshire were transferred to Fairfax's command and assigned new quarters. In due time the bulk of his foot regiments were merged with those of Maj. Gen. William Crawford. Essex complied with the committee's commands—some of which he personally executed—despite the fact that they had undermined his authority.

Yet, at the same time, he continued to exercise authority within the framework of his original commission. He corresponded with those governors he had appointed. He arranged for the exchange of prisoners. At the behest of the Committee of Both Kingdoms, he granted Colonel Massey a broad commission to command the

[62] Whitelocke, *Memorials*, p. 132.
[63] *Ibid.*
[64] *Ibid.*

forces in Gloucestershire, Herefordshire, Monmouthshire, and three Welsh counties. He also promoted some officers to higher ranks and upon occasion assembled a Council of War to conduct a court-martial. The lord general did not relinquish his military authority upon the passage of the New Model Ordinance, as his enemies had no doubt hoped he would; rather he stubbornly clung to his commission-granted power until the bitter end.

That came during the first week of April. On 25 March the House of Lords obtained from the House of Commons an ordinance granting Fairfax his general's commission. Upon comparing this commission with his own, received in 1642, Essex discovered that the significant clause calling for *"the preservation of the King's person"* was omitted in Fairfax's.[65] Essex and his faction in the Upper House took exception to this deliberate exclusion. Questions were asked. The measure was delayed for several days. Finally, on 1 April after Bolingbroke switched sides, the controversial commission—minus the crucial clause—won approval in the House of Lords. This omission represented a radical shift in the character of the war in Essex's eyes.

On the next day Lord General Essex offered to surrender his original commission.[66] He was joined, probably by prearrangement, by the Earl of Manchester and the Earl of Denbigh. The majority in the Upper House accepted his offer and immediately arranged for a conference with a delegation from the House of Commons. During the ensuing meeting the former lord general read a prepared statement explaining his action:[67]

Having received this great charge in obedience to the command of both Houses, and taken their sword into my hand, I can with confidence say, that I have, for now almost three years, faithfully served you, and I hope without loss of any honor to myself or prejudice to the public, supported therein by the goodness of God, and the fidelity and courage of a great many gallant men. . . .

I see, by the now coming up of these ordinances, that it is the desire of the House of Commons that my commission may be vacated; and it hath been no particular respect to myself, whatever is whispered to the contrary,

65 *Lords Journal*, vol. 7, pp. 287–90. Emphasis added.

66 Rushworth, *Historical Collections*, 6: 15. Also see *Lords Journal*, 7: 299; *Commons Journal*, 4: 96; Sanderson, *A Compleat History*, p. 799; and Whitelocke, *Memorials*, p. 134.

67 *Lords Journal*, 7: 300. It is reprinted in Devereux, *Lives and Letters*, 2: 454.

that hath made me thus long omit to declare my readiness thereto . . . I do now do it, and return my commission into those hands that gave it me; wishing it may prove as good and expedient to the present distempers as some will have it believed, which I shall pray for with as hearty a zeal as any that desire my doing this which now I do.

Essex graciously accepted his eclipse and stepped aside like a gentleman.

The lord general did not step aside without pleading the cause of his subordinates, however:

I think it not immodest that I intreat both Houses that those officers of mine which are now laid by, might have their debentures audited, some considerable part of their arrears paid them for their support, and the remainder secured them by public faith, and that some of them that remain questioned, may be brought to some speedy trial, whereby they may receive either punishment or the justification that is due to them . . . I hope that this advice from me is not unseasonable, wishing myself and my friends may, among others, participate the benefit thereof; this proceeding from my affection to the Parliament.

This well-phrased and restrained statement was subsequently released to the printers of London for publication and distribution.

The timing of Essex's public resignation was most significant. The New Model Ordinance had passed. Fairfax, his controversial commission approved, was preparing to march against the Royalists. There was little doubt in Essex's mind, apparently, that the new Self-Denying Ordinance would pass its final reading in the Upper House. He evidently realized that his party could no longer prevent its passage. Rather than sustain a political defeat which would compel him to surrender his commission Essex decided to bow out honorably and thus forestall more controversy which might further humiliate him and adversely affect his soldiers still in the field. Bulstrode Whitelocke sensed this when he wrote in his *Memorials*: "Some of Essex his Friends were against his laying down of his Commission, but others told him that mischiefs and contests might arise if he kept it, whereof himself was sensible; and as he had great stoutness of spirit, so he had great goodness of nature, and love to the publick, which perswaded him to lay down his Commission."[68]

Essex's resignation marked a pivotal turning point in the struggle between King and Parliament. Before his resignation the aristocrats

[68] Whitelocke, *Memorials*, p. 135.

possessed a voice in the management of the war, the conduct of peace negotiations, and the determination of a settlement with the enemy. Thereafter the Lords offered only token opposition to measures passed in the House of Commons: their effective power was gone. Henceforth the Independent majority in the House of Commons would wage war more militantly, negotiate with less liberality, and determine a final settlement unilaterally, with little reference to the opinions of the Lords. The eclipse of Lord General Essex, in retrospect, foreshadowed the abolition of the House of Lords and the execution of the King.

The Earl of Essex, having surrendered his commission, immediately dropped his opposition to the Self-Denying Ordinance. On 3 April the controversial ordinance won approval with little or no resistance.[69] Essex was acclaimed for his selfless devotion to Parliament. Later that day he held court at Essex House while members of both Houses lauded him for faithful military service. The immediate effect of the new Self-Denying Ordinance upon the House of Lords was now inconsequential. Except for the Earl of Warwick all the peers holding commissions in the army had already tendered their resignations. Warwick, Lord Admiral of Parliament's fleet, surrendered his commission several days later.

The ordinance actually had a greater impact upon the commoners, for it affected Cromwell, Waller, Stapleton, and Meyrick. Within approximately one week all these officers except Oliver Cromwell turned in their commissions. Fairfax wanted him to remain on the field, so Cromwell insisted upon retaining his commission. How long Parliament would tolerate this exception remained a moot question.

Essex's military career ended with this capitulation to Cromwell and the Independents. Henceforth he would participate in decisions made in the Committee of Both Kingdoms and in Parliament. He would read about the war in newsbooks or hear about it from others. His fighting days were over. He was no longer the lord general or His Excellency, but simply the Earl of Essex. "And here ended the first scene of our Tragick Civil Wars," wailed Whitelocke, "in the Exit of this brave person Essex."[70]

[69] Firth and Rait, *Acts and Ordinances*, 1: 665.
[70] *Memorials*, p. 135.

CHAPTER 19

Coda

I

AT THE TIME of his resignation the Earl of Essex was fifty-four. The future held little promise. Nonetheless, in the months following the passage of the Self-Denying Ordinance, the former commander did not fade completely into obscurity, as some authors have claimed; rather he stayed in London to support the cause of the Presbyterians in Parliament and take care of unfinished business.[1] He continued to attend the deliberations of the Committee of Both Kingdoms, but records show that he went less frequently and lost interest as the year wore on.[2] Essex was present at the debates at the House of Lords very regularly, still taking part in the deliberations and serving on committees of various types. He remained committed to parliamentary government until his death.

Shortly after resigning, Essex participated in a move to bolster the House of Lords and ensure the preservation of the aristocracy. Many peers feared—and not without reason—that the war, now that the Independents predominated, might well turn into a full-fledged revolution. Vane considered deposing the King; Cromwell criticized the aristocracy and its privileges; and some radicals, like Henry Marten, spoke in terms of a republic. The changing complexion of the Lower House, moreover, increased the plausibility of integral innovations. Beginning as far back as the latter part of 1644, the House of Commons had begun to fill the vacancies caused by death or delinquency with newly elected members.[3] These "recruiters," tending to be more radical in both political and religious matters, included extreme Independents, like Henry Ireton, and republicans, like Edmund Ludlow.

[1] See Devereux, *Lives and Letters*, 2: 455–57.

[2] See *C. S. P. Dom., 1644–1645*, pp. 379 ff.

[3] R. N. Kershaw, "The Recruiting of the Long Parliament, 1645–1647," *History* 8 (1929): 169–79; and Douglas Brunton and D. H. Pennington, *Members of the Long Parliament* (London: George Allen and Unwin, 1954), pp. 21–37.

To counteract these changes, Essex and his compeers wanted to strengthen their position in the body politic. In mid-April they made a successful bid to retain a voice in the direction of naval affairs. Within a week of Lord Admiral Warwick's resignation, after a compromise was worked out with the Commons, Parliament brought into being an Admiralty Commission composed of six peers, including Essex,[4] and twelve commoners. The Lords held out for a single commander of the fleet, probably hoping to reinstate Warwick or some other aristocrat, but the Lower House requested a committee of three. After more debate in Parliament the Lords won their point, whereupon the Commons proceeded to appoint William Batten, an experienced naval officer who had served under Warwick, to command the fleet. To soften this blow, Warwick was named chairman of the Admiralty Commission. In that capacity he continued to exercise a great amount of influence over naval operations and the selection of personnel.

Essex also sought to achieve complete conformity to the Self-Denying Ordinance. In the Upper House, after Warwick submitted his resignation, there was no problem, because all peers had complied with the terms of the ordinance; but in the Lower House it was a different story. Waller did not yield until the middle of the month—and then reluctantly—and Cromwell never did. On 10 April the Lower House excused Cromwell from attending Parliament and allowed him to serve as Lieutenant General of the Horse in the New Model Army for forty more days, despite the Self-Denying Ordinance, and the House of Lords concurred with the action.[5] Throughout the remainder of his days Essex contended with Cromwell. Cromwell's retention of his commission, according to Whitelocke, "was much spoken against by Essex and his party as a breach of that Ordinance, and a discovery of the Intentions to continue who they pleased, and to remove the others from Commands, notwithstanding their former self-denying pretences."[6] Each time that Cromwell's temporary exemption came up for reconsideration Essex opposed it—each time without success.

The former general likewise devoted much time to unfinished business growing out of his military administration. The humiliating defeat in Cornwall still haunted him, apparently, for in the weeks

4 Powell, *Navy*, pp. 90–94.

5 Whitelocke, *Memorials*, p. 140.

6 *Ibid.*

following his resignation Essex sought the trials of several officers who had faltered there. In mid-April the Upper House, led by Essex, requested the Lower House to proceed against Commissary General Lionell Copley, Col. James Butler, and Col. John Dalbier, all of whom had been taken into custody and charged with violating the *Lawes and Ordinances*.[7] Nothing happened in the Lower House. On 29 April, Essex again moved that the Commons bring the accused officers to trial, and was so ordered in the Upper House, but a week later Copley was released by the Commons and the charges against Butler and Dalbier were dropped. All of Essex's attempts to redeem his reputation through parliamentary means were thwarted by his political enemies in the Lower House.

Soon after the passage of the Self Denying Ordinance most of the remaining units of Essex's army were incorporated into the New Model.[8] Most rank-and-file soldiers took the transfer in stride, but those officers who lost their commands reacted differently. Some of the displaced officers returned to London rather than accept a lower rank. Others petitioned Parliament and complained to the Committee of Both Kingdoms. The fate of Essex's life guard hung in the balance for several weeks. When it became evident that they might be cast aside, the members drafted a petition calling for their transfer to the New Model and presented it to the House of Commons, which in turn referred it to a select committee. On 25 April, Parliament resolved that the elite unit would be assigned to the New Model and that it would serve Fairfax in the same way it had served Essex for several years.[9]

The mergence of Essex's army with the New Model was accompanied by several disturbing developments.[10] Many disgruntled soldiers, especially the commissioned officers, took the law into their own hands. Some defected to the Royalist army, others deserted. To forestall further desertions, Parliament passed an ordinance which treated as criminals those who harbored such offenders. In the following weeks there was increasing discontent among the demoted officers who had served under Essex. Some troops mutinied. Others threatened to do so if their demands were not met. To counter these threats and to better maintain order,

---

[7] *Ibid.*, pp. 141–42.

[8] Davies, "Parliament's Army," p. 46.

[9] Whitelocke, *Memorials*, p. 139.

[10] Holles, *Memoirs*, pp. 208–9.

General Fairfax reissued Essex's military code, the *Lawes and Ordinances*, and made it the law of the New Model Army.[11] A new edition was published. In December 1645, Major General Skippon, upon being appointed governor of Bristol, was also directed to put Essex's military code into effect.

During the following months Essex used his political influence and personal prestige to secure the back pay of countless soldiers who had fought under his colors. Essex also had much money coming to him. He had invested upwards of forty-five hundred pounds of his personal funds without any compensation and he had not received the per diem pay, which amounted to over ten thousand pounds. Parliament appointed a special committee to deal with this matter.[12] While Essex sought funds for his unpaid subordinates, in mid-June 1645, as a result of his influence, the House of Lords responded favorably to the petition of some demoted officers who were in arrears. In due time the House of Commons appropriated the funds. Parliament also voted back pay to several officers in Essex's staff. In September, Sir John Meyrick was granted five hundred pounds and in November, Lord Robartes was allowed two thousand pounds to cover his pay claim.[13]

On several occasions the former general took public stands on crucial issues of the day. In the summer of 1645, after the New Model Army won several engagements, Essex came out in favor of bargaining with the King. He pushed for a negotiated settlement in the Upper House and backed those in the Lower House who wanted a compromise. On 5 July 1645 he was appointed to a committee authorized to draw up instructions for the negotiators.[14] These measures were unproductive, however, for they were opposed by the Independent majority in the House of Commons. The following March, Essex clashed with Sir Harry Vane over the fate of the King. During the winter months Sir Harry had suggested to the Scots the possibility of deposing Charles. The Covenanters were violently opposed to this proposition; they stood firmly behind the principle of monarchy and reaffirmed their support of the Stuart dynasty. When the Royalists heard of Vane's scheme they immediately protested. In letters addressed to Vane, the King and

11 Firth, *Cromwell's Army*, pp. 282–85.
12 Whitelocke, *Memorials*, p. 141.
13 *Ibid.*, p. 188.
14 *Lords Journal*, 7: 478.

his secretary, Sir Edward Nicholas, registered their opposition to both abdication and deposition. When in mid-March Essex learned of Vane's plan and the correspondence with the King, he immediately brought the matter to the attention of the House of Lords and objected to the idea of deposing Charles.[15]

During the last year of his life Essex received recognition for his service to Parliament. In June 1646 he was featured in a broadside entitled *A Perfect list of the Many Victories Obtained (through the Blessing of God) by the Parliaments Forces under the Command of his Excellency, Robert Earl of Essex.*[16] A woodcut portrait in the center of the broadside showed Essex mounted on his charger, with a battle formation in the background. The author, Josiah Ricraft, included Essex's insignia and a list of the important battles of his Civil War career. Later in the month the same author published a more complete version, entitled *A Perfect Table of Two Hundred and ninety-nine victories obtained since the King's attempt to enter Hull.*[17] Essex was credited with 179 victories, Fairfax with the remaining 120. In the following months this pamphlet was further modified and enlarged several times. Essex remained newsworthy until his demise.

After his resignation the former generalissimo finally received compensation for services rendered to the cause of Parliament. On 20 April 1645 the House of Commons empowered a special committee to determine the amount of back wages due Essex and to devise methods for paying the same.[18] The committee decided to first compensate Essex in cash for his arrears and then to arrange for an annuity to cover the material losses he sustained in Staffordshire. Parliament awarded him fifteen hundred pounds on 22 May and two thousand pounds on 4 June.[19] On 25 September, after much discussion, Parliament passed an ordinance which established an annuity amounting to ten thousand pounds a year.[20] It was financed from lands sequestered from the following Royalists: Lord Capel; Sir John, Sir Thomas, and Sir Charles Lucas; Thomas Fanshawe; William Peter; Sir Thomas Glenham; and the Earl of

---

[15] Bray, *Diary of John Evelyn*, pp. 811–12.

[16] This pamphlet was dated 9 June 1646 by Thomason.

[17] Thomason dated this pamphlet 30 June 1646.

[18] Whitelocke, *Memorials*, p. 141.

[19] *H. M. C. House of Lords Manuscripts*, 6: 60.

[20] *Lords Journal*, 8: 290, 319.

Saint Albans and Clanricarde. From his half brother, called a papist in the ordinance, Essex obtained some English holdings, including the manor of Somerhill, located near the watering place of Tunbridge Wells and once the favorite residence of their mother.

Essex spent his last days in London. He kept on attending the parliamentary deliberations with his usual diligence. He was overshadowed by others—Northumberland, Saye, and Warwick—but he did not take a back seat in the Upper House. He served on a committee authorized to investigate and reform the abuses in the heraldry practices of the day and was assigned to the all-important Committee for Sequestrations. On several occasions in 1646 he registered formal protests against measures passed by Lord Saye's majority. In April, for example, he spoke twice against the passage of an ordinance establishing martial law in London. In May, Essex had the satisfaction of receiving the proxy of the Earl of Mulgrave and of using it to defeat Lord Saye on a close vote dealing with peace propositions.[21] The following month Essex sat on a committee empowered to hear the cause of rabble-rouser John Lilburne, who had been imprisoned for subversive activities, and in July he was appointed to serve on a committee authorized to reform the University of Oxford.

Essex continued to live in the elegant style expected of an aristocrat.[22] He purchased a new coach. He bought new clothes. He retained a large staff of household servants at Essex House. He purchased some of the latest books and pamphlets. He kept his wine cellar well-stocked. There was nothing ascetic about this retired Puritan general. He was a conspicuous consumer, addicted to fashionable and ostentatious dress, and he continued to reside in a large mansion that far exceeded his needs. Like many of his enemies attached to the Court he "drank" tobacco. His household possessions included large quantities of silver plate, oriental rugs from Turkey, imported furniture from Spain and the Near East, and rich tapestries.

Essex had few connections with his family. His estranged spouse was living in Oxford, presumably with her paramour. His elder sister Lady Dorothy had died during the war and his favorite

21 *Ibid.*, p. 490.

22 British Museum, Additional MSS, 46,189. This paragraph is based on an inventory of his possessions and unpaid bills.

nephew and ward, Sir Charles Shirley, passed away in the early months of 1646, leaving only Robert Shirley at Essex House. Essex remained more or less alienated from his Royalist relatives, the Marquess and Marchioness of Hertford, the Earl and Countess of Clanricarde, the Marquess and Marchioness of Winchester, and the children of each family. Those closest to him during the last year of his life were two cousins, the Earl of Warwick and the Earl of Holland; a more remote relative, the Earl of Northumberland; Denzil Holles; Sir Philip Stapleton; Sir John Meyrick; and his domestic servants.

The Earl retained his reputation for liberality until his death. He maintained a large table. He provided for the lodging and education of his nephew Robert Shirley. He extended to the Marquess of Hertford an invitation to reside at any of his many country estates. Toward the less fortunate Essex was charitable. He bestowed many pounds sterling upon the poor and needy soldiers. He also received and acted upon many petitions from veterans who had fought under his colors. He listened to the pleas of war widows. He sometimes used his influence in the House of Lords to obtain justice. In August 1646, shortly before his death, the Earl received a petition from a Lt. Col. William Allen, an indebted veteran who desired release from prison. Essex presented the case before the Upper House and backed the petitioner. His peers went along with his request, and Allen was freed. Two days later Essex received a letter of appreciation from his onetime subordinate.

Essex remained physically active until his last days. After resigning his commission he occasionally went to the countryside on week ends for recreation. He sometimes stayed away from Parliament to escape the heat and the plague. There is no record of his returning to Chartley, but he did frequent his park and lodge at Eltham.

The Earl pursued his last stag in Windsor Forest on 10 September, when he overexerted himself and suffered a stroke.[23] He was immediately taken to Essex House and placed under the care of Dr. John Clarke. During his last days Essex was attended by close friends and relatives, including the Earl of Holland and his favorite sister, the Marchioness of Hertford. He died in the evening hours of 14 September 1646.

[23] Sanderson, *A Compleat History*, p. 928.

II

THE FOLLOWING morning the members of both Houses of Parliament learned of the death of their colleague. "The Lords," reported a contemporary newspaper, "being acquainted with the death of the E. of Essex, and being much grieved at the sad news Ordered to adjourn their House until the next day, and that Message should be sent to the House of Commons to acquaint them with the same."[24] The Lower House, now dominated by a Presbyterian majority, responded similarly to the news. Out of respect to their former generalissimo, the Commons adjourned for the day after passing the following resolution: "Resolved that this House doth declare, That when the Body of the Earl of Essex shall be carried to the Interring that the House shall accompany it."[25]

The impact of Essex's demise concerned several contemporaries. The Scottish divine Robert Baillie remarked that "the unexpected death of the brave Earle of Essex has wounded us exceedingly. He was the head of our partie here, keeped all together, who now are like by that alone to fall in pieces: the House of Lords absolutely, the City very much, and many of the Shyres depended upon him."[26] Edmund Ludlow, the cantankerous republican, felt that "his death was a great loss to those of his party."[27] To diarist Ralph Josselin, a hero-worshipping soldier, it spelled "a great weakening to the Peerage of England."[28] To Edward Hyde, who had just commenced writing his *History of the Great Rebellion*, the death proved most untimely, for Essex took with him invaluable eyewitness information about the causes and course of the Civil War.[29]

For the Devereux family Essex's death signalized tragedy. He died without a male heir. Thus the earldom of Essex, which had been in the Devereux family for nearly a century, passed into extinction, and the baronies of Ferrers of Chartley, Bourchier, and Louvaine into abeyance between his two sisters and their heirs. For the Countess of Essex the death promised more misery and misfortune; a delinquent Royalist, she was denied her rightful

24 *Perfect Diurnal*, 15 September 1646, p. 1313.

25 *Commons Journal*, 15 September 1646, 4: 697.

26 Baillie, *Letters*, 2: 401.

27 Ludlow, *Memoirs*, 1: 145.

28 Ernest Hockliffe, *The Diary of Rev. Ralph Josselin, 1616–1683*, Camden Society (London: Royal Historical Society, 1908), p. 35.

29 Ogle, *Clarendon State Papers*, 1: 342.

share in the estate. The Devereux inheritors, especially Essex's sisters and their heirs, fell into a long, bitter dispute over the disposal of the estate. Litigation, which became involved in the conflicting jurisdictions of courts and even Parliament, plagued the claimants for a generation. While his body lay in state at Essex House, the grasping claimants were already bidding for their share of the inheritance.[30]

On 16 October, Sir Walter Devereux, who descended from a collateral line of the Devereux family, made a visit to Essex House to secure from the late Earl's lawyer, Zacheus Isham, the legal documents for his inheritance. Isham flatly refused to surrender the titles, however, claiming it was not within his power to do so. This action came to the attention of the Marchioness of Hertford, who lived in the western wing of Essex House. Fearful, no doubt, of losing her own inheritance, she called Isham into her chambers late that same night for a long conversation about the disposal of the estate. While Isham was thus engaged, some of the Marchioness's hirelings pilfered the eastern wing of Essex House for valuables. They forced their way into the study and seized the late Earl's writings, jewels, plate, and coin valued at over thirty-seven hundred pounds, plus other goods of worth, which they turned over to the Marquess of Hertford for safekeeping.

Devereux learned of the midnight seizure the next morning. He promptly appealed to Parliament, personally presenting his grievance to the House of Commons. Isham also gave evidence. To redress the wrong, the Lower House appointed a committee composed of Oliver Cromwell, John Selden, Henry Vane the Younger, and several others to investigate the incident. Upon the recommendation of this committee the Marquess of Hertford was compelled to return to the executors of Essex's estate all the seized goods. The Lower House also ordered that Hertford, previously designated the chief mourner at Essex's funeral, should be denied the honor. Both he and his wife were forbidden to attend the public rites at Westminster Abbey.

Meanwhile, preparations for the state funeral went forward. Parliament appropriated five thousand pounds for burial expenses.[31] The façade of Essex House was draped with mourning cloth. An

[30] For the incident that followed see *Perfect Diurnal*, 15–22 September 1646, pp. 1317, 1350, 1353.

[31] *Mercurius Civicus*, 1 October 1646, p. 2403.

elaborate, newly constructed hearse was placed in Essex House. Out of respect to the deceased, the Commons closed its doors and ordered all members to attend the state funeral.

At the appointed hour of ten o'clock on 22 October the dignitaries convened at Essex House to participate in the most grandiose funeral since that of James I.[32] To prevent any disorderly demonstrations, five regiments of soldiers were posted along both sides of the route between Essex House and Westminster Abbey. Leading the processional were the Marshal of London and his retinue, four regiments of foot soldiers—some with their pikes trailing, others with their muskets in a funeral posture—and three hundred-sixty field officers. Next came the Earl of Essex's standard, his personal servants and chaplains, and his horses, covered with richly adorned black cloth and bearing the family arms. This colorful display of Devereux glory was followed by a contingent of fifty field soldiers, mostly colonels who had served under Essex's command, each dressed in mourning attire. Not the least of these was Gen. Oliver Cromwell, the ambitious soldier-politician who had succeeded in ousting Essex from his command. Then in order came the knights; the baronets; the younger sons of nobles; the chief mourning horse, covered with black velvet; Richard Vines, the preacher; and several heralds. Following them were seventy paid mourners, poor men clad in black cloaks, behind whom came twelve almsmen from the Abbey. Interspersed throughout the procession were fifers, drummers with black-covered drums, and trumpeters.

A richly adorned funeral chariot bearing the body of the deceased came next. The chariot was drawn by six horses, each covered with black velvet reaching to the street and garnished with plumes and escutcheons, and each led by a groom. A funeral effigy, mounted on the velvet-canopied hearse, depicted Essex in his buff-colored military coat, scarlet breeches, blue stirrup stockings, white boots, and parliamentary robes, with his coronet on his head, his staff in his hand, and his gilt sword at his side. At the foot of the effigy sat Master Thomas Pudsey, the late Earl's favorite servant.

---

[32] My description of the funeral is based upon the following accounts: *The True Mannor and Forme of the Proceeding to the Funeral of the Right Honourable Robert Earl of Essex* (London, 1646); *A Funeral Monument: or the Manner of the Hearse of the Earl of Essex* (London, 1646); Richard Vines, *The Hearse of the Renowned Right Honourable Robert Earl of Essex* (London, 1646); and Daniel Evance, *Justa Honoraria* (London, 1646).

Bringing up the rear of the cortege were some of England's most distinguished public figures. The supporters of the pall included Henry Howard, Denzil Holles, George Montagu, Charles Rich, and Thomas Sheffield, second sons of the Earls of Suffolk, Clare, Manchester, Warwick, and Mulgrave, respectively. The armor bearers were Sir William Balfour, Sir Philip Stapleton, Sir John Meyrick, and Major General Skippon, each of whom carried a different piece of Essex's personal armor. These men were followed by eight bearers of the bannerets, the Garter King of Arms, and the gentleman-usher. Finally came the principal mourner, Sir Walter Devereux, the new Viscount Hereford, and his train. With him were some of Essex's closest friends and political allies: the Earls of Northumberland, Pembroke, Suffolk, Warwick, and Holland; Lord Lisle; Oliver St. John; and Robert Shirley. Following them were the members of the House of Lords and the House of Commons, the aldermen of London, and the divines from the Westminster Assembly.

Westminster Abbey was specially decorated for the last rites of the Earl of Essex. From the floor to the roof, black hangings covered the interior of the sanctuary. The pews, too, were covered with black cloth. In the center of the chancel, near the communion table, stood a specially prepared hearse, modeled after that of James I. The Abbey was so crowded with people that the Puritan officials who had brought up the rear of the cortege were compelled to push their way into the church and stand behind the effigy. Conspicuously absent were the late general's spouse; his sister and brother-in-law; his Catholic half brother, the Earl of Clanricarde; and his half sister, the Marchioness of Winchester, all of whom were Royalists. The absence of Charles I and members of the royal family, of any bishops and deans, and of any courtiers underscored the Puritan tone of the gathering.

Vines, rector of Essex's parish church, Saint Clement Danes, officiated at the funeral ceremony. A Puritan of Presbyterian persuasion, he sat in the Westminster Assembly. For his text the Calvinist preacher selected 2 Samuel 3:38:

> Know ye not that there is a prince, and
> a great man fallen this day in Israel?

Just as Abner, a renowned Biblical warrior, had delivered the Israelites from the tyranny of King Saul, so Lord General Essex had led the English people against Charles I, he explained. Just as Abner had subjugated all Israel to the scepter of David, so Essex had reduced England to the sovereignty of Parliament. Both warriors, though separated by millenia, were God's chosen instruments in a providential universe. Just as General Abner was solemnly buried in Hebron, the royal city of Israel, so was His Excellency, the Earl of Essex, laid to rest in Westminster.

Vines believed that the Earl of Essex should be placed within the ranks of the great men of history. He deserved a niche along side of Alexander, Pompey, and Caesar. He was a warrior like them; but instead of using his sword to subjugate a foreign people, Essex used his sword to defend "the liberty and property of the subjects of England."[33] Unlike Caesar and Pompey, Essex was not seduced by political and military glory; hence he did not fall from the good graces of God or betray the English people. Essex, in Vines's eyes, was England's deliverer in her worst hour of history.[34] He was a dedicated warrior. "His monument needs no inscription, for his Epitaph is written in the Hearts of Men. Nothing but Essex, the Great, the Valiant, the Faithfull, the Parliament's Essex, the Essex of England."[35]

The funeral ceremony ended in a manner befitting a king. As the last words of the peroration fell from the lips of the Puritan preacher, the coffin was carried to the freshly dug grave in Saint John the Baptist Chapel, located off the ambulatory along the north side of the Abbey choir. Nearby were the graves of several other notables: Lord Huntingdon, cousin of Good Queen Bess; the Earl of Exeter and his wife; Sir Francis Vere, the famed Elizabethan general; and John Pym, the masterful Parliamentarian who had been Essex's political ally in the House of Commons. The attendant heralds then broke their white staves and cast them into the grave. While the gravediggers buried the coffin, the trumpeters played a solemn burial call. As the mourners withdrew into the muddied streets the air was filled with the mingled sounds of rattled muskets, the tolling bells of Saint Margaret's, and the booming of the great guns of the Tower of London.

"Such a Subject's Funeral hath not been seen in the memory of man," reported the *Perfect Occurrences*.[36] According to the *Scottish*

---

33 Vines, *The Hearse*, p. 39.

34 *Ibid.*, p. 40.

35 *Ibid.*, p. 41.

36 See the 23 October 1646 issue.

Dove, "no subject of England was ever attended to the grave with more state nor greater honour."[37] Several accounts of the funeral, some embellished with wood cuts, came off the presses shortly thereafter. Vines published his funeral sermon at the request of the Upper House. Daniel Evance brought into print two poems, while a contemporary anagrammarian reduced Essex's name to a simple rhyme.[38] Before the end of the year Essex's life was twice told. In *A Brief and Compendious Narrative of the Renowned, Robert, Earl of Essex*, an anonymous pamphleteer published a short sketch of Essex's life and death, including a pedigree, a description of his military exploits, and several woodcuts portraying various phases of his life. Robert Codrington, a friend of the deceased Earl, rendered a more balanced and detailed account in his *The Life and Death of the Illustrious Robert, Earl of Essex*, but he too left much untold.

England's engravers seized the opportunity to strike some commemorative medals.[39] One, executed by Thomas Simon, portrayed the deceased hero in armor, with a scarf across his body, and honored him with a Latin legend which translates Robert, Earl of Essex, General for the King and Parliament. Inscribed on the reverse side were a coronet, a skull and crossbones, and Essex's arms within a garnished shield. The obverse side of a second medal depicted Essex with a mantle over one shoulder; the reverse side, with an allegorical scene with Grief seated in the ruins and weeping over a broken column, contained the Latin inscription which translates His Fortitude sustained the Commonwealth.

To further perpetuate the memory of their late leader, the revolutionary government turned Westminster Abbey into a Puritan shrine. Parliament passed an order that the funeral hearse remain in the chancel indefinitely to accommodate all those Englishmen who wished to pay their last respects to the Puritan generalissimo. Daily they came in large numbers to view the funeral effigy. There the Puritan pilgrims could see the relics of their foremost crusader. There they could admire the costly catafalque designed by England's foremost architect, Inigo Jones, who used that of James I as his model.[40] There John Aubrey, a gossipy

37 *The Scottish Dove*, 8–15 October 1646, p. 1.

38 Daniel Evance, *To the Most Fragrant Dust of my Deceased Master* (London, 1646); and *Justa Honoraria* (London, 1646).

39 Hawkins, *Medallic Illustrations*, 1: 326.

40 See Andrew Clark's edition of *Aubrey's Brief Lives*, 2 vols. (Oxford, 1890), 2: 10.

antiquarian, could gape with amazement and make a sketch for posterity of the tomblike structure built, not for a king or an emperor, but for a rebel. There for many weeks the Puritans paid tribute to their deliverer.

On 26 November an embittered Cavalier by the name of John White entered the Abbey to execute a well-planned mission of destruction.[41] He eluded the concierge by hiding in a pew near the pulpit until shortly after midnight, at which time he proceeded to Essex's grave. There he vented his wrath against Essex by mutilating the catafalque with an ax he had purchased from a Ludgate ironmonger. He chopped the head from the effigy with seven or eight blows; he ripped the buff-colored coat worn by Essex at the battle of Edgehill; and he slashed the scarlet breeches and white boots. In a final act of defiance the frenzied iconoclast stole Essex's gilt sword.[42]

White eluded the city authorities for over two weeks, but he was eventually tracked down, imprisoned in the Gatehouse, and turned over to the House of Lords for questioning. The examination revealed him to be a poor farmer from Dorset, who in his own words was "moved by an angel" to destroy the image of Essex.[43] In addition to confessing his "heinous crime" against the Earl, White also admitted that he had unintentionally broken off the nose of a statue of Sir William Camden, the learned antiquarian who had been buried in the Abbey in 1623, and damaged the stone likeness of Camden's *Britannia*. He then begged the House to forgive him and release him. The Lords denied his plea and let him starve in the Gatehouse.

To preserve Essex's effigy from further mutilation by enraged Royalists, Parliament ordered that the figure of the late Earl be reclothed and placed in a glass case near that of the Earl of Lennox in Henry VII's chapel. For the next fifteen years those who shared John White's sentiments were powerless against their Puritan rulers. The Royalists did, however, ridicule Essex in song, in verse, and in prose.[44] They took his name in vain. They denounced him as a

[41] For this incident see *Whole Proceedings of the Barbarous and Inhuman demolishing of the Earl of Essex Tomb on Thursday Night Last, November 26, 1646* (London, 1646).

[42] *Perfect Diurnal*, 23 October 1646, p. 1397.

[43] Main Papers, House of Lords Record Office.

[44] Essex figured in the satirical anti-Puritan Rump songs. See MSS collection, HM 16522, Huntington Library.

rebel and a traitor. But they could not remove him from Westminster Abbey. Only after the death of Oliver Cromwell and his
son; after the restoration of Charles II; after the radical republicans
were tried, drawn, and quartered; after Cromwell was removed
from his final resting place—only then did the Royalists secure their
revenge against the Earl of Essex. In June 1661, Charles II ordered
the removal of Essex's effigy from the Abbey.[45] However, in contrast to Cromwell's body, which was exhumed and decapitated in a
fit of vengeance, Essex's corpse was unmolested. The deceased was
soon forgotten. His grave remained unmarked until the mid-
nineteenth century, when it was rediscovered by Dean Stanley, who
had Essex's name carved on the stone.[46]

III

It remains now to appraise Essex's career and fix his place in
history. The biographer is invariably tempted to exaggerate the
significance of the man he portrays, and even when that temptation
is resisted he is very likely to make a stronger case when his subject
has never been treated in a full-length biography. Let it be emphasized at the outset, then, that Essex was not a great man in the
Carlylean sense. He did not embody the spirit of an age like Elizabeth I or Louis XIV. He did not establish a new order like Cromwell.
He did not leave a permanent imprint on posterity like Frederick
the Great or Lenin. Nor did he create any lasting monuments
like Cellini or Milton. Rather, his influence was—like that of most
other rebels in history—primarily negative and ephemeral in
nature.

Yet during the reign of Charles I, the third Earl of Essex was a
prominent aristocrat whose significance has been underrated and
frequently misunderstood. The hundreds of Londoners who
attended his funeral rites in Westminster Abbey and the thousands
who braved the rain to glimpse his cortege attest to his renown in
Puritan England. Essex was in his day a famous man: he possessed
what his contemporaries called common fame. He was a high-
ranking lord at a time when lords—even those who led rebellions—

45 *H. M. C. Fourth Report*, app. 180. He seems to have acted upon the suggestion
of Sir Philip Warwick and the Duchess of Richmond.

46 Arthur P. Stanley, *Historical Memorials of Westminster Abbey*, 2 vols. (New
York, 1882), 1: 206.

were loved and idolized. His family name and title were well-known to his countrymen, especially his fellow citizens in London, and his activities were always newsworthy. His public image brought back memories of medieval and Elizabethan times. He was, in short, a public figure whose *aura popularis* expanded with the times.

Essex's popularity, propelled by a legend associated with his father and enhanced by his own exploits, stemmed from the fact that he was a living link between the abortive *coup d'état* of 1601 and the Great Rebellion. He came to personify the spirit of discontent and the hope for change which hovered over England in early Stuart times. His significance was, therefore, partly symbolic in nature. Essex did not discourage the spread of the legend which made his father a marred hero rather than a traitor, nor did he disassociate himself from those Englishmen who helped perpetuate the legend. On the contrary, he accepted and fostered the story, and befriended the survivors of the Essex conspiracy and their heirs. Doing so changed his own public image from that of son of a traitor to that of heir of a popular martyr.

This notoriety had several consequences. Essex acquired an international reputation. He was a favorite of the swordsmen. He attracted hundreds to his banner when a volunteer in the Thirty Years War and he filled his ranks with considerable ease when serving as lord lieutenant. Moreover, he won the admiration and support of many gentry in the countryside and the masses in London. It is not surprising that his military services were sought by several European princes, by the Venetians, by his own king and even Buckingham, and, finally, by the opposition leaders of the Long Parliament. Both the man and the legend which was greater than the man served as a rallying point for those in opposition to the King and inspired many to fight for the "good old cause."

Essex's political importance must be characterized as negative: he had little constructive influence on English political development. He produced no new constitutional theories or political doctrines and had little to do with the administration of Charles's government. He successfully managed his own estates and fulfilled his duties as lord lieutenant in Staffordshire over a great number of years. Although he served as Lord Chamberlain, his tenure was brief and his authority limited in scope. Similarly, his advisory role in the government amounted to little. Unlike his father, the third Earl of

Essex never played the courtier; in fact, he was virtually excluded from the Caroline establishment.

The constructive influence Essex exercised occurred within the framework of Parliament. He participated in all the sessions from 1614 through 1646, including the historic one which passed the Petition of Right, and took his legislative duties very seriously. He attended the daily meetings and sat on the most important committees in the Upper House. Dedicated to the deliberative process, he upheld the central place of Parliament in the English constitution, asserted the power of the House of Lords, and defended the rights and privileges of his peers.

Nevertheless, even in Parliament, the third Earl is most remembered for his opposition activities. He associated with the opponents of James and became one of the most persistent critics of Charles. He objected to some of the royal policies, called for the removal of "evil councilors," and eventually became distrustful of Charles and regarded him as a stubborn and weak monarch. Essex's opposition was more often than not indirect in nature. Instead of speaking out in Parliament, he relied upon committees, procedures, votes, and extraparliamentary meetings with other peers of like mind. More important, he worked very closely with several leaders in the Lower House and established a political alliance with John Pym.

From the trial of Strafford to the death of Pym, the Earl of Essex was influential in Parliament: he was the man of the hour, the uncrowned "king." He had a bloc, or faction, supporting him in the Upper House, had the backing of Pym's majority in the Lower House, and enjoyed popular support from London. During these crucial years of the Great Rebellion, Essex's aims remained mainly negative in character. He demanded the removal of more councilors, successfully sought to abolish the prerogative courts, and struck out against extraparliamentary taxation. He destroyed; he removed; he abolished; he reformed. In short, he labored to limit the power of the English sovereign—to limit him by Parliament—and his labors were not completely in vain, for most of the remedial changes wrought between 1640 and 1642 remained on the statute book long after Essex's death.

To preserve these changes, however, Parliament assumed police powers, established an army independent of the sovereign, and appointed a commander to defend itself and the King. When Essex accepted Parliament's commission to raise an army, he became, in effect, a rebel; and a rebel he remained until his death. Like those of his medieval prototypes who led rebellions, Essex's political and military objectives remained limited and somewhat ill-defined. He hoped to defeat the Royalists in battle and secure guarantees from Charles relating to the limitation of royal power. He wanted to retain the monarchy, even the Stuart dynasty, the aristocracy, and the established church. When these limited goals did not satisfy the majority in the Lower House, especially after Pym's death, he experienced the gradual diminution of his power in Parliament. Essex the rebel ended his political career, ironically, by defending the kingship and the king from political attacks made by Puritan revolutionaries.

Essex is best remembered as a soldier, as Parliament's generalissimo, and yet this aspect of his life remains difficult to assess. He received much training in the military arts in his younger days, and he possessed the military virtues associated with successful generalship. He fought in several campaigns on the Continent and faithfully carried out his local military obligations, but his reputation in military matters was undoubtedly inflated or at least distorted by the Essex legend. He was not a full-time professional soldier, as were some of his contemporaries who participated in the Thirty Years War, nor was he a master of strategy. During the first Civil War, Essex had little occasion to make strategic decisions, for they were made collectively by Parliament or one of its agencies. It is clear that he preferred a defensive type of war with limited objectives: on the field Essex was cautious, slow, and very conventional. Toward the end of 1644 he became war-weary, disillusioned, and eventually bedridden. For these and other reasons he was castigated by his political enemies—even as he has been criticized by latter-day historians.

Much of the criticism, whether direct or implied, has missed the point. Essex possessed the social rank and prestige essential for commandeering. He enjoyed a good reputation, and could point to long experience as an officer. Who among his peers could muster better credentials? Moreover, Essex did display proficiency in tactics on several occasions: his capture of Newcastle, his maneuvers before Reading and Oxford, and his Gloucester campaign all were well executed and won him praise. Yet Essex must be remembered chiefly as the organizer of England's first "national" army. He did not rely upon armed retainers. He did not look to the local militia. Through the auspices of Parliament he mobilized an army—the the largest to that date—and he successfully defended London and the Southeast against the Royalists until his eclipse in 1644.[47]

More important, Essex stood for certain principles which have been ignored by posterity. He attempted to maintain the unity of command; but although he had the backing of Pym, Essex sought in vain, for Parliament eventually permitted both the division of command and sectional armies, and in so doing paved the way for the advent of Oliver Cromwell. Most important of all, Essex accepted the principle of civilian control over the military. To be sure, Essex switched his loyalty in 1642 from the King to Parliament— at least he placed Parliament on a higher plane—but then he abided by Parliament's decisions. He disliked many of those decisions, especially those which emanated from his political enemies, but he did not challenge them or treat Parliament lightly. Nor did he, after sustaining a series of political and military reversals, resort to force and try to establish a military dictatorship. For these principles involving the relationship of military and civilian authority—which eventually became enshrined as part and parcel of the constitution—Essex has been all but forgotten.

Essex was a rebel, an aristocratic rebel, hopelessly caught between the crosscurrents of the Puritan Revolution. To the bitter end his objectives remained moderate and conventional. He possessed no compulsive drive to construct a New Jerusalem in Stuart England. Rather, he fought for a limited government in which the King would be more responsive to Parliament than the early Stuarts had been. Parliament, conversely, would have a larger voice in the affairs of state, in such matters as war, royal education, foreign policy, and the succession. In that Parliament, the aristocracy would enjoy a central, pivotal place between the King and the Commons. It is no mere coincidence that some of these ends and means bore the stamp of medieval times, for Essex possessed a decided reactionary bent, or that, on the other hand, some of his

[47] This interpretation of Essex's military career, especially his important role during the Civil Wars, corresponds with that of Col. H. C. B. Rogers in *Battles and Generals of the Civil Wars* (London: Seeley Service, 1968). Unfortunately, I received Rogers's work too late to incorporate his revisionist views in the narrative.

aims and methods bore a resemblance to those of Augustan England, for Essex would have been pleased with the Glorious Revolution and content with the resultant settlement.

The third Earl of Essex, like most other rebels, repudiated the present and turned to the past and the future for salvation, only to discover himself impotent to establish enduring alternatives. Though a product of his troublesome times, he rejected his age; though failing to achieve personal fulfillment, he succeeded in unleashing social forces which eventually consumed him. Such was the fate of the last of the Devereux.

Index

Where the title Essex appears in the following index, it refers to the subject of this biography, Robert Devereux, 3rd Earl of Essex.